PIDGINIZATION AND CREOLIZATION
OF LANGUAGES

PIDGINIZATION AND CREOLIZATION OF LANGUAGES

PROCEEDINGS OF A CONFERENCE HELD AT THE UNIVERSITY OF THE WEST INDIES MONA, JAMAICA, APRIL 1968

EDITED BY
DELL HYMES
Professor of Anthropology, University of Pennsylvania

CAMBRIDGE UNIVERSITY PRESS

Published by the Syndics of the Cambridge University Press
Bentley House, 200 Euston Road, London NW1 2DB
American Branch: 32 East 57th Street, New York, N.Y.10022

© Cambridge University Press 1971

Library of Congress Catalogue Card Number: 77–123672

ISBNS
0 521 07833 4 hard covers
0 521 09888 2 paperback

First published 1971
First paperback edition 1974

First printed in Great Britain by
Alden & Mowbray Ltd
at the Alden Press, Oxford
Reprinted in Great Britain by
Redwood Burn Limited
Trowbridge & Esher

CONTENTS

I. PREFACE AND INTRODUCTION

II. A PIDGIN (AND TWO CREOLES)

III. GENERAL CONCEPTIONS OF PROCESS

v

VI. DISCIPLINARY PERSPECTIVES

I
PREFACE AND INTRODUCTION

PREFACE

DELL HYMES

The languages called pidgins and creoles have long been a stepchild, so far as serious attention, either public or scientific, is concerned. The interest and activity reflected in this book suggest that the stepchild may prove a Cinderella.

Pidgin and *creole*, as types of languages, first were effectively distinguished less than forty years ago (Bloomfield 1933: 472–4, Reinecke 1937, 1938; for the prior situation cf. Reinecke 1969 [1935]: xii, xvi, 1938). Distinguishing them, Reinecke also kept them together, under the rubric of 'marginal languages'. Pidgins arise as makeshift adaptations, reduced in structure and use, no one's first language; creoles are pidgins become primary languages. Both are marginal, in the circumstances of their origin, and in the attitudes towards them on the part of those who speak one of the languages from which they derive.

Marginal, one might have also said, in terms of knowledge about them. These languages are of central importance to our understanding of language, and central too in the lives of some millions of people. Because of their origins, however, their association with poorer and darker members of a society, and through perpetuation of misleading stereotypes – such as that a pidgin is merely a broken or baby-talk version of another language – most interest, even where positive, has considered them merely curiosities. Much of the interest and information, scholarly as well as public, has been prejudicial. These languages have been considered, not creative adaptations, but degenerations; not systems in their own right, but deviations from other systems. Their origins have been explained, not by historical and social forces, but by inherent ignorance, indolence, and inferiority. Not the least of the crimes of colonialism has been to persuade the colonialized that they, or ways in which they differ, are inferior – to convince the stigmatized that the stigma is deserved. Indigenous languages, and especially pidgins and creoles, have suffered in this respect. Rarely would a speaker of a pidgin or creole think the idiom deserving of the prestige of being an object of serious description, of being written and studied.

A generation or so ago the situation was not much better among scholars. The scientific significance of pidgins and creoles was recognized by a few pioneers – notably Schuchardt, Jespersen and Hjelmslev among linguists, Herskovits and Reinecke among social scientists – but available descriptions seldom went beyond vocabularies and occasional texts, most often attempting to represent the language in some other language's conventional orthography (cf. Goodman 1964:109). Even an objective view toward such languages seems to begin only in the late nineteenth century, as when Brinton (1889) praised the simplicity of pidgins as efficiency and a high point, not a nadir, in linguistic evolution.

In the 1930s the objective spirit began to be combined with the descriptive field techniques of anthropological linguistics (Jacobs 1932, 1936; Herskovits 1936). The scattered literature on the many pidgins and creoles of the world was organized for the first time (Reinecke 1937). Terminology and definitions that were to become standard for 'pidgin' and 'creole' emerged (beside Reinecke 1937, 1938, cf. Bloomfield 1933; Hockett 1958; Hall 1966). Stereotypes began to be effectively attacked. Their languages represented 'the blind groping of minds too primitive for expression in modes of speech beyond their capabilities' – that was the 'hypothesis most commonly met with in discussions of Negro pidgin speech dialects and Negro speech variants', among many scholars as well as the public (Herskovits 1936:117; on Herskovits's role in combating such stereotypes, cf. Dillard 1964 and Mintz 1964:809, and on stereotypes, see Dillard's paper in this volume).

Since the 1940s, modern descriptions have appeared in some number, spearheaded by the extensive work of Hall (1942 et seq.), joined by that of Taylor in the Caribbean (1947 et seq.). No earlier theory has been accepted as sufficient to explain all the similarities among the world's pidgins and creoles, or to provide a model of their origins. Convergence through reduction to minimal linguistic universals (Hjelmslev), parallel evolution due to parallels, colored by prejudice, in the relation between superior and subordinate (Bloomfield; cf. Hall 1966), African retentions, so far as the New World is concerned – all have a point, but none the whole story. Indeed, this book, particularly Parts III and IV, testifies to the controversial status of any single explanatory theory.

Controversy stemming from concern to explain origins, particularly of the Caribbean creoles, however, has vivified the field – first, around the claim that the various creoles could be classified genetically as branches of the Indo-European language families to which they are linked – Haitian Creole a branch of North-Gallo-Romance, for example, Dominican Creole of English and Germanic, etc., and then around the rapid development of the hypothesis of descent of pidgins and creoles throughout the world from an early original Portuguese pidgin.[1] These controversies have stimulated scholars with the central importance of pidgin and creole studies to linguistic theory (cf. Hymes 1959), and have brought scholars working with various languages to consciousness of participation in a common field. (On this development since the 1950s, see DeCamp's Introduction; cf. also Valkhoff 1966:36.)

This surge of activity and interest, and its implications, has not been widely recognized in general linguistics, let alone beyond. Yet the origins, description, and social roles of pidgins and creoles pose in particularly clear form the kind of problem with which the emerging field of sociolinguistics is concerned. On the one hand, these languages deeply implicate the processes that underlie the single world society that is now emerging. Their very existence is largely due to the processes – discovery, exploration, trade, conquest, slavery, migration, colonialism, nationalism – that have brought the peoples of Europe and the peoples of the rest of the world to share a common destiny. More than any other variety of language, they have been part of these activities and transformations, and their future is bound up with the course social change in the 'third world' now takes. And while these languages have come into being and existed largely at the margins of historical consciousness – on trading ships, on plantations, in mines and colonial armies, often under the most limiting or harshest of conditions – their very origin and development under such conditions attests to fundamental characteristics of language and human nature.

On the other hand, the processes of pidginization and creolization, by which these languages are formed, seem to represent the extreme to which social factors can go in shaping the transmission and use of language. Linguists often find it possible to take social factors for granted in analyzing present structure and the results of past change. They proceed as if the sample of speech provided by one or a few informants could be assumed to represent a norm identical throughout a community, and as if something that can be called 'normal transmission', a sort of seamless continuity, from one generation to another, could be taken for granted. That these assumptions are ever fully justified is doubtful. It is clear that they must be questioned when the language to be described or classified historically is a pidgin or creole. These languages demonstrate dramatically the interdependence of language and society. Their study opens up new possibilities for integration of linguistic and social research.

Some have defined sociolinguistics as the study of linguistic diversity, or variation. This definition fits much of the current field, and certainly pidgins and creoles challenge our ability to deal with linguistic diversity, to discover its systematic basis from the standpoint of social life. I would predict that the future of sociolinguistics lies in a still more widely defined concern, namely, explanation of the origin, maintenance, change and loss of specific *means of speech*. The concern would be with the structure of variation, not for its own sake, but as part of human adaptation. It would be part of the general problem of the social sciences, the maintenance and transformation of social and symbolic order. Well known problems of the evolution and adaptation of lexical and syntactic means, of semantic domains and categories, on the one hand, and of verbal genres, literary and conversational, on the other, would be part of this wider concern. Equally important would be study of the emergence and adaptation of the phenomena variously identified as code-repertoires, registers, speech levels, speech styles, and the like. In all these respects, pidgin and creole languages are of special importance, since their very existence poses the question of the relation of means of speech to social needs. Any theory of linguistic varieties, genres and semantic features as adaptive means must deal with the reduction that leads to the one (pidgins) and the expansion that leads to the other (creoles).

For reasons such as these, the planning of an international conference on pidgin and creole languages was initiated by the Committee on Sociolinguistics of the Social Science Research Council (U.S.). The conference was co-sponsored by the University of the West Indies, and held at the campus of the University in Mona, Kingston, Jamaica, on 9 – 12 April, 1968. Jamaica and the University have been a principal focus of creole studies, and by meeting there it was possible to benefit from the participation of a number of Caribbean scholars for whom creole languages are of personal and practical, as well as scientific, importance. Some of the discussion had a depth and realism that reflected their presence.

The principal contributions of the conference, sometimes considerably revised, are presented here.[2] They are organized in terms of the major needs of the field. In addition to the main papers, a number of other contributions made available to the participants are represented in briefer form, and a map and list of pidgin and creole languages, especially prepared for this volume, have been included as an appendix.

David DeCamp had circulated to participants before the conference a survey of the study of pidgin and creole languages. He has revised it especially for this book in the light of the conference discussions, so that it provides, uniquely, an introduction to the concepts of pidgin and creole, an overview of the widespread occurrence of such languages in the world today, and a history and review of the field and its major problems. From the vantage point of a leading participant, he vividly describes the emergence of a field of creole studies, and comments on the origin of pidgins and creoles, both in general and in relation to historical linguistics; on the survival of such languages, including the phenomenon of 'decreolization', in relation to sociolinguistics; on description of pidgins and creoles; and finally, on the implications of creole studies for the understanding of 'black English'.

Perhaps the greatest need is the elementary one of adequate linguistic descriptions of pidgins and creoles. Part II, 'A Pidgin (and Two Creoles)', symbolizes this need, and illustrates the character of pidgins and creoles with a concrete case of each.

Part III, 'General Conceptions of Process', reflects the need for fresh theoretical work, for the development and testing of models adequate to explain the origins and characteristics of these languages. The papers demonstrate the inability of any previously received theory adequately to discriminate and explain all relevant cases. This is not to say that the contributions are negative. Rather, each develops a line of work needed to arrive at an adequate theory, sharpening concepts on the one hand, and showing their place within broader frames of relevance on the other. Together they place the study of pidginization and creolization within the context of the general process of hybridization, simplification, convergence, and acculturation.

Here indeed is the major consequence of what is presented: that pidgins and creoles are part of a much broader subject, that of the processes of pidginization and creolization, or, more generally, of the reduction and expansion of languages in structure and function. The standard definitions of pidgins and creoles point out the center of a field of study, but do not wholly delimit it. The awkward but accurate title of this book stems from that realization. (Below and in the Introduction to Part III I sketch my own view of this problem.)

Theories and explanatory models depend not only on descriptions and analytical concepts, but also on much careful work of historical inference and reconstruction. Whether or not pidgin and creole languages generally are to be explained in terms of ordinary genetic relationship, their individual histories require much application of the tools of historical and comparative linguistics. The interpretation of a given case as transmogrified pidgin Portuguese, brusquely restructured English (say), or neither, depends very much on the careful assessment of particular details, both as to words and as to populations, concerning their occurrence in space and time. Major problems of historical analysis and inference are presented in Part IV, in connection with new results and hypotheses.

While much can be learned from descriptions along usual linguistic lines – would we had many more of such! – there remain problems that can be solved only on the basis of descriptions that are *socio*linguistic, that capture the socially governed variation and stratification of language in a community. In Part V, 'Variation and Use', the need for sociolinguistic models of description is shown in connection with the range and relevance of these problems to creolized English, in the Caribbean, Pacific, and United States. The section takes up questions of the emergence and decline of differentiation; juxtaposes alternative models for the description of complex variation; and relates creole varieties to religion, social interaction, poetry, education, and race relations. The New World focus is in keeping with the site of the conference in the Caribbean. Cases chosen from Africa, or from Oceania, would display problems of equivalent scientific and social significance.

A basic motivation for the conference and this book has been the belief that pidgins and creoles require the joint skills and knowledge of linguistics and the social sciences. The final section, Part VI, 'Disciplinary Perspectives', is an attempt to contribute to this union. It must frankly be said that only a small beginning has been made. Most of the participants, as most of the specialists in the field, are linguists. Although many of these have had some background in social science, and one of four participants was in fact affiliated with social science, discussion was dominated by the present status of problems from a linguistic standpoint. Social scientists usually know little about such languages, and when they do know something, may be reluctant to deal with them because of lack of linguistic sophistication.[3] (It is less common for a linguist to hesitate from a sense of a lack of social science sophistication.) And it is the recent history of the subject among linguists that has constituted it a field; the initial sense of transcending marginality and isolation, of achieving communication and wider relevance, is still very much to the fore.

Understandably, then, the larger framework of comparison most in evidence is that of language history, a perspective concerned with the provenience of linguistic features, more than with the recurrence of social (or sociolinguistic) processes. Just the need for the latter perspective, however, is made salient in the two concluding contributions by Grimshaw and Mintz. Each suggests criteria for a general typology of cases, and Mintz sketches a controlled comparison, transcending linguistic provenience, of the Caribbean as a region with a particular social history. In the spirit of broader relevance, Hoenigswald and Labov consider the ways in which pidgin and creole languages require linguists to transcend the significance commonly attached to the notions of 'genetic relationship' and 'system'.

The Mona conference, and this book, symbolize recognition of the legitimacy and importance of the study of pidgin and creole languages, and reflect the extension of linguistic work, descriptive and historical, that is already under way. The next major step for the field of pidgin and creole studies is clear. It is research dictated by needs beyond the description and history of particular languages and linguistically related groups of languages, research required for the sort of controlled comparison needed to achieve an adequate model of the formation of pidgins and creoles. There should be comparisons, for example, of cases because of their common social features, rather than because of linguistic connection; or comparison of cases just because a linguistic connection appears to be absent (the Sudan-Arabic that flourished in the southern portion of the then Anglo-Egyptian Sudan for some half century (1870–1920), for example, with Sango of the Central African Republic and Vietnamese Pidgin French (Tây Bôi)). There should be comparison of true pidgins and creoles with cases in which pidginization began, but did not result in a pidgin; in which creolization has begun, but not continued; in which one of the diagnostic traits of a true pidgin or creole is absent.

It would be natural enough for specialists in pidgin and creole languages to let the subject develop along the lines of other specialities, historically or areally defined, such as 'South Asian languages' or 'Germanic linguistics'.

Certainly there is need for specialization in, say, the Atlantic English creoles. It is the claim of this book, however, that the basic questions of the subject cut deeper, and that explanation, like description, must draw upon models more fully developed in the social sciences.

Pidgins and creoles raise questions vital to the integration of linguistic and social theory, and to the foundations of theory; and their study has practical as well as scientific importance. To realize their potential contribution, however, we must here, as in other areas of language, transcend a deep-seated limitation of linguistic work. Social aspects of language have typically been treated only when they intruded into the ordinary work of the linguist. When social status, or sex, or the like, intruded into the core of grammar, or phonology, then it would be described, and the language in question marked as a special case of a 'status language', 'men's and women's speech', or the like. But adequate information, a set of cases sufficient to analyze and explain such phenomena, would have to comprise cases as well in which social status, or sexual role, did *not* intrude into grammar or phonology in the ordinary sense, but was marked in some other way. One would have to begin with the general phenomenon of the expression of social status, or sexual role, in speech, and consider the conditions under which its expression would take now one form, now another. (Obviously it is not the case that there are languages whose use does *not* ever signal social status or sexual role.) Just as ordinary linguistic description must comprise both grammar and lexicon, because, the great pioneer of structural linguistics, De Saussure, remarked, the same linguistic meaning is expressed in some languages in one, in some languages in the other, so a sociolinguistic description must comprise the full range of means by which social meanings are conveyed, meanings that will sometimes be found in grammar, sometimes not. It is the same with the formation of pidgins and creoles. The processes of which they are the culmination are universal tendencies in the use of speech.

There are in effect four distinct 'moments' which a theory of pidgin and creole languages must integrate: (1) the universal tendencies to adapt speech, and varieties of a language, by simplification in some circumstances, expansion in others; (2) the occurrence of these tendencies in situations of language contact, so as to give rise to partial confluence of linguistic traditions; (3) the conditions, linguistic and social, under which forms of speech so adapted and influenced become and remain independent of the norms of any contributing tradition;[4] (4) the subsequent histories of languages so formed. We enter the study of pidgins and creoles ordinarily with the last of these four moments, and try to infer or speculate about the rest. Our strategy must include ways of direct access to all, and can, if all are recognized as part of the field of study. Work of this sort, indeed, is already reflected here, not only in the essays by social scientists, but in the model proposed by Whinnom, the attention of

Samarin to pidginization as a general process, the typological thrust of
Ferguson, the exploration of universals of pidgin vocabulary by Cassidy.

If this book reflects the great progress that has been made in the last
decade, it reflects also a sense of urgency, of research that is greatly needed,
descriptive, historical, analytical. In short, there is a hope that the next decade
will see as great a transformation of our knowledge as has the last.

The conference at Mona was made possible by a grant of the Social Science
Research Council from the National Science Foundation, and by funds
allocated by the University of the West Indies. The conference was organized
in collaboration with Dr. Gertrud Buscher of the University of the West
Indies. All of us are indebted to our hosts at the University of the West Indies,
and particularly to Dr. John Figueroa for an evening of Creole poetry on the
eve of the conference. Without the care and efforts of Dr. Buscher, and of Dr.
Elbridge Sibley of the Social Science Research Council, neither the conference
nor this book would have been possible. Professor Robert Le Page is owed a
special debt of thanks for his help in arranging publication.

We should like to recognize the role of three senior scholars in pioneering
the serious study of pidgin and creole languages, and wish to dedicate this
book to them: John E. Reinecke, Robert A. Hall, and Douglas Taylor.

January 1971   DELL HYMES

NOTES

1 This view was put forward by Hall (1950, 1955), challenged by Taylor (1956;
cf. 1945); defended by Hall (1958); and mediated in terms of convergence areas
by Weinreich (1959). The controversy has a good deal of methodological
importance. Hall maintains the universal application of the principles of
historical linguistics formulated in the neo-grammarian tradition, while Taylor
employs a new method of grammatical reconstruction to question them. Either
view can have liberal social and political connotations. Classification as Indo-
European perhaps unconsciously is intended to rescue the languages from
denigration as 'bastards'. Interpretation as discontinuous, new entities necessarily stresses the continuity of non-European structures and the positive,
creative role of the non-European speakers.
2 A report of the conference, 'Pidginization and creolization of languages: their
social aspects' has appeared in *Items* 22 (2): 13–18 (1968). This preface and
some of the introductions to follow draw upon it. References in the preface are
to be found with the bibliography to the Introduction (Part I) by David DeCamp.
A list of participants in the conference is given as an appendix.
3 I recall one sociologist (not at the conference) objecting to a conference on
'pidgins' and 'creoles', and asking for substitute terms, on the ground that

sociologists did not know them. One social scientist was reluctant to participate because of his lack of linguistic training; I learned later that one of the most knowledgeable linguists had been hesitant to speak on a subject because of the same person's awesome knowledge of relevant social information.

4 Become, in the case of crystallization of a pidgin; remain in the sense of maintenance beyond an initial moment of formation, particularly by becoming general in a group. True pidgins may be formed in individual relationships but not survive them; and the technical creolization of a language as first language of children in a family whose parents speak it as a pidgin may not outlast exposure to schooling – the children may in effect have 'learned a second language first'. The essential thing is survival without reabsorption by a contributing tradition. A pidgin may remain either as a pidgin (escaping de-pidginization) or by transformation into a creole. A creole in continuing contact with a dominant contributing tradition is likely to undergo 'decreolization' even to the point of reabsorption. (Cf. papers on Jamaica in Part v and Dillard there.)

INTRODUCTION: THE STUDY OF PIDGIN AND CREOLE LANGUAGES

DAVID DECAMP

The study of pidgin and creole languages is not new. Most of Hugo Schuchardt's pioneering *Kreolische Studien* were published in the 1880s, and significant studies have appeared in every decade since then. (On Schuchardt, see p. 31 below.) Nor are many of the current issues in creole studies really new. The current debate over the theory of a Portuguese origin of non-Portuguese creoles, for example, is usually dated from the 1950s. Yet Dirk Christiaan Hesseling's famous and controversial *Het Afrikaans*, in which he attributed the origin of Afrikaans to creolization under the influence of a Malayo-Portuguese trade jargon, was first published in 1899.

Since the second world war, and especially within the past decade, however, the nature of pidgin and creole studies has indeed radically changed in several ways. First, the field has become unified. Before the 1950s very few linguists dealt with both pidgins and creoles. Very few studied more than one geographical area or more than one creole language. For example, Chinese pidgin English, Hawaiian English, Gullah, Jamaican Creole, and West African Krio were all treated separately but never as a single field. This compartmentalization is now rapidly breaking down. Linguists now view pidgins and creoles as two phases, perhaps even as only two aspects, of the same linguistic process. The geographical and interlingual barriers have so eroded that although a linguist may think of himself as primarily a Caribbeanist or a French creolist, he can no longer ignore work in other areas and other languages. Students of Haitian French and of Trinidadian English realize that they are dealing not with similar linguistic problems, but with the same linguistic problem. There is an increasing tendency to speak not of *creoles* but of *creole*, or even of *pidgin-creole*.

Second, pidgin-creole studies have become a respectable academic field. No longer are young linguists advised not to waste their time on such peripheral subjects but to study 'real' languages if they wish to get on in the academic world. Beginning in 1969, the Modern Language Association's annual bibliography groups pidgin-creole studies together in a new and separate division rather than treating them as subordinate appendages to French, English, Spanish, etc. The first international conference on creole language studies was held in 1959. During that five-day meeting in Jamaica, the generative-transformational theory, at that time a new and controversial approach, only two years after the publication of Chomsky's *Syntactic structures*, was first applied to creole languages. Sociolinguistic concepts such as diglossia and continuum were discussed. The Portuguese-origin hypothesis had been advanced sixty years earlier by Hesseling, but not until 1959 was it seriously considered and discussed from a general pidgin-creole point of view, and only then were its implications apparent: the possibility of a monogenetic theory of pidgin-creole origin. The proceedings of this conference (Le Page 1961) have formed the basis of much of the research and discussion since 1961. The greatest contribution, however, was the recognition by a group of scholars that they were in fact 'creolists'. The birth of the field of pidgin-creole studies may be dated from that April afternoon in Jamaica, when Jack Berry suddenly remarked, 'All of us are talking about the same thing!'

If pidgin-creole as a separate discipline was born in 1959, then it came of age in 1968. The second international conference, also held in Jamaica, revealed how much the field had grown in the intervening nine years. The second conference was attended by several times as many scholars as the first, representing a much greater number of territories and interests. Some of the topics discussed in 1959 – e.g. the question of origin and genetic classification – reappear in the papers in this volume, but at a much more advanced and sophisticated level. Other topics – e.g. the consideration of American Negro non-standard English as a creole – are new since 1959. To an extent not dreamed of in 1959, these papers draw upon the concepts of related fields: theoretical linguistics, anthropology, and sociology. Sociolinguistics is still predominantly an empirical study. If a genuine sociolinguistic theory ever does appear, it will certainly be indebted to pidgin-creole studies such as those presented at this conference.

This introduction will attempt to outline the current issues in creole studies, to summarize the progress so far, and to suggest approaches which are being made or which might be made to creole linguistic problems. It is not intended for the specialist but for the student of anthropology, sociology, or general linguistics. So that it may serve as a bibliographic guide to any reader interested in further study of creole, I have provided rather extensive citation of sources. The bibliography is representative, not exhaustive. Many important works have been omitted, and I am well aware that another author with different interests might recommend a very different list. The beginning student would do well to begin with such standard bibliographic guides as *Bilingualism in the Americas* (Haugen 1956) and *Languages in contact* (Weinreich 1964) and with the relevant papers in anthologies such as *The ethnography of communication* (Gumperz and Hymes 1964), *Language in culture and society* (Hymes 1964), and *Readings in the sociology of language* (Fishman 1968). It is now expected that the major bibliographical guide by Reinecke (1937) will be revised and published.

Characteristics and definitions

The terminology of pidgin-creole studies reflects the traditional classification and theory of origin of these languages. Each pidgin or creole has been traditionally classed as a deviant dialect of a standard language, usually European, with English, French, Portuguese, Spanish, and Dutch the most frequent. A creole which shares most of its vocabulary with English is traditionally called an *English-based creole* or *creolized English*. The origin of pidgins and creoles is indeed controversial, however, and many linguists would hotly deny that French-based creole is 'genetically' related to French in the same sense that French is related to Italian. These terms must be understood as purely descriptive labels which refer primarily to similarities in vocabulary, not to basic structural similarities or to genetic classification. Pidgins and creoles are also often called *mixed languages*, an even more dangerous term, for it not only begs the historical question but is also descriptively misleading, suggesting that a pidgin or creole is only a potpourri with no uniform coherent structure of its own. These are genuine languages in their own right, not just macaronic blends or interlingual corruptions of standard languages.

The traditional etymology derives *pidgin* from English *business*, and indeed expressions like 'That's my pigeon!' (i.e. that's my own private affair) are still common in Sino-English. Although the etymology has been challenged (Kleinecke 1959; cf. Hall 1966:7), the word in this sense was first applied to Chinese pidgin English, and later to any language of similar type. A pidgin is a contact vernacular, normally not the native language of any of its speakers. It is used in trading or in any situation requiring communication between persons who do not speak each other's native languages. It is characterized by a limited vocabulary, an elimination of many grammatical devices such as number and gender, and a drastic reduction of redundant features. This reduction has been often called simplification, but it is now considered debatable whether the less-redundant pidgin is simpler or more complex than the standard language.

The term *creole* (from Portuguese *crioulo*, via Spanish and French) originally meant a white man of European descent born and raised in a tropical or semi-tropical colony. Only later was the meaning extended to include indigenous natives and others of non-European origin, e.g. African slaves (Cassidy 1961:21–3, 161–2). The term was then applied to certain languages spoken by creoles in and around the Caribbean and in West Africa and was later extended to other languages of similar types. Most creoles, like most pidgins, are European based, i.e. each has derived most of its vocabulary from one or more European languages. Creole French (also called *patois*) and creole English are the most frequent in West Africa and the New World, but Spanish,

Dutch, and Portuguese creoles are common in other parts of the world and, as I will later discuss, are of great importance in the historical development of pidgins and creoles. By no means all of the vocabulary of a creole is shared with its corresponding European language, however, and in both phonology and syntax the differences between a creole and a standard are usually so great as to make them mutually unintelligible. Some pidgins and creoles are not European based. The famous Chinook Jargon, once used for trading by north-western American Indians, was a pidgin (Jacobs 1932; Boas 1933; Grant 1945; Kaufman ms.); and there are non-European creoles flourishing today in Africa (Samarin 1962; M. Goodman 1968; Polomé 1968).

Unlike a pidgin, which functions only as an auxiliary contact language, a creole is the native language of most of its speakers. Therefore its vocabulary and syntactic devices are, like those of any native language, large enough to meet all the communication needs of its speakers. In West Africa and in the Caribbean there is a small but growing literature written in creole languages. (See the Sranan poem presented by Voorhoeve, and Figueroa's comments, in this volume.) A creole, like a pidgin, tends to minimize redundancy in syntax. For example, although English pidgins lack any plural marker for nouns, creole English has a plural suffix or enclitic -dem (derived from the English demonstrative them). This suffix is normally omitted when redundant, i.e. when plurality may be inferred from other signals. Thus the standard English the boys, the three boys, and those boys would appear in creole as di bwai-dem, di trii bwai, and dem bwai; neither *di trii bwai-dem nor *dem bwai-dem would occur unless unusual emphasis on the plural was intended.

A creole is inferior to its corresponding standard language only in social status. A pidgin, however, is so limited, both lexically and structurally, that it is suitable only for specialized and limited communication. Pidgins are therefore short lived. Rarely does a pidgin survive for a century, and there is no parallel to the longevity of Sabir, better known as Mediterranean Lingua Franca, which survived from the middle ages until the twentieth century (Schuchardt 1909; Reinecke 1938; Whinnom 1965). If the interlingual contact ends, the pidgin usually also ends (cf. Reinecke, this volume); there is no longer a need for it, and there are no sentimental attachments or nationalistic motivations for preserving a dead pidgin. If the interlingual contact is maintained for a long time, usually one group learns the standard language of the other, as the American Indians learned English (Leachman and Hall 1955). The only way in which a pidgin may escape extinction is by evolving into a creole; i.e. the syntax and vocabulary are extended and it becomes the native language of a community. After this metamorphosis, it may survive long after the termination of the interlingual contacts which had maintained the pidgin. In fact we can never know how many of the 'normal' languages of the world originated via this pidgin-creole process. It was apparently Bloomfield

(1933:474) who first suggested this historical relationship between pidgin and creole. Robert A. Hall, Jr., has carried the idea much further, however; he makes a pidgin origin an essential feature of his definition of creole and postulates a sort of linguistic 'life-cycle' beginning with a spontaneous generation of a pidgin, followed by evolution to creole (Hall 1953, 1962, 1966).

Present distribution of pidgin and creole languages

Creoles are spoken today by more than six million persons in and around the Caribbean and by smaller and more scattered groups of speakers in West Africa (especially Sierra Leone and the Camerouns), South Africa (i.e. Afrikaans), and in South and South-east Asia (e.g. India, Macao, and the Philippines). Because a pidgin is an auxiliary rather than a native language, estimates of total numbers of speakers are difficult and unreliable, but one could safely say that two or three million persons daily use some form of pidgin in at least some language situations. World-wide there are more pidgin-creole speakers than Swedish or Czech speakers, perhaps even as many speakers as Serbo-Croatian or Persian. (*Languages of the world* 1964; Whinnom 1956; Le Page 1957–8:54–62; Hall 1966; Stewart 1962.)

Numerically the largest are the French-based creoles, perhaps totalling 4,500,000 speakers. There are four major dialects of French creole in the Caribbean (all mutually intelligible): Haiti, French Guiana, Louisiana, and the Lesser Antilles (i.e. the French islands of Guadeloupe, Les Saintes, Marie-Galante, and Martinique, and the once French but later British islands of Dominica, Trinidad, Grenada, and St Lucia). Creole French is also spoken on the French island of Réunion and the British island of Mauritius, both in the Indian Ocean (Richardson 1963a). These creoles have long co-existed with standard French or standard English and (in the British islands) with English-based creoles, all with surprisingly little interlingual influence (Stewart 1962; M. Goodman 1964).

English-based creoles are used in West Africa, in the Camerouns and in Sierra Leone (Berry 1961, 1962). They are also spoken by at least a million and a half speakers in Jamaica and by smaller numbers in Trinidad and Tobago, Guyana (British Guiana), British Honduras, Barbados, St Lucia, St Kitts, Anguilla, Nevis, and the Netherlands Antilles. Sranan (also called Sranan Tongo or Taki-Taki) and Saramaccan, two mutually unintelligible English-based creoles are still spoken by about 80,000 in Surinam, even though that territory passed from British to Dutch hands in 1667 (Voorhoeve 1961b, 1962). Gullah, once widely spoken in Georgia, South Carolina, and the nearby Sea Islands, is now nearly extinct on the mainland and becoming rare on the islands (Turner 1949), although William Stewart claims to have located numerous mainland Gullah speakers and even reports a Gullah-speaking community in Texas. (Neo-Melanesian (New Guinea pidgin English) may be undergoing creolization among some thousands of speakers (Wolfers, this volume), and pidgin English is undergoing creolization in the Northern Territory of Australia (Jernudd 1969:151, 153).)

Negerhollands, still spoken by a few persons in the U.S. Virgin Islands, is not an English but a Dutch creole, long antedating the American purchase of these islands in 1916 (Hesseling 1905). The most important Dutch creole is Afrikaans, spoken by three million persons in the Union of South Africa (Valkhoff 1960, 1966; Hesseling 1923).

Spanish-based and Portuguese-based creoles are widely used in Asia (Whinnom 1956; Frake 1968), and Stewart (1962:53) reports creole Portuguese still in use on three islands off the West African coast: Cape Verde, Annobón, and São Tomé. The only example in the Caribbean is Papiamento, spoken by about 200,000 in the Dutch ABC islands (Aruba, Bonaire, and Curaçao) in the southern Caribbean. The Spanish and Portuguese elements in Papiamento are both so pervasive and so intermingled that its classification is disputed. Since the islands were acquired by the Netherlands in 1634, it has been so influenced by other languages, especially Dutch and English, that it now resembles a sort of creolized Esperanto (van Wijk 1958; Navarro Tomás 1951).

European-based creoles are used also in other widely scattered areas of the world, such as Hawaii (Reinecke and Tokimasa 1934; Reinecke and Tsuzaki 1967; Carr 1962; Tsuzaki 1968a), and Pitcairn Island (Ross and Moverley 1964). Pitcairnese is the creole descendant of the pidgin English used by the original *Bounty* mutineers who reached the island in 1790. Non-European-based creoles are less common, but Samarin (1962) reports them from Africa. (See also Polomé on creolization of Swahili in Katanga in this volume, Polomé 1963 on Swahili and Kituba in the Congo, and Wurm (1964:34) on creolization of Police Motu in Papua.) Furthermore, many other 'mixed languages' not usually thought of as creoles, e.g. Yiddish, Indonesian (Hall 1966:18), Marathi (Southworth 1968), and Swahili (Polomé 1968), have many creole characteristics. (A map and list of pidgins and creoles, provided by Ian Hancock, can be found at the end of this volume.)

The origin of European-based pidgins and creoles

Within the past decade a controversy has arisen between monogenetic and polygenetic theories of origin for pidgins and creoles. Do all pidgins and creoles have a common 'genetic' ancestor from which they have diverged in the traditional stammbaum sense? Or is each different pidgin and creole — perhaps even the pidgin or creole of each different speech community — the result of a separate act of creation and process of development? In other words, is general pidgin-creole a single language which has developed distinct and mutually unintelligible varieties (French, English, Portuguese, etc.) under the influence of the relevant standard languages? Or is each pidgin and creole genetically related to the corresponding standard language, from which it diverged under the influence of a similar sociolinguistic situation?

Until recently, the controversy was among competing polygenetic theories. The earliest of these was incredibly naive but unfortunately is still held by some reputable scholars. (It seems to persist in part in the only modern general book on the subject (Hall 1966:5, 86).) According to this theory, each pidgin and creole began as a sort of baby-talk used by masters, plantation owners, and merchants to communicate with their servants, slaves, and customers. Each speaker deliberately mutilated the standard language by eliminating all grammatical inflections, reducing the number of phonological and syntactic contrasts, and limiting the vocabulary to a few hundred words. The resulting structure was described by many scholars as a 'corruption', a 'minimum grammar', a return to an 'archaic state', etc. (e.g. Göbl-Galdi 1934). Even Jespersen described pidgins as 'minimal' and 'makeshift' languages (1922:ch. XII). Some scholars (e.g. Hjelmslev 1939) inverted the invidious value judgments, describing pidgin structure as 'optimum' rather than 'minimum' grammar, but still espoused the simplistic baby-talk theory and denied to pidgins a status as true languages. Bloomfield (1933:472–5) most fully developed the baby-talk theory, seeing in the process of pidgin creation a recursive series of imitations; i.e. the standard English speaker would contemptuously imitate the native's 'desperate attempt' to imitate standard English. The native would then imitate the imitation of his imitation, and so on.

The baby-talk theory is easily refuted. First, all the early accounts (dating from the eighteenth century in Jamaica, for example) report that the white planters and their families were learning the creole from the slaves, not vice versa (Cassidy 1961:21–3). Furthermore, if each European had indeed improvised his own variety of baby-talk to communicate with his servants and slaves, how could one explain the fact that all dialects of creole French, including those in the Indian Ocean, are mutually intelligible? The typological similarities shared by creole French, English, Spanish, etc., are too great for coincidence, and when we consider that these creoles also share many common vocabulary words, including syntactic function words, the baby-talk hypothesis completely collapses (Valdman 1964:85; Taylor 1956, and in this volume; cf. Alleyne's critique in this volume).

These similarities were explained by many writers as a result of languages in contact; i.e. Haitian French is similar to Jamaican English because the slaves there were also Africans. The planter in Jamaica not only taught English, in a simplified form, to his slaves; he also learned from them, and the resulting language was a blend of English and African elements. Le Page, for example, saw the phonemic structure of Jamaican creole as reflecting 'the process of translation by West African ears' (Le Page and DeCamp 1960:118). But Africa, even West Africa, is anything but a linguistically uniform area. Slaves were brought from many areas speaking many different languages of widely different type. No one African language can account for all or even a majority of the 'African' elements in Caribbean creole, nor is any significant 'African' feature in creole shared by all or even a majority of the native languages of the slaves (for the ethnic backgrounds of West Indian slavery, see Le Page and DeCamp 1960:ch. IV; Cassidy 1961:15–19; and now Curtin 1969). Furthermore, plantation owners deliberately acquired slaves with the greatest possible variety of languages in order to make native-language communication among slaves impossible and thus reduce the risk of insurrection. Thus there could not have been any significant systematic African 'substratum'. If we assume that the language-mixing process was eclectic, taking one feature from this African language, another from that one, we are still unable to explain the similarities between all Caribbean creoles and the remarkable uniformity of French-based creole. That each group would just happen to choose the same features from Twi, the same from Hausa, etc., would stretch coincidence too far. Finally, as Le Page pointed out in an attack on the African substratum theories of Herskovits (Le Page 1957–8:374–5), many of the common features of Caribbean and African creoles are also shared by other creoles such as Pitcairnese, where there have been no African influences, only English and Polynesian (see also Ross 1962). (This is not to deny significant, particular African influences on particular languages (cf. Hall 1966:108–9; 1968:365, and Daeleman and Taylor in this volume).)

The most vigorous defender of polygenesis today is Robert A. Hall, Jr. He insists that all creoles have evolved from pidgins and may evolve further into 'normal' languages, thus completing a 'life-cycle'; pidgins, on the other hand, appear by spontaneous generation whenever and wherever the need for them arises.

A pidgin normally owes its origin to relatively casual, short-term contact between groups which do not have a language in common . . . a pidgin can arise – on occasion, even in the space of only a few hours – whenever an emergency situation calls for communication on a minimal level of comprehension. (Hall 1962:152.)

Whenever guide meets tourist, employer meets employee, or shopkeeper meets customer, Hall claims, a new pidgin is likely to arise if the two do not share a common language. The pidgin will draw its minimal vocabulary from both languages. The phonology and syntax will be stripped not only of redundancies, but also of many essential features, so that the pidgin is suitable only for minimal and specialized communication. 'Me Tarzan, you Jane!' is the prototype pidgin situation. Most such pidgins are ephemeral and disappear as quickly as they arise. If the interlingual contact is prolonged and institutionalized, however, as in the case of slavery, the presence of foreign military troops, or the marriage of Tarzan and Jane, then the pidgin becomes fixed, and newcomers to that interlingual scene must learn it as they would learn Esperanto. The pidgin may then be expanded to make it suitable for a greater variety of speech situations, either externally by borrowing additional features from the standard language or internally by analogical improvizations on the resources of the original pidgin − and so begins the process of evolution which may someday result in a creole if speakers begin using it as a native language.

Note that Hall's theory provides not one but two mechanisms for the appearance of a pidgin or creole in a given community: either the spontaneous generation of a new pidgin or the extension to a new community of an already established pidgin or creole (e.g. the spread of pidgin English throughout Melanesia). If we find a similar creole in two communities, we would assume that the latter process (diffusion) has operated, for two different tourists would hardly improvise the same interlingual pidgin to communicate with their guides. Thus we could explain the uniformity of the French creoles by assuming that creole French had become institutionalized and followed the flag to the colonies. But what about the similarities between creoles whose sets of original interlingual components apparently had nothing in common, e.g. the English creole of the Caribbean and the Spanish creole of the Philippines? These similarities are too great for coincidence: elimination of inflections for number in nouns and for gender and case in pronouns, identity of adverb and adjective, use of iteration for intensification of adverb-adjectives, development of compound prepositions using the Portuguese *na* and *de*, use of verbal aspects marked by syntactic particles rather than true tenses, etc. (Taylor 1957). If we were also to explain these similarities as the result of diffusion, we would be moving rapidly toward a monogenetic theory, and we might well wonder whether the spontaneous generation alternative had much relevance except in trivial situations like the tourist and his guide.

Whinnom (1968) has now suggested that the tourist and his guide are not the persons likely to use a pidgin at all. The languages which we today recognize as pidgins, he points out, are not spoken by foreigners nor even primarily by dominant speakers of a standard language, but by natives in subordinate positions who do not share a common language among themselves. Thus Chinese pidgin English is not spoken between English and Chinese speakers, but rather among Chinese of different and mutually unintelligible dialects. Because the occasion which necessitates the use of the interlingual pidgin is the bringing together of different Chinese speakers under the domination of English speakers (Americans in Taiwan, Englishmen in Hong Kong, Singapore, and old Shanghai), the pidgin will contain a great deal of English vocabulary. Rarely does the Englishman or American take the time and effort to learn pidgin as he would have to learn any foreign language. Though he may claim to speak pidgin, it is more likely only a baby-talk English larded with bits of Chinese and of real pidgin. The speakers of genuine pidgin English, the Chinese, treat this improvised interlingua with contempt. If the Englishman or American overhears his servants speaking pidgin English to each other, he will probably not recognize it and assume that they are speaking Chinese. If Whinnom's observation on the present function of pidgins is valid and general (cf. the analogous situation described by Wolfers for Neo-Melanesian), it suggests that two languages in contact can result in an interlingual improvisation like those described by Hall, but that more than two languages in contact are required for the birth of a true pidgin. The common people who are to be the pidgin speakers must come from two or more different and mutually unintelligible language backgrounds, and there must also be a dominant (and usually alien) language which supplies much of the vocabulary. (Cf. now Reinecke 1969 on immigrant labourers for the sugar plantations, especially Portuguese, after the Reciprocity Act of 1876, as precipitating crystallization of a pidgin-creole out of what had been a bilingual situation (Hawaiian, English) with makeshift intermediary forms (hapa haole, 'half-white').)

During the 1950s several scholars became increasingly dissatisfied with polygenetic theories. In 1951 Navarro Tomás argued that Papiamento was not an indigenous Caribbean blend of Portuguese and/or Spanish with African elements, but rather had its origin in the Portuguese pidgin used as a trade jargon in West Africa during the slave trade. He was by no means the first to point out the key importance of Portuguese in the history of pidgin-creole. Schuchardt had stressed the role of Portuguese, and Hesseling had seen it as the origin of both Afrikaans and Negerhollands. Hesseling's theory was violently opposed in the Union of South Africa on political grounds, however, and even the 1923 reprinting of his *Het Afrikaans*, though it stirred considerable controversy, did not succeed in establishing the theory of Portuguese origin (Valkhoff 1960). In the 1950s, however, the theory won many converts. In 1956 Keith Whinnom proved that four Spanish creoles of the Philippines were not independent developments, but had all diverged from a common source in the Moluccas, and that underlying these Spanish creoles was a Portuguese pidgin very similar to that of Goa in India (Whinnom 1956, 1965).

This Portuguese pidgin during the sixteenth century replaced Arabic and Malay as the trade language of the Far East. It was used by traders of all nationalities, from India to Indonesia and as far north as Japan. It became clear that the Asian Spanish creoles were not simply 'restructured' Spanish, but rather were Portuguese pidgin 'relexified' under later Spanish influences. And when arguments were later presented that the Chinese elements in pidgin English might be only secondary and that pidgin English was very possibly also a relexification of pidgin Portuguese, the case was then indeed strong for monogenesis of all the Far Eastern pidgins and creoles (Whinnom 1965:519–221; according to one eighteenth-century account cited by Whinnom in a private communication, the earliest pidgin English in use in China was a 'broken and mixed dialect of Portuguese and English'.

In the Caribbean, Douglas Taylor (1956, 1957, 1960, 1961) emphasized the similarities among the Caribbean creoles and their many parallels with the creoles of the Far East, and suggested that both Papiamento and Sranan were also relexifications of pidgin Portuguese. R. W. Thompson (1961) argued for a parallel development of all the pidgins and creoles, Caribbean, African and Far Eastern, from Portuguese sources (see also Cassidy 1962). William Stewart (1962) discussed the functions of structure and lexicon in linguistic relationships and concluded that the divergent relexification (i.e. a wholesale shift of vocabulary) of a single proto-pidgin was a more tenable hypothesis than the convergent restructuring of a whole group of separate languages. (The theory has since been supported with regard to Spanish-based creoles by Granda (1968a).) And Whinnom (1965:522–7) then suggested that Sabir, the famous Lingua Franca of the Mediterranean, was the proto-creole, the source of all the European-based pidgins and creoles of the world. Sabir is as least as old as the Crusades; texts survive from the early sixteenth century; the language became moribund after the French conquest of North Africa but was still alive when it was described by Schuchardt in 1909. Though its vocabulary was drawn from almost every language in the Mediterranean, the proportions of the mixture varied from place to place. It is very possible that a predominantly Portuguese version of Sabir (or a Portuguese relexification of it) was indeed that pidgin which in the sixteenth century was carried to the Far East, where it developed into the Portuguese and so-called Spanish creoles and perhaps also pidgin English, and was carried to West Africa, where its creole descendant is still spoken on Cape Verde and other islands, and thence to the New World, where it formed the basis not only of Papiamento but also of the English, French, and Dutch creoles.

Historical linguistics and pidgin-creole studies

The supporters of monogenesis would thus have us think of Anglicized creole rather than creolized English. As yet, the theory rests on many assumptions and very little documentary evidence, but it has a great deal to recommend it. Even if we were to assume that the lexicon and the structure of a language were equally susceptible to change, relexification would still be a better explanation than restructuralization for the development of pidgins and creoles; for the influences which could bring about a wholesale adoption of French vocabulary in French territories, English vocabulary in British territories, etc., are clear and obvious, whereas there is no known sociolinguistic influence which could explain why the structures of five different European languages should have been modified in precisely the same direction (for further discussion of the problems of convergent development and genetic relationship, see Weinreich 1958).

The weaknesses in the monogenetic theory are first a very sketchy historical documentation, second the controversial status of Far Eastern pidgin English (which lacks many of the features shared by other pidgins and creoles), and third the problem of certain pidgins and creoles which clearly developed without any direct Portuguese influence; these include not only the non-European-based pidgins like Sango and Chinook, but also some of the European-based like Pitcairnese and Amerindian pidgin English. At least some of these were certainly independent creations, and probably no monogenetic theory will ever account for absolutely all the pidgins of the world. Hall's theory of spontaneous generation indeed must apply to some cases, though the area of applicability has dwindled as a result of the research of the past decade. It is significant that the non-European-based pidgins are very different in structure from the European-based, much more complex and lacking even the typological features common to the European-based pidgins. Creoles such as Pitcairnese which had no direct Portuguese influences yet share many common creole characteristics, may have arisen by stimulus diffusion rather than by either direct descent or totally independent creation. If a person with even a casual familiarity with any form of pidgin participates in the spontaneous creation of a new pidgin, the resulting language will not be a random improvisation but will inevitably be influenced by the pattern of the pidgin already known. If an American tourist in Mexico has previously learned pidgin English in the Far East, his interlingual improvization with a Mexican taxi driver will be influenced by it. It is probable that many of the English speakers who participated in the development of Pitcairnese and Hawaiian English had already had some contact with other pidgins.

No theory yet proposed can fully account for the special similarities between some creoles. The English creoles of Jamaica and Trinidad (on equivalent socio-economic levels) are mutually intelligible and are remarkably similar to Sierra Leone Krio in Africa. Saramaccan (in Surinam) is markedly different, however, and is perhaps more similar to Cameroun creole. This might indicate only that more conservative varieties of creole have survived in Surinam and the Camerouns (some of the very old and isolated speakers in Jamaica might then be the link between the two English creole types), or it might indicate a dual origin for Atlantic English creole, with a significant difference in African provenience. Studies of Kongo etymologies in Saramaccan carried on by Jan Daeleman of Louvanium University in the Congo (see his report in this volume) may help to decide this issue. Among those who dispute the Sabir monogenetic hypothesis are Mervyn Alleyne (1968) and Ian Hancock (1968), who have applied the traditional methods of comparative reconstruction to the English creoles and suggest an Eastern Caribbean origin.

Apparently the rate of linguistic change for a pidgin-creole may change greatly from time to time. The almost total relexification of a pidgin or the extensive structural and lexical expansion which accompanies creolization may take place within a few decades. The rapid growth of Bahasa Indonesia as the Indonesian national language is by no means a unique phenomenon resulting from modern linguistic engineering. The total evolution of the Caribbean French creoles, for example, took place almost entirely within the first half century of French settlement there (Jourdain 1956). The English creoles of Surinam developed within one generation (Voorhoeve 1962). (So also apparently did the Hawaiian pidgin-creole English (Reinecke 1969:166).) This fact casts considerable doubt on the reliability of basic vocabulary and *a fortiori*, glottochronology, for sub-grouping related languages, if there is no way of knowing whether a language of unknown history has ever passed through the pidgin-creole cycle and thus been subject to these enormously accelerated changes (Hall 1959). If Jamaican English and Haitian French are indeed genetically related through a common pidgin ancestor, the time depth must be less than four hundred years, but normal estimates of rate of lexical change would enormously exaggerate this figure, given the great divergence in their vocabularies. For this reason, ethnolinguists such as Dell Hymes (1959) give high priority to the search for typological characteristics (either linguistic or sociocultural) of a creole or post-creole language, so that one might determine whether a pidgin-creole cycle with its accelerated changes has been a part of the history of any given language. (Cf. Southworth in this volume on possible linguistic criteria, Whinnom, Mintz and Joos in this volume on linguistic and sociological conditions, and cf. Diebold 1961 on the necessarily sociological basis for absence of Indian-Spanish pidgins in Mexico (1954:503).) At present, however, there is no certain way of identifying as a creole a language whose history is unknown.

Sociolinguistics and pidgin-creole studies

Once a pidgin has been created or imported into a community, its continued survival and its evolution toward creole status and beyond both depend primarily on its role in the society, not on its inherent structure. The drastically limited vocabulary and syntactic devices of a pidgin need not in themselves lessen the chance of survival – though they may condition adverse social prejudices which can indeed threaten its survival – in so far as any pidgin is capable of expansion whenever changing social conditions call on it to perform a role greater than minimal interlingual communication, just as

B

any 'dialect' or language is inherently capable of expanding its vocabulary to become a national cultural language when the need arises. The limited resources of a pidgin will be the very cause of its survival if the need for a minimal pidgin persists in the community. Sango has outlived and largely replaced the language from which it took its name (Samarin 1967). Pidgin English is indeed limited, yet it has survived for centuries, and one variety, Neo-Melanesian, was even given official status under the German rule and may now be about to become a national language (Hall 1966:11; cf. Wurm 1966; Wolfers, this volume). On the other hand Negerhollands, a creole so 'developed' that it boasts a translation of the Bible, is now nearly extinct; and of course many 'normal' languages, including culture languages, have become extinct.

If the interlingual situation which first brought a pidgin into a community remains unchanged, the pidgin will normally also remain, and with very little change. If not, then its subsequent development depends mainly on two factors: the social status of the pidgin *vis à vis* the standard language of the community, and the variability of both the language and the culture. A pidgin or creole almost invariably has low social status. If the equivalent European language is also the standard language of the community, the creole is especially unlikely to be granted status as a real language. Rather it is thought of as merely a barbarous corruption of the standard language. In Jamaica, for example, most educators persist in treating the 'dialect problem' as if it were a problem of speech correction, attributing it to careless, slovenly pronunciation. The few exceptional teachers who see it as a foreign-language problem (or a quasi-foreign-language problem) are considered dangerously radical by many Jamaicans. The creole is inseparably associated with poverty, ignorance, and lack of moral character. This association is, of course, a half truth for the poor, the uneducated, and the unambitious do speak the broader varieties of creole, whereas the bright young boy with a chance at education and a white-collar job strives diligently to acquire the Kingston middle-class standard. However it is the social prejudice against creole which is partially responsible for continued poverty, ignorance, and lack of ambition. The overwhelming majority of the population are told every day of their lives that they will never amount to anything because they 'talk like Quashie', and the nouveau-rich middle class lead lives of desperate linguistic anxiety, loudly proclaiming the superiority of their own 'standard' English while nursing inward doubts about whether their English is really sufficiently standard. The written compositions of schoolchildren are dull and vapid because the children are so fearful of lapsing into their native creole that they cannot express themselves freely. (Similar cases are found as between standard and dialect in, for example, England. Figueroa and Craig in this volume broach some of the educational problems.) Some middle-class speakers become almost inarticulate in the presence of anyone of higher social status.

Similar situations occur in other creole areas (Hall 1955: ch. 3; Efron 1954). Relative status in a creole society is not always a simple two-valued system. In some areas, e.g. Sierra Leone (Berry 1961:5 note), a nationalist reaction against the oppressive corrective pressures from the standard language results in 'hyper-creolization', an aggressive assertion of linguistic discreteness and superior status for creole. Hyper-creolization is usually limited to small dissident groups, however, and an attitude of mutual tolerance is even more rare. Church Creole in Surinam originated in the use of Sranan by Moravian missionaries in the eighteenth century and later gained acceptance for use in many formal secular situations, inferior to Dutch in status but superior to common Sranan. Ironically it is a hyper-creolization movement which is now threatening Church Creole with extinction (Voorhoeve 1968). A pidgin which is developed by elites for interlingual communication of limited duration and in prestigious circumstances, e.g. university students at an international conference or expert technicians working with foreign counterparts in a foreign aid program, may enjoy high status within that in-group; it may even function as what Malinowski calls 'phatic communion', with members proudly using it at later reunions as a nostalgic assertion of membership (J. S. Goodman 1967). Such a pidgin is not valued by the larger community outside the elite in-group, however, and is usually short lived. With very few exceptions, every pidgin, and often a creole, must survive despite the diffidence of its speakers and hostile invective from the authorities. One of the difficulties in doing fieldwork in creole is the fact that a creole speaker who also speaks the standard is usually offended if anyone speaks to him in creole, and that one who is not offended may yet conceal the depth of the creole he knows (cf. Reisman 1968).

As we have seen, pidgins and creoles are capable of sudden and massive changes, especially in vocabulary. Their degree of divergent development and consequent variability is therefore potentially very great. Their variability is the result of social forces, however, not their inherent structures or their mixed origins, for some are far more uniform than others. The French creoles of the Caribbean and of the Indian Ocean are all mutually intelligible. Within each community the French creole is also quite uniform and contrasts sharply with standard French. In fact a speaker's shift from the creole to the mutually unintelligible standard French is much like a shift to a totally foreign language, a situation known as 'diglossia' (Ferguson 1959). The Spanish and Portuguese creoles are also relatively uniform (though not mutually intelligible) and in sharp contrast with the standard languages, though few of them now co-exist in a community with standard Spanish or Portuguese. English creoles, however, are extremely variable. Even the two principal varieties in Surinam (Sranan, Saramaccan) are mutually unintelligible and unintelligible to speakers of other English creoles.

Isolation from the unifying effect of the standard language has been sug-

gested as one cause of this variability. Most creole French areas have long had
contact with France and standard French, whereas the official language of
Surinam has been Dutch since 1667. Grenada, however, has been in British
hands for two centuries, yet the creole French there is not substantially
different from that spoken on islands which have always been under French
rule. And the extreme varieties of Jamaican English are mutually unintelligible
even though English has been the only official language since the Spaniards
were all evicted in 1655. A mere change of official language probably has
relatively little immediate effect on a pidgin or creole. The development of a
rigid caste system in the formative years of most (perhaps all) creole societies
minimized European influences except for vocabulary. This supports Stewart's
relexification hypothesis (1962), for lexical borrowing probably does not
require so intimate a contact as does phonological or syntactic influence. In
such cases it is not the function of a pidgin or creole to bridge the gap between
the social castes, as Hall has claimed. Rather, it is to provide a stable medium
for communication between members of the subordinate caste (Whinnom
1968). Although this communication takes place within a society dominated
by the higher caste, the pidgin-creole is not necessarily spoken by the elites,
nor is the standard language spoken or even frequently heard by the lower
caste. A rigid system of caste isolation is more likely to unify than to diversify
a pidgin-creole. It is significant that the linguistic diversification of Jamaica
is largely the result of increased, not decreased, influence of standard English
and that this resulted from the breakdown, not the development, of caste
isolation.

Let me exemplify these problems from the situation I know best. In
Jamaica, linguistic diversification now operates in two dimensions. First,
there is geographical dialect variation, especially in vocabulary, with many
localisms totally unknown even in adjacent villages. As in Surinam, this
resulted from barriers to communication in the formative years: lack of
adequate roads, the dense forests of Surinam and the rugged mountains of
Jamaica, and the development of a plantation system which discouraged or
prohibited creole speakers from traveling (Voorhoeve 1962: 234–7; DeCamp
1961:61–3). Second, and apparently unlike Surinam, there is also a socio-
economically-oriented linguistic continuum in Jamaica, a continuous spectrum
of speech varieties whose extremes are mutually unintelligible but which also
includes all possible intermediate varieties (Le Page 1957–8:380; Le Page
and DeCamp 1960:116–17; DeCamp 1961:80–4). At one end of this continuum is the speech of highly-educated Jamaican leaders, many of whom
claim to be speaking standard British English but who are actually using what
seems to be evolving into a standard Jamaican English; it is mutually intelligible with but undeniably different from standard British. At the other
extreme is the so-called 'broad creole' or 'broken language', the variety which

so far has received the most attention from linguists (e.g. Cassidy 1961, 1962; B. Bailey 1966; Cassidy and Le Page 1967). Each Jamaican speaker commands a span of this continuum, the breadth of the span depending on the breadth of his social activities; a labor leader, for example, can command a greater span of varieties than can a sheltered housewife of suburban middle class. A housewife may make a limited adjustment downward on the continuum in order to communicate with a market woman, and the market woman may adjust upward when she talks to the housewife. Each of them may then believe that she is speaking the other's language, for the myth persists in Jamaica that there are only two varieties of language – standard English and 'the dialect' – but the fact is that the housewife's broadest dialect may be closer to the standard end of the spectrum than is the market woman's 'standard'.

Because of this lack of clear separation between speech varieties, some writers have called Jamaican English an English dialect system rather than a true creole (Stewart 1962:50–1; Taylor 1963; Alleyne 1967). Stewart went so far as to make a clear separation from standard, i.e. a structural gap between the two at some point, a defining criterion of a creole. This seems unjustifiably arbitrary, however, and if, as some creolists believe (e.g. Reinecke and Tokimasa 1934; Tsuzaki 1968a, 1968b), continuing corrective pressures from schools and other institutions can turn any creole community into a dialect continuum, then we have in Jamaica only a creole in a late stage of development, comparable to the creole English of Hawaii. Whenever a term is needed to distinguish the kind of situation in Jamaica from that in Surinam and Haiti, then I would speak of a *post-creole* community. Hawaii, the Gullah areas, and the other British West Indies (British Honduras, Guyana, Trinidad, Barbados, etc.) are probably also post-creole areas.

It would appear that a speech community can reach post-creole status only under two conditions. First, the dominant official language must be the same as the creole vocabulary base; if it is different, then the creole either persists as a separate language with little change (e.g. the English creoles of Surinam and the French creole of St Lucia and Grenada) or becomes extinct, as Negerhollands is now doing. Second, the social system, though perhaps still sharply stratified, must provide for sufficient social mobility and sufficient corrective pressures from above in order for the standard language to exert real influence on creole speakers; otherwise the creole and the standard remain sharply separated as they do in the French areas. These corrective pressures (radio, television, internal migration, education, etc.) do not operate uniformly on all speakers, of course; otherwise the result would be a merger of the creole with the standard rather than a continuum. Rather the educational and occupational opportunities and the necessity of learning a more nearly standard variety of English in order to get a better job all act on individual speakers, pulling them in differing degrees toward the standard end of the continuum.

Both the creole diglossia and the post-creole continuum require further study. Even in Haiti, which has been the most extensively reported of the French creole areas, the functional distribution of standard and creole French is so complex that it is by no means understood (Efron 1954; Stewart 1963; Valdman 1968). The simple statement that standard French dominates creole in a relation of diglossia does not begin to describe the complex factors which determine which language will be used in a given situation. Similar complexity in the choice of language has been reported from Surinam (Eersel 1968). Karl Reisman (1968) has examined the linguistic values of an Antiguan village in terms of cultural values and reports a complex of interrelationships that no one had expected on a small island. My own linguistic and cultural survey of 142 Jamaican communities (in preparation) has provided a rough outline of the geographic and socio-economic patterns of linguistic diversity, but much more needs to be studied, especially the cultural functions of language in the Jamaican speech continuum. Few creolists have been adequately trained in sociology or anthropology and, until recently, few sociologists and anthropologists were interested in the linguistic problems of creole areas. Consequently we hear debates on Parsonian equilibrium versus Furnivall's pluralism as a theoretical model of West Indian society (Smith 1965), yet neither we linguists nor the sociologists really know the relevance of creole language studies to such questions. We need carefully controlled experiments to determine the linguistic behavior of both groups and individuals under varying circumstances (e.g. experiments of the type reported by Labov 1966). The political implications of a linguistic continuum have received almost no attention: Alleyne (1963) has published one paper on the sociolinguistic factors in a Jamaican election, and I included a few questions on political attitudes in my linguistic survey. It is clear, however, that a command of the creole can be an asset to a politician. The phenomenal political success of one Jamaican leader is at least partially due to his conscious and successful efforts to learn the speech and the social mores of the people in his slum constituency; despite his white middle-class background, he is able to talk with the people, not at them. It is worth noting that before entering politics he had been a publishing scholar in anthropology. Finally, although the problems of multilingualism in newly-emerging nations have drawn the attention of linguists (e.g. Symposium 1964; Le Page 1964; Wurm 1966), the relationships between creole diversity and emergent nationalism are largely unexplored.

Descriptive linguistics and pidgin-creole studies

Allusions, travelers' accounts, and even fragmentary texts of pidgins date back to the middle ages. Historians in the eighteenth century 'described' the Caribbean creoles. But such early accounts were generally limited to invectives and parodies, providing little information beyond the fact that the author had contempt for the pidgin or creole. Objective description began in the later nineteenth century. In 1868 Russell published the first reliable and extensive account of Jamaican Creole. In 1869 Thomas did the same for the French creole of Trinidad. In the 1880s and 90s there appeared many scholarly accounts of pidgins and creoles from all over the world, including Louisiana, the Virgin Islands, Mauritius, and Melanesia (see the bibliography in Hall 1966:163–77).

The greatest of these early scholars and the undisputed father of pidgin-creole studies was Hugo Schuchardt (1842–1927). This remarkable man, perhaps more generally known for his contributions to Romance philology and to Basque studies, published dozens of papers on a great variety of pidgin and creole languages, including his nine *Kreolische Studien* (a good sample of this work is conveniently available in the *Schuchardt Brevier* 1928 edited by Leo Spitzer). Schuchardt, basically an historical philologist, was a leader of the opposition against the Leipzig school of 'neo-grammarians', who had adopted a 'family tree' model of language classification and held that every language had genetically descended from its ancestors on the family tree by means of deterministic sound changes, changes which could be formulated into 'laws' which operated without exception. Like many linguists to follow him (e.g. Weinreich 1958), Schuchardt found in pidgin-creole good ammunition against the neo-grammarian or any other simple genetic system of classification. Some creoles, he pointed out, have completely changed their affiliation (e.g. from Portuguese to Dutch), and others are so mixed as to defy classification. It was Schuchardt who associated the term 'Mischsprache' with pidgin-creole, a term which was later to be so often misinterpreted as a macaronic blend, a mish-mash with no real structure of its own.

After the turn of the century, the neo-grammarian controversy abated, and the number of studies of pidgin-creole languages also dwindled. The historical philologists lost interest in them, and, until World War II they were generally ignored by the new structural linguists, most of whom professed more interest in 'real' languages than in odd dialects (there were, of course, notable exceptions, e.g. Jacobs 1932 and Boas 1933 on Chinook Jargon, and Reinecke and Tokimasa 1934 on Hawaiian English). The war brought a change of attitude, however, and there soon appeared structural descriptions of Melanesian Pidgin, of Taki-Taki (Sranan) in Surinam (Hall 1948), of Gullah (Turner 1949), of Haitian creole (Hall 1953), and of pidgin English (Hall 1955); and Taylor published two structural sketches of 'Caribbean creole' (1947, 1951; the progress during the 1940s and 1950s is summarized in Cassidy 1959).

In the past decade pidgin-creole studies have become respectable and the research has intensified. For Jamaica alone we now have a structural sketch (Le Page 1957–8), a generative syntax (B. Bailey 1966), a set of edited texts in phonemic transcription (Le Page and DeCamp 1960:125–79), an account of the cultural setting of the language (Cassidy 1961), a major historical dictionary (Cassidy and Le Page 1967), and an attempt at a description of the highly complex suprasegmental phenomena (Lawton 1963). The Cassidy-Le Page dictionary is particularly notable; containing more than fifteen thousand entries, it is a Jamaican supplement to the *Oxford English Dictionary* comparable in scope and in scholarship to the *Dictionary of American English*. A beginning has been made in linguistic geography in the British Caribbean generally (Le Page 1957–8), in Jamaica (DeCamp 1961), and in the creole French areas (M. Goodman 1964). The recognition that creoles are genuine languages has stimulated efforts in applied linguistics. Peace Corps language training materials have been prepared for Jamaican Creole (Bailey 1962; Lawton 1964) and Sierra Leone (Krio manual 1964), and the first part of a modern programmed course in Haitian creole French is now available (Valdman 1967). In 1964 a conference of linguists and educators was held in Jamaica (for the proceedings, see Faculty of Education 1965) to summarize and attempt to apply the results of creole research to the many special problems of language teaching in the West Indies. Research was presented there which proved conclusively that the inability of West Indian schoolchildren to express themselves adequately in the standard language is at least partly a foreign language problem, not merely cultural deprivation.

Bailey's *Jamaican Creole Syntax* (1966) is the first major transformational attempt on a creole (preceded only by a few somewhat transformationally oriented articles: Voorhoeve 1961a; DeCamp 1962, 1963) and is the most extensive syntactic study to appear so far. Although it is based on the pre-1960 formulation of generative theory and therefore sometimes seems unnecessarily cumbersome and complex, this book, like the Cassidy-Le Page dictionary, provides a badly needed 'ideal-type' description of creole, i.e. the language described is a composite of all the non-standard features in the continuum. More recently, Bailey has been working on a technique for classifying speech varieties on the continuum in terms of number of deviant rules (Bailey 1968).

Other linguists have also been working on the problems of applying generative theory to the linguistic diversity of creole or post-creole communities. I have demonstrated that any linear speech continuum such as that in Jamaica is subject to Guttman scalogram analysis. The cutting points in this analysis can then be used as a schema of variable features in a generative grammar, thus permitting a single set of rules to characterize simultaneously all of the speech varieties in the continuum (DeCamp 1968, 1969). Charles-James

Bailey (1969) has now extended this approach to the more general problem of characterizing all the dialect variants of a language, and Labov (1968) has worked out a set of variable rules to account for copula-deletion in nonstandard Negro English, a feature which was probably inherited from creole.

Concluding note

As pidgin-creole studies have grown and matured, they have been extended into areas whose relevance has only recently been discovered. Many sociolinguists now see in American Negro English a linguistic continuum similar to that in the West Indies, and some even hold that both are only parts of a general New World Negro linguistic and cultural continuum, with standard English (British or American) at one end, and at the other something like Bailey's ideal-type creole. If American Negro English is indeed a creole with varying degrees of acculturation to standard English, rather than a divergent dialect with varying degrees of deviance from standard English, the social and political implications will be great indeed. The Negro will then be sociolinguistically comparable to the Chicano, who is also approaching the general Anglo-American linguistic and cultural norms but who has long been aware that his 'other heritage' includes a respectable language and culture, Spanish. The black nationalist movement in the United States has told the Negro that he is 'black and beautiful' and has tried to give him pride in his heritage. Until now, language has not been included as an aspect of that heritage. If the creole-origin hypothesis for Negro English is confirmed and if the Negro, like the Chicano, really does have a genuine linguistic heritage rather than merely a substandard deviant dialect of English, a great many people, both black and white, will have to revise drastically their attitudes toward Negro English. At the Center for Applied Linguistics and at several other research centers, creolists are now engaged in the task of verifying and documenting this hypothesis (Dillard 1968; Stewart 1967, 1968). Until recently, pidgin-creole studies were often considered only a whimsical and useless hobby, not to be taken very seriously. Their significance to general linguistics, anthropology, and sociology has now been established. The issues raised by creolists working on American Negro English now give to pidgin-creole studies a practical and topical relevance which was inconceivable only a decade ago.

REFERENCES

Alleyne, Mervyn 1963. 'Communication and politics in Jamaica', *Caribbean Studies* 3:22–61
  1967. 'Review of *Jamaican Creole syntax*, by Beryl L. Bailey', *Caribbean Studies* 6:92–4

[1968]. 'The cultural matrix of Caribbean dialects', Mona, Creole Conference paper. [Revised version, this volume]

Bailey, Beryl L. 1962. *A language guide to Jamaica*, New York, Research Institute for the Study of Man

1966. *Jamaican Creole syntax: a transformational approach*, Cambridge, Cambridge University Press

[1968]. 'Jamaican Creole: Can dialect boundaries be defined?' Mona, Creole Conference Paper. [Revised version, this volume]

Bailey, Charles-James N. 1969. 'The integration of linguistic theory: internal reconstruction and the comparative method in descriptive linguistics', *Working Papers in Linguistics*, 2, Honolulu, University of Hawaii, Department of Linguistics

Berry, Jack 1961. 'English loanwords and adaptations in Sierra Leone Krio', in Le Page (ed.), *Proceedings*, pp. 1–16

1962. 'Pidgins and creoles in Africa', in [Symposium], pp. 219–25

Bloomfield, Leonard 1933. *Language*, New York, Holt

Boas, Franz 1933. 'Note on the Chinook jargon', *Language* 9:208–13

Brinton, D. G. 1889. *Aims and traits of a world language*, New York

Carr, Elizabeth 1962. 'Bilingual speakers in Hawaii today', *Social Process in Hawaii* 25:53–7

Cassidy, F. G. 1959. 'English language studies in the Caribbean', *American Speech* 34:163–71

1961. *Jamaica talk: three hundred years of the English language in Jamaica*, London, Macmillan

1962. 'Toward the recovery of early English–African pidgin', in [Symposium], pp. 267–77

Cassidy, F. G. and R. B. Le Page 1967. *Dictionary of Jamaican English*, Cambridge, Cambridge University Press

Curtin, Philip 1969. *The Atlantic slave trade. A census*, Madison, University of Wisconsin Press

DeCamp, David 1961. 'Social and geographical factors in Jamaican dialects', in Le Page (ed.), *Proceedings*, pp. 61–84

1962. 'Creole language areas considered as multilingual communities', in [Symposium], pp. 227–31

1963. 'Review of *Jamaica Talk*, by F. G. Cassidy', *Language* 39:536–44

[1968]. 'Toward a generative analysis of a post-creole speech continuum', Mona, Creole Conference paper. [Revised version, this volume]

1969. 'Diasystem versus overall pattern: the Jamaican syllabic nuclei', in *Studies in the language, literature, and culture of the Middle Ages and later*, Austin, Texas, University of Texas Press

Diebold, A. Richard 1961. 'Incipient bilingualism', *Language* 37:97–112. (Reprinted in Hymes 1964:495–506)

Dillard, J. L. 1964. 'The writings of Herskovits and the study of the languages of the Negro in the New World', *Caribbean Studies* 4(2):35–41

1968. 'The creolist and the study of Negro non-standard dialects in the continental United States', Mona, Creole Conference paper. [Revised version, this volume]

Edwards, Jay [1968]. 'Social linguistics on San Andres and Providencia islands', unpublished research report presented to the annual meeting of the American Anthropological Society, Seattle

Eersel, Christian [1968]. 'Questions of prestige in language choice in a multilingual setting', Mona, Creole Conference paper. [Précis, this volume]

Efron, E. 1954. 'French and creole patois in Haiti', *Caribbean Quarterly* 3:199–214

[Faculty of Education] 1965. *Language teaching, linguistics and the teaching of English in a multilingual society*, Kingston, Jamaica, University of the West Indies

Ferguson, Charles A. 1959. 'Diglossia', *Word* 15:325–40, reprinted in Hymes 1964:429–39

Fishman, Joshua A. (ed.) 1968. *Readings in the sociology of language*, The Hague, Mouton

Frake, Charles O. 1968. 'Lexical origins and semantic structure in Philippine Creole Spanish', Mona, Creole Conference paper. [Revised version, this volume]

Göbl-Galdi, L. 1934. 'Esquisse de la structure grammaticale des patios français-creoles', *Zeitschrift für französische Sprache und Literatur* 58:257–95

Goodman, Morris 1964. *A comparative study of creole French dialects*, The Hague, Mouton

[1968]. 'The strange case of Mbugu', Mona, Creole Conference paper. [Revised version, this volume]

Goodman, John Stuart 1967. 'The development of a dialect of English-Japanese pidgin', *Anthropological Linguistics* 9:43–55

Granda, German de 1968a. 'La tipologia "criolla" de dos hablos del area lingüistica hispánica', *Thesaurus* 23:3–15, Bogota, Instituto Caro y Cuervo

1968b. 'Sobre el estudio de las hablas "criollas" en el area hispanica', *Thesaurus* 23:64–74

Grant, Rena V. 1945. 'Chinook jargon', *International Journal of American Linguistics* 11:225–33

Gumperz, John, and Dell Hymes (eds.) 1964. 'The ethnography of communication' (*American Anthropologist* 66(6), Part 2), Washington, D.C., American Anthropological Association

Hall, Robert A., Jr. 1948. 'The linguistic structure of Taki-Taki', *Language* 24:92–116

1950. 'The genetic relationships of Haitian Creole', *Ricerche Linguistique* 1:194–203

1953. 'Haitian Creole: grammar, texts, vocabulary' (American Anthropological Association, *Memoir* 74), Washington, D.C.

1955. *Hands off Pidgin English!* Sydney, Pacific Publications

1958. 'Creole languages and genetic relationships', *Word* 14:367–73

1959. 'Neo-Melanesian and glottochronology', *International Journal of American Linguistics* 25:265–7

1962. 'The life cycle of pidgin languages', *Lingua* 11:151–6

1966. *Pidgin and creole languages*, Ithaca, Cornell University Press

1968. 'Creole linguistics', *Ibero-American and Caribbean linguistics*, ed. by T. A. Sebeok *et al.*, 361–71 (Current Trends in linguistics, 4), The Hague, Mouton

Hancock, Ian F. 1968. 'A provisional comparison of the English-based Atlantic creoles, with accompanying word-lists', Mona, Creole Conference paper. [Précis, this volume]

Haugen, Einar 1956. *Bilingualism in the Americas: a bibliography and research guide* (American Dialect Society, Publication 26), University, Alabama, University of Alabama Press

Herskovits, M. J. 1936. *Suriname folk-lore*, New York

Hesseling, Dirk C. 1905. *Het Negerhollands van de Deense Antillan. Bijdrage tot de geschiedenis der Nederlandse taal in Amerika*, Leiden

1923. *Het Afrikaans; Bijdrage tot de geschiedenis der Nederlandse taal in Zuid-Afrika*, 2nd ed., Leiden

Hjelmslev, Louis 1939. 'Caractères grammaticaux des langues créoles', Congrès international des sciences anthropologiques et ethnologiques, compte rendu de la 2ᵉ session, Copenhagen

Hockett, C. F. 1958. *A course in modern linguistics*, New York, Macmillan

Hymes, Dell 1959. 'Genetic relationship: retrospect and prospect', *Anthropological Linguistics* 1(2):50–66

(ed.) 1964. *Language in culture and society*, New York, Harper and Row

Jacobs, Melville 1932. 'Notes on the structure of Chinook Jargon', *Language* 8:27–50

1936. *Texts in Chinook jargon* (University of Washington Publications in Anthropology 7(1):1–27), Seattle

Jernudd, Bjorn H. 1969. 'Social change and aboriginal speech variation in Australia', *Working papers in Linguistics* 4:145–68, Honolulu, University of Hawaii, Department of Linguistics

Jespersen, Otto 1922. *Language, its nature, development and origin*, London, Allen and Unwin

Jourdain, Elodie 1956. *Du français aux parlers créoles*, Paris

Kaufman, Terence [1968]. 'Chinook jargon vocabulary with grammatical notes', unpublished

Kleinecke, David 1959. 'An etymology for "pidgin"', *International Journal of American Linguistics* 25:271–2

[Krio Manual] 1964. *Introductory Krio language training manual*, Bloomington, Indiana, Sierra Leone Peace Corps training project

Labov, William 1966. *The social stratification of English in New York City*, Washington, D.C., Center for Applied Linguistics

[1968]. 'Contraction, deletion, and inherent variability of the English copula', unpublished

[Languages of the World] 1964. 'Ibero-Caucasian and Pidgin-Creole', fascicle one, *Anthropological Linguistics* 6, No. 8

Lawton, David L. 1963. 'Suprasegmental phenomena in Jamaican Creole', unpublished doctoral dissertation, Michigan State University

1964. 'Some problems of teaching a creolized language to Peace Corps members', *Language Learning* 14:11–19

Le Page, Robert B. 1957–8. 'General outlines of creole English dialects in the British Caribbean', *Orbis* 6:373–91, 7:54–64

(ed.) 1961. *Proceedings of the conference on creole language studies* (1959), (Creole Language Studies 2), London, Macmillan

1964. *The national language question: linguistic problems of newly independent states*, London, Institute of Race Relations

Le Page, Robert B. and David DeCamp 1960. *Jamaican Creole* (Creole Language Studies 1), London, Macmillan

Leachman, D. and Robert A. Hall, Jr. 1955. 'American Indian pidgin English: attestations and grammatical peculiarities', *American Speech* 30:163–71

Navarro Tomás, T. 1951. 'Observaciones sobre el papiamento', *Nueva revista de filología hispánica* 7:183–9

Polomé, Edgar [1968]. 'The Katanga Swahili Creole', Mona, Creole Conference paper

Reinecke, John 1937. 'Marginal languages: a sociological survey of the Creole languages and trade jargons', unpublished Ph.D. dissertation, Yale University

1938. 'Trade jargons and creole dialects as marginal languages', *Social Forces* 17:107–18. [Reprinted in Hymes 1964:534–546]

1969. *Language and dialect in Hawaii. A sociolinguistic history to 1935*, Honolulu, University of Hawaii Press

Reinecke, John, and Aiko Tokimasa 1934. 'The English dialect of Hawaii', *American Speech* 9:48–58, 122–31

Reinecke, John E. and Stanley M. Tsuzaki 1967. 'Hawaiian loanwords in Hawaiian English of the 1930's', *Oceanic Linguistics*, 6(2):80–115

Reisman, Karl [1968]. 'Linguistic values and cultural values in an Antiguan village', Mona, Creole Conference paper. [Précis, this volume]

Rice, Frank A. (ed.) 1962. *Study of the role of second languages in Asia, Africa, and Latin America*, Washington, Center for Applied Linguistics

Richardson, Irvine 1961. 'Some observations on the status of Town Bemba in Northern Rhodesia', *African Language Studies* 2:25–36

1963a. 'Evolutionary factors in Mauritian Creole', *Journal of African Languages* 2(1):2–14

1963b. 'Examples of deviation and innovation in Bemba', *African Language Studies* 4:129–45

Ross, Alan S. C. 1962. 'On the historical study of pidgins', in [Symposium], pp. 243–9

Ross, Alan S. C. and A. W. Moverley 1964. *The Pitcairnese language*, London, Deutsch

Russell, Thomas 1868. *The etymology of Jamaica grammar*, Kingston, Jamaica

Samarin, William J. 1962. 'Lingua francas, with special reference to Africa', in Frank A. Rice (ed.), *Study of the role of second languages*, pp. 54–64. [Revised, expanded, and reprinted in Fishman 1968:660–72]

1967. *A grammar of Sango*, The Hague, Mouton

Schuchardt, Hugo 1909. 'Die Lingua franca', *Zeitschrift für romanische Philologie* 33:441–61

1928. *Schuchardt-Brevier: Ein Vademecum der allgemeinen Sprachwissenschaft*, ed. Leo Spitzer, 2nd edn., Halle, Niemeyer

Smith, M. G. 1965. *The plural society in the British West Indies*, Berkeley, California, University of California Press

Southworth, Franklin [1968]. 'Prior pidginization: an analysis of criteria and the historical origins of Marathi', Mona, Creole Conference paper. [Revised version this volume]

Stewart, William A. 1962. 'Creole languages in the Caribbean', *Study of the role of second languages in Asia, Africa, and Latin America*, ed. by Frank A. Rice, pp. 34–53, Washington D.C., Center for Applied Linguistics

1963. 'The functional distribution of Creole and French in Haiti', *Linguistics and language study* (13th Georgetown round table meeting), ed. by E. D. Woodworth and R. J. Pietro, 149–62 (Monograph Series on Languages and Linguistics, 15), Washington, D.C., Georgetown University Press

1967. 'Sociolinguistic factors in the history of American Negro dialects', *Florida FL Reporter* 5(2):1–4

1968. 'Continuity and change in American Negro dialects', *Florida FL Reporter* 6.2

[Symposium] 1964. Symposium on multilingualism (Brazzaville 1962), (CSA/CCTA Publication No. 87), London, Commission de cooperation technique en Afrique

Taylor, Douglas 1947. 'Phonemes of Caribbean creole', *Word* 3:173–9

1951. 'Structural outline of Caribbean creole', *Word* 7:43–59

1956. 'Language contacts in the West Indies', *Word* 12:391–414

1957. 'Review of *Spanish contact vernaculars in the Philippine Islands*, by Keith Whinnom', *Word* 13:489–99

1960. 'Language shift or changing relationship?' *International Journal of American Linguistics* 26:155–61

1961. 'New languages for old in the West Indies', *Comparative studies in society and history* 3:277–88 [Reprinted in Fishman 1968:607–19]

1963. 'Review of *Jamaican Creole*, by Robert B. Le Page and David DeCamp', *Language* 39:316–22

Thomas, J. J. 1869. *The Theory and practice of creole grammar*, Port-of-Spain, Trinidad

Thompson, R. W. 1961. 'A note on some possible affinities between the creole dialects of the old world and those of the new', in Le Page (ed.), *Proceedings*, 107–13

Tsuzaki, Stanley M. [1968a]. 'Problems in the study of Hawaiian English,' Mona, Creole Conference paper. [Revised as 1968b]

[1968b]. 'Coexistent systems in language variation: the case of Hawaiian English'. [This volume]

Turner, Lorenzo Dow. 1949. *Africanisms in the Gullah dialect*, Chicago, University of Chicago Press

Valdman, Albert 1964. 'Du créole au français en Haiti', *Linguistics* 8:84–94

1967. *Haitian creole basic course*, Part 1, Bloomington, Indiana

[1968]. 'The language situation in Haiti', Mona, Creole Conference paper. [Précis, this volume]

Valkhoff, Marius F. 1960. 'Contributions to the study of creole', *African Studies* 19 (2): 77–87

1966. *Studies in Portuguese and creole, with special reference to South Africa*, Johannesburg, Witwatersrand University Press

Van Wiijk, H. L. 1958. 'Origenes y evolución del Papiamento', *Neophilologus* 42

Voorhoeve, Jan 1961a. 'Linguistic experiments in syntactic analysis', in Le Page (ed.), *Proceedings*, 37–60

1961b. 'A project for the study of creole language history in Surinam,' in Le Page (ed.), *Proceedings*, 99–106

1962. 'Creole languages and communication', in [Symposium], pp. 233–42

[1968]. 'Church Creole and languages of concealment in Surinam', Mona, Creole Conference paper. [Revised version, this volume]

Weinreich, Uriel 1958. 'On the compatability of genetic relationship and convergent development', *Word* 14:374–9

1964. *Languages in contact*, The Hague. Mouton [Originally published as Publications of the Linguistic Circle of New York, No. 1, 1953]

Whinnom, Keith 1956. *Spanish contact vernaculars in the Philippine Islands*, London and Hong Kong, Hong Kong University Press

1965. 'The origin of the European-based creoles and pidgins', *Orbis* 14: 509–27

[1968]. 'Linguistic hybridization and the "special case" of pidgins and creoles', Mona, Creole Conference paper. [Revised version, this volume]

Wurm, S. A. 1964. *Motu and Police Motu: a study in typological contrasts* (Linguistic Circle of Canberra Publications, Series A, Occasional Papers 4), Canberra

1966. 'Pidgin—a national language', *New Guinea and Australia* 7:49–54.

1970. 'Pidgins, creoles and lingue franche', *Linguistics in Oceania*, ed. by T. A. Sebeok *et al.* (*Current Trends in Linguistics* 8), The Hague, Mouton

II
A PIDGIN (AND TWO CREOLES)

INTRODUCTION

Pidgin and creolized languages – their existence and nature – are the heart of the matter. And there is great need for descriptions of them. These things are symbolized by this account of Tay Boi (Tây Bồi). It is a preliminary sketch, it is technical, and the form of speech it treats must be investigated now largely from recollection – not characteristics, it would seem, that make a strong beginning for a book. In just these respects, however, the account brings home the issues that attach to the study of pidgins.

Reinecke plans to follow the present sketch with further work on the syntax of the language, on its historical background, and on its relation to other French-linked pidgins; yet more knowledge of contemporary Tay Boi is already provided here than has hitherto reached print. In the century since the inception of the language only eleven pages altogether have been published.

Though preliminary, the sketch is sufficiently detailed and comprehensive to show the 'classic' features of a true pidgin. Here is a variety of speech whose vocabulary is mostly from one language, its sentence structures often from another, and yet distinct from both; restricted in vocabulary and structure, variable in pronunciation; restricted in function, and used by a community for none of whose members is it a first language. Although Tay Boi has been sufficiently stereotyped to be cited in comic strips, it has remained quite variable throughout the range of its use, both geographical and social. Its lexicon is almost wholly from the dominant language (French); morphology almost does not exist; syntax shows some carry-over perhaps from French word order, a good deal of carry-over from the indigenous language (Vietnamese), and a good deal that may be due to neither, having emerged in the language's own development. Phonetics have been essentially those of a user's primary language (French or Vietnamese).

It is in the nature of the case for full-fledged pidgins not often to arise, and, when they do, not to survive indefinitely as such, but to either develop into a fuller language or to disappear. Indeed, crystallization and persistence of pidgins may depend upon circumstances of communication – limited yet mandatory among people of diverse languages – that are likely with intermittent trade, mercantilism, slavery, and colonialism, but not with the forms of economic and political organization that increasingly dominate the world today. Industrialization and nationalism that require literacy and developed lingua francas, as well as the means of international and internal communications now available, make the survival of true pidgins, let alone the emergence of new ones, increasingly unlikely (with the possible exception of pidgin-like argots, used as languages of concealment).

The end of the open colonialism that gave rise to Tay Boi, and on which it depended, is not to be regretted, but does limit what we can learn of the language's origin and use. Given its obsolescence, it is fortunate that Reinecke found and accepted the opportunity to work with it. (Tay Boi is not known to have influenced limited forms of communication between Vietnamese and the American military personnel, but the matter should be investigated, while still possible.)

Tay Boi underscores the urgency of research, both field work and philology, on pidgins. Beyond standard linguistic description, there is even greater need for precise accounts of pidgins in use in their local settings. Such hardly exist.

Some pidgins do continue in use without immediate danger of extinction, although without promise of expansion either, e.g. Fanagalo in Johannesburg gold mines, Beach-la-mar in the New Hebrides and Fiji, Solomon Islands Pidgin, Police Motu in Papua. *Ad hoc* pidginization does continue to occur, as in the German of immigrant labourers in Germany (Clyne 1968), although not necessarily to the point of precipitating a true pidgin. And some pidgins undergo technical creolization, through use as a mother-tongue, on a smaller or larger scale: Police Motu is the mother tongue of a number of individuals, mostly children of native constables whose parents have Police Motu as their only common language (Wurm 1964:34); so also Pidgin English in the Northern Territory of Australia (Jernudd 1969:153), and Neo-Melanesian (New Guinea Pidgin (English)), e.g. in Manus (Capell 1969:112). Neo-Melanesian is expanding as a primary language in another sense as well, through its use in government and Parliament in New Guinea. Sango is likewise expanding in both respects (first language, a primary public language) in the Central African Republic (Jacquot 1961; Tonkin 1969).

A particularly important and complex case of contemporary creolization is that of Swahili in the former Belgian Congo. Swahili, itself a creole in origin, has undergone reduction, reshaping, and expansion in function to be recreolized as the first language of a number of younger people in Katanga. The East Coast Swahili norm dominates the written use of the Katangese variety, but the spoken form, Polomé reports, is quite distinct. The case resembles that of the post-creole continuum in Jamaica, discussed in this book by DeCamp. The case is particularly important because the linguistic varieties and the dominant norm involved are not Indo-European. Thus comparison of cases such as the Jamaican with the Katangan would permit control over what is specific to the languages and what is general in the process. The complexities of the social history and linguistic composition of Katangese Swahili are described from first-hand research and experience in the work by Polomé summarized here.

Obsolescent cases, such as Tay Boi, and cases of ongoing pidginization and creolization, such as in Katanga, constitute urgent research for pidgin and creole studies, but there is much to be done with established languages too. These needs exist even with regard to one of the most studied creoles, that of Haiti, as Valdman's statement here shows.

REFERENCES

Capell, A. 1969. 'The changing status of Melanesian Pidgin', *La mondo lingvo-problemo* 1:107–14

Clyne, M. 1968. 'Zum Pidgin-Deutsch der Gastarbeiter', *Zeitschrift für Mundartforschung* 35(2):130–9

Jacquot, André 1961. 'Notes on the position of Sango in Bangui', *Africa* 31(2):158–66

Jernudd, Björn H. 1969. 'Social change and aboriginal speech variation in Australia', *Working Papers in Linguistics* 4:145–68, Honolulu, University of Hawaii, Department of Linguistics

Tonkin, J. E. A. 1969. 'Coastal pidgins in West Africa', paper presented to the Association of Social Anthropologists, University of Sussex

Wurm, S. A. 1964. 'Motu and Police Motu: a study in typological contrasts' (Linguistic Circle of Canberra Publications, Series A, Occasional Papers, 4), Canberra, Australian National University

TÂY BÔI: NOTES ON THE PIDGIN FRENCH OF VIETNAM

JOHN E. REINECKE

with the assistance of

Phan thi Thúy Nường *and* Tôn nũ' Kim Chi

General background

In 1888 Hugo Schuchardt published a brief paper on 'the Annamite French jargon' that had been spoken for about twenty years at Sàigòn between French colonials and 'such natives as are in frequent or permanent contact with foreigners – servants, sailors, etc.' (1888:230).[1] The pidgin had gotten its start in the French garrisons in what was then Cochin China in the 1860s; where the garrisons came from, and whether they had brought with them some sort of military pidgin, as a stimulus or model, is not at present known to me. Until about 1960 the pidgin was spoken rather extensively in Sàigòn and other places of French concentration in Vietnam, and until 1954 it was used in the armed services. With the departure of nearly all the French it is now almost extinct. (Tây Bôi has not survived in use between Vietnamese and American military personnel, nor has it influenced the Pidgin English that now has its place, apart from a word or two (*beaucoup, fini*). The Pidgin English of Vietnam derives from Pidgin English used by American forces previously in Japan and Korea (personal communication from Mr Saul Broudy to the editor).)

Schuchardt thought the jargon might be a creole in the bud. To the end, however, it remained purely a pidgin, used chiefly in the armed services, the police, the lower ranks of government service, and between masters and servants in French households.

The low esteem in which the pidgin was held is reflected in its nickname, Tây Bôi, French as spoken by *boys* (servants). The two nationalities remained decidedly distinct from each other. French was the language of command, and few Frenchmen learned more than the most rudimentary Vietnamese (VN). A very small minority of Vietnamese received formal instruction in standard French (SF). The few who attended secondary schools and colleges learned to speak it well; those who attended only the elementary schools spoke it imperfectly but not in pidginized form. Most soldiers, policemen, and domestics, learning purely by ear from Frenchmen or from their fellows who had been longer in service, acquired only the pidgin.

This PF was standardized enough to be used – in VN orthography except for some words left in French spelling for 'atmosphere' – in comic strips in VN newspapers. The PF speaker in the strip might typically be a Vietnamese soldier addressing his French officer. Both of the collaborators on this article, however, are emphatic in insisting that there was great variation in vocabulary, pronunciation, and sentence structure among the speakers of the pidgin. It is their impression that the PF of the armed services was more fluent and closer to SF than that of the domestic servants, for association of French and Vietnamese soldiers (including many from tribal linguistic minorities) was more extended and intimate than that between masters and servants. The collaborators' observations have been chiefly of Tây Bồi as they used to hear it spoken by servants in Sàigòn and Huế.[2] No PF-speaking informants being available, they have had to rely upon their memory. The result is a generalizing description, doubtless colored by interference from their SF and VN speech habits, which obscures the actual variety of PF.

Phonology

Although French masters deliberately simplify morphology and syntax and use scraps of VN in speaking to their servants, they depart little from SF pronunciation. On the other hand, while some servants try to pronounce SF, most of them disregard any sound which they cannot easily approximate in VN. They wreak special havoc on final consonant clusters, as in *piastre* [bi át] and *ordre* [ɔt]. (The French used to call the Vietnamese *mangeurs de syllabes*.) But sometimes a coda may be split into two syllables, as *apte* [ap tɣɯ]. Most initial and medial clusters are reduced to a single consonant as in *s'il vous plait* [sin wʊu~vʊu leı] or broken by a vowel, usually [ɣ(ɯ)]. Liaison is greatly reduced, though kept in a few phrases such as *fait-il* [fɛə tin], and individual syllables stand out distinctly in PF. This distinctness is heightened by the ending of many syllables by a consonant instead of by a vowel as in SF, as *argent* [ak rɐŋ~žɐŋ] and *frapper* [fɣɯ rap beı]. All final consonants are unreleased. Back unrounded vowels and the schwa, often in diphthongs, are common in PF as in VN. The nasalized vowels are replaced by vowel + nasal. Imploded [ɓ] and [ɗ] and otherwise initial vowels are normally preglottalized, and vowels in the *ngã* tone are glottalized in the Huế dialect. Stress is more marked than in SF. The five tones of Sàigòn VN are carried into PF, though without phonemic function.[3] All these features make Tây Bồi sound very un-French and close to VN.

The following partial list of sound changes from SF to Vietnamized PF is only approximate, for it takes little account of the variety due to VN dialects and other factors, or of many exceptions to the generalizations. (Some differences between Sàigòn and Huế pronunciation are indicated by (S) and

(H) respectively.) We have not attempted to state the rules governing sound changes, e.g. one pointed out by Thompson 1968: that final [t] and [n] are kept only after high front vowels, otherwise they become [k] and [ŋ].

French phonemes and clusters are enclosed by slashes; an asterisk indicates those which are not approximated in VN.

CONSONANTS   Initial /p/* and /b/ > (ʔɓ), as *pas* and *bas* [ba]. Final /p/ and /b/* > [p⁻], as *arbre* [ap], sometimes > [k⁻], as *le-herbe* [lɣɯ ɛ́ək]. Final /t/ generally > [t⁻] (often nearly [c⁻]), as *huit* [wɨt (S) ~ wit (H)], but also > [k⁻], as *côte* [kɔ́k (S) ~ kok (H)]. Final /d/* > [t⁻], as *sud* [sit]. Final /k/ > [k⁻], rarely > [t⁻], as *biftek* [bít tɛt ~ tət]. Initial /g/ > [gʻ] (S) ~ [ɣ] (H), as *gaz* [gʻ a ~ ɣa]. Final /g/* > ø, as *figue* [fɨi]. Final /n/ > [n⁻], but following /ɔ/ > [ŋ⁻ ~ ŋm⁻], as *personne* [bɛək sɔŋ (S) ~ bɛə(t) sɔn͡m (H). Final /ɲ/ > [n⁻], as *insigne* [ɛn sin]. Final /f/* > [p⁻], as *neuf* [nɣp], rarely > [t⁻], as *biftek*. Initial /v/ > [w] (S) ~ [v] (H), as *avec* [awɛ́ək ~ avɛk]. Final /v/* > ø, as *cave* [ka], but may become initial [v], as [ká vɣɯ]. Final /s/* > [t⁻], as *bus* [bit], sometimes approaching [c⁻], as *six* [sɨt (S) ~ sit (H)]. Initial /z/ rarely > [s], as transit [traŋ sit]. /z/* > ø, as *rose* [rov (S) ~ žov (H)]. Final /š/* and /tš/* > [t⁻], as *riche* [rit (S) ~ žit (H)] and *sandwich* [sɛŋ wit]. Initial /ž/ > [ž] (H) or [r] and sometimes [j] (S), as *Jean* [žɛŋ ~ rɛŋ ~ jɛŋ], also [š] (S), as *déjà*[deɪ ša ~ ža]. Final /ž/* > ø ~ [j] (glide), as *âge* [a: (H) ~ aj (S)]. Initial /R/ > [r] (S) ~ [ž] (H). Final /R/* > ø, as *écrire* [eɪ kɣ ʼrɨi], but is often replaced by [ə], as in *mourir* [muə riə (S) ~ mʊu žiə (H)], or by a stop (depending upon the initial consonant of the next syllable), as in *personne*. Final /l/* > [n⁻], as *quel* [kɛn]. In Sàigòn initial /j/ and /dj/* > [j], as *Dieu* and *yeux* [jɣɯ], but in Hué /dj/* > [d]. Final /j/* > ø, as *fille* [fɨi], also [i], as *combien* [kɣm biəŋ]. /y/* > ø ~ [w], as *lui* [lɨi (S) ~ lwɨi (H). The VN phonemes *kh* [x] and *th* [tʻ] are not carried into PF, nor is [h] except very rarely, as in *Haut les mains!* [hov leɪ mɛa (S) ~ mɛn (H)].

VOWELS   /i/ sometimes > [ɨ] (S) and often approaches [ɪ]; final /i/ normally > [ɪi]. /y/* > [i], but sometimes [u], as *dur* [duə]. Final /e/ normally > [eɪ]; also final /ɛ/ sometimes > [eɪ], as *filet* [fɨí leɪ]. /ɛ/ has several variations: *bête* [bɣt (S) ~ bɛt (H)]; *paix* and *père* [bɛa (S) ~ bɛ: (H)]; *sept* [sɣt ~ sət (S) ~ sɛt (H)]. /ɛ̃/* > [ɛn⁻], as *fin* [fɛn] and *ainsi* [ɛn sɨi], or [əŋ⁻], as *chien* [šiəŋ], sometimes > [ɔŋ⁻], as *soin* [sɔŋ]. /ø/* and /œ/* > [ɣ] medially and [ɣɯ] finally. /œ/* > [ɔŋ⁻], as *lundi* [lɔŋ dɨi]. SF /a/ and /ɑ/ coalesce in PF, being distributed according to the VN distribution of allophones; both often > [ɐ], as *local* [lov kɛn] and *tasse* [tɐt]. /wa/ > [ɔ ~ɔə] (S) ~ [wa] (H), as *toi* [tɔ ~ tɔə ~ twa]. /ã/* > [ɛŋ⁻], as *tant* [tɛŋ]. Final /o/ > [ov] (H) ~ [oɪ] (S), as *chose* [šov ~ soɪ]. Medial /ɔ/ and /o/ appear to be interchangeable as between dialects and perhaps within the same dialect, as *stop* [sì tɔ́p (S) ~ si top (H)] and *côte* [kɔ́k (S) ~ kok (H)]; also /ɔ/ sometimes > [ɣ], as *comme* [kɣm]. /ɔ̃/* > [ɔŋ⁻] (S) ~ [oŋ⁻] (H), as *bon* [bɔŋ ~ boŋ], [ʌʊn͡m⁻] (H), as *bonbon* [bɔ̀ŋ bɔŋ ~ bʌʊn͡m bʌʊn͡m], or [aʊ̆n͡m⁻], as *garçon* [gʻiặk saʊ̆n͡m (S) ~ ɣạ(t) saŭ͡m̄ (H)]. Final /u/ usually >[ʋu], as *tout* [tʋu]. /ə/ often > [ɣ~ɣɯ], as *le-riz* [lɣɯ rɪi].

Lexicon

Tây Bồi is a true pidgin, with the inadequacy of lexicon emphasized by Whinnom (1968). Often in trying to translate short sentences from SF or VN the junior collaborators found that an idea which appeared simple was hard to express exactly in PF, largely because of inadequate lexicon. *Bao ngày ông đi khỏi, tôi vẫn ở nhà*, 'However many days you are away, I'll still be at home', emerges as *Vous partir, moi ici maison* [wʋu bạ tiə, mɔ isi mɛ~mɛ̃ə sʌʋ͡m̄]. Meaning is often eked out by gestures and intonation, especially when asking questions. There is some onomatopoeic imitation: a PF speaker may indicate 'fowl(s)' by either *con poulet* [kɔŋ bʋu leɪ] or *con ò ó o ò o*. Circumlocutions are common, e.g. *(couteau) pas bon* [kʋu toʋ] for 'dull', *comme ballon* [kɣm ba lʌʋ͡m̄] for 'to swell', *pas bon* instead of *mauvais*, *pas même chose* [ba mɛm soɪ~šou] instead of *différent(es) chose(s)*. *Peau* (boʋ) serves for both 'bark' and 'skin', *manger* [mɐn žeɪ] for 'bite' and 'eat'. Since a limited number of adverbs and prepositions and almost no conjunctions have been carried from SF into PF, a few words, like *beaucoup* [boʋ kʋu] and *avec*, are overworked. *Le mari obéit à sa femme* becomes *Mari docile avec femme* [marɪi doʋ sin awɛək fam].

Remarkably few VN words are used in PF. Not a single VN word appears in Swadesh's 200-word list (Swadesh 1955:133–7) as translated into PF. My collaborators could think of no PF equivalents for about eight words in the list, and for about twelve more the PF differs from SF. 'Stand', for example, is illustrated by *Moi debout ici* [mɔ dɣɯ bʋu isi], 'I am standing here'. In short, almost 94% (180/192) of the PF equivalents to the 200-word list are from SF. This criterion of basic vocabulary, if used alone, would place PF as a contemporary dialect of French (if a phonologically quite divergent one).

Most of the VN words in PF are names of foods and plants, such as *củ khoai* alongside *patate* [ba tɛ́t], or of distinctive features of Vietnamese life such as the *xe kéo*, 'pedicab', and the *chị vú*, 'nursemaid'. A few are onomatopoeic names of animals, such as *mèo*, 'cat', and *chút chít*, 'mouse'. A noteworthy feature of PF is the use of some VN classifiers (Thompson 1965:193–7, Emeneau 1951:101–13) with French nouns. Most common is *cái*, the general classifier: *Cái robe sale* [kái rɣp sɐn), 'The dress(es) is/are dirty' or 'The dirty dress(es)'; *cái trois tasse* [kái trɔ~twa tɐt], 'the three cups'. Also used are *bộ* 'set': *bộ pyjama* [boʋ bi ja~ža ma], 'the suit of pajamas'; *con*, 'living non-human being': *con cochon* [kɔŋ koʋ šɔŋ], 'the pig(s)'; *chiếc*, 'item', especially in sets of two: *chiếc sabot* (ciɔ̃k sa boʋ], 'the wooden slipper(s)'; *trái*, 'fruit': *trái coco* [trái koʋ koʋ], 'the coconut(s)'. To point to an object, however, French words are used: *ce robe ci sale*, 'this dirty dress here'.

The foreign words in PF mentioned by Schuchardt appear to have been dropped. A new one probably introduced during the Japanese occupation is *yotonai* < Jp. *yokunai*, 'no good'.

A few French words have acquired special meanings approaching slang, as *local*, 'of poor quality, bogus', etc., applied to products and persons alike. *Lui zéro* [sɪi rov] expresses SF *C'est un homme bon à rien*. Some children's words are used, e.g. *tata* for *tante* and *tonton* [tɔŋ tɔŋ] for *oncle*.

Morphology and classes of words

Reduplication, prominent in many pidgin and creole languages, is lacking in Tây Bồi, even though it is virtually the only morphological feature of VN (Emeneau 1951:159–200, Thompson 1965: 151–78).[4] Except for a few isolated set forms, SF inflection has been dropped and has not been replaced by new formations as in many creole dialects. Most PF words, however, on the basis of derivation and function, can be fitted more or less into the traditional SF parts of speech.

NOUNS are generally used without an article, gender is disregarded, and number is inferred from the context. There are a few partial exceptions such as *la-robe*, *la-maison*, *le-riz*, *le-herbe*, and the set expressions *tous les jours* [tʊu leɪ ruə ~ žuə] and *Haut les mains*! The prefixed articles conspicuous in French creole dialects are lacking. *Nhomme* [nom] sometimes alternates with *homme* and *narbre* with *arbre*, but no one ever says **trois narbre*.

ADJECTIVES are almost always masculine, e.g. *cái robe blanc*, 'the white dress' or 'The dress is white'; *Elle femme sot* [ɛn fam sov], 'She is a stupid woman'. Only one pair is distinguished, *petit garçon* [tɪ gɪak saŭŋ͡m] versus *petite fille* [tit fɪi]. But such a pronunciation as [lʊɔk] for *lourd* may perhaps show influence of the feminine form.

PERSONAL PRONOUNS, unaffected by the VN pattern of status pronouns (Emeneau 1951:114–36), follow the SF. Often, though, no pronoun is used, reference being inferred from the context, as in *Combien jour finir travail?* [fɪi nɪi trà weɪ-veɪ], 'How long will it take you/him/etc. to finish the job?'

moi [mɔ ~ mɔə ~ mwa]	*nous* [nʊu]
toi [tɔ ~ tɔə ~ twa]	*vous* [wʊu ~ vʊu] (also as polite
tu [ty] (master to servant)	singular to the master)
lui [lɪi ~ lwɪi] (either sex)	*eux* [ɣɯi] (either sex)
elle [ɜn]	*elles* [ɛn]
	zautre [zɔt] < *eux autres*
	lui + number, as *lui cinq*

In a few set phrases, almost all of them impersonal expressions, the SF forms are kept, e.g. *J'ai faim* [reɪ ~ ʒeɪ fɛn ~fɛa] alongside *Moi faim*; *Il pleut* [in lɣɯ~in bɣɯ lɣɯ]; *Il fait froid/chaud* [in fɛə fɣ̀ù rɔ/šov]; *Quel temps fait-il?* [kɛn tʟŋ fɛə tin]; *Il est deux heures* [in lɛə dɣɯ zɯə].

Three POSSESSIVE PRONOUNS are carried over from SF: *mon* [mʌʋ͡m], *ton* [tʌʋ͡m], *son* [sʌʋ͡m]. Personal pronouns serve for the others, e.g. *nous chien*, [nu šɪən] 'our dog(s)', and sometimes for the first three as well, as in *Lui moi enfant* [ɐŋ fɐŋ], 'He/she is my child'. The possessive with *à* or *de* is very rare. *Cette tasse est à moi* > *Moi tasse* or simply an emphatic *Moi!*, 'mine!'

Of the other pronouns the only ones commonly used are *qui* [kɪi], *quoi* [kɔ (S) ~kwa (H)], *personne*, *rien* [rɪəŋ], and *tout*. *Quel* is used only as an adjective. *Que* occurs only in comparisons: *Mon garçon grand que mon fille* [mʌʋ͡m g'ạk saṳ͡mgɣɯ rɐŋ kɣɯ mʌʋ͡m fɪi].

NUMERALS The cardinal numerals from 1 to 10 are French: [ɔŋ], [dɣɯ], [trɔ ~twa], [kɐt], [sɐn], sɨt ~sit], [sʌt ~ sɛt], wɨt ~wit], [nɣp], [dɨt~dit]. But, following the VN way of counting, 11 is *dix-un*, etc., up to 20, which may be either *deux-dix* or *vingt* [wɐn]. The system continues, *trois-dix*, etc., up to *cent* [sɐn] and *mille* [min]. The only fractions used are *demi* [dɣ̀ù mɪi] and *quart* [ka]. VN *ruở'i*, 'and one half', is not translated into PF, which expresses 150 by *cent cinq-dix*, not *cent demi. Pour cent*, however, is commonly used; *cent pour cent* [sɐn buə sɐn) signifies 'first rate'.

Ordinals and multiplicatives are lost in PF. *Elle/lui soeur* [sɯə] *deux moi*, 'She is my second sister'; *Moi aller* [a leɪ] *Saïgon deux déjà*, 'I have been to Sàigòn twice already'.

VERBS The PF verb is invariable. It regularly derives from and approximates the SF infinitive. Since many common indicative and imperative forms as well as the vast majority of infinitives end in [e], PF speakers 'hear' [e ~eɪ] as the appropriate ending for some verbs not derived from first conjugation infinitives. Thus *bouver* (bʋu weɪ ~veɪ] is used instead of *boire*, *cuiser* [kwɪi seɪ] instead of *cuire*, *vouler* [wʋu ~vʋu leɪ] instead of *vouloir*, *aver* [a weɪ ~veɪ] instead of *avoir, recever* [rɣ seɪ weɪ ~veɪ] instead of *recevoir*, *saver* [sa weɪ ~veɪ] instead of *savoir*, *vender* [wɐŋ deɪ] instead of *vendre*, *ouvrer* [ʋu wɣ reɪ] for *ouvrir*, and *vener* [wɣɯ neɪ] alongside *venir* [wɣɯ nɪə]. The participle *compris* [kɣm bɣɯ rɪf] is used instead of *comprendre* and *promis* [bɣ rov mɪi] for *promettre*.

In a few instances a related SF noun functions as a verb. *Moi contrôle tout* [mɔ kʌʋ͡m trovn tʋu], 'I'll take care of everything'. *Lui aver permission repos* [bɛk mit sʌʋ͡m rɣw bov], 'I let him rest'. *Moi question lui venir café, oui ou non* [mɔ kɛ(t) sʌʋ͡m lɪ̃ wɣɯ nɪə ka feɪ, wɪi ʋu nʌʋ͡m], 'I'll talk to him if he comes to the café'. *Demain moi retour campagne* [dɣ mɐn mɔ rɣɯ tuə kɐm bɐn], 'Tomorrow I'll return to the country'. *Vous pas argent, moi stop travail*, 'If you don't pay [me], I won't work any longer'.

Two verbs, besides *il-faut* noted below, derive from common indicative forms, *peut* instead of *pouvoir* and *veux* [wyɯ∼vyɯ] alongside *vouler*: *Moi peut parler français* [mɔ byɯ ba leɪ fyɯ rɐŋ sɛə]; *Lui veux/vouler toi ici* [lĩ wyɯ/wʋu leɪ tɔ isi], 'He wants you to stay'. According to Thompson (1968), however, *vouloir* is usually expressed by *content*: *Monsieur content aller danser?* [mʌʋɲm̃ sɯə kʌʋɲm̃ tɐŋ a leɪ dɐŋ seɪ], (polite) 'Do you want to go dancing?' Likewise *pouvoir* is expressed by *moyen* [mɔ j ɛn]. 'Dinner is served' is announced by *Moyen manger*, '[You] can eat'.

Time and aspect are inferred from the context or indicated, often vaguely, by adverbs of time. *Moi bouver thé* [teɪ], 'I drink/am drinking tea'; *Moi bouver thé jour avant* [a wɐŋ∼vɐŋ], 'I drank/was drinking tea yesterday' (or in the recent past); *Demain moi bouver thé avec ami*, 'Tomorrow I shall drink tea with my friend(s)'. If anything, PF is even more indeterminate than VN.[5] Though VN distinguishes between ordinary past and recent past, PF reduces them both to such a form as *Mois avant moi arriver Saïgon* [mɔ a wɐŋ mɔ a rɪi weɪ sàɪ gòŋ], in which *mois* means time generally. VN *Nhà cháy rồi*, 'The house has burned already', becomes *Maison au feu* [oʋ fyɯ]. In PF as in VN there is no distinction of voice. *Lui là frapper*, 'He was/has been/is being beaten by somebody' ∼ 'He was/has been/is beating [someone or something]'.

No restructured system of verbal auxiliaries has been developed as in the creole dialects. The nearest approach is *il faut*, often employed according to its SF model: *Il-faut couper arbre* [in foʋ kʋu beɪ ap], 'The tree must be/had to be/etc. cut down'; *Moi il-faut ici*, 'I must/had to/etc. remain'; *Il-faut lui venir* to express SF *Il faudrait qu'il vienne*.

There are a few set phrases with SF indicative or subjunctive forms, such as *s'il vous plaît*. Frenchmen sometimes address their servants in the second person plural, coupling it with the singular pronoun, as in the question *Quel âge avez toi?*

The invariable verb (which may happen to coincide with the SF imperative) is employed for orders and requests. *Va au marché* becomes PF *Toi/vous aller marché* [ma(t) šeɪ]; *Allons-nous au marché* > *Vous, moi aller marché*. *Prends-moi cette assiette* > *Donner moi assiette* [dõn neɪ mɔ a(t) sɛt] with an accompanying gesture. However, *Allons-nous en* > PF *Va-t'en* [wa(S)∼va(H) tɐŋ].

Except in a few set phrases there is no copula, neither *être* nor any substitute.

Syntax

Except for circumlocutions caused by lack of vocabulary, PF cuts structure to the bone. It is generally more concise (and less precise) even than VN. SF *Il vaut mieux ne pas y aller* translates as *Bon pas aller*; VN *Chia hai bánh này cho đều*, 'Divide these two cakes equally', as *Couper deux ce gâteau* (kʋu beɪ dyɯ syɯ g'a toʋ]. Although it is probable that explicit subjects, objects, and verbs appear oftener in PF than in VN, very often they are not expressed; and there are many minor sentences. The following are typical: *Pas même chose*, '[It's] another matter'. *Ici le-riz*, 'Here [is] the rice'. *Assez, pas connaître!* [a sei, ba kɔn nét], 'Enough! [I] don't know'. *Maître dur* (or *mechant*) *partout* [mɛt duə/mɛ̀ sɛŋ bạt tʊu]. *Vietnam beaucoup riz*, 'Vietnam is rich in rice'. *Lui pas bon sens* [sɛŋ], 'He [has] no common sense'. *Moi voir rien* [mɔ wa riəŋ]. 'I see/have seen nothing'.

Often the PF is a word by word translation of VN, as *Tôi đi chợ = Moi aller marché*. But the French words which translate VN particles of time and place often do not follow the same order. *Tôi sẽ đi*, 'I subsequent-time go', becomes *Moi aller ce soir* [syɯ sɔ ~swa] (or some other specific future time). *Ông đi đâu?* may be translated in either VN or French word order, *Monsieur aller où?* or *Où monsieur aller?*

Questions depend primarily on intonation and stress to distinguish them from statements. 'Are there any oranges?' would probably be asked as *Encore orange?* [ɛŋ kɔ ɔrɛŋ] and answered as *Pas orange dans* [dɛŋ] *la-maison, Pas d'encore*, or most likely *Fini orange* [fiɪnɪɪ ɔrɛŋ]. In some questions the subject precedes the verb or complement, in others it follows, without necessarily corresponding to either SF or VN order. *Toi saver dame-là?* [dam la], 'Do you know that lady?' *Toi Hué garçon/fille?*, 'Are you a native of Hué?' *Quel robe toi content?* ,'Which dress do you prefer?' *Aller (toi) marché acheter fruit, legume?* [frɯ rɪi, le ˈgim], 'Are you going to the market to buy fruit and vegetables?'

The lack of conjunctions, the absence of *que*, the invariable form of the verb, and VN influence cause ideas in PF to be juxtaposed rather than subordinated. Typical is *Moi compris toi parler* [bạt lei] *qui*, 'I know what you want to say'; less typical, *Si toi pas chapeau, prendre chapeau ton frère* [sɪi tɔ ba ša bʊʊ, byɯ rɛŋ ša bʊʊ tʌʊɲ̃m fyɯ vɛə], 'If you [have] no hat, take your brother's', *Vous faire ceci, faire connaître* [wvu feə syɯ sɪi, fɜə kɔn nɛt] translates closely VN *Có làm sao, nói làm vậy*, 'Whatever [you] do, [you] should make it known'.

Simple comparison such as *Moi (pas) beaucoup vieux* [jˈɣɯ (S) ~ viɣɯ (H)] *avec toi*, 'I am younger/older than you', is easily expressed. 'Paul is the laziest of his class', however, is *Paul plus paresseux dans classe* [bɔn bɣ lɪi ba rɛ syɯ dɛŋ kɣ lɛt]. SF *Il est plus bon qu'intelligent* loses its exactness as *Lui bon mais pas intelligent* [lɪĩ bʌʊɲ̃m mɛ̀ə ba ɛn tei lɪi rɛŋ ~žɛŋ].[6]

Addendum: A policeman's text

The following text was furnished from memory by Miss Nương's mother. A policeman has arrested a man without an identification card and is reporting to his superior.

La quanh [province] *Sa-đec vener la quanh Tân-an, trois jour déjà, pas travail;*

moi demander sa carte; lui dire n'a pas; moi signaler M. le Commissaire. [la wɛn sa dɛ́k wɣɯ neɪ la wɛn tʌŋ aŋ, trɔ ruə deɪ ša, ba trà wɛɪ; mɔə dɣɯ mɛŋ deɪ sa kat; lɪ̃ díə na ba; mɔə sɪɪ ɲa leɪ mʌuɲ̃m suəlɣɯ kɣm mit sɛ̀ə.]

Free translation: He came from Sa-dec province to Tân-an province, has been here three days already, has no job. I asked for his card; he said he did not have one; so I am reporting to M. le Commissaire.

NOTES

1 Schuchardt quotes a brief notice of the pidgin from Saint-Martin (1879:762b) Schuchardt notes a few Pidgin English, Malay, and Tamil words, but the pidgin appears to have been almost wholly an *ad hoc* creation of the Vietnamese and the French.

2 Miss N'ương has lived most of her life in Sàigòn, Miss Chi most of hers in Huế, a city with a much smaller French community, although she has also lived in Sàigòn. The senior author knows the PF only from their description of it.

3 We use a broad transcription, without indicating glottal stops, implosion, unreleased consonants, niceties of vowel position, or (usually) vowel length or stress. Tone is indicated as in VN orthography: à, á, ạ, ã (for coalesced *hỏi* and *ngã* tones), with *ngang* tone unmarked. Transcriptions are divided by syllables, since the Vietnamese think of words in syllabic units.

Emeneau 1951 and Thompson 1965 discuss VN phonology at length. We are greatly indebted to Professor Thompson for calling attention to omissions and correcting errors in our original transcription. Remaining faults are the responsibility of the senior author.

4 There is at least one instance of reduplication, playful rather than functional, in which a VN emphatic (Thompson 1965:154–68) has been coined: *même chose xén* [mɛm soɪ sɛ̀eŋ] 'the same thing'. Stageberg (1956:168) also points out the repetition of *ti* (<*petit*) for emphasis.

5 Nguyễn Đăng Liêm (1966: xvi–xviii) characterizes VN as governed by the law of indeterminacy and the law of simplicity, with extreme dependence upon context of utterance.

6 Stageberg's sketch (1956) of PF as spoken at Haiphòng about 1945 came to our attention after this article was written. Misses Nương and Chi characterize many of Stageberg's examples as 'high class' pidgin, the sort used by persons who perhaps have a smattering of formal instruction in French: for example, *livre à moi* instead of *mon livre* or *moi livre*; *il a* instead of *déjà*; *Moi il n'y a pas ami* instead of *Moi pas ami* 'I have no friend'. All of Stageberg's examples would be understood in the south but several would seldom be used. In the south, for example, *moyẹn* indicates ability to do; so, *Toi dire encore ca va?* would be used rather than *Toi dire encore moyen?*, and *oui ou non?* rather than *moyen pas moyen?* would be added to a statement to turn it into a question.

REFERENCES

Emeneau, M. B. 1951. *Studies in Vietnamese (Annamese) grammar*, Berkeley and Los Angeles, University of California Press (University of California Publications in Linguistics, vol. 8)

Nguyễn Đăng Liêm 1966. *English grammar . . . A contrastive analysis of English and Vietnamese*, vol. 1 (Linguistic Circle of Canberra, Publications, Series C: Books, No. 3), Canberra, The Australian National University

Saint-Martin, Vivien de 1879. *Nouveau dictionnaire de géographie universelle* (Cited by Schuchardt)

Schuchardt, Hugo 1888. 'Kreolische Studien VIII, Über das Annamito-französische', *Sitzungsberichte der k. k. Akademie der Wissenschaften zu Wien* (Philosophisch-historische Klasse) 116:227–34

Stageberg, Norman C. 1956. 'Pidgin French grammar: a sketch', *Modern Language Journal* 40:167–169

Swadesh, Morris 1955. 'Towards greater accuracy in lexicostatistic dating', *International Journal of American Linguistics* 21:121–37.

Thompson, Laurence C. 1965. *A Vietnamese grammar*, Seattle, University of Washington Press

— 1968. Personal communication

Whinnom, Keith 1968. 'Linguistic hybridization and the "special case" of pidgins and creoles', paper prepared for the Mona Conference

STATEMENTS AND PRÉCIS

THE KATANGA (LUBUMBASHI) SWAHILI CREOLE[1]

EDGAR POLOMÉ

Multilingualism was a common practice in Katanga before European penetration. The way was opened up for Swahili by the BaYeke people, whose chieftain Msiri was assisted by a group of Swahili speakers in his conquest of Katanga; some BaYeke themselves used Swahili. Further spread of Swahili in Katanga was favoured by Belgian occupation after 1891, by recruitment of most soldiers in Zanzibar and use of Swahili in the training of soldiers until World War I, but especially through the development of the Union Minière du Haut-Katanga and its extensive recruitment of outside labour. At its peak by 1928, the African personnel of the Union Minière was more than four times the population of the district in 1904. In a town such as Elisabethville only 16% of the population come from neighboring rural districts. On the eve of Congolese independence, the Katanga mining district was one of the most important urban concentrations in Central Africa.

The new population came from all neighboring areas, but principally from three: the Kasayi, the northern and western districts of Katanga itself, and Rwanda-Burundi. The latter immigrants usually knew Swahili, if familiar with any language other than their own, as it had been, for decades, the lingua franca of trading centers. Labour supplied by Rhodesian firms from rural areas would know a smattering of English, but the Rhodesians, until the depression of the 1930s, came as transients on short-term contracts and could not influence the lingua franca of the mining centers very greatly. Although large numbers of them still resided in Elisabethville and Jadotville in later years (10,000 and 3,500, respectively), they were greatly outnumbered by the migrants from the Kasayi (Luba-speaking) and from Luba-speaking areas of northern Katanga itself. In 1955 there were 40,000 from the Kasayi in Elisabethville, and 20,000 in Jadotville, i.e. about a third of the African population in both towns, and there were at least as many from Luba-speaking areas within the province.

Migrants from the Luba-speaking areas, having had a higher degree of education in the missions in the Kasayi, secured the best jobs as clerks, teachers, etc., so that the African middle class was predominantly Luba-speaking before the tribal conflicts following Independence. The baLuba acquired the Swahili lingua franca quickly as a second language and greatly influenced it. Two-thirds of the instructors who teach the younger generation, using French and Swahili, are native Luba-speakers.

At present, in Katangese urban communities, as in many other towns in Central Africa, the mother tongue is usually retained at home, except in intertribal marriages, but the younger generation drift away from it toward the lingua franca, even among others of their age group from the same tribal background. In social intercourse, the Katangese variety of Swahili is commonly used, knowledge of it varying with education and length of residence in the urban community. French is the prestige language, used at all levels of education and administration. Public notices and documents for general use are bilingual (French and Swahili). Apart from a short revival after Katanga's Independence, the teaching of Swahili seems to be generally discontinued in towns. Swahili is found in the local press, containing numerous French words. Swahili material is used in religious instruction, mainly by Protestant missions. In current speech and in folk-literature, such as popular plays, 'poto-poto-Swahili', as some call it, is resorted to. With the growing number of young people who use it as their first language, Swahili has become a 'creole' in Katanga, as has kiTuba in Leopoldville province. An inquiry among school children in a suburb of Elisabethville in 1963 showed that only very recently arrived children were not fluent in Katanga Swahili and did not use it as their second language, and that about 11% did not know any other African language.

Katangese Swahili has diverged rather sharply from Congo Swahili, i.e. the language of the Arabized Africans in Maniema and the northeast. Only educated people with some training in Swahili grammar and idiom can understand without trouble texts in East Coast Swahili (ECS). (There has also developed a French-Swahili kitchen *Mischsprache*, through extensive borrowing of words from each into the other, during long coexistence.)

The major influences on the formation of Katangese (Lubumbashi) Swahili can be summarized as follows:

Phonology

(1) *Luba*: reorganization of dental order of consonants; neutralization of voiced/ voiceless distinction in velar stops except after nasal (also occurring in KiNgwana the Swahili dialect of Maniema and the North-East); occasional devoicing of *v* to *f*; palatalization of *s* to *š*, of *z* to *ž*, and occasionally of *t* to *tš*; by-forms with initial *nz*- for *nj*-.

(2) *Local (Central Bantu) dialects*: substitution of *l* for *r*; breaking up of consonant clusters by inserted vowels.

Morphology

Local (Central Bantu) dialects: change in shapes of class prefixes; use of *ka*- to form diminutives; loss of locatives in *-ni*. The difference between ECS and the local Bantu dialects has led to structural simplification of the whole morphological system, with a result that is different from either ECS or the local dialects. There has been complete disruption of concord system, entailing (a) replacement of complex rules of class agreement for possessives in noun phrases with animate nouns in ECS with one stereotyped prefix, (b) invariance of adjectives, usually with stereotyped prefix, (mostly *mu*-), (c) replacement of ECS adverbials with *vi*- or *u*- by *mu*- adjectives, (d) invariance of numerals, (e) invariance of demonstratives, (f) replacement of all pronominal affixes for 'things' in verbs by one stereotyped affix (*i*); reduction of whole conjugation of indicative verbs practically to three main tenses (present *-na*-, past *-li*-, future *-ta*-), e.g. replacement of 'completive' *-me*- tense by a periphrastic form; whole complex of aspectual meanings (marking dependence of realization of a process on certain conditions) lost; for the functions of the copula in the present, generalization of the quasi-verbal complex *iko* 'there is' with prefixes for personal subject as well as with locative *ku*- (the third person prefix, however, showing zero in place of *a*-), this same

-iko complex combining with connective *na* to mark possession and translate 'to have'; loss of relative forms in speech (occasional retention in writing). The derivational system of applicatives, causatives, passives, statives, remains remarkably operative, due presumably to the striking correspondences between ECS and the local dialects.

Syntax

(1) *Local (Central Bantu) dialects*: see under 'Morphology' above. Syntax, in the sense of word order and idiom formation, has not diverged considerably from the ECS patterns, which are basically similar to those of Central Bantu.

(2) *French*: literal translation has led to the carryover of some French patterns.

Vocabulary

(1) *Local (Central Bantu) dialects*: some substitution of local dialect forms for ECS cognates (essentially substitution of phonological shapes); a considerable number of words from local dialects introduced in process of reBantuization; semantic changes in Swahili words common both to local dialects and ECS.

(2) *East Coast Swahili*: continuity of much vocabulary (but see just above).

(3) *French*: loanwords, connected with colonial administration, partial Westernization, material culture, etc.

(4) *English*: old English loans in ECS; new loans via Rhodesians.

NOTES

1 Summary of two papers, 'The position of Swahili and other Bantu languages in Katanga', prepared for the Second International Congress of Africanists (Dakar), and distributed to the conference in advance, and 'The Katanga Swahili Creole', presented in a provisional version at the conference. The first paper appears in *Texas Studies in Language and Literature* 11 (2): 905–13 (1969), and the second in *Journal of African Languages* 7 (1): 14–25 (1968). It is very much regretted that health and unexpected duties prevented Professor Polomé from preparing the full-length revised study he had intended. This résumé was prepared by the editor, and approved by him. On the general linguistic situation in the Congo, see Polomé, 'Cultural languages and contact vernaculars in the Republic of the Congo', *Texas Studies in Literature and Language* 4(4):499–511 (1963), from which two or three points have been taken.

THE LANGUAGE SITUATION IN HAITI[1]

ALBERT VALDMAN

A review of currently available research on the language situation in Haiti shows that problems which need study or re-examination may be grouped in four main areas: (1) descriptive studies of Creole and French in Haiti; (2) the sociolinguistic relationship between Creole and French in Haiti; (3) variation within Creole and its consequence for several problems of language engineering; and (4) the genesis of Creole.

(1) With regard to existing descriptions of Creole French, the principal needs are for lexicographic studies and grammars that attempt to interrelate superficially different forms and constructions. For instance, a more coherent description of Creole syntax results if reduplicative constructions of the type *Sé manjé l ap manjé*, 'He's really eating' or *A a bèl li bèl*, 'Is she ever beautiful' are treated as special cases of embedding.

(2) The most striking feature of the relationship between French and Creole in Haiti is the diglossia which characterizes the speech of the elite (Stewart 1963; Valdman 1968). Typically, educated, diglossic Haitians will shift from French to Creole in the middle of a sentence, and these shifts are signals of subtle shifts of roles and attitudes between interlocutors. Creole is the repository of folk culture and the outsider who does not know Creole will be denied entry to many aspects of Haiti's culture. Thus in Haiti full participation in the total life of the community requires knowledge of the vernacular as well as knowledge of and literacy in the official language. On the other hand, the majority of Haitians are monolingual speakers of Creole and are totally excluded from participation in official matters, for these are carried out in French.

(3) Haitian Creole exhibits considerable variation. In addition to geographically determined dialect variation, there is considerable variation in the form of lexical items due to borrowing from French on the part of semi-literate urban (chiefly Port-au-Prince) speakers of Creole. Together with numerous lexical items, these speakers borrow cliché phrases and isolated syntactical constructions as well as, perhaps, phonological features. For instance, the vowel system of urban Creole contains front rounded vowels /y/, /ø/, and /œ/. However, these vowels are also found in some rural varieties of Creole and it would be safest to assume that apparent loans from French have a double source: the French spoken by the elite and conservative rural dialects. The important fact is that features which monolingual Creole speakers attribute to French enjoy considerable prestige and should be adopted in the elaboration of a normalized Creole usage which would be employed, for example, in literacy programs. Early literacy workers, unaware of the prestige factor in language variation, adopted a rural innovating norm rather than an urban or a conservative rural norm. This no doubt has contributed to the resistance against the creation of a suitable writing system for Creole on the part of the Haitian elite and reduced the motivation for the acquisition of literacy on the part of the illiterate masses (Hall 1953; Pressoir 1947).

(4) While it is clear that African languages have contributed considerably to the development of Creole, perhaps through the intermediary of an Afro-

Portuguese pidgin transported to the New World by African slaves and European slave traders, the contribution of French to the grammatical structure of Creole should not be underrated. Features which superficially resemble those found in West African languages are found in North American French dialects and can be shown to be derived from French. For instance the post-position of determiners (Creole *ti moun-mouen*) is generated by a set of rules which also yield popular French *un ami à moi*.

Another fact which has not been given sufficient importance by creolists is that Creole served as a means of communication among segments of the white population of the West Indian island colonies. Still today one finds in Saint-Bart two white groups each speaking Creole French dialects and the only monolingual speakers of Creole in Reunion island, off the east coast of Africa, are poor whites living in the island's highlands (Deltel 1967). The hypothesis that Creole was born of the contact between a 'maximalized' overseas northern French, used in French ports serving the colonies and in the colonies themselves, and an Afro-Portuguese pidgin is well worth serious consideration.

NOTES

1 Valdman (1969).

2 The concluding quotation of this article, although attributed to Bloomfield, actually is from the Introduction to Part VII of Hymes (ed.), *Language in culture and society* (New York, Harper and Row, 1964), in which Bloomfield's paper is reprinted.

REFERENCES

Deltel, J. 1967. 'Le Créole de la Réunion', Unpublished License thesis, University of Aix-Marseilles

Hall, Robert A., Jr. 1953. 'Haitian Creole' (American Anthropological Association, Memoir 74) Washington, D.C.

Pressoir, Charles-Fernand 1947. *Débats sur le créole et le folklore*, Port-au-Prince, Imprimerie de l'État

   1969. 'The language situation in Haiti', *Research resources of Haiti*, ed. by R. Schaedel, 155–203, Research Institute for the Study of Man, New York

Stewart, William A. 1963. 'The functional distribution of Creole and French in Haiti', *Linguistics and language study* (13th round table meeting), ed. by E. E. Woodworth, 149–62 (Monograph Series on Languages and Linguistics, 15), Washington, D.C., Georgetown University Press

Valdman, Albert 1968. 'Language standardization in a diglossia situation: Haiti', *Language problems of the developing nations*, ed. by J. A. Fishman, C. A. Ferguson, and J. Das Gupta, 313–26, New York, John Wiley[2]

   1969. 'The language situation in Haiti', *Research resources of Haiti*, ed. by R. Schaedel, 155–203, Research Institute for the Study of Man, New York

III
GENERAL CONCEPTIONS OF PROCESS

INTRODUCTION

I

These contributions treat pidginization and creolization, not as unique and marginal, but as part of our general understanding of linguistic change. They show that what may be called the 'formative' period of modern pidgin and creole study has come to an end. It was necessary a generation or so ago to delimit 'pidgin' and 'creole' by a standard definition, as against confusion with any and all simplification and admixture in language. Just so modern linguistics began by limiting its attention to certain properties of sounds and forms. Once established, the logic of its own development has led linguistics again into broader concerns, re-establishing old links and forging new ones (cf. discussion in Hymes 1968, 1971). The same has become true of pidgin and creole studies. Having 'crystallized', they depend for future progress, like the languages of their concern, on an expansion of content and role. Indeed, they promise to be an important focus of the broader integration of linguistics as a field with regard to processes of change and use.

The general field within which pidgin and creole studies now find their place may be described as having to do with four kinds of change, two structural, two functional: change in scale (reduction, expansion, simplification, complication) of linguistic make-up; change through confluence of different linguistic traditions; change in scope (reduction or expansion) of use; and change in status as a norm. Pidgin and creole studies are specifically concerned with the interaction of these processes, as they entail the emergence (and loss), wholly or partially, of autonomy as a norm for some variety of language, within the repertoire of a community or person. The papers in this part each place the problem of the formation of pidgins and creoles with respect to some aspect of this more general field.

II

PIDGINIZATION, DISTANCE FROM A NORM, AND PRE-PIDGIN CONTINUA

Whinnom examines pidginization in the context of a general analysis of language contact. Because of the checkered history of biological analogy in linguistics and social science, the notion of hybridization, with which he begins, may put some readers off; if so, they will miss an analysis that has already begun to reshape thinking in this field (Wurm 1970). The separation of cultural from biological sciences early in this century has in fact been followed by a rebuilding of ties in studies of ecology, adaptation, and evolution; and problems of taxonomy, differentiation, and distribution do provide a common ground on which differences and similarities alike may be instructive. In any case, Whinnom restricts the scope of the biological parallel quite clearly, and the proof of its value is in the result.

Two important assumptions should be noted: (1) the change that differenti-
ates communities is continuous with the change that goes on within them, and
(2) it is not the mixing of traditions, but the maintenance of boundaries between
them, that requires explanation.[1] Whinnom considers four types of barrier to
hybridization: 'ecological' (having to do with the nature of the contact),
'emotional' (having to do with attitudes), 'mechanical' (outer linguistic form),
and 'interspecific' or 'conceptual' (inner linguistic form). Whinnom rejects the
widespread notion of 'reinforcement of error' (a speaker's simplifications or
baby talk being imitated, the imitation itself being imitated by speakers of the
dominant source, etc.). Pidginization is neither arbitrary simplification nor
mechanical mixing, but an adaptation, a selective change to certain ends, and
what crucially needs explaining is not the occurrence of the component processes (simplification, mixture), but that these processes should result in a
distinct, stable new form of speech. The processes are common; their concurrence so as to result in crystallization of a true pidgin is very rare.

To clarify his point, Whinnom analyzes three cases. With regard to an
Italianized Spanish of Argentina (cocoliche), and the 'thought-experiment' of
the French used between schoolboys whose native languages are English and
German, he asks us to consider why either result is *not* a pidgin. (So also with
regard to stereotyped 'stage-Irish' forms of speech.) With an undoubted
pidgin, Chinese Pidgin English, he stresses that it has been stabilized at a very
low level of intelligibility to speakers of either English or Chinese, such that it
must be learned by either, and that it is maintained as a lingua franca among
speakers of different dialects by the Chinese themselves.

Whinnom concludes that 'it may well be that no simple bilingual situation
ever gives rise to a pidgin'. Only in a multilingual situation, with one or more
third parties, will a true pidgin emerge. Only by use by speakers without access to
the language(s) being pidginized, and without (or in need of) other means of
communication among themselves, can account for the crystallization of a novel
form of speech, characterized, in Whinnom's words, by the stability, unintelligibility, impoverishment, and simplification of pidgins.

Whinnom points out that a pidgin, once formed, may play a part in the formation of other pidgins, as the notion of 'relexification' entails, and as would seem
clearly to have happened in some cases (e.g. the probable line of development
from Chinese Pidgin English used in sea trade between China and Pacific
islands in formation of Beach-la-mar (named after a delicacy that was a focus of
the trade), and of Beach-la-mar in the development of other Pacific forms of
Pidgin English). Here the 'mechanical barrier' may be of special importance,
i.e. relexification of an earlier Portuguese pidgin seems more plausible in the
case of subsequent Spanish and French pidgins and creoles, than with English.
And the 'emotional' and 'ecological' barriers must be carefully specified – one
might imagine the Chinese users of Pidgin English to have had the option of
dialect levelling, of developing a koiné. Further, as Whinnom grants, pidginization might occur, not between but within groups, not out of communicative
necessity, but for ritual or play. His main thesis remains: in an ordinary bilingual situation one side will learn the other's language, or continue to produce
afresh cocoliche-like unstable varieties, so long as a model and a motive for
improved facility is present. In other words, the decisive factor is relationship to,
or better, distance from, the norm(s) of the language(s) being adapted, as this
distance is affected by the various kinds of barrier.

This last way of formulating Whinnom's point may seem innocuous or vague, but the generality is in fact essential. For one pidgin to derive from another by 'relexification', for example, there would have to be distance from the norm of the new source of lexicon of the sort required in the original formation of a pidgin. Otherwise, the result would be merely English, or French, or Spanish, or whatever, with perhaps a pidgin flavor. And with both pidgins and creoles it is tempting to seize upon too specific a formulation. Where such languages are known to have crystallized in approximately a generation – Fanagalo in Africa (from about 1860), Hawaiian Pidgin (from 1876), Lumumbashi Swahili (from about 1900?), Chinook Jargon (from about 1800?) and Sranan (from 1667) – the cause seems very likely the intrusion of third parties who learn and stabilize a form of the existing mixture without access to the norms of its source(s): Indians in Africa, immigrant labourers of many origins in Hawaii, immigrant labourers in Katanga, European traders and missionaries in the Pacific Northwest, perhaps new slaves (or children) in seventeenth-century Surinam. And when one creole remains sturdily distinct, as Sranan in Surinam, and a related creole does not, as is the case with Jamaican, the cause again seems clear: absence, or presence, of a dominant related source. Sranan struggles against Dutch, but Jamaican against English, so that one situation is language contact, another dialect levelling.[2]

For both pidgins and creoles, however, the general formulation, in terms of distance from a norm, is needed. With regard to pidgins, one must consider the possibility that some specialized varieties, such as the 'very fragmentary Malayalam' spoken by Toda diviners during possession (Emeneau 1942:174), seventeenth century Island Carib 'men's speech' (Taylor 1968 [1961]:607), contemporary Pennsylvania Dutch, and the uninflected variety of Anglo-Romanes (Hancock 1970) should be defined as pidginized. That is, these varieties show simplification in outer form, reduction in inner form, and restriction in role, together with a confluence of traditions that distinguishes them from, say, the rote Arabic of prayer among the Minangkabau of Indonesia.[3] They have become stabilized and autonomous, but their restricted role is internal, not external; they have become separate from the norm of a source not by intrusion, but exclusion, not by creation of a new variety so much as by loss and dissociation of an old one.

With regard to creoles, notice that Haitian, like Jamaican, continues in the presence of a related, dominant source (French), indeed borrows from it extensively, but although one finds varieties of creole full of gallicisms and varieties of French full of creolisms (Taylor 1968 [1961]:616, n. 14), and although Haitian Creole may even be experiencing decreolization (Goodman 1964:116, 135), its status as a distinct language is not in doubt, whereas that of Jamaican Creole has been denied (Taylor, *idem*). There is clearly a difference, one that does not depend on the relatedness of the dominant language, but on whatever social factors have underlain the difference in degree, and perhaps the timing, of the stabilization of the creole.

Whinnom makes sharply clear the difference between pidginization and a pidgin, not to separate, but to clearly relate the two. He thus is able to encompass the extreme variability of the one and the stability that it is essential to recognize in the other. Quantity becomes quality, as it were, when distance from a norm becomes autonomy. Notice that *cocoliche* is a counterpart to the post-creole continuum of present-day Jamaica, Antigua or Hawaii. It might be termed a *pre-pidgin continuum*. Another instance of a pre-pidgin continuum would be the *hapa haole* ('half white') of mid-nineteenth century Hawaii (Reinecke 1969). Both types of continuum are unstable in virtue of movement toward an external norm (what Stewart 1968:535, n. 11, calls 'heteronomy'). In the pre-pidgin continuum autonomy has not been achieved, while in the post-creole continuum it has been lost. (Nothing perhaps more clearly establishes the basis in social norms of the possibility of homogeneity in language, whether in a synchronic system or diachronic change.)

A continuum may seem only a lack of structure often ascribed to pidgins and even creoles themselves, but the problem of description posed by such continua is quite general. Creolists (Whinnom, De Camp) have brought the significance of these two types of continuum to the fore, and the problem has been generalized to all multilingual communities by another (Le Page 1969). The problem may be found in monolingual situations as well. It is a fundamental principle of sociolinguistics that the same functional relation may involve means of diverse scale and provenience in different situations. Sometimes a situation may be defined as formal or informal by *switching* between unrelated languages (Spanish, Guarani in Paraguay), distinct dialects (standard, local Norwegian in Hemnes, Norway), or style of speech within one language (Burundi, Africa (Albert 1970)). A situation may also be defined as more or less formal by *ranging* across the distance between distinct languages (*créole française, français créolisé* in Haiti), distinct dialects (the fading effect and methods of speech disguise employed between the English and Creole poles on Antigua (Reisman 1970), or between levels or styles within a single variety. (Such movement is reported from one level of respect to another in languages such as Japanese, where the system of politeness (cf. Neustupný 1968) comprises a number of individually variable features, and between levels of intimacy, from standard to colloquial Czech (Kučera 1955).) It is also, of course, a principle that the same sort of linguistic means may reflect different functional relations. Graduated variation may reflect an effort to define or express situations and relationships, but also an effort to achieve a more prestigeful norm, or purely an effort for the sake of intelligibility. Such variability may be entirely within a homogeneous variety, but often involves heterogeneous adaptation of means in situations other than those of pidgins and creoles. The Jamaican continuum can be compared to the fact that 'increased eloquence is in Eastern Yiddish associated with a rising frequency of the Hebrew-Aramaic component, in Western Yiddish an analogous stylistic effect is achieved by an increase in the German component' (Hutterer 1969:2 – assuming for the moment that Yiddish is not creolized), or to the use of the Greco-Latin stratum in English. *Cocoliche* can be compared to modes of use of Danish and Swedish (Haugen 1966:295–6).

Style-ranging poses analogous problems of description wherever found, problems that have hardly been satisfactorily solved (see discussion in Part v and by Labov). It may be that the salience of the phenomenon in pidgin and creole studies will stimulate development of methods that can deepen understanding in other circumstances.

Whinnom raises the question of the adequacy of creole languages, and suggests that their relation to standard European languages is analogous to the relation between the vernacular ancestors of these same European languages and pre-modern Latin. In each case one is comparing a language adapted to local needs with a language serving the gamut of cultural and international needs of its time. Such evolutionary questions are generally tabu in linguistics, but need to be confronted. The present analogy, of course, takes into account only referential content and use, and has to do only with the resources of the languages in general, not with the competence with which they may be utilized by individuals. And in fully assessing the adequacy of languages, of course, social and expressive uses would have to be taken into account as well, together with the possibility that a referentially more complex language might be inadequate in other respects (cf. Reisman 1970).

III

THE SCOPE OF SIMPLIFICATION

Whereas Whinnom is concerned to explain the occurrence of pidgins as something rare, Samarin focusses upon the process of pidginization as something quite widespread. He considers first the status of pidgin languages, and the ways in which linguists have saved generalizations by the expedient of ruling cases such as pidgins out of court, as not normal, not languages. Samarin finds, as against some writers, that a pidgin is not normal, but also, as against others, that it is a language. The goal he sets is to distinguish what is notable, but perhaps superficial and intermittent, from what is universal and presumably essential, indeed, constitutive of the class, pidgin.

Agreed upon measures for complexity, simplicity, functional load of languages hardly exist. Part of the challenge of pidgins to linguistic theory is to show the need for such measures if the defining criteria of reduction in form and use are to have any power. Samarin here explores some properties that might characterize pidgin texts. The results are only suggestive, but what they suggest is important. Since pidginization is a process more general than crystallization of pidgins, and since pidgins, once formed, may be elaborated in content and use, while remaining pidgins, the characteristics found in development to, and of, a pidgin admit of degrees. Indeed, pidgins and pidginization are instances *par excellence* of variable adaptation of means to an audience and situation. To analyze them, and to place them among other types of language and language use, quantitative measures are essential.

Samarin's discussion is informed throughout by his close knowledge of Sango, the national language of the Central African Republic. Sango's relation to its source, Ngbandi, as a result of reduction, is noted in some detail. Samarin stresses the emergence of novel features (cf. Reinecke on Tây Bồi and Hall 1966:109–110), and that pidgins cannot be seen as merely combinations or least common denominators, but reflect creative adaptation and innovation. Like Whinnom, Samarin finds the common 'reinforcement of error' model inadequate – it would seem to have no place in the origin of Sango – but whereas imperfect learning of a second language is set aside by Whinnom, for Samarin, it, memory loss of one's language, field work jargons, argots, restricted codes (Bernstein), and the like are all of interest, inasmuch as they are instances, not of pidgins necessarily, but of a process of pidginization, which he defines as any consistent reduction of the functioning of a language both in its grammar and its use. In complementary fashion, Samarin examines *koinés*, because they exhibit the other main type of process found in pidgins, confluence of different linguistic traditions, often with simplification, and by definition through the contact of members of different speech communities.

Whinnom's analysis of the emergence of a true pidgin as rare conflicts with Samarin's broad use of 'pidginization', but the conflict can be resolved by recognizing both a 'perfective' and an 'imperfective' sense of the term. If 'full' or 'completed' pidginization, or some equivalent, will serve for the former, then plain 'pidginization' can be used for a general process, one which may be carried through to different degrees, and have diverse outcomes, depending on configurations of forces such as Whinnom analyzes.

Many scholars still would not join Samarin in equating pidginization with simplification (reduction). Memory loss (Samarin's Auca case), and other reductions through acculturation and obsolescence – Bloomfield's 'threadbare' Menomini (1964 [1927] – cf. discussion in Hymes 1967), the truncated forms in which some other Amerindian languages survive (e.g. 'dog Wasco', as some members of the older generation call the Chinookan of their children) – would be excluded. So would 'baby talk' and other conventionally simplified forms, internally used, of the sort analyzed by Ferguson. Even the Australian 'in-law' language discussed by Samarin, which may indeed have arisen through a special kind of deliberate 'relexification' (or, adlexification) from surrounding languages, and argots, such as *caló*, the Anglicized Spanish of Tirilones in Texas (Coltharp 1965), showing mixture as well as reduction, but used only internally, are novel candidates for the title, 'pidgin'.[4] Simplified 'foreigner talk' might be considered an example, especially if reciprocated by those to whom used, and compromise forms of simplified speech with foreigners, perhaps even without admixture, would be called pidginized or even pidgin (Clyne 1968). *Cocoliche* and *hapa haole* certainly would be considered instances of (imperfective) pidginization, as the term *pre-pidgin continuum* has assumed.

In short, simplification itself is only salient pidginization. Use of 'simplification' in a substantive sense had implied the concurrence of simplification and other properties, particularly, admixture, and use between groups with different primary languages. Use of 'pidginization' for any of the three alone would be inadequate, however; not even the salient property of being no one's mother tongue would suffice to delimit pidgins – until recently Hebrew was such a language (Blanc 1968:237)). Admixture of course refers to phenomena far more widespread than pidginization, and so, indeed, does simplification. There is need for greater precision in the use of this and other terms for the changes that occur in pidginization, but not for another name for pidginization. To make any one term, and concept, tautologous with pidginization would be the converse of what is needed, namely, to recognize pidginization as a complex process, comprising the concurrence of several component processes.

In this respect, it seems desirable to make the component processes terminologically distinct. For change in complexity of outer form, one can speak of *simplification* and *complication*. For change in the scope of inner form, one can speak of *reduction* and *expansion*. For change in the scope of use of a variety of language, one can speak of *restriction* and *extension*. Many writers have used 'simplification' or 'reduction' (or both) for both the first two kinds of change. But while use of word order rather than inflection, of syntax rather than morphology, is a kind of simplification in outer form common to pidgins, to treat it as diagnostic of pidginization (or of previous pidginization) would make Chinese a creole and former pidgin. Such mistaking of part for whole does in fact continue to occur (cf. Bickerten and Escalante 1970:262, where it is maintained that a heavy functional load of syntactic as opposed to morphological resources 'ought to qualify it [Palanquero] as a creole by the most stringent criteria'). Palanquero may well be a pidgin or former pidgin, perhaps by internal processes – it seems to be used primarily as a boundary-maintaining device, and to be learned as a second, not first language—but this argument has the effect of equating pidginization with change to an analytic type of structure. The terminological distinctions introduced here may help retain recognition of the generality of the component processes that enter into pidginization, while keeping clear the distinction between them and the complex, specific process of pidginization itself.

Where simplification is joined with intergroup use, the relevance to pidginization is clear (cf. Ferguson's 'foreigner talk'). Even here, one would want to specify restricted intergroup use. Whether the other two pairs of properties (simplification and admixture; admixture and inter-group use) could be taken as implying pidginization is less certain. (An overall view of the taxonomic problem can be gained from Table 1.) In any case, it is Samarin's great merit to show that discussion in which the concurrence of the three properties is taken for granted will not do. The relevant meaning of each of the three must be specified – how much, and what kind, of each is to count? Does the case of the Australian in-law language, for example, show that to equate lack of a language in common with *ignorance* of a common language, as is usually done, is superficial? That the essential property is simply the *unavailability* of a language in common, for which the cause may be a social definition of the situation as one in which the ordinary language both parties share is not to be used between them? What is salient, what is substantive, in the standard definition of the properties of pidginization is far from resolved. And the various kinds of relation into which the properties may enter, each pair, and all three together, must be studied. Only thus can the complex process that is pidginization proper be adequately understood.

TABLE I

	Reduction	Admixture	Inter-group Use
1. Pidginization	+	+	+
2. X-ized Y		+	+
3. Foreigner talk	+		+
4. *caló* (argot)	+	+	
5. Lingua franca			+
6. Diffusion	–	+	–
7. Reduction	+	–	–

SOME SOURCES OF SIMPLIFICATION

In recognition of just such a need, Ferguson has taken up the matter of purposeful simplification in overt grammatical form, selecting the trait perhaps most often associated with simplification, absence of copula. (The trait has had great attention also with regard to Black English, on the one hand, and the influence of language on philosophy (as between Aristotle in Greek and in Arabic for

example) as well.) Ferguson's gift for careful typological analysis, both of
linguistic and cultural detail, is brought to bear on the difference between absence of copula as a salient trait, characteristic of one type of normal language,
and absence of copula as a putative substantive universal of pidginization. His
analysis touches on important, unresolved questions as to simplicity, natural-
ness, and universality in language, and leads to two specific hypotheses to be
tested.

Ferguson stresses the need to take into account the existence, prior to
pidginization, of conventional notions and practices as to how to talk simply.
Such folk-notions and varieties may not coincide with linguistic analyses of
simplicity, as studies of some baby talk have shown, but they no doubt influence
the form of a language that is proffered in situations that lead to pidginization.
Recognition of this fact is of course quite different from positing it as a general
theory, claiming it to be the sole source of what is proffered and acquired in
pidginization.[5]

This analysis re-establishes the place of typological convergence in explaining
resemblances among pidgins and creoles. (The typology is in part sociolinguistic:
deletion of copula may point to an original equivalence of register, rather than
unity of language, behind diverse pidgins.) Other features of pidgins and
creoles may reflect limited grammatical possibilities, once certain means are
adopted. The recurrent preference for word order, over inflection, is a typological convergence and at the same time a possible cause of other similarities
(the possibilities of word order being limited by universal constraints). Ferguson
points out that predictions must be probabilistic, rather than absolute, recalling
Samarin's point that reduplication, although common among pidgins, is not
universal, being absent in Sango, although present in its source, Ngbandi. (So
also Tâi Boy in relation to Vietnamese, suggesting that reduplication, where not
of West African provenience, may be characteristic of English pidgins because
English speakers put it there. Cf. Hall 1966: 65, 121, and Goodman 1967, on
introduction of reduplication into Japanese Pidgin English, as perhaps reflecting
an American assumption as to what is simple.)

Ferguson's study of course can only broach the general question of the kinds
and sources of simplicity in verbal form. From the standpoint of general
linguistics, one must not confuse simplicity of form with simplicity of content.
There are well-known contrasts between elaborate and simple styles, such as
the Asianic and Attic in classical Greek, wherein the simpler style would not be
obviously simpler in content. There is selective simplicity of form that compacts
a great deal of meaning – many lyrics, for example. There is simplicity of form
which is elliptical, to which the relevant contrast would be, not complexity,
but explicitness. There is the difference between what is simple for the speaker
and what is simple for the hearer, in terms of ease of production vs. ease of
interpretation. All these matters have to do with what the speaker and hearer
may have in common as a basis for interpreting what is said. As Samarin has
pointed out, there are kinds of simplification internal to a group involving loss
or attenuation of knowledge, and concealment. The kinds of talk, or register,
discussed by Ferguson, and the kinds of simplification immediately pertinent
to external pidginization, have to do with cases in which speaker and hearer
share a minimum of linguistic competence, and perhaps a minimum of common
cultural understanding as well. Simplification of outer form is here an adaptation to that constraint. (This functional condition, and any concomitants it

may have in linguistic form, may serve to distinguish 'ordinary', external pidginization from the internal kind.)

Invariance in form, rather than allomorphic variation; an invariant relation between form and grammatical function, rather than derivational and inflectional declensional and conjugational variation; largely monomorphemic, rather than inflected and derived words; reliance on overt word order; all have in common that they minimize the knowledge a hearer need have, and the speed with which he must decide, to know what in fact has grammatically happened. They minimize the knowledge a speaker need have, and his task in encoding, to say something within the rules of the code being used. Such simplification maximizes the role of the sector of language an outsider is most likely to encounter, and to find easiest to acquire, namely, items of lexicon. In this respect, the heart of pidginization is a focus on words and their order in situational context. Given the circumstances of use, the purpose is to make what means of communication are shared or sharable as accessible as possible.

It is a fair question whether this analysis does not have another side. If simplification, at least in the case of pidgins, reflects an interest in making messages, and codes, accessible, may not complication of outer form, at least in some cases, reflect an interest in making messages, and codes, *in*accessible? (I owe this suggestion to Franklin Southworth.) It is commonly observed that in communities with 'high' and 'low' linguistic varieties, it is the 'high' variety which is more complex in outer form. A similar relation might hold for whole languages, as between communities. If the simplification of pidgins is a means of transcending language boundaries, might not the complication of some languages in outer form, such as those of many small American Indian communities of the Pacific Coast, be a means of maintaining boundaries? Within a small community, sharing a maximum of knowledge and experience, variation in form, variable relation between form and grammatical function, syntagmatically complex words, reliance on inflational and covert relations might more easily develop. Such development could at least have the effect of maintaining boundaries between small autonomous communities. Such an effect might be welcomed, even cultivated, especially where one's language is regarded as the vehicle of indispensable lore, where it might serve to discriminate against persons who marry in, etc.

In short, the study of pidginization, by requiring us to study simplification, may lead to recognition of a sociolinguistic universal. Simplification may prove to be, not an isolated phenomenon, but one pole of a continuum applicable to outer form in all languages.

The view is widely held today that there is a natural universal form underlying all languages, a form to be taken as part of the description of each language. Departures from the natural universal form, requiring to be stated in individual descriptions, represent 'costs'. What current linguistic theory seeks to characterize and use as explanation is the natural universal form. The fact that all languages depart from that form, and pay such costs, is left unexplained. Closeness to or distance from such an underlying universal form, and 'payment' as it were of 'costs' for departure, may depend in part on the role a language or language-variety has played in maintenance of social boundary and communicative distance. If so, there would here be a case in which pursuit of explanatory adequacy within linguistics, narrowly conceived (cf. Chomsky 1965, pt. 1), has posed a problem whose explanation lies in sociolinguistics.

Ferguson thus poses problems wherein sociolinguistic description and general
linguistic theory intersect. He suggests that baby talk and foreigner talk are
based in part on universal characteristics of language acquisition, but their
presence or absence, and makeup, depend upon sociocultural processes as
well.[6]

IV

THE CRITERION OF CONVERGENCE OR MIXTURE

Where Samarin and Ferguson examine reduction and simplification, Gumperz
and Wilson, and Alleyne, examine convergence and mixture, particularly with
regard to creolization. Gumperz and Wilson show first of all how misleading for
the study of change is a view of a language as a homogeneous, isolated unity.
In Kupwar, as in some other places in India, one could come close to describing
the linguistic competence of the community with three lexicons attached to a
single grammar and phonology. Not to do so, indeed, would, from the standpoint of the speech community, be to fail to 'capture' a quite significant
generalization. Their work demonstrates clearly that the step from a feature or
component of a linguistic system to the system of which it is part is empirical and
problematic, and that ready recourse to a familiar, 'named' linguistic entity
('Urdu', 'English', etc.) can seriously mislead (cf. Le Page 1968:206–8).
    Gumperz and Wilson start from the view that the great need is to examine
ongoing sociolinguistic processes in the context of actual (not definitional)
speech communities. Only thus can one arrive at satisfactory explanations of
change. In Kupwar they find a situation in which lexical distinctness has been
maintained, but in which phonological and grammatical convergence has been
massive, the one reflecting the privacy and sanctity of the home, the other mutual
adaptation in communication outside the home. It would be important to know
the nature of the Marathi that is used in work groups by speakers of other languages – it might show pidginization – but the character of the natively-used
languages is clear. The mutual adaptation of all of them is reflected in the fact
that most changes simplify surface structure, or outer form, rather than complicate it, and bring about convergence of inner form. The changes are all
convergences among all three of the languages, rather than between just some pair.
    If one of the Kupwar languages were compared to its cognates outside the
village in isolation from its congeners within, past restructuring through some
radical discontinuity of tradition might be inferred. Analysis of the speech community as a whole enables us to see the continuity and mutual adaptation that
explain the present outcome.
    Clearly Kupwar represents a type of linguistic change for which one will
want a name, so as to identify it elsewhere, and for whose instances one will
hope eventually to have a comparative analysis. But is the Kupwar type a type
of creolization? A distinctive lexicon deployed in a grammar shared with other
languages does make one suspect creolization. Such convergence is a 'salient'
trait. Is it a substantive trait? That might be challenged. The standard definition
of a creole as a pidgin that has become a primary language refers only to
expansion. Expansion need not entail convergence. One can, for example,
imagine a case in which a much reduced, stable form of a language is used exclusively in intergroup communication, by both parties. Probably one would
accept such a variety as a pidgin. One can then imagine such a variety as the

initial language of children whose parents had only it in common, and as being expanded by the children toward the norm of the full language, if one parent was a speaker of the latter. (Such might occur in marriage between a German woman and immigrant labourer knowing German in the form described by Clyne 1968.) The expanded language of the children would be hardly distinguishable among other dialects of the full language. But – and here, I think, is the rub – it would also not seem a useful or interesting example of creolization. Although the initial process of acquisition might be fascinating, it would seem strange to insist on defining the later speech of the children as creolized.

In sum, although definition of a creole as an expanded pidgin says nothing of admixture, common usage implies that we think of convergence as a creole's most salient property. Not all kinds of convergence are usually in mind. We readily relate a case of convergence to creolization, when, if three components converge with those of another linguistic tradition and one distinctively persists, the distinct component is lexical, a convergent component grammar, as in Kupwar. Not so, where the distinctively retained component is phonetic, as in Anglo-Indian Speech (Spencer 1966, tracing the distinctive phonetics to Bengali). Such a case is usually referred to 'substratum' effects or the like. No doubt the difference is due to the central place we assign grammar; for convergence in it we reserve a special term.

If we generalize consideration of convergence to the whole of a language, then the possibilities with respect to differential persistence and convergence of components are numerous. If a language is considered to comprise four components, phonetics, lexicon (Gumperz' and Wilson's morphophonemics), syntax, and semantics, and the components are taken in all-or-nothing fashion, there are fourteen possibilities, as shown in Table 2 (using A to indicate persistence, B convergence).

TABLE 2

	Phonetics	Lexicon	Syntax	Semantics	Example
1.	B	A	A	A	North Pacific Coast
2.	A	B	A	A	Relexification
3.	A	A	B	A	Mbugu?
4.	A	A	A	B	European intertranslatability
5.	B	B	A	A	
6.	B	A	B	A	
7.	B	A	A	B	
8.	A	B	B	A	
9.	A	B	A	B	
10.	A	A	B	B	
11.	B	B	B	A	
12.	B	B	A	B	
13.	B	A	B	B	Kupwar; Island Carib 'men's speech'
14.	A	B	B	B	Anglo-Indian English
15.	A(b)	AB→C	Ab	?	*caló*

The separability of components in change must be recognized, and does often make it reasonable to talk of them as persisting or converging independently – to talk, as one may do, of 'lexicon' versus 'grammar', of phonetics versus the rest, etc. And an inexplicit criterion of significant degree is of course implied. One loanword does not a convergence make. Yet it is essential to take different degrees and consequences of convergence into account. They may differ as between components, and also may cut across components. (Inflectional elements especially may intersect components and participate in innovations.) Indeed, when we think of creolization and convergence as kin, we often seem to think of more than convergence in the strict sense of approximation of one variety to another. We have in mind mingling, coalescence, even fusion, of two varieties, especially as involves grammar. The prime candidate for consideration as creolization is convergence that is, as it were, internal rather than external. The grouping together as 'mixed languages' of Yiddish and other Jewish languages, Gypsy languages, creoles, and pidgins, in an international linguistic bibliography some years back perhaps reflects this tendency.[7] Creolization as convergence implies not only approximation, nor mixture even, but creativity, the adaptation of means of diverse provenience to new ends.[8] The Anglicized Spanish argot, *caló*, for example, might be characterized by the formula at the bottom of Table 2. English influence has introduced allophonic variants in pronunciation (A(b)); lexicon shows considerable English borrowing, together with innovations reflecting interaction of Spanish and English elements (AB→C); syntax shows less English influence (Ab); semantic influences are uncertain (?), since much of the continuing slang-like innovation may be new shapes for persisting meanings (Coltharp 1965:78–81). In Yiddish, 'an interpenetration of the different components [referring here to linguistic traditions, particularly Hebrew and German] took place in the language as a whole with the resultants afterwards undergoing an internal development of their own' (Weinreich 1968 [1953]:399).

The full number of possible patterns of convergent change, and the number actually attested, remains to be established, as does the sector of such a general field that is to be considered relevant to creolization. Gumperz and Wilson anticipate that the difference between creolization and other processes involving convergence will prove one of degree (cf. Goodman 1964:13, and the model proposed by Southworth, and Hoenigswald's conclusion, in this volume).

The question remains, to what extent is Kupwar a case of creolization? Kupwar shows use between speakers of different languages, admixture, some simplification in form, some restriction in role. The result is not a pidgin, because none of the languages has been severely reduced or lost its role as a primary language. Some pidginization in work groups may occur and play a part in convergence, but no shared, separate norm appears to be established. Nor are the languages creoles, in the sense of the standard definition of resulting from expansion of a pidgin. Behind the process of change has not been need to create a language (pidgin or creole) in the absence of one, but need to retain ritual separations of language in the presence of multiple multilingualism.

The requirement of a pidginized starting-point for a creole can be questioned (as will be seen with Alleyne's paper), but not the requirement of expansion. Change in scale and scope are essential criteria, if pidginization and creolization are to be distinguished from other processes, and from each other. Convergence is found apart from either, after all, and as a part of both. Kinds of convergence that are part of change in scale and scope (whether reduction or expansion) may differ less from each other than do both differ from kinds of convergence that are not part of such change. The same gross analysis of convergence at least seems to apply both to pidginization and to creolization (the inclusion of *caló* in Table 2 has implied as much). In short, convergence does not distinguish pidgins or creoles from other languages. Change in scale and scope does not distinguish pidgins and creoles from each other without specification of direction of change. If 'creolization' is to have a significant meaning, and if an important series of cases is to be properly distinguished, creolization, like pidginization, must be understood as a complex process, involving the concurrence of three components, here expansion, and extension in role, as well as convergence. It is not reducible to any one of them. Creolization, then, is expansion in content, with convergence, in the context of expansion in use. A creole is the result of such a process that has achieved autonomy as a norm.

In equating pidginization with simplification, Samarin has carried out the logic of equating the converse, creolization, with expansion. Neither equation is adequate, but in each the component process singled out is indispensable to the fuller process of which it is a part. To isolate simplification for study is important, as the work of Samarin and Ferguson shows. A corresponding analysis of expansion is greatly to be desired.

In sum, the work of Gumperz and Wilson shows the need for an analysis of the component processes of creolization, comparable to the analysis broached for pidginization by Whinnom and Samarin. And their work exemplifies the sort of field investigation that must be done, if we are to be able to specify the relationships between mechanisms of convergence, their settings, and their outcomes, so as to place creolization properly. Kupwar is not full creolization, but it is the kind of case that is indispensable to the understanding of full creolization.

V

CREOLIZATION, DISTANCE FROM A NORM, AND EXPANSION

Alleyne challenges the application of the standard definition of creoles to the classic set of cases, those of the Caribbean. By implication, he challenges the adequacy of the definition as well. Alleyne argues that the Caribbean languages have *not* developed from pidgins. He regards them as having arisen as part of an acculturative process in which the conditions specified by Whinnom for crystallization of a pidgin did not obtain. (In Whinnom's terms, the Caribbean languages are viewed as having originated in 'secondary', not 'tertiary', hybridization.) While there was some initial reduction of form and use, no doubt, and considerable African admixture, what was spoken was always a variety of the European language in question (Alleyne has English and French particularly in mind). The subsequent development of the culture contact situation, and particularly differences as to distance from the standard norm, both as between areas, and as between social positions (e.g. house slaves versus field slaves), has been crucial to the range of outcomes now found in the Caribbean. But, if one can so phrase Alleyne's view, the Caribbean shows the result of creolization with perhaps some prior pidginization, a pre-pidgin continuum, but without a prior pidgin. Put the other way round, pidginization may have as an outcome the crystallization of a creole. Initial reduction may be followed by expansion and admixture in primary use within a group, such that there emerges a distinct variety of speech, but one that has never been autonomous of the norm of a dominant source. The process begins and ends as technically a matter of dialect. The distance from the dominant norm is so great as to produce rapidly a distinctive variety, but the distance never becomes a break.[9]

Alleyne may have in mind especially the English creoles of Barbados and Jamaica, and certainly his analysis would explain the different contemporary situations in Jamaica and Haiti. In Jamaica, one would infer, the continuum has been present, without break, from the start.

Alleyne's view implies that of Whinnom, namely, that a full pidgin results only rarely under quite specific circumstances. The two differ as to the nature and origin of the Caribbean languages, Whinnom, like Cassidy, assuming relexification of an earlier Portuguese pidgin; Hancock (Part IV) differs yet again, agreeing with Whinnom and Cassidy in the prior existence of a pidgin, but in effect agreeing with Alleyne, in considering the pidgin English. Hancock thinks that the initial stage of the language was not highly Africanized and was to some extent comprehensible to a speaker of English, the extensive Africanization coming in the process of creolization in use between Africans. On Hancock's view, creolization began on the West African coast where there were English factories and settlements for many years.[10]

Much further empirical work (including study of the West African situation, such as undertaken by John Spencer, Elizabeth Tonkin, and others) is necessary to resolve the historical issues, but the present situation already makes two things clear. The inferences depend on social history and theory, not linguistic comparison alone (*contra* the implication of Hall 1966:120; cf. n. 3) – Alleyne's insistence on anthropological theory of cultural change is invaluable in this regard. And analytical work is needed too. A linear model of two discrete steps, as implied by the standard conception of pidgin and creole, may oversimplify the complexity of the historical cases to the point of distortion, and in itself contribute to the difficulty of interpreting the evidence. Within a single region there may coexist, contiguously, more than one stage of development. And there may indeed be more than two stages – a pre-pidgin continuum, a crystallized pidgin, a pidgin undergoing de-pidginization (reabsorption by its dominant source), a pidgin undergoing creolization, a creole, a creole undergoing decreolization. All six types are not likely to occur together, but some certainly do co-occur, e.g. a pidgin and the same pidgin undergoing creolization (Neo-Melanesian, and Police Motu, in New Guinea and Papua) – such cases motivate some authors to use the term 'pidgin-creole' (Voegelin and Voegelin 1964); a creole and a pidgin sustained by the creole (so some interpret the Cameroons situation); a pidgin, a creole, and a creole undergoing decreolization (at least as ideal types, if Tsuzaki is right) in Hawaii, to which cf. Southworth's model of the development of Marathi (Part IV)). In the circumstances of the West African Coast and Caribbean, and elsewhere, groups and individuals may well have experienced different configurations of development with regard to the same base language.

Just as Whinnom raises the question of varied outcomes for pidginization, so Alleyne raises the equally fundamental question of varied starting points for creolization. The most important point in this regard is perhaps the relation between creolization and the processes by which standard languages and koinés are sometimes formed. Expansion in content, admixture, and expansion in role as a primary language are found in both. After centuries of use only in liturgy and literature, as no one's first language, for example, Hebrew began to acquire native speakers, who number by now something like a million. Over some three generations the expansion of function led to a compromise form of speech based on several literary dialects and the speech of various communities immigrant to Israel. A standard has begun to emerge. The initial process has been termed 'koineizing' (Blanc 1968) – cf. Dillard (1964:38) for reference to 'trade pidgins and slave koinés'. Again, after the Norman conquest English was subordinate, limited in function. It subsequently expanded in function, replacing French (in the law courts for instance) and replacing, or rivalling, Latin too. (On English as inadequate and in need of expansion in the eyes of its own users, see Jones 1953.) It expanded in inner and outer form as well with considerable mixture of sources, both of English dialects and of other languages, notably Latin and French, quite as Neo-Melanesian now draws on English. (Note the complexities introduced into the analysis of English by the Romance component.) In each case, of course, Hebrew and English, the starting point of expansion and admixture was not a pidgin; in that fact lies presumably an essential difference. How much a difference, however, will be clear only after recognition of the similarity has led to careful comparison of the two kinds of cases for the light each can shed on the other.

Recognition that the starting point of creolization is problematic cuts deeper yet. A feature held in common by emerging standards, koinés, and creoles is that each entails some stabilization and awareness of a new norm. (On standards in this regard, cf. Garvin 1964 [1959].) A stabilized pidgin too, whatever the loyalty it may or may not enjoy, is something that must be learned. It is in fact important to remember that a pidginized form of speech, once initiated, may elaborate and stabilize to various degrees without becoming a creole in the usual sense (Reinecke 1964 [1938]:537).[11] This may occur before it becomes stabilized as a pidgin, or without stabilization as a pidgin occurring. A koiné or a standard language may expand and become stabilized through the interaction of adults and without being learned as such by children; why not a pidgin? Here again the standard definition of pidgin and creole, and the life cycle model it assumes, is too narrow and mistakenly concrete. Technical creolization defined as acquisition as a first language by children, might not in fact lead to expansion, if a second language were acquired at school age, and the infant creole was developed no further or abandoned. On the other hand, considerable expansion in form might result from expansion in role, through use as a lingua franca, quite apart from any acquisition as a first language. Such seems to be the case with Neo-Melanesian, which is developing into a national language in New Guinea. In sum, it is expansion in functional role that is at stake, not a particular route. What counts is what may be said to be status as a *primary* language (functionally) in a community. Autobiographical priority, as first language learned, is a possible route to primary status, but neither necessary nor sufficient. Just as the reduction of pidginization need not be external, between groups, so the expansion of creolization need not be internal, but may occur in use as a lingua franca.

Alleyne does not deny the distinctive character of what has emerged in the Caribbean as a result of the process he analyzes, but he does object to the term 'creole', especially where autonomy as a norm has been achieved and maintained (e.g. Sranan in Surinam). Invidious public associations with both 'pidgin'

and 'creole' do present a problem, especially where they imply a status as less
than true languages for both; and 'pidgin' may remain attached to a language
after it has been creolized, as sometimes in West Africa and as perhaps will be
the case in New Guinea. Replacement of a demeaning individual name has been
necessary, e.g. of 'Taki taki' by 'Sranan', and the attempt to replace 'Pidgin'
by 'Neo-Melanesian'. It may be generally necessary to avoid either 'pidgin' or
'creole' in the local name of an individual language. Scholars still will find the
descriptive terms of the type Surinam Creole English, Melanesian Pidgin
English, Philippine Creole Spanish, useful, especially where, as in the last case,
no substitute is at hand. For types of language, *pidgin* and *creole* remain indispensable, unless equivalents can be found, for specific outcomes of the processes discussed here. The trouble, of course, is not in the linguistics but the
social situations of discrimination and prejudice, and perhaps no names can be
wholly acceptable so long as there is bias toward that which they name.

CLASSIFICATION: A FOURTH DIMENSION

The problem of invidious association extends to classification. Alleyne grants
that to assign creoles genetically to other than their European sources would
seem indefensible, yet notes that it seems absurd to call the African element
borrowing. He dismisses the question of genetic classification as unanswerable
or irrelevant. The question misses the point, which is the novel integration that
has come about. One should note that some scholars may classify pidgins and
creoles as Indo-European perhaps unconsciously for liberal motives – not to
deny a creative role to their non-European speakers and sources, but to rescue
them from stigmatization as 'bastards'. As with names, there is no simple
solution, so long as social prejudice is a factor. But whereas not to use descriptive
names for languages may seem to inconvenience the scholar, downgrading of
genetic classification is a necessary step toward clarity. On Alleyne's own showing, Jamaican could be classified as a continuation of a variety of English, and
in turn, Germanic, Indo-European, and someday perhaps, of a wider relationship involving Semitic or Finno-Ugric. That shows how little such classification
explains. After all, if to place a pidgin or creole genetically sufficed, there would
be no special subject of pidgin and creole. In fact, genetic classification explains
no more than a fraction of the history and formation of a language, however
indispensable that fraction may be to understanding the whole. Indeed, the
kind of classification to which the genetic model is appropriate has to do principally with a period of human history – mass migration and the peopling of the
regions of the world – that is past. Genetic diversification may never occur again.
The kind of classification, and the associated models of explanation, required
by pidgins and creoles are in fact the kind required by the process of reintegration of social groups and linguistic varieties now prevalent in the world.

All this shows the failure of the approach to language history that has been
dominant, especially in American work, and especially regarding pidgins and
creoles. There is first of all the failure to deal with some of the outcomes of
linguistic change as emergents, as discontinuities. The dogma of continuity
has led some linguists of late even to the extreme of denying the possibility of
periodization in the history of language, or of distinguishing any valid break in
the line that runs from, say, modern Jamaican or Lancashire English back to
the beginning of human speech, so far as it can be traced. Despite the documented evidence of emergence of distinct, unintelligible new varieties in a generation

in the case of pidgins and creoles, the issue is evaded with a phrase. One refers to the special rapidity, 'intensity', 'brusque restructuring' of the change. Such rapidity is diagnostic of these languages, true, but it is not an explanation. Were unique rate of change taken seriously, scholars presumably would make a general glottochronology, comprising the special rate of formation of pidgins and creoles, their active concern. As it is, those who refer to such a rate as if it were an explanation seem to be in the position of maintaining that there is a set of languages defined by a trait which is (1) unique, (2) proof of their normality, and (3) not needing to be studied. Such attempts to preserve the gradualist, narrowly uniformitarian assumptions of the 'neo-grammarian' tradition treat as merely quantitative changes that have a qualitative result. Rate of change in pidgins and creoles, as elsewhere in languages, is a manifestation of underlying sociolinguistic forces. It may prove an invaluable diagnostic tool, covarying with different configurations of underlying forces, but it is in analysis of the configurations that explanation lies.

Recent discussion of the rate of extensive change through pidginization apparently has neglected what may be a critical difference from 'normal genetic transmission'. For the latter, in cases in which questions of 'substratum' and convergence do not arise, the transmission is to children. There is acceptance in a few years of most of the basic vocabulary and most of the basic grammar of a linguistic variety. Even if the children are multilingual (as many children are), it would seem that normally they segregate the form and use of their various language varieties. It seems likely that this depends upon acquisition in a period of life biologically favourable to the acquisition of language. Moreover, from the standpoint of the community, the process is a continuous, hardly visible one, one year's cohort of children overlapping another. The normal communication of the community goes on, and the induction of children into it is without end, and, in a sense, often without beginning. (Replacement, obsolescence, and generational stratification of languages of course can be dated.) Children's speech is recognizable as degrees of approximation to a pre-existing, comprehensive norm.

By definition, a pidginization situation principally involves adults. (Were the participants children, we would call it incipient creolization.) The process does not have the maturational basis of childhood acquisition, but is learning and adaptation, a *selective* acceptance of lexicon and grammar, so far as any one source is concerned, in a context of limited opportunity, limited need, and, as adults, of more limited ability. From the standpoint of the community or group, the process is a visible one of sharing in the *ad hoc* adaptation and creation of a novel means of speech.

To insist in the face of such considerations that transmission and kind of relationship of linguistic varieties does not qualitatively differ, according to sociolinguistic configurations, is to assign to 'genetic relationship' a 'mystical', 'metaphysical', quality, an unconditioned magic, of the sort adherents of the universality of normal genetic transmission have sometimes liked to attribute to other points of view.

To speak of sociolinguistic forces is to point to a second, or more precisely, a general failure – inability to deal with linguistic change as something on-going, observable, and motivated. Historical linguistics developed in the context of a search for origins, and in connection with a view of language as an organic whole (or at least a view in which some part, such as grammar, could stand for the whole). It has bequeathed a perspective so pervasive that one hardly thinks to question it. When we seek to classify a language or elements of a language, we think unreflectingly of having three choices, choices which amount to three alternative sorts of origin. Can resemblances with another language be due to chance convergence or language universals? If not, are they due to borrowing or to retention from a common ancestor? That is, are the languages to be classed together as only members of the same formal type (convergence without historical contact), as members of the same language area (due to borrowing) or of the same language family (through retention)? A very great part of the literature on pidgin and creole languages is concerned with questions within the limits of this frame of reference – the celebrated exchange between Taylor (1956) and Hall (1958), for example, or the argument over whether there can be such a thing as 'mixed languages' (for recent observations, see Goodman 1964:136–7 and Dalby 1966:175).

These three alternatives are inadequate to pidgin and creole languages (and beyond that, to languages generally), because they omit a fourth source of resemblance, social role. There are studies of what languages share because they are of the same formal type, of the same area, and of the same family, but only very recently has the general question of what languages share because they occupy the same functional role been broached (Hymes 1968:363–4 and Greenberg 1968:133). Of course a great portion of this book is concerned with what languages may have in common as a result of use as a pidgin, or, after reduction, use as a primary language. Much discussion of pidgins and creoles has indeed been of this sort, but, it has tended to be couched typologically in terms of formal universals, rather than social process. Moreover, the lack of a general framework within which to discuss all languages in these terms has been a handicap. Just because such functional discussion, inevitable with regard to pidgins and creoles, did not fit the usual trinity of family, area and type, it probably contributed to the marginal status of pidgin and creole studies. The growing sense of the general relevance of pidgin and creole studies today has in part to do with recognition that *all* languages exist as (one or more) functional varieties, and that questions of the classification and consequences of such functions must be raised for all.

One and the same language may of course be classifiable in more than one way, perhaps in all four ways. With most languages scholars are content to place genetic classification first, to say of a language that it is English, or Germanic, or Indo-European, and then to discuss borrowing or formal typology or functional role against that background. There is considerable utility to such an approach (else it would not have persisted). But pidgins and creoles are languages, *par excellence*, in which the several kinds of origin combine, and combine in a way that is essential to the nature of what is being classified. (Discussion of 'mixed languages' has been an attempt to face this fact within the older frame of reference.) Classification as to kinds of origin misses the very essence of the phenomenon. The vantage point of classification must be that of a group of persons moving toward the future, making the best of a current situation with the linguistic resources at hand under one or another set of conditions.

Genetic classification by its nature is concerned with the oldest stratum discernible in a language, subject to some kind of weighting as to significance as part of the core of the language. Inevitably it treats as basic what has been, not what is coming into being, and traces the most arbitrary, least adaptive features. (Cf. Hall 1966:110–11, and for a factual critique, Goodman 1964:134, n. 26.) It was once of great cultural importance to Europeans to trace origins, language was a major clue, useful because of its long persistence in detectable form; and nineteenth century linguistics answered the call of its culture, sometimes to liberal effect, as in demonstrating the unsuspected kinship of the English and Irish. It is now of great importance to analyze adaptation and meaningful integration, but linguistics has lagged. We need to develop modes of functional classification, taking as basic the ways in which linguistic means are organized for social ends, and extending the scope of classification from individual lines of historical transmission to the linguistic repertoires of persons and communities.

VI

TAXONOMIES, MODELS, AND DEFINITIONS

The study of pidgin and creole languages especially needs the development of a new, sociolinguistic form of taxonomy, in which origin or provenience of linguistic means is but one dimension among others. The dimensions of such a taxonomy are brought out in the papers presented here, and have been reflected in this introduction. They are:

(1) scale of linguistic means with regard both to outer form (simplification, complication) and inner form (reduction, expansion);

(2) provenience of linguistic means, that is confluence, or not, of traditions;

(3) scope of social role (restricted, extended), with regard to use both between groups, and within a group, as primary or secondary means of communication;

(4) context, with regard to the barriers analyzed by Whinnom; motivation and identifications of persons involved (cf. Le Page 1969); the linguistic repertoires of the persons involved; and, particularly, relation to existing linguistic norms.

A great many types could be placed in terms of such dimensions: lingua francas, koinés, various kinds of argot, languages of special function, obsolescent languages, international auxiliary languages, restricted codes, foreigner talk, and of course, pidgins and creoles, including all the permutations one might wish to ring on the general formula represented in 'Chinese Pidgin English': Pidgin X (if one wishes to retain 'Pidgin' (or 'Pidginized') for cases of severe reduction of a single language in intergroup use); Y Pidgin X (Chinese Pidgin English); Y Creole X; and the intermediate degrees of Y Pidginized X (Hawaiian Pidginized English, *hapa haole*),Y creolizing X (Melanesian creolizing English, where that is occurring in New Guinea), Y-ized X (*français créolisé*), etc.

Beyond taxonomy is explanation, and new models, and a new approach, are needed in the study of pidgins and creoles, in order to transcend the 'all-or-nothing' choice with which one would seem to be presented today (either parallel development or relexification, most notably). One needs a model designed to deal with the integration of processes of change in relation to types of outcome – simplification, imperfect learning, borrowing, etc. What would be constant would be the fundamental terms, or variables, and variables they would be, such that differences in their values would result in differing outcomes. Put the other way round, different outcomes, either of degree or of kind, do not require different underlying models, but different values of one model.

Whinnom's analysis of pidginization in relation to a pidgin as outcome is in effect such a model. The taxonomic dimensions just listed could provide such a model, if the several properties were stated in terms of *change in* scale of linguistic means, *change in* provenience, and convergence, *change in* scope, in relation to context, itself subject to change. The models presented by Southworth (Part IV) and Mintz (Part VI) might be interpretable as specifications of such a general model for particular historical cases.

Only extensive empirical and analytical work can determine what specific values the dimensions must be given; at the same time, the theoretical possibilities of the dimensions may point to otherwise unnoticed types. In sum, the deeper study of pidginization and creolization implicates the general study of sociolinguistic change.

Much of what has been argued in this Introduction can be summed up in the following definitions and comments.

Pidginization is that complex process of sociolinguistic change comprising reduction in inner form, with convergence, in the context of restriction in use. A *pidgin* is a result of such a process that has achieved autonomy as a norm. The context of restricted use in pidginization need not be external, but may be internal to a speech community instead (or as well). The result of pidginization may acquire a name, but not an independent life, that is it may be a pre-pidgin continuum.

Creolization is that complex process of sociolinguistic change comprising expansion in inner form, with convergence, in the context of extension in use. A *creole* is the result of such a process that has achieved autonomy as a norm. The context of expanded use in creolization need not be internal to a speech community, but may be external instead (or as well). The starting point of creolization need not be a pidgin, but may be a pre-pidgin continuum, or a subordinated language-variety of some other sort.

Pidginization is usually associated with simplification in outer form, creolization with complication in outer form.

The component processes of pidginization and creolization occur generally in languages. For pidginization and creolization, and *a fortiori*, pidgins and creoles, to be adequately understood, we require both study of the component processes in their own right, and study of the ways in which they combine. These processes are interdependent with sociocultural factors. The study of pidginization and creolization is thus an essential part of the general study of language from a sociolinguistic point of view.

Four short contributions bearing on questions of process are included in this part. In the succinct hypotheses which he noted down at the conference, and has kindly permitted to be published here, Joos stresses social solidarity as the key variable affecting pidgins and creolization. This emphasis is particularly valuable because attitudes toward these languages have sometimes been taken for granted, whereas Joos formulates hypotheses to be tested.[12] Voorhoeve shows that the impossibility of inference as to reduction and expansion in many historically known cases makes mandatory field study of ongoing processes, e.g. the incipient creolization of Cameroons Pidgin English, if satisfactory models of explanation are to be had. Silverstein focusses attention on lexicon as crucial to pidgins, proposing that at least some pidgins are constituted wholly by their lexicons, supported by independently converging, rather than shared, grammars. His thesis would make a considerable difference to the likelihood of relexification as a source of pidgins. The illustration of energetic communication with a pidgin reminds us that language is not the only medium available, and that reduction in overt linguistic form is not certain indication of reduction in underlying structure, or of the limits of what may be conveyed. Lawton suggests that Puerto Rican Spanish is an instance of creolization without prior pidginization.

NOTES

1 The first indeed was Sapir's view, as it is that of Hoenigswald and Labov in this volume (Sapir 1949 [1916]:425). The view has important implications for a theory of the nature of culture (cf. Sapir 1949 [1938], and discussion in Hymes 1964:29, n. 8, and 1967). On the theoretical implications of the second, cf. Barth 1969.

2 A valuable comparison could be made to the development of Yiddish, where Eastern Yiddish developed in Slavic and other non-German environments, while Western Yiddish never lost contact with German. From a purely linguistic point of view, the contact was similar in the two areas, the literary and vernacular language of the environment coming to be interwoven with the system of Yiddish. 'But while such interweaving produced a specific form of language synthesis in Slavic surroundings, it led to a step-by-step absorption of German norms by Yiddish in completely German environments' (Hutterer 1969:3). In the transitional area, especially in Hungary, the situation was more complex, and after German lost its role as a model, Yiddish was not reshaped on Hungarian models (as happened in Slavic surroundings), but replaced by Hungarian, except as the process was restrained by subsequent presence of German as an important lingua franca in the Carpathian region (Hutterer 1969:4).

3 Island Carib men's speech consists largely of Karina (Carib) lexemes, used with Arawakan phonemes, inflexion and syntax. Taylor suggests that it was a former lingua franca and pidgin, made necessary, if tradition is correct, by Carib conquest and killing of all indigenous Arawakan-speaking males. The pidginized variety of Anglo-Romanes apparently arose through formation of gangs containing both Gipsy and English members within a dozen years after the landing of the Gipsies in the mid-fifteenth century in England. The pidginized variety is essentially exotic lexemes in an English matrix, having lost phonological contrasts and word-class suffixes. Note that the most reduced and converged variety is used in initial contact with non-Romani travellers or other families, a 'deeper' variety being retained by many Romani families among themselves.

4 Voegelin and Voegelin (1964:69–70) deny the pidgin status of the *pachuco* of Arizona and California, and by implication, that of the *caló* of El Paso, Texas. In point of fact, users of the *caló* do not consider it *pachuco*, a word which to them identifies people from California (Coltharp 1965:74). Voegelin and Voegelin argue that a person bilingual in English and Spanish could with sufficient context interpret the calquing and loanwords that make the language unintelligible to native speakers of ordinary Spanish. The *caló* in fact is restricted to use by males (although it may be understood passively by females in the group) and changes steadily to preserve its role as a language of concealment. (Notice a process of relexification for the sake, not of convergence, but of divergence.)

Of approximately 700 entries given by Coltharp, most are specific to the argot. A count of over one-third (those in A–C, some 276) shows only 25 % to be shared with the *pachuco* of Tucson, Arizona, as recorded by Barker; not quite 15% to be found in a regional Spanish dictionary; no more than 10 or 11% to be found in the relevant dictionaries of Americanisms and Mexicanisms in Spanish. It is not clear how many ordinary Spanish elements may be in use, since Coltharp excludes forms with the same shape and meaning in the dictionary of the Real Academia Española, but about one-third of the forms were not to be found in the standard dictionary at all, even in varied shape or meaning, or both. The unintelligibility, restricted function, simplification in form (most verbs end in the one inflection, -*ar*), and admixture strongly suggest a process of internal pidginization. It is noteworthy that the term accepted by speakers for the language, *caló*, is defined in the Academy dictionary as language or dialect of the Gipsies, adopted in part by people of the lower working class. The relations of creoles, pidgins, and argots, as languages of concealment, and languages sometimes concealed, have yet to be systematically explored.

5 That view is implied by Hall (1966:120), when he writes that the Proto-Pidgin-English lexicon he reconstructs is 'essentially an approximation of such features of lower-class seventeenth-century English speech as its speakers saw fit to use in their contacts with non-Europeans in the course of their trading, "blackbirding", and colonizing activities'. This is to inflate a partial reconstruction and process into the whole story. Goodman (1964:124) notes that the French Creole forms of personal pronouns and verb constructions do reflect an effort of French speakers to avoid or to simplify inflectional complexities, but that other Creole forms show traces of inflection that indicate simplification was far from thorough-going, and that those acquiring the French played an active part. (Cf. also Goodman 1964:27–8, 123, 133, n. 26.) Clyne (1968) reports that the imperfect German of immigrant labourers is a compromise between their own simplified forms and the ideas as to simplification of German speakers.

6 Revill (1966:251, 252) reports a feature (a final vocalic element) used both to foreigners and children to insure better understanding, and a feature (absence of elision) used only to foreigners, not to children.

7 Linguistic Bibliography for the year 1953 [also, 1954, 1955, 1956, 1957]. Published by the Permanent International Committee of Linguistics with a grant from Unesco. Paris. Since 1957 there has been a division, 'Creolized Languages' (cf. Valkhoff 1966:37). Comparative study of the Jewish and Gipsy languages, and the argots to which they have sometimes given rise, is in fact important to clarification of the factors determining salient and substantive pidginization and creolization.

8 Cf. Craig (Part v) on mutation as well as mixture in the post-creole continuum of Jamaica; and Taylor (1964:436) on 'remodelling' as between Portuguese, Dutch and English affinities of forms in Saramaccan; and Reisman (1970:131–2), quoting Taylor, on reshaping and reinterpretation as ongoing, creative processes. Especially in such cases, 'typological' thinking in terms of whole languages, or parts of languages as surrogates for the whole, must be replaced by 'stylistic' models, concerned with fashions of speaking, or speech styles. Such styles would be defined by rules of co-occurrence and co-variation, and by contrastive alternation with other styles, and would be capable of dealing more directly and empirically with change in terms of features and limited configurations of features. Cf. Labov 1970 (1965), Le Page 1968, and Rowe 1959.

9 Just such a process of pidginization and subsequent expansion in internal use, accompanied by admixture, but without crystallization of a pidgin, may have occurred in the formation of Yiddish, which must have begun as a limited form of German used outside the home by speakers of Romance dialects of eastern France and northern Italy and writers of Hebrew. On the possibility of direct creolization, cf. Reinecke 1964 [1938]:539 on 'settlers' creole dialects', and Valkhoff 1968: 'there is also the possibility – left unmentioned by Hall – that a Creole variety of the cultural language was born directly, usually in the close contact between European colonists and their male and female slaves, who first spoke various African languages and then resorted to the new tongue that was thrust upon them.' Valkhoff cites the Dutch linguist Hesseling, his predecessor in study of the influence of a Portuguese creole on the formation of Afrikaans.

10 Hancock, personal communication. I am indebted to Hancock also for the quotation from Valkhoff (n. 7) and discussion of Anglo-Romanes.

11 Cf. Epstein (1968 [1959]:322): 'Despite its many inherent limitations, Fanagalo is not a completely impoverished jargon. Among skilled speakers it lends itself readily to fluent and intelligent conversation on a wide variety of subjects.' Cf. also Hooley (1962:127): 'Contrary to expectation, it was found that while Neomelanesian is sharply reduced in structure and vocabulary, there are nevertheless considerable transformation possibilities.'

12 Note contrasting attitudes, although for similar motives, with regard to Fanagalo and Police Motu. Fanagalo 'remains essentially the language of command and direction ... associated with European racialist attitudes ... [so that] in the sphere of Black-White relations, Fanagalo is the mark of social distance, English is the mark of social acceptance and even equality' (Epstein 1968 [1959]:322). In contact in New Guinea between speakers of Roro, Makeo and Kovio in town there is a tendency for the language nearest the coast to be used, but this may imply something of a superior-inferior relationship, and, if one wishes to avoid this, Police Motu, if available is used (Taylor 1968:46–7).

While creoles are often regarded as inadequate and inferior, there are instances of pride and preferred use. There is the incipient standardization of Sranan, associated with the nationalist movement Wie Eegie Sanie (Our own things) (cf. Part v); and there is what Berry (1961:5, n. 1) calls 'hypercreolization', an inordinate use of Africanisms, and a keen awareness of early patterns of phonemic integration, in movement *away* from English norms. There are the loyalties and attitudes reflected in such situations as Hall reports (1966:133): 'For the normal, unpretentious Haitian, use of Creole is the symbol of truth and reality, and French is the language of bluff and mystification and duplicity, as shown by such expressions as ... 'I'm talking Creole [that is, straightforwardly, honestly] to you, am I not? '[and] ... 'to speak French', i.e. 'to offer money [or a bribe] to someone'. Creoles may be preferred for structural reasons. Speakers of Timne, an indigenous language of Sierra Leone, may use Krio when they wish to be able to discuss contemporary topics without the problem of integrating loanwords into the Temne gender system (David Dalby, personal communication).

REFERENCES

Albert, Ethel 1971. 'Cultural patterning of speech in Burundi', *Directions in Sociolinguistics*, ed. by J. Gumperz and D. Hymes, New York, Holt, Rinehart, and Winston

Barth, Fredrik (ed.) 1969. *Ethnic groups and boundaries. The social organization of cultural difference*, Bergen/Oslo, Universitetsforlaget; London, George Allen and Unwin

Berry, Jack 1961. 'English loanwords and adaptations in Sierra Leone Krio', *Proceedings of the conference on creole language studies (1959)*, ed. R. B. Le Page, 1–16, London, Macmillan

Bickerten, D. and A. Escalante 1970. 'Palanquero: a Spanish-based creole of northern Colombia', *Lingua* 24:254–67

Blanc, Haim 1968. 'The Israeli Koine as an emergent national standard', *Language problems of developing nations*, ed. by J. A. Fishman, C. A. Ferguson, J. Das Gupta, 237–51, New York, John Wiley

Bloomfield, Leonard 1964 [1927]. 'Literate and illiterate speech', *Language, in culture and society*, ed. by D. Hymes, 391–6, New York, Harper and Row. [Originally, *American Speech* 10:432–9]

Chomsky, N. 1965. *Aspects of the theory of syntax*, Cambridge, M.I.T. Press

Clyne, M. 1968. 'Zum Pidgin-Deutsch der Gastarbeiter', *Zeitschrift für Mundartforschung* 35:130–9

Coltharp, Lurline 1965. *The tongue of the tirilones: a linguistic study of a criminal argot* (Alabama Linguistic and Philological Series, 7), University, Alabama, University of Alabama Press

Dalby, David 1966. 'Levels of relationship in the comparative study of African languages', *African Language Studies* 7:171–9

Dillard, J. L. 1964. 'The writings of Herskovits and the study of the languages of the Negro in the New World', *Caribbean Studies* 4(2):35–41

Emeneau, Murray B. 1942. 'Language and social forms: a study of Toda kinship terms and dual descent', *Language, culture, and personality*, ed. by L. Spier, A. I. Hallowell and S. S. Newman, 158–79, Menasha, Wisconsin, Banta

Epstein, A. L. 1968 [1959]. 'Linguistic innovation and culture on the Copperbelt, Northern Rhodesia', *Readings in the sociology of language*, ed. by J. A. Fishman, 320–39, The Hague, Mouton. [Originally, *Southwestern Journal of Anthropology* 15:235–53]

Garvin, P. L. 1964 [1959]. 'The standard language problem: concepts and methods', *Language in culture and society*, ed. by D. Hymes, 521–3, New York, Harper and Row. [Originally, *Anthropological Linguistics* 1(2):28–31]

Goodman, Morris 1964. *A comparative study of creole French dialects*, The Hague, Mouton

Goodman, J. S. 1967. 'The development of a dialect of English-Japanese pidgin', *Anthropological Linguistics* 9(6):43–55

Greenberg, J. H. 1968. *Anthropological linguistics*, New York, Random House

Hall, R. A., Jr. 1958. 'Creolized languages and "genetic relationships",' *Word* 14:367–73

 1966. *Pidgin and creole languages*, Ithaca, Cornell University Press

Hancock, Ian 1970. 'Is Anglo-Romanes a creole?' *Journal of the Gypsy Lore Society* 49 (1/2):41–4

Haugen, Einar 1966. 'Semicommunication in Scandinavia. Explorations in sociolinguistics', ed. by S. Lieberson, 280–97, *Sociological Inquiry* 36(2). [Also: *International Journal of American Linguistics* 33(2), pt. II (1967)]

Hooley, Bruce A. 1962. 'Transformations in Neomelanesian', *Oceania* 33:116–27

Hutterer, C. J. 1969. 'Theoretical and practical problems of Western Yiddish dialectology', *The field of Yiddish, third collection*, ed. M. I. Herzog, W. Ravid, U. Weinreich, 1–7, The Hague, Mouton

Hymes, Dell. 1964. 'Introduction', *The ethnography of communication*, ed. by

J. J. Gumperz and D. Hymes, 1–34, Washington, D.C., American Anthropological Association

1967. 'Why linguistics needs the sociologist', *Social Research* 34:632–47

1968. 'Linguistics – the field', *International Encyclopedia of the Social Sciences* 9:351–71, New York, Macmillan

1971. 'Sociolinguistics and the ethnography of speaking', *Linguistics and social anthropology*, ed. by E. Ardener. London, Tavistock

Jones, R. F. 1953. *The triumph of the English language*, Stanford, Stanford University Press

Kucera, H. 1955. 'Phonemic variation of spoken Czech', *Word* 11:575–602

Labov, W. A. 1971 [1965]. 'Mechanism of linguistic change', *Directions in sociolinguistics*, ed. J. J. Gumperz and D. Hymes, New York, Holt, Rinehart, Winston. [Originally, *Georgetown University Monograph on Languages and Linguistics* 18:91–114]

Le Page, R. B. 1969. 'Problems of description in multilingual communities', *Transactions of the Philological Society (1968)*, 189–212

Neustupny, J. V. 1968. *Politeness patterns in the system of communication*, Eighth International Congress of Anthropological and Ethnological Sciences, Tokyo and Kyoto

Reinecke, John E. 1964 [1938]. 'Trade jargons and creole dialects as marginal languages', *Language in culture and society*, ed. by D. Hymes, 534–42, New York, Harper and Row. [Originally, *Social Forces* 17:107–18]

1969. *Language and dialect in Hawaii*, Honolulu, University of Hawaii Press

Reisman, Karl 1970. 'Cultural and linguistic ambiguity in a West Indian village', *Afro-American anthropology, contemporary perspectives*, ed. by N. E. Whitten, Jr., and J. F. Szwed, 129–44, New York, The Free Press. [Précis, this volume]

Revill, P. M. 1966. 'Preliminary report on paralinguistics in Mbembe (E. Nigeria)', *Tagmemic and matrix linguistics applied to selected African languages*, by K. L. Pike, 245–54, Washington, D.C., U.S. Dept. Health, Education and Welfare, Office of Education, Bureau of Research

Rowe, J. R. 1959 'Archaeological dating and cultural process', *Southwestern Journal of Anthropology* 15:317–24

Sapir, Edward 1949 [1916]. 'Time perspective in aboriginal American culture: a study in method', *Selected writings of Edward Sapir*, ed. by D. G. Mandelbaum, 389–462, Berkeley and Los Angeles, University of California Press. [Originally, Ottawa, Canada, Dept. of Mines, Geological Survey, Memoir 90]

1949 [1938]. 'Why cultural anthropology needs the psychiatrist', *Selected writings of Edward Sapir*, ed. by D. G. Mandelbaum, 569–77, Berkeley and Los Angeles, University of California Press. [Originally, *Psychiatry* 1:7–12]

Spencer, John 1966. 'The Anglo-Indians and their speech: a socio-linguistic essay', *Lingua* 16:57–70

Stewart, William A. 1968. 'A sociolinguistic typology for describing national multilingualism', *Readings in the sociology of language*, ed. by J. A. Fishman, 531–45, The Hague, Mouton

Taylor, Andrew J. 1968. 'A note on the study of sociolinguistics, with particular reference to Papua-New Guinea,' *Kivung* (Journal of the Linguistic Society of the University of Papua and New Guinea) 1:43–52

D

Taylor, Douglas 1956. 'Language contacts in the West Indies: I, A case of intimate borrowing; II, On the classification of creolized languages', *Word* 12:399–414

    1959. 'On function versus form in "non-traditional languages",' *Word* 15:485–9

    1963. 'The origin of West Indian creole languages: evidence from grammatical categories', *American Anthropologist* 65:800–14

    1964. 'Review of A. Donicie and J. Voorhoeve, *De saramakaanse woordenschat*', *International Journal of American Linguistics* 30:434–9

    1968 [1961]. 'New languages for old in the West Indies', *Readings in the sociology of language*, ed. by J. A. Fishman, 607–19, The Hague, Mouton. [Originally, *Comparative studies in society and history* 3(3):277–88]

Valkhoff, Marius 1966. *Studies in Portuguese and Creole. With special reference to South Africa*, Johannesburg, Witwatersrand University Press

    1968. 'Review of R. A. Hall, Jr., *Pidgin and creole languages*', *African Studies* 27:47–9

Voegelin, C. F. and Voegelin, F. M. 1964 'Pidgin-creoles', *Anthropological Linguistics* 6(8):39–71

Weinreich, Max 1968 [1953]. 'Yidishkayt and Yiddish: on the impact of religion on language in Ashkenazic Jewry', *Readings in the sociology of language*, ed. by J. A. Fishman, 382–413. [Originally, Mordecai M. Kaplan Jubilee Volume, 481–514, New York, Jewish Theological Seminary of America]

Wurm, Stefan A. 1970. 'Pidgins, creoles, and lingue franche', *Current Trends in Linguistics* 8, *Linguistics in Oceania*, ed. by T. A. Sebeok *et al.* The Hague, Mouton

LINGUISTIC HYBRIDIZATION AND THE 'SPECIAL CASE' OF PIDGINS AND CREOLES

KEITH WHINNOM

The terms 'hybrid', 'hybridize', and 'hybridization' are used more frequently in biology than in linguistics. However, not only is there no other wholly satisfactory term for the phenomenon of language-mixing, but, *mutatis mutandis*, the biological and linguistic processes of hybridization are closely comparable if not mechanically identical; the theoretical problems of evolution, taxonomy, and hybridization have been discussed in enormous and sophisticated detail by biologists; and, provided that the analogies are properly applied, a 'biological' approach to the problems of linguistic hybridization can, I believe, prove fruitful. I do not propose to argue further the following propositions:

1. That in terms of the respective hierarchies, biological-linguistic correspondences are valid at only two levels: at that of species-language (and race-dialect) and at that of the minimal genetic-linguistic unit. Consequently, the analogy of two languages 'mating' to produce a hybrid offspring (a pidgin or creole) is quite false,[1] since this is to equate a language with a biotype which (a) is on a different hierarchical level, and (b) has in fact no linguistic equivalent (since the theoretical 'idiolect' is non-comparable).

2. That evolutionary processes in biology and linguistics are explicable and describable in terms of minimal mutations (allowing for pleiotropic effects), whether intrusions from outside or generated within the system, whose spread is controlled by factors of 'advantage' or lack of disadvantage, which are measurable only relatively, by reference to the environment.

Primary and secondary hybridization

The term 'primary hybridization' is used by biologists (and it always seems to come as a surprise to linguists) for a phenomenon which linguists would call 'fragmentation', i.e. the breaking up of a species-language into races (incipient species)/dialects. Given that all linguistic changes start with individual speakers (even if a weakness in the system may result in polygenesis of analogical formations), the spread of such innovations can clearly be considered as a form of hybridization. So, for instance, among Spanish dialects, Castilian can be defined sufficiently characteristically (even if it is not most satisfactorily defined) in terms of innovations accepted from outside (e.g. the reduction of

-MB- to -m-, which is of eastern origin, and the modification of PL-, CL-, FL-, which is of western origin). Secondary hybridization refers to the inter-breeding of distinct species, and is what is usually intended by the unqualified 'hybridization'.

In biology, primary and secondary hybridization can easily be distinguished by the nature of the bridge between the two homogeneous species: smooth intergrading (comparable with linguistic geographical band-frontiers), due to the effect of waves of minimal mutations, indicates primary hybridization, while secondary hybridization produces a plethora of variant forms, and the bridge-population cannot be arranged in a smoothly intergrading series of types. The biological indications of secondary hybridization are virtually unmistakable and readily explicable theoretically in terms of Mendelian genetics, and I believe they are exactly paralleled in certain linguistic situations (naïve foreign-language learning, 'bilingualism'), which might therefore be identified as situations of 'secondary hybridization'.

The barriers to hybridization

It is generally held (and it has been argued that it is one of the points at which the biological-linguistic analogy breaks down) that all languages are capable of hybridizing with all other languages. But even though they may be capable of doing so (and it is a proposition which needs careful shading), since languages have not evolved into one great linguistic stew, it is obvious that there are barriers to hybridization.

Interlinguistic barriers (and, for that matter, intralinguistic barriers) are of at least four main types and can be arranged in a graded sequence correspond-ing (approximately, perhaps) to the generally recognized and graded ecological, ethological, mechanical, and genetic interspecific barriers. (A convenient résumé, with references, of the biologists' thinking on the subject may be found in Mayr 1942.) While it is never easy to provide wholly adequate three-dimensional models for processes such as these, I think it is important to conceive of the barriers to hybridization *not* as a succession of fences, but perhaps as so many superimposed, horizontal, penetrable layers; the resistance of any layer can at any point become critically severe, in some cases insuper-able, and the effect of a barrier, once penetrated, does not at any point stop entirely.

THE 'ECOLOGICAL' BARRIER: FACTORS OF CONTACT

For the first barrier it may be advisable to retain the label ECOLOGICAL, since to define it in other terms (of geographical distance, political separation, and the like) is more complex and requires a series of qualifications. The essential point (and it is elementary) is that linguistic hybridization cannot take place without CONTACT (not necessarily, of course, the personal contact of individuals, but only because there exist non-personal media of communication). Although we are concerned only with languages in contact, with situations in which the ecological barriers have already been breached, this does not mean that we can neglect their operation. The extent, nature, and intensity of the hybridization are influenced by the extent, nature, and intensity of the contact. Total contact, for instance, would have, ultimately, results different from partial contact: the assimilation of linguistic units from another language may be confined to one sub-population, without affecting the entire population and whole language, and these units may then reach metropolitan speakers from the colonial population, or be eliminated from the dialect in response to the resistance of the metropolis. Sixteenth-century Caribbean Spanish, for instance, contained, on the evidence of Fernández de Oviedo and Las Casas, a vastly greater number of Indian words (Arawak, Carib) than were assimilated by Peninsular Spanish or than now survive in modern Caribbean Spanish. Clearly other factors (the operation of other barriers) were also at work, but the ecological factor cannot be ignored.

THE 'ETHOLOGICAL' (EMOTIONAL) BARRIER: FACTORS OF ATTITUDE

The second barrier (ETHOLOGICAL) might be relabelled EMOTIONAL if we are prepared to allow a certain latitude in the interpretation of that term. It concerns the *attitude* of the speakers of one language to another foreign language (or perhaps even to the speakers of another foreign language).[2] There are well-known sociolinguistic situations (discussed by Weinreich 1953, *passim*) in which a population of speakers will be particularly tenacious of their language, concerned for its 'purity' and so on (when a hostile environment promotes in them feelings of insecurity but, culturally different, allows them to feel superior to that environment), and, at the other extreme, situations of cultural shock in which populations are unresistant to, and even eager to accept, the most sweeping linguistic innovations. The conditions of contact of course may shape attitudes (see Dozier 1956 for contrasting cases).

It is clear too that different linguistic items carry, as it were, different emotional charges, and that emotional resistance is modified by practical considerations of utility. It is notorious that a population will be most tenacious of its place-names (particularly of natural features like rivers) and proper names (exceptions to the rule, like personal names in the Philippines, require explanation in terms of specific pressures) and least resistant to accepting foreign labels for new and unfamiliar objects – which is why philologists interested in classifying or determining the root-stock of languages used to set great store by the evidence of such unequivocal and basic words as *sand* or *grass*.

Indubitably factors of attitude must be taken into account in trying to solve the puzzle of why pidgins arise in certain places and at certain times and not in other circumstances. But after we have exhausted the plausible arguments from emotional resistance (and it is often not easy to see why pidgins should not have arisen when all attendant circumstances seem identical with those in which they did arise) we need to seek other explanations.

THE 'MECHANICAL' BARRIER: FACTORS OF 'OUTER FORM'

The equivalent of the mechanical barrier relates, I would suggest, not to the whole of the linguistic system as such, but to its 'outer form', namely its phonological structure. But since linguistic hybridization can take place by means of media other than the oral-aural, writing-systems can also assume a certain importance in certain circumstances, and I should again be inclined to retain the term MECHANICAL, to include both aspects of the phonological-grammatological barrier.

The case of Chinese is extremely instructive for our present purposes. The Chinese, with their monosyllabic lexemes of very simple phonological structure, are (nowadays) extremely resistant to accepting neologisms from other languages. The Chinese linguistic system demands that a word like 'telephone' be rendered as *tê-lü-fêng* 德 律 風 (each syllable in a different tone), that is by three monosyllables which have each independent meanings, and which can be transcribed (the writing-system is a factor of importance) by three separate logograms arbitrarily selected from several possible, and which could be read as 'power-law-wind'. A polysyllable causes difficulty to the hearer, and, expressed by a string of characters, even more to the reader, whose first impulse is to find some thread of meaning in the series. Modern Chinese has in fact replaced *tê-lü-fêng* by *tien-hua* 電 話, 'electric speech'. Now, in replacing the clumsy polysyllable borrowed from English by the neater native compound (involving in this instance the revival of a classical word for 'lightning'), which is the solution which modern Chinese has in general adopted for the new vocabulary of science and technology,[3] there are four separate factors operating, involving the four major barriers to hybridization. Because *contact* is tenuous and often through the medium of writing, the conceptual content of the labels of Western technological innovations tends to assume more importance than their phonetic form (so that, for instance, there never was any attempt to do more than 'translate', into new Chinese compounds, words like 'railway' and 'steamship'). Secondly there is an *emotional* barrier, a basic psychological resistance, or at least reluctance, to borrowing anything from the barbarians; for in the old days of Buddhism, i.e. in the first century, the Chinese made no bones about borrowing, from Sanskrit, and despite all the attendant mechanical difficulties, a large number of barbaric polysyllables, so that the difference between the prolific borrowing from Sanskrit and the modern reluctance to borrow from English must be explained primarily in emotional terms. A severer barrier, breached nevertheless when there is a positive emotional incentive to do so, is the *mechanical* barrier. The difficulty of adjusting /elek'trisiti/ to the Chinese phonological system is enormous, entailing alternatively the addition of two support-syllables or the elimination of several consonants. (But the difficulties of adapting Sanskrit *upadhyâya* were scarcely less great.) And there is a final barrier at the CONCEPTUAL level (see below) in that one borrowed word has to become five, six or seven Chinese words (a crude statement which will serve for the present).

The effectiveness of the mechanical barrier is subordinate to the effectiveness of the emotional barrier. While one might, therefore, like the Prague phonologists, construct schemes of relative phonological incompatibility which could be useful, they have only relative value because of the preconditioning variable of the emotional barrier. (Both are taken into account by, e.g. Martinet (1951–2), but he does not clearly establish the operational priorities.) Perhaps an even more convincing illustration of the fact that the emotional barrier must be taken into account earlier than the mechanical barrier is provided by a comparison of anglicisms in Argentine and Peninsular Spanish (or at least Peninsular Spanish twenty years ago): Argentine speakers, in contrast with Peninsular Spaniards, were prepared to accept the most blatant *extranjerismos* like (to stick to horse-racing) *el betting, el starter, el winning-post*, etc., even though these terms were practically not needed (providing only snob satisfaction), for there existed and exist the perfectly good Spanish *apuestas, abanderado, meta*, etc. (see Entwistle 1936:275–6).

Seemingly extreme phonological incompatibility will not prevent a population of speakers in a state of cultural shock from adopting neologisms incompatible with the native phonological system, and if necessary such a population may even acquire new sounds, as the Guaranís learned the *elle* or Nahuatl-speakers /r/ and /ñ/. Linguists would normally regard the restructuring of the phonological system as an extreme case, but instances in which speakers of a given language learn a new sound and incorporate it into their phonemic system in order to assimilate new lexical items are in fact far more numerous than is generally admitted. Coseriu (1965–8) reaffirmed a thesis concerning possible and impossible developments in a given language; while justifiable for most practical purposes, it is nevertheless finally highly misleading to speak of any 'impossible' developments, since these 'impossibilities' cannot be more than highly improbable. Though structuralist analyses of English often fail to reveal the fact, English-speakers have in fact acquired a number of exotic phonemes (the uvular fricative for Scottish words with graphic CH, nasalized vowels, etc., for French words) to accommodate foreign lexemes in their vocabulary. And the modern tendency in Peninsular Spanish (see Lorenzo 1966, *passim*) is no longer to adjust English borrowings to the Spanish sound-system but to accept them (with minor phonetic adjustments of the kind usually described as 'accent') with new phonemes (as for English graphic sh) and with new phonotactic patterns (totally unfamiliar and in 'Spanish' 'impossible' consonantal clusters which traditionally require supports vowels, such as sc^{ons} without the prothetic e-, or final -rd, -ts, -lms, etc.). The boundaries of the phonemic system of any language are usually a good deal more fluid than structuralists tend to admit. It may be worth noting at this point that the phonological system of creole languages in many instances does not appear to be the 'highest common factor' of the sound-systems of the 'parent languages', so that, for instance, both Spaniards and Tagalogs must acquire new phones to pronounce Ermiteño or Caviteño; but the conclusions to be drawn from this fact could be misleading if we do not accept that a language can acquire new phonemes.

While we have here phenomena of hybridization, most linguists would be reluctant to call the language which assimilates lexical or phonetic items from a foreign language a 'hybrid'. They would argue that because we say 'kinkajou' and 'jaguar' it does not follow that English would be accurately described as a 'hybrid' of English and Guaraní. But while it may upset traditional notions of the classification of languages, I see no sound reason, if all languages hybridize with other languages (is there any language without loan-words?), for shying away from the term 'hybrid' for all languages.[4]

THE (CONCEPTUAL) BARRIER: FACTORS OF 'INNER FORM'

I do not think it is necessary to distinguish a morphological barrier. Morphemes can be regarded as lexical items, and there is clearly no lexemic barrier as such; or, as inflectional particles, they can be regarded as forming part of the grammatical rules. In lexical borrowing, as I suggested in referring to Chinese, there is, below the barrier of phonological incompatibility, a still stronger barrier at a lower level. *Words*, for instance, are not readily transferred to or from a language which has no words in the Indo-European sense, if there is no one-to-one conceptual equivalence, or from a polysyllabic to a monosyllabic language. Flexion or infixation will not, of course, inhibit borrowing if there is one simple and statistically frequent form in which a word occurs – as witness Spanish borrowing from Nahuatl – but the more lexemic variants a word has, the more difficult the transfer will be, and the flexions, inflective or derivational affixes for instance, and grammatical particles, are very rarely transferred at all. I would suggest that the analogue of the fourth and ultimate biological barrier is conceptual: it is the mode of perception of reality which is conditioned primarily by the individual's native language, acquired in childhood, conditioned most notably by the semantic and syntactical structure of his language (ideas of hierarchy, contrast, relationship, etc., and of the analysis of events). This cognitive conditioning forms what might be called the CONCEPTUAL barrier.[5]

In biology, when the first three barriers are overcome (sometimes by artificial means) it is found that there are degrees of genetic incompatibility. Between what are good species, on the biological definition, one can find everything from total genetic incompatibility, i.e. the failure to produce offspring at all, through the production of weak, sterile, or deformed offspring, to the production of successful, fertile offspring which may be capable of breeding only with one or other species of the parent stocks, with either, or with one another, to a point at which 'hybridizing forms must be regarded as having combined to form a new species'.[6] Similarly with languages, the conceptual, like the phonological barrier, should be expected to show degrees of incompatibility.

Secondary hybridization, cocoliche, and the mechanism of pidginization

It is a now despised formula of 'primitive' creolistics that a pidgin is made up of the vocabulary of one language and the grammar of another. The observation may be faulty but it reflects a basic reality. It is, moreover, a description which fits very well certain linguistic phenomena ('secondary languages') associated with naïve language-learning. We talk very readily of an Englishman's speaking 'French' or 'Spanish'. It is the everyday way – it is the only conveniently brief way – of referring to a common phenomenon. But no descriptive linguist would dream of basing his description of a language on information elicited from a non-native speaker, and strictly we ought not to call such secondary languages 'French' or 'Spanish', but specify: 'French as spoken by an Englishman', 'Spanish as spoken by a Tagalog', or whatever. Few of the manifestations of this phenomenon have been distinctively named,[7] but one such is *cocoliche*, the study of which is highly instructive. (I propose to regard this imperfect code-switching as a case of 'secondary hybridization'.)

Cocoliche (once extensively spoken by Italian immigrants in Argentina, but not by Argentines) was an open system which had, theoretically, every grade of a finite but huge number of series of continua ranging from (usually substandard) Italian to non-native *porteño* Spanish (Entwistle 1936:274–5). Though little solid work has been done on *cocoliche* – the hispanist-philologists never felt it was worth bothering about – one can say with fair security that it displayed broadly coincidental spectra of innovations as follows:

1. At the level of least intense hybridization Spanish lexical items (nouns, adjectives, verb-radicals) were imported into an Italian morpho-syntactical system without their being allowed to interfere with the native phonological system (*viejo* /bjexo/ > *vieco* /vjeko/ etc. – *vecchio* presumably accounts for the

retention of /v/); but at this level, whenever the native Italian lexeme presented no serious obstacle to understanding by Spanish-speaking Argentines it stood unmodified (*amico* for *amigo*, *dovia* for *debía*, etc.). The level of intensity of hybridization is broadly measurable by the quantity of Spanish lexemes employed (a) absolutely, and (b) in comparison with native Italian lexemes.

2. There are singularly few phonological contrasts between Italian and Argentine Spanish, so that evidence of phonetic innovation is scant; unfamiliar phonemes (such as the *jota* /x/) were acquired only after massive lexical borrowing (though it would be easy to draw misleading conclusions from this observation[8]).

3. Morphemes and particles were among the last items to be transferred. Pluralization with -*s* in fact appears quite early, but a scale of degree is perceptible not in its presence as such, but in the accuracy with which it is employed: at 'low' levels of hybridization its use is subject to gross error, being tacked at random on to singulars (which suggests a conceptual failure). Italian particles, and particularly those which lack one-to-one translation equivalents, such as *ne* and *vi*, tend to be preserved intact at quite high levels, again suggesting conceptual failure.

Cocoliche was completely 'unstable' in given individuals, since there was almost invariably continuing improvement in performance in achieving communication with Spanish speakers (and the succeeding generation acquired native Spanish). Furthermore the acquisition of lexical, phonological, morphological, and syntactic material must with each individual speaker have been subject to chance, so that the speech of no two individual *cocoliche*-speakers was ever quite identical (this is a consistent phenomenon of secondary hybridization). Nevertheless, the system as a whole, however ephemeral in given individuals, and however broad a series of spectra it encompassed, was fairly clearly *predictable* and was continuously renewed in recognizable and labellable form from year to year and from generation of immigrant to generation of immigrant.

But now, at the risk of labouring the obvious, let us consider in the light of these facts what would be the result if the behavioural barrier had been breached from the other side. One might with fair confidence predict – it would be interesting to have a study of an actual case – the stages in the linguistic development of a native Spanish-speaker in an Italian-speaking environment. The earliest stage would be marked by the acquisition of discrete lexical items (but he would tend to keep *amigo* for *amico*); the acquisition of new phonemes (such as /v/) would follow, but would be postponed because of the relative compatibility of the two sound-systems; he would adopt, making many mistakes, only a few Italian morphemes; and the modification of his Spanish syntactic structures might be indefinitely postponed. At no point in the resultant continuum of systems should we find anything recognizable or definable as *cocoliche*. Moreover it is obvious that the 'marriage' of *cocoliche* with this its 'mirror-image' could not result in a pidgin.[9]

'Stable' is, of course, a highly relative term. But we can surely agree that by the standards of *cocoliche* any pidgin is relatively stable. For *cocoliche* to become a pidgin, it would have to be stabilized in two ways: (a) the dynamic processes which in given individuals consistently exert pressure on them further to modify their *cocoliche* in the direction of standard Spanish would have to be arrested; and (b) the innumerable varieties of *cocoliche* would have to be reduced to comparative uniformity.

To consider first the function of the ecological barrier: one might suppose that arrestation of the dynamic processes could occur if there were no intimate convivence of the populations, if the speakers of the superstrate (or target) language withdrew from contact, withdrawing simultaneously the target language. It is, of course, a pidginist cliché that the speaker of the socially 'superior' standard language simplifies his speech when addressing speakers of the 'inferior' foreign language, and that this happens is incontrovertible (see Valkhoff 1966:120–1); but its significance may not have been correctly assessed. Simplification can contribute, I would suggest, only to the retardation of the learning-process. If the speaker of the standard language reduces the range of his vocabulary, avoids complex syntactical structures, etc., he could be said to deprive the substrate speaker of a model on which to improve his performance in the standard language; but with multiplicity of contacts the target cannot be removed entirely, the simplified model will vary from speaker to speaker, and simplification is *not* pidginization. Obviously in Argentina (or in the United States) there is no withdrawal of the target. But I think it is obvious that while social distance tends to *perpetuate* bilingualism, preventing or slowing the assimilation of substrate speakers, it will not explain alone the origin of a pidgin.

Other ecological factors worth considering concern the extent of the contact. In Argentina the situation which produced *cocoliche* was constantly renewed by the arrival of fresh immigrants from Italy. If the Italian population of Buenos Aires had been cut off from Italy, the result of the contact situation would have been different only to the extent that *cocoliche* would have been eliminated in one generation. Conversely if the Spanish-speaking Argentines had had no external contacts with other Spanish-speakers, their language might have been modified by the acceptance of Italianisms to a far greater extent than it has been (*ciao*, etc.). But even in greatly modified circumstances (the fusion of the two communities, for instance) there is not the slightest reason to suppose that a pidgin would have emerged: *cocoliche* could have become an entirely viable primary language comparable with Middle English,

the referential adequacy of its lexicon nowise impaired, its phonological
system enriched, and its morphology pruned (if at all) only of redundancy.

Emotional factors must also be taken into account. Even in the Argentine
context, some Italian immigrants reached a point at which for them the
reward began to be outweighed by the effort. Planning to accumulate some
capital and retire to southern Italy, they had no overwhelming desire to
integrate themselves into the Spanish-speaking community (and may have
regarded integration as ultimately impossible); and, able to preserve uncontaminated part of their linguistic system, they could fall back on an immediate
Italian-speaking community for emotional satisfaction. Similar pressures must
also operate in preventing the evolution of a pidgin or creole towards a
standard (effort versus reward, the possession of a complete and functionally
and emotionally adequate native language, etc.). Clearly the speakers of the
pidgin have to reach only a minimal degree of functional adequacy in the
context in which the language is used for the strength of the motives for
improved performance to be seriously weakened. But again such factors
explain only the slowing of a process of development and not the establishment
of a *uniform* system.

The third set of factors to consider is secondary interference in the mixed
system. I inferred that in Argentina the breach of the ethological barrier was
one-sided, and there is in fact no 'mirror-image' of *cocoliche*. But Spanish-
speaking Argentines, without attempting to enter into real functional communication with the immigrants, 'learned' their mixed dialect by casual
observation, formed a somewhat stereotyped notion of what it was like, and
even wrote it (in newspaper columns) for comic effect. The result is, inevitably, no more 'authentic' *cocoliche* than stage-Irish ('would you be after having
a drink?') is Anglo-Irish (and similar examples could be multiplied of this
distinctive but still anonymous linguistic phenomenon).[10] Entwistle (1936:274)
says that the Italian appears to mistake the quality of the Spanish atonic /o/
and substitutes /u/ (*dun* for *don*, etc.); but he is relying on newspaper speci-
mens of the dialect composed by Argentines, and what must actually happen
is that it is the Argentine who mistakes the Italian substitute /o/ for the
equivalent of a Spanish /u/. Similarly while the Argentine observers noted
that the immigrants tended to preserve Italian particles and verb-flexions,
their imitations of Italian usages are often mistaken and do not represent the
usage a native Italian would actually make of these particles, even attempting,
unsuccessfully, to speak Spanish.

Since the most usually accepted theory of pidginization depends on the
'stage-Irish' proposition, namely, that the substrate speakers imitate the
superstrate speakers' imitation of the substrate speakers' imitation of the
superstrate language,[11] it will be worth considering in greater detail how
plausible this notion is. Fortunately in looking at *cocoliche* or at pidgins we

do not have to bear in mind the complications which arise with formal language-instruction – when, for instance, a linguist will early point out, from his own peculiar vantage-point, phonological or conceptual incompatibilities which might otherwise pass unperceived or be badly misunderstood and misapplied (such as, for English-speakers, the distinction between /r/ and /rr/ or between *ser* and *estar* in Spanish). Naïve language-learning, as is evident from the case of *cocoliche*, concentrates on acquiring lexemes with scant regard for pronunciation or grammar. But in this second-degree language-learning, the scale is reversed. The English speaker observing a foreigner's attempts to speak English will note immediately failures of acoustic equivalence (as there are novelists who indicate a French accent by rendering every definite article as 'ze') or an unaccustomed sequence of semantemes (so that the English-speaker's version of a German's English is liable to place *all* verbs at the end of the sentence). But in the lexicon, though there are bound to be innumerable failures in employing words correctly, the English-speaker fails to perceive the total pattern of the underlying semantic-conceptual structure (he will never discover, for instance, why a Frenchman says now 'he' and now 'she' for 'it'), and reproduces only occasionally, anecdotally as it were, some of the failures, such as comically colourful periphrases, which seem to him funny.

But before considering the possible systemic effect of the superstrate speaker's defective mimicry of the substrate language-learner, we should bear in mind a behavioural barrier. Though linguistic errors almost invariably strike the native speaker as amusing, he will tend to want to share his amusement with those who can appreciate the joke, i.e. other native speakers, and will not in fact believe that the reproduction of *these* mistakes is the way to achieve improved communication with the foreign speaker of his language, though he may certainly modify his own speech in other ways. This point may be arguable (some fool *might* say 'ze feesh' to a Frenchman), but it is only one of several which make me sceptical of the traditional explanations of the mechanism of pidginization.

Suppose that the immigrant *cocoliche*-speakers *were* deprived of access to the target-language, and had as a model *only* the Argentines' versions of *cocoliche*, in which Argentines actually did address immigrants. Certain 'mistakes' (/oko/ for /oxo/, *dovia*, etc.) would certainly be reinforced. But it is extremely difficult to see how a stable and drastically simplified pidgin might emerge from this situation. To take the lexicon alone, the Argentine's vocabulary, a macaronic mixture of Spanish and Italian, would encourage the Italian to maintain Italian lexemes, and, as we know, the vocabularies of pidgins are characteristically homogeneous and borrowed from the superstrate language (Hall 1964:381, etc.).[12] It is clear, of course, that *cocoliche* is an inadequate model of a 'pre-pidgin' but why it is inadequate is interesting and it can still provide some instructive contrasts with genuine pidgins.

No pidgin arose or was ever likely to arise in Argentina, and the most obvious differences between the Argentine situation and situations in which we know pidgins did arise appear to be the following:

1. In Argentina there was ample opportunity for members of the substrate population to go on improving their performance in the target language. Pidgins have arisen where there was restricted contact, whether the superstrate was a resident minority of high social status (as in the plantations) or a transient minority of equivocal social status (as with visiting traders).

2. In Argentina there was very strong motivation for improved performance in the target language. The superstrate was a majority, and, as with immigrant communities in the United States, complete social assimilation (promotion from second-class to first-class citizen) was a not impracticable objective. Where the superstrate is a transient or socially superior minority to which the substrate speakers do not aspire to assimilate themselves, there is (a) reduced motivation for improved performance, and (b) simultaneously, a more limited area of mutual interest in which a defective language can be functionally adequate.

3. In Argentina there is no secondary interference of consequence. (Indeed Argentine newspaper-*cocoliche*, by holding errors up to ridicule would, if anything, have *prevented* reinforcement of those errors.)

These are not, in fact, the only differences, as we shall see.

Chinese Pidgin and the mechanism of pidginization

One must assume that Chinese Pidgin is now, in Hong Kong, a dying language;[13] and it could be argued that present conditions in Hong Kong are dissimilar from those in which Chinese Pidgin was formed. But the modern situation offers some thought-provoking features.

1. The Chinese community in Hong Kong cannot be treated as a whole. There is, as it were, a 'substrate section' of the community in which pidgin is maintained, most notably among servants, taxi-drivers, small shopkeepers, and the like. Middle- and upper-class Chinese speak Chinese or English, but never pidgin, which they despise as the mark of a socially inferior class. At the same time, farmers, fishermen, and coolies, who have very restricted contact with Europeans, do not speak pidgin. It is necessary therefore, in one instance at least, to refine the concept of a 'substrate' population. The concept must also be further refined linguistically: there is no single substrate 'Chinese' language, but, and especially among the service community (in contrast with the stable peasant and fisher communities) a variety of Chinese dialects.

2. The rewards in Hong Kong for superior performance in English are considerable, and a good deal of very active language-learning and language-teaching must be one of the principal reasons for the slow decline in the use

of pidgin. At the same time, this very fact demonstrates that in the context of Chinese–European communication pidgin is now contextually inadequate, or adequate only in a very restricted context (though its inadequacy need not be systemically but might be ethologically defined).

3. There is no secondary interference of any significance on the part of the 'superstrate' speakers. Certainly the fact that a pidgin-speaker discovers that gross phonological distortion need not lead to unintelligibility (/bafu/ for '*bath*', etc.) reinforces him in these 'errors'. But one observes about the present situation the following extraordinary facts:

(a) While it is notorious that many creoles, which may be assumed to have evolved, are unintelligible to the speakers of the superstrate languages from which they derive their lexicon, rapidly spoken Chinese Pidgin is also quite unintelligible to the newcomer from England. To make themselves understood pidgin-speakers adopt precisely the same measures as in the alleged behaviour of master to slave, i.e. they speak slowly and distinctly, repeat carefully phrases and sentences obviously not understood, seek periphrases, resort to gestures, etc. (Cf. the pains taken by Chinook using jargon to foreigners, cited by Silverstein, this section.) For intercommunication between Chinese and colonial Englishmen, pidgin, like French Creole, has been stabilized at an extraordinarily low level of intelligibility (and is thus quite different from the Argentine's *cocoliche* or stage-Irish).

(b) The superstrate community does not speak pidgin. Except possibly for the merest handful of 'old China hands', born in Shanghai or Hong Kong and brought up by Chinese amahs, the resident superstrate population of administrators and merchants does not use pidgin (they learn Chinese or use interpreters). The transient population of soldiers and sailors, who can scarcely differ greatly from their predecessors of previous centuries, acquire perhaps half a dozen elementary phrases but no facility in the dialect, and derive some amusement from instructing unsuspecting natives in obscenities or comically grotesque locutions (for a polite formula of greeting 'Oh, my aching back'), when (as with stage-Irish or Argentine *cocoliche*) the real intended recipient of the communication is a native speaker of the language which is being abused.

While Chinese may still purchase in Hong Kong manuals for speaking pidgin (done entirely through the medium of Chinese logograms used to indicate the meaning and the pronunciation of pidgin words and phrases), there exist only one or two nineteenth-century manuals of pidgin directed to English speakers (inevitably they also contain comic poems), with sample dialogues which seem to indicate that the English-speaker expected to have some acquaintance with the dialect was primarily the mistress of the household, who is to give orders to the servants and call on her dressmaker. What fluency nineteenth-century ladies actually achieved is doubtful. Furthermore, it is quite clear that pidgin was a stable dialect which they were expected to *learn* (as Australian policemen learn New Guinea Pidgin), and so, that, unlike *cocoliche*, it was early recognized that it was not a language one 'picked up' by casual observation or could improvise.

(c) Pidgin is the language of Chinese. The only speakers of the dialect who handle it with fluency, with unhesitating command of its limited resources, and without corrective or hyper-corrective error, are the Chinese servants and shopkeepers, who will address Europeans in it, but who are able to deploy the full battery of its resources and make no allowances for difficulties of comprehension only with *other Chinese*. It is the language in which the amah from Canton communicates with the cook-boy from Shanghai, and in which the shopkeeper will address a fellow-trader from Fuchow.

(d) Finally, one finds a kind of bilingualism: the more educated, intelligent or ambitious amah or shopkeeper may possess two varieties of English, a more or less imperfect non-native English used to address English-speakers, and an apparently uncontaminated and stable pidgin in which to talk to Chinese from other regions (or in which, when occasion arises, to retreat and baffle a native English-speaker who is proving troublesome).

It may not be admissible to argue that conditions were always similar; but there is no good evidence that they were ever fundamentally different, and since it would appear to be true that no pidgin has ever consolidated itself in other than a multilingual situation (New Guinea Pidgin, Hawaiian Pidgin, the Caribbean Creoles, Sango, Chinook, etc., etc.), it may well be that no simple *bilingual* situation ever gives rise to a pidgin. The perhaps inadequate evidence that we have suggests that in a simple two-language context (in which there is not total swamping of one community): (a) there cannot be any really effective withdrawal of the target language, and the substrate speakers will continue to improve their performance in it; (b) a second-degree secondary hybrid dialect (a 'stage-Irish' type) is not actually employed as a medium of communication from superstrate to substrate; and (c) even where such a dialect existed it is very difficult to see how it could have stabilized the first-degree hybrid (e.g. *cocoliche*) which it mimes at the low level of intelligibility to superstrate speakers characteristic of pidgins, or, for that matter, how it could have stabilized the dialect at all.

The origin of pidgins

The essential differences between a pidgin proper and a secondary 'language' like *cocoliche* seem to be (a) that the linguistic product of a process of simple secondary hybridization exhibits the same characteristics as biological hybrid populations, namely a plethora of variant forms which fill a series of spectra between one language and another, whereas a pidgin exhibits variation no greater than a 'primary' language;[14] and (b) that several pidgins, unlike *cocoliche*, contain linguistic items (structures, etc.) which are not *immediately* assignable to the native or to the target language, even though they could and have been argued (by a series of linguists) to be attributable to 'internal linguistic factors'.

It seems to me that there are two conceivable processes by which pidgins could come into being: 'tertiary hybridization' (it is necessary to invent this term because the simple biological analogy does break down here, for reasons I explain below), and 'relexification'.

TERTIARY HYBRIDIZATION

This first process is precisely the kind of process by which new breeds of domestic animal, or new plant populations in the wild, are formed. Once again it is important to get the biological analogues right, since the hybrid biotype has no linguistic counterpart and the bilingual (in contradistinction to the secondary *language*) has no biological equivalent. A *population* of hybrids resembles a secondary language; breeding back to either parent stock decreases somewhat the spectra of variation (stage-Irish, newspaper-*cocoliche*);[15] but a distinct new hybrid species does not emerge until the hybrids interbreed with each other, until barriers to continued hybridization with the parent species have developed, and until in successive generations the distribution of variant forms stabilizes itself at a sort of mid-term, i.e. until the *cocoliche* proto-pidgin is used as a medium of communication with other proto-pidgin speakers (and this does *not* include the superstrate 'stage-Irish' speakers).

Now with languages this 'tertiary hybridization' simply cannot occur between speakers of the simple secondary hybrid, because, unlike the biological hybrids of fixed genetic inheritance, these speakers possess simultaneously another much more viable system in common, namely their mother tongue, which they will in fact use (as the Argentine Italians use Italian) for communicating with each other.[16]

Surely it is obvious that a French-'based' pidgin (i.e. a pidgin whose proto-pidgin target was French) is unlikely to arise in stable form from, say, the communication of an English-speaking schoolboy with a French schoolboy (Hall 1966 repeatedly denies this, but I think there is simply a difference over terminology, in that he seems to be prepared to call all 'mixed languages', including secondary languages, 'pidgins'); whereas a French-based pidgin could easily arise from the communication of an English schoolboy with a German schoolboy, given that they had no other common language. Perhaps the most essential of sundry differences between these two situations is that, in the second, the target-language, French, is removed from consideration. Neither speaker has any model on which to improve his performance in

French, nor any motive to improve it. Their motive can only be improved communication with each other, the inhibitions of the native who fears ridicule from speakers of the target-language are removed, and one can easily see how and why certain essential pidgin features could be produced:

1. The vocabulary of their exchanges would be reduced to the words known in common, and a series of semantic discriminations would be obliterated (terms of approval and disapproval, for instance, might well be reduced to *bon* and *pas bon*), while unusual concepts for which 'the French word' was not known would be rendered by periphrases, soon agreed and formalized, employing known words. (The system is never, of course, entirely closed, but renewal of the lexicon from the 'base'-language is of necessity restricted.)

2. Though both would have acquired and would maintain phonemes foreign to their native systems, their mispronunciations of French words, intelligible to each other and reinforced by repetition, might soon render their 'French' unintelligible to a native speaker.

3. It might be further predicted that they would also soon discover that communication was impaired more by, for instance, mishandled verb-forms (when neither was quite sure of how to conjugate '*savoir*') than by the use of a simple infinitive; and neither would care very much about getting genders right.

Obviously the illustration is crude and the actual mechanism of pidginization, with whole communities of speakers involved, more complex; but this model (which in fact matches the sociolinguistic circumstances of present-day Chinese pidgin) accounts for the *simplification, impoverishment, unintelligibility*, and *stability* of pidgins which the usual theory of 'reinforcement of error' by the superstrate speaker will not, it seems to me, explain. If this explanation is correct, Hockett's formula for designating pidgins and creoles as X Pidgin/Creole Y (Y being the primary source and X the secondary source, Hockett 1948:424) is not entirely satisfactory. It works for 'Chinese Pidgin English', for example, only because 'Chinese' can stand, and, I should argue, in this instance *does* stand, for more than one language. In another circumstance, it is obvious that one could not have, for instance, simply a Twi Pidgin English (cf. Hancock's summary of his work on the Atlantic English-based creoles in this volume). If in fact a pidgin always arises, as I suggest, from a situation involving a target language and two or more substrate languages, then one requires *at least* three terms to formulate a wholly exact description. A general formula might be represented by:

$$\frac{\text{Target language}}{\text{Substrate languages A} \times \text{B} \, (\times \, \text{C} \dots)}$$

My hypothetical French pidgin could then be represented as

$$\frac{\text{French}}{\text{English} \times \text{German}}$$

The difficulty about extending the formula to actual existing pidgins is that the subordinate or substrate languages can rarely be designated so precisely or so economically: the 'denominator' for Hawaiian Pidgin English, for instance, would be exceedingly complex (involving, presumably, Hawaiian, Chinese, Japanese, Korean, Filipino languages, Portuguese, etc.). But in this particular case, the term 'Hawaiian' might well serve, since there is not too much danger of its being read as a simple linguistic term, rather than as a geographical term indicating an area in which several linguistic influences were at work. In general, perhaps the most convenient and least ambiguous designation for pidgins and creoles would be one that was always partly geographical: China Coast Pidgin English (avoiding the ambiguous 'Chinese'), Caribbean Pidgin/Creole English, Manila Bay Creole Spanish, etc.

RELEXIFICATION

The above is not, of course, how several 'European-based' pidgins actually arose.[17] The Philippine creoles (at the very least) are known to have been initially Portuguese pidgins or creoles (Whinnom 1956), and I need not set out again the reasons for supposing that other pidgins and creoles may have been 'relexifications' of Portuguese pidgins (Thompson 1961; Stewart 1962, etc.) or that medieval Sabir may stand at the origin of them all (Whinnom 1965). This latter innocuous hypothesis – my intention was stated to be merely to set out the possible case in detail, and it has, after all, some irrefutable basis in historical fact – has already been subjected to attack (Vintila–Radulescu 1967), but while I am not wedded to the theory, I am highly sceptical of some of the arguments advanced to refute it. To describe a pidgin as a simplified language is a gross oversimplification. Even if we consider only its 'simplicity', it is my own experience, repeatedly confirmed, that no one *pidginizes* his own language without very considerable linguistic awareness (just as the subliterate cannot write telegraphese) or even perhaps without some experience of pidgin (even if only at the comic-book level). If one does not posit 'relexification' for, say, the French creoles, one must at least allow something for stimulus diffusion (Kroeber 1940) of a principle. But 'simplification', even if one were to concede that this might be a universal intuitive notion for all speakers of all languages (and I am not convinced of that), is the least of it. One must also account satisfactorily for the stability, the *grammaticality*, the stabilization at such a low level of intelligibility to the superstrate speaker, and the phonemes, structures, and particles common to neither 'parent' language, which are also quite characteristic of pidgins.

With this second theory one might, in other words, allow that a pidgin could result from first-degree secondary hybridization (a *cocoliche* situation) provided that the target offered consistently by the superstrate speakers was itself a stabilized pidgin (deriving, at whatever remove, from a pidgin created by 'tertiary hybridization'), and that one accepts that the substrate speaker achieves, not some mid-term degree of proficiency (which would coincide with no other mid-term achieved by fellow-speakers) but almost complete proficiency.

Impoverishment and repair

Biological hybridization often results in infertility or deformity because of minor degrees of genetic incompatibility resulting in genetic loss. Similarly a failure of matching in languages at the conceptual level results in loss, since the simpler – and cruder – system always prevails, from whichever linguistic system it originates (so that, for instance, the naïve native English-speaker blurs simultaneously when speaking Spanish both the Spanish distinction between *saber* and *conocer*, *este*, *ese*, and *aquel*, etc., and his original native distinction between *house* and *home*, *story* and *history*, *packet* and *parcel*, etc. – to cite only the cruder cases). But the deficiencies of a linguistic, unlike a genetic system, can be repaired; and it is now fairly well established that every creole language of which we have early texts appears to have repaired many of the deficiencies of its parent pidgin by reconstructing a more elaborate and more flexible syntax, and reintroducing in the verbal system, for instance, distinctions of, and methods of marking, tense, aspect, mood, and so on.

Without for the moment attempting to define the term, it is clear that pidgins are 'defective' languages of inferior flexibility and adaptability ('genetic plasticity'), which because of peculiar circumstances (and this is the heart of the problem) have temporary advantages over their rivals and so survive. The further question is whether creoles derived from them are also in some way deficient. The older linguists like Sapir felt obliged to inveigh against misguided notions about 'primitive' languages; and most modern linguists would tend to subscribe to the view that all languages are equally interesting, and, in some metaphysical sense, 'equal'. Stewart (1962:52) makes the point that a series of despective comments on the Caribbean Creoles 'are almost word for word counterparts of what was once said in Europe about the Standards themselves, back when these were as yet unstandardized and occupied an inferior social position with respect to standardized and written Latin'. I assume this is to be read as a kind of rhetorical question; but there is a suppressed premise in this syllogism (namely that the despective comments on the medieval 'Standards' were unjustified) which requires inspection. In brief, few hispanist-philologists, even while recognizing the enormous achievement of Alfonso X in 'creating' Castilian prose, would attempt to argue that thirteenth-century Spanish had achieved parity of adequacy with Latin. One may argue, of course, about criteria of adequacy; but at least three of those commonly adduced seem to me questionable.

One is the criterion of 'contextual adequacy'. Chinese Pidgin can be argued to be adequate 'in its context'; but this is circular. If a language exists it must be grossly adequate in its context; if it is not it is developed or dies. A second is 'referential adequacy'. Though languages obviously differ greatly in their referential adequacy, it can be argued that this is not an *inherent* inadequacy and that it can easily be repaired. It is certainly true that referential inadequacy can be repaired with astonishing speed. I might cite the case (since I have a book on the subject) of Sr Francisco Bernís who single-handed and at one fell swoop repaired the referential adequacy of Spanish with regard to bird-names (Bernís 1955; Whinnom 1966:7–9). Any pidgin or creole (or 'primitive' language) can repair its referential inadequacy when it is a question of naming *objects*, and does so when the pressure of its inadequacy is felt. And the third criterion often mentioned is the use of a creole for 'literature'. Literature, and most especially lyric poetry, can be produced in languages adequate for day-to-day intercourse and quite inadequate for literary criticism (or linguistics).

The main differences between the adequacy of thirteenth-century Spanish and medieval Latin are (a) the greatly reduced possibilities of sophisticated semantic distinctions in Spanish (Alfonso X borrows freely from Latin, and glosses his borrowing, but the relative inadequacy of thirteenth-century Spanish is betrayed by a phrase like *tirano, que quiere dezir rey cruel*); and (b) the enormously less flexible and subtle repertoire of subordinating conjunctions (Alfonso struggles with concepts like 'in spite of the fact that', 'even though', 'with the result that', 'in order that', but usually relies on an all-purpose and inevitably ambiguous *que*). Even so there is a further difference between medieval Spanish (which took several centuries to match the flexibility and sophistication of Latin) and creole languages, since one feature which appears to be seriously impaired by pidginization is the capacity for word-coinage from within the resources of the language: in the European-'based' pidgins and creoles, derivational prefixes and suffixes seem to have lost their original conceptual content and become fossilized. Obviously there are other devices for word-formation and we are all familiar with the ingenious periphrases of pidgins, but what cannot be generated very successfully by the combination of concrete words is abstract terms, in which it is notorious that pidgins and creoles are deficient. And there are probably upper limits to the number and length of such periphrases.

In other words, there may be some reason to suspect that the creole-speaker is handicapped by his language. Creolists have had a hard enough struggle to justify the respectability of their discipline, and modern linguists are rather more sensitive than nineteenth-century linguists to patronizing and despective attitudes to creole languages (partly perhaps because of a well-intentioned but mistaken failure to distinguish between attitudes to languages and attitudes to speakers of those languages); but, without wishing to spark an emotionally loaded discussion, I feel that someone should venture the suggestion that modern linguists may have been dangerously sentimental about creole languages, which, with only a few notable exceptions, constitute in most communities a distinct handicap to the social mobility of the individual, and *may* also constitute a handicap to the creole-speaker's personal intellectual development.

The point perhaps merits amplification. First, there can be no doubt about the limitations of a pidgin. This, of course, says nothing about the user of the pidgin who, by definition, has a native language of his own, and whose intellectual and communicative capacity cannot be judged from his fluency in the pidgin. But a recently creolized pidgin is a different matter. Again by definition, the starting point *cannot be* adequate. And the early period of creolization would involve (and on what historical evidence we have has invariably involved) a process of 'repair', of fashioning a more adequate instrument capable of meeting (at least roughly) the needs of the community. And from what we know of the role of language in intellectual development, one would expect the speakers of these primitive creoles to be intellectually handicapped. Two separate issues arise here: first, it is wrong to jump to the defence of a language (or its speakers) in terms of the potential equality of all languages or all mankind, refusing to consider the possibility of actual inequality (confusing, that is, potential with actual adequacy); and, secondly, while adequacy may be assessed in relation to the context of the language, it may also be assessed against a less restricted scale. If we concede (as we must) that languages adapt to needs, it follows, on any reasonable evolutionary view, that before the adaptation the language is not as well adapted as after it. And it then becomes an empirical question as to how far and how successfully adaptation has gone, and with what consequences for the individual speakers of the languages. This is a problem for the psychologists and the educationalists; at present I should go no further than to say that linguists do not have the evidence to assert with confidence that speakers of creole-languages are not handicapped by their language, and should not, while any doubt remains, make unsupported assertions to the contrary.

The classification of pidgins and creoles

Linguists have been exercised for a long time over the problem of 'classifying' creole languages (Hjelmslev 1939, etc.). No one ever caught a zoologist arguing about whether a mule was a horse or an ass, and I doubt that discussion of whether Haitian is to be classed as an African language (Sylvain 1936) or as French (Hall 1953) is any more relevant. Nor does the existence of pidgins and creoles mean that linguists have totally to revise their ideas on the classification of languages (tigons and ligers have not upset the Linnaean system); but they do need to clarify their ideas about hybridization.

The fact is that linguistic hybridization is not the exception but the rule. 'Spanish' has an enormous number of hybridizing dialects (Gibraltar, British Honduras, New Mexico, Texas, the Philippines, etc., etc.) which customarily do not figure at all in histories of the 'Spanish language'. But they should. And structuralists should pay a little more attention to the dubious fringes of the linguistic sub-systems.

I would suggest that the bulk of linguistic phenomena of hybridization – all those cases indeed in which the languages involved are not *sympatric* – should be regarded as cases of *primary* hybridization, on the same level as ordinary dialectal fragmentation (this is of course the same as Jakobson's proposition 1944:193), and that these 'primary' languages can be classified by the normal phylogenetic criteria; that all language-*switching* constitutes secondary hybridization (so that we do not have to attempt to classify the French spoken by an English-speaker as either French or English) and that, apart from formal language-learning, this is also the phenomenon associated with 'bilingualism' and the geographical superimposition of languages (*cocoliche*, etc.); and that the puzzle of the pidgins may be solved if we accept that they are *tertiary* languages, linked to the primary languages by secondary languages (i.e. non-natively learned foreign languages). A creole, despite its mixed inheritance – of which we should need to remind ourselves in any phylogenetic classification – must be regarded as a primary language: *the hybrid has become a new species*.

One final point: there is a sense in which it *is* meaningful to speak of Jamaican Creole as a dialect of English. Stewart (1962:51) proposed that the existence of what DeCamp has now called a 'post-creole speech continuum' meant that Jamaican Creole was not a creole in the proper sense of the term. The idea has met with support and opposition; and I would suggest that both sides are partly right. Not all evolutionary processes lead to divergence, and there is a comparatively rare biological phenomenon known as *de-speciation*: the barriers (normally ecological) separating incipient (or even apparently separate) species are removed, and the populations reintegrate. The biological analogue is not exact; but clearly one must allow, in any sophisticated taxonomy, for the process of *decreolization*, which can in time transform a creole into something linked by a smoothly intergrading bridge to the original target-language of the parent pidgin – transform the creole, in effect, into a 'dialect' of the standard. It would be wise, however, not to lose sight of the fact that there are dialects which originate by a simple process of primary hybridization, and 'dialects', like Jamaican Creole, which arise from a more complex sequence of secondary hybridization, tertiary hybridization (pidginization), creolization, and decreolization (which is a process of primary hybridization).

NOTES

1 Biological analogies have not infrequently been applied by linguists with utter confusion of the hierarchies. Meillet (1921: I, 83) calls the Western European languages 'parthenogenetic'! (A possible linguistic analogue of the agamospecies might be a 'dead' language.) And this misapplication of the analogies has led, unfortunately, to the almost total discrediting of any attempt to apply them.

2 Linguists, from the time of Hempl (1898), have tended to lump together the ecological and ethological factors as 'external', i.e. non-structural, circumstances, and the distinction is not, perhaps, of great moment, even though 'ecology' preconditions 'attitude'.

3 An elementary account of the problems may be found in Forrest (1948:237–47). Chinese is still obliged to treat foreign names (Washington, Johnson, etc.) by the syllabizing method, which Purcell (1936) argued, somewhat unconvincingly, was the superior method of assimilating the vocabulary of Western technology.

4 The term does not then become merely tautologous, since one can distinguish (a) degrees of intensity of hybridization, and (b) primary, secondary, and tertiary hybridization.

5 Of course we at once come up against the hoary old philosophical problems of language and thought, heredity and environment. How much of children's conceptualization is governed by language is still something of an open question. (See, e.g. Watts 1944:18–25, Piaget 1955: 350–86.) It is not 'Whorfianism' to suggest that linguistic acculturation can be affected by this 'conceptual barrier'. (See Lyons 1963:38–44.)

6 It is my impression that many linguists seem unaware that the possibility is admitted by the taxonomists. I quote Cain (1954:95).

7 They tend to acquire distinctive names, of course, only when they are perceived to be linguistic phenomena associated with a specific, self-contained, identifiable community of speakers.

8 I mean that while phonological innovation appears invariably to occur later than *some* lexemic borrowing, the postponement of the adoption of phonetic innovations is probably aided by the compatibility of two sound-systems, i.e. the possibility of finding, easily, acceptable substitute phonemes.

9 Since the proposition has never been seriously advanced, it is scarcely worth wasting time over; but, essentially, a pidgin would not result because the situation, though more complex, would still be a *cocoliche* situation. The two groups of bilinguals could not be brought together except in a cultural situation which would determine which was the superstrate target language, and there is no factor inherent in the double-bilingual situation which could introduce stability into any hybridizing dialect which might result from the contact.

10 It comprises the code-varieties produced by speakers of the target-language in attempting to reproduce the mixed language produced by the speakers of another language in attempting to communicate with the speakers of the target-

language by means of the target-language. The purpose of those who produce these varieties is communication not with the speakers of the mixed language but with fellow target-language speakers, for purposes of entertainment. Though almost wholly neglected as a group, they are important, for almost all our early records of pidgins and creoles are of this type, and comparisons of superstrate copies with the genuine articles could be instructive in enabling us to determine more accurately the validity of such evidence. (One might refer to these varieties as *stereotyped* (cf. Labov 1965:102) and adapt a formula devised by Hockett for pidgins and creoles (e.g. Chinese Pidgin English), thus designating English Stereotyped Irish English, Argentinian Stereotyped Italian Spanish (or *cocoliche*), etc.)

11 This does not quite translate Bloomfield's (1933:473) 'a foreign speaker's version of a language and a native speaker's version of the foreign speaker's version and so on' for it omits that crucial 'and so on'. But the images which that 'and so on' suggests: of an oscillation's coming to rest, of the successive corrections of the undershooting and overshooting of a target, are not, I think valid ones, though plausible at first sight. The vibration of a string *starts from* a static mid-term and returns to it, the gunner is *aiming at* a fixed point. I suggest that the plausibility of this formula rests solely on the plausibility of the concealed analogues, which are false. There is no reason why the 'imitation of the imitation', *ad infinitum*, should not give linguistic results which go on swinging indefinitely between extremes, like the booms and recessions of an uncontrolled economy, or, indeed, swing ever more wildly until the wobble becomes a crash, i.e. until the mixed language is abandoned entirely for one or other of the stable systems.

12 On the evidence of Terrence Kaufman and W. J. Samarin, this does not appear to be true of Chinook or Sango; but in the case of Charles Frake's Zamboangueño one might easily postulate a historical process of repair, the deficiencies of the pidgin vocabulary being supplemented from the substrate native language, and it remains in general true that the lexicon of a pidgin is not macaronic.

13 David DeCamp has pointed out that my original statement, that Chinese Pidgin is a dying language *tout court*, is wrong, in as much as it appears to have acquired a new lease of life in Taiwan where, also, it is the language of maids and cab-drivers.

14 I mean that there is, in most pidgins, a stable norm, with a very restricted range of alternative ways of saying the same thing, and, among their speakers, at least some notion of 'grammaticality'. The well-documented fact that there was never a single norm of *pronunciation* among Chinook-speakers (Indians and traders using distinct phonologies adapted from their native languages) or, on Reinecke's evidence, among French and Vietnamese speakers of Tây Boi (this volume) does not invalidate this generalization.

15 The Argentines who imitate *cocoliche* (like the Uruguayans who imitate in Montevideo newspapers the mixed Spanish-Portuguese dialect of the Brazilian frontier) use neither an all-Spanish nor all-Italian lexicon. Much of the comic effect depends on the macaronic juxtaposition (almost alternation) of Spanish and Italian forms. They aim, that is, about the middle of the spectrum; but this does not mean that any consistency is achieved, or that variation is drastically reduced, since one is likely to find (although I invent these examples) *el muchacho ha fame* alongside *il ragazzo tiene hambre*.

16 Dell Hymes, in a private communication, has suggested that there might be situations in which speakers of the same language could stabilize a secondary language among themselves as a pidgin, if, for instance, cut off from models of it, they had a special role for it, as in a ritual. I should not discard this possibility. There is no essential difference between secondary and tertiary hybridization (any more than between hybrids and the offspring of hybrids) except a process of intercommunicating/interbreeding which reduces the range of variability, and a process of hardening of the barriers between the secondary language and the model (as between the population of hybrids and the parent species). There does seem to be something of a gap between the confused spectra of imperfectly acquired foreign languages and the grammaticality of pidgins, but there may be no really hard-and-fast dividing line.

17 And probably not how Chinese Pidgin arose, since we have records of a *mixed* Portuguese-English 'jargon' (Noble 1762), intermediate between the known use of Portuguese Pidgin as a means of communication between *English* and Chinese (Hamilton 1727) and the rise of pidgin proper. I can find no documentation to support Hall (1966:8) in his assertion that 'the English established their first "factory" or trading post at Canton in 1664, and *immediately a variety of Pidgin English grew up there*' (my italics).

REFERENCES

Bernís, Francisco 1955. *Prontuario de la avifauna española . . . con los nombres científicos y españoles . . . Lista patrón de la Sociedad Española de Ornitología*, Madrid, Soc. Esp. de Ornitología

Bloomfield, Leonard 1933. *Language*, New York, Holt

Cain, A. J. 1954. *Animal species and their evolution*, London, Hutchinson

Coseriu, Eugenio 1968. 'Sincronía, diacronía y tipología', *Actas del XI Congreso Internacional de Lingüística y Filología Románicas, Madrid 1965*, Madrid, Consejo Superior de Investigaciones Científicas

Dozier, Edward P. 1956. 'Two examples of linguistic acculturation', *Language* 32:146–57

Entwistle, William James 1936. *The Spanish language*. London, Faber and Faber

Forrest, R. A. D. 1948. *The Chinese language*, London, Faber and Faber

Hall, Robert A., Jr. 1953. 'Haitian Creole: grammar, texts, vocabulary', (*American Anthropological Association, Memoir* 74), Washington, D.C., American Anthropological Association
    1964. *Introductory linguistics*, Philadelphia, Chilton Books
    1966. *Pidgin and creole languages*, Ithaca, New York, Cornell University Press

Hamilton, Alexander 1727. *A new account of the East Indies, being the . . . remarks of Capt. A. H. who spent his time there from . . . 1688 to 1723*, Edinburgh, J. Mosman

Hempl, G. 1898. 'Language-rivalry and speech-differentiation in the case of race-mixture', *Transactions of the American Philological Association* 29:31–47

Hjelmslev, Louis 1939. 'Études sur la notion de parenté linguistique: Relations de parenté des langues créoles', *Revue des Études Indo-Européennes* 2:271–86

Jakobson, Roman 1944. 'Franz Boas' approach to language', *International Journal of American Linguistics* 10:188–95

Kroeber, A. L. 1940. 'Stimulus diffusion', *American Anthropologist* 42:1–20

Labov, William A. 1965. 'Stages in the acquisition of standard English', *Social dialects and language learning*, ed. by Roger Shuy, 77–103, Champaign, Illinois, National Council of Teachers of English

Lorenzo, Emilio 1966. *El español de hoy, lengua en ebullición*, Madrid, Gredos

Lyons, John 1963. *Structural semantics*, Oxford, Blackwell

Martinet, André 1951–2. 'The unvoicing of Old Spanish sibillants', *Romance Philology* 5:133–56

Mayr, Ernst 1942. *Systematics and the origin of species*, New York, Columbia University Press

Meillet, Antoine 1921. *Linguistique historique et linguistique générale*, 2 vols., Paris, Société de Linguistique de Paris

[Noble, Charles Frederick] Anonymous 1762. *A voyage to the East Indies in 1747 and 1748*, London, without imprint

Piaget, Jean 1955. *The child's construction of reality*, London, Routledge and Kegan Paul

Purcell, Victor 1936. *Problems in Chinese education*. London, Kegan Paul and Co.

Stewart, William A. 1962. 'Creole languages in the Caribbean', *Study of the Role of Second Languages in Asia, Africa, and Latin America*, ed. by Frank A. Rice, 34–53, Washington, D.C., Center for Applied Linguistics

Sylvain, Suzanne 1936. *Le créole haïtien: Morphologie et syntaxe*, Port-au-Prince, Wetteren

Thompson, R. W. 1961. 'A note on some possible affinities between the creole dialects of the Old World and those of the New', *Creole Language Studies II*, ed. by R. B. Le Page, 107–13, London, Macmillan

Valkhoff, Marius F. 1966. *Studies in Portuguese and Creole with special reference to South Africa*, Johannesburg, Witwatersrand University Press

Vintila-Radulescu, Ioana 1967. 'Remarques sur les idiomes créoles', *Revue Roumaine de Linguistique* 12:229–43

Watts, A. F. 1944. *The language and mental development of children*, London, Harrap

Weinreich, Uriel 1953. *Languages in contact: findings and problems*, New York, Linguistic Circle of New York

Whinnom, Keith 1956. *Spanish contact vernaculars in the Philippine Islands*, Hong Kong, Hong Kong University Press

1965. 'The origin of the European-based pidgins and creoles', *Orbis* 14: 509–27

1966. *A glossary of Spanish bird-names*, London, Támesis Books

SALIENT AND SUBSTANTIVE
PIDGINIZATION

WILLIAM J. SAMARIN

There was some question at one time as to whether or not pidgins were languages. This was an era when decisions were being made about the use of pidgins in business, government, and education in former colonial territories throughout the world. There was always a superfluity of languages, and in the keen competition that characterizes multilingual areas, the pidgins were outclassed; they hardly 'made the leagues' at all. In the contest with the natural languages, both indigenous and imported, they showed up very poorly, having no supporters with mother-tongue loyalties. Of course, the arguments given – when they were not simply disregarded – were mainly linguistic: pidgins have vocabularies and grammars so restricted as to be inadequate for communication. Seldom did anyone observe that they actually were in widespread and successful use. Without them communication would, in many areas, be severely hampered or almost impossible. But still, they were not languages.

The usefulness of pidgins is clear, but there seems to be very little more support for them now than there was ten or twenty years ago. This is certainly true of the Central African Republic which has been independent since 1960. Four months of close observations in 1967 (June–September), three of which were spent in the capital, Bangui, convinced me that although Sango was still the *langue nationale* (French being *langue officielle*) nothing official was being done to develop its use. There was a government-appointed Sango committee, but it has met only a few times since its establishment in 1962, and very little has come of the meetings. It made no recommendations for the use of the several thousand dollars earmarked by Unesco for developing Sango during the fiscal year 1966–7 and linguistic studies were sacrificed to musical instruments in the subsequent requests from the C.A.R. delegation. Some of the Central African members of the committee, for there are some European members as well, are mildly nationalistic about Sango, attributing to it value as a symbol of independence. The last meeting of the committee in August 1967 favored the adoption of a standard orthography and spelling before further work, meaning a grammar and dictionary (independent of the American publications), be taken up. Since then the chairman of the committee, whose official position was Directeur de l'Enseignement, and the Minister of Interior were removed, the President retaining this ministry's

portfolio himself. In any case, the committee could only act in an advisory
capacity; decisions had to be made by the President. (Sango will be further
characterized below.)

The situation is different now, but only partly. What makes the difference is
that linguists have taken up the study of pidgins with the seriousness that
hitherto characterized only the investigation of natural languages.[1] The increase in the number and variety of publications on this subject is witness to
this fact. (Not all of this has had scientific motivations, of course. The U.S.
Office of Education, which has subsidized much of the work on pidgins, is
concerned with the preparation of language teaching material. It obviously
has nothing to say to the foreign countries about the use of pidgins and must
rely on informed observers for information about the usefulness, *for Americans*,
of this or that pidgin.)

Distinctiveness of pidgins

But have we proven that pidgins are indeed languages? No one has addressed
himself to this task with greater vigor than R. A. Hall, Jr. *Hands Off Pidgin
English!* (1955, and the exclamation point is part of the title) is not just a
grammar of Melanesian Pidgin; it is also a brief for the social and linguistic
legitimacy of the language. His *Pidgin and Creole Languages* (1966) does not
alter his stand. It is one thing to say, however, that pidgins deserve linguistic
investigation or that they manifest the kinds of structures that we find in
natural languages and another thing to say that they are (real) languages in
any very precise sense. Linguists clearly should investigate various types of
semi-languages for the information they can give us about the place of
languages in human communication.[2]

It is clear that pidgins are different from natural languages in several significant respects. Even Hall recognizes the fact that the life history of pidgins
is different (Hall 1962). Historically, that is, genetically, they may be even
more different than he is prepared to admit, if relexification is accepted as the
best hypothesis (Whinnom 1965).[3] In Stewart's scheme, creoles and pidgins
are also distantly removed from standard languages, because a pidgin, for
example, has no 'codified set of grammatical and lexical norms which are
formally accepted and learned by the language's user', no 'existing community
of speakers', and lacks 'homogenicity' (its 'basic lexicon and basic grammatical
structure [are not] both from the same pre-stages of the language') (1962).

Many other characteristics of pidgins have been mentioned, but they are as
varied as the two kinds of observations referred to in the preceding paragraph.
There has been little concern with distinguishing between superficial features
and defining characteristics. This is the fundamental problem in taxonomy.
Although most people can recognize a cow when they see one, they could not

tell what distinguishes a cow from a goat, and it is, in fact, very difficult to define *cow* without appeal to characteristics which are not immediately apparent, e.g. the dentition. In pidgins there may be a striking amount of reduplication or iteration, but it is doubtful, as far as I am concerned, that reduplication is a defining characteristic of these languages.[4] This morphological characteristic is probably due to the source languages. In itself it helps us to recognize most pidgins, but not to distinguish them from other kinds of languages. Reduplication is therefore a *salient* feature of pidgins, not a *substantive* one.

Salient pidginization describes the striking concomitant changes that natural language A (A_n) experiences in the process of becoming a pidgin (A_p). One of these is, or may be, a very high rate of borrowing – so high that a pidgin is sometimes automatically called a mixed language. (Many have used 'creole' with this meaning.) *Substantive pidginization*, on the other hand, is the set of changes that characterizes all pidgins. One of these, perhaps the most important one, is simplification. For example, the total lexical inventories of pidgins are known to be impoverished by comparison with those of natural languages.

If we can agree on what constitutes substantive pidginization, we will have agreed on what is a pidgin. We will also have agreed on whether or not pidgins are languages. For example, does Sango's restricted vocabulary make it a non-language? Haugen thought so (Samarin 1966a:209). There may have been some misunderstanding, however, about the total morphemic inventory of Sango. If the figure of 489 is given for 'Sango' words (Samarin 1966a:188), as opposed to French borrowings, this is not to ignore the many French words that have become fully naturalized – *mɛrdée* 'to bother', for example. Taber's dictionary (1965) lists 186 such borrowings: 123 nouns, 40 verbs, 9 adjunctives, and 14 connectives and particles. Still, the total is somewhere between 700 and 1,000 morpheme-words. Although this is quite low when compared to the inventory of English or even Zulu, it is not so striking when compared with Caucasic languages (e.g. Kuipers 1960). (And it is of the same order of magnitude as the number of fundamental word-forming elements that Swadesh has found characteristic of all languages (including Mayan and Aztec) not enlarged with an exogenously-derived learned vocabulary (the world languages of modern science such as English and Russian especially).) This is to point out that it is not simply the size of a pidgin's inventory that may be significant, but its character.

The nature of pidgins

In trying to determine what kinds of languages pidgins are we can take two avenues of investigation.[5] We can first proceed by examining the assertions that have been made about languages in general, sometimes without any thought given to pidgins, to determine the measure of their applicability to pidgins. We can also proceed in the other direction, by comparing pidgins with natural languages.

Let us look first at four assertions about natural languages. Two have to do with language use and two with characteristics of language systems.

Chomsky believes, along with Humboldt, that language is primarily a 'means of thought and self-expression' (1966:21). This being true, 'The purely practical use of language is characteristic of no real human language, but only of invented parasitic systems' (22), adding in a footnote, 'For example, the *lingua franca* of the Mediterranean coast', probably referring to Sabir (for which, see Whinnom 1965). A pidgin is therefore a parasitic form of speech whose primary function is not the expression of thought but that of practical interchange. (The paraphrase is my own.) Chomsky is led to this assertion by his commitment to the Cartesian principle, so named by him, that language is a human species-specific endowment that liberates man from contextual restraints and stimuli and permits him to freely encode his own experience. He does not suggest how thought and self-expression are to be measured, and he surely could not deprive my Central African assistant of these gifts when he and I discuss cultural relativity and the importance of saying 'Thank you' in Western society! Still, we know what Chomsky is driving at.

There are two assertions by Joos that apply to pidgins, only the second of which I will consider in any length. First, ' . . . all languages are as complex as is biologically tolerable, and hence all are equally complex . . . It is to the advantage of every community to make its language as complex as biologically possible . . .' (1964:191).[6] This is patently inapplicable to pidgins, for they are far less complex than normal languages. It might, in any case, be more appropriate to say, as suggested by Gleason (in conversation), that complexity in language, whose function is the resolution of conflicts between various functions of language, is limited only by the ability of the pattern-setting speaker to cope with it.

The second of Joos' claims has to do with *hapax legomena*. He believes that the number of types in any natural-language text long enough to deserve the title 'text', say 500 words long or more, that occur only once 'always falls between 46% and 48%' (personal communication, but cf. Joos 1936 and 1937–8 and Hanley 1937). The corollary of this assertion is that figures that diverge greatly from these would belong to 'pseudo-texts' or 'pseudo-languages'. In James Joyce's *Ulysses* the *hapax legomena* are 50·5% of its vocabulary and one Esperanto text of about 20,000 tokens had a figure of 63%. But a Basic English text of a size similar to the Esperanto one had 38%. Joos concludes: 'Neither Basic English nor Esperanto is a language.'

When applied to other languages for the present study the test produced ambiguous results. Only in the case of Sango, where 31·5% of the types are *hapax legomena*, is it validated. One would have expected similar results for Police Motu, another pidginized *lingua franca*, but the percentage is 42·94%. The figure for Jamaican Creole is as high as one expects for natural languages (46·48%), but this may only show that the text is closer to English than other varieties of JC are. On the other hand, the figures for Ngbandi (32·09%), Gbeya (40·89%), and Cashinawa, a language of Peru (34·21%), are lower than one expects for natural languages. The skewing factor here may be in the size rather than in the kind of texts that were obtained, but since the Ngbandi text is a portion of the Bible translated by a missionary, we may have to deal with inadvertent pidginization. The figure is low in the highly inflected Cashinawa language perhaps because all morphemes are lumped together.

In any case, Gleason suggests (in conversation) that such gross calculations are not going to prove as diagnostic as some other kinds. It may be just as important, if not more important, to see the curve of the percentages and their dispersion. The hypothesis put forth by him is that a pidgin will have a sharper drop in a text of a given size than a natural language. [That is, an element is not only more likely to recur, but also to do so in a shorter interval.] He experimented with Kâte, a natural language from New Guinea. Five passages of 200 words each from five stories in *Wowose Tikihata Buk I* and one passage of 600 words from *Harinkec Ere Binan* were counted. The percentage of *hapax legomena* falls as the sample gets larger and the dispersion appears to become less. Nothing is said about how this compares with a pidgin language.

Only a few comprehensive statements of the above-mentioned kind are necessary to illustrate both their value and their limitation. On the one hand, they set off pidgins in a class of languages different from natural ones. On the other hand, they do not contribute to our understanding of the pidgins themselves. This remaining class of unnatural languages is really no class at all. It is simply comprised of what is left over after other forms of speech have passed the test of normality. Since this is true, the comprehensive statements (if not the ones referred to, then others) are weaker than they ought to be. The inclusion of the term 'normal' is only a device to save the statements from invalidation. Implied is the following: 'If one finds a language where this generalization does not apply, it is probably not normal.'

The term 'normal' occurs in the fourth statement considered in this discussion. Hymes, in writing about the varieties of language that humans use, asserts that 'No normal person, and no normal community, is limited in repertoire to a single variety of code [implying that a code could have more than one variety], to an unchanging monotony which would preclude the possibility of indicating respect, insolence, mock-seriousness, humor, role-distance, etc., by switching from one code-variety to another' (1967:9). Does this apply to pidgins? No, since Hymes is talking, not about particular kinds

E

of linguistic systems, but about language *use*. This is to say that a speaker of a pidgin, as a *normal* human being in a normal society, can be expected to have more than one code-variety for different uses. The pidgin, on the other hand, is not normal, and when a person is speaking a pidgin he is limited to the use of a code with but one level or style or key or register, to cite some terms used for this aspect of the organization of language. (One might speak here of a 'monostratic', 'monoclaval' or 'monotonic' code.) In other words, he does not have the rich variety of language styles from which to choose whatever is appropriate to the context, situation, or person (or people) to whom he is talking.

(What happens to pidgin – or for that matter, an artificial language – in a normal society where a plurality of functions is universally characteristic of language is, of course, another matter. Is it inevitable, for example, that people who are limited to a pidgin somehow contribute to the evolution of a language that will respond to socially significant differences in human behavior? And even if this is inevitable, there are many who would like to know what the behavioral and psychological consequences are of being restricted to a pidgin or other type of 'monoclaval' language.)

The crucial term in the immediate discussion is *code*. We mean, of course, a clearly defined and integrated array of linguistic features, opposed to another similar array. Precisely what is needed to produce a 'code-variety' is unclear. It is probably something more than a single feature. Thus, it would seem ill-advised to suggest two code-varieties for Sango just because of the use of the second/third person plural pronoun (*ála*) in politely addressing another individual or referring to him. Deference to an elder is not indicated in any other ways in the language itself. (The use of *babá* and *mamá*, with the obvious meanings, is not really parallel.) In fact, it would be possible to describe *ála* as being the morphemic realizate of the semons of person and number/age-with-respect-to-speaker. (Politeness is an attitude, not necessarily a part of the semantic structure of language.) It should further be noted about *ála* that not all Sango-speaking people use it in the way described here. It is the Gbaya-Ngbaka-Manza who use *ála* deferentially, with interference from their own languages (cf. Gbeya *wi* 'second person plural' and *wa* 'third person plural'). It is very significant that although the President is called by many lofty titles in Sango and French on the Sango radio broadcasts, he is never referred to by *ála*.[7]

In summary, the pidgin-speaking community is not normal from a sociolinguistic point of view. Neither is the language normal. A pidgin is a language, but a different kind of language.

Diagnostic tool for normality

What is needed is a clearer understanding of what linguistic abnormalcy is.

More specifically, how can we best describe pidginization? (The use of this process noun is deliberate. I think that pidginization is a common phenomenon in human language and that pidgins are only special cases of it. The study of both will obviously go on together.)

There might be considerable value, for example, in the establishment of a recognition procedure for pidgins (or pidginization). On the basis of a certain amount of connected discourse which is subjected to a particular kind of analysis, we would hope to determine, with a reasonable margin of error, whether or not the text was normal. There should be no *a priori* reason why texts from marginal languages (in Stewart's term) should be excluded. The processing of a great variety of data would have the value of breaking us of some of our prejudices and expanding our knowledge of what constitutes pidginization.

Another value of a pidgin-diagnostic tool would be to free us at least in part from dependence on accidents of historical information. We are at the moment concerned with contemporary pidgins and creoles, cases known today to be such. This is understandable, for there is still a great deal to learn about them. For example, I should very much like to know more about the origin of Sango: the amount of multilingualism in the Ubangi basin, the human relationships that existed between the speakers of vernacular Sango and other people of the area, the identification of the carriers of Sango and the channels that characterized its use, the relative importance of African (both indigenous and foreign – e.g. from Senegal, Congo, etc.) and European (French, Portuguese, Greek) carriers of the language, etc. But the time ought to come when other languages will be examined in the light of these cases. This may not be easy, for if pidgins survive, they apparently adapt themselves to the needs of their speakers; they become naturalized, although not necessarily to the same degree. If we examine a language at a very great time after its pidginized era, we might have to be less dogmatic about its past than we would like to be. (See Southworth's study of Indo-Aryan in this volume.) I therefore agree with Le Page when he writes that 'Many of the world's languages have probably undergone some degree of creolization at one time or another; by studying what is happening under our noses at the present day we should get a much better idea of what has happened . . . in the past' (1966:vii). Investigators should be encouraged to suggest some possibilities. There has perhaps been too much timidity. How widely is it known among pidginists, for example, that 'Oceanic Melanesian represents a pidginized form of Austronesian grafted onto basically non-Austronesian languages' (Capell 1966:537)?

If a new approach to pidgin studies can free linguists from historical constraints, thus contributing to the rigor of their methodology, it may at the same time make a contribution to historical reconstructions. The new approach may help us to understand better what we observe and to reveal what we do not even suspect. Thus, if we can determine a set of linguistic characteristics that evince rapid (or traumatic) social changes, we may be able to increase our ability to reconstruct the histories of societies.[8] If, for example, among related languages A, B, C, and D, A reveals some of our diagnostic traits, we would be justified in seeking evidence for the kinds of social changes they are associated with. This at least, is a task to which sociolinguistics should seriously address itself.

A linguistic diagnostic tool for 'pidginness' would be applied to a corpus, as was mentioned above. Therefore the selection of this corpus must be pursued with the utmost deliberation. As in all linguistic investigation we must be concerned with the sampling technique as well as the kind and quantity of the corpus collected.

Simplification

Let us now return to comparison of pidgins with natural languages. We need to examine the concept of simplification. The following represents the common belief:

From a structural point of view, the essential characteristic of a pidgin language is that it is sharply reduced in its pronunciation and grammar and in its vocabulary. In general, this reduction is in the direction of whatever features are common to the language of all those using the pidgin, for mutual ease in use and comprehensibility, thus arriving at a kind of greatest common denominator (Hall 1966:25).

Two things are wrong with this characterization of pidgins: the notions of commonality and reduction are both imprecise.

As for *commonality*, what is implied here is that the pidgin AB results when speakers of A seek to learn B but fail to acquire the use of some features of B, certain grammatical categories, for example (and conversely, of course, for speakers of B learning A). The following grid shows the set of theoretical possibilities. ($+$) marks the presence, ($-$) the absence, of a feature. Rows 1a, b are for features present in both A and B, rows 2a, b for features present only in A, rows 3a, b for features present only in B, and rows 4a, b for features present in neither. In these pairs (a) represents the case in which the outcome is the presence of the feature in AB, (b) the case in which it is not.

	A	B	AB
1a	+	+	+
1b	+	+	−
2a	+	−	+
2b	+	−	−
3a	−	+	+
3b	−	+	−
4a	−	−	+
4b	−	−	−

Hall's statement implies that a pidgin language will have features (here, grammatical categories) that reflect the possibilities represented by 1a, 2b, 3b (and probably 1b), as well as of course 4b. The features positively present in the pidgin will be those represented by 1a, features present in both sources (the common denominator). From this point of view, a pidgin is not expected to be as complex as A or B (even though the grid shows four plus marks in each column), though balancing features from both (2a, 3a); and the possibility that the formation of a pidgin could involve innovation (4a) is not even considered. But it is possible for the pidgin to have a category which was absent in the two languages in contact. I believe that there are examples of it (4a) in Sango. The most notable one is the existence and use of *ɛkɛ* 'to be'. In Sango it is used both as a kind of auxiliary verb to mark progressive aspect (*lo ɛkɛ tɛ kóbe* 'he is eating') and as a copula (*lo ɛkɛ makunzi* 'he is a village-headman'). No such verb has yet been found in Ngbandi (in the absence of data on vernacular Sango or Yakoma). Moreover, in that language, identification is expressed by the juxtaposition of two elements.

Ngbandi   Sango

é ázì 'we are people' (lit. 'we people')   *i ɛkɛ ázo*
lò nà tá tí nkpç 'she had a pot of oil.'   *lo ɛkɛ na ta tí mafuta*
(lit. 'she with pot of oil')

In Sango juxtaposition is limited to only certain kinds of constructions: e.g. *só zo wa* 'who is this person?' *só makunzi* 'this is the village-headman' or *lo ɛkɛ makunzi*. Let this example illustrate the much-overlooked innovative powers of a pidgin.

Of much more interest is the concept of *reduction*. We are generally led to believe that what is involved in reduction is primarily a decrease in the number of linguistic elements, whether phonological, morphological, or lexical. And Le Page, agreeing with Hall in principle, further restricts the concept of reduction by adding that 'since the *inflectional* structures of two languages in a contact situation rarely coincide, inflection is the commonest casualty in a contact situation' (1967:86). Such a narrow view of simplification is unfortunate although it is understandable. Both Le Page and Hall are thinking too much about pidgins they are most familiar with, the ones that are closely linked to European languages. This view ignores the possibility that pidginization could occur without the drastic reduction of an inflectional system. Moreover, pidginization can certainly occur when the source language has very little inflection. Sango is a good example of this kind of development. In the source language what are commonly called verbal categories are marked by co-occurrence patterns of tone in verbs and pronouns (and the subject marker *a-*). Thus, future time or anticipatory aspect is marked by pronoun set 3 (with high tone) and verb tone set B (but there are eight classes of verbs): e.g. *é fɔnɔ* 'we will walk' (Nelson 1952). In Pidgin Sango, verbs and pronouns are invariable, but some of the inflection remains with subject marker *a-*: *fadé i fɔnɔ* 'we will walk,' *i fɔnɔ awɛ* 'we have walked' (literally 'we walk it-is-finished').

Both Hall and Le Page seem to have forgotten (or rejected?) the notion of purposeful simplification on the part of B-speakers (that is, of the language being learned). It has generally been held that B-speakers both simplified their language to make it easier for the learners and also imitated the learners in the simplifying changes they were making. A single term covers both kinds of behavior, but they are fundamentally different. Simplification on the part of A-speakers involves the inability (a) to infer linguistic structure from random utterances, and (b) to remember both the elements and the rules. Simplification on the part of B-speakers, on the other hand, is self-motivated. It assumes either some kind of notion, albeit extremely naïve, of what is difficult in their language or enough acquaintance with language A to realize what the learning difficulties are going to be, or both. I would not expect the second kind of knowledge on a large enough scale to account for pidginization. (But for its possible role, see Ferguson's paper in this volume.) The first kind, if it were entirely self-motivated, would be extremely interesting. Would we find, perchance, that there was a universal intuitive notion of simplification? Would the speakers of vernacular Sango, for example, have deliberately eliminated tonal inflection?

A broader concept of reduction will comprehend more linguistic phenomena, thereby establishing relationships that have gone unnoticed. I should like to suggest that there is something in pidgin languages, imperfect learning of a second language, loss of one's own language, and restricted codes, that is common to them all. These are only examples; the list can undoubtedly be lengthened, and with the larger number will come the need for establishing a more refined typology of pidginization than I can offer at this time.

Reduction in functions

The fundamental characteristic of pidginization is indeed reduction or simplification, and it need not be 'drastic' or 'sharp' at all. Moreover, it is not necessarily a purely linguistic phenomenon. Pidginization should be seen as *any consistent reduction of the functions of language both in its grammar and its use.*[9] The key word here is 'functions'. With reference to the various uses to which language is put, this characterization means that a language is used to talk about less topics, or in fewer contexts, to indicate fewer social relations, etc. Imagine the whole gamut of uses to which any specific language is put, and a pidginized form of that language would have fewer such uses.[10] This function reduction is what is indicated in the term 'trade language', but many other restricted uses are obviously possible. A speaker whose proficiency in a second language is primarily in some specialized area of learning or human activity (sports, religious ritual, hunting, farming) speaks a pidginized form of the language. Boys who learn Yiddish to talk about the Talmud and Molokan young people in America who learn to talk Russian to take part in Molokan religious life are sometimes examples of such speakers. And most of us who only occasionally speak a second language probably have a limited world of discourse. This kind of pidginization therefore comprehends the limitations implied in the statements by Chomsky and Hymes referred to above.

Reduction in language use probably always has some repercussions on language output. When they are massive, a pidgin language results. Limited pidginization is much more common. It is common, for example, in linguistic field work and in the making of bilingual dictionaries of preliterate languages. In the initial stages of field work one chooses to elicit utterances which will reveal just as much information as can be controlled by the investigator. One permits the linguistic structure to drip out, so to speak; one does not turn on the faucet wide open. This means use of the same constructions again and again. Even if one attempts to vary them, as generative grammarians claim to do, they will vary in only a few ways. The same kind of stereotypy is found in dictionaries, even those as good as Lekens' *Dictionnaire Ngbandi* (but not his *Ngbandi Idioticon*). This dictionary illustrates the meanings of words with very few kinds of syntactic constructions, showing a preference for pronoun subjects and one of the past tenses. Unwittingly much of the language structure is amputated.

It is choice that both requires and permits a language-learner to pidginize. He is faced with options between which he has to decide. Some of these are, for the native speakers, stylistic choices, others are to avoid ambiguity (Gleason 1965:440ff). To the learner they are just a headache. Thus, if he has difficulties with arranging pronouns in a French sentence, he may avoid constructions like *je ne lui en ai pas donné* 'I didn't give him any of it' for those like *je ne lui ai pas donné de ça* (or the named object). American speakers of Sango have further pidginized this pidgin by ignoring the (stylistic?) option between sentences like *lo gá apɛ, téné aɛkɛ apɛ* ('he come not, word is not') and *tongana lo gá apɛ, téné aɛkɛ apɛ* both of which mean 'If he doesn't come, it's all right'. They use only the second one, presumably because it is closer to English, which has a subordinating conjunction. The statistical differences in the incidence of *tongana* in African and American texts probably also indicates other significant differences in encoding. So striking are the differences that I can on the basis of the use of *tongana* alone unerringly identify a Central African who has lived in a very dependent relationship on English-speaking missionaries.

The case of *tongana* in Sango is evidence for options in a pidgin, but Sango has fewer of them than one expects in a natural language. (The use or nonuse of the copula in *só aɛkɛ yɛ̧* or *só yɛ̧* 'what is this?' is another example.) Thus it should be possible to identify pidginness on internal evidence alone. Be that as it may, we have in the reduction of options a means for characterizing historical pidginization. By way of illustration let us look rather closely at the Sango connective *ti* (*na* could also be used). Both of these occur in the source language with the same general functions they have in Sango, but their uses are not identical. Moreover, the total number of connective types is greater in the source language than in Sango.[11]

Ngbandi has two connectives comparable to Sango's *ti*. They are *tɛ́* and *ti* with varying tone. Both of them mark possession:

> *zàmà ti mbi* 'my knife'   *dà tɛ́ lò* 'his house'
> *ágbia tí kɔdɔlɔ* 'village chiefs'   *Lo-gbia tɛ́ Nzàpa* 'kingdom of
> (Mark 14:53)   God'   (Mark 14:25)

Examples like these suggest that there is no restriction on the use of either *tɛ́* or *ti*, but the corpus gives some indication that there may be a semantic difference; if not, I would assume a stylistic one. In other constructions there are clear (as far as our corpus is concerned) differences of use. Only *tɛ́* is used to 'intensify' the subject: *álà kpɛ́ tɛ́ 'là* 'they fled' (literally 'they flee of them'). Only *ti* is used with the interrogative substitute *nɛ̀* 'what?' and to introduce verbs or nominalized verbs: *tɛnɛ tɛnɛ ti nɛ̀* 'say what?' (literally 'say word of what?'), cf. *tɛnɛ ti nvɛ̀nɛ̀* 'falsehood' ('word of lie'), *tɛnɛ tɛ́ 'là* 'their word'; *tongɔ lo mɛ̀ tí lìa bɛ* 'raillerie (qui lèche le cœur) amère', *à léngbì ti vɔ̧ngɔ* 'can sell' ('equal to the selling') (Mark 14:5). However, *ti* is absent in some such cases for no apparent reason, marked by (): *à nɔ* () *'bâ nyì lo* 'il est allé en visite chez sa fille', *lò bàbà* () *lingɔ kwà* 'il continue à travailler ('he continued doing work'). On the other hand, *ti* (or *tɛ́* or both) is consistently omitted in constructions marked by what one can call inalienable possession:

ngú lɛ̀   'tears' (cf. *ngú tí le kɛkɛ* 'fruit juice', Mark 14:25)
lì lò   'his head'
pɛ̂ lo   'after him'
kɔ́ lò   'her husband'
sà ndo   'forest animal(s)'
ngò 'dɔ   'axe handle'

It is possible to have three and even four nouns in a possessive series: *olo mɛ́nɛ tɛ̀lɛ́ mbi lǎ* 'this is my blood' ('blood of body of me').

In Sango the picture is considerably more simple. There is only one unvarying connective which marks possession, and it is used with none of the restrictions found in Ngbandi. There is still, however, some option with inalienable possession. I should guess that the farther one got away from

Bangui, where Sango–Yakoma still exerts a little influence on the *lingua franca*, the fewer would be the options. The following phrase illustrates not only the single option that is possible but also the reason for the high frequency of *tí*: *mɛ́rɛngɛ́ (tí) kɔ́li tí ita tí mbi tí kɔ́li* 'my brother's son' ('child of male of sibling of me of male').

What is significant about *na* and *tí*, both of which have a high incidence, is not simply their frequency. Yet it was their frequency that attracted my attention and led to the formulations being presented in this paper. I started with very different goals, however. I had assumed that they might lead me to evidence of significant semantic and syntactic reorganization. I was looking for something characteristically pidgin about paraphrasis, for example. Instead, something else was found. So striking are the statistics that it is worth saying something about them.

In a corpus of 37,217 words and morphemes there were 11 connective types (i.e. different words), making up a total of 6,940 tokens or occurrences of all connectives. This represented 20.4% of the non-French part of the corpus, itself representing 33,990 tokens. But *na* and *tí* together account for 81.5% of all the Sango (non-French) connectives, the other 9 accounting for only 1,281 tokens. As is indicated in Table 1, these two words represent 15·19% of the total Sango corpus. The figure can be higher than this in random portions of text. For example, in the 100-word microcorpus from text N80 (from Samarin 1966b), *tí* represents 16% and *na* 6%. In other words, in a running microtext where there were only 32 types, 2 of them together accounted for 22% of all the tokens.

TABLE 1. *Incidence of 'na' and 'tí' in a Sango corpus*

	Tokens	Non-French tokens 33,990	All tokens, including French 37,217
tí	3,056	8·99%	8·20%
na	2,603	7·64%	6·99%
Totals	5,659	16·63%	15·19%

The lesson that these facts teach is clear: we must refrain from assuming that the salient features of a particular pidgin are a characteristic of pidginization itself. Even if we found that connectives had a higher incidence in pidgins than in natural languages, we would be obliged to seek the causes. The effects of pidginization might be similar and the causes quite different. And while we are suggesting the exercise of caution, we might add that we must distinguish what is the result of pidginization from what is accidental in the text, whether because of the way it was obtained, the topic, the genre of discourse, the style, etc. For example, the rather uninteresting narrative style of Sango, with clauses strung along in a close parallel to the actual events that took place, is very much like the narrative style of Tonga, another African, but Bantu and natural, language. What characterizes Tonga is a redundant style which uses four devices: staging, overlapping, repetition, and synonymous expressions (Jones and Carter 1967). For what is translated as 'The whites followed us to the Bembezi and there was a great battle, Tonga has the following:

. . . again we ran away, we came here to the Bembezi. When we had come here to the Bembezi, the whites followed us, and came and found us at the Bembezi. They found us at the Bembezi, there was a very great battle (Jones and Carter 1967:112).

Other kinds of pidginization

In illustrating the concept of reduction in pidginization, we have been talking primarily about language learning, but two other instances of pidginization were earlier mentioned. The first is loss of memory, not that kind that is treated medically or psychiatrically, but the more normal kind, particularly when it is associated with 'disculturation', that is, losing the knowledge of and feeling for one's former existence. I should imagine that it is common among immigrants and people whose former way of living has been destroyed (e.g. American Indians). The only documentation of pidginization by memory loss known to me is that of an Auca Indian. The following is a description of her 'language' based on data that were elicited only with great difficulty. For 17 years she had not spoken her language; while living among the Quechua, to whom she had fled when she was 15 years old, she had deliberately tried to repress all she knew of her Auca existence.

. . . the verb suffixal system was impoverished, but supplemented by occasional Quichua [sic] affixes. The native pronominal set (apart from the honorific and the first-person exclusive plural forms) seems to have been complete. Most of the tense or aspect group was found, but only three occurred with normal frequency. The modal system was impoverished. Modal suffixes indicating uncertainty, doubt, probability, intention, negation, and obligation, were used so rarely as to be outside her effective control. Modal enclitics indicating derision, disgust, satire, extreme emotion, and emphatic negative seem to have been completely missing. Of the imperative system, only one of several suffixal combinations was used (Saint and Pike 1962:28–9).

The second is in restricted codes, as opposed to elaborated codes. These are constructs of speech forms suggested by the sociologist Basil Bernstein to account for linguistic variables correlative with different forms of social relations or qualities of social structure (see Bernstein 1967 with bibliography). In one sense the speech forms are determined by the roles the speaker assumes, and a role is a set of shared and learned meanings through which a person inter-acts with others. Bernstein asserts that the role is therefore a 'complex coding activity' that controls the production of speech. The codes thus generated are discoverable in terms of the probability of predicting what form of speech a speaker will use. Of these two codes it is the restricted one that seems to reveal features of pidginization. Linguistically, it is characterized by verbal planning that is 'confined to choice of sequence rather than selection and organ-ization of the sequence' (128). This apparently means that the speaker has fewer options. He has less freedom in organizing his utterances on the basis of greater vocabulary and syntactic patterns. A restricted code is best com-prehended in its pure form 'where all the words, and hence the organizing structure, irrespective of its degree of complexity, are wholly predictable for speakers and listeners' (127). From a sociological point of view, in this code speech 'is not perceived as a major means of presenting inner states to the other' (130; cf. the statement by Chomsky above).

If, as Bernstein suggests, the pure form of restricted codes would be ritualis-tic modes of communication, then *glossolalia* ('speaking in tongues') is the epitome of such a code. What he says of relationships regulated by protocol and cocktail party routines is eminently true of this form of nonsense language. He writes:

In these relations individual difference cannot be signalled through the verbal channel except insofar as the *choice* of sequence or routine exists. It is trans-mitted essentially through variations in extraverbal signals. Given the selection of the sequence, new information will be made available through the [with following emphasis added] *extraverbal channels*, and these channels are likely to become the *object of special perceptual activity* (1967:127–8).

Glossolalia must be characterized both as a restricted code and as a highly pidginized form of speech because of its predictable form, using Bernstein's criterion, and because it represents the nearly maximal amount of reduction that language can experience and *still sound like* language. With a very restricted number of consonants and vowels a limited number of syllables is produced and arranged in a highly predictable order. Imposed on this segmental phonology, however, is a suprasegmental structure that is equally expressive as that of the native language of the speaker.[12]

There are, of course, very important differences between glossolalia and the kinds of restricted codes set up by Bernstein. For one thing, they are, or can be, extemporaneously generated; yet all the glossas – glossolalic 'languages' – so far studied have revealed a remarkable similarity of general structure (Samarin 1968). Moreover, there is no cognitive semantic encoding, at least of the normal type. That is to say, there is no correlation of the segmented stream of speech with units of meaning. There is meaning of a very different kind – the meaning of function; glossolalia provides phonological material that is the vehicle of affect without the distraction of semantic content. This is not far from the extemporaneous pidgins that one devises when, knowing less than the rudiments of Portuguese or Serbo-Croatian, he seeks to establish rapport with peasants who speak these languages.

Closer to the speech forms Bernstein is focussing his attention on are jargons and secret languages. They too are pidgin languages or are pidginized forms of other languages. Having collected some samples of the 'secret' language of the Gbeya grass-hunting Ngaragé society (Samarin 1959), for whom the speaking of Sango and Gbeya is proscribed during the hunting season, I would suggest that it is similar to Sango in having a limited inventory of lexical units and syntactic patterns, with one exception: it does not borrow from French as Sango does.

Another kind of 'exotic language' that displays features of pidginization is the special language used in Australia by the Dyirbal in the presence of certain in-laws. According to Dixon (1971), this language, called Dyalŋuy, has the same grammar and phonology as the everyday language, but is lexically more parsimonious. There is as a rule a one-many correspondence between items from the two vocabularies. For example, whereas the normal language (Guwal, or Dyirbal) has names for specific kinds of grub, Dyalŋuy (which Dixon dubs 'mother-in-law language') has only one generic term; and whereas there are three verbs in Guwal to denote different kinds of cutting, there are but two in Dyalŋuy. If one must be specific in the latter about a certain kind of grub, one uses a relative clause with the generic term.[13]

All of this is paralleled in pidgins. What is particularly interesting about the Dyirbal in-law language is that it is a pidgin (in my opinion) that, in the first place, is not used as a second language by a society, and, in the second place, does not appear to be derived by process of pidginization, as ordinarily understood. It is even possible, Dixon suggests (personal communication) that the language evolved from a collection of lexical items borrowed from neighboring languages. Guwal and Dyalŋuy are not 'cognate' lexically, and multilingualism within groups is common in Australia. The in-law language would thus appear to be reduced, both in structure (lexicon) and use, and a mixture as well (Dyirbal grammar and phonology, exotic lexicon), not through exigencies of contact, but as a deliberate creation; not as an unrespected compromise, but specifically to express respect. In any case, Dyalŋuy and languages like it may force us to redefine pidgin, and certainly require the distinction between pidgin and pidginization.

The pidginized nature of a restricted code is seen in the extent to which the full potential of language, as revealed in an elaborated code, is contracted. Bernstein sees this as a result of the major function of the code, which is to 'define and reinforce the form of the social relationship by restricting the verbal signalling of individual experience' (128). But we need not accept his interpretation of the linguistic facts. He may profit as much from a consideration of pidginization as we from a consideration of restricted codes sociologically defined. I believe that we are looking at similar phenomena from two very different points of view.

As compared to pidgins, restricted codes have a different genesis. Pidgins result from language learning situations whereas restricted codes are part of the shared and learned behavior of a social group. There is no suggestion that an elaborated code was reduced, no matter how slowly, to the level of a restricted code. It could very well be that the latter is a lineal descendant of a certain form of speech. If it proves to be very much like other forms of speech in other societies, we may have to conclude that it is not pidginized at all but that it is normal language. If this be the case, then the elaborated code is the innovation, like – in a weak simile – the improved fruit on a grafted tree. One would expect, for example, that as a society's culture becomes more complex (i.e. 'richer'), as the language is forced to serve more functions (e.g. oratory or art), and as individuals acquire more and more functions, there would be a concomitant elaboration of the code. But would the contrary occur? If not for whole societies, at least for segments? This is what may produce restricted codes in complex societies and pidgins in multilingual ones.

Koinés

One type of language that has been excluded from the discussion to this point is the koiné. The reason is that koinés, like the Common Greek (so called by the Greeks themselves) *lingua franca* of the Mediterranean basin from which our technical term is derived, have never (at least to my knowledge) been considered pidgins. Unlike pidgins, koinés are not drastically reduced forms of language in spite of the fact that some simplification can be expected in them (Samarin 1962b). For example, Cohen (1956:310) talks about the 'élimination d'un nombre de ses traits propres' in Attic as koiné developed from it. What characterizes them linguistically is the incorporation of features from several regional varieties of a single language. This kind of amalgamation (or dialect mixing) can lead to a certain amount of heterogeneity. That is, a koiné, caught at an early stage of its history, might consist of many kinds of speech that are not easily correlated with non-linguistic factors like region, function, social status, etc. In time, however, the mix might jell, not without varieties of speech like those characteristic of any normal speech community: the gelatin is more like head-cheese than a dessert jelly. Some such development may be part of the history of Standard Macedonian with a base of what Lunt calls 'interdialects' (1959:23; see Samarin 1966a:199). Another feature that distinguishes koinés from pidgins, a feature that is implied in what has just been said, is that they are never detached from the languages they issue from. That is, Common Greek as spoken at the beginning of the Christian era (but already 300 years old) in Jerusalem, Corinth, and Rome, would not be discontinuous from Attic Greek which was its base. (Those who insist on the continuity of, say, Jamaican Creole with English and Haitian Creole with French, might want to reexamine their positions with koinés in mind.)

Macedonian has just been mentioned as illustrating the process of koineization; but other examples should also be cited. (For information about the following I am indebted to J. Edward Gates for access to the file of the 'Dictionary of Linguistic Terminology' at the Centre for Linguistic Studies, University of Toronto, formerly at the Hartford Seminary Foundation.) Among the five 'style variations' of Spoken Arabic is 'the koineized colloquial', 'a plain colloquial into which leveling devices have been more or less liberally introduced' (Blanc 1960:85). This leveling is described by Blanc (82) in the following way:

> In certain situations, usually interdialectal contact, the speaker may replace certain features of his native dialect with their equivalents in a dialect carrying higher prestige, not necessarily that of the interlocutor . . . Moreover leveling devices may be called into play without the speaker's actually stepping out of his native dialect, but by selecting from among a number of equivalent features available to him those which are more general or more urban and suppressing those which sound local or rustic . . . In general, leveling often takes place not so much in imitation of a specific dialect as in an attempt to suppress localisms in favor of features which are simply more common, more well known.

Although this description might give the impression that koineization is an impromptu thing, Blanc makes it clear elsewhere (1953:2-3) that the koiné is widely spread, found even among village dwellers. (He also mentions a 'pidgin' Arabic that is 'almost always easily recognized' which is also used when one wants to avoid using one's local dialect with strangers.) This colloquial koiné should not be confused with the one discussed by Ferguson.

> . . . Most modern Arabic dialects descend from the earlier language through a form of Arabic, called here the koine, which was not identical with any of the earlier dialects and which differed in many significant respects from Classical Arabic but was used side by side with the Classical language during early centuries of the Muslim era (1959:616).

The Italian of late fourteenth-century Naples might also have been a kind of koiné based on the speech of other regions Hall (1949:154). No such qualifications are made by Karlgren (1949:45) about the language of northern China which was a 'real' koiné in the seventh to the tenth centuries. For a contemporary koiné we can go to Yugoslavia where one of the two standard varieties of Serbo-Croatian is a Belgrade-based koiné (Bidwell 1964:532).

The koinés mentioned in the preceding paragraphs all seem to be languages that evolved through one channel only, the spoken one. Others have evolved through the medium of writing. Atkinson cites the Ionic idiom in which Herodotus wrote as a kind of literary koiné (1933:248). 'Standard Yoruba', a koiné based on the Oyo dialect, might be another example since it is the language used in education, writing, and, of course, contact between people speaking different dialects of Yoruba (Bamgboṣe 1966:2). Since writing implies, at least for some cases, a certain amount of conscious 'engineering' of language (like the creation of 'union languages'), it is not surprising to find that the koiné which arose from the Tupi-Guarani group, the Lingua Geral, 'was the work of missionaries' after the conquest (Entwistle 1936:233). Vachek goes so far as to suggest that the important function of a literary language 'has always been to serve as a kind of koiné' (1966:98). However, we must remember the motivations suggested by Lunt and Blanc for the emergence of koinés, a topic about which Marouzeau is explicit:

La manie de copier le bourg, la petite ville, le chef-lieu, la capitale, tout cela contribue à fixer et à répandre une langue-modèle; les habitudes de langage se communiquent et s'imposent comme les idées et les préjugés, comme la mode et la façon de s'habiller; ainsi se crée ce qu'on appelle une langue commune . . . (1950:96).

The distinction between pidgins and koinés presented here differs from implications made in an earlier paper (Samarin 1966a). There I said that 'Town Bemba must certainly be considered a kind of pidgin language' (201n.) on the basis of Richardson's characterization of Town Bemba as having a 'tendency to indeterminacy in most departments of the language' (1963:145). Richardson, however, did not challenge this assertion in his comment on my paper, and in fact he said 'the parallel drawn...between Sango and Town Bemba in no way disagrees with the sense of my articles on the linguistic effects of urbanization' (Samarin 1966a:207). But he went on to say (208) that the real difference between Town and Village Bemba was in lexicon and style, implying that there was no reduction of the kind that I now use in characterizing a pidgin. (My purpose in that paper, of course, was something other than trying to characterize pidginization.) I would now say that Town Bemba might be a kind of koiné with pidgin features. If not, it might prove in any case to have features of salient pidginization with only a minimal amount of substantive pidginization. What kinds and degrees of pidginization occur in koinés still remain to be determined.

Conclusion

The terms 'pidginized', 'restricted', and 'elaborated', are stative terms by grammatical definition, but they are dynamic by implication. That is, something *was* pidginized, restricted, or elaborated. The terms need not be taken too literally. There is value in using them in a purely descriptive way in formulating a taxonomy of language varieties and language functions. But they also have the value of reminding us that language is not static, no more so than societies are. It is the responsibility of linguistics therefore to address itself to the sociological dimensions of both synchronic and diachronic dynamism.

NOTES

1 It was just eight years ago that an African linguist of European extraction said to me, 'You talk as if you *like* Fanagalo.' In our conversation, I thought that I was simply asking the kinds of questions any linguist might ask about another language.

2 Recent investigations of glossolalia show clearly its value, though it is not a language in any ordinary sense of the term. See below.

3 This hypothesis is being attributed to several people. If someone deserves the honor of having first suggested it, we ought to have the detective work done once and for all. But perhaps there is convergence as well as diffusion in the explanation of the distribution of this idea.

4 Sango is one of the exceptions to the putative generalizations. Although repetition is used in the language, it is not found as a characteristic of a large number of words, as one finds in Jamaican iteratives (De Camp 1967). When one compares Sango with the source language, he sees what has happened: most of the ideophones have been lost in the process of pidginization. It is in these words that most of the reduplication occurs in Adamawa–Eastern languages. (Thomas (1963) seems to believe otherwise, but see my review (1965).) The result is that it is the *loss* of reduplication which is characteristic of the pidginization of vernacular Sango, not its presence.

5 We shall no longer pretend that pidgins are not languages. Up to now we have indulged in a bit of rhetoric. That pidgins are languages is beyond question; what we have to determine is what *kind* of language they are. There may be some forms of speech that are outside the range of linguisticality, but they are not illustrated by pidgins.

6 Le Page might disagree with this statement, for he writes that 'the grammar of a language is the sum total of *all* its relational devices and this sum total must be roughly constant. In other words, if you don't manage to get something across by one means, you will by another' (1967:86). He does not seem to exclude pidgins from this generalization. In fact, the next sentence limits grammatical simplification in pidginization to inflectional structures.

7 The monostratal nature of Sango seems to have a strong equalizing function. It certainly had on one particular occasion. I paid a call one day in New York City on a very high-ranking member of the C.A.R. delegation to the United Nations. The language we used was French, and our behavior was appropriately formal. We were naturally using *vous* with each other, and I, not certain what protocol required under the circumstances, was tossing in *votre excellence* from time to time. The introduction of Sango into the interview, but not by myself, completely altered our relationship. In Sango it was inappropriate to refer to 'his excellence'. For the remainder of the appointment we became casual, if not a bit intimate, with each other. And then, on parting, we switched back to the formulas that French provides for such occasions.

8 This linguistic diagnostic tool would obviously not tell us more than it was designed for. It could hardly tell us, for example, whether or not Afrikaans owes its existence to the use of Portuguese Creole in South Africa in the seventeenth and eighteenth centuries, as is suggested by M. F. Valkhoff (1966, and Samarin 1967a). But if we had a good sample of local and colloquial seventeenth century Dutch spoken by the indigenous population and foreign residents, his interests and ours would both be served. (On the general point, however, cf. Hymes (1959), discussing Taylor (1956).)

9 For what immediately follows I profited from a stimulating conversation with my colleague, H. A. Gleason, Jr.

10 Le Page also may be talking about non-linguistic (or sociolinguistic) pidginization in the following statement. The important expression is 'mode of behavior': '. . . one should . . . think of a pidgin as a mode of behavior which results when speakers of A [the learners of B] meet speakers of B [the language being learned] under certain social conditions . . .' (1967:86).

A diagnostic device that relies on measuring the kinds and number of options in a language obviates the difficulty of measuring redundancy. Although one might like to talk about redundancy being reduced in a pidgin in comparison with the languages in contact, this is difficult to maintain in the absence, as Le Page admits (1967:86), of any means to measure redundancy itself.

11 For the sake of convenience we shall call the source language Ngbandi, partly to avoid confusion between the names of the vernacular and the pidginized languages and partly because our best source of information about the Ngbandi–Sango–Yakoma dialect cluster is on Ngbandi itself. See the works by Lekens, Nelson, and the *Gospel of Mark* published by the British and Foreign Bible Society (1959). Nelson is the translator of *Mark*. Differences between Lekens and Nelson seem to be their differences, not the language's. I have tried with little success to get a corpus from vernacular Sango. I do have three 8-inch (78 r.p.m.) records of a religious nature produced by Gospel Recordings Incorporated (146 Glendale Boulevard, Los Angeles 26, California). They are labeled 'Sango: Ubangi', 1408-1A-LA3865 to 3870 and are not of high quality. The recording was made at Libenge, Republic of Congo (Kinshasa), around 1957. Rev. Richard B. Anderson, missionary of the Evangelical Free Church, who was there at that time, informs me that Sango fishermen lived on the sand-banks during the dry season, some of whom came from as far away as the confluence of the Uele and the Mbomu rivers. There was also a permanent Sango village on the banks of the Ubangi river not far from Libenge. Sango is spoken by about a million inhabitants of the Central African Republic and the adjoining parts of the Chad, Cameroun, and Congo (Kinshasa) republics, mostly as a second language. There is an increasing number of people for whom it is a first language, and for these it would be considered a creolized language, using the term in one of its senses. Whatever one says about the classification of Sango, Ngbandi is an Eastern (or as I prefer to call it, Ubangian) language of Joseph Greenberg's Adamawa–Eastern family, itself a part of Niger–Congo.

12 One person, eventually a glossolalist himself, characterized the tongues he heard at a religious retreat in the following way: '. . . I listened intently to the beautiful, expressive flow of language. Although I could not understand a word, it was unmistakably reverent and adoring, and something within my own spirit responded to that adoration' (Donald W. Basham, 'Keeping a divine appointment', in *Full Gospel Business Men's Voice*, December 1967, p. 26).

13 Dixon accounts for the similarities and differences in terms of nuclear and non-nuclear words, a taxonomy of the lexical inventory of languages that he suggests for incorporating the advantages of both the componential and definitional approaches to semantic description. Nuclear words are those that cannot be defined in terms of other lexical words and must be defined componentially; non-nuclear words, on the other hand, are defined in terms of the nuclear words utilizing the full grammatical possibilities of the language in the formulation of these definitions. Thus, nuclear terms are fewer in number but generally more frequent in occurrence than the non-nuclear ones. Since this is true of all natural languages, it is true of Guwal, but it is not true of Dyalŋuy: the latter has equivalents for Guwal's nuclear words but only a handful of non-nuclear items; and the non-nuclear words of Guwal are 'defined' in Dyalŋuy in terms of one or more nuclear words. Dixon finds the 'mother-in-law language' very helpful as a source of clues to semantic relations within the everyday language.

REFERENCES

Atkinson, B. F. C. 1933. *The Greek language*, London, Faber and Faber

Bamgboṣe, Ayọ 1966. *A grammar of Yoruba* (West African Language Monograph Series, No. 5), London, Cambridge University Press

Bernstein, Basil 1967. 'Elaborated and restricted codes: an outline', *Explorations in sociolinguistics*, ed. by Stanley Lieberson, 129–33, Bloomington, Indiana University Press, and The Hague, Mouton

Bidwell, Charles E. 1964. 'The Serbo-Croatian verb', *Language* 40:532–50

Blanc, Haim 1953. 'Studies in North Palestinian Arabic', *The Israel Oriental Society*, no. 4

1960. 'Stylistic variations in Spoken Arabic: a sample of interdialectal educated conversation', *Contributions to Arabic linguistics*, ed. by Charles A. Ferguson, 79–161 (Harvard Middle East Monograph Series, 3), Cambridge, Harvard University Press

British and Foreign Bible Society 1959. 'Nzɔ pà à sú na tí Malako' [The Gospel according to Mark], London

Capell, A. 1966. 'Discussion' [of Population distances, by W. W. Howells], *Current Anthropology* 7:537–8

Chomsky, Noam 1966. *Cartesian linguistics*, New York and London, Harper and Row

Cohen, Marcel 1956. *Pour une sociologie du langage*, Paris, Albian Michel

De Camp, David 1960. 'Four Jamaican Creole texts', *Jamaican Crole*, ed. by R. B. Le Page and David DeCamp, 127–79 (Creole Language Studies, 1), London, Macmillan

[1967]. 'Vocalic alternation in Jamaican Creole iteratives', paper read at the forty-second annual meeting of the Linguistic Society of America, Chicago, Illinois

Dixon, R. M. W. 1971. 'A method of semantic description, illustrated for Dyirbal verbs', *Semantics: an interdisciplinary reader in philosophy, linguistics, psychology and anthropology*, ed. by Danny D. Steinberg and Leon Jakobovits, Cambridge University Press

Entwistle, W. J. 1936. *The Spanish language*, London, Faber and Faber

Ferguson, Charles A. 1959. 'The Arabic koiné', *Language* 35:616–30

Gleason, H. A., Jr. 1965. *Linguistics and English grammar*, New York, Holt, Rinehart and Winston

Hall, Robert A., Jr. 1949. 'Nasal plus homorganic plosive in Central and Southern Italy', *Archivum Linguisticum* 1:151–6

1955. *Hands off Pidgin English!* Sydney, Australia, Pacific Publications

1962. 'The life-cycle of pidgin languages', *Lingua* 11:151–6

1966. *Pidgin and creole languages*, Ithaca, Cornell University Press

Hanley, Miles L. 1937. *Word index to James Joyce's 'Ulysses'*, Madison, University of Wisconsin Press

Hymes, Dell 1959. 'Genetic relationship: retrospect and prospect', *Anthropological Linguistics* 1(2):50–66

1967. 'Models of the interaction of language and social setting, *Journal of social issues* 23:8–28

Jones, A. M. and H. Carter 1967. 'The style of a Tonga historical narrative' (*African language studies*, 8, ed. by Malcolm Guthrie, 93–126), London, School of Oriental and African Studies, University of London

Joos, Martin 1936. 'Review of *The psycho-biology of language*, by George K. Zipf', *Language* 12:196–210

1937–8. *Word index to James Joyce's 'Ulysses'*, Madison, University of Wisconsin Press

1964. 'Discussion' [of Bastian *et al.*], *Linguistics and language study* (Fifteenth round table meeting), ed. by C. I. J. M. Stuart, 189–91 (Georgetown University Monograph Series on Languages and Linguistics, 17), Washington, D.C., Georgetown University Press

Karlgren, Bernhard 1949. *The Chinese language*, New York, Ronald Press

Kuipers, Aert H. 1960. 'Phoneme and morpheme in Kabardian' (*Janua linguarum*, 8), The Hague, Mouton

Lekens, Benjamin 1952. *Dictionnaire ngbandi* (*Annales du Musée du Congo Belge, Sciences de l'Homme, Linguistique*, 1), Anvers, Éditions de Sikkel

Lekens, Benjamin, and Gerebern Mens 1958. 'Ngbandi-idioticon II' (*Annales, Sciences de l'Homme, Linguistique*, vol. 3, tome 2), Tervuren, Musée Royal du Congo Belge

Le Page, Robert B. 1966. Foreword, *Jamaican Creole syntax*, by Beryl L. Bailey, v–viii, Cambridge, Cambridge University Press

1967. 'Review of *Pidgin and creole languages*, by R. A. Hall, Jr.', *Journal of African Languages* 6:83–6

Lunt, Horace G. 1959. 'The creation of Standard Macedonian: some facts and attitudes', *Anthropological Linguistics* 5(1):19–25

Marouzeau, J. 1950. *La linguistique ou science du langage*, Paris, Librairie Orientaliste Paul Geuthner

Nelson, Quentin D. 1952. 'Linguistic problems in Ngbandi', *The Bible Translator* 3:39–45

Richardson, I. 1963. 'Examples of deviation and innovation in Bemba', *African Language Studies* 4:138–45

Saint, Rachel, and K. L. Pike 1952. 'Auca phonemics', *Studies in Ecuadorian Indian languages* 1, ed. by Benjamin Elson, 2–30, Norman, Summer Institute of Linguistics of the University of Oklahoma

Samarin, William J. 1955. 'Sango, an African *lingua franca*', *Word* 11: 254–67

1958. 'The phonology of pidgin Sango', *Word* 14:62–70

1959. 'Ngaragé, a Gbeya society', *African Studies* 18:190–6

1961. 'The vocabulary of Sango', *Word* 17:16–22

1962a. 'Une *lingua franca* centrafricaine', *Colloque sur le multilinguisme* (Brazzaville 1962), 257–65, Brazzaville, Commission de Coopération Téchnique en Afrique

1962b. '*Lingua francas* with special reference to Africa', *Study of the role of second languages in Asia, Africa, and Latin America*, ed. by Frank A. Rice, 54–65, Washington, D.C., Center for Applied Linguistics

1963. 'Questions and orthography in Sango', *The Bible Translator* 14:30–3, reprinted in *Orthography studies*, ed. by William A. Smalley, 161–4, 1964, The United Bible Societies

1965. 'Review of *Le parler Ngbaka de Bokanga*, by J. M. C. Thomas', *Journal of African Languages* 4:231–4

1966a. 'Self-annulling prestige factors among speakers of a creole language', *Sociolinguistics*, ed. by William Bright, 188–213, The Hague, Mouton

1966b. *A grammar of Sango*, The Hague, Mouton

1966c. *The Gbeya language: grammar, texts, and vocabularies* (University of California Publications in Linguistics, 44), Berkeley and Los Angeles, University of California Press

1967a. 'Review of *Studies in Portuguese and Creole*, by Marius F. Valkhoff', *Lingua* 19:105–9

1967b. Basic course in Sango: vol. I, *Lessons in Sango*: vol. II, *Readings in Sango*, duplicated at Hartford Seminary Foundation for U.S. Office of Education

1968. 'The linguisticality of glossolalia', *The Hartford Quarterly* (Hartford Seminary Foundation) 8(4):49–75

1970. *Sango, langue de l'Afrique Centrale* Leiden, E. J. Brill

Stewart, William A. 1962. 'An outline of linguistic typology for describing multilingualism', *Study of the role of second languages in Asia, Africa, and Latin America*, ed. by Frank A. Rice, 15–25, Washington, D.C., Center for Applied Linguistics

Taber, Charles R. 1964. 'French loan words in Sango: a statistical analysis of incidence' (Hartford Studies in Linguistics, 12), Hartford, Connecticut, Hartford Seminary Foundation

1965. *A dictionary of Sango*, duplicated at Hartford Seminary Foundation for U.S. Office of Education

Taylor, Douglas 1956. 'Language contacts in the British West Indies I; A case of intimate borrowing II; On the classification of creolized languages', *Word* 12:399–414

Thomas, Jacqueline M. C. 1963. *Le parler ngbaka de Bokanga: phonologie, morphologie, syntaxe*, Paris and The Hague, Mouton

Vachek, Josef 1966. *The linguistic school of Prague: an introduction to its theory and practice*, Bloomington, Indiana University Press

Valkhoff, Marius F. 1966. *Studies in Portuguese and Creole with special reference to South Africa*, Johannesburg, Witwatersrand University Press

Whinnom, Keith 1965. 'The origin of the European-based creoles and pidgins', *Orbis* 14:509–27

Wurm, S. A., and J. B. Harris 1963. *Police Motu* (Linguistic Circle of Canberra Publications, Series B, Monographs, 1), Canberra, The Australian National University

ABSENCE OF COPULA AND THE NOTION OF SIMPLICITY

A Study of Normal Speech, Baby Talk, Foreigner Talk, and Pidgins

CHARLES A. FERGUSON

The purpose of this paper is to examine one feature of human language in a general typological framework in order to obtain some insights into the notion of grammatical simplicity. The feature in question is the presence in some languages, or special varieties or registers of a single language, of an overt connecting link, or COPULA, between nominal subjects and complements in equational clauses of the type X *is* Y[1] as compared with the absence of such a link in other languages or other varieties of the same language. Thus, English *My brother is a student* and Japanese *Ani wa gakkusee desu* differ from Russian *Moj brat student(om)* or Arabic *'Axī tilmīðun* by having a copula (*is, desu*) which has no overt equivalent in the latter two languages. Similarly, English *Your mother is outside* or *has gone out* may correspond to baby talk *Mommy bye-bye* with no copula, or French *La machine est grande* 'The machine is big' corresponds to Haitian Creole *Machin-nâ gro*.

Normal speech

It may safely be assumed that all natural languages have grammatical machinery for equational clauses, but the details vary considerably from one language to another. There has been very little systematic study of clause types across languages, and future investigations may show the inadequacy of the crude classification used here, but it seems helpful for the purposes at hand. There seem to be two main types of language as far as equational clauses are concerned. Type A has a copula in all normal neutral equational clauses; the absence of the copula is limited to certain set expressions or signals a particular style or register, such as proverbs (e.g. *Nothing ventured, nothing gained*). In such languages the copula generally functions very similarly (i.e. has similar patterns of allomorphs, exhibits similar grammatico-semantic categories, occurs in similar constructions) to the members of the major word class of verbs. It generally differs from verbs, however, in certain respects, in some languages so much as to constitute a separate word class, in other languages in such a way as to belong to a distinct sub-class of verbs ('auxiliaries'). In Indo-European languages of type A the copula typically has a unique pattern of suppletion (e.g. Latin *es-~fu-*). In type A languages the copula often appears also in existential clauses of the type *There is/are X*, although they may have special constructions with the copula (e.g. English *there is/are*), or not use it at all (e.g. French *il y a*), in such clauses.

Type B languages normally have no copula in equational clauses. The copula is invariably absent in a main clause when both members of the clause (subject and complement) are present, the clause is timeless or unmarked present in time, the complement is attributive (i.e. adjectival rather than nominal), and the subject is third person. In many type B languages the absence of a copula goes beyond these minimum limits. For example, probably in most type B languages the copula is absent with first and second person subjects as well as third (e.g. Russian *Ja student* 'I am a student'), although in some the absence is limited to the third person (e.g. Hungarian *Én diák vagyok* 'I am a student' but *Ö diák* 'He is a student').[2] In many type B languages the copula is absent also when the complement is a noun or pronoun, as in the Russian and Arabic examples previously cited, although in some the absence is limited to adjectival complements (e.g. Haitian Creole *Chwal yo parésé* 'The horses are lazy' but *Chwal yo sé étalô* 'The horses are stallions' (McConnell 1953:20). Again, many type B languages have no copula in either main or dependent clause but some have it only in dependent clauses, e.g. Bengali *Se chatro* 'He is a student' but *Se jodi chatro hɔĕ. . .* 'If he is a student. . .' (Sableski 1965).

In all type B languages there seem to be conditions under which a copula must be used. The most widespread such condition is when a tense other than present is called for. Thus, English *My brother was a student* has Russian and Arabic equivalents with an overt *was* in *Moj brat byl student*, *'Axī kāna tilmīðan*.[3] Also, most type B languages seem to use a copula if only one member of the equational clause (subject or complement) is present, or if because of an inverted word order the copula would be in an 'exposed' position.[4] Thus, Haitian Creole *Machin nâ gro* 'The machine is big' but *Sé gro* 'It is big' (with copula *sé*); *Chwal yo nâ châ* 'The horses are in the field' but *Koté chwal yo yé?* 'Where are the horses?' (with copula *yó*). Finally, in type B languages when emphasis is put on the semantic link, as in definitions and exclamatory pronouncements, a copula equivalent is used, either a special verb (e.g. 'stands', 'is found') or a pronoun (e.g. 'he', 'they'), or a verb 'to be' which is normally used in other tenses or in existential clauses. Thus, Russian *čto jest' istina?* 'What is truth?'.

In type B languages there is often a special negative construction used in equational clauses without copula and not elsewhere in the language. Thus Arabic and Bengali have special negative copulas, *lays-~las-* and *nɔ-~no-* respectively, which are used only here: Arabic *Laysa (lastu) tilmīðan* 'He is not (I am not) a student'; Bengali *Se chatro nɔē* 'He is not a student', *Ami chatro noǐ* 'I am not a student'. Some, however, have the same negative formative in these clauses that appears in the negation of verbal predicates (e.g. Russian *Ja ne student*, Haitian Creole *Machin nâ pa gro*).

Type B languages typically have a different verb or verb equivalent for existential clauses, e.g. Bengali *ach-* 'exist, be', Russian *jest'* 'there is/are', Haitian Creole *gê*, and sometimes they have still another special form of clause negation for this, e.g. Bengali *neǐ*, Russian *net*, Haitian Creole *nâ pwê*. Bengali illustrates the full range of possibilities here (cf. Sableski):

eṭa boǐ this is a book	*eṭa boi nɔe* this isn't a book
ekhane boǐ ache there are books here	*ekhane boǐ neǐ* there aren't any books here

Simplified speech

It may be assumed that every speech community has in its verbal repertoire a variety of registers, that is, modes of speech, appropriate for use with particular statuses, roles, or situations (cf. Halliday *et al.*, 1967, ch. 4). It may further be assumed that many, perhaps all, speech communities have registers of a special kind for use with people who are regarded for one reason or another as unable to readily understand the normal speech of the community (e.g. babies, foreigners, deaf people). These forms of speech are generally felt by their users to be simplified versions of the language, hence easier to understand, and they are often regarded as imitation of the way the person addressed uses the language himself. Thus, the baby talk which is used by adults in talking to young children is felt to be easier for the child to understand and is often asserted to be an imitation of the way the children speak. Such registers are, of course, culturally transmitted like any other part of the language and may be quite systematic and resistant to change. Unfortunately they have not been studied very much; for summary and references on baby talk, cf. Ferguson 1964.

A register of simplified speech which has been even less studied, although it seems quite widespread and may even be universal, is the kind of 'foreigner talk' which is used by speakers of a language to outsiders who are felt to have very limited command of the language or no knowledge of it at all. Many [all?] languages seem to have particular features of pronunciation, grammar, and lexicon which are characteristically used in this situation. For example, a speaker of Spanish who wishes to communicate with a foreigner who has little or no Spanish will typically use the infinitive of the verb or the third singular rather than the usual inflected forms, and he will use *mi* 'me' for *yo* 'I' and omit the definite and indefinite articles: *mi ver soldado* 'me [to-] see soldier' for *yo veo al soldado* 'I see the soldier'. Such Spanish is felt by native speakers of the language to be the way foreigners talk, and it can most readily be elicited from Spanish-speaking informants by asking them how foreigners speak.[5]

Similarly, Arabs sometimes use a simplified form of the language in talking to non-native speakers, such as Armenian immigrants. This form is sometimes referred to as the way Armenians talk and can be elicited by asking for Armenian Arabic. It is characterized by such features as the use of the third person masculine singular of the imperfect of the verb for all persons, genders, numbers, and tenses (e.g. *ya'rif* 'he knows' for 'you know', 'I know', etc.) and the use of the long forms of the numbers 3–10 with a singular noun instead of the normal contracted form of the number with a plural noun (e.g. *tlāte sā'a* for *tlat sā'āt* 'three hours'). Some Armenians and other non-native speakers of Arabic do sometimes use these expressions, but it is not clear whether this comes as a direct result of interference from their own languages or results at least in part from imitation of Arabs' use of foreigner talk.

In both baby talk and foreigner talk the responses of the person addressed affect the speaker, and the verbal interaction may bring some modification of the register from both sides. The normal outcome of the use of baby talk is that as the child grows up he acquires the other normal, non-simplified registers of the language and retains some competence in baby talk for use in talking with young children and in such displaced functions as talking to a pet or with a lover.

The usual outcome of the use of foreigner talk is that one side or the other acquires an adequate command of the other's language and the foreigner talk is used in talking to, reporting on, or ridiculing people who have not yet acquired adequate command of the language. If the communication context is appropriate, however, this foreigner talk may serve as an incipient pidgin and become a more widely used form of speech.

Baby talk and foreigner talk are not the only forms of simplified speech. English, for example, has special usages for telegrams and formal instructions which resemble baby talk and foreigner talk in omitting definite article, prepositions, and copula, and the resemblance of these usages to early childhood language behavior has been noticed (Brown and Bellugi 1964:138–9). The conventional nature of these usages, which native speakers explain as being more economical of space, time, or money, is shown by their use where the limitations are irrelevant, as with instructions printed on a package where there is plenty of empty space or choices of wording in telegrams where either wording is below the number of words allowed at minimum cost.

Simplicity

The notion of simplicity in language and language description has been a perennial issue in linguistics as in other disciplines, and there is little agreement on what constitutes simplicity. Some recent work in linguistics has been concerned with a 'simplicity metric' in evaluating alternative grammars or partial grammars. The notion of simplicity in language itself, however, is only indirectly related to this. In the present paper we are concerned with the concept of simplicity in language, i.e. the possibility of rating some part of a language (e.g. a paradigm, a construction, an utterance, a clause type, a phonological sequence) as in some sense simpler than another comparable part in the same language or another language. For sample statements of this sort, cf. Ferguson (1959:333–4).

The notion of simplicity in language is important in several ways, since it may be related to theories of language universals, language acquisition, and language loss. Jakobson and others have assumed that, other things being equal, the simpler of two comparable features is likely to be the more widespread among languages of the world, the earlier acquired in child language development, and the later lost under pathological conditions. Even though the last of these assumptions may offer great difficulties because of the varied nature of pathological conditions, there seems to be some validity for the first two.[6] Accordingly, the creation of taxonomies involving the dimension simple–complex and investigation of these across many languages offers promise in the development of the general theory of language.

Also, any full-scale description of a language should identify simple versus complex (i.e. primary versus derivative) along a number of dimensions and thus offer predictions about possible orders of acquisition of the respective features. This process of prediction and empirical confirmation offers an opportunity for checking the validity of grammars which goes outside the linguists' intuitions about languages. For examples of predictions of this kind, cf. Ferguson 1966.[7]

The present paper suggests an additional approach to the study of simplicity in language, viz. the investigation of simplified registers, such as baby talk and foreigner talk, which give some indication of what folk grammatical analysis rates as relatively simple or easy versus complex or difficult. For discussions of simplicity in pidgins, see Samarin (1962:59–60), Ferguson (1963:119–20).

Hypotheses

Even on the basis of the largely impressionistic and anecdotal accounts of simplified speech now available, it is possible to hazard some universal hypotheses. For example, 'If a language has an inflectional system, this will tend to be replaced in simplified speech such as baby talk and foreigner talk by uninflected forms (e.g. simple nominative for the noun; infinitive, imperative, or third person singular for the verb)'. Several such hypotheses might even be subsumed under a more general hypothesis of the form: 'If a language has a grammatical category which clearly involves an unmarked–marked opposition,[8] the unmarked term tends to be used for both in simplified speech'. This general hypothesis may raise more problems than it solves at this point in our understanding of grammatical systems, but it illustrates the kind of hypotheses which may be generated in the study of language universals. A fairly specific kind of universal hypothesis is the central point of this paper.

In pairs of clauses differing by presence and absence of a copula in a given language, speakers will generally rate the one without the copula as simpler and easier to understand. Also, studies of child language development seem to show that children, apart from some marginal cases, first make equational clauses without a copula and only later – if the language has a copula – acquire the construction with the copula. Thus, even though the linguistic analyst may find that in the full normal speech absence of the copula is to be regarded as a deletion and hence grammatically more complex than its presence, and even though languages which lack a copula in equational clauses may have quite complicated patterns of allomorphy and distribution of synonyms in verbs 'to be', it seems wise to make the assumption that other things being equal absence of the copula is simpler than presence of the copula.[9]

Therefore, given that languages can be classified into two types according to their equational clauses, type A with copula and type B without copula, then:

Hypothesis 1   In languages of type A, the copula in equational clauses will tend to be omitted in simplified speech such as baby talk and foreigner talk.

Although this hypothesis says nothing about equational sentences in languages of type B, it predicts that speakers of a language of type A will tend to omit the copula when they are attempting to simplify their speech. Specifically it predicts that simplified registers in regular use in the speech community will tend to omit the copula, e.g. baby talk, foreigner talk, telegraph language, newspaper headlines. Going a step further, the hypothesis would suggest that a pidgin language whose lexical source was a type A language would tend to omit the copula.

The wording of the hypothesis in terms of possibility ('will tend to') rather than in absolute terms ('will') is based on the existence of empirical data showing considerable variation in the extent to which the copula is actually omitted. For example, in French baby talk the copula seems to be omitted much less often than in English baby talk, although *être* as an auxiliary is often left out (*Papa parti* 'Daddy bye-bye'). Also, of the Portuguese-based creoles used in the Far East in the sixteenth century some apparently had a copula while others did not (Whinnom 1965).

A further subhypothesis can be made with regard to the degrees of likelihood of omission of the copula under different conditions. This hypothesis is based on the descriptive statements made about type B languages, although their relation to the notion of simplicity is unclear.

Hypothesis 2 In simplified speech of languages of type A, the copula is more likely to be omitted under each of the following conditions than otherwise:

> main clause
> subject and complement both present
> non-emphatic
> timeless or unmarked present
> third person subject
> adjectival complement
> non-exposed position

The presentation of these two hypotheses constitutes in effect the outline of a research project to examine the omission of copulas in baby talk, foreigner talk, and pidgins to find the extent to which the hypotheses would be disconfirmed, confirmed in principle, or even quantified. Some encouragement as to possible results comes from recently presented evidence (Labov 1967) that certain varieties of English which frequently omit the copula do not do so in clauses where the standard language does not permit contraction, i.e. in instances of emphasis, exposed position, or absence of one member of the clause.

Concluding observations

For the linguist interested in typology and language universals this paper suggests the usefulness of a taxonomy of copula and copula-like constructions in the world's languages and the elaboration of hypotheses of synchronic variation and diachronic change in this part of language. The copula seems of particular interest because of the universality of equational clauses, the widespread patterns of polysemy and suppletion and possible exceptions to general hypotheses of the status of markedness in grammar.

For the linguist interested in child language development, the paper repeats earlier suggestions that the notion of simplicity may be a useful one in accounting for the development of grammar in the child, repeats the point (Ferguson 1964) that baby talk is largely initiated by adults on the basis of existing patterns, and suggests further that the telegraphic style used by young children may in part be based on the fact that adults in their attempt to simplify their speech (i.e. use baby talk) tend to omit items such as the copula, prepositions, articles, and inflectional endings.

For the linguist interested in pidgins and creoles, the most important suggestion of the paper is probably the view that the foreigner talk of a speech community may serve as an incipient pidgin. This view asserts that the initial source of the grammatical structure of a pidgin is the more or less systematic simplification of the lexical source language which occurs in the foreigner talk register of its speakers, rather than the grammatical structure of the language(s) of the other users of the pidgin. Such a view would not, of course, deny the grammatical influence of the other language(s), but would help to explain some of the otherwise surprising similarities among distant creoles by setting the starting point in a universal simplification process. It differs from the view held by some scholars from Schuchard to the present that 'the Europeans deliberately and systematically simplified and distorted their language to facilitate communication with the non-Europeans' (Goodman 1964:124) by emphasizing the conventional, culturally given aspect of the linguistic simplification and by recognizing with Bloomfield the interaction 'between a foreign speaker's version of a language and a native speaker's version of the foreign language' (quoted in Goodman 1964:12).

NOTES

1 The equational clause type includes a number of semantic (and in some languages grammatically distinct) sub-types such as identity (*Her father is the President of the University*), class membership (*Your friend is a fool*), attribution of a property (*The towel is wet*). For the purposes of the present article these distinctions are generally disregarded, and the terms 'equational clause' and 'copula' are used to refer to any or all of them unless otherwise specified. For discussion of equational clauses, see Elson and Pickett (1962:112–13); sample definitions in specific languages, cf. Sableski (1965); Sebeok (1943).

2 It has been pointed out that in those early Indo-European languages which have equational clauses without copula, this is normal only in the third person. Cf. Meillet (1906–8:20).

3 Bally called attention to this feature of languages without copula in a more general discussion of zero and ellipsis (Bally 1922:1–2).

4 For the term 'exposed', cf. Hall (1953:66n.); for *latter* read *former*.

5 For examples of this kind of Spanish, see Lynch (1955), in which an Englishman is portrayed as using this kind of foreigner's Spanish; e.g. *Osted moi buena conmigue . . . Mí no olvida nunca.* 'You very good with me . . . Me not forget(s) never' (187).

6 On the question of order of acquisition, it is, of course, necessary to recognize that other things are not equal and that acquisition may run not only from simple to complex but from less effort to more effort, from heavy affect to light affect, or from high frequency to low frequency, and that interference from other parts of the language or another language may be involved.

7 The possibility must be noted that the speaker may, in the case of language development, reorganize his internal grammar in such a way that what was previously primary may become derivative and vice versa. Thus a speaker who learns *Handschuh* as a monomorphematic lexical item meaning 'glove' may later identify it as *Hand* 'hand' plus *Schuh* 'shoe' in a compound-word construction. Similar reorganizations of grammatical constructions make it hazardous to relate a line of derivation or the ordering of a set of rules to an actual developmental sequence, but the grammar will surely offer clues which can be checked against empirical data.

8 For an extensive discussion of marked–unmarked categories in grammatical universals see Greenberg (1966: 25–55).

9 In making this judgment of simplicity on the basis of certain phenomena of child language development and 'simplified' registers, no claim is made about simplicity in grammar writing or in cognitive adequacy. To say a certain construction is 'simpler' in the sense used here says nothing directly about its value in communication or other language functions: no one would maintain that Russian and Arabic in which the copula is omitted are less adequate or more 'primitive' than Japanese and English which regularly use the copula.

REFERENCES

Bally, Charles 1922. 'Copula zero et faits connexes', *Bulletins de la Société Linguistique de Paris* 23:1–6

Brown, Roger W. and Bellugi, Ursula 1964. 'Three processes in the child's acquisition of syntax', *Harvard Educational Review* 34:133–51. (Reprinted in *New directions in the study of language*, ed. by E. H. Lenneberg, Cambridge, Massachusetts, M.I.T. Press, 1964)

Elson, Benjamin and Pickett, Velma 1962. *An introduction to morphology and syntax*, Santa Ana, California, Summer Institute of Linguistics

Ferguson, Charles A. 1959. 'Diglossia', *Word* 15:325–40. (Reprinted in *Language in culture and society*, ed. Dell Hymes, New York, Harper and Row, 1964)

    1963. 'Linguistic theory and language learning', *Linguistics and language study* (14th round table meeting), ed. by R. J. DiPietro, 115–24 (Monograph Series on Languages and Linguistics 16), Washington, D.C., Georgetown University Press

    1964. 'Baby talk in six languages', *The ethnography of communication*, ed. by John J. Gumperz and Dell Hymes, 103–14 (*American Anthropologist* 66(6), pt. 2), Washington, D.C., American Anthropological Association

    1966. 'Linguistic theory as behavioral theory', *Brain function III, Speech, language and communication*, ed. Edward C. Carterette, 249–61, Berkeley and Los Angles, University of California Press

Goodman, Morris F. 1964. *A comparative study of Creole French dialects*, The Hague, Mouton

Greenberg, Joseph H. 1966. *Language universals*, The Hague, Mouton

Hall, Robert A., Jr. 1953. 'Haitian Creole' (*American Anthropological Association, Memoir* 74), Washington, D.C., American Anthropological Association

Halliday, M. A. K., McIntosh, Angus and Strevens, Peter 1964. *The linguistic sciences and language teaching*, London, Longmans

Labov, William 1969. 'Contraction, deletion and inherent variability of the English copula', *Language* 45:715–62

Lynch, Benito 1955. *El Inglés de los Güesos*, Mexico City

McConnell, H. Ormande and Swan, Eugene, Jr. 1953. *You can learn Creole*, 2nd ed., Port-au-Prince

Meillet, A. 1906–8. 'La phrase nominale en indo-européen', *Memoires de la Société Linguistique de Paris* 14:1–26

Sableski, Julia A. 1965. 'Equational clauses in Bengali', *Language* 41:439–46

Samarin, William J. 1962. '*Lingua francas* in Africa', *Study of the role of second languages in Asia, Africa, and Latin America*, ed. by Frank A. Rice, 54–64, Washington, D.C., Center for Applied Linguistics

Sebeok, Thomas A. 1943. 'The equational sentence in Hungarian', *Language* 19:162–4

Whinnom, Keith 1965. 'The origin of the European-based creoles and pidgins', *Orbis* 15:509–27

CONVERGENCE AND CREOLIZATION

A Case from the Indo-Aryan/Dravidian Border in India

JOHN J. GUMPERZ AND ROBERT WILSON

Introduction

Historical linguists frequently point to bilingualism as a major determinant of language convergence. It is assumed that the greater the number of individuals who control two or more of the varieties spoken in a linguistically heterogeneous region and who use them alternatively in the course of their daily routine, the greater the likelihood that features from one system will diffuse into another. Studies of such diffusion processes during the last few decades have revealed some striking cases of grammatical borrowing among otherwise unrelated languages, both in India and elsewhere around the world. Although lexical items are by far the most frequently borrowed, it seems clear that borrowing extends to all aspects of the grammatical systems. As Weinreich (1952) points out: 'language contact can result in such far reaching changes that the affected language assumes a different structural type'. There seems to be no reason therefore to draw an *a priori* distinction among pidginization, creolization and other diffusion processes; the difference may be merely one of degree.

Students of bilingualism and language contact so far, have concentrated primarily on the end effects of these diffusion processes. There has been almost no direct investigation of the actual mechanisms involved. The principal goal has been to explain the historical origin of particular items of lexicon, phonology or grammar. To this end texts or interview material in a given language are searched for deviant features. If these features cannot be explained on the basis of normal intra-language change and show similarities to a language with which the first is in contact, the deviant features are said to be the result of convergence. It is assumed, however, that the varieties involved are distinct systems and that apart from the convergent feature they will remain distinct.

The present paper takes a somewhat different approach. Rather than concerning ourselves with the historical origin of deviant features, we focus on interacting social groups, as they alternate among varieties in their linguistic repertoire (Gumperz 1964) in the course of natural conversation. The data derives from a study designed to specify some of the linguistic skills involved in this code-switching process. (A model, based on recent work in machine translation, was constructed to simulate the operations performed by speakers in converting from one code into another (Gumperz 1967).[1] In the present paper the local varieties are compared with the varieties of the standard language that are also used in the village. Our concern is essentially ethnographic, rather than historical: analytic, rather than normative. We start with the local varieties LV1 and LV2 and compare the corresponding St1 and St2 to them, rather than the reverse. Furthermore, we match sentences drawn from natural conversations rather than isolated forms. This procedure brings out similarities as well as differences and provides better insight into communication processes. We can of course lay no claim to reconstructing exactly what has happened. Our goal is to elucidate the sociolinguistic nature of the convergence processes.

Sociolinguistic setting

Kupwar village is located in Sangli district, Maharashtra, approximately seven miles north of the Mysore border. It has a population of 3,000 and four languages. Village lands are controlled largely by two land-owning and cultivating groups, *Kannada*-speaking Jains, who form the majority, and *Urdu*-speaking Moslems. There are furthermore, large contingents of *Kannada*-speaking Lingayats – largely craftsmen, *Marathi*-speaking untouchables and other landless laborers, as well as some *Telugu*-speaking rope makers.[2]

As Indian villages go, Kupwar is well integrated into the regional communication system. Sangli, the district capital, where Marathi is the dominant language, is only three miles away by a fairly good unpaved road. Kupwar has both a primary school and a junior high school, the latter founded and controlled by local Jains. Village milk and produce are regularly sold on the Sangli market. A number of village leaders have been prominent in regional Congress politics ever since the days of Indian independence and many Jain and Muslim families have members who hold relatively high positions in State service.

Marathi is the principal literary language. It is also spoken in the neighboring urban bazaars as well as in many surrounding villages. In Sangli there is an Urdu medium high school controlled by Muslims, but very few villagers attend it. With increasing education during the last twenty years, literary forms of Marathi and Urdu have become better known in the village. They are used in written communication and increasingly also in conversation with educated visitors. Although we have no exact figures literacy is almost certainly above the national average. Those who are literate tend to be literate primarily in Marathi and secondarily in one of the several varieties of Hindi-Urdu or in English. Only one or two Jain priests read Kannada although Kannada is taught in schools across the Mysore border, where many local residents have close relatives.

As far as can be determined, almost all local men are bi- or multi-lingual.

Marathi serves as the main local medium of intergroup communication. Jains, for example, use it in talking to their Muslim or untouchable field hands. We furthermore have recorded conversations where Jains discussing business affairs seem to be switching freely between Kannada and Marathi.

There is every indication that the Kannada-speaking Jain cultivators and the Marathi-speaking service castes have both been in the region for more than six centuries. The Urdu-speaking Muslims date from the days of the Moghul domination three or four centuries ago. Bilingualism in Kupwar is therefore a long standing tradition. Why has it been maintained for so long? Why has regular and frequent interaction among local residents not led to the 'triumph' of one language?

Information obtained from living in the village over a period of several months suggests that the major factor in language maintenance is that the local norms or values require strict separation between public and private (intra-kin group) spheres of activity. There is considerable interaction with members of other groups at work and in the public areas of the village, but a person's home is pretty much reserved for the members of his extended family and for close friends who tend also to be close relatives. Village residences are distributed in such a way that each major caste or group of castes such as the Jains, Muslims, Lingayats, Untouchables has its own neighborhood. During our residence in a village Jain home we observed few if any non-Jain visitors. Those strangers who did visit could immediately be distinguished from relatives by their stiff and somewhat distant demeanor. The separateness of the home environment and of the home-group is symbolized in dress and posture as well as in language. Speech in the home, especially speech to women and children, is exclusively in the home-group language.

There are also some communication situations outside the home in which code-switching is not common and in which only one language is appropriate. Religious rituals for Kannada speakers, for example, are conducted in Kannada, and for Marathi speakers in Marathi.

When a Kannada-speaking Jain employs Urdu and Marathi speakers in his work group, all three local varieties of these languages may be heard. Now, there is little reason to doubt that his non-Jain co-residents would understand directions given in Kannada. The extensive bilingualism among men and the intertranslatability that has come about (see below) indicate as much. For the Jain to address one of these others in Kannada, however, would be tantamount to saying, I consider you a potential member of my home and friendship group. Marathi, the normal language for intergroup contact, does not carry such a connotation in work situations, and is therefore preferred in them. The fact that Marathi is *not* the home language of the vast majority of local residents, nor of either socially dominant group, makes it socially neutral. As long as ethnic separateness of home life is valued, then, and language remains

F

associated with ethnic separateness, there is little reason to expect multi-lingualism to disappear.

Intertranslatability

The constant code-switching required by the daily interaction routine has had some far reaching effects on local grammatical systems. When considered alone, to be sure, each local variety seems distinct. A historical linguist would readily identify particular texts as from a deviant dialect of Kannada, Marathi or Urdu. What would be missed is that sentence-by-sentence comparison of natural conversation texts in all three main local varieties reveals an extra-ordinary degree of translatability from one local utterance to the other. This translatability can be illustrated by the following example, which is taken from a corpus of almost 10,000 words of text tape recorded in natural settings during a three-month period.[3]

(1) 'I cut some greens and brought them.'

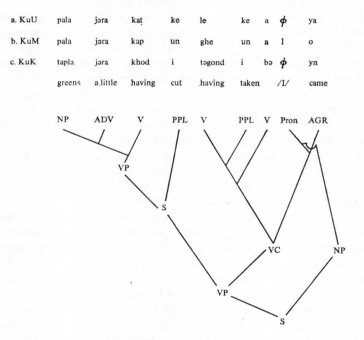

a. KuU	pala	jɔra	kaṭ	ke	le	ke	a	φ	ya
b. KuM	pala	jɔra	kap	un	ghe	un	a	l	o
c. KuK	tapla	jɔra	khod	i	təgond	i	bə	φ	yn
	greens	a little	having	cut	having	taken	/I/		came

The sentences in this example are lexically distinct in almost every respect, yet they have identical grammatical categories and identical constituent structures (as shown in the rough constituent structure diagram above). It is possible to translate one sentence into the other by simple morph for morph substitution. Contrast the way in which predication is expressed in the English translation to the equivalent expressions in the three Indian languages. English is historically related to Indo-Aryan Marathi and Urdu and Kannada is not, but English is nevertheless radically different, and in the same way, from all three local varieties. So great is the similarity among Ku grammatical structures that we were able to analyse an extensive corpus of bilingual texts involving all three local varieties without having to postulate syntactic categories or rules for one language which were not present in the other language. We may say, therefore, that the codes used in code-switching situations in Kupwar have *a single syntactic surface structure*.

Work still in progress further indicates that the three local varieties are also identical in phonetics although they have different morphophonemic rules (Gumperz 1967). What seems to have happened in these informal varieties is a gradual adaptation of grammatical differences to the point that only morphophonemic differences (differences of lexical shape) remain.

Convergent changes

The co-existence within the same community of standard varieties not directly affected by convergence along with maximally similar local varieties presents a special opportunity to examine changes generated by code-switching.

The remainder of this paper will examine the most important of these changes as they are revealed in the syntax and semantic structure of Ku varieties. The emphasis will be on KuU since it has changed most radically. Relevant features of the standard languages will be discussed first, followed by Ku equivalents.

GENDER

Urdu nouns and pronouns fall into two gender classes: masculine and feminine. Gender classification of nouns is based on (a) the phonological shape of plural suffix allomorphs, and (b) agreement markers (A) occurring in subject-verb constructions and elsewhere, which will be discussed further below. Most, but by no means all, animate nouns denoting females are feminine, and most nouns denoting males are masculine. Inanimate nouns are predictably assigned to either gender. Moreover, the masculine category is unmarked since it occurs in constructions where gender is otherwise unspecified or where agreement is blocked by syntactic rules. Urdu gender is therefore a syntactic category in spite of the fact that there is some correlation with sex. Marathi also has grammatical gender defined by similar criteria. There are, however, three gender categories: masculine, feminine and neuter, of which the latter is unmarked.

Kannada nouns fall into three gender-like classes characterized by the shape of plural suffix allomorphs and by agreement markers. Kannada gender, however, is semantically determined. All nouns denoting male humans are masculine, all nouns denoting female humans are feminine and all other animate and inanimate nouns are neuter.

The Ku gender systems are semantically based and closely resemble that of Kannada. KuK is identical with K. In KuM non-human nouns which correspond to M masculines or feminines appear as neuter. Only human males are masculine and human females feminine. The system has therefore become isomorphic with KuK and K. In KuU all U non-human nouns are merged into the unmarked masculine, so that only human females remain as a special gender category. Thus both KuM and KuU have enlarged their unmarked category, so as to make the remainder (one category, feminine, in Urdu; two categories, masculine and feminine, in Marathi) semantically determined, as are all gender categories in KuK.

(2) 'There was a flood'

a.	HU	wəhã	nədii	a-*ii*
b.	KuU	hwa	nədi	ay-*a*
c.	KuM	tith	nədi	al-*ə*
d.	KuK	yəlli	hwəLi	bət tu
		there	river	came

Note that in HU the noun *nədii* takes feminine agreement -*ii*, KuU has the unmarked masculine agreement marker -*a*, and KuM the neuter marker -*ə*.

AGREEMENT

HU verb constructions of the structure Vb-T-A Aux-T-A, containing a verb stem (Vb) inflected for tense (T) followed by a tense-inflected auxiliary (Aux) show agreement (A) in two positions. In all Ku varieties as in K there is only one agreement marker which occurs at the end of the verb phrase: Vb-T Aux-T-A.

(3) 'He went to graze the buffalo'

a.	HU	wo	[bhæs	cərane – ke	liye]	gəya th – *a*
b.	KuU	o	gəe	t – *a*	[bhæs	carn – e – ko]
c.	KuM	tew	gel	hot – *a*	[mhæs	car – ay la]
d.	KuK	aw	hog	id – *a*	[yəmmi	mes – ø – k]
		he	go	past (A)	[buffalo	graze (obl) to]

The verb complement phrase ['to graze the buffalo'] is included here primarily for the sake of meaning. In the text it is preceded by a slight pause and appears to be phonologically separate from the first. Note how KuU follows the common Ku work order (Subject Verb Phrase Complement) and thus contrasts with the normal HU order (Subject Complement Verb Phrase).

In HU the past auxiliary ('were') is marked for gender but not for person. KuU seems to have restructured the gender agreement into person agreement in this case.

(4) 'Where did you go'

a.	HU	kəhã	gə-ya	th-a	tu	(to a man)
			gə-ii	th-ii	tu	(to a woman)
b.	KuU	khã	gəe	te	tu	
c.	KuM	kəṭṭə	gel	hotas	twa	
d.	KuK	yəlli	hog	idi	ni	
		where	gone	were	you	

Note the KuU form *te* in agreement with the second person *tu* which contrasts with KuU ta in *o gəe ta* 'he was gone'.

In constructions of the type Vb Tp A the U future verb constructions show person agreement (Tp) where K has only the invariable tense marker. KuU in this case again follows K, as shown in the example below.

(5) 'I'll go tomorrow'

a.	HU	məy	kəl	ja	-ũg-	a	(man
				...	ii	(woman)
b.	KuU	məy	kəl	jya	-ẽg-	a	(man or woman)

Note the U first person future marker *-ug-* where KuU has invariable future marker *-ẽg-*.

In HU and in M in a sentence of the structure NP_1 NP_2 VP, if the verb is transitive and in the past tense, then NP_2 takes an agentive post-position (HU *-ne*, Marathi *-nə* or *ni* or zero). When NP_2 is human it takes the dative suffix and NP-VP agreement is blocked (i.e. the VP has no grammatical subject with which to show agreement). If NP_2 is not human, VP shows agreement with NP_2. In K, as elsewhere in Dravidian languages, the VP in NP_1 NP_2 VP constructions uniformly show agreement with NP_1 (when agreement markers are permitted by syntactic rules) regardless of the tense or transitivity of the verb. KuU and KuM again follow K in this case.

(6) 'Hey, fellow, did you sell the mare'

a.	HU	kya	bhaii	ghoṛii	beč dii	kya
b.	KuU	kya	baba	ghoṛi	di-ya	kya
c.	KuM	kay	baba	ghoṛi	dil-as	kay
d.	KuK	yan	əppa	kudri	kwaṭṭ-i	yan
		what	fellow	horse	gave – you	what

The NP_1 is the optional pronoun 'you' which is deleted here. Note that the HU verb shows agreement with NP_2 *ghoṛii*, while all Ku verbs agree with the second person pronoun *tu*, as would be the case in K.

In HU variable adjectives, demonstratives, possessive forms of pronouns and modifier constructions consisting of noun plus genitive post-position all show agreement with the case number and gender of the noun head. In K as well as in all Ku varieties this type of agreement does not occur. The relevant KuU forms show masculine suffix allomorphs while KuM forms have neuter endings.

(7) 'The mare which was sent to the cultivated fields'

a.	HU	bag mẽ	dii huii	ghoṛii
b.	KuU	bag-mi	dieso	ghoṛi
c.	KuM	maḷi-aa	dilvalə	ghoṛi
d.	KuK	maḷi-ay	kwattind	kudri
		garden in	given	mare

PRONOMINAL AND ADJECTIVAL USE OF POSSESSIVES AND
DEMONSTRATIVES

In all languages concerned, demonstratives or possessives may occur either as noun modifiers or in predicate position. In K as in other Dravidian languages forms in predicate position show a nominalizing suffix. In all Ku dialects, as in HU and Marathi, there is no phonological difference between forms occurring in the two positions.

(8) 'This house is yours'   'This is your house'

a.	K	*ii*	məne	*nim-də*		*i-du*	*nim*	mənə	
b.	KuK	*id*	məni	*nim-d*	eti	*id*	*nim-d*	məni	eti
c.	KuM	*he*	ghər	*tumc-ə*	hay	*he*	*tumc-ə*	ghər	hay
d.	KuU	*ye*	ghər	*tumhar-a*	həy	*ye*	*tumhar-ə*	ghər	həy
		this-one	house	yours	is	this-one	your	house	is

Note that in KuK it is the predicate form that is generalized and not the adjectival form.

DATIVE AND ACCUSATIVE POST-POSITIONS

Standard Kannada along with other Dravidian languages has a special accusative post-position contrasting with the dative. HU and M both show only dative post-positions for a human object in sentences like those below. Ku dialects including KuK follow Urdu and Marathi. This accusative post-position can on occasion be elicited in Kupwar, but it is always substitutable with the dative.

(9) 'Seeing the poor man, he gave'

a.	HU	gəriib	admi-*ko*	dekh-kər	diy-a	th-a
b.	KuU	gərib	manus-*ko*	dekh ke	die	ta
c.	KuM	gərib	mansa-*la*	bəg un	dil	hota
d.	KuK	gərib	mansya-*gə*	noḍ i	kwaṭṭ	ida
		poor	man – to	having seen	he gave	

NON-FINITE VP'S AND COMPOUND VERBS

Standard Marathi and Kannada and other Dravidian languages have a non-

finite verb form which we can call the *past non-finite*. It is used in two different
types of sentence constructions which are sometimes difficult to distinguish.
One is the very common pan-Indian sentence with one or more non-finite
verb phrases ended by a finite verb phrase (e.g. 'Having done the work,
having eaten, I'll go home.'); the other is the verb phrase ending with a compound verb, which serves about the same function as prefixing does in Indo-
European languages. Compound verbs differ from the former type of construction because only a very small class of verbs can serve as the second (i.e.
compounding) element.

Urdu has different verb forms here. In KuU, as in the other Kupwar
languages, the past non-finite is usually used for both types of construction, as
stated above for Marathi and Kannada.

(10) 'I cut some greens and brought them'

a.	HU	pala	jəra	kaṭ-kər	*le a-ya*	
b.	KuU	pala	jəra	kaṭ ke	*le – ke a-ya*	
c.	KuM	pala	jəra	kap un	*ghe – un al-o*	
d.	KuK	təpla	jəra	khod i	*təgond-i bə-yn*	
		leaves	a few	having cut	*taking (I) came*	

COPULA CONSTRUCTIONS

In HU and M both 'NP – is – NP' constructions like 'That is a table' and
'NP exists' constructions like 'Is the table here?' contain a copula 'is'. In
standard Kannada as in other Dravidian languages NP-NP constructions
contain no copula. In 'NP exists' constructions there is a form of 'be'.

(11) 'Your house is big'

a.	HU	tumhar-a	ghər	bəṛ-a	hay
b.	K	nim	məne	doḍdu	
c.	KuU	tumhara	ghər	bəḍa	hay
d.	KuM	tumcə	ghər	moṭhə	hay
e.	KuK	nimd	məni	dwədd	eti
		your	house	big	is

All Ku varieties including KuK show the HU, M pattern.

THE SUBORDINATING CONJUNCTION KI AND ITS SYNTAX

In Urdu and Marathi, direct quotations and quotations of questions are introduced by the subordinating conjunction *ki* 'that' as follows:

S₁	ki	S₂			
—	—	—	He said	that	'I'm going now'
			I don't know	*that 'Where is he?'*	

In Kannada the order in introducing quotations is the reverse of that
described above, and the conjoining element is a form of the verb 'say':

S₂ *conj* S₁   *'I'm going now'*   *so saying*   *he said.*

All Ku varieties show the HU, M pattern.

(12) 'Tell (us) where you went yesterday'

a.	HU	bol-o	*ki*	kəhã	gəy-a	tha	kəl
b.	KuU	bol o	*ki*	khã	gəe	te	kəl
c.	KuM	sang a	*ki*	kuṭṭə	gel	hota	kal
d.	KuK	heḷ ri	*ki*	yəlli	hog	idi	ninni
		tell	*that*	where	did (you)	go	yesterday

INTERROGATIVE VERBAL SUFFIXES

HU and Marathi form 'yes or no' questions with the interrogative 'what'. Kannada has a verb suffix -*a* which forms 'yes or no' questions. In U 'what' can occur in several positions in the verb construction. In Marathi 'what' is always final. All Ku dialects (a) have 'what' and (b) have it in final position as in Marathi. Kupwar Kannada speakers reject the -*a* suffix as ungrammatical.

(13) 'Did you sell the horse'

a.	HU	*kya*	ghoṛii	dii
b.	KuU	ghoḍi	di ya	*kya*
c.	KuM	ghoḍi	dil əs	*kay*
d.	KuK	kudri	kwaṭṭ i	*yan*
		the horse	gave (you)	what?

SOME INSTANCES OF SEMANTIC CHANGE

In Marathi and Kannada the general meaning of V plus oblique plus dative is 'for doing—— in order to do ——.' HU would use V plus oblique plus *ke liye* in equivalent constructions. KuU follows M and K here.

(14) 'He went to graze the buffalo'

a.	HU	wo	bhəys	car-n-e	ke	liye gəy-a
b.	KuU	o	gəe	ta	bhəys	car ne ko
c.	KuM	tew	gel	hota	mhays	car-ay-la
d.	KuK	aũ	hog	ida	yəmmi	mes ka
		he	go	did	buffalo	graze to

In Marathi and Kannada the present verb stem plus genitive suffix is used as a noun modifier. In HU this construction occurs as a noun modifier and in negative constructions of the 'should not' type. KuU forms are structurally identical with KuM and KuK and follow Marathi and Kannada.

(15) 'What should (you) do'

a.	HU	kya	kərna		
b.	KuU	kya	kar	ne	ka
c.	KuM	kay	kar	ay	cə
d.	KuK	yan	maḍ	o	d
		what	to do		

Inclusive and exclusive 'we' pronouns: Kannada and Marathi have two 1st person pronouns each, one meaning 'we but not you' and the other 'we including you'. HU does not make this distinction. KuU uses *apun* as the inclusive and *ham* as the exclusive 'we'.

Borrowing

Our data on borrowing of morphs confirms the findings of Weinreich, Emeneau and other students of language contact who maintain that both lexical and grammatical items can be borrowed, and that content word borrowings are more frequent. Within the realm of borrowed grammatical items some further finer distinctions can be drawn. Next after content words in order of frequency are adverbs, conjunctions, post-positions and other similar function words. Derivative suffixes are third. Here are some striking examples of this.

Marathi has a verb suffix *-u* which is used in constructions like *ja-u syɔk -t- o* '(he) can go' or *ja-u-n-ko* 'Don't go'. The standard Urdu 'can+Vb' construction is the verb root plus *sɔk-*.

All four Kupwar languages have the construction *Vb-u-syɔk(s)-*. The *-u* suffix has clearly been borrowed from Marathi.

(16) 'I can go'

a.	HU	məy	ja		sək-t-a	
b.	M	mi	ja	u	šək	t	o
c.	KuU	məy	jya	u	syək	t	u
d.	KuM	mi	ja	u	syək	t	o
e.	KuK	na	hog	u	syəks	t	yən
		I	go		can	

Inflectional morphs forming part of closed paradigmatic sets such as person and gender agreement or tense markers are almost never borrowed. Only in one or two instances did such borrowings occur. Here is one example:

(17) 'He even said something'

a.	KuK	aw	bi	yanr	mataḍ *ya*
		he	even	something	told

The Kannada past ending *-da* would be expected here; *ya* is a past marker in Kupwar Urdu and Telugu.

(18) 'Cousins came to call us from there'

a. KuU hwa – si həm – *na*   bula ne – ko pəwne ae
there – from us – *to*   calling – for cousins came

In the above case the KuU dative suffix *-ko* would be expected; *-na* is one of the Marathi allomorphs of the dative suffix.

In contrast to other borrowings which were freely elicited, items like the above, when heard on tape, were regarded as wrong or funny by natives. They were not repeated voluntarily. Such paradigmatically structured inflectional morphs seem to be at the core of the native speakers perception of what constitute 'different languages'.

Compare the above with examples from another language contact situation where ethnic identity is similarly marked by language distinctions. The languages here are HU and Punjabi (P), which although historically and typologically quite closely related are, nevertheless, officially recognized as separate languages.

(19) 'He doesn't eat'

> a. HU wo nəhii kha-*t*-a
> b. P o nəii kha-nd-a

Here, aside from minor features of phonology, the only difference lies in the phonological realizations of the participal endings respectively -*t*- and -*nd*-. It seems that in each of these cases, and quite possibly elsewhere, wherever social norms favor the maintenance of linguistic markers of ethnic identity, and where there are no absolute barriers to borrowing of lexicon and syntax, these morphophonemic features take on the social function of marking the separateness of two language varieties. In some cases they seem to remain as the last barriers to complete language shift or creolization.

Discussion

What can one say about the nature of the processes of language change illustrated in our case study? It is obvious that it is KuU which has undergone the greatest changes. It has adapted its gender system and radically restructured its system of agreement markers, in some cases even to the point of reshaping gender agreement markers into person agreement markers. It has further given up such typical HU features as verb compounding and has also undergone a number of semantic changes including the creation of a new distinction between exclusive and inclusive personal pronouns. KuK has also changed considerably. It has adapted to Marathi in that it has lost the distinction between pronominal and adjectival possessives and dative and accusative postpositions. Copula constructions, interrogative suffixes, and sentences with subordinating conjunctions have been restructured. KuM by contrast has changed least, though with major changes in gender and in agreement markers.

In sum, KuU has changed altogether in 11 of the cases discussed, KuM and KuK in 6 each (taking 2 a–c to apply to Marathi in the same way as to Urdu). Conversely, there have been no changes toward KuU, 1 toward KuM, 6 toward KuK, 4 toward KuK, KuM jointly, and 5 toward KuU and KuM jointly. Thus, if we assume for the sake of argument that the varieties involved in the diffusion process can be treated as independent entities, change has been toward KuU altogether in 5 of the cases discussed, KuK in 10, and KuM in 10.

These relations among the languages can be summarized as follows:

HU, M→K	1, 2a–e	6
K→HU, M	3, 4, 6, 7, 8a	5
HU→K, M	5, 9a–c	4
HU, K→M	8b	1

While we have no way of weighting the relative significance of the changes, the rough numerical relationships themselves are revealing. There are 12 possible relations of change among the three varieties: each variety toward each of the other two, or toward the other two jointly ($3 \times 3 = 9$), and each pair toward the third (3). Of these 12 possibilities, only 4 are found. (See Table 1.) As noted, KuK and KuM do not change toward KuU, singly or

	U	K	M	U,K	U,M	K,M
U						4
K					5	
M						
U,K			1			
U,M		6.				
K,M						

jointly. There are in fact *no* instances of changes involving just two of the varieties to the exclusion of the third. *All* changes are convergences involving the three varieties as a set, being changes either of one toward the other two, or of two toward the other one. The largest number of changes, and the only major case of two adapting to one, are of KuU and KuM toward KuK in semantic determination of gender, and in surface structure syntactic agreement (1, 2a–e). With the exception of the position of the interrogative marker (8b), all other changes discussed are of KuU toward KuK, KuM, where those two agree, and of KuK toward KuM, KuU, where those two agree. (Not, notice, of KuM toward KuK and KuU where those two may agree).

That KuM has been much more changed toward (where it agrees with one of the other languages) than changed from, despite its home group of speakers being a subordinate minority in the village, reflects the position of Kupwar within the regional communication network. Marathi is and has been for several centuries the dominant regional language, being spoken in Sangli, the district capital, as well as by the majority of cultivators in several adjoining villages. Since Kupwar residents are well integrated into the political and social life of the area there is no reason to treat the village as a self-contained isolate. On the contrary the Kupwar Jain's need for communicating with Marathi-speaking business men and neighboring cultivators provides the most reasonable explanation for the use of Marathi as a medium for inter-group communication in the village also.

The pattern would appear to be striking indication that the changes are based in mutual adaptation within the village. The equivalent roles of the language of the large majority, and of a minority of untouchables, reflect no doubt the status of the language of the latter outside the village, but that status is itself involved in what is the key to the whole, the norms governing choice of alternative variety in social situations. To what extent the adaptation in each language has been initiated by its home-group speakers, under the influence of their knowledge of the languages of others, and to what extent adaptation has been initiated by others, using a language *to* its home-group speakers, or, in the case of Marathi, to others, we are not able to say.

The present-day conditions after all reflect processes which must have taken place over a period of several hundred years during which time there have also been deep changes in power and prestige relationships. Notice, however, that almost all the changes can be interpreted as reductions or generalizations that simplify surface structure in relation to underlying categories and relationships. The semantic convergences of 9a–c, to be sure, would seem to reflect simply joint pressure on Urdu of Marathi and Kannada, and 9c entails a new distinction. The change in gender categories, though, results in making gender form predictable semantically. (In KuU there is a binary choice: [+human, +female] or not; in KuM a ternary choice: [+human, +female], [+human, −female], [−human].) The other changes show reduction in number of positions in which a category is marked (2a, 8b); reduction of number of categories marked (2c, 2b (where implicit gender of addressee is replaced by redundant surface agreement), 2e, 3, 4, 5); generalization of a surface form (without addition of a contrast) (some of the preceding, and 6); and changes that arguably are toward simpler, or more 'natural' surface structure relationships (2d, 7, 8a).

The most striking result of the various changes the dialects have undergone is the creation of three parallel creole-like local varieties. This linguistic situation seems uniquely suited to the social situation discussed at the beginning of the paper. Speakers can validly maintain that they speak distinct languages corresponding to distinct ethnic groups. While language distinctions are maintained, actual messages show word-for-word or morph-for-morph translatability, and speakers can therefore switch from one code to another with a minimum of additional learning.

The trend towards word-for-word translatable codes also explains many of the syntactic changes that the languages concerned have undergone. There are several instances where two grammatical categories in one language correspond to a single category in the other languages, as for example with Kannada dative and accusative and where the marked category in the first language is lost and the unmarked category is generalized. This same pressure for translatability of local codes further explains the many instances of restructuring of phonological materials by loan translation-like processes to fill categories in other local varieties.

Historical linguists as well as students of creolization in the past have had a tendency to think of standard languages as basic and to regard pidgins as relatively marginal or impermanent phenomena. For Kupwar, at least, and possibly for elsewhere, our situation would suggest a reversal of emphasis. If there is anything about the Kupwar linguistic situation that all speakers share it is the common Ku syntax. It is this syntax which is learned in childhood and in playgroups. Standard languages are superimposed on this system through formal education and other forms of contact with the outside. Knowledge of these languages is unevenly distributed, and is a function of an individual's socio-economic position. For many Kupwar residents, especially men, a model of linguistic competence must comprise a single semological, a single syntactic, and a single phonetic component, and *alternative* set of rules for the relation of semantic categories to morphemic shapes.

The Kupwar varieties have processes of reduction and convergence suggestive of pidginization and creolization. To say that the varieties have in fact undergone those processes would of course be misleading, if creolization is defined as requiring a pidgin as its starting point. We have no evidence of a pidgin-stage in the history of the village, or reason to suspect one. The adaptations involved are the result of several centuries of language contact. The present state of the varieties is creole-like, in that one finds grammatical structure and lexical shape pointing to different sources, quite like the stereotype of a pidgin or creole as the words of one language used with the grammar of another. And in Kupwar, whatever the exact historical circumstances, clearly the social basis for such striking convergence has been an important part of the same type as that associated with the changes that create a pidgin and persist in a creole. The need for constant code-switching and for mutual adaptation within a situation in which home languages are maintained has led to reduction and adaptation in linguistic structure. Historically viewed, moreover, where one is used to thinking of grammar as most persistent, lexicon as most changeable, in the normal development of a language, in Kupwar it is grammar that has been most adaptable, lexical shape most persistent. Kupwar, by the way, is not unique in this respect. Similar findings have been reported for other parts of India (Pandit in press). To be sure, while it has been proposed that the major process of change for pidgins in new settings has been re-lexification, the local Kupwar varieties might be said to have undergone 're-syntactification' (if the term may be excused for the sake of the contrast). On the other hand, if Kupwar Urdu were examined in isolation from other Kupwar varieties, and the identity and history of its speakers, and compared only to Standard Urdu, it might be thought that its deviance was due, not to adaptation by a continuous line of native speakers, but to a discontinuity, to 'substratum' or creolizing influence from a community to whom it was not at first a native language. Standard Urdu and Kupwar Urdu would stand in a relation analogous to that of Standard French and Haitian Creole, for those for whom the latter is a drastically reshaped French dialect.

That Kupwar Urdu might be suspected of having undergone pidginization and creolization indicates that these processes are not different in kind from other processes of language contact and adaptation. The main difference between KuU and a creolized language may be, as Hymes suggests, that its starting point was not a pidgin. The Kupwar situation points up the urgent need for direct investigation of actual mechanisms of linguistic change in their actual settings, leading to a theory of the relations between the two and their possible results.

NOTES

1 Field research and analysis of the data were financed by grants from the National Science Foundation, the U.S. Office of Education and the Institute of International Studies, University of California, Berkeley, whose support is gratefully acknowledged. We are grateful to Dell Hymes for extensive comments.
2 Kannada and Telugu are members of the Dravidian family of languages. Marathi and Urdu are members of the Indo-Aryan branch of the Indo-European family, but are not directly related. Urdu, now the national language of Pakistan, and Hindi, the national language of India, are distinct politically and culturally and have different scripts but linguistically almost identical. Following recent scholarly practice we use the term Hindi-Urdu to refer to these common features, while the term Urdu, as used here refers more specifically to the speech of local Muslim groups.
3 The following abbreviations are used in this and all following examples: Standard Hindi-Urdu, HU; Standard Marathi, M; Standard Kannada, K. The corresponding local varieties of each language in Kupwar are indicated by the prefix Ku, thus Kupwar Urdu, KuU; Kupwar Marathi, KuM; Kupwar Kannada, KuK. Each example is preceded by an idiomatic English equivalent in quotation marks. A literal English translation is given at the bottom.

REFERENCES

Gumperz, John 1964. 'Linguistic and social interaction in two communities. The ethnography of communication', ed. by John Gumperz and Dell Hymes, *American Anthropologist* 66(6), pt. 2, 137–54

1967. 'On the linguistic markers of bilingual communication. Problems of bilingualism', ed. by J. MacNamara, *Journal of Social Issues* 23(2):48–57

Pandit, P. B. 'The Grammar of Number Names in a Bilingual setting' (typescript)

Weinreich, Uriel 1952. *Languages in contact*, New York, Linguistic Circle of New York (2nd printing, 1963)

ACCULTURATION AND THE CULTURAL MATRIX OF CREOLIZATION

MERVYN C. ALLEYNE

Introduction

It is no surprise to find that the basic view of the definition of so-called 'creole' languages which still obtains is inherited from Leonard Bloomfield (1933). Apart from the current debunking of Bloomfieldian linguistics by the transformationalists, almost all of modern linguistics, as practised by Western Hemisphere linguists, gets its cues from Bloomfield. And even so, the transformationalists, in their wholesale slaughter of structuralists, usually spare the grand old man, even if only as part of their strategy of elevating non-contemporary linguists. Of course no one can deny the exciting insights that Bloomfield had into all aspects of language. But this does not mean that we should continue to do Bloomfield the disservice of perpetuating opinions which he expressed tentatively in the absence of a sufficient body of information, and not take the time to substantiate them properly or else modify them.

I shall try to extract from a series of different writings those features that are generally considered to underlie the definition of 'creole' languages and which have been basically inherited from Bloomfield:

   (i) A 'creole' is a 'pidgin' that has nativized itself;
  (ii) A 'pidgin' or 'creole' is a reduced or simplified form of another language (in our case, European); because,
 (iii) Speakers of the upper language (in our case, European) are much involved in the emergence of the 'pidgin' or 'creole';
 (iv) A 'pidgin' becomes fixed or conventionalized very rapidly.

One must admit that there have been some recent expansions of these notions, one at least of which has gained very wide acceptance. By the application of the comparative method, which assumes that systematic correspondences between languages cannot be explained by chance, but should be explained by the languages in question being outgrowths of some common ancestral stock, it has been postulated that 'creole' languages or dialects of West Africa, the Caribbean, and the Far East, are all descendants of one common ancestor, identified as a Portuguese 'pidgin', the first of its type to appear on the coast of Africa when the 'Age of Discovery' set in.

The fact is, however, that very few systematic correspondences have been explicitly pointed out which have any possible relationship with Portuguese. It turns out indeed that in the case of Caribbean dialects the vast majority of correspondences (or perhaps, more properly, structural similarities) can be plausibly shown to be West African in origin; while others, like the preposition *na*, and the verbal particle *ka*, attributed to Portuguese, can be shown to have West African etymologies as plausible as the Portuguese ones put forward. Thompson (1961) recommended the carrying out of what we would suppose to be the next logical step in support of the Portuguese pidgin notion, namely the reconstruction of the proto-language. But this has not been done, nor even attempted, to my knowledge.

Another expansion of the Bloomfieldian notions attempts to strengthen the hypothesis that 'pidgins' or 'creoles' are, to a large extent, in their genesis, European phenomena. Accepting the notion of stimulus diffusion developed by Kroeber (1948), some linguists, in particular Whinnom (1965) and Thompson (1961), attempt to relate the Portuguese pidgin to *Sabir*, the *lingua franca* of the Mediterranean which predates the presence of Europeans in Africa. I shall not attempt a discussion of this latter expansion, as I do not think it is necessary for explaining the genesis of 'creole' dialects, nor do I think that a convincing case has been made for it. It is a reassertion rather than a substantiation of the European-base hypothesis.

This paper will attempt to point out the deficiencies in the Bloomfieldian or post-Bloomfieldian argument. It will then propose a different framework in which one might more fruitfully examine the origin and development of languages and/or dialects spoken in the Caribbean and traditionally referred to as 'creoles'. 'Creoles' or 'pidgins', spoken in the Caribbean, show evidence of considerable variation from their inception rather than early and rapid crystallization. This paper considers that such variation can be better explained within the general framework of differential acculturation among Africans placed in contact with European culture. From the outset, a kind of linguistic syncretism took place out of the clash with West African languages of certain West European languages in their full morphological and syntactical forms. The precise nature and degree of this syncretism depends on the ways in which the cultural situation developed in each area in the Caribbean and elsewhere.

This paper discusses correlations between the language situation and other aspects of culture in the areas where 'creoles' are spoken. It points out the fact that there are similarities in the linguistic forms of West Africa which survive in the Caribbean area, as well as similarities in the other cultural forms which survive from West Africa. To account for this, the paper discusses the significance of the existence of a basic cultural uniformity in West Africa, as well as the significance of the notion of parallel development used in cultural anthropology.

Creole as nativized pidgin

As far as the notion of a 'creole' as the nativization of a 'pidgin' is concerned, it is clear that there do exist forms of speech which appear to be native to no group of speakers and which later appear to become mother-tongues. This view, however, fails to consider the very important question of the assigning of speech forms to particular identifiable and designated languages. It implies that, as far at least as the 'pidginization' of European languages in West Africa is concerned, a static linguistic situation rapidly developed in which three discrete types of expression coexisted: European language(s), African language(s), and 'pidgin'. To state a very simple example, when a Yiddish speaker says 'now is gebusted the cup', or 'like a can from sardines was gepacked the train' (Weinreich 1953), is he speaking English, Yiddish, or a 'pidginized' version of one or the other? Is this kind of linguistic phenomenon ever static? Or is it not rather subject to variation determined by a whole series of factors? Some instances of variation could be described as 'English with a Yiddish accent'; but other very deviant instances are less easily classifiable by linguist or by layman, and give rise among the latter to designations such as 'broken English', 'bastard English', 'Yidlish', etc . . . Were the first attempts by Celts or Iberians to communicate with Romans ascribable to the Latin language or to a 'pidginized' version of it?

Of course one finds in the literature on 'creole' languages frequent mention of a possible more inclusive reference for the term 'pidgin'. That is to say that writers, without wanting to explore it too far[1], speculate on the possibility that quite a number of languages, some of them European (especially English), may have started out as 'pidgins'. Whether it is useful to make this speculation or not, we cannot discuss here. But it is certain that in these cases, and too, as I shall attempt to show, in those we are discussing in this paper, what is crucial is *the later development of the cultural contact situation.* In some cases, this situation develops in such a way as to allow the members of the 'lower' culture to acquire habits of speaking the 'upper' language which are undistinguishable from those of its native speakers, while the language then undergoes regular slow historical change (presumably the case of Romance languages). In other cases, there is no wholesale attempt at learning the 'upper' language, but rather a massive incorporation of lexical items from the 'upper' language into the 'lower'; these bring with them derivational affixes which even become productive in the 'lower' language, and perhaps inflectional affixes as well, and cause the morphological system and therefore the syntactical system to undergo a kind of restructuring that very much resembles simplification (presumably the case of English in contact with Old Norse and Norman French).[2] The nature of the cultural contact situation in which languages and dialects of the Caribbean, commonly referred to as 'creoles', emerged will be discussed later. We must now deal with the other notions underlying the definition of 'pidgin' and 'creole'.

The notion of simplification

Simplification, like its sociological correlate of 'language without native speakers', may be inherent in any culture contact situation. On the one hand, speakers of one language may simplify their language and supplement it by recourse to other communication media (signs especially); while speakers of the lower language in their first clumsy attempts to speak the 'upper' language may so interpret it, either through the medium of their own native language or through simple inaccurate reproduction, that the results do appear to be a simplification of the 'upper' language. Even if this is so, it is difficult to accept that such simplification on the part of speakers of the 'upper' language might be either systematic and consistent or widespread and continuing.

In the case of 'creole' languages, certainly those of English and French lexical bases, there is no linguistic evidence to support this idea of simplification. There is on the other hand strong linguistic evidence that English and French in their full morphological systems were used in the contact situation. The survival in French-based 'creoles' of the French articles *la*, *l'*, *du*, *des*, (*lafimẽ* 'smoke', *laž* 'age', *diri* 'rice', *dlo* 'water', *zami* 'friend') suggests that the basic structure of the noun phrase of French was used. The survival of the feminine forms of the adjective as well as masculine forms indicates no simplification as far as the flexional system of adjectives is concerned. The 'irregular' French plural is there in *zye* 'eye', and the existence of *dot*, *lot*, *zot*, 'other', shows that the complex morphological variation determined by the use of the negative was much a part of the French language used in the contact situation. One finds in French-based 'creoles' everywhere *vle* (<*voulez*), *pe* (<*peut*), *met* (<*mettre*), *mete* (<*mettez*), *ped* (<*perdre*), *pedi* (<*perdu*), *konẽ* (<*connaît*), *konet* (<*connaître*). The form of the conditional in French, *serait*, survives in Louisiana *sre* (obsolete), Haiti *sre* (obsolete), and in Antilles *sre* (obsolete) and *se*. The expression *mwẽ malad* looks like a simplification of French by the omission of the verb 'to be'. But there also exists *usa li ye* or *kote li ye* 'where is he?' *kazen-na se you pil ti roch žon* 'the barracks is a pile of yellow pebbles', *mãže se-te piti mi ak pwa* 'the food was little millet and beans', all of which show that the verb 'to be' is not absent from creole but only cut up into different semantic and syntactic categories. As far as the choice of the flectionally invariant verb form is concerned, Goodman (1964) sums up the situation as follows: 'If the French infinitive and past participle are phonologically identical, or if they would become so due to regular phonological developments in Creole, such as the loss of syllable final *r* or the change of *ü* to *i*, then it is the form which virtually without exception becomes the invariant Creole verb. If these conditions do not hold, then Creole sometimes adopts the infinitive, sometimes the past participle, and sometimes a finite form.'

As far as the English-based dialects are concerned, the comparative work parallel to Goodman's for French is lacking.[3] But we can already observe that the survival of *brok* 'to break', *lef* 'to leave', *los* 'to lose', shows that the English verb system with strong preterites was in use in the contact situation. If this kind of morphological formation was in use, there is no reason to suppose that the few other inflections of English were simplified. Certainly in the case of the weak preterites, certain phonological reinterpretations of English final consonant clusters would have rendered the majority of these forms undistinguishable from the infinitive or the present.

It has not been clarified, to my knowledge, which features of the syntax of 'creoles' represent simplifications or reductions. The verbal system is perhaps, if anything, an *expansion* of the verbal systems of some Indo-European languages. I shall venture to guess at what is presumed to represent simplification. The frequently cited omission of the verb 'to be' is really, as I have said, a non-starter. The verb 'to be' is not omitted in 'creoles'. The predicative use of adjectives in expressions such as *mwẽ malad, mi sik*, can be shown to have West African models: Ewe *gli la keke* 'the wall is broad'. There are in fact African models for the precise 'creole' dissection of 'to be' into (i) 'to be a quality', (ii) 'to be', as copula, (iii) 'to be' locational (see Turner 1949). Juxtaposition may be another feature of 'simplification'. But here again there are African models: Ewe *fia dada* 'the chief's mother'; Gã *kofi wolo le* 'Kofi's book'; Twi *Ata ne nã* 'Ata's mother' (lit. 'Ata his mother').

One can of course anticipate a counter-argument that the presence of almost the full set of inflected morphemes as fossilized forms without grammatical function is due to later contact with English or French in the respective areas outside Africa where these languages were used side by side with their 'creole' offspring. The fact, however, that the majority of these forms are common to all the dialects involved suggests that they spring from one common source and that these fossilized inflections and other features existed at the very inception of the life of these languages.[4] The other explanation for their presence over widely separate geographical regions, i.e. parallel development, is, I suggest, unsatisfactory when applied to details of morphology such as *vle, sre, ye*, etc. Its relevance in accounting for broader structural patterns (such as the predicative use of adjectives) will be discussed later.

Pidgins as fixed, discrete systems which emerged rapidly

Another notion implicit in the writings about Caribbean 'creole' dialects is that the pidgins (or pidgin) from which they are alleged to have developed emerged abruptly, acquired their essential features very quickly, and became discrete linguistic systems. We would therefore have had a situation in which there were European languages, African languages, and 'pidgins' of English, French and Portuguese lexical bases, these last either having all emerged independently or else the first two being 'relexifications' of the third. There is no convincing evidence, first of all, that there was any connection between the three types except for lexical borrowing that might have come from close proximity on the African coast. Indeed, and this is what interests us at this point, there is no evidence that there were any discrete systems of the third type based on English or French. What at that time characterized these emergent forms of expression and what has characterized them throughout all their history, wherever they were used side by side with the European language from which they derive their vocabularies, is the high degree of variation, rather than discreteness and stability, within them.

For example, the evidence suggests that at the beginning there was apparently free variation between the forms of the noun showing agglutination of French articles and forms without agglutination before the distribution became relatively fixed. A number of variant forms of the personal pronouns evidently existed in some variety of speech taken from Africa to the French colonies in the Americas and the Indian Ocean: *mo, mwe* (first person), *to, twe* (second), both with optional nasalization and optional elision of *mo, to,* causing loss of vowel;[5] *i, li, so* (possessive).[6] The verbal system so characteristic of all 'creoles' was most evidently there in the pre-colonial period. But its precise form in each colony became fixed only after the dialect was implanted in particular specific areas. For the non-perfective aspect, there seems to have been an alteration of *après* (in its several forms) and *ka. ape* survives in Louisiana, Haiti, Indian Ocean; *apre* in the Indian Ocean; *ap, apr, apo* in Haiti; *ka* in the French Antilles and Guyana. For the future tense, *a, va, ava* are competing forms which remain so in Haiti, Louisiana, Indian Ocean, but have become obsolete or rare in the French Antilles and Guyana. The picture then is that variants have become more or less eliminated once the dialect is established in any one territory. But they sometimes persist, as one observes, for example, in the treatment of the *schwa* vowel of French, for which 'it is impossible to formulate any clear cut rule, either for Creole as a whole or for any particular dialect' (Goodman 1964: 33). The variants *u, i, e, o,* reflect not only variation within the French language spoken by Frenchmen, but also undoubtedly variation in the interpretation of the vowel by Africans of different linguistic backgrounds. One can multiply the examples.

Nature of the contact situation

This high degree of variation within a norm of uniformity, the treatment and interpretation of French forms, can best be accounted for, not by any special appeal to notions of 'pidginization' and 'creolization' as they have been formulated so far, but rather *within the framework of language change as merely one aspect of culture change arising out of culture contact.*

The establishment of European communities (fortresses and factories for trading in slaves) created a situation of culture contact, as a result of which Africans began to be involved in processes of deculturation and acculturation. The locus of contact was within the fortresses and factories, but also, and perhaps more significantly, within the African towns that sprung up outside the factories. It was therefore not a question of a trade jargon that had to be in some way invented to deal with a rigidly circumscribed area of contact. It was rather a question of two types of communities in contact without serious attempts at social integration, and of one type, African, seeing it in their interests to learn the languages of the other type of community (European).

In fact, it was nothing more than the classical contact situation (Latin with Celtic, Iberian, or Italic) with differences in the degree of social integration, in the quality of the learning situation, and especially differences caused by the diverse ways in which the European/African contact situation later developed. These differences account for the greater and more persistent transfer of native speech habits into the learning of the new languages in Africa than is usually accepted in the case of the learning of Latin by Celts and Iberians.

What may have been another difference between the two contact situations, with corresponding results in cultural changes that followed, is that in any one factory and in the towns adjacent to them, there may not always have been a homogeneous African type of culture but rather representatives of different cultural or sub-cultural types. This does not unquestionably constitute a difference from the classical type of contact situation, because cultural divergences, linguistic or otherwise, within Gaul and within Iberia (with the exception of Basque) have either not been properly established or else not used fundamentally in the discussion of language change in Gaul or Iberia.[7] Moreover, one factor which evidently counteracted divergence in both cases was the common base which underlay surface cultural differences in West Africa, and presumably in Gaul and Iberia.[8]

Basic cultural uniformity of West Africa

This basic cultural uniformity of West Africa can account for similarities found in New World cultures that were created by the importation of slaves from West Africa.

The similarities are numerous in folklore, religion, kinship structure, music, as well as in language. Some similar features may of course have come to particular territories by cultural diffusion. But other similarities must be explained by the relative basic homogeneity of the cultural area of West Africa. In these latter cases, similarities go back to very generalized items, not

directly referable to a specific tribe or a definite area.[9] In yet other cases however, specific areas in West Africa can be shown to be responsible, and we
have to account for this. It seems that as far as language is concerned, the
Akan and Ewe groups were predominantly responsible for many of the
structural similarities found within English-based 'creoles' and within French-
based 'creoles', as well as similarities across the two groups. It was there that
the English and French companies did the bulk of their trading and the very
early trading in the case of the English company (cf. Patterson 1967:134).
The predominance of the Akan culture in the English contact areas in the
West Indies is also sometimes attributed to certain psychological and cultural
traits possessed by the Coromanti. They certainly seem to have been everywhere leaders of slave revolts.

Another interesting phenomenon to account for is that everywhere we find
similarities in the specific aspects of West African culture that survive and in
the specific aspects that undergo extinction in favour of European forms.
Thus everywhere African forms of technology, political organization, clothes,
left little or no trace in the new cultures of the New World, while everywhere
religion, magic, music, superstition, forms of amusement of Africa survive
either in a pure state or syncretized. In language the correlates may be considered to be the deep structure which is African-derived and persists, and
the surface structure (or from a different point of view, the lower order elements) which is everywhere European-derived. Even within the lexicon which
is generally European-derived, we may find that there are everywhere the
same kinds of survivals of African words that belong to a semantic category
that can be generally described as *private* in contrast with the broad semantic
category of European-derived words that may be termed *public*. That form of
citation is used elsewhere. If details are needed, the reference is to the précis
in Part v, 'Variation and Use.'

The problem of genetic classification

The question of the genetic classification of 'creole' dialects and languages
has been the subject of a fair amount of comment, beginning with Antoine
Meillet and Hugo Schuchardt in the thirties and later Hall, Hymes, Taylor
and Weinreich in the fifties. Nothing resembling agreement has been reached
and this lack of agreement as to the genetic classification of 'creole' languages
reflects the current lack of agreement as to the conditions which must be
fulfilled before genetic relationships between languages can be accepted.
From the 'continuity of morphology' of Antoine Meillet to the scant lexical
evidence accepted by lexicostatisticians, there have been as many theories as
interested scholars.

The 'creole' language field has been made further difficult by the absence of detailed historical studies. R. A. Hall, Jr., arrived at the rather *a priori* conclusion that there are systematic correspondences between French 'creoles' and French in all aspects of their structure. But I have shown (1966) that at least so-called phonological correspondences are the necessary result of the use of lexical items from French and that these correspondences say nothing for the historical origin of the phonological system. Another question that needs clarification is that of the identification of borrowings. It seems absurd, especially if one looks at the total cultural situation in the Caribbean, to call the African element in 'creole' language borrowings. Yet this is precisely what strict uncritical adherence to the notion of 'pidgin' induced R. Hall, Jr., to do. On the other hand, the European element in some 'creoles' seems on superficial study so important that to deny its existence and assign 'creoles' genetically to some other parent would seem to be indefensible. It must however be admitted that a historical study of Caribbean cultures suggests that a process of cultural change took place in which an African type of culture has been overlaid partially by a European type.

It must be carefully noted that the problem is not whether certain dialects of common lexical base, e.g. those referred to as 'French creoles', are historically or genetically related to each other. The problem is first their genetic relationship in the 'parent/daughter' sense; and secondly whether 'creoles' of different lexical bases can be considered to be genetically related to each other, a problem which the notion of a 'Portuguese pidgin' is alleged to answer.

It would be useful to comment here on one aspect of 'creole' languages before going any further. The comparative study of French-based creoles demonstrates, quite incontrovertibly I believe, that all these dialects are in some way historically related. The impression is that they go back to one basic source. This is indeed the conclusion of Goodman's study. The geographical location of the basic common source is problematic. If one follows the external history of these dialects in the Western Hemisphere, one can establish fairly convincingly that St Kitts was, as it were, the cradle of French-based 'creoles', and that from there they spread to other parts of the hemisphere as the French colonial empire grew. The gross deficiency of this view is that it does not account for the Indian Ocean dialect, which is clearly related historically to the others, and, surprisingly, apparently more related, according to Goodman, to Louisiana dialect. This seems to transfer the location of proto-French-based 'creole' to West Africa. The same applies to the English-based dialects. In the Western Hemisphere, their source may be traced to Barbados which, like St Kitts for French, was the stepping stone for the English colonization of the Americas. But it does not account for Krio and other English-based vernaculars spoken on the West Coast of Africa, one of which, used in the Camerouns, has been recently honoured with a name Wes Kos.[10] We are obliged to conclude, tentatively, that the English-based 'creoles', which like the French-based ones, resemble one another not only in broad structural patterns but also in morphological and phonological detail, spring from one basic common source and that the geographical location of it was West Africa.

Everywhere in the New World we find that specific cultures have emerged which in some ways pose the same problems of genetic identification that the linguistic forms pose. Some forms may be considered to be pure European in their derivation, and others pure African, but the majority are reinterpretations. It is not always clear what determines the reinterpretation. Is Pocomania an African cult influenced by Christian worship, or Christian religious practice reinterpreted and restructured in the mould of African cult? The question may, like the question of the genetic classification of linguistic forms, be unanswerable or irrelevant. What is interesting however is Herskovits's analysis of the Toco (Trinidad) family which concludes with the following statement (Herskovits 1947: 296): 'In considering the forms taken by the family and the behaviour associated with it, we are faced with a retention of African custom that has been reinterpreted so drastically as to make the resulting institutions not only susceptible of description as pathological manifestations of the European family but ones which have been frequently so described.'

The notion of parallel development

Implicit in the anthropological approach to cultural similarities is the acceptance of the idea of parallel development, not only arising out of the survival of specific or generalized aspects of West African culture, but also determined by the parallel conditions existing in each area. In fact the notion of common ancestor has not been used in anthropology in the same way that it has been used in linguistics by the supporters of the Portuguese 'pidgin' theory. Notions of deculturation and acculturation, restructuring and reinterpretation, along parallel lines, are used in examining cultural phenomena in the New World. It must be admitted however that the most recent views on New World culture are moving away from a too generalized 'African' explanation to other causation alternatives. It has always been accepted that the survival of particular African phenomena (cf. the animal trickster hero in folklore) as against the non-survival of others was due to conditions inherent in the new situation in the New World. Some anthropologists are even now considering that some phenomena which had been previously thought to be African-derived have absolutely nothing to do with Africa, but are caused by particular social and economic conditions that can exist elsewhere with similar results. Thus the particular structure of the Negro family, thought by many to be descended from an African type of family system, is now thought to be the product of a certain set of socioeconomic conditions, and Oscar Lewis (1961) shows how this family structure exists among some Mexican families and is a product of what Lewis calls the 'culture of poverty'. But this by no means constitutes a debunking of the 'African survival' notion, supported chiefly by M. Herkovits. It merely recommends caution and shows the dangers of over generalization.

Parallel development is certainly not as unsound a notion for the anthropologist as it has appeared to be for the linguist.[11] It seems reasonable to ascribe a common historical source to details of lower order linguistic elements that show similarity over a number of geographically related dialects, and it has been suggested that dialects of French lexical base can be assumed to have had a common origin. The comparative historical work for English-based dialects remains to be done, but the present evidence points to a common origin with later separation due to special political factors in each case. Certain similarities across dialects of different lexical bases can be shown to have West African historical models and it seems to be more valuable heuristically to consider whether they cannot be accounted for by the notion of parallel development, by parallel retention of generalized features of West African syntax, bearing in mind that the similar socio-economic conditions in Western Hemisphere plantation societies might explain some similarities.

The total acculturative process

It is in its approach to the total acculturative process that anthropology can interest us most. Linguistic adaptation, which expresses itself almost exclusively on the lexical level, may be seen as merely one instance of a very general process of partial adaptation to European culture. This adaptation began in Africa in the factories and in the towns surrounding them. And from the very beginning of contact, the important thing is that variations in the degree and precise nature of adaptation begin to appear. When we attempt to determine the extent to which initial contact may have influenced the later process, one of the things we should consider is the size of these communities. Unfortunately it is impossible to say what their numerical strength was. It is still more difficult to estimate what percentage of the African population coming out as slaves to the New World had already embarked on this linguistic acculturation. The evidence of course is very strong that the majority of slaves in the English and French factories, on ships, and on plantations early in their existence, were speakers of African languages only.[12] Other factors are however equally important, especially the fact that persons, however relatively few, who were involved in the initial contact and who were the first to acquire skills in the European language, were either used formally as interpreters or became informal interpreters aboard ship and on plantations in the New World. What is important then is that persons involved in the acculturative process in

Africa would have attracted newcomers into it and would have served as their model. Thus persons who had first contact with Europeans served as carriers of the new developing culture of later arrivals.

The variations in the degree and quality of acculturation were conditioned by several factors which it will be impossible to discuss in detail here. It will be sufficient to mention the salient points. As a very general rule, degrees of closeness of contact with Europeans correlated with degrees of acculturation. And this was clearly the major factor in one kind of linguistic variation. So that persons in close contact with Europeans achieved a high level of accurate performance of the European culture in general, and a high level of accuracy in the reproduction of the structural patterns of the European language. Others with little contact and subject to poor learning conditions saw their attempts at reproducing English or French patterns subject to interference from their native languages. In the West Indies, contact was determined primarily by occupation; on the other hand our knowledge of the social and economic structure of towns that sprung up outside European factories is not great enough to allow us to state clearly the sociological determination of variations in degrees of contact. In the New World, on sugar plantations, production was organized on the basis of a kind of occupational stratification according to which field slaves were most numerous and were furthest removed from contact with Europeans. Social intercourse of the field slaves was almost exclusively confined within the group; and so, among them, linguistic forms showing a high degree of divergence going back to the incipient culture contact situation in Africa, were able to crystallize and achieve the appearance of stability. The fact is however that in the areas where the same linguistic model continued to exist, there is no real stability but a continuing variation caused by increasing modification in the direction of the model language.

We must mention one other very important factor which must have helped some degree of stability to develop in field slave language; that is the group consciousness of field slaves and those who identified with them. There may have been positive refusals to become totally acculturated to the European way. This would be a further example of the psychological duality of the New World negro wishing to participate in the European way, but yet wishing to preserve something of a separate identity. This duality, this public/private dichotomy or ambivalence is very characteristic of present-day Caribbean peoples. M. G. Smith (1953) has commented on the 'reluctance among slaves to let white people know more about their behaviour and institutions than was strictly necessary'.

In descending order of numerical strength and ascending order of degree of contact were artisans, freedmen, and house slaves. Among these we have from the beginning a greater and more rapid departure from an African form of culture and speech. And of course there were many persons in Africa and in the West Indies in whom the acculturative process was almost complete or who learned English quite effectively as a second language. This is confirmed by the many references to the use of interpreters who are variously described as speaking 'good', 'pretty good', or 'very good' English. This was the basic picture. There are certain refinements and nuances to be introduced, and these have been dealt with by Herskovits (1942). We have to examine the continuing nature of the contact situation to understand the precise linguistic and the general cultural configuration that developed in each territory. We have Barbados, the U.S.A., Antigua, on the one hand, where conditions favoured the greatest departure from African modes of life; on the extreme we have the Bush negroes of Surinam and perhaps the inhabitants of the Gullah area (the Sea Islands) of North America, where, certainly in the case of the former, it is hardly possible to speak about acculturation except in the most tenuous of ways. The culture of the Saramaccans has very little, if anything, to do with Europe; and similarly with the language, which has distinctive tone, prenasalized stops, coarticulated stops, syllables with vowel finals, and African-derived words in its basic vocabulary. Thus if we consider all the English contact areas together, we find that we can construct a scale starting with Saramaccan and ending with Barbadian English and passing by varying degrees of retention or elimination of African speech habits. If we consider one territory such as Jamaica or Antigua, this scale is microcosmically represented in the continuum type structure existing there.

The correlations of this linguistic picture with other aspects of culture are numerous. Take the example of religion. African religion survives in its pure state in cults like *Cumina* in Jamaica; it survives in a syncretized form in cults like *shango* (Trinidad) manifested in several areas of the New World including Brazil without necessarily having been diffused from one place to another. This kind of worship is entirely absent from the modern United States of America or Barbados, although we might speculate that similar forms of religious practice existed there previously. In any one territory possessing some form of *shango*, we find at the other end undiluted forms of Christian worship in the European manner; and in between are cults like the Shouters of Trinidad, representing a reinterpretation of African cult organization and cult belief within the framework of Protestantism.[13]

The French contact areas seem to present a greater degree of homogeneity than the English contact areas. This however is readily understood when one considers first the fact that the colonial history of the French territories was quite uniform as compared with the diverse kinds of conditions existing in the English contact areas. In Surinam, the contact with English was lost very early; Barbados enjoyed (*sic*) unbroken English contact from the 1620s which was always close and intense. Secondly for reasons probably related to differences in colonial policy and the psychology of the people, the French elite adopted to a large measure the dialect of the African-derived sector of the population, whereas there is no evidence for the English elite doing the same.[14] This must have given a greater solidity and stability to the French-based 'creole'. It must be pointed out here however that it is wrong to believe, as seems to be sometimes believed, that the kind of continuum structure existing in Jamaica is absent from the French contact territories. There are in fact intermediate varieties sometimes designated *créole francisé* or *français créolisé*, as against *le gros creole*. The reasons why the intermediate varieties seem less prevalent in the French contact areas than in Jamaica is first because basic Jamaican has itself moved closer to English than, say, Haitian has in relation to French; and secondly because the demographic strength of intermediate varieties in Jamaica is much greater than in Haiti. There are undoubtedly reasons of linguistic typology as well, but they cannot be supported without more research.

Summary

The argument then is that in attempting to speak English or French, Africans in Africa, as well as in the New World, interpreted English or French structural patterns in terms of native patterns. Socio-cultural factors everywhere determined the degree of interference, from one territory to another and also within any single territory. This resulted in linguistic variation and instability which is characteristic of any dynamic acculturative process. Because field slaves constituted the greatest numbers and were in effective contact only with themselves, a linguistic medium, commonly referred to as 'creole', appears to have become crystallized within that group. At the beginning of the process, this creole was in fact everywhere only a major segment of a continuum of variation and marked the first stage in the process of adaptation to a cultural model.

In two outstanding cases in the Caribbean – Surinam and the Netherland Antilles – the linguistic model is suddenly withdrawn and the movement of linguistic acculturation ends. A new elite language, Dutch, is introduced and a simple bilingual situation develops. This situation is interesting in that it records very vividly the manner of emergence of a new *language*. In other cases, Barbados, North America, and maybe too the Latin American Caribbean, and Brazil, conditions allow the almost total linguistic acculturation of the African-derived population. As far as the Latin American Caribbean is concerned, the relevant question is not why something called a 'creole' did not develop, but what conditions allowed the African-derived sector of the population to eliminate substratum features from their speech,[15] as the Barbadians have done.

Where continua still exist, there will be a tendency for the segment called 'creole' to become more and more modified in the direction of the model language and to disappear as the acculturation process continues. This, as I have said, is what has happened in Barbados where nineteenth-century texts attest to the existence of a dialect variety very similar to Jamaican. It will also undoubtedly happen in Jamaica and Antigua, unless a new cultural and political movement reverses the current process of change. The same applies to the French territories, except that there, it seems that a slightly different set of conditions has caused a relatively solid crystallization of the 'creole'.

I can see no value whatever in calling Sranan and Papiamentu 'creoles'. They are merely languages, which carry low status because their speakers belong to a culture which occupies low status in the hierarchical arrangement of world cultures at the present time. Dialectal varieties showing greatest degrees of divergence from standard languages of Europe in the dialect complexes of Haiti, Jamaica, etc., may, I suppose, be called 'creole' dialects; but the only value the term can have so used is one derived from the contrast of that dialect situation with other social dialect situations. The contrast lies firstly in the fact that in Haiti and Jamaica the variety of maximum divergence is not only a sociological variant, as say *cockney* is in England, but is also a cultural variant; and secondly, and this is the linguistic correlate of that cultural fact, in the fact that the standard European language and this variant of maximum divergence cannot be compared for the purpose of reconstruction of any common ancestral stock, as presumably can be done in the case of RP and *cockney*. That is to say that Jamaica and Haiti are in a sense plural societies, culturally segmented. One culture (or sub-culture) is in a very dynamic state, as is the language which conveys it, and represents in some way the interaction of European forms and African forms. It may be useful to characterize this special kind of dialect variation by calling one variant, the one of maximum divergence from the standard, the 'creole' dialect. But here the anthropologists and the linguists will differ. The former use 'creole' and 'creolization' to refer to the common value system that seems to be emerging in Caribbean territories where the plural society is breaking down and an integrated one ensues. The parallel in linguistic terms would be the intermediate varieties which in fact are becoming most prevalent in places like Jamaica and Guyana. To explore further the value which the term 'creole' might have, it may be that we might wish to refer to Jamaican as the 'creole dialect' of English, and Sranan as a 'creole language', using 'creole' to express the historical connection between the two. But since we shall have to refer to Haitian as the 'creole dialect' of French, we would also be suggesting that Haitian has some historical connection with Sranan, for which we have no real justification.[16] It may be best indeed to leave the languages Sranan and Papiamentu alone, and, if we wish to continue to use 'creole' in reference to Jamaican or Haitian, to seek some common understanding with the anthropologists.

Postscript

This paper, it will have been noted, deals with French- and English-based 'creoles', and not at all with Portuguese. I have neglected Portuguese because of my unfamiliarity with the structure of Portuguese 'creoles'. I may however permit myself some observations in this regard. I have not found any reference in accounts of the English slave trade to the use of a Portuguese 'jargon' or any other form of Portuguese, other than that called simply 'Portuguese', in English factories. I have met references to the use of African languages and to the use of all sorts of English, including 'broken'. Linguists often refer to the systematic separation of slaves of the same tribal origin in factories, aboard ship, and in the New World, so as to minimize the possibility of revolt. Some of the same linguists subscribe to the idea of a widespread Portuguese 'pidgin'. The two seem to be incompatible. That is to say, if the Portuguese 'pidgin' was indeed widespread, there would have been no point in recommending the separation of slaves. Persons responsible for the conduct of the trade were therefore not envisaging slaves being able to communicate in any 'pidgin' in widespread use. The question of the origin of Portuguese elements in Sranan and Saramaccan is really a non-question in the way that it is usually formulated. The two arguments (Portuguese 'pidgin' direct from Africa or Portuguese from the Brazilian Sephardic Jews) are not mutually exclusive. Slaves going early to Surinam may have come from Portuguese contact areas in Africa, and then later met others brought from Brazil by their owners, both groups speaking undoubtedly the same variety of Portuguese. Research on this point should be directed to discovering what aspects of the new environment in Surinam are conveyed in Sranan and Saramaccan by Portuguese-derived words. If we find that there are relatively many, we would conclude that the influence of the Sephardic Jews and their slaves was very important in the establishment of Portuguese elements in the two languages.

A variety of Portuguese seems to have been taken to the Far East. We need studies, such as Goodman's, to establish the precise relationship between the eastern varieties and those of West Africa and elsewhere. My own feeling is that in time Portuguese sailors learned the West African variety of Portuguese, and, assuming that it would be a variety commonly more intelligible to all non-European peoples, they used it in some form in the East. The Portuguese, much more than other Europeans, settled in West Africa and, like the French elite in the New World, may have adopted the local linguistic norm, in the same way that they are known to adopt the general cultural norms of the colonial territories. We should then attempt to discover, if it is at all possible, whether Portuguese going to the East were recruited from among settlers on the West African coast. It seems reasonable to expect that this should be so, but the research must be done.

NOTES

1 Jean daCosta has made a very comprehensive and enlightening examination of the question in a paper read to the Linguistics Seminar of the University of the West Indies.

2 Another example of this is the kind of restructuring that immigrant languages undergo in the United States of America: massive lexical borrowings from English; morphological 'simplification', loan translations from English.

3 The author of this paper is at present undertaking the comparative study of Saramaccan, Sranan, West Indian dialects, and Krio.

4 For example, one notes the startlingly high degree of coincidence in the 'creole' forms that show agglutination of the French articles.

5 This sometimes functions like a two case system of nominative and accusative (in eighteenth century Haitian, Louisiana, Indian Ocean), but *mo* could also merely be a morphophonological variant in preconstruction (Goodman 1964:35). However in French Guiana, *mo*, together with *m* by elision, is the only form used.

6 Today, *so* (French 'son', 'sa', 'ses') survives only in Louisiana, French Guiana, Indian Ocean.

7 It is nevertheless still accepted in some circles as a reasonable hypothesis that dialect divisions in Spain and France were influenced by subcultural divisions in Gaul and Iberia. This will remain nothing more than a plausible hypothesis in the absence of any record of such cultural divisions.

8 See, for example, Forde (1960); and Elkins (1963:93).

9 Thus Patterson (1967) comments: 'It is impossible to locate the particular areas in West Africa from which the different funeral rites described above came. It is more fruitful to regard the rites as syncretisms of what existed all over Africa.' I was forced to arrive at a similar conclusion in examining the origin of the phonological system of Haitian (Alleyne 1966).

10 It is convenient but not strictly acceptable to assume that Krio was brought to Africa by Jamaicans who were 'repatriated' there in the eighteenth century. The dialect brought to Sierra Leone by Jamaicans may have found a similar English-based dialect existing there. My work, as well as that of Ian Hancock, I believe, suggests that the dialect brought by Jamaicans found another similar English dialect already existing in Sierra Leone (See Hancock, App.).

11 Not all linguists are frightened by it. I once heard Angel Rosenblat make a convincing case for parallel development in examining the phenomenon of *seseo* in Latin America.

12 The evidence is in the weight of references in the literature to the need for interpreters both on the coast of Africa, on the ships, and in the New World, and to the variety of African languages spoken.

13 It is also interesting to observe that this picture of a continuum holds good for physiological characteristics such as skin pigmentation and hair texture.

14 The use of 'creole' by the highest circles of French colonists in the French West Indies has been pointed out in Alleyne (1961).

15 'Negro' Spanish has to be more carefully studied. Manuel Alvarez Nazario (1961) has done the preliminary work which should be followed up. See also the review by myself (1963:96).

16 In a sense Haitian and Sranan do have a very important historical connection. And that is their common West African base, plus the broad similarities in the process of development of the socio-cultural context in which they emerged. 'Creole' does not seem to be an appropriate term to refer to this.

G

REFERENCES

Alleyne, Mervyn C. 1961. 'Language and society in St Lucia', *Caribbean Studies* 1:1–11

1963. 'Review of M. Alvarez Nazario, *Elemento afronegroide en el español de Puerto Rico*' (San Juan, Puerto Rico, 1961), *Caribbean Studies* 3:96–8

1966. 'La nature du changement phonétique', *Revue de Linguistique Romane*, 30:279–303

Bloomfield, Leonard 1933. *Language*, New York, Holt

Elkins, Stanley 1959. *Slavery*, Chicago, University of Chicago Press

Forde, C. Daryll 1960. 'The cultural map of West Africa', *Culture and societies of Africa*, ed. by Simon Ottenberg, 116–38, New York, Random House, New York

Goodman, Morris 1964. *A comparative study of creole French dialects*, The Hague, Mouton

Hall, Robert A., Jr. 1966. *Pidgin and creole languages*, Ithaca, New York, Cornell University Press

Herskovits, Melville S. 1942. *The myth of the Negro past*, New York, Harper and Brothers. (Reprinted, Boston, Beacon, 1958)

1947. *Trinidad village*, New York, Knopf

Kroeber, A. L. 1948. *Anthropology*, New York, Harcourt, Brace

Lewis, Oscar 1961. *Children of Sanchez*, London, Secker & Warburg

Nazario, Manuel Alvarez 1961. *Elemento afronegroide en el español de Puerto Rico*, San Juan

Patterson, H. Orlando 1967. *The sociology of slavery*, London, McGibbon and Kee

Smith, M. G. 1953. 'Some aspects of the social structure in the British Caribbean about 1820', *Social and Economic Studies* 1(4):55–79

Thompson, R. W. 1961. 'A note on some possible affinities between the creole dialects of the Old World and those of the New', *Proceedings of the conference on creole language studies (1959)*, ed. by Robert B. Le Page, 107–13 (Creole Language Studies II), London, Macmillan

Turner, Lorenzo Dow 1949. *Africanisms in the Gullah dialect*, Chicago, University of Chicago Press

Whinnom, Keith 1965. 'The origin of the European-based creoles and pidgins', *Orbis* 14:509–27

Weinreich, Uriel 1953. *Languages in contact: findings and problems* (Publications of the Linguistic Circle of New York, 1), New York, Linguistic Circle of New York (Republished, The Hague, Mouton, 1964)

STATEMENTS AND PRÉCIS

HYPOTHESES AS TO THE ORIGIN AND MODIFICATION OF PIDGINS[1]

MARTIN JOOS

For present purposes, 'text' is defined as a stretch of speech considered as repeatable: 'What did he say? – and remember that you are under oath!'

The skeletonizing/skeletonized pattern of pidgin-formation [what is referred to as pidgin defect/deficiency] emerges automatically from lack of actual/prospective social solidarity between speaker and addressee. Is this notion testable?

Hypothesis I: Solidarity and redundancy tend to be in equilibrium, as each promotes the other. [Intra-text redundancies are: phonological, e.g. phonotactic constraints are redundant to distinctive-feature marking; grammatical, e.g. concord is redundant to regime; semological, e.g. idiomatic congruity is redundant to logical collocation.] Equilibrium (mutual promotion between solidarity and redundancy) adds, to the surface value of the message transmitted *this time* (*this* command, *this* piece of information, *this* request or query), the societal benefits of at least *phatic communion* ('we speak the same language' = I can cooperate with him) and (for 'younger addressees') *enculturation* – short-range and long-range survival-values.

Hypothesis II: Incipient solidarity tends to convert pidgin into creole, as (more) redundancies emerge and lexicon is elaborated; styles begin to differentiate and to get stratified; literature can begin.

Hypothesis III: Literature (in the broad sense) tends to convert creole into mature ('natural') language by infusing traditions/values into idiom: CODE[1] (as in 'encoding/decoding') becomes CODE[2] (as in 'ethical code'); the result is now at last *inter-text* redundancy, e.g. *allusion* and *education*.

Hypothesis IV: Hypertrophy of literature (including technical texts) leaves lacunae in personal competences; this tends towards degeneration: language→creole→pidgin→blank.

Hypothesis V: [New problems of institutionalized education.]

Hypothesis VI: [New problems in literature: failure to communicate.]

Hypothesis VII: [General breakdown in the community: riots, etc.]

NOTE

1 Written during a session of the Mona conference by Dr Joos and conveyed then to Dr Mintz, who included it as a footnote in the first draft of his report. The editor is grateful to Dr Joos and Dr Mintz for agreeing to its inclusion in this section of the book.

A NOTE ON REDUCTION AND EXPANSION
IN GRAMMAR

JAN VOORHOEVE

All specialists seem to agree that creoles originated in pidgins. All seem to agree that pidgins are characterized by a process of reduction or simplification. This does not mean that pidgins are simpler languages than non-pidgins, but that they seem simplified in comparison to their model. Creoles are characterized by a subsequent process of expansion. This again does not mean that creoles are more complex than non-creoles, but only more complex than their pidgin origin.

The process of reduction can be studied in the case of pidgins only if their model is known. We are sure, for example, that Djuka Creole in Surinam served as model for the trade language between Djuka Bush Negroes and Trio Indians. We may study the process of reduction in comparing this trade language with Djuka Creole. We cannot, however, study the process of expansion by comparing the same languages.

In comparing, say, French creoles to French, nothing can be learned about the process of reduction. We assume a process of reduction between French and an unknown historical French pidgin (if this ever existed), and a process of expansion between this unknown French pidgin and the actual French creole. Every speculation about a process of reduction between French and French creole is based on false grounds. We are not even sure of the existence of an intermediate French pidgin stage. If the theory of relexification holds true, a historical Portuguese pidgin has been relexified in contact with French masters, without passing through an intermediate French pidgin stage.

Finally, the process of expansion cannot be studied directly in the case of creoles, insofar as the preceding pidgin stage disappeared from the scene as soon as it became the mother tongue of a community of speakers.

Something may be done by means of historical reconstruction, but the main thing, if we want to understand these processes, must be to study them as they take place. The Cameroons pidgin is a case in which expansion could be studied for example, because it is becoming the first language of children of plantation workers.

LANGUAGE CONTACT AND THE PROBLEM
OF CONVERGENT GENERATIVE SYSTEMS:
CHINOOK JARGON[1]

MICHAEL SILVERSTEIN

For about a hundred years, the Chinook Jargon was the principal medium of trade communication on the North-west Coast, among speakers of various European and American languages, such as English, French, Nootka, Chinook and Salish dialects. The lack of prestige, capability of being rapidly acquired, and limited social uses of Jargon indicate that its very general structural features are not to be sought in any one of the component languages to the exclusion of the others. Such an 'imperfect acquisition' of one of the grammars involved for example in a 'creole' is not the basis of the Jargon, since the reason for its existence is a lack of linguistic and social subordination of any of the parties entering into the contact situation.

For purposes of limited communication, we can expect a highly redundant extralinguistic context, and hence the Jargon can seize on this freedom from lexical specification to increase the grammatical information of each minimal unit. As Horatio Hale noted (1890: 18–19): 'We frequently had occasion to observe the sudden change produced when a party of natives, who had been conversing in their own tongue, were joined by a foreigner, with whom it was necessary to speak in the Jargon. The countenances, which had before been grave, stolid, and inexpressive, were instantly lighted up with animation; the low, monotonous tone became lively and modulated; every feature was active; the head, the arms, and the whole body were in motion, and every look and gesture became instinct with meaning. One who knew merely the subject of the discourse might often have comprehended, from this source alone, the general purport of the conversation.'

Examining the Chinook Jargon sentences of native speakers of different languages, we find a tremendous range in phonetic realizations of the same items, not consistent with one sound system for Jargon. Each speaker apparently uses the native system minus the highly specialized sounds, e.g. Chinook /ƛ'/→[tl] or [kl], Nootka /n'/→[n]. Thus Jargon phonology is in some sense closer to universal phonetic categories. Similarly, the grammatical oppositions of Jargon sentences show an elimination of such features as dual number or gender-classification of Chinook, or progressive/non-progressive verb-phrase constructions in English. Indeed, this total generality of the grammatical system of Chinook Jargon makes it possible to construct sentences with a reduced grammatical system of any of the component languages.

This can be illustrated with Chinook and English, whose deep structures at a comparable depth of analysis look totally different, Chinook being an 'ergative' language and English an 'objective' one. From either of these deep structures, for a given sentence, by universal reductions in surface specializations, we can arrive at an acceptable Chinook Jargon sentence. This leads us to believe that in learning a jargon the speaker of a given language learns the interlingual *signans* to be identified with his native *signatum* and uses an attenuated form of his native grammatical knowledge to produce jargon sentences.

In this view, it is the psychological economy of such a situation, not the economy of any abstract grammatical structure we might construct for Chinook Jargon itself, which explains the facts. Therefore the equation of 'linguistic community' with 'people with the same grammar' seems to be too strong here.

NOTE

1 Summary of an unpublished paper.

REFERENCE

Hale, Horatio 1890. *A manual of the Oregon trade language or 'Chinook Jargon'*, London, Whittaker and Co.

THE QUESTION OF CREOLIZATION IN
PUERTO RICAN SPANISH[1]

DAVID LAWTON

From the evidence available, it appears that Puerto Rican Spanish did not pass through a pidgin stage and become a full-fledged creolized language as such a language is defined by Bloomfield (1933:474) and Hockett (1958:423). It is suggested that the reason for this lies in the system of colonization used by the Spaniards whose socio-political policies were different from those of the English in the British colonies of the West Indies. The Spaniards stressed early conversion to Christianity, Spanish as the vernacular, and permitted racial assimilation. Further, the slave population did not so increase as to outnumber the non-slave during the nineteenth century in Puerto Rico.

Today, in Puerto Rico, linguistic artifacts remain only in Taíno Indian place-names and Africanisms in folklore and references to personal characteristics. Phonologically, creolizations are evident in such items as [-x-] in *carro* > [káxo], [-l-] in *izquiérdo* > [iskyɛldo], -ø ~[-ɛ] in *noche* > [noč]~[nóčɛ], -ø- for [-d-] in *pelado* > [pɛláo], and in the pitch accent on such free morphemes as *mangó* [maŋgó], *bembú* [bembú], *mariyandá* [mariyandá].

It is suggested that 'creolization' as a conceptually and linguistically adequate term applied to languages whose lexemic bases are of English, Dutch, Portuguese, Spanish, or other derivation be examined from three viewpoints: (1) linguistic, (2) sememic, (3) sociolinguistic. Such an approach would enable one to reach interesting conclusions about aspects of creolization which involve morphological changes in free forms, and syntactic changes in phrase structure.

In Puerto Rico, given the above criteria for typological decisions, the suggestion is that two major languages – English and Spanish – in contact are producing a creolized language whose intonation is Spanish, whose lexicon is drawn from English and Spanish, and whose morphology shares inflectional features of the two languages. Spanish verbs have consistent inflectional loss of the final consonant where such consonants normally occur. Spanish nouns sometimes have no final vowel as in *noč* for *noche*, or the final vowel may be [ə]. English verbs are simplified to a single form (*have* < *has*; *walk* < *walks*), and English nouns have Spanish inflections as in *rufo* 'roof'. Syntactically, *el* and *la* 'the' are in free variation. Word order increasingly tends to follow the English pattern.

Sociolinguistically, speakers who have Spanish as a first language, but have acquired or are acquiring the emerging 'dialect' do not function effectively on an intellectual level in either Spanish or English.

In general, there is no hard evidence to support the thesis that creolized languages emerge from pidgins, although this thesis is apparently accepted by many linguists. Oddly enough, however, few if any of these linguists have approached the problem from the viewpoint of the specialist in second, or foreign, language learning, which gives a different insight into the problem of deciding the source of creolized languages. From what we know of language learning, it would seem more plausible to argue that creolized languages do indeed develop from contact situations rather than from pidgin languages.

The present paper presupposes the idea that creolizations need not be historically derived from pidgins. The general question of pidgin theory will be dealt with in another paper.

NOTE

1 Summary of a paper of the same title presented at the conference.

REFERENCES

Bloomfield, Leonard 1933. *Language*, New York, Henry Holt
Hockett, Charles F. 1958. *A course in modern linguistics*, New York, Macmillan

IV

PROBLEMS OF HISTORICAL
RECONSTRUCTION

INTRODUCTION

Two main questions confront the creolist, where historical reconstruction is concerned: how have languages known to be pidgins and creoles developed? have other languages, not directly known to be creoles, actually developed in the same, or a related, way?

Historical research and general theory are inseparable in either case. Findings as to known pidgins and creoles are evidence with which to evaluate competing models of the formation of such languages – crucial evidence, because most of the cases on which theory can be tested have probably already occurred. In assessing the claim (or denial) that a language has a 'pidgin in its past' (e.g. Germanic (Hall 1966:190)), theory must provide the criteria.

Cassidy presents representative examples and general principles from his analysis of the lexical development of Jamaican Creole English. Progress is slow – 'each word has its own history' and there are nearly five centuries of history to trace – but the work is exemplary and essential. Cassidy makes clear that the history is *socio*linguistic. Time, place, numbers, sources of settlement and contact were determinants of what occurred, and knowledge of social history is as necessary as knowledge of the European dialects and African languages spoken by sailors and slaves. Cassidy makes equally clear that the possibility (and necessity) of using the methods of comparative and historical linguistics is quite independent of the claim that the European-linked creoles are to be classified genetically with branches of Indo-European, or even to be classified genetically at all (Hall 1966:119–20). Reconstruction and its interpretation are controlled by socio-historical context; one's assumptions and knowledge about that context are an independent factor. Cassidy himself works on the assumption that Jamaican Creole was formed by lexical replacement from a prior Portuguese pidgin.

Having specified methodological canons for historical inference from Caribbean creoles, Cassidy takes up cases representative of the three possible types of lexical provenience: Portuguese pidgin (e.g. *savvy*, *pickaninny*), English pidgin (e.g. *by-and-by*, *too-much*), and native New World (e.g. possibly *coco*). Provenience is not inferred for its own sake, but to lay the basis for (1) retracing the steps by which the pidgin developed lexically, and (2) inferring the lexical characteristics universal to pidgins, as governed by a particular relation of linguistic means to social needs. While the first goal requires comparison of related languages (as the paper illustrates), the second requires comparison of (more or less) unrelated languages. Such comparison is broached in an appendix, where Melanesian Pidgin English (Neo-Melanesian), Chinese Pidgin English, French Pidgin Sango, and English Pidgin Chinook (Chinook Jargon) are compared in terms of the 100-item list of basic vocabulary devised by Morris Swadesh for glottochronology. (Note that the percentages, as between Neo-Melanesian and English, are counts of etymological connection, not of equivalence of form and meaning as required in glottochronology.)

Frake's firsthand study of Philippine Spanish-linked creoles shows that lexical origins may be important to general theory in quite a different, unexpected way. As Frake observes, it may be the case that 'languages don't mix' – and the basic vocabulary of Zamboangueño is after all 90% or more Spanish in provenience – but Zamboangueño displays a remarkable integration of Spanish and Philippine elements.

Frake emphasizes first two historical puzzles: the primary Philippine element is much greater in Zamboangueño than in the other dialect, Manila Bay Creole, and it does not come from the Philippine languages with which Zamboangueño is now in contact. Beyond the particular history, there is the striking outcome of that history. Because Zamboangueño is no longer in contact with either of its original sources, its original lexical strata can be discerned much more easily than often is the case with creoles (e.g. Jamaican Creole). And the relations among these strata violate conventional wisdom as to the nature of lexical borrowing; there is here evidence of a creative use of diverse linguistic means that may prove unique to creolization.

The Spanish and Philippine elements in Zamboangueño do not sort according to respectively foreign and indigenous referents, or domains of reference. They are integrated within one and the same domain, such as personal pronouns. And, Frake concludes, Philippine provenience is in effect a marked feature of a Zamboangueño word. The Philippine form will designate (if there is a contrast with a Spanish form) the marked member – something smaller, closer, lesser, female, junior, or plural, where referential meaning is involved. Where social meaning (speech style) is involved, the Philippine form (if there is a choice) will be the one for unmarked normal conversation, the Spanish alternate the form for formal situations or politeness.

Zamboangueño raises questions as to the adequacy of current linguistic theory of markedness, since it separates as marked in one respect (referential meaning) and unmarked in another (social meaning), rules which have clearly the same motivation, an association of lesser evaluation with the Philippine form. At the same time Frake's work shows the productive application of markedness to an entirely new problem. His findings must be tested in all other situations of creolization and suspected creolization. The nature of the marking itself speaks volumes as to the process of adaptation by which the new language was formed.

Notice that the glottochronological lists provided by Frake support his finding that the language is a true creole. The glottochronological distinctiveness of pidgins and creoles was first discovered by Hall (1959), who showed that Neo-Melanesian had diverged from its base language, English, at a rate far exceeding that normally found. Whereas glottochronology normally errs in the direction of underestimating the time depth of divergence between languages, here it greatly overestimates the time-depth. The list of Spanish glosses provided by Samarin (1967) shows 78 clear equivalences to Frake's Zamboangueño list, or a divergence of 821 years and a date of A.D. 1147. Calculations could vary according to choice of items on the Spanish list; and if one includes two or three cases where Spanish forms are listed before Philippine synonyms in Frake's list, there are 81 equivalences, or 668 years of divergence and a date of A.D. 1300. On either count, the divergence is greater than the time depth actually possible (after A.D. 1500).

Goodman calls to our attention a type case of what a 'mixed language' often has been taken to be, the vocabulary of one language in the grammar of another.

Much more needs to be known about Mbugu, through field work and comparison, but essential facts are clear: the grammar and grammatical affixes are mostly of Bantu origin, the basic vocabulary mostly is not (and has significant affinity to the Iraqw and Cushitic language groups). As Hoenigswald brings out in his contribution in the final part of this book, a genetic classification can be assigned, by relying on basic vocabulary, but that fact shows how little a genetic classification explains.

Goodman himself does not wish to say that Mbugu reflects pidginization and subsequent creolization, for in its morphological complexity it differs from the known contemporary cases involving Bantu languages (e.g. Fanagalo). One might invoke pidginization at an earlier time, followed by a 'decreolization' such as Jamaican Creole is now undergoing in relation to English, or such as Katangese Swahili probably is undergoing with respect to the East Coast Standard. One could still wonder (as does Goodman) as to the identity of a third party, such as Whinnom's theory makes necessary to the crystallization of a true pidgin. On the other hand, the mutual convergence suggested by Goodman might be supported by appeal to the type of case described from India by Gumperz and Wilson, or constructed as a model by Southworth.

Mbugu clearly reflects some form of creolization, if the term is to have any linguistic significance. The puzzle it provides points up the need for more information, including ethnographic study that could provide clues as to the social process that has brought it into existence. The case points up also the need for comprehensive analytic typology of situations in which 'hybrids' can emerge. Together, specific research and comparative theoretical work may yet enable us to choose among models to explain a case such as that of Mbugu.

Southworth's study of Marathi is intended precisely as a contribution toward a more adequate sociolinguistic typology of such outcomes. Such a typology is needed for creole studies, but it is needed as well in general linguistics, and may be the special contribution that creole linguistics makes to the general field. Hall has cited the exceptional status of pidgins against use of glottochronology; the estimates of the latter cannot be validly employed if one does not know whether or not pidginization has occurred in the history of a language, and for most languages we have no documentation to tell us. The difficulty attaches to more than glottochronology. Often the internal relations of a series of languages can be ascertained only on the basis of vocabularies (that being the only evidence at hand). To group languages on the basis of the proportion of vocabulary they share is to make (only inexplicitly) the same assumption as glottochronology, namely, that lexical change has some normal relation to time. Many other studies and inferences one wishes to make in historical linguistics implicitly assume that pidginization and creolization have not intervened. If cases of prior pidginization and creolization cannot be detected, much more than the 'upstart', glottochronology, is in trouble. Consider Hall's own reconstruction of a proto-Pidgin English (1966:119). If this 'proto-language' in fact was once Afro-Portuguese, rapidly relexified with English items, as Cassidy assumes, how can the results of the comparative method itself give any more assurance than Hall finds for glottochronology?

It seems likely, in fact, that the formation of true creoles (as distinct from the general processes of simplification and expansion) is a quite unusual thing, dependent upon specific kinds of social relationship, such as would not have obtained, for example, among hunting-and-gathering peoples such as the North

American Indians. Intertribal trading leading sometimes to the formation of pidgins, yes, as Chinook Jargon seems to attest; but not plantations or mines or conquest such as would lead to a creole as the primary language of a subordinate group. In general, it would seem that in favorable cases our knowledge of linguistic relationships and social history would permit us to decide whether or not creolization had occurred.

Even so much has been doubted or denied by some linguists. And not all cases would be favorable. It remains that pidgins and creoles show the study of linguistic change without reference to its social context to be untenable. The several individual processes of change may be universal, sound change, analogy, borrowing, and the like, but their patterning and the patterns they produce in a language, and among the components of a language, covary with social factors. We must become able to identify a 'Marathi-type' of change, a 'Mbugu-type', a 'Zamboangueño-type' perhaps – or whatever the names of the best type cases will prove to be. The key will be to view change from the standpoint of the linguistic repertoire of a community or group, and in terms of the maintenance (or loss) of group identity, whether between communities and societies, or between strata within them.

Southworth reviews the social history, and the linguistic characteristics, that make Marathi a candidate for what he calls a quasi- or *semi*-creole (or an instance of 'X creol*ized* Y'), and for whose formation he provides an important model in his conclusions. The model that he suggests for Marathi has analogues to the probable development of Hawaiian Pidgin-Creole English, to the creolization of English that is occurring now in the Northern Territory of Australia, and in part to the 'decreolization' so salient in Jamaica. A pidgin, a creolizing pidgin, and a decreolizing creole could well have been contemporary, differently located in social and geographical space. Either the indigenous internal social stratification, or intermarriage, or both, might have provided for the third party that Whinnom's theory would require. (Southworth points out that the Dravidian-speaking communities into which Indo-Aryan came probably were already internally stratified, readily permitting forms of diglossia, if such did not already obtain (personal communication).)

An important point is that there is a continuum with regard to the phenomena that imply creolization, both within the Marathi area, and among the Indo-Aryan languages as a whole. In short, the Indo-Aryan languages in India appear to illustrate precisely the perspective of this volume: a quite general process of sociolinguistic change, the specific outcome of which is determined by, and differs according to, specific socio-historical factors.

Painstaking historical work is greatly needed for all pidgins and creoles. The main lines along which such work is now proceeding are shown by the reports with which this part concludes. There is first of all work from the standpoint of the formation of a single pidgin or creole, as in Kaufmann's study of major lexical strata in Chinook Jargon, and in Tsuzaki's concern for the provenience of features distinctive of Hawaiian Pidgin-Creole English, where a given language is compared to all known or possible sources. There is exploration in detail of the role of some one source, as in Father Daeleman's discoveries as to African (Kongo) correspondences, including tone, to elements in Sranan, the Creole English of Surinam, and the investigations into earlier French dialects by Valdman (see the fourth section of his precis in Part II). (One must also note here the historical significance of fresh analysis of the underlying structure of a source that puts comparisons in a new light (Berry, Valdman).) This is comparison of several creoles presumed to have a common historical source, with the goal of reconstructing that source, a kind of work pioneered in modern terms by Goodman (1964) for the French creoles, employed by Cassidy here as a necessary methodological step, and pursued for its own sake in Hancock's ambitious study of English-based Atlantic creoles. Finally, there is also comparison across the lines of the major source, or base, of a language to reveal features common to several creoles and independent of a given 'base' (Taylor).

These lines of work complement each other, obviously enough in regard to the first three types, but also in regard to the fourth. More than one source for a feature may be possible, and rival possibilities must be assessed (as Cassidy shows with lexical elements). The force of evidence such as Taylor presents can quite be missed (e.g. Goodman 1964:630) if one thinks only in terms of a single line of origin, as the framework of genetic classification tends to induce. The grammatical parallels that Taylor has shown to cut across English or French base for Caribbean creoles equally require historical explanation. Indeed, the ultimate goal, as Cassidy states, is not provenience and retrospective classification as to origin, but integration and 'prospective' classification as to type of formation. The distinctive interaction of diverse lines of linguistic tradition, after all, is what constitutes pidgin and creole studies a field.[1]

NOTE

1 On the view of historical linguistics and linguistic change presupposed here, cf. Hymes 1964:450–2, and the major theoretical study by Weinreich, Labov and Herzog (1968).

REFERENCES

Goodman, Morris F. 1964. *A comparative study of Creole French dialects*, The Hague, Mouton

Hall, Robert A., Jr. 1959. 'Neo-Melanesian and glottochronology', *International Journal of American Linguistics* 25:265–7

    1966. *Pidgin and creole languages*, Ithaca, Cornell University Press

Hymes, Dell (ed.) 1964. *Language in culture and society*, New York, Harper and Row

Samarin, William 1967. *Field linguistics*, New York, Holt, Rinehart and Winston

Weinreich, Uriel, William Labov, and Marvin I. Herzog 1968. 'Empirical foundations for a theory of language change', *Directions for historical linguistics: a symposium*, 97–195, Austin, University of Texas Press

TRACING THE PIDGIN ELEMENT IN JAMAICAN CREOLE

(*with notes on method and the nature of pidgin vocabularies*)

FREDERIC G. CASSIDY

The following is a very small sample of a larger study upon which I am engaged. It follows up what I began in a paper written for the 1962 Brazzaville Conference on Multilingualism in Africa (Cassidy 1964). When that paper was under preparation certain ideas about the relationships of various Caribbean and other creoles were just beginning to take shape.[1] Probably the name of Douglas Taylor (1951, 1956) should head the list of those who further clarified these ideas, but Wallace Thompson (1961), Keith Whinnom (1956), and William Stewart (1962) must also be mentioned. Nor dare we forget the earlier study of Papiamento by Navarro-Tomás (1951) which showed how lexical replacement[2] occurs, and how a creole based on one language can be made over under the influence of another.

Today the thesis is defensible that in modern times, from the second half of the fifteenth century when the Portuguese began trading along the West African coast, there came into existence a trade language drawing its European elements basically from Portuguese; that the Portuguese themselves carried this in the sixteenth century to East Africa, India, and the China Coast; and that when other Europeans began to follow their lead they used this Portuguese Pidgin (PgP)[3] as the basis and model for pidgins of their own. English, French, and Dutch Pidgins then, to mention only the most important, appear to have been formed partly by direct adoption of PgP elements, partly by replacement of others, and partly by new addition from various sources.

In my 1962 paper I gave evidence to suggest that this was the case with regard to the origins of English-based creoles in the Caribbean. By comparing common features of Jamaican Creole (JC), Sranan (Sr), and Cameroons Creole (CamC) I argued for the existence of an English pidgin (EngP) used along the African coast before the settlement of the Caribbean colonies.[4] This contact-language would naturally be brought with slaves to the New World and become the source of English-based creoles. In addition to PgP, Pg elements already a part of this EngP would be brought to the Caribbean, along with African and English ones. Transportation of EngP to the new colonies would inevitably lead to a phase of change and growth as American Indian languages entered the picture and many new situations required linguistic expression. The culmination of the new phase would be creolization as the plantation system became fully established, African languages faded out, and the new generations could speak only such English as the situation permitted them to learn.

In the present paper I shall attempt no more than a sketch of what will require far more detailed study before it can be formally presented. I think it may be possible ultimately to separate, out of JC as it exists today, those elements which belonged to PgP and EngP. The latter I assume to have been virtually the same throughout the English settlements when they were being founded; and I would attempt to separate them from the creole elements added later, many of which are the same in all the English-speaking colonies, though others have developed locally in separate colonies. In other words, I am interested in seeing how a pidgin becomes a creole, and think that the stages of this process can be followed by the normal methods of comparative linguistics.

The Jamaican situation

The situation which makes this possible is an interesting one. In JC as it exists today we have an example of a spectrum of variant features. At one end of this spectrum is a very conservative, countrified, socially isolated form of speech, a true creole, preserving the best evidence of pidgin connections. This has been little influenced until recently by the 'good English' of schools, printing, and upper-class speakers because of the long-standing and virtually unbridged social and economic gap existing between the small-settler and village dweller, on the one hand, and on the other the urbanized, educated, professional or upper business type, who speaks with local colonial variations a form of Standard English (StdE) representing the other end of the language spectrum. Speakers are distributed at any and every point along this spectrum, though most may be seen to lean one way or the other according to background and occupational demands. The details of this spectrum, both linguistic and social, have not been fully described, though David DeCamp is now engaged on this task. It should also be mentioned that almost any Jamaican can speak or at least understand more than one type of the local speech, moving to left or right along the spectrum as occasion requires. When native upper-class Jamaicans protest that they cannot understand the Creole, this is usually a defensive attitude expressed to outsiders which yields to the practical needs of the marketplace.

The existence of this spectrum in Jamaican English is clearly the result, I think, of two conditions: first, for JC to have come into existence the slaves must have been brought in such large numbers, so rapidly, and from so many places, that they could neither preserve a functioning African language nor learn English fully. The demographic evidence bears this out. The English took the island in 1655; three years later the Negro population was 24%. But seven years later a charter was granted to the African Company to supply 3,000 slaves per year, and the trade increased rapidly. By 1673 the Negro population had risen to 53%, by 1690 it was 82%, and by the time the colony was only half a century old, it had risen to more than 90%, below which figure it has never fallen since. The policy was to mix slaves of differing African languages as a precaution against insurrection. Thus everything was in favor of the expansion of the first pidgin language, perhaps adequate to handling raw field hands on plantations, into the new and much fuller native speech of Jamaican creoles. A further evidence of the conditions under which JC was formed is the large number of Africanisms that survive in it even today, after more than a hundred years since immigration from Africa ceased (Cassidy 1961:394–7).

The second condition leading to the existence of the present spectrum is that the Creole speech became so fully established that it could function adequately alongside British English or even in defiance of it. There is ample evidence that this was indeed the case on plantations during the eighteenth century. The island-born whites became so creolized in their habits and speech that those not sent to England for education never did learn to speak proper British English. Yet however firmly the Creole was established, it has always been thought of as intrinsically less good (not to say *bad*), and every kind of preferment has been correlated with some command of educated English. The profound social changes of the past thirty years have accentuated this further: upward movement in Jamaican society, accelerating rapidly, has distributed speakers in ever larger numbers along the language spectrum toward the educated end. The features distinctive of Creole are therefore more and more mixed with those of this 'good' or Standard English as an increasing amount of the latter is adopted by speakers traditionally attached to the former. The gradual *restructuring* of Creole under the influence of Standard is now giving way to *displacement* of Creole by Standard. Enough of the older Creole features, phonological, grammatical, and lexical subsist, however, so that not only they but even certain pidgin features can be detected.

Method pursued

My method of arriving at originally pidgin features will be by comparison. One should have in mind the formation of PgP, probably beginning in the fifteenth century; of EngP beginning in the sixteenth; the introduction of EngP to the Caribbean in the seventeenth century; and its subsequent development into various creoles: Jamaican Pidgin (JP) becoming JC (with similar forms in Barbados, the Lesser Antilles, Guyana, Trinidad, etc.), Sranan (Sr), Saramaccan (Sara), Gullah (Gul), and so on. Especially useful will be the comparison between JC, a developed creole, and Sr, a conservative one.[5] Though these two creoles must have been virtually identical in the pidgin stage, they have evolved in decidedly different ways. Once the English took Jamaica (1655) it remained thereafter in their hands: JC has had three hundred uninterrupted years under the influence of English. Borrowing must have been vigorous during the first stages of creolization, to judge by the large number of English dialectal and archaic words it preserves today (Cassidy 1961:397).

Surinam, on the other hand, settled only three years before (1652), was given up to the Dutch after fifteen years and has remained Dutch almost without interruption since. The English-based pidgin or creole established in Surinam survived this change of government, for the Dutch did not seek to eradicate or replace it. (Nonetheless, it has undergone a good deal of influence from the Dutch language, increasingly visible today.) Sr, cut off thus from its connection with English, has remained relatively undeveloped and archaic – much closer in form than JC to its early state. Thus it may be used to show, in many cases, what JC would have been like in its early phase, hence the features which have changed in JC, and the respects in which they have changed. Features common to JC and Sr, barring evidence to the contrary, may be taken as going back to the time when the two separated. By further comparisons with English-based and other pidgins and creoles it should be possible to arrive at some original PgP elements, some elements both of archaic English and of African source belonging to EngP, and some New World features that entered as creolization proceeded. Since morphological features have already been outlined by others, I shall limit myself chiefly to lexical ones.

The following working assumptions or principles are used:

1. Among related P/Cs, historical priority sets up the sequence of possible influence. (PgP developed before other European P/Cs, hence it is more likely to have influenced them than the contrary. In a pidgin of mixed European components, a Pg element would presumably be the oldest.)

2. Among P/Cs of the same base, the one having the greatest number of conservative forms is an index to the earlier state of its less conservative cognate(s). That P/C in which more words have been replaced is the less conservative. (So Sr and Sara are guides to the earlier stages of JC.)

3. When P/Cs of the same base preserve related forms in similar meanings, these are presumably among the earliest or most basic components of the ancestor. (So cognate English forms in Sr and JC probably go back to EngP.)

4. In P/Cs of the *same* base, the presence of different words with similar meaning implies replacement (in the less conservative). In P/Cs of *different* base, the presence of different words with similar meaning implies either replacement or new borrowing.

5. In any P/C, the components which have undergone the most phonetic erosion and the most semantic development (in which the basic meaning has been notably enlarged or extended) are probably among the oldest.

6. Very simple or essential conditions of communication lead to the emergence of components having the same or similar meaning even in totally unrelated P/Cs. (The limits of this coincidental expression may be approached by comparing the structures and lexicons of P/Cs unrelated in place, time, or base language. See last section and App.)

7. Reinforcement of elements in a P/C is a possibility not to be overlooked; it depends on new contact with speakers of the language which originally furnished the P/C component. (Reinforcement presumably works against replacement.)

Words of Portuguese Pidgin provenience

The Pg element in JC could have entered as a part of PgP spoken in the Caribbean: it formed the basis of Papiamento (Pap). The English learned sugarcane culture from the Portuguese and spread it from Barbados to their other colonies. When the English took Jamaica some Portuguese Jews opted to stay in the island rather than follow the Spanish to Cuba, where their religion was not tolerated. These people might have been a direct source, or their Pg might have reinforced words that entered otherwise. But some of the 'Portuguese' Jews were actually Spanish who, expelled from Spain in 1492, moved to Portugal and respelled their names. In any case, Le Page has shown (1960:5–7) that these people were less numerous in Jamaica than some have thought – not a very likely source of Pg elements in JC. This may be the place to mention also Voorhoeve's (1960) evidence that the Jewish planters in Surinam, though they came early, were never numerous, and that their relative numbers decreased. Thus one should probably not look to direct contact with colonial speakers of Pg but to an earlier and more basic influence: that of PgP.

If PgP had left its traces in JC there are still two routes by which they could have come: directly from PgP to the Africans later transported to Jamaica, or indirectly to them as an element adopted into EngP when that was formed. And if the latter, the learning of this PgP element could have taken place in Africa or later in Jamaica. Finally, some PgP, but much more likely EngP, could have been brought by the Surinam settlers.[6] The problem is to sort out these possibilities and arrive at the best probability.

SAVVY Taking the bull by the horns, let us look first at *savvy*, to know. This has found its way into most European-based pidgins and creoles; it has even become an established English colloquial word since the eighteenth century, associated with the broken English of foreign places (OED). On sheer grounds of form it could equally well come from Pg or Sp *saber*, but since it turns up in Africa, India, China, and the South Pacific, places chiefly outside the Spanish orbit, Pg is by far the more probable. In English-based pidgins and creoles it has a *b*-form *sabby* and a *v*-form *savvy*. Either *could* have come from Spanish, which has [b]; the *b*-form is more likely from Pg. The *v*-form implies influence from Fr *savoir*: compare Fr Guiana *save*, Martinique *sav* (Goodman 1964:71); besides, Englishmen more often knew Fr than Sp or Pg. Further, these *v*-forms come later.

I take it that *sabe* was one of the earliest PgP words: it survives in the Crioulo of Guiné (Wilson 1962:19) as *sibi*; in St Thomas, Principe, and Annobón as *sebe* (Valkhoff 1966:106, etc.); in Pap as *sa* (no doubt reinforced by Spanish). It surely entered EngP: the *b*-form has left traces in Krio and Biafran Creole as *sabe*, in CamC as *sæbi-am*; also in Chinese Pidgin (ChP) and Beach-la-Mar (BlM) as *sabby, sabe*. But these last two also have the *v*-form as do Hawaiian 'Pidgin' (HawC) and Neo-Melanesian (NeoM), all probably brought in later *via* English.

The fact that both JC and Sr have *sabi* indicates that the word came to the Caribbean no later than the mid-seventeenth century, *via* PgP or EngP or both. It was certainly a component of JaP. However, it should be noted that the presence of *b*-forms in JC and Sr does not guarantee direct Pg source: /v/ was absent from English creoles in the Caribbean; /b/ took its place in borrowed words, and JC /v/ is a recent acquisition. During the development of JC, *sabi* has been largely replaced by *know*. *Mi no sabi* would be archaic today; *mi no nuo* is normal JC.

PICKANINNY   A word of similar history is *pickaninny*, usually meaning small, and by no means limited to children or even living things; in JC, *píkni*, earlier *píkini*. This *could* be from Sp *pequeñino* but since it is found in Africa, the South Pacific, and China, Pg is pretty surely the source. Pg has two forms, both with pidgin descendants: *pequeno*, small and diminutive *pequenino*. The latter is clearly the source of Eng *pickaninny*, used in the American colonies and in slave days given its narrower meaning, a black child. The OED first example is from Barbados (Ligon 1657:48), refers to a newborn baby, and says that its mother called it so. This form is found in ChP, BlM, and NeoM, *pikinini*. The shorter form appears in Sr *pikíen*, with second-syllable stress like Pg *pequeno*, and in both meanings, 'small' and 'small child'. In CamC it is *píkin*, with first syllable stress, probably due to English influence, and also with the English limitation of meaning to offspring, though this is extended metaphorically. In Jamaica there are an older form *píkini* (more likely reduced from *pikinini* rather than coming from *pequeno*) and the current form *píkni*, which most often refers to small offspring. In sum: PgP probably contained both *pequeno* and *pequenino* with the broad meanings 'small' and 'very small'. Both entered EngP, which however ultimately favored the long form and spread it, especially in the Pacific, in the narrower meaning of 'small child'. Judging by the closeness of the Sr form and meaning to Pg, it and the Jamaican forms came while the PgP influence was still strong in EngP. After *piccaninny* became a StdE word, its prestige and the general analogy of English stress patterns produced the first-syllable stress of the JC (and CamC) forms.

DOBL   An example of a word which might ultimately come from any of several sources is JC *dobl*, though proximately it reflects English *double*. Sp has *doble*, Fr *double*, Dutch *dubbel*; Pg has *dobro*, but since the l/r alternation is very common in Caribbean Creoles the Pg form is not excluded as a possible source. The uncertainty is resolved by Sranan, which has *dóbru*. Though this *might* be another case where /r/ took the place of /l/, its closeness to the Pg form seems inescapable. If JC and Sr had the same origin it was, for this word, PgP, and the present JC *dobl* is an English replacement of *dobro*. Sr *dóbru*, by the way, has resisted the influence of Du *dubbel*. CamC has *dəbu*, more plausibly explained by the /u/ standing for vocalized /l/ than by loss of Pg /r/-in other words, by coming directly from English. Nevertheless it could be a replacement of PgP by English, as JC *dobl* is.

CANDLE   One good indication of Pg source for a JC word would be that the Pg original had entered some African language as a loan, especially if this occurred outside the Pg orbit. An example is the simple word *candle*, JC *kyanggl*, with the Creole phoneme /ky/ for Engl /k/ and the common substitution of /g/ for Engl /d/ before /l/. In short, the word is proximately from English. Pg has *candéia* or *candéa*, a lamp. (All forms go back to Lat *candela*, of course.) In the Ghana language Twi, which was not under direct Pg influence, two distinct forms have been borrowed ɔ-*kanéa*, which is probably earlier judging by its form, and *kàndère*. The first probably represents Pg *candéia*, the second Engl *candle*. Since more JC words are drawn from Twi than from any other African language (Cassidy 1961) it is *possible* that either or both loans were brought to Jamaica. PgP certainly contained a word meaning candle or lamp; it is equally certain that *candle* in some form was in the vocabulary of EngP, and would have come to Jamaica. What light is cast by Sranan? Its form is *kándra*, which might at first seem to reflect Pg *candeiro*; but the stress shows English influence, /r/ regularly substitutes for /l/ in Sr, and the final /a/ probably reflects an African language requirement. Twi words, for example, cannot end in a consonant, except /n/ – hence *kàndère* from Engl *candle*. In Sr therefore the ultimate source is almost certainly English. Probably the PgP forms were displaced in Africa within the English orbit and it was Twi *kàndère* and Engl *candle* that produced the Caribbean Engl forms. It is likely that early JP had *kandra* or *kandre*, later creolized as *kyanggl*.

PAEN   A word found only once in the Ja literature and now out of use is *paen*, a sort of petticoat worn by slave children. This is ultimately from Pg *panho*, the older form of MnPg *panno* (Sp *paño*, Fr *pagne*, Du *paan*). The JC form is difficult to explain unless it reflects an old sense of *pane*, a panel or strip of cloth, which OED documents to the end of the sixteenth century. The MnE dictionary form is *pagne*, from Fr, which is in turn from Sp *paño*, cloth, corresponding to Pg *panho*. Presumably the Pg took this word to Africa with the trade article it named. Sr *pángi* probably represents the Pg and suggests that the word existed early in JC but must have been replaced by *shift*, *petticoat*, or some other word still current in Jamaica. Incidentally, *panho* survives in the BIM form *pam*.

SAMPATA   Another curious JC word is *sampáta*, a rough sandal, appearing in numerous folk-etymologized forms: *sand-patta*, *sand-platter*, *slampatta*, *shampatta*, etc. This clearly goes back to Pg *sapato*, but how the nasal got into the first syllable, and why the /s/ and /š/ forms, is the question. This time Twi and Temne (Sierra Leone) furnish the solution since they borrowed the Pg word: Twi as *asepâteré*, Temne as *a-sampatha* (Wilson 1962:48). This explains the final syllable (Eng -*er* is regularly reduced to /a/ in JC). The /m/ or /n/ of *sam-*, *san-*, probably consonantizes the nasalization common in Twi; it developed also in the Temne form, more likely the direct source for the JC forms. Most initial unstressed syllables of African words taken into JC were lost (aphetized) as here. The /s/ varying with /š/ is probably also of African source though more difficult to assign and not supported by the Twi or Temne forms. It is altogether possible – even likely – that in the Caribbean there was some reinforcement from Sp *zapato*. English influence appears only in the several attempts to rationalize the strange word. The most recent is *shoe-patta*. In sum, *sampáta* is ultimately a Pg word which came *via* Africa into JC, brought by the slaves, not the English.

Words of English Pidgin provenience

The English element could have come into JP as a part of EngP (most probable) or as a part of current English used during the establishment of the colonies (probable also). In either case there was no doubt some lexical replacement of earlier Pg elements. Reinforcement of some features may well have occurred: many of the British colonists spoke archaic dialects.

GLASS, TUB   Such words as JC *glaas*, glass, and *tob*, tub, must have been quite independent of Pg influence even though already known in Africa before the settlement of the English Caribbean colonies. These name common trade objects; they have no Romance language cognates; and both were borrowed into Twi, respectively as *giraasè* and *topóo*. Here they acquired the final vowels which turn up in Sr *grâsi* and *tóbo*. An important part of the decreolization of JC has consisted in the loss of these final vowels when, as here, they are unsupported by StdE.[7] Hence JC *glaas* and *tob*. The fact that the stressed vowels of these words are phonetically regular for JC removes the unlikely possibility that they might be recent acquisitions. They are undoubtedly old, going back to Africa to the Twi or EngP forms.

BY-AND-BY   An example of a phrasal word which has found its way into many pidgins and creoles is *by-and-by*, in JC *bambai*, now a trifle archaic but common in narration. In the U.S. it is familiar in the Uncle Remus tales as *bimeby*. The Sr form is *bámbai*. I have no evidence from Africa but would be surprised if it were not in Sierra Leone and Ghana, at least. It has certainly gone all over the Pacific: BIM *bymby*, Pitcairnese ˌ*bem'bei* (Ross 1964), NeoM *baimbai*, etc. Possibly this is a replacement of Pg *logo*, which Whinnom (1956) has noted in Macanese as a not quite regular verbal marker of futurity. I do not know of *bimeby I come* having turned into a regular future construction, but one can see how it well might, so far as the meaning is concerned. Merely as a time expression *by-and-by* has gone throughout the English orbit and no doubt came into JC via EngP.

TOO-MUCH   Another English phrase reduced to a word with change of sense is *too much*, JC *túmoch*, meaning 'very much'. The sound /č/ was not adopted at first; its presence is evidence of continued or more recent influence from English. Sr has *túmusi* or *túmsi*, CamC has *tuməš*, ChP has *too-muchee*, NeoM has *tumas*; but BIM is closer to StdE with *too-much*, and JC, which was once like Sr *túmusi*, long ago lost the final /i/ and acquired /č/: *tumoch*. As an EngP word, however, in all these Creoles it still means not 'too much' but 'very much, a great deal'; even when the form approaches StdE this sense remains the mark of pidgin origin. To mean 'too much' JC uses *too* by itself with emphatic stress: *tú – yu tú lob moni*, you love money too much.

SOMETHING   A similar skewing of meaning is found in the word *something* used to mean merely 'thing'. This too must have been in EngP: it is found in JC, Sr, BIM, and NeoM among others. In MnE the word is frequently reduced in pronunciation to *sunthin, suthn, sumpm*, etc. Since it was no doubt learned by pidgin speakers from heard forms, it is no surprise to find it reduced in Sr to *sani*. Thus JC *sinti* or *sinting*, the older forms; the more modern *somting* shows influence of StdE and perhaps of writing and school emphasis. BIM and NeoM *samting* similarly. The concept of 'thing' would seem to be a basic one, hence should be found in pidgins generally. I have no evidence on how 'something' came to express it in EngP.

A word of New World provenience

Let me take as a last example a word which entered English creoles and perhaps EngP in the New World colonies. In JC the edible rootstock or tuber of *Colocasia esculenta*, the *taro* or *kalo* of Polynesia, is called *koko*; the plant likewise. Where this word comes from is uncertain; perhaps from Polynesia as did other JC plant names: breadfruit, roseapple, Otaheite apple, and so on, for special kinds imported. It could have been a West Indian creation perhaps connected with the *coco* of *coconut*, itself probably from Pg. And there are other possibilities (Cassidy–Le Page, 1967). The important point is, however, that the root was taken from Jamaica to Africa (Christaller 1933:243) and the name borrowed into Twi as *kóokó, koókó*; perhaps also Fanti *koko*. The first record of the word is from Jamaica, 1740; but similar araceous roots were in use from before the end of the seventeenth century – specifically *taya*, of Tupí or Cariban origin (Sloane 1696:62). Since Sr has *taya* but not *coco* in this sense, *coco* is probably later and perhaps came into existence in Jamaica. It may have been too late to enter EngP; there is no question that it was an important word in early JC, that it went abroad and was productive.

Conclusions and a codicil

To follow the emergence of a creole lexicon through elaboration of the underlying pidgin is a slow business. As Gilliéron put it, 'every word has its history' – and each has to be followed separately. Yet our study of the lexicon's development as the pidgin becomes a creole necessarily brings into focus the important social dimension, showing the numerous currents and cross-currents that mingled to produce the creole. Our few examples should serve to present the problems involved, a method of attacking them, and some tentative solutions. But one further important point needs to be made.

Though similarities in pidgins are often the result of their being historically related, and though the replacement of words and phrases in them as they come under later influences cannot be denied, some of the similarities are just as certainly due merely to their simplicity. Any language at its inception is necessarily simple; if a number of pidgins develop independently out of similar demands of communication, it should be no surprise that they arrive at similar linguistic solutions. In short, in a pidgin one reaches a sort of core: the universals of communication. The test of this notion is to compare pidgins that arose independently. Up to a point one might expect totally unrelated auxiliary trade-languages – say Chinook jargon (Chk), Chinese Pidgin, and Sango – to require, hence to produce and contain, many words and expressions for the same operations and 'ideas'. Both syntax and lexicon, reduced to essentials, should share a good deal of semantic ground. Lists such as Hancock's[8] show the common element in *related* creoles; another kind of test should come from comparing the *unrelated* pidgins or creoles just mentioned.[9] But before making this test it would be interesting to consider in a purely speculative way what an initial pidgin situation might require.

If the typical situation which produces a pidgin is contact for purposes of trade between speakers of mutually unintelligible languages, there would initially be a good deal of gesture accompanying speech; this would be reduced, though probably never eliminated, as the pidgin took shape. Gestures would accompany the first exclamations: shouts to attract attention (arm waving), more restrained greetings (salutes, beckoning to approach, signs to stop, parting signs). Exclamations or interjections expressing surprise, fear, amusement, warning, anger, might be accompanied by gestures – which can only be guessed at. (Cf. 'Lexicon' in Reinecke, and Silverstein, in this volume, on Vietnamese Pidgin French and Chinook Jargon respectively.) (Nevertheless, many interjections are culture-oriented, traditional, and tenacious. A number traceable to Twi and related languages are still current in Jamaica; they certainly came with the slaves and must have been present in JP.)

A first necessity in communication is to establish identifications for the two parties: the 'inside' group, natives or home people, and the 'outside' group, the travelers or in-comers. Thus the Portuguese and Negroes in Africa, the English and Chinook on the North Pacific coast of America, and so on. Not only would names for the interlocutors be necessary, but very soon a pronominal system to designate a *thou-you* party and an *I-we* party, switching identities according to who was speaking. (Gestures here, of course.) These would probably precede the designation of a *he-they* party. (Further elaboration, as for gender or case, would be unlikely, and indeed seems to be lacking even in European-based creoles.) Though the first pronouns would doubtless be personal, a demonstrative would soon be necessary to point out people and things. If more than one developed, the first distinction to be expressed would probably be of the near-far, *this-that* type.

Among relationships early needing distinctive forms would be statements, questions, commands or requests. At first, prosodic features and voice qualifiers would no doubt be sufficient: changing the 'tone of voice', a statement becomes a command (firm, short), a request (soft, wheedling); it becomes a question through intonation or some added functional marker, perhaps one showing affirmation or negation – ideas which would also have to be verbalized early. (Yes-no gestures already conventionalized by the parties might differ but could be readily learned.) Interrogative words would soon develop (who, when, why, what-kind), and an asseverative word or phrase (sure, the-very-same, just-so).

The next necessity would be to name things (cf. *something* above), especially trade objects, again with gestures (food, water) or by exhibiting and naming them (mirrors, axes, cloth, etc.). These last would be in the 'outside' language; local foods and products unfamiliar to the outsiders would first have the native names (e.g. *ananas*), later perhaps outside ones (*pineapple*). Trade objects sought by the outsiders would probably take outside names (pepper, gold, sandalwood) which the insiders would have to learn in order to trade in them.

Names for local trade objects would vary according to their region or origin, hence be the least general or predictable part of the pidgin lexicon.

But apart from trade objects there would have to be names for certain essential things or concepts – among the most basic: *Natural materials* (water, stone, fire, etc.); *Physiography* (mountain, river, sea, etc.); *Time* (yesterday, month, midday, etc.); *Numbers* (at least to ten, and some multiples); *Weights and Measures* (bundle, jarfull, arm's-length, etc.); *Colors* (black, white, and a few more of broad range); *People, kinship* (father, sister, son, child, chief, hunter, etc. – a large group); *Body parts* (head, hand, heart, eyes, teeth, skin – a large group); *Weapons, utensils* (spear, gun, stool, pot, hammer, bottle – a very large group); *Clothing* (shoes, shirt, dress, bracelet, etc.); *Foods* (general word, meat, oil, sugar, beverage, etc.); *Animals, birds, plants, fish*; *Buildings* (house, door, cart, bridge); *Emotion, morality* (fear, joy, lying, theft).

The number of words used currently in these and other categories would depend on the degree of communication established, but even the most elementary trade could hardly be carried on without words for times, places, quantities, and the things being traded: nominal ideas. Similarly certain verbal ideas would have to be expressed: *Thought, communication* (know, say, name, forget, etc.); *Bodily motion* (walk, stand, come, etc.); *Physical action* (do, give, eat, cut, look, strike, fasten, etc. – a very large group); *Feelings* (want, like, wonder, distrust, etc.). The idea of equating need not at first require formal expression: things can be associated with properties by simple juxtaposition without a copula. (In English-based creoles when a copula is used it is not necessarily *be*; *stand, stay, sit*, and other words may be made to serve. The sense for this goes back very far: Romance *estar, essere, être*, etc. < Lat. *stare*, and Germanic **standan-*, both < IE **stā-*. Pidginized reductions of *estar* and *stand* could meet again in the coincidence of *sta*.)

The relationship of modification would soon demand expression, not necessarily in terms of adjectival or adverbial words: formal marking of the parts of speech as in full languages should not be expected – on the contrary, functional shift without change of form. Basic modifying ideas would include: *Size* (big, long, wide, thick, deep, etc., and their contraries); *Quality* (good, strong, heavy, hot, quick, sweet, etc., and their contraries); *Condition, manner* (ill, asleep, dead, wet, hard, etc., and their contraries; also blind, deaf, dumb, crippled, etc.); *Shape* (round, long-and-thin, straight, flat, wavy, etc., many with contraries); *Position, direction* (high, far, seaward, upstream, at-center, above, etc., and their contraries – a large group); *Time* (right-now, in-a-while, after, always, etc.).

Once pidgins were established, the next step would no doubt be toward refinements or elaborations, to sharpen distinctions and avoid confusion. Verbal expressions would at first lack tense or aspect, getting along with time-words: You come yesterday/today/tomorrow/all-the-time/no-more. But certain common verbs might quickly attain auxiliary status as markers of performance (do, make, put) or of change (go, come) and would form paradigms in combination with other verbs. Thus the idea of burning could be expressed directly by converting *fire* to a verb, or making the phrase *do fire*: burn. Quantities, qualities and the rest would need to be compared, hence the use of increment words (more, most, very, much, plenty, all-gone). Plurality, at first indicated with number-words, might acquire some particle as a general marker.

Non-factual statements (possibilities, contingencies, etc.) are necessary to even very elementary communication. One would accordingly look for use of words meaning if, perhaps, provided that. Causal relationships similarly should demand words meaning because, and adversative or concessive relationships words meaning but, although, yet. (Note that some of these English words originated as phrases; similar combinations could be and are made in pidgins.)

Some metaphors or descriptions are so obvious that they may be expected to turn up by coincidence or 'reinvention' in unrelated pidgins. They are formed simply by combining noun (or verb) and modifier: iron rope = chain, dog child = puppy, tree skin = bark, shut ear = deaf, boat tail = rudder. From phrase to word is a common semantic track. Pidgins may be expected to use the more basic word-forming devices: echoism, phonosymbolism,[10] iteration (Cassidy 1957), to express repetition, continuation, increment, essentiality, and the like.

The point of this rather lengthy speculation is that solutions proposed by invoking replacement or 'relexification' must not be too easily accepted. Independent expression of corresponding features becomes more and more possible as communication is reduced to essentials. A basic lexicon may be increased by combination along expectable lines: some coincidences need not indicate historical relationship. What the basic requirements of a pidgin are can be established up to a point by the kind of comparison I have suggested. The relative age of individual items, or the stage at which they must have entered the pidgin, can be judged by frequency or extent of use, and this in turn by the changes they have undergone: development of syntactic markers by reduction of full words (e.g. verbs to auxiliaries, pronouns to particles), or elaboration of the range of meanings – e.g. the sense of *go, leave* becoming *part with* (emphasizing separation) then *remove, throw away, turn out, get rid of* (involving causation), all which meanings developed when Fr *marche* was taken into Chinook Jargon.

In trying to get at what any specific pidgin was like, its process of formation, one has to work not only with specific data, historical and linguistic, but also to keep in mind what may be established about pidgins as a linguistic type

Structures that grow up in pidgins may reflect the underlying structure of related base-languages, but they may also testify to still deeper universals of human communication.

APPENDIX

Following is Swadesh's corrected list of 100 basic words, taken from Hall (1959:265), with Hall's list of equivalents from NeoM, to which I have added (so far as I could find them) the equivalents in three other P/Cs: ChP, Sango, and Chk. Sources are Hall 1959; Mihalic 1957; Leland 1910; Samarin 1967; Taber 1965; Gibbs 1863; Shaw 1909. Though the list was made for use in glottochronology and is not so used here, it is adopted for convenience, merely as a very limited but well known sample.

Comparison of the lists shows considerable differences. In NeoM the English element is 94%, Pg 1%. In ChP the Engl element is 85% (probably more, since 20 words could not be found in the glossary or texts). In Sango 99% are African (3 words could not be found; 3 others are French loans). In Chk 70% are Chinook and other Indian languages (5 words could not be found, 20 are English, 9 French loans). Clearly, European contact with Sango has been too recent and limited to be profound; in Chk it was much greater at the time of full use, and the jargon has since died, displaced by English; the other two pidgins were English based with small elements from other sources (Pg, Chinese, Melanesian, etc.).

The native numerals are preserved in Sango and Chk, not in the others. Surprisingly, the Fr element in Chk and Sango is almost wholly for parts of the body (in the sample lists). It is also surprising to find Engl loans in Chk for such basic things as stone, fire, moon, smoke. The differences from pidgin to pidgin are no doubt due to 'social' factors inherent in the type of contact which produced the language.

Simple referents are not necessarily expressed by simplexes: complex words or phrasal constructions appear in all these P/Cs (least in Sango). Notable are the use of -fɛlə (or -pɛlə) as an adjective marker and -im as a transitive verb marker (NeoM). An interesting coincidence occurs in the descriptive phrases or metaphors used for *feather*: grass-of-bird (NeoM), hair-of-bird (Sango), leaf-of-bird (Chk), which can hardly be historically connected. Similarly the words for *heart* emphasizing its audible pulsation: clock (NeoM) and *túmtum* (Chk); and for *bark*: tree-skin (Chk) and skin-of-tree (NeoM).

Despite the simplicity or broadness of the concepts expressed in this list, some words in the P/Cs are even broader: *sun* also means day and day's time (ChP, NeoM); *chuck* means not only water but river, lake, etc. (Chk). Also, certain words quickly enter into combination: *diwaj*, tree (NeoM), foot-of-tree for root, skin-of-tree for bark; *stick*, tree (Chk), *stick-skin* for bark, tree-under-at-ground for root.

Affixal elements are apparently added to loans to adapt them to the receiving language: -ee, -(l)o in *bitee, doggee, dielo, longo*, etc. (ChP). All lists include examples of iteration and echoism, though in non-coinciding positions in the lists.

It would obviously be of value to carry the comparison much farther, extending the lists to 500 or more items, though at present the available sources are quite unequal. Some further coincidences would no doubt appear;

not many should be expected, however. Nevertheless, it would become more apparent that when the basic vocabulary is separated from the rest, it will contain, in historically unrelated P/Cs, some evidences of obvious and expectable metaphor. Much further work is needed before firm conclusions can be drawn from this kind of comparison.

Engl	NeoM	ChP	Sango	Chk
1 all	ɔlgedər	állo	kóé	kónaway
2 ashes	æšıs			
3 bark	skın bilɔŋ diwaj			stick skin
4 bell	bɛl	bell	ngbéréná	tíntin
5 big	bıgfɛlə	big	kótá	hyás
6 bird	pıǧın	bird(ee)	ndɛkɛ	kalákala
7 bite	kajkajım	bitee	tɛ	múckamuck
8 black	blækfɛlə	black	(zo) vɔkɔ́	klale
9 blood	blʊt	blood	ménɛ́	pilpil
10 bone	bon		bíó	stone
11 burn	bonım	burn	zɔ́	mamook piah
12 cloud	klawd		pupu	smoke
13 cold	kilfɛlə	colo	dé	cole, tshis
14 come	kəm	li	gá	cháhko
15 die	daj	dielo	kúí	mémaloost
16 dog	dɔg	doggee	mbo	kámooks
17 drink	drıŋk	dlinkee, haw	yç	múckamuck
18 dry	draj	dly	kúrú, ole	dely
19 ear	ir	ear	mɛ́	kwolánn
20 earth	grawn	glound	sése	íllahie
21 eat	kajkaj	chowchow	kóbe, tɛ	múckamuck
22 egg	kiaw		párá	le sap
23 eye	aj	eye	lé	seáhhost
24 fat	gris	fat, glease	mafuta	glease
25 feather	gras bılɔŋ pıǧın	fedder	kɔ́á tí ndɛkɛ	kalákala yaka túpso
26 fire	fajr	fai, hwan	wá	píah
27 fish	fıš	fishee	susu	pish
28 fly	flaj	fly	uru	kawák
29 foot	fʊt		gɛ́rɛ́	le pée
30 give	gıvım	pay	fú	pótlatch
31 good	gʊdfɛlə	how, ut	nzoní	klose, kloshe
32 green	grinfɛlə	gleen, lu	vɔkɔ́ kété	pechúgh
33 hair	gras bılɔŋ hɛd	hair	kɔ́á	yákso
34 hand	hæn	hand, sho	mabɔ́kɔ	le máh
35 head	hɛd	headee	li	la tet
36 hear	hirım	hearee	má	kúmtuks kopa kwolánn
37 heart	klak	heart	coeur	túmtum

H

Engl	NeoM	ChP	Sango	Chk
38 I	mi	my, woa	mbi	níka
39 kill	kɪlɪm	killee	fáa	mamook méma-loost
40 know	save	savvy	hínga	kúmtuks
41 leaf	lif	leaf	kugbé	túpso
42 lie (down)	slip		sέ	mitlite
43 liver	lεwa		bέ	
44 long	lɔŋfεlə	chee, longo	yɔngɔ́rɔ	yóutlkut
45 louse	laws			éenapoo
46 man	mæn	man	kɔ́lĭ	man
47 many	plεntɪ	plenty	míngi	hyiú
48 meat	abus		yama	ítlwillie
49 mountain	mawntεn	mountain	hɔ́tɔ́	la mónti
50 mouth	maws	mout'h	yángá	la boos
51 name	nem	name	éré	nem, yahhul
52 neck	nεk		gɔ́	le cou
53 new	nufεlə	new	finí	chee
54 night	najt	naiti	bí	pólaklie
55 nose	nos	peedza	hɔ̃	nose
56 no	no	na	non	wake
57 one	wənfεlə	one piecee	ɔ́kɔ́	ikt
58 person	mæn na meri	person	zo	tíllikum
59 rain	ren	lin	ngú	snass
60 red	rεdfεlə	hoong, lüt	bingbá	pil
61 road	rod	load	lége	wáyhut
62 root	fʊt bɪlɔŋ diwaj		mbutu	stick kéekwulie kopa íllahie
63 sand	wajtsæn		pupusése	póllalie
64 see	lʊkɪm	look-see	baa	nánitsh
65 seed	sid		lé	
66 sit	sindawn	sittsik	dutí	mítlite
67 skin	skɪn		póró	skin
68 sleep	slip	shleep	lángó	móosum
69 small	lɪklɪk	likki	kété	ténas
70 smoke	smok	smoke	gúrú	smoke
71 stand	sænəp	stand	lutí	mítwhit
72 star	star		tɔngɔro	tsiltsil
73 stone	ston		témέ	stone
74 sun	sən	sun	lá	sun, ótelagh
75 swim	swɪm	swim	sa (ngu)	sítshum
76 tail	tel	tail	dambá	ópoots
77 there	εm . . . lɔŋ hæf	t'hat-side	ká	yáhwa, kopáh
78 this	dɪsfεlə	t'his	sɔ́	ókoke
79 thou	ju	nee	mɔ	míka
80 tongue	təŋ	tongue	méngá	la lang
81 teeth	tit	teeth	pémbέ	le táh
82 tree	diwaj	tlee, shoo	kéké	stick
83 two	tufεlə	two	óse	mokst

Engl	NeoM	ChP	Sango	Chk
84 walk	wɔkə-bawt	walkee	tambéla	klatawa kopa la pée
85 warm	hɔtfɛlə	warm	wá	waum
86 water	water	wata, shooey	ngú	chuck
87 we	mifɛlə	woamun	í	nesíka
88 what/which	wɔnəm	wat, kali, shummo	yɛ̧, wa	íktah
89 white	wajtfɛlə	white	vurú	t'kope
90 who	husæt	who	yɛ̧, wa	kláksta
91 woman	meri	nüyen	wálē	klóotshman
92 yellow	jɛlə		bingbá	káwkawak
93 talk	tɔk	talkee	tɛnɛ	wáuwau
94 moon	mun	moon	nzɛ	moon
95 round	rawnfɛlə	lound		loló
96 full	fʊləp	full	sí	pahtl
97 knee	skru bɪlɔŋ lɛg		genou	
98 claw	kapər bilɔŋ fɪŋgər bɪlɔŋ lɛg	claw	nzɛné	
99 horn	kom		dede, nzá	stone
100 breast	susu		libɛ́, mɛ	totóosh

ABBREVIATIONS

BlM	Beach-la-Mar	Krio	(Sierra Leone) Krio
CamC	Cameroons Creole	NeoM	Neo-Melanesian
Chk	Chinook Jargon	OED	Oxford English Dictionary
ChP	Chinese Pidgin	Pap	Papiamento
EngP	English Pidgin	P/C	pidgin or creole language
Gul	Gullah	PgP	Portuguese Pidgin
HawC	Hawaiian Creole	Pit	Pitcairnese
JC	Jamaican Creole	Sara	Saramaccan
JP	Jamaican Pidgin	Sr	Sranan Tongo

NOTES

1 Bailey 1953, a MS, did not get much circulation, though I had been fortunate enough to see it. Hall 1966 was not yet in print and I did not see the MS till 1965.

2 The recent term 'relexification' seems to me both clumsy and unnecessary. The established term 'replacement' is quite adequate and does not have the sweeping implications of the other.

3 Abbreviations are listed at the end of the paper (p. 219).

4 Two papers circulated in preliminary form at the Conference on Pidginization and Creolization in Jamaica, 1968, deserve notice here: Ian F. Hancock's parallel lists of corresponding words in six English-based creoles (450 item's), and checklist of 15 features characteristic of 13 creole languages, French-,

English-, Dutch-, and Iberian-based; and Dr Voorhoeve's summary of a paper by Jan Daeleman, S.I., Kongo words in Saramaccan Tongo.

5 Sources used for Sranan are Focke 1855, and Echteld 1962.

6 In 1675 a group of 250 planters arrived in Jamaica from Surinam, bringing 950 Negroes and 31 Indians (presumably Arawak), and settled the 'Surinam Quarters', in present Westmoreland parish. They are a possible source of PgP, EngP, and African and Indian language features.

7 A very few have survived as archaisms today: *rata*, rat, *wara*, what, etc. (Cassidy 1961:403).

8 See note 4 above.

9 See App.

10 Phonosymbolism differs from echoism in not being an imitation of a sound heard, but the use of sounds to suggest more abstract notions: stop sounds for abruptness, ablaut series to show gradations of one kind or another, close versus open vowels (or front and back) correlated respectively with small versus large, or other properties, etc. (Sometimes called sound-symbolism, or less satisfactorily phonesthesis.)

REFERENCES

Bailey, Beryl L. 1953. 'Creole languages of the Caribbean area', M.A. thesis, Columbia University, New York

Cassidy, Frederic G. 1957. 'Iteration as a word-forming device in Jamaican folk speech', *American Speech* 32:49–53
  1961. *Jamaica talk*, London, Macmillan
  1964. 'Toward the recovery of early English-African pidgin', *Symposium on multilingualism* (*Brazzaville 1962*), 267–77 (Conseil Scientifique pour Afrique–Commission de coopération technique en Afrique, publication 87), London

Cassidy, Frederic G. and Le Page, Robert B. 1967. *Dictionary of Jamaican English*, Cambridge, Cambridge University Press

Christaller, J. G. 1933. *Dictionary of the Asante language, called Tshi* (*Twi*), Basel, Evangelical Missionary Society

Echteld, J. J. M. 1962. *The English words in Sranan*, Groningen, Wolters

Focke, J. C. 1855. *Negerengelsch woordenboek*, Leiden, Van den Heuvell

Gibbs, George 1863. *A dictionary of Chinook jargon or trade language of Oregon* (Smithsonian Miscellaneous Collections, 161), Washington, Smithsonian Institution

Goodman, Morris 1964. *A comparative study of creole French dialects*, The Hague, Mouton

Hall, Robert A., Jr. 1959. 'Neo-Melanesian and glottochronology,' *International Journal of American Linguistics* 25:265–7
  1966. *Pidgin and creole languages*, Ithaca, Cornell University

Leland, Charles G. 1910. *Pidgin-English sing-song*, London, Kegan Paul

Le Page, Robert B. 1960. *An historical introduction to Jamaican creole* (Creole language studies I, pt. 1), London, Macmillan

Ligon, Richard 1657. *A true and exact history of the island of Barbados*, London, Moseley

Mihalic, Francis 1957. *Grammar and dictionary of Neo-Melanesian*, Techny, Illinois, The Mission Press

Navarro-Tomás, T. 1951. 'Observaciones sobre el papiamento', *Nueva revista de filología hispánica* 7:183–9.

Ross, Alan S. C. 1964. *The Pitcairnese language*, London, André Deutsch

Samarin, William 1967. *A grammar of Sango*, The Hague, Mouton

Shaw, George C. 1909. *The Chinook jargon and how to use it*, Seattle, Rainier

Sloane, Sir Hans 1696. *Catalogus plantarum quae in insula Jamaica sponte proveniunt*, London, Browne

Stewart, William 1962. 'Creole languages in the Caribbean', *Study of the role of second languages*, ed. by F. A. Rice, 34–53, Washington, Center for Applied Linguistics

Swadesh, Morris 1955. 'Towards greater accuracy in lexicostatistic dating', *International Journal of American Linguistics* 21:121–31

Taber, Charles R. 1965. *A dictionary of Sango*, Hartford, Connecticut [Duplicated at Hartford Seminary Foundation for the U.S. Office of Education]

Taylor, Douglas 1951. 'Structural outline of Caribbean creole', *Word* 7:43–59
　1956. 'Language contacts in the West Indies', *Word* 12:391–414

Thompson, R. Wallace 1961. 'A note on some possible affinities between the creole dialects of the Old World and those of the New', *Proceedings of the conference on creole language studies*, ed. by R. B. Le Page, 107–13 (Creole Language Studies II), London, Macmillan

Valkhoff, Marius F. 1966. *Studies in Portuguese and creole*, Johannesburg, Witwatersrand University Press

Voorhoeve, Jan 1960. Personal letter to F. G. Cassidy

Whinnom, Keith 1956. *Spanish contact vernaculars in the Philippine islands*, Hong Kong, Hong Kong University Press
　1965. 'The origin of the European-based creoles and pidgins', *Orbis* 14:509–27

Wilson, W. A. A. 1962. *The crioulo of Guiné*, Johannesburg, Witwatersrand University Press

LEXICAL ORIGINS AND SEMANTIC STRUCTURE IN PHILIPPINE CREOLE SPANISH

CHARLES O. FRAKE

Introduction

ABSTRACT

Work still in progress on the Zamboangueño dialect of Philippine Creole Spanish has revealed that Zamboangueño differs from other dialects of Philippine Creole Spanish and from European-based creoles in general in having a prominent and clearly identifiable non-European lexical component whose distribution across semantic domains is not that normally associated with lexical borrowing.[1] With reference to general problems of language contact and creole language properties, this paper is concerned with establishing the uniqueness of Zamboangueño among dialects of Philippine Creole Spanish, with identifying the sources of the non-Spanish portion of the lexicon, with interpreting the distribution of non-Spanish forms as semantically marked and stylistically unmarked, and, finally, with comparing the semantic structure of Zamboangueño with that of its Spanish and non-Spanish source languages. The results conflict with a number of accepted assumptions about lexical borrowing. A brief historical account precedes the discussion of these problems.

HISTORY OF PHILIPPINE CREOLE SPANISH

The linguistic consequences of Hispanicization in the New World and in South-east Asia differed markedly. In the Philippines, in spite of rapid Spanish conquest, almost total conversion to Christianity, and over three hundred years of occupation, the Spanish language failed to establish itself. Spanish replaced no indigenous Philippine language, and its role as an auxiliary language was sufficiently tenuous that it was quickly supplanted by English after the American occupation. Today, apart from the many Spanish loan words in Philippine languages and a few speakers of Spanish in the upper echelons of society, the linguistic legacy of Spain in the Philippines is limited to the existence of several communities that speak a Spanish creole language as their mother tongue. Philippine Creole Spanish is not simply a Philippine language with unusually heavy Spanish lexical influence, nor is it Spanish with a large number of Philippine loan words. It is a distinct language, easily distinguishable from both its Romance and its Austronesian progenitors. As

implied by the name I have given it,[2] Philippine Creole Spanish shares enough
in common with the classic creoles of the Caribbean that no one, whatever his
position in the various controversies on the subject, would, I think, challenge
its assignment to the category 'creole language'.

Philippine Creole Spanish (PCS) known in the Philippines as Chabacano,
is spoken as the native language of over 10,000 people in several communities
along the south shore of Manila Bay and by over 100,000 people in Zamboanga City and Basilan Island in the southern Philippines.[3] In the latter region,
an area of great linguistic and ethnic diversity, it is also an important auxiliary
language. The speech of Zamboanga (Zamboangueño, Zm) represents a
distinct dialect of PCS opposed to the dialects of Manila Bay Creole (MBC)
spoken in Ternate (Ternateño, Tr), Cavite City (Caviteño, Cv), and formerly
in the Manila district of Ermita (Ermiteño).[4] Speakers of MBC dialects can
be found in a number of other towns in Cavite Province and once inhabited
the fortress island of Corregidor at the entrance to Manila Bay (B&R 36:237)[5]
(See map.) These locations suggest something about the origin of PCS.
Zamboanga, from the beginning of the seventeenth century to the end of the
nineteenth, was a Spanish military base in the heart of hostile Moslem territory. Cavite was a major naval base and shipyard; Ternate and Corregidor
guarded the entrance to Manila Bay against Moslem raiders (de la Costa
1961:475, B&R 36:237). Although I have found no direct evidence in the
Spanish literature, it seems reasonable to assume that Spanish military and
naval units in the Philippines, known to have been composed of men speaking
diverse Philippine languages and officered by Spaniards, used a Spanish-
based pidgin for communication. Such a military pidgin could then have been
creolized as the native language of certain permanent garrison communities.

Also suggestive is the name of the Philippine town of Ternate, and here we
have both historical documentation and local Ternateño tradition to go on.[6]
There is an island named Ternate in the Moluccas which in the sixteenth and
seventeenth centuries was the focus of Portuguese, Spanish, and Dutch
conflict for control of the spice trade. In 1606 the Spanish captured Ternate
from the Dutch, who had recently taken it from the Portuguese, but evacuated
it, as well as their garrison in Zamboanga, in 1663 in order to concentrate forces
in Manila against a threatened attack by the Chinese warlord Ch'eng-kung
(Koxinga). From Ternate the Spanish took with them a group of local
Christians, the product of Jesuit missions in the Moluccas and northern
Celebes, and allowed them to settle in a community, which they named
Ternate, near the Tagalog town of Maragondon on Manila Bay. These people,
known as Márdikas,[7] frequently served in Spanish military forces and were
responsible for guarding the entrance to Manila Bay. Soon after their arrival
they are reported to have spoken their 'own language', Tagalog, and Spanish
(B&R 24:41, 36:237). Eventually they came to speak PCS as their native

tongue. Whether they invented it themselves, adopted a Philippine Spanish
military pidgin, or relexified a Portuguese pidgin brought from the Moluccas
is not known. The Spanish reoccupied Zamboanga in 1718. I have not yet

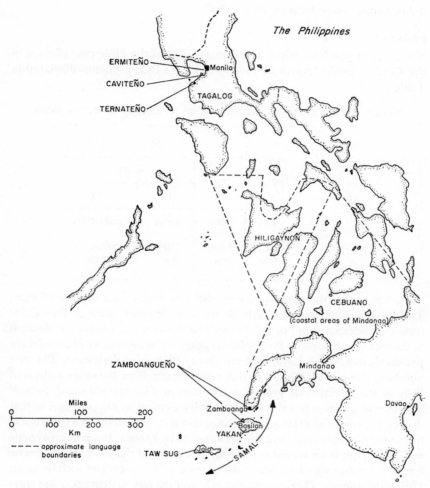

Philippine Creole Spanish dialects and relevant Philippine languages.

found any record or tradition of native creole-speaking Márdikas participating
in the resettlement of Zamboanga and thereby being responsible for the
establishment of a dialect of PCS there. Zamboangueño may represent an
independent creolization of the same pidgin. The similarities between Zm

and MBC, however, are such to make historically independent derivation from Spanish unlikely. I have yet to find any texts, descriptions, or even explicit reference to Zamboangueño in Spanish sources other than statements such as Montero y Vidal's (1888:37): 'Los naturales de Zamboanga hablan todos, aunque imperfectamente, español'.

PROBLEMS

The kinds of problems raised by a consideration of the Philippine element in the Zamboangueño lexicon are illustrated by the PCS pronouns displayed in Table 1.

TABLE 1. *PCS pronouns: full nominative stylistically unmarked forms*

| | Sg | | Pl | |
| | | | MBC | |
person	PCS	Zm	Cv	Tr
1	yó	kamí	nisós	mihótroh
1 + 2		kitá		
2	tú	kamó	busós	buhótroh
3	ʔéle	silá	ilós	nótroh

First note that the plural pronouns differ in each of the dialects of PCS. The Cv and Tr forms all clearly derive from Spanish although they differ from the corresponding Spanish forms. The Zm plural pronouns are identical to those of several Central Philippine languages. The attributive forms of these plurals (ʔámon, ʔáton, ʔínyo, ʔíla) are also of Philippine derivation. The first question, then, is: (1) 'Does Zm differ consistently from the other dialects of PCS in the direction of greater penetration of Philippine-derived forms?' The second question is: (2) 'If the Philippine element in Zm is unique to that dialect, then from what language or languages does it derive?' The latter question cannot be answered from the data present in Table 1, but it is answerable and the answer is somewhat surprising. It will reveal that, not only is Zm no longer in contact with Spanish, it also is not in effective contact with its major Philippine sources. There is consequently no difficulty in delimiting Zm from other linguistic codes used in the area – there is no Jamaica-like continuum from creole to standard language (cf. Cassidy and Le Page 1961) – and one can consider separately the contact situation which gave rise to the language and the contact situation which is influencing it now.

Thirdly consider the distribution of Philippine-derived pronouns within this semantic domain. The set of personal pronouns in Zm, as in most

languages, shares distinctive semantic, syntactic, and morphological properties, and its members appear with high frequency. It certainly cannot be considered a peripheral part of the lexicon. Yet the set is split right down the
middle between forms of Spanish and of Philippine derivation. We all
know, of course, that 'languages don't mix', but this must be one of the closest
existing approximations to that impossible state. The third question, then, is:
(3) 'Is this a random mixture or is it interpretable according to some kind of
pattern? If so, is this pattern one that corresponds to traditional theories of
lexical influence of one language upon another?' Such questions are not so
easily raised with other creole languages. The prominence and clear identifi-
ability of the Philippine element, not only in Zm lexicon, but also in syntax,

TABLE 2. *Zm second person pronouns: stylistic alternatives*

		Sg	Pl
respect	+	?usté	?ustédes
	o	tú	bosótros
			kamó
	—	?ebós	

morphology, and phonology, contrast sharply with the situation of Caribbean
creoles where the nature and extent of African substratum influence, if any, is
a subject of considerable controversy. Actually there are two aspects to this
question. One concerns the distribution of Philippine forms across semantic
domains, across the topics of speech if you will. The other concerns the distribution of Philippine forms across speech events, the selection of expressions
at a level of formality appropriate to the situation. In pronouns the latter consideration is relevant to the selection of second person forms, members also
of the domain of terms of address (see Table 2). (Note the discrepancy in
respect usage between the singular and plural pronouns and the participation
of a single Philippine form in the latter set.)

Finally, note the semantic structure of the domain of pronouns in Zm. The
differentiation between the inclusive and exclusive first person plural and the
lack of sex or gender distinctions in the third person correspond to Philippine
rather than Spanish pronominal semantics. On the other hand, the differentiation of second person pronouns by the degree of respect they accord the addressee is more complex than that of any Philippine language I know of, and
it does not quite correspond to Spanish usage. Comparisons of the semantic structure of given domains in Zm with corresponding domains in Spanish

and in the relevant Philippine languages provide a nice test case of language-culture interrelations. Speakers of Zm share a basically common culture with other Christian Filipino groups and with them belong to the same larger sociopolitical system. Yet unlike other Christian Filipinos, they do not speak one of a closely related group of Austronesian languages. To the extent that the semantic structure of a language mirrors culture, one would expect the semantics of Zm and other PCS dialects to resemble that of Philippine languages rather than that of Spanish. This is something that cannot be tested with Caribbean creoles since their speakers no longer participate in the same culture and society as their West African ancestors.

Data relevant to each of these questions will now be presented.

Data

COMPARISONS BETWEEN ZM AND MBC

The two variants of PCS share enough distinctive differences from regular Spanish or regular Philippine usage that they must be considered historically related dialects of the same language. There is some evidence that the Spanish-derived element in PCS underwent some revision in Zm. Where Spanish-derived forms in Zm differ from those in MBC, the Zm forms generally more closely correspond to the shape of the form in modern Spanish. But the most conspicuous difference between the two dialects is the much larger number of Philippine derived forms in Zm and the deeper penetration of these forms into core grammatical and semantic sets. About 20% of the total vocabulary of Zm collected thus far (1,000 out of 5,000 words) and 10% of the 200 words Swadesh list is of Philippine origin. Philippine forms occur among the high frequency adverbial enclitics, conjunctions, negatives, and pronouns. The productive derivational affixes of Zm are almost all of Philippine origin. Although comparable data for MBC are not yet available, the much lesser impact of Philippine languages on these dialects is readily apparent from casual inspection of texts.

One cannot explain the more prominent Philippine element in Zm by postulating that Zm has suffered much more intensive language contact *in situ* with Philippine languages. If anything the reverse is the case. MBC speech communities are, and presumably always have been, tiny islands in a Tagalog speaking sea. Probably almost all of its speakers are bilingual and use Tagalog daily.[8] Zamboangueño, on the other hand, is the dominant language of the Christian population of Southwestern Mindanao and of Basilan Island. Its local competition is divided among a half dozen other Philippine languages. But, more significant, it is not the languages with which Zm is in contact locally that are responsible for its Philippine element.

PROVENIENCE OF PHILIPPINE-DERIVED FORMS IN ZM

Before the intrusion of the Spanish, the Zamboanga–Basilan area was occupied by speakers of Samalan languages, a clearly distinct sub-group of Philippine languages. The early Christian community in Zamboanga, prior to its evacuation in 1663, included Samal-speaking converts (de la Costa 1961: 445, 451). The development and spread of Zamboangueño Creole in the area, which probably began after the re-occupation of Zamboanga in 1718, took place in the midst of a Samalan-speaking area. Zamboangueños remain in close contact with, and in many communities in almost symbiotic economic relations with, Samalan speakers. Yet Samalan languages have had little discernible influence on Zm.[9] It is readily apparent from inspection that the Philippine element in Zm is drawn from one or more languages of the Central Philippine (or 'Tagalic') subgroup of Philippine languages, a group including Tagalog, the 'Bisayan' languages of the Central Philippines, and Taw Sug, the language of Joló and an auxiliary language for Moslems throughout the south-western Philippines. Of these Central Philippine languages, Zm is in contact with Taw Sug, a competing auxiliary language in Christian–Moslem interaction, with Cebuano Bisayan the dominant language of Christian areas throughout most of the rest of Mindanao as well as the native language of the majority of recent immigrants to the Zamboanga area, and with Tagalog, which through school instruction, movies and popular magazines, is gaining utility as an auxiliary language among Christians. This role of Tagalog in the area is a recent one and does not involve extensive contact with native speakers of the language. Until the twentieth century, Zamboangueños were not in direct contact with any Central Philippine language other than Taw Sug.[10] Since then the major new contact has been with Cebuano Bisayan.

Determination of the specific Central Philippine languages responsible for the Philippine element in Zamboangueño is obscured by the lexical similarities among the relevant languages. Nevertheless, a determination on linguistic grounds is possible. By plotting the occurrence of Zm forms among Central Philippine languages, one can formulate a minimal set of Philippine languages necessary to account for the Philippine-derived portion of the Zm lexicon. This procedure has been completed only for about three hundred of the about one thousand Philippine-derived forms in Zm so far collected. It is clear, however, that Hiligaynon (Ilongo) Bisayan is undoubtedly the major source of the Philippine-derived element in the Zm lexicon.[11] Tagalog is an important secondary source. These two languages are sufficient to account for the overwhelming bulk of Philippine forms in Zm. The local contact languages, Cebuano, Samalan, and Taw Sug have all contributed forms, but their discernible impact has been and continues to be surprisingly small.[12] The major language influencing Zm today is English.

The Tagalog element, especially in the very basic areas of Zm vocabulary, can be attributed to the probable role of this major Philippine language in any early Philippine military pidgin or creole. But what about Hiligaynon Bisayan, a language we have had no occasion to mention when describing past or present language contact in Zamboanga? This is a language spoken in Eastern Panay and Western Negros (see map). Although there are Hiligaynon speaking immigrants in Zamboanga and elsewhere in Mindanao, nowhere outside of its home area is the language a lingua franca of importance. Presumably Hiligaynon speakers played a major role in the early settlement of Zamboanga, but I have not been able to find any historical documentation of this. We know only that 'Bisayans' participated in many of the Spanish campaigns in Mindanao and Sulu. In any case Hiligaynon at some time had a profound impact on Zamboangueño that subsequent language contact has not obscured.

DISTRIBUTION OF PHILIPPINE-DERIVED FORMS ACROSS SEMANTIC DOMAINS

The situation presented by Zm pronouns where Philippine and Spanish-derived forms participate as contrasting items in a single semantic domain is repeated over and over in the Zm lexicon. Take common indigenous biota for example. Coconut, bamboo, and ratan are Spanish; bananas, sugar cane, and egg plant are Philippine. Rice is Philippine when growing in the field, Spanish when milled, and Philippine again when cooked. Pigs are Spanish, chickens Philippine. Trees and grass are Spanish; vines are Philippine. Primary forest is Spanish; secondary forest is Philippine. Mature leaves and blossoms are Spanish; young leaves and buds are Philippine. Because of the preponderance of Spanish-derived words in the total lexicon there are, of course, many contrast sets made exclusively of Spanish forms – color terminology for example – , but it is extremely difficult to find even two member sets made up exclusively of Philippine forms. Although there is some skewing in the distribution of Philippine forms across semantic domains – in plant and animal terminology the Philippine element exceeds 50% – it is still fair to say that Philippine forms in Zm do not sort by semantic domain as one expects of loan words. Nor do they sort by provenience of the objects they denote. If one were to separate indigenous from introduced plants, a favorite goal of loan word studies, by the etymologies of their names in Zm, one would have the Spanish bringing coconuts (*kóko*) to the Philippines and discovering chili peppers (*katumbal*) there.

At first sight it appears that Spanish and Philippine forms were distributed through the Zm lexicon by some random device that produced five Spanish forms to every Philippine form. A possibility, however, of some pattern to this distribution is suggested by the Zm pronouns. The distribution of pronouns of Philippine origin coincides with that of the semantic feature of plurality. Philippine derivation marks pronoun plurality (among stylistically unmarked forms). Zm nouns and adjectives are not inflected for plurality, but, following Greenberg (1966), we can generalize the contrast 'singular-plural' as a case of the contrast 'unmarked-marked'. Semantic marking appears in a variety of lexical domains. Among adjectival contrast pairs, there is a polarity whereby terms such as 'tall', 'big', 'far', 'fast' are linked as opposed to 'short', 'little', 'near', and 'slow'. The members of the former set are of positive (unmarked) polarity, the latter set of negative (marked) polarity.[13] Various criteria have been given in the literature for sorting out polarity (Greenberg 1966:90, Bierwisch 1967, Lamb 1964:218–23). Osgood (1964) factors out three dimensions of adjective polarity, activity, potency, and evaluation, which he feels are universal. If one lists Zm adjectival contrast pairs in which one member is of Spanish origin and the other member of Philippine origin, then, where there is a clear case of a marked-unmarked contrast, the Philippine-derived form will represent the marked member. Examples are listed in Table 3A. No clear counter-examples have been found, though there are a number of ambiguous cases where the direction of polarity is arguable or where it may differ on different dimensions.[14]

Kinship, generation, and growth stage reciprocals also fit the pattern. Philippine forms designate the younger member of the pair (Table 3B). I have only one case in which a Spanish and a Philippine form are opposed by sex, but in this case the Philippine form designates the marked (female) sex (Table 3B).

Extending this argument to taxonomic relations we would, at first sight, expect that, when Spanish and Philippine-derived forms occur at different hierarchical levels, the Philippine form would label the subordinate (marked) category. Examples conforming to this expectation can be found, but so also can counter-examples. One can easily find hierarchical series in which Spanish and Philippine forms alternate. What makes the construction of such series possible is that the typical situation throughout the lexicon has Philippine forms contrasting with Spanish forms at the same level. Each successive contrast set in a taxonomy frequently has both Philippine and Spanish terms. Given this pattern, Philippine-derived forms cannot consistently mark subordinate relations (Table 4).

Through much of the lexicon, where there is no clear marking or polarity involved within a contrast set, no patterning in the occurrence of Philippine forms is discernible. Why a roof is Spanish and a wall Philippine, or why wind and thunder are Spanish, rain and lightning Philippine, I cannot imagine. But we can make the following generalization: where a Philippine and a Spanish-derived form participate in a marked-unmarked relation in the same contrast set, the Philippine form will designate the marked category: it will signify lesser magnitude, shorter distance, worse evaluation, female sex, junior generation, or plurality.

Consider now the distribution of Philippine-derived forms across speech

TABLE 3. *Some Zm contrast pairs of contrasting etymology*

A. Adjectives contrasting in magnitude and/or evaluation

< Sp	< Ph		
+	−		
gránde	dyútay	large	small
ʔálto	pandak	tall	short
lihéro	mahínay	fast	slow
kórre	pátaʔ	fast	slow
mapwérso	malúya	strong	weak
ʔárde	ʔamamaluŋ	bright	dim
ʔapretáo	halugaʔ	tight	loose
ʔagúdu	mapurul	sharp	dull
líso	makasap	smooth	rough
sabróso	mataʔbaŋ	tasty	tasteless
dúlse	mapaʔit	sweet	bitter
madúru	mahilaw	ripe	raw
mánso	maʔilap	tame	wild
buníto	ʔumálin	pretty	ugly
límpyo	buliŋ	clean	dirty
kláro	lubug	clear	turbid
deréčo	tikuʔ	straight	bent
balyénte	mahuyaʔ	bold	shy
ʔumílde	hambuk	modest	vain
byého	bátaʔ	old	young
nwébo	dáʔan	new	old

B. Nouns contrasting in generation, age, or sex

< Sp	< Ph		
+	−		
byého/a	bátaʔ	old man/woman	child
lólo/a	ʔapu	grandfather/mother	grandchild
táta/nána	ʔanak	father/mother	son, daughter
ʔóhas	talbus	mature leaf	young leaf
plóres	putut	blossom	bud
soltéro	dalága	bachelor	unmarried girl

events, their selection according to style levels. The crucial data here are those cases of synonyms or near synonyms in which one term is Spanish, the other Philippine. Such pairs are not invariably differentiated by style level, but, when there is a clear difference, it is the Spanish-derived term that is appropriate to formal situations or which indicates politeness towards the addressee. The Spanish term is marked for formality whereas the Philippine term is the stylistically unmarked, normal conversational form. No counter-examples have yet been found; however, the investigation of synonymous pairs has only begun.

In many languages semantic marking may also be used as stylistic marking. It is quite common that plural (semantically marked) pronouns are used as second person respect terms in the singular. Such is the case in Tagalog where, in the second person, *kayo* contrasts with *ʔikaw* in being either semantically marked as plural or stylistically marked as polite. In the latter case it

TABLE 4. *Partial taxonomy of some Zm meal constituents (Philippine-derived forms italicized)*

1.	komída	'food'
1.1.	*kánon*	'main dish'
1.1.1.	*kánon* (de arros)	'cooked rice'
1.1.2.	mais	'maize'
1.2.	*ʔúlam*	'side dish'
1.2.1.	kárne	'meat'
1.2.1.1.	*manok*	'chicken'
1.2.1.1.1.	galyina	'hen'
1.2.1.1.2.	*dumalága*	'pullet'
1.2.1.2.	pwérko	'pork'
1.2.1.2.1.	*butakal*	'uncastrated boar'
1.2.1.2.2.	lečon	'suckling pig'
1.2.2.	*gulay*	'vegetables'
1.2.2.1.	prehóles	'string beans'
1.2.2.2.	*patáni*	'lima beans'
1.2.3.	peskáo	'fish'
1.2.3.1.	*tulíŋan*	'tuna'
1.2.3.2.	kabályas	'mackerel'

can be used to address one person. European examples are of course familiar (Brown and Gilman 1960). There is probably no language in which a singular pronoun is marked for respect in contrast to a plural. The second person pronouns in Zm (Table 2), however, contain an anomaly in this regard. There are separate three-member sets of second-person pronouns, differentiated by respect, in the singular and in the plural. But the pattern of differentiation does not match. In the singular, *tú* is unmarked, *ʔuste* is marked for respect, and *ʔebos* may be said to be marked for lack of respect or intimacy. In the plural, *kamo*, a Philippine form, is the stylistically unmarked equivalent of *tú*, whereas *bosótros* and *ʔustédes* are marked for increasing degrees of respect. Given the matching of *kamo* and *tú*, it would seem more reasonable if *bosótros* were the plural equivalent of *ʔebos* so that respect discriminations would match in the singular and plural. This arrangement, however, would place a Philippine form at a higher respect level than a Spanish form. Given the fact

that the marking for pronoun plurality is designated by Philippine provenience, a feature carrying with it stylistic unmarking, then any Spanish plurals
added to the set must rank higher in formality.

STRUCTURE OF SEMANTIC DOMAINS IN ZM

To the extent that semantic structures link language with other cultural
systems, Zm semantics should parallel that of other Philippine languages
more closely than that of Spanish. Nothing like a definitive statement on this
problem is possible at this point. Not only are comparable data from the
relevant languages lacking, but also the current state of semantic theory – of
whatever variety – does not yet make it clear how one goes about describing
the semantic structure of a language in anything approaching an exhaustive
way. Current theoretical and methodology proposals are backed only by
illustrations of semantic relations in some few domains that have proven tract-
able to analysis by the procedures proposed. I have nothing better to offer
here. Limited, and admittedly superficial comparisons of a few domains,
however, suggest some tentative generalizations.

The Zm pronouns (Table 1) fulfill the expectation that Zm should exhibit a
Philippine semantic structure. Apart from the style differentiations in the
second person, Zm pronouns can be matched semantically one-to-one with
pronouns in a language like Hiligaynon or Cebuano. A cultural explanation of
this matching, however, is jarred by the MBC dialects, which, although their
speakers participate in the same culture, fail to make the distinction between
exclusive and inclusive that is universal in the Philippines. There are other
examples of similar contrasts between Zm and MBC. In distinguishing short
of stature (*pandak*) from short of length (*kórto*), old of objects (*dáʔan*) from
old of persons (*byého*), full of containers (*lyéno*) from full of food (*busug*),
negation of completed events (*nway*) from negation of non-completed events
(*hindiʔ*),[15] Zm has typical Philippine distinctions lacking in MBC (Table 5).
In all of these cases, Zm also has Philippine derived forms, lacking in MBC, to
mark these distinctions. Where Philippine derived words are lacking in Zm,
Philippine semantic distinctions may also be lost. Unlike Philippine languages,
for example, Zm represents both 'low' and 'shallow' with one form (*báho*).
What seems to lend a Philippine-like semantic structure to these domains is
not the Philippine culture of the Zamboangueños but the Philippine derivation of much of their lexicon. Comparisons between MBC and Zm suggest
that Zm semantic structure in these domains has accommodated to the lexicon
rather than the lexicon accommodating to some pre-existing semantic structure.

A counter example to the preceding generalization would be provided by a
domain with Spanish-derived forms representing a Philippine-like semantic
structure. Unfortunately, good test cases are hard to find. Among domains of

easy cross-language comparability, some, such as the terminology of spatial orientation and of color, are exclusively Spanish, but there are no striking contrasts between Philippine and Spanish systems. Zm and Spanish share a three-point system of spatial position deictics ('here', 'there', 'elsewhere'); Philippine languages have three or four (with inclusive and exclusive 'here') point systems. In spatial movement deictics, Zm, like Spanish, makes only a

TABLE 5. *Verb inflection and negation*

A. Zamboangueño

ʔaykome yo	I will eat
hindiʔ yo aykome	I will not eat
takome yo	I am (was) eating
hindiʔ yo takome	I am (was) not eating
yakome yo	I ate
nway yo kome	I did not eat
kome	Eat!
no kome	Don't eat!

$\left\{\begin{array}{l}\text{kyére}\\\text{sábe}\\\text{pwéde}\end{array}\right\}$ yo kome   I $\left\{\begin{array}{l}\text{want to}\\\text{know how to}\\\text{can}\end{array}\right\}$ eat

no $\left\{\begin{array}{l}\text{kyére}\\\text{sábe}\\\text{pwéde}\end{array}\right\}$ yo kome   I $\left\{\begin{array}{l}\text{don't want to}\\\text{don't know how to}\\\text{can not}\end{array}\right\}$ eat

tyéne komída	There is food
nway komída	There is no food

B. Caviteño negation

no yo dikumi	I will not eat
no yo takumi	I am (was) not eating
no yo yakumi	I did not eat
no kumi	Don't eat!
nway kumída	There is no food

two-way contrast ('come' and 'go'), whereas in Philippine languages this set parallels, generally by inflection of the positionals, the three or four point distinctions of the positionals. The terminology of time deixis, the universal labeling of 'day-night' units preceding and following the time of the speech event, provides the clearest case of Spanish-derived forms adapted to a Philippine semantic pattern. In Spanish, as in English, the starting point of the system is 'today' (Sp 'hoy'), the unit *encompassing* the time of the speech event. 'Yesterday' is the unit preceding 'today'; 'tomorrow' is the unit following 'today'. In all dialects of PCS and in the relevant Philippine languages, there is no 'today' (Sp 'hoy' does not occur in PCS). The starting point of time deixis is 'now' (Zm *ára*, MBC *agóra*). All units preceding and following 'now' have distinctive terms. In Zm, (*en*)*denántes* labels the period from the last previous sunrise until 'now'; *lwégo* labels the period from 'now' until the next sunrise. English 'this afternoon' translates into Zm as *lwégo tárde* or *endenántes tárde* depending on whether the time of the speech event (*ára*) is prior to or subsequent to 'this afternoon'. 'Last night' is *anóče*; 'yesterday' is *ayer*; 'tomorrow' is *manyána*. The only Philippine-derived term in the system is *aga* 'morning', removing the ambiguity of Spanish 'mañana'. The orientation of named day-night units (days of the week) is marked by a contrast between genitive definite and locative: *del lúnes* 'last Monday', *na lúnes* 'next Monday'. Compare Hiligaynon *say lúnis* (gen. def.) 'last Monday', *sa lúnis* (loc.) 'next Monday'. (Wolff, pers. com.).

All of the domains discussed thus far are of dubious cultural sensitivity. Presumably one can participate in Philippine culture equally well however his particular language structures such domains. In searching for domains of undisputed cultural sensitivity and yet still of cross-cultural comparability, one immediately thinks of kinship terminology, a favorite among anthropologists just because it combines features of sensitivity and comparability. Unfortunately in the structuring of genealogical dimensions, Central Philippine and Spanish systems are practically identical. They both sort kin by generation and by collaterality but ignore sex of linking relatives. Where they differ is in distinguishing sex of kinsmen. Spanish makes such distinctions consistently; Central Philippine languages consistently ignore them outside of the first ascending generation (sometimes sex of spouse is distinguished as well). Despite the presumed greater cultural significance of this domain, the semantic pattern of Zm kinship terminology is much like that of the domains discussed previously. Zm distinguishes sex of relative where it has Spanish-derived terms and fails to do so where it has Philippine-derived terms. The Philippine-derived terms are those for the *marked* member of lineal reciprocal pairs, i.e. 'child' and 'grandchild'.[16]

All languages spoken by Christian Filipino groups, including PCS, appear to share similarly structured sets of address terms extendable on the basis of sex, age, and assessed status to non-kin, including strangers (cf. Geoghegan 1968). The details of these systems have yet to be worked out. They would undoubtedly provide some very fruitful comparisons. Interestingly, most of the terms used in all of these languages, although varied, derive from Spanish, generally in phonologically and semantically altered form. A typical example is *manoy/manay* (<Sp ermano/a) addressed to older siblings and to non-kin of comparable seniority throughout much of the Christian Philippines. Unlike Philippine kinship terms of reference, these address sets among Christians consistently distinguish sex of addressee.

When one considers domains of less comparability but of very clear cultural relevance, such as plant and animal nomenclature, vegetation types, agricultural techniques, and meal constituents, Zm, as expected, displays Philippine-like semantic structures. Some of these domains are similarly structured in Philippine English and Philippine Spanish as well (Table 6).

TABLE 6. *Rice and food in the Philippines*

	Zamboangueño	Hiligaynon	Tagalog	Phil. Spanish	Phil. English
1	paláy	pálay	pálay	paláy	paláy
2	ʔarros	bugas	bigas	arroz	rice
3	kánon	kanʔun	kánin	morisqueta	food
4	ʔúlam	sudʔan	ʔúlam	vianda	viand

1	rice plant, unmilled grain
2	milled rice
3	cooked rice, main dish
4	side dish

Conclusions

A fundamental problem presented by most creole languages is that of accounting for the apparently divergent sources of the lexicon on the one hand and the grammatical system on the other. Lexicons themselves rarely show any appreciable mixture and there is no internal evidence that the lexicon was ever anything other than what it is today. Zamboangueño provides a special case among creoles where something has happened to the lexicon. It may not be mixture and it may not be relexification, but it does seem to me to be a unique kind of lexical impact, one that differs in many respects from that ordinarily associated with the acquisition of loan words in situations of language contact. Consider the Zm data with respect to the following generally accepted assumptions about lexical borrowing (cf. Weinreich 1953:56–61).

1. High frequency portions of the lexicon are relatively impermeable to borrowing. In Zm, Philippine-derived forms occur among the pronouns, adverbial particles, conjunctions, negatives, and derivational affixes. Some 20 words in the Swadesh 200 word list are of Philippine origin.

2. Loan words are accommodated to existing phonological, and semantic systems. With Zm one can make the reverse argument that phonology and semantics have been accommodated to the acquired lexicon. Zm phonology enables the rendering of both Spanish and Philippine forms much as they are rendered in their respective source languages. Since it is a combination rather than a simplification of source language phonology, the Zm sound system is difficult to master both for a speaker of a Central Philippine language, who has

trouble with initial clusters, palatalized consonants, trilled r's, and five vowels; and for the Spaniard faced with ŋ's, glottal stops, medial clusters, and final consonants.

In semantics we have noted cases where the structure of certain domains parallels that of Philippine languages rather than Spanish. This result is to be expected of a language spoken by native actors in Christian Philippine culture. However, in many of these same domains the semantic structure of the MBC dialects does not exhibit these Philippine features; yet speakers of MBC dialects have been for centuries more fully immersed in the heartland of Christian Philippine culture than the Zamboangueños. Until the present century, Zamboanga was an isolated outpost of Christianity in a Philippine Moslem world. One can, then, propose the following argument: In those domains with a Philippine-like structure in Zm and a Spanish-like structure in MBC, the Zm domain will show Philippine semantic features where it has Philippine-derived words to mark these features. In other words the more Philippine-like nature of Zm semantics is the product of the adoption of Philippine words and their associated meanings, but these words were not originally adopted in order to make semantic distinctions necessary for participation in Philippine culture.

3. Loans words are adopted to name new concepts; consequently they should sort out by semantic domain. In Zm, on the other hand, Philippine and Spanish derived terms typically participate together as contrasting items in a single domain. Basic concepts like 'rain', 'worry', 'ugly', and 'not' have Philippine-derived labels.

4. If the adoption of loans cannot be explained by the need for new labels, then it can be expected that the use of loans from the particular source language confers prestige upon the speaker. In Zm the use of a Philippine form rather than a Spanish derived alternative never confers prestige. If there is a difference among alternatives in the direction of prestige, politeness, or formality it is always the Spanish form that ranks higher.

5. Lexical borrowing results from the proximity and interaction of adjacent speech communities. Zm has suffered relatively little lexical influence from neighbouring Philippine languages but a heavy impact from geographically remote languages, one of which Tagalog, has failed to make a corresponding impact on the PCS dialects in the midst of its own territory.

6. Apart from stylistic considerations the etymology of a linguistic form is irrelevant to its role in a synchronic grammatical description of the language.[17] In Zm the source of a word is pertinent to a synchronic description of the language. Being of Philippine provenience is a recognizable and linguistically significant attribute of a Zm morpheme. It is like an affix that marks the form. Like many affixes it often has no discernible semantic content, but, when it does, it typically signifies something smaller, closer, less valued, of lesser

generation or sex than its Spanish-derived opposite. Its most widespread meaning seems to be lesser evaluation, a meaning that relates perhaps to the appropriateness of a Philippine word to less formal speech situations than its Spanish-derived stylistic alternative. As an affix, Philippine provenience resembles the affix of morpheme duplication common in all Philippine languages including Zamboangueño. Sometimes, as where there is no corresponding non-duplicated form, duplication signifies little if anything. Generally, however, it denotes something smaller, less real, more intimate, or more numerous than the corresponding non-duplicated form. In other words duplication marks a form for a range of meanings from diminutive through plurality not unlike that marked by a Philippine form in contrast to a Spanish form.

NOTES

1 Current research on Zamboangueño is being supported by the National Science Foundation. I have been using Zamboangueño and collecting data on it incidental to work (supported by the National Institute of Mental Health) on other languages in the Zamboanga–Basilan area since 1962. The arguments of this paper will be documented in a monographic description of Philippine Creole Spanish now in preparation. I am grateful to the following persons for very helpful comments on an earlier version of this paper: Harold C. Conklin, Michael Forman, Dell Hymes, Carol Molony, Keith Whinnom, and John Wolff.
2 This label for the language is composed according to principles suggested by Hockett 1958:424.
3 The literature has Zamboangueño on the verge of extinction with only 1,300 speakers (cf. Taylor 1957:489; Voegelin 1964:49). Their source, Whinnom (1956), must have relied on the 1939 census which reported only 1,290 speakers of 'Chabacano' in Zamboanga. This figure is corrected in the 1948 census to 100,645 with the note: 'The phenomenal increase of the number of persons able to speak Chabacano is due to the instruction given to census enumerators to report as able to speak Spanish only those persons who speak the pure language of Cervantes' (Philippines 1954). Actually it does not require such a lofty standard to distinguish Zamboangueño from Spanish. The 1960 census lists 110,376 native speakers of Zamboangueño and 10,628 native speakers of 'Caviteño' (including Ternateño) (Philippines 1962–3). Another listing based on the 1960 census gives 126,500 and 13,500 native speakers of Zamboangueño and Caviteño respectively (Wernstedt and Spencer 1967:620–1). Zamboanga 'City', it should be noted, is a political unit encompassing 546 square miles, mostly rural.
4 The name 'Manila Bay Creole' is my own invention. All dialect names ending in *-eño*, as well as the name 'Chabacano' for any or all dialects of the language, are used locally. I have as yet made only brief visits to Cavite City and Ternate. Information on these dialects and their speakers presented here must be considered preliminary and subject to correction. I have no first-hand information on 'Davaoeño', a creole or pidgin reportedly once spoken in Davao City, Mindanao, where Cebuano Bisayan is now the dominant language (cf. Whinnom 1956).
5 'B&R 36:237' represents Blair and Robertson (1903–9), vol. 36, p. 237.

6 Philippine Ternateños recount a story of the original settlement of their community by 'Márdikas' from Moluccan Ternate that follows closely the accounts in historical sources (B&R 28:100; 36:237; 38:167, 177, 203, 220; 42:124, 251, 269; 44:29).

7 *mardika, merdeka, merdeheka* are Malay variants of a Sanskrit loan (Skr *maharddhika*) meaning 'freedom in contrast to servitude' (Wilkinson 1932, 2:134). Tagalog has *maharlika?* 'aristocratic', 'high class' from the same source. The etymological meaning of *márdikas* is not known in Philippine Ternate today but is given in seventeenth-century Spanish accounts (see references, note 6).

8 According to the 1960 census, 95% of the residents of the municipality of Ternate speak Tagalog, the *lowest* percentage for any municipality in Cavite Provence (Philippines 1962–3).

9 Identified Samalan loans include terms for Moslem religious practices and Moslem titles, fishing and nautical terms, possibly the word for 'secondary forest' and, from Yakan, a Samalan language of Basilan, the word for 'bandit' or 'pirate'.

10 I am ignoring Subanun, a peripheral member of the Central Philippine Sub-group spoken by pagans in the interior of Zamboanga Peninsula. This language has had no discernible influence on Zamboangueño.

11 As John Wolff has emphasized to me (personal communication), the dialect variation within Bisayan languages is complex and not fully mapped out. Moreover forms now diagnostic of particular languages or dialects may be of recent currency (e.g. modern standard Tagalog *hindi?* 'not' which has replaced an earlier form *díli?* identical to the current form in modern standard Cebuano. H. C. Conklin, personal communication). Nevertheless, it is clear that the sources of the bulk of the Philippine element in Zm were Bisayan dialects more closely related to modern standard Hiligaynon than to the modern standard Cebuano with which Zm speakers are now in contact.

12 This data contradicts Whinnom's (1956:14) conclusion, which accords with local statements about the language, that the sources of the Philippine element in Zamboangueño are Tagalog and Cebuano.

13 The difference between 'and' and 'but' reflects this polarity. 'And' links adjectives of the same polarity, like 'beautiful and smart', whereas 'but' links adjectives of opposite polarity like 'beautiful but dumb' (cf. Osgood, cited by D'Andrade and Romney 1964:240). Logicians usually define 'but' as 'and' plus surprise, but there is nothing surprising in my experience about the combination 'beautiful but dumb'.

14 The apparent discrepancy between the pair *nwébo-dálan* 'new-old' and *byého-báta?* 'old-young' (Table 5A) perhaps reflects the priority of evaluation over other dimensions of polarity. In terms of evaluation *nwébo* and *byého* are both positive (unmarked).

15 The formal distinction of aspect among negatives, together with the use of the word for 'none' to negate completed aspect, is characteristic of Hiligaynon, Cebuano, and many other Philippine languages, but not of Tagalog. In phonemic shape, on the other hand, the Zm negative *hindi?* is identical to the modern standard Tagalog form but differs from Hiligaynon *?indi?* and Cebuano *díli?* (but see note 11).

16 Zm parental and grandparental terms (Table 5 B) are derived from Spanish terms frequently used as terms of address in Philippine languages spoken by

Christians. Other Zm kin terms, including terms for step and god-kin are identical to Spanish with the addition of a low frequency Philippine form *balá?i* 'child's spouse's parent'.

17 Generative phonologists, however, are now proposing features such as 'Church Slavonic $\left(\begin{bmatrix} +\text{Slavic} \\ -\text{Russian} \end{bmatrix}\right)$' in the synchronic description of languages such as modern Russian (Chomsky and Halle 1968:373).

REFERENCES
(Including dictionaries consulted but not cited in the text)

Bierwisch, Manfred 1967. 'Some semantic universals of German adjectivals', *Foundations of Language* 3(1):1–36

Blair, E. H., and J. A. Robertson, eds. 1903–9. *The Philippine Islands*, 55 vols , Cleveland, A. H. Clark Co.

Brown, R. W., and A. Gilman 1960. 'The pronouns of power and solidarity', *Style in Language*, ed. by T. A. Sebeok, 253–76, Cambridge, Mass., MIT Press

Cassidy, F. G. and R. B. Le Page 1961. 'Lexicographical problems of *The Dictionary of Jamaican English*', *Proceedings of the conference on creole language studies*, ed. by R. B. Le Page (Creole Language Studies, 2), London, Macmillan

Chomsky, Noam, and Morris Halle 1968. *The sound pattern of English*, New York, Harper and Row

de la Costa, H. 1961. *The Jesuits in the Philippines 1581–1768*, Cambridge, Mass., Harvard University Press

Cruz, M. and S. P. Ignashev 1959. *Tagal'sko-Russkii Slovar'*, Gosudarstvennoye izdatel'stvo inostrannikh i natsional'nikh slovarei, Moskow

D'Andrade, R. G. and A. K. Romney 1964. 'Summary of participants' discussion', *Transcultural Studies in Cognition*, AA 66(3), pt. 2, 230–42

Felix de la Encarnacion 1885. *Diccionario Bisaya-Espanol*, Tercera Edicion, Aumentada . . . por J. Sanchez, Manila [Cebuano]

Geoghegan, William 1968. 'Information processing systems in culture', *Explorations in mathematical anthropology*, ed. by Paul Kay, Cambridge, Mass., MIT Press (in press)

Greenberg, Joseph H. 1966. 'Language universals', *Current Trends in Linguistics*, ed. by T. A. Sebeok, vol. III, Theoretical Foundations, The Hague, Mouton

Hermosisima, T. V. and P. S. Lopez, Jr. 1966. *Dictionary Bisayan-English-Tagalog*, Manila, P. B. Ayuda [Cebuano]

Hockett, C. F. 1958. *A course in modern linguistics*, New York, Macmillan

Jakobson, Roman 1939. 'Signe zéro', in *Mélanges de linguistique*, offerts à Charles Bally, 143–52, Geneva, Georg
    1957. *Shifters, verbal categories and the Russian verb*, Cambridge, Mass., Harvard University, Russian Language Project

Kaufmann, J. n.d. *Visayan-English dictionary*, Iloilo, La Editorial [Hiligaynon and Hiniraya]

Laktaw, Pedro Serrano 1914. *Diccionario Tagalog-Hispano*, Manila

Lamb, Sydney M. 1964. 'The sememic approach to structural semantics', *American Anthropologist* 66(3), pt. 2, 57–78

Montero y Vidal, Jose 1888. *Historia de la pirateria malayomahometana*, vol. 2, Madrid, M. Tello

Osgood, Charles E. 1964. 'Semantic differential technique in the study of cultures', *American Anthropologist* 66(3), pt. 2, 171–200

Panganiban, Jose Villa 1966. *Talahuluganang Pilipino-Ingles*, Kagawaran na Edukasyon, Surian ng Wikang Pambansa, Manila, Kawanihan ng Palimbagan [Tagalog dictionary]

Weinreich, U. 1953. *Languages in Contact*, New York, Linguistic Circle of New York

Wernstedt, F. L. and J. E. Spencer 1967. *The Philippine Island world: a physical cultural, and regional geography*, Berkeley, University of California Press

Whinnom, K. 1956. *Spanish contact vernaculars in the Philippine Islands*, Hong Kong, Hong Kong University Press

Wilkinson, R. J. 1932. *A Malay-English dictionary*, Mytilene, Greece

Wolff, John 1967. 'History of the dialect of the Camotes Islands, Philippines, and the spread of Cebuano Bisayan', *Oceanic Linguistics* 7:63–79

THE STRANGE CASE OF MBUGU

MORRIS GOODMAN

Background and Sources

Mbugu is a language spoken by about 12,000 people (according to the 1948 census) in the Usambara district of north-eastern Tanzania very near the Kenya border. The indigenous ethnic name is Maanthi according to Meinhof (1906) but Ma'a according to Copland (1933–4) and subsequent writers. Like ethnic names in Bantu languages, it is preceded by the appropriate prefix to designate the language (*ki-*), the people (*wa-*), etc. The name Mbugu is used by neighboring Bantu peoples, such as the Shambala. The earliest documentation of the language is a list of approximately 130 words compiled by Archdeacon Farler appended to Shaw (1885). On the title page the language is called Kibwyo but elsewhere in the text the people are referred to as Wambugu. Farler states that, 'Their language is unlike any other I know, but certainly more Bantu in form than anything else. Some words are like Kikwavi [i.e. Masai], but very few; they are certainly not like Swahili.' (p. 204). Cust in a brief introduction to the book merely states that 'it is not known to what family or group it belongs'.

The language was next mentioned by Sir Harry Johnston (1886) who, on the basis of Farler's work and, apparently, some additional investigation, notes that, 'the language they [the Wambugu] speak (which has recently been brought to light by Archdeacon Farler of Magila) is a thorough enigma. While possessing Bantu prefixes and using them as they are used in Bantu languages, its word roots with one or two exceptions, are unlike anything we have yet met with. The exceptions are a few terms taken from Masai, Ki-Kamba, and KiSambara [i.e. Shambala]' (p. 403). He provided, however, no illustrations of the language.

Shortly thereafter, a group of four closely-interrelated languages of north-central Tanzania became known, which proved to have significant lexical affinities to Mbugu. These are Iraqw (or Mbulu), for which the entire group is named, Gorowa (Fiome), Alagwa (Wasi), and Burunge, spoken respectively by approximately 100,000, 15,000, 11,000, and 9,000 (according to the 1948 census). The earliest account of them is in Baumann (1894) who classified them as Hamitic, evidently at the suggestion of Leo Reinisch. Those linguists who next dealt with them, Seidel (1900) and Meinhof (1906), accepted this designation, the former suggesting a particular relation to Galla, the latter to Somali.

Meinhof (1906) was also the next to investigate Mbugu, publishing the earliest phonological and grammatical sketch of the language as well as a list of approximately 300 words, Mbugu to German and vice versa, and he was the first to call attention to the lexical resemblances of Mbugu to the Iraqw languages as well as to their presumed relatives, Galla and Somali. He also noted, however, a few similarities to such West African languages as Twi, Ewe, and Gã and to a few less well known languages of the upper Nile region, whose names are difficult to identify, but which apparently belong to Greenberg's Central Sudanic group. On the basis of these similarities and the fact that Mbugu has many monosyllabic verb roots and no inflectional morphology apart from that of Bantu origin, he arrived at the conclusion that it was originally an isolating Sudanic language which came in contact with one or more Hamitic languages (i.e. the Iraqw group and perhaps Somali and Galla), resulting in significant lexical borrowing but no evident grammatical influence, and subsequently with one or more Bantu languages, resulting in profound grammatical influence but only slight and non-basic lexical borrowing.

The next writer to deal with the language was Copland (1933–4), who published the only continuous text ever recorded in the language but no linguistic analysis. He claims that, '[Meinhof's] theory of the origin of the language is confirmed by their tribal history, a summary of which I obtained in Mlalo, Usambara (May, 1933) (p. 241)'. Thereafter almost nothing was said of Mbugu until a brief grammatical sketch and word list appeared in Tucker and Bryan (1957), who categorized it as 'partly Bantu', but recognized lexical affinities with the Iraqw group.

The most recent study of Mbugu and, in general, the most informative is by E. C. Green (1963). This contains a comparative word list of 136 items with English glosses, given in Mbugu, Iraqw, Masai, and two neighbouring Bantu languages, Asu and Shambala. Although the latter, for whom the district of Usambara is named, are the Bantu people with whom the Mbugu have been in closest contact since they came to the attention of Europeans and probably long before that, it is evident from their traditions, as documented by Copland and Green, that their previous habitat had been the neighboring Pare district to the west, inhabited by the Asu, whose language is similar to but distinct from Shambala. These are the two Bantu languages whose grammatical and lexical similarities to Mbugu should be examined most closely. My principal sources for them are Seidel (1895) and Kotz (1909).

Three years earlier, W. H. Whiteley, who had access to Green's then unpublished manuscript, and who, himself, had done the most important work to date on the Iraqw group (1958) published a note (1960) using the example of Mbugu to justify the concept 'linguistic hybrid'. He wrote as follows:

While the material available on the language is not as full as one would wish, the broad characteristics of the language as spoken at present emerge clearly.

These characteristics may be briefly summarized. The system of affixes associated with nouns, adjectives, and verbs can be regularly correlated with the systems operating in neighboring Bantu languages, and indeed with those operating over the whole Bantu field. The stems and roots of the language, however, cannot be correlated with the Bantu stems and roots, nor, in fact, are there regular correspondences with any other language families. There are a few correspondences with the Iraqw group of languages spoken nearly 200 miles to the west, and this is not inconsistent with oral tradition; there are also a number of Asu and Shambala words consistent with borrowing. The language would, therefore, appear to be an amalgam of a Bantu and a non-Bantu language, and merit Guthrie's term 'Bantoid'. Tucker and Bryan prefer the term 'Partly Bantu language' while Greenberg categorically labels it 'Cushitic' (p. 96).

Greenberg (1955, 1963) followed Meinhof and others in including the Iraqw languages within the Cushitic branch of Hamito-Semitic along with Somali, Galla, etc., but he is alone in grouping Mbugu together with them. It would seem advisable therefore, to take a closer look at it in order to determine as precisely as possible the sources of its structure and vocabulary.

Structure

As in the Bantu languages, every Mbugu noun belongs to a concordial class, which determines (a) its prefix, henceforth referred to as the nominal prefix, (b) the prefix (identical with the nominal prefix) of any variable adjective which modifies it; invariable adjectives take no prefix, (c) the appropriate prefix of any verb whose subject or object it is, henceforth referred to as the pronominal prefix (this is identical with the nominal prefix in some classes, different in others), (d) the particle linking it to the dependent noun in the genitive construction (this consists of the pronominal prefix, undergoing various modifications and reductions, plus the vowel *a*).

The noun classes play a more restricted role in Mbugu, however, than they do in most Bantu languages. For example, the demonstratives, and the pronominal possessives (e.g. 'my, mine', etc.), which take concordial agreement in Bantu, do not in Mbugu. Furthermore as Meinhof and Green have pointed out, the prefix of the noun, particularly if it is a singular, is frequently omitted, whether randomly or on the basis of style, idiolect, or context is not entirely clear.

All noun classes except 15 (see below) are paired so that singular nouns belong to one member of the pair, while their plural counterparts belong to the other. Some plural classes (notably numbers 10 and 8; see below) are paired with more than one singular, but not vice versa. All nouns denoting humans, and only those, occur in classes 1 (as singulars) and 2 (as plurals). All those denoting trees, but many others as well (e.g. 'hand', 'fire', etc.), occur similarly in classes 3 and 4. Class 15 includes only verb infinitives and, therefore, is not part of a singular-plural pair.

The other classes are more difficult to categorize semantically, although generally mass nouns occur in class 6 (normally plural) and abstract nouns in class 14 (normally singular). Being non-denumerable, these have no corresponding forms in the other member of the same pair, classes 5 (singular) and 10 (plural) respectively. The noun classes, appropriately paired, are listed below as given by Green (1963). They are numbered according to the system conventionally used in comparative Bantu linguistic studies and identified by the nominal prefix; the pronominal prefix, where different, is listed adjacently in parentheses. In classes 1 and 2, unlike the others, the pronominal prefix functioning as subject differs from that functioning as object; the former is listed first.

sing. 1: *mu* (*e*/*mu*) 3: *mu* (*u*) 5: *i* (*li*)   7: *ki* 13: *ka* 9: ø (*i*) 11: *lu* 14: *vu* 15: *ku*
plu. 2: *va* (*ve*/*va*) 4: *mi* (*i*) 6: *ma* (*ya*) 8: *vi* 8: *vi* 10: ø (*zi*) 10: ø (*zi*) 10: ø (*zi*)

It should be pointed out that the above cited pronominal prefixes, when functioning as the subject or object of a verb are in actuality indicators of the third person, chosen from class 1 (singular) or 2 (plural) if the referent is human, from one of the other classes if it is not. If the referent is other than third person, the following pronominal prefixes are used, which are the same whether functioning as subject or object.

	sing.	plu.
1st	*ni*	*tu*
2nd	*u*	*mu*

Like the prefixes of the noun class system they are clearly of Bantu origin.

The noun class system, fairly uniform throughout Bantu, is so similar in Shambala and Asu (and Mbugu as well) in the shape and functioning of the prefixes and the pairing and semantic content of the classes, that it is difficult to connect Mbugu more closely to one than to the other. However, certain features point towards Asu. For example, the pronominal subject prefixes of classes 1 and 2 as given by Green, *e* and *ve* respectively, occur in Asu but not Shambala. The situation is complicated by the fact that these are the subject prefixes for certain tenses only in Asu; *a* and *va* are used with the others. Furthermore, Meinhof as well as Tucker and Bryan, as opposed to Green and Whiteley give the Mbugu subject prefixes as *a* and *va*. Copland's text clarifies the matter to some extent, however. The Mbugu prefixes seem to vary according to tense, likewise, although some forms are unclear, and to agree largely with Asu in the choice of prefix. This will be demonstrated in greater detail when the tenses are examined.

The nominal prefix of class 5 in Asu is *i* as in Mbugu, whereas the Shambala prefix is generally o (zero); it is *i*, however, with monosyllabic stems (e.g. *i-gi* 'egg') and *zi* before stems whose initial vowel is *i* (e.g. *zino* < *zi* + *ino* 'tooth'). Likewise, the pronominal prefix of class 5 in Mbugu, *li*, agrees with

Asu, whereas in Shambala it is *dji*. The former is much more widespread throughout Bantu, however, and need not be related exclusively to Asu. On the other hand, the Mbugu pronominal prefix of class 6, *ya*, as given by Green and Whiteley agrees with Shambala, whereas, in Asu it is *e* or *a* alternating on much the same basis as the prefix of class 1. However, Copland's text shows the Mbugu prefix to be *e* in his only relevant example '*ma'aze ekutaxo* "days passed" ', where *ma'aze* (with nominal prefix *ma*) is a class 6 (plural) noun and the *e* of *ekutaxo* the corresponding pronominal prefix functioning as the subject of the verb. The other writers (i.e. Meinhof and Tucker and Bryan) are silent on this point.

The Mbugu pronominal prefix of class 10, *zi*, as given by Green, resembles Shambala but the forms listed by other writers, *dji* (Meinhof) or *dyi* (Tucker and Bryan) point to Asu, where it is *ži*. So does the prefix of class 14, *vu*, which in Shambala is *u*. On the other hand, the pairing of classes 8 and 10 as the plurals of 13 and 11, respectively, points to Shambala, since in Asu the corresponding plural classes would be 14 (otherwise a singular class) and 6. However, only one Mbugu noun, *kawaha/viwaha*, 'knife' occurs in the noun class pair 13 (singular) and 8 (plural), and Meinhof records its plural as class 14, as it would be in Asu.

Finally, among non-third person pronominal prefixes, Asu and Shambala differ only in the first person plural; *tu* in the former, as in Mbugu, and *ti* in the latter. Thus, on the basis of the earlier descriptions (Meinhof, Copland, and Tucker and Bryan), the Mbugu nominal and pronominal prefix system resembles Asu rather than Shambala in almost every instance where these two differ. The more recent descriptions (Green and Whiteley) are less conclusive, however, indicating that Mbugu may be changing under the influence of the latter.

Like the noun class system, the verb construction in Mbugu is clearly of Bantu origin. Here, however, since individual Bantu languages differ from one another to a greater extent, a much closer resemblance to Asu is easily demonstrated even though Mbugu differs from both of them in some respects, perhaps as a result of independent developments or affinities to yet another Bantu language. The Mbugu verb consists of a series of affixes to the verb stem occurring in the following order:

1. The negative prefix *te*, used in conjunction with all the negative tenses noted below, is the same in Asu; its Shambala counterpart is *nka*.

2. The pronominal subject prefix, as discussed above; these coalesce with the preceding negative prefix in the following cases: *te + ni* (1st sing.) > *si*, *te + u* (2nd sing.) > *tu*, *te + e* (class 1) > *te*, as in Asu, although Shambala *nka + ni* > *si*, likewise.

3. The tense prefix, of which the following are like those of Asu:
(a) The affirmative past, *a*; Shambala has a present but not a past formed with *a*, its past is formed otherwise.

(b) The 'not yet' negative *na*.

(c) The affirmative and negative future, *ne* and *ka*, respectively.

(d) The affirmative narrative past, *ka* (not to be confused with the *ka* of the negative future, however); this is not attested by Green but occurs in Copland's text and takes *a* and *va* rather than *e* and *ve* as the pronominal subject prefixes of classes 1 and 2 respectively.

(e) The o (zero) prefix of the present affirmative and negative tenses; this might also be connected with Shambala, however.

(f) The affirmative conditional *ku*, unlike the others, however, not identical with any Asu or Shambala prefix, although possibly related to *eki* of the former or *ki* of the latter, similar in function.

4. The pronominal object prefix; this may be omitted if the noun object is expressed.

5. The verb stem; unlike those in most Bantu languages, this need not end in *a*, nor does it undergo any grammatically-determined final vowel change.

6. The tense suffix *ye*; this is virtually the same as the Asu perfect tense suffix *ie*, developing from its Bantu prototype *ile*, which has a different form in Shambala. The function of the suffix is somewhat specialized in Mbugu, however. It occurs in a negative and an affirmative conditional tense in conjunction with the tense prefix *se*, which is of uncertain origin, and it occurs with the zero tense prefix in the negative past, whose affirmative counterpart is formed with *a* (see 3(a)). This usage corresponds to that of Asu.

There are also three derivational suffixes to the verb stem, which are clearly of Bantu origin, the stative *ka*, the passive *wa*, and the causative *(i)ja*, of which the first two could be connected either with Asu or Shambala (or many other Bantu languages), but the third seems most likely to come from Asu *(i)ža*. Two common Mbugu connectives are, likewise, clearly Bantu, *ni* and *na*. The former functions as the copula and introduces the agent of a passive verb, the latter conjoins noun phrases and sentences and introduces the goal of a verb of motion. Both of these are used precisely as in Asu.

Vocabulary

Contrasting with this overwhelmingly Bantu grammar, corresponding, in particular, to Asu, but with a few specific resemblances to Shambala and possibly other Bantu languages, are the non-Bantu independent and possessive pronouns and a basic vocabulary (including the numerals 'six' and below), only a small percentage of which can be traced unambiguously to any source.

The pronouns are listed below as given by Green:

	Independent		Possessive	
	sing.	plu.	sing.	plu.
1st	*ani*	*nine*	*go*	*kanu*
2nd	*ari*	*kuni*	*ke*	*kago*
3rd	*hu*	*kini*	*ku'u*	*kini*

The possessives are postposed immediately to the possessed noun without any linking element (cf. Copland *mburi kanu* 'our plan'), but the fact that all begin with *k* (the only exception is the first person singular, *go* which Meinhof records, however, as *koo*) may indicate that this consonant at one time had the status of a separate morpheme. It may be possible to relate it to a *k* in Iraqw prefixed to the possessive suffixes when used predicatively (e.g. 'mine', etc.); some nouns, however, require *t*, evidently a gender distinction. The following are the Iraqw independent and possessive pronouns; those of the other members of the Iraqw group are quite similar:

	Independent		Possessive	
	sing.	plu.	sing.	plu.
1st	*ani anī anin*	*atenī at*	*ee*	*ren*
2nd				
m	*kuī kun*	*kunga*	*ok*	*hun*
f	*kiī kin*	*kinga*	*ok*	*hun*
3rd	*inosī inus*	*ino'in*	*os*	*in*

The most striking similarity to Mbugu is the first person singular independent pronoun *ani*, but similar forms for this pronoun occur so widely that it proves very little (e.g. the comparable forms of the Nilotic and Nilo-Hamitic languages and the first person singular pronominal prefix of Bantu and Mbugu, *ni*). Cushitic languages, such as Somali and Galla, which very likely are related to Iraqw, likewise have such a form and also a second person singular independent pronoun *ati* (Galla), *adi* (Somali), which might possibly be connected with Mbugu *ari*. The Mbugu independent second person plural pronoun *kuni* may be related to its Iraqw masculine counterpart *kunga* and even to the widespread second person pronominal element *k* of Cushitic and Hamito-Semitic as a whole. This family likewise has a widespread pluralizing pronominal suffix *n*, which might possibly be related to the *ne/ni* endings of the Mbugu plural personal pronouns. Nevertheless, it must be admitted that no convincing systematic resemblances can be demonstrated between the independent and possessive pronouns of Mbugu and those of any other language to which a relationship has been suggested.

Mbugu has two demonstratives, which, unlike those of Bantu, have no noun class concord, nor do they distinguish singular from plural. They are, according to Green, *hu* 'that, those', identical with the third person singular independent pronoun, and *iya* 'this, these' instead of which, however, Meinhof records *ka*. The latter could be related to either of two Iraqw forms, *ka* 'these' (plural only) or *qa* 'that, those' (invariable for number and gender), but there are other Iraqw forms for 'this', *wi* (masculine) and *ti, ri* (feminine). The other Mbugu demonstratives are of uncertain origin, but might possibly be related to Bantu forms, though I am inclined to doubt it. Compare Asu *uu* 'this' for singular noun classes 1 and 3 only and *io* 'that, those' for classes 4 and 9 only.

The numerals of Mbugu according to Green are as follows: 1. *we*, 2. *nnu*, 3. *xai*, 4. *hai*, 5. *kooi*, 6. *matisu*, 7. *mfungate*, 8. *mnane*, 9. *kenda*, 10. *ixadu* or *xademu*, 11. *ixadu* or *xademu na we*, etc., 20. *maxadu* or *maxademu na nnu* (*mixademu minu* according to Meinhof), 100. *gana*. Only two Iraqw numerals bear any resemblance to these, 1. *wäk* (*ä* = low central vowel) and 5. *ko'an* (compare also *qonoin* in Danakil, a Cushitic language), while 10 might possibly be related to Galla (Cushitic) *qudan*. Numerals 7–9 and 100, on the other hand, are identical with those of Shambala and nearly so with those of Asu. At least some of the numerals take the concordial nominal prefix when modifying nouns, as in Bantu generally, and the prefix *ka* when used in counting, precisely as in Asu and Shambala. The connective *na* 'and, with', discussed in the preceding section, is used in composite numerals and is clearly of Bantu origin.

Although the evidence presented thus far of Iraqw influence in Mbugu is so negligible, that the few above examples could be dismissed as mere coincidence, a more extensive examination of the vocabulary presents a different picture. The following is virtually an exhaustive list of clearcut previously-recorded Mbugu and Iraqw equivalents (given in that order, preceded by the English gloss): (1) 'body' *m-sako* (Farler) : *hlaqwa* pl. *hlaqo*; (2) 'bone' *i-fuara* : *fara*; (3) 'breast' *i-asema* : *iseema*; (4) 'cow' *de* (*ele* Meinhof) : *hle*; (5) 'to die' *ga* : *gwa'a* (see 'to kill'); (6) 'eye' *i-ila* : *ila*; (7) 'fire' *mw-ahla* : *ahla*; (8) 'firewood' *habi* : 'charcoal' *xabi*; (9) 'hill' *ana* : *on* (Burunge); (10) 'human being' *mu-he* : *he*; (11) 'to kill' *ga'a* : *gaas* (see 'to die'); (12) 'milk' *i-iba* : *iliba* (a Burunge form); (13) 'moon' *m-hlihle* : *hlehey* (Alagwa); (14) 'nose' *nunga* : *dunga*; (15) 'tree' *mu-xatu* : *xaimu* pl. *xatlin* (Meinhof; a Burunge form). In the above examples, Mbugu noun prefixes have been separated by a hyphen; *tl* and *hl* are voiceless laterals, the former preceded by stop release. Unless otherwise noted, the Mbugu forms are from Green, and those of the Iraqw group from Whiteley (1958).

Further investigation might reveal additional cognates, which may have diverged considerably in either sound or meaning. For example, Mbugu *ximeno* and Iraqw *tsir/i* (Burunge *tcira/a*); / = pharyngal plosive) 'bird' have little in common phonologically, but the Cushitic equivalents *qimbire* (Danakil), *šimbiro* (Galla), etc., suggest an earlier form which may have developed into those of Mbugu and Iraqw. There are, furthermore, a few clear similarities between Mbugu and Cushitic languages, not shared by the Iraqw group, notably Mbugu *mu-harega* and Galla *harqa* 'hand' and Mbugu *aro* and Galla *arba* 'elephant'. Vocabulary resemblances to Bantu languages scarcely touch basic vocabulary with one or two exceptions (e.g. the adjective stem *-le* 'long'), but include a few names for wild and domesticated animals, cultural items, and the numerals 7–9 (but not 10) and 100 which, where decidable, resemble Shambala, by and large, rather than Asu, in contrast to the grammar. Vocabulary resemblances to other languages (e.g. those of West Africa and the upper Nile pointed out by Meinhof) are too sporadic to allow any conclusions to be drawn. Additional investigation may throw more light on the sources of the Mbugu vocabulary, but at present they are largely obscure.

Interpretation

All that one can say with certainty about the origin of Mbugu is that at some time a Bantu and a non-Bantu language came into contact. The Bantu language may have been Asu, but just as Shambala grammatical elements now appear to be slowly replacing those from Asu in Mbugu, so may the Asu forms have replaced those from another Bantu language of even earlier contact, just as such forms are replaced when one Bantu language comes into contact with another (e.g. Swahili in the Congo in contact with local Bantu languages). This may explain certain Mbugu verb affixes apparently neither of Asu nor Shambala origin. The non-Bantu language may have been related to the Iraqw group, but this is not certain, although there was undoubtedly some sort of affinity. One can only speculate as to how the language developed its present form. I offer the following tentative suggestion. In the course of contact the Bantu language incorporated a number of words from the non-Bantu language and adapted them to the Bantu grammatical system, precisely as has happened to Arabic words in Swahili, for example, where borrowed nouns acquired Bantu prefixes and appropriate concords, either by reanalysis (e.g. *ki-tabu/vi-tabu* 'book/books' from Arabic *kitab*) or by accretion (e.g. *m-tini/mi-tini* 'fig tree/trees' from Arabic *tin* 'fig'), while verbs acquire Bantu derivational affixes (e.g. *fahamika* 'to be understandable' derived from *fahamu* 'to understand', a Swahili verb borrowed from Arabic) and are conjugated, of course, on the Bantu model. On the other hand, Bantu words were borrowed into the non-Bantu progenitor of Mbugu with some variation in their affixes according to grammatical function. A superficial parallel would be the use of Bantu prefixes with Bantu ethnic names in English. Thus one might say that someone is a mu-Ganda, a member of the ba-Ganda people, who inhabit the kingdom of bu-Ganda, and speak lu-Ganda. Furthermore, sporadic concord may have developed if Bantu adjectives were borrowed (e.g. *-le* 'long', which actually occurs in Mbugu).

The Bantu and the non-Bantu language may have gradually become ever more alike until they were little more than stylistic variants, depending on who was speaking to whom. Those who have described the language, notably Meinhof and Green, have noted, for example, as was already mentioned, a certain tendency to omit class prefixes, particularly of singular nouns. In addition, Bantu and non-Bantu alternatives exist for a number of words (e.g. 'elephant', 'meat'). It is possible that these were once more numerous, but that gradually the non-Bantu forms were favored, perhaps to make the language less comprehensible to the surrounding Bantu peoples. It is conceivable, furthermore, but not demonstrable, that a third and totally different linguistic group entered into this bilingual situation and in trying to learn both other languages contributed substantially to mixing them, since it is far more common to confuse two imperfectly-learned second languages than a person's native tongue and one that has been subsequently acquired.

Is Mbugu, then, a linguistic hybrid, a true mixed language? This would depend upon one's definition, but it clearly challenges the presupposition that one can unambiguously determine the linguistic antecedence of every language. Whiteley (1960) speculated that:

> It is possible, however, that one is not recording evidence of a unique contact situation, but of a more usual situation, which for one reason or another, has been protracted over a long period. There are certainly other examples in East Africa of groups changing their language completely in the way that small sections of Bantu-speaking Kuria and Gusii have become assimilated by the Nilotic Luo, and similar small groups of Iraqw have become assimilated by Barabaig, who speak a Nandi-type language. Here [i.e. in Mbugu] it is certainly true that the affix system is better established among the younger people than among the older generations, and it may well be that if they do not become wholly assimilated by the Shambala, they will in time not only operate the affix structure of a Bantu language but will also acquire a sufficient number of Bantu stems and roots for them to be considered speakers of a Bantu language (p. 96).

There is no evidence, however, that widespread bilingualism in a speech community in the process of giving up one language in favor of another is normally accompanied by the sort of linguistic interpenetration found in Mbugu. Furthermore, this language appears to have remained relatively unchanged in its present state for a considerable period, since its Bantu elements point more to Asu, a language with which it is no longer in intense contact, than to Shambala. Rather, it appears to have developed its present form as a result of a particularly intense contact situation, which has subsequently disappeared. The changes that Mbugu has been undergoing since then are of a more 'normal' and gradual nature. There may be other languages as mixed as Mbugu, but they are not common or typical.

Can Mbugu be considered an instance of pidginization and subsequent creolization? It is not always easy to draw a clear line between these processes and other types of linguistic change resulting from intense language contact. Nevertheless, one feature which is virtually universal to those languages generally classified as pidgins and creoles is the drastic reduction of morphological complexity and irregularity. For example, those pidgins which have developed from Bantu languages, such as Fanagalo (the mining pidgin of South Africa), Lingala, or 'up-country' Swahili, have lost most of the Bantu noun class system and, in particular, its concordial features, the very Bantu elements which are most conspicuous in Mbugu. If Mbugu has undergone pidginization, it is of a very different type from that undergone by known pidginized varieties of Bantu languages.

Can Mbugu, on the other hand be considered a Bantu language which has been 'relexified' with a non-Bantu vocabulary? A comparison of the Bantu and non-Bantu portions of the Mbugu vocabulary shows that the former is, in general, more likely to have been borrowed than the latter. For example, the numerals 1–6 are not of Bantu origin, whereas 7–9 and 100 are; 10, on the other hand, is not, nor are 20–90, which are derived from it. If Mbugu were a 'relexified' Bantu language, one would expect the reverse situation, since higher numerals are more readily borrowed than lower ones. Thus, the development which Mbugu has undergone defies easy categorization; it remains a unique linguistic specimen.

REFERENCES

Baumann, Oskar 1894. *Durch Massailand zur Nilquelle*, Berlin

Copland, B. 1933–4. 'A note on the origin of the Mbugu, with a text', *Zeitschrift für eingeborenen Sprachen* 24(4):241–4

Green, E. C. 1963. 'The Wambugu of Usambara, with notes on Kimbugu', *Tanganyika notes and records* 175–88

Greenberg, Joseph H. 1955. *Studies in African linguistic classification*, New Haven

1963. *The Languages of Africa*, Bloomington

Johnston, Sir Harry H. 1886. *The Kilimanjaro expedition*, London

Kotz, Ernst 1909. *Grammatik des Chasu in Deutsch-Ostrafrika* (Archivum des Studium der deutschen Kolonial-Sprachen, 10), Berlin

Meinhof, Carl 1906. 'Linguistische Studien aus Ostafrica: X Mbugu, XI Mbulunge', *Mitteilungen des Seminars der orientalischen Sprachen* 9(3):293–323, 324–33

Seidel, August 1895. *Handbuch der Schambalasprache in Usambara, Deutsch-Ostafrika*, Dresden

1900. 'Die Sprache von Ufiomi in Deutsch-Ostafrika', *Zeitschrift für afrikanische und ozeanische Sprachen* 5:165–75

Shaw, A. Downes 1885. *A pocket vocabulary of the Ki-Swahili, Ki-Nyika, Ki-Taita, and Ki-Kamba languages; also a brief vocabulary of the Kibwyo dialect, collected by Archdeacon Farler*, London

Tucker, A. N., and Bryan, M. 1957. *Lingustic survey of the northern Bantu borderland*, vol. IV, Oxford University Press

Whiteley, W. H. 1958. *A short description of item categories in Iraqw, with material on Gorowa, Alagwa, and Burunge* (East African linguistic studies, 3), Kampala

— 1960. 'Linguistic hybrids', *African studies* 19(2):95–7

DETECTING PRIOR CREOLIZATION

An analysis of the historical origins of Marathi[1]

FRANKLIN C. SOUTHWORTH

Introduction

The processes known as pidginization and creolization occupy a unique position in the theory of linguistic change. Most of the known cases have occurred within the last 400 years, under well-documented social circumstances. Though linguists often suspect that the same thing may have happened on other occasions in the more distant past, such suspicions must remain pure speculation unless supported by historical documentation – or unless it is possible to establish a set of criteria which would prove the likelihood of pidginization having occurred at an earlier period in history. With this purpose in mind, this paper proposes to examine various criteria which might be used in testing hypotheses of prior pidginization, and apply them to a specific case, Marathi, which has traditionally been considered an Indo-Aryan (Sanskrit-derived) language showing extensive influence from the neighboring Dravidian languages (Bloch 1919:33).

The initial period of contact between Indo-Aryan and the indigenous languages of India goes back some three millennia, and even for the Marathi area one must assume a minimum time-depth of about two millennia. At such long range, can we find evidence to distinguish between the results of pidginization (and subsequent creolization) and other kinds of contact? Is it possible that, over long periods, the same kind of results could be produced by other processes? Is pidginization a unique process, fundamentally distinct from other types of contact, or is it an extreme point in a continuum whose opposite pole is 'normal' transmission? Seeking the answers to these questions may help us to understand the importance of pidginization and related processes in the history of human society.

The most common type of linguistic interference, known as borrowing, involves primarily the transfer of lexical items from one language to another, though extensive borrowing may also contribute to structural changes of various kinds. Even extreme cases of borrowing produce no interruption of ongoing speech behavior, and leave intact the signs of genetic affiliation, such as basic vocabulary and high-frequency inflectional morphemes and function words. Pidginization, as a process, is distinct from borrowing in that it involves a sharp break in transmission and the creation of a new code, which serves for communication between groups which previously had no common language. Pidgins are popularly thought to combine the vocabulary of one language with the grammar of another. Obviously this is an oversimplification (Hall 1952), but there appear to be numerous cases of languages which are like pidgins in that they can be given an unambiguous genetic classification on lexical grounds, but at the same time show extensive non-lexical resemblances to other languages which cannot be explained as borrowing in the usual sense. Goodman's Mbugu is such a case; in the Indo-European family, French and the Germanic family are also possible candidates. Marathi, even in its oldest known form (tenth century A.D.), also presents such a picture: grammatical and semantic resemblances with Dravidian are massive, but there are few actual lexical items from Dravidian sources. The vague term 'influence' is often used to describe such phenomena; Boas's phrase, 'the diffusion of grammatical processes over contiguous areas' (1929:6) is equally unhelpful in contributing to our understanding of the social processes involved. Clearly, not all cases of influence imply pidginization, and as this question is pursued more deeply it becomes clear that we need a more precise sociolinguistic typology of outcomes of language contact. This investigation of Marathi is intended to be a step in that direction.

Socio-historical background

Figure 1 shows the present distribution of the major Indo-Aryan and Dravidian languages; Munda languages are nowadays limited to a few scattered locations in central and eastern India. The original speakers of Indo-Aryan began to make their appearance in the western borderlands of the subcontinent somewhere around 1500 B.C. (Wheeler 1959:22). Current archaeological opinion holds it unlikely that there was anything resembling an Aryan 'invasion', but rather that there was a series of small-scale movements which went on over a long period (Fairservis, personal communication). On entering India, the Aryans encountered a once highly-developed urbanized civilization in an advanced stage of decay and dissolution (Wheeler 1959:114ff; Fairservis 1967:16): this was the famous Harappan civilization of the Indus Valley. Though there is no positive evidence to link this civilization with the Dravidian peoples, the present distribution of Dravidian languages is compatible with the hypothesis that they covered most of northern India at an earlier period (Emeneau 1956:6): non-literary Dravidian languages still appear in the Hindi and Oriya-speaking areas, as well as in western West Pakistan (Brahui). Furthermore, their present distribution appears on the basis of genetic subgrouping to reflect the older distribution (Dyen 1956). Thus most of the present area of Indo-Aryan speech would appear to represent absorption of earlier Dravidian speakers, and the notion that the Dravidians were forced to retreat southward en masse before the oncoming Aryans has little to support it. If we add to this the evidence of current research in physical anthropology, which indicates a continuity in dominant physical type on the subcontinent from the late stone age up to the present day (Kennedy 1965), it seems highly inappropriate to speak of the Aryanization of India as having involved the physical displacement of one group by another.

FIGURE I. *The principal languages of the Indo-Pakistan subcontinent*

Notes: The Urdu-Hindi area also includes: Iranian languages (such as Pashto, Balochi) in the western part of West Pakistan; Rajasthani, a distinct variety of Hindi (or a distinct language?) in the area north of Gujarat; distinct varieties of eastern Hindi such as Bhojpuri and Maithili; Sindhi (formerly in the southern part of West Pakistan, though many Sindhis have now settled in India).

The dotted lines mark the boundaries between India and Pakistan.

The line north of Kannada and Telugu is the boundary between Indo-Aryan and the major Dravidian languages, though some non-literary Dravidian languages are spoken in the Indo-Aryan area also.

The newcomers spoke 'an Indo-European language, later to be called Sanskrit' (Emeneau 1954:282). The oldest known form of this language is that of the Vedic rituals; a somewhat evolved form became the language of the epics, the classical language of poetry and drama, and later (and to some extent still today) the vehicle of scholarship and literature, much like the Latin of medieval Europe. The earliest actual written records in Indo-Aryan (the

Ashokan inscriptions of the third century B.C.) are not, however, in this language, but in a series of dialects known as Prakrits, which are substantially different from Sanskrit but historically derivable from it in most essential aspects. At the point when these inscriptions appear, it is clear that Sanskrit had attained the status of a learned language. Thus from an early period we have evidence of the existence of a functional diglossia involving the co-existence of Sanskrit (literally the 'refined' language) and Prakrit (the 'natural' or 'crude' speech), the former being used for ritual and formal occasions and the latter for the casual routine of worldly life. Indian grammarians tell us that the Brahmin who talks Sanskrit to the gods during the Vedic sacrifice uses ordinary language at other times; we have essentially the same phenomenon in modern India, where the ability to use the formal variety of a language (such as the /sadhu bhaṣa/ or 'decent language' of Bengali) is one of the essential marks of a cultured man. It seems probable that the elaborate techniques of memorization developed for the preservation of Vedic texts, and in fact the whole Hindu grammatical tradition, had as its primary motivation the maintenance of the purity of this ritual language – and also the status and prestige of its speakers. That there was a social aspect to this diglossia is shown by the use of Prakrit by the lower characters in Sanskrit dramas; its persistence in modern India is documented by studies such as Gumperz 1958. Pandit (1963:79–80) suggests that one of the main functions of Sanskritic or Sanskritized speech is to accentuate socially important distinctions, though nowadays English has taken over this function for many Indians. At the same time, the Sanskritization (or Anglicization) of one's speech is an important ingredient in the competition for social status, except for the elite who do not need to compete.

It is likely that the groups of incoming Aryans achieved a dominant status in the communities they entered, by virtue of their well-developed rituals and their knowledge of advanced metallurgical techniques, military arts and horsemanship. At the time they first appeared on the scene they were primarily a pastoral people (see Emeneau 1954:284–5), but they were entering an area of fairly advanced sedentary cultivators. Ultimately the Aryans must have been integrated (and interbred) with the indigenous upper class; the stratified nature of the pre-Aryan local society is suggested by the technological advancement of the Harappan sites, as well as the existence of advanced agricultural techniques elsewhere in the subcontinent. The language of highest prestige under these circumstances (apart from Sanskrit, used extensively only by the priestly class) would have been the colloquial Aryan speech, or rather the closest approximation to it which an individual speaker could produce; if his native speech was not Aryan, then his ability to approximate it would vary in direct proportion to his geographical and social proximity to the nearest Aryan speakers. Obviously, this could range from near-native control (in cases of intimate contact) to a true pidgin (which would be the most likely result in the case of lower-class individuals), and it is possible that the whole range existed. While this cannot be proven, there is evidence (particularly phonological) to show that a socially differentiated continuum still exists which could well be the remnant of such an earlier spectrum (see *Social variations* below). (It should be noted also that these circumstances were partially duplicated during the British period, resulting in just such a linguistic spectrum, running from foreign-sounding English – the familiar Indian English of the educated Indian – to the rural varieties which are totally incomprehensible to the newly-arrived American or Englishman.) The propagation of Indo-Aryan speech, like English, was probably facilitated by economic factors, such as the development of north–south trade routes and the existence of widespread trading communities such as the modern Marwaris or Chettis.

One aspect of the Indian diglossia is important in predicting the outcome of this situation: the upper class, while fiercely maintaining the purity of their ritual language, can often afford to take a much more relaxed attitude about their language of worldly intercourse, which has no religious or intellectual significance; it is the language used for talking with ordinary people about ordinary things. Thus we can expect to find the upper class much more tolerant of modifications in Prakrit introduced by others, and less motivated to preserve its purity; this, in fact, coincides with the attitudes of modern educated Indians. The non-appearance of extreme pidginized forms of Indo-Aryan in early texts is accounted for by the fact that all writing and scholarship has traditionally been in the hands of Brahmins, the guardians of the purist tradition.

The above shows that the conditions for pidginization, or something closely akin to it, were present in the initial period of Aryan-Dravidian contact. For a pidgin to develop into a creole, there must be factors which lead to its taking over new functions. In many of the known cases, the motivation for forsaking the native language in favor of the pidgin seems to have been the sheer need for social and physical survival (as in the case of groups of slaves who had no other common language). In the present case, the eclipse of Dravidian speech in most of the present Indo-Aryan area is probably due to a combination of the factors of prestige and the military dominance of the northern, Aryan-oriented urban centers which developed in the first millennium B.C. (Wheeler 1959: 132ff; Subbarao 1958: 156-7). With the gradual southward extension of this sphere of influence, there were presumably increased opportunities and pressures for people to adopt their version of Prakrit in more and more aspects of their lives. The probable linguistic outcome of this situation is taken up again in the *Conclusion*, following a presentation of the linguistic situation in Indo-Aryan, and particularly Marathi.

Linguistic evidence

Linguistically, pidgins have certain distinguishing features, some of which have been commented on in other papers in this volume. Synchronically, the most obvious characteristic is that they make use of limited resources, and lack certain types of complexity. While this might be a useable criterion for identifying pidgins, it is not of much help in identifying creoles, since these are usually normal full-sized languages in all respects. Diachronically, both pidgins and creoles are recognizable as deviant in certain respects when compared with their predecessors, at least in cases where the time-depth involves only a few centuries. This subject has been discussed by Hall in a number of publications; the main features which he has noted are the *reduction* of the resources of the model language[2] (loss of phonological contrasts, merging of morphological categories, extreme generalizations of semantic range of lexical items) and the *brusque restructuring* of features of the model language at all structural levels (examples below). He also points out that many of the changes which take place in the formation of a pidgin are indistinguishable at long range from normal changes, though they take place abruptly and often involve a whole set of interrelated items at once (such as a whole vowel system, or a whole category of inflectional affixes). In the following paragraphs Marathi is briefly compared to earlier Indo-Aryan with respect to phonological and grammatical structures; following this, some semantic similarities between Marathi and Dravidian are presented, and the evidence of vocabulary replacement is considered.

PHONOLOGICAL CHANGES

A number of sweeping changes took place throughout Indo-Aryan by the third century B.C., as evidenced by the Ashokan inscriptions; these changes include: the assimilation of the many and varied consonant clusters of Sanskrit (e.g. *sapta-* 'seven' → *satta-*, *švašru* 'father-in-law' → *sassu*); the loss of final consonants, followed later by the loss of all final short vowels, with disastrous morphological consequences; loss of the variable pitch accent of Vedic; a number of unconditioned phonemic mergers (e.g. *š, ṣ, s* → *s*; *ai, e* → *e*; *au, o* → *o*); spirantization and/or loss of most single intervocalic stops; loss of medial *h* in certain areas under certain conditions (see below). By the time of the earliest Marathi texts (tenth century A.D.), Marathi has undergone a number of additional reductions such as: loss of nasal consonants before voiceless stops; loss of medial *h* in further positions; additional phonemic mergers (such as *ch, s* → *s*; *i, ī* → *i*; *u, ū* → *u*); loss of unaccented /i/, /u/, and short /a/ (Southworth 1958:152–3). While these changes drastically altered the appearance of the language, they do not in themselves constitute evidence of any abnormal processes of change; they are no more extreme than the changes undergone by other Indo-European languages, for example. In fact, it is worth noting that there are some close parallels between the Indo-Aryan case and some of the European languages such as Germanic (loss of final consonants and vowels) and French (the fate of medial consonants and consonant clusters). It will be remembered, however, that these are two of the cases where abnormal processes of change have been suggested, and the possibility should not be ruled out that certain types of phonological change may correlate with specific kinds of social upheaval. For the present purpose, however, there is nothing further that can be said about these cases, except that they need further study.

RESTRUCTURING

Under the heading of restructuring the most important change, which affected almost all of Indo-Aryan, was the development of a set of retroflex consonants contrasting with the dentals inherited from Indo-European. All modern Indo-Aryan languages except Assamese have a distinction between *t d* (with primarily dental allophones) and *ṭ ḍ* (with varying degrees of retroflexion), occurring both aspirated and unaspirated; some languages (e.g. Marathi, Gujarati, and some varieties of Panjabi) have also *ṇ* and *ḷ* distinct from *n* and *l*. These contrasts are virtually universal in Dravidian, and must be reconstructed for proto-Dravidian (Emeneau 1956:7); they are frequent in Munda languages, but were probably not present in proto-Munda (Zide 1958: 47, n. 10). In tracing this development from the earliest period in Indo-Aryan, it seems probable that the retroflexes originated as allophonic modifications of original dentals, which came into contrast as a result of subsequent changes. Another important general change is the modification of syllable structure which results from some of the changes mentioned above, and which ultimately brings Indo-Aryan to resemble Dravidian in a general way (since the contrast between single and double stops is no longer present, as in proto-Dravidian and in the inherited portions of most Dravidian languages). Restructurings restricted (mainly) to Marathi include: change of the (phonetically predictable) word-stress of Prakrit to the initial syllable (Southworth 1958:143 ff.); the development of dental and palatal sets of affricates, which contrast in Marathi (and occur in the neighboring Kannada, Telugu, and Oriya, mostly in non-contrastive distribution) (Emeneau 1956:7–8); '. . . la diphtongaison de *e* et *o* initiaux prononcés *ye-* et *wo-*' (Bloch 1919:33), a well-known Dravidian phenomenon. These changes, as well as those of the preceding paragraph, all show that Indo-Aryan has been heavily modified in the direction of Dravidian. The crucial evidence for pidginization, however, is not provided by such changes, as long as there is nothing to show whether they took place gradually or suddenly. Both possibilities are open.

SOCIAL VARIATIONS

Very little material is available on social variation in Marathi, but such as there is suggests strongly that the speech of the uneducated (particularly the non-Brahmins) is consistently less Sanskritized, or more Dravidianized, than that of the literary standard. This shows up in two ways: (1) changes in the direction of Dravidian are often carried through more consistently in non-standard speech; (2) old Indo-Aryan contrasts which were eliminated by phonological change are reintroduced in Sanskrit loans in educated speech only. An example of the first type concerns the changes $e \rightarrow ye$ and $o \rightarrow wo$ mentioned by Bloch, which do not show up in educated urban speech nowadays except in a few cases, but are the regular representations in rural uneducated speech (see, for example, Chitnis 1964:3, 5). Examples of the second type include the reinstatement of the contrasts between i and $\bar{\imath}$, u and $\bar{u}$, and the reintroduction of the palatal and retroflex sibilants of Sanskrit in such learned words as $\bar{a}\check{s}\bar{a}$ 'hope', $ru\d{s}i$ 'seer'. More significant in the present context is the case of the aspirated consonants, which Marathi has inherited from early Indo-Aryan. Since these are not proto-Dravidian (and in fact occur only in very Sanskritized forms of Dravidian languages), their survival in Marathi could be construed as evidence against the hypothesis of pidginization, and therefore they require some comment here. On the whole, initial aspiration is well preserved in Marathi, but medial and final aspirates are as likely to be lost as retained (Bloch 1919:99ff.; Panse 1953:46–7). The aspirates of modern Sanskrit borrowings are accurately reproduced by educated speakers, but this is scarcely different from what is observed among educated speakers of Malayalam or Telugu.[3] Master (1964:15) points out that in Old Marathi texts 'There is a tendency to drop the aspirates of aspirated consonants or to aspirate unaspirated consonants'. This of course refers to scribal practice, but probably reflects fluctuation in the spoken language of the period. Non-standard Marathi in many areas lacks the aspiration (Apte 1962:9). In the uneducated speech of Phaltan, real contrast between aspirated and unaspirated consonants occurs only in word-initial position (M. Berntsen, personal communication). All this suggests that the original aspiration was on its way to disappearing from Marathi at some point in history, and that it may actually have been lost in some varieties. The current speech of uneducated low-caste individuals probably represents dialects which lost the aspiration, and partially reinstated it under the influence of educated (Brahmin) speech.

PHONOLOGICAL IRREGULARITY

Pidginization is usually pictured as taking place under circumstances which give rise to extensive mishearing, without subsequent opportunity for correction. Thus we should expect that pidgins would show more random variation, or phonological irregularity, than languages transmitted normally. This notion should of course be tested with a large number of languages, including known creoles as well as those languages assumed to have developed via normal processes of transmission only (if these can be identified with confidence). A comparison between Marathi and Hindi in this respect shows Marathi to have considerably greater irregularity. On the basis of a 200-word basic vocabulary list, approximately 32% of Marathi words and 44% of Hindi words can be derived by regular sound-change from the earliest (Sanskrit or Prakrit) forms of the words, whereas forms showing non-systematic sound change amount to 21% for Marathi and 13% for Hindi. The ratio of irregular to regular would be, then, 21/32 or 0.66 for Marathi and 13/44 or 0.30 for Hindi. (A count of items in Hall's Melanesian Pidgin glossary (1943) yields a figure of about 0.40.)

GRAMMATICAL CHANGES

Since a full presentation of the grammatical evidence for the influence of Dravidian on Marathi would require a large monograph, it will suffice here to mention briefly two important areas, postpositions and verbal sequences. Both of these features involve intimate parts of the grammatical structure, of the type traditionally thought of as relatively secure from outside influence. Both features show non-lexical influence, that is the use of inherited Indo-Aryan morphemes (in most cases) according to completely Dravidian patterns. The features mentioned here also appear in the other Indo-Aryan languages, but are more marked in Marathi: i.e. either they appear with higher frequency, or else they show more detailed similarity to their Dravidian equivalents. This type of resemblance can be considered necessary, though not sufficient, evidence in the present context; its relevance to the pidginization hypothesis is spelled out in the *Conclusion*.

Most of the languages of the subcontinent use postpositions to the complete exclusion of prepositions: e.g. Marathi *mumbaī lā* 'to Bombay', Hindi *dillī mē* 'in Delhi', Tamil *bambāy-le* 'in Bombay', Kharia (Munda) *og-te* 'to the house', *mAra-te* 'to the cave'. Many if not most of the postpositions of modern Indo-Aryan are traceable to morphemes of earlier Indo-Aryan, but not to earlier prepositions (most cases appear to go back to nominal or verbal forms). For example, a Marathi *rāmā pāśī* 'with Ram, in Ram's possession' reflects a Sanskrit *rāmasya* (genitive 'of Ram')+*pārśve* (locative of a noun which originally meant 'rib, side of the body' and later 'side, vicinity') 'at Ram's side'. It is particularly striking that some of the most common postpositions are not cognate from one Indo-Aryan language to another, even though they fill very similar functional slots. For example:

'Dative' = Marathi *lā* : Hindi *ko* : Panjabi *nu* : Nepali *lāi* : Bengali *ke* : Gujarati *ne*

'Genitive' = Marathi *cā* : Hindi *kā* : Panjabi *dā* : Nepali *ko* : Bengali *(e)r* : Gujarati *nā*[4]

While these suffixes can be considered as the functional replacements of the older Indo-Aryan suffixes (which were lost along with other word-finals, as noted above), their postnominal position and their probable origin suggest that they are actually based on Dravidian models. No satisfactory etymologies have been proposed for any of these suffixes, but the most likely candidates for their ancestors within Indo-Aryan are the earlier past participles of certain high-frequency verbs such as *kar-* 'do, make', *de-* 'give' (occurring throughout modern Indo-Aryan), Marathi *ne-* 'bring', Hindi *le-* 'take'. When the loss of earlier endings rendered the old genitive and dative homonymous, the same distinctions could be expressed by paraphrases of the type 'made for Ram' (Skt *rāmāya kṛtaḥ* → Pkt *rāmā kiya* → Hindi *rām kā* 'Ram's'), 'acquired for Ram' (Skt *rāmāya citaḥ* → Pkt *rāmā ciya* → Old Marathi *rāmā ciyā* → Marathi *rāmā cā* 'Ram's'), 'given to Ram' (Skt *rāmāya ditaḥ* → Pkt *rāmā diya* → Panjabi *rām dā* 'Ram's'). Although these paraphrases make use of inherited Indo-Aryan material, the presence of a Dravidian model is indicated by such examples as Tamil *rāman-oḍiya*, Malayalam *rāman-ḍe* 'Raman's' (probably originally 'Raman-owned', cf. the now obsolete Tamil verb *uḍaiya* 'to own'). These cases seem to be directly comparable with such typically pidgin developments as that of English *belong* in Melanesian Pidgin (as in *ars bIlɔŋ tri* 'bottom part of a tree', *kajkaj bIlɔŋ ju* 'your food').

Languages of all three families in the subcontinent have very frequent constructions involving sequences of verbs ending in a finite form, the preceding ones generally being bare stems or infinitival forms (Emeneau 1956:9ff; Southworth 1961): e.g. Marathi *zā-u lāgto* 'go-Aff begins' – 'begins to go', Hindi *jā-nā cāhiye thā* 'go-Aff needed it-was' = '(someone) needed to go', Tamil *pōh-a māṭān* 'go-Aff won't' = 'he won't go'. Emeneau remarks of this phenomenon: 'It is one of the syntactic features of Sanskrit that distinguishes it from other Indo-European languages . . . We must look to the syntax of the non-Indo-European languages of India for the stimulus that brought about this re-use in India of older material' (1965:9). A particular feature of these sequences in Dravidian languages is the use of negative auxiliaries in the final position (e.g. Tamil *pōh-a māṭen* 'I won't go', *pōh-a māṭānga* 'they won't go', *pōh-a le* 'didn't go', *pōh-a kūḍādu* 'shouldn't go'). Marathi alone among the Indo-Aryan languages has developed a whole set of negative auxiliaries on the Dravidian pattern: cf. *zā-t nāhi* 'doesn't go', *zā-t nāhit* 'they don't go', *zā-u nako* 'don't go' (imperative), *zā-t nasel* 'probably doesn't go', *zā-u naye* 'shouldn't go', etc. Again, these Marathi forms consist mainly of inherited Indo-Aryan material (including the initial morpheme *na-*, of Indo-European origin), but have clearly been remodeled on the prevailing Dravidian pattern. Other similarities in this area of grammatical structure could be cited (cf. the semantic parallel in the next section), but the above are sufficient to indicate the extent of interpenetration.

SEMANTIC SIMILARITIES

The most important resemblances between Marathi and Dravidian are found in the realm of semantics, in the sense that morphemes with closely similar ranges of meaning, and similar semantic distinctions, are found in both. (Marathi is not alone among Indo-Aryan languages in showing such resemblances, but it appears to have a greater number of them than, for example, Hindi.) Very few of these similarities can be attributed to lexical borrowing, since the overwhelming majority of morphemes involved are either derived from early Indo-Aryan or are of obscure origin. For the present purpose, primary interest would focus on those cases which show deviation from the oldest Indo-Aryan meanings in the direction of Dravidian models; only further research (especially on the Dravidian side) will make it possible to estimate how many cases of semantic convergence are of this type. The following brief list includes some prominent cases which fall in this category, and which are also significant in terms of frequency and/or cultural content.

1. The so-called 'plural of respect' occurs in languages all over the subcontinent in both second and third person – e.g. Marathi *te* = Tamil *avanga* 'they; he (formal)'.

2. Marathi, like most Dravidian languages, distinguishes in the first person plural pronoun between inclusive[5] (*āpaṇ*, cf. Tamil *nāma*) and exclusive (*āmhi*, cf. Tamil *nānga*) forms. This distinction is Proto-Dravidian, but is lacking in Sanskrit and elsewhere in modern Indo-Aryan.

3. Both Dravidian and Indo-Aryan languages have copulative verbs, but in equational sentences which identify one NP with another, it is common in Dravidian languages to have no copula (e.g. Tamil *avar enga appā* 'he our father' = 'he is our father'). Such sentences normally have a copula in Indo-Aryan languages (as in Hindi *vo hamāre pitāji haĩ* 'he our father is'), but in Marathi the copula is optional, and perhaps only occurs when emphasis is intended: *te āmce vaḍil (āhet)* 'he our father (is)'.

4. In Tamil and Malayalam (descriptions for other Dravidian languages are not sufficiently explicit) a common verbal suffix used to refer to future time can best be described as meaning 'event which is expected to occur, but under circumstances which cannot be specified' (Southworth 1968). Thus this suffix is not only appropriate to future time, but to events regarded as probable or contingent in present and past time as well. The so-called 'future' forms of Marathi and Hindi (and perhaps other Indo-Aryan languages) cover this same range of meaning.

5. The English verb *have* (in the meaning 'possess' or 'own') translates into a number of Indian languages with expressions containing the post-

position which also has the meaning 'near', e.g. Marathi *mājhā kade pustak āhe* 'me near book is' = 'I have a book', and similarly Tamil *en kiṭṭe pustagam irukkadu*, Hindi *mere pās kitāb hai*, etc. Most of the other meanings of English *have* are expressed similarly by post-positions in languages of both families.

6. In languages of both families, there are a number of morphemes which function both as main verbs and as non-initial elements in verbal sequences (see above), known as verbal operators. Often the meanings of the same form in these different usages seem totally unrelated, but the semantic shifts involved are so similar in different languages that they can hardly be ascribed to independent development. For example:

(a) Marathi *ghe-* 'take': as verbal operator, *kar-un ghe* 'do something to oneself' (cf. Tamil *koḷ-* 'take': as operator, *vāng-i ko* 'buy for yourself' or 'buy according to your wish');

(b) Marathi *ṭāk-* 'throw, get rid of': as operator, *khā-un ṭāk* 'eat up, get done eating' (cf. Tamil *viḍ-* 'leave, abandon': as operator, *pō-i viḍu* 'beat it, get out');

(c) Marathi *zā-* 'go (away)': as operator, *visr-un zā* 'forgot completely' (cf. Tamil *pō-* 'go': as operator, *oḍanj-u pō-cci* 'It's completely broken');

(d) Marathi *ṭhev-* 'put, place' (← Skt *sthāpayati* 'cause to stand'): as operator, *sāng-un ṭhev* 'tell (someone something) for future reference, tell once and for all' (cf. Tamil *vecc-* 'put, insert': as operator, *soll-i vecc-* 'tell for future reference').

7. In a large number of cases, semantic distinctions are made between particular pairs of words which have no early Indo-Aryan parallels (though the morphemes involved often have Sanskrit cognates); for example:

(a) Marathi *nes-* 'wear, put on' (used only for the traditional unstitched one-piece garments, the *sari* and the *dhoti*): *ghāl-* 'put; put on, wear' (other clothing, e.g. stitched garments, shoes); Tamil *kaṭṭ-*: *pod-* express the same distinction; Hindi has a single verb; *pahan-*, to cover all varieties of clothing;

(b) Marathi *zunā* 'old, of long standing', (used e.g. for inanimates or for persons of long-standing status, as in *zunā mitra* 'old friend'): *mhātārā* 'old, aged' (of chronological age of animates); the same distinction is communicated by Tamil *paṛayya*: *keṛavan*, Hindi *purānā*: *būṛhā* (← Skt *vṛddha-* 'grown, increased');

(c) Marathi *bhāt* 'cooked rice' (← Skt *bhakta-* 'eaten'): *tāndul* 'uncooked, husked rice' (as bought in the market): *dhān* 'paddy'; similarly Tamil *sora* (Brahmin *sādam*): *arisi*: *nellu*; cf. Hindi *cāwal* 'rice' (in any form);

(d) Dravidian languages in general distinguish lexically between younger and older siblings (cf. Tamil *annan* 'elder brother', *tambi* 'younger brother', *akkā* 'elder sister', *tange* 'younger sister'); Marathi normally makes the distinction by using one of the adjectives *thorlā* 'elder' (*thorlā bhāu* 'elder brother', *thorli bahin* 'elder sister', *thorlā mulgā* 'elder son', *thorli mulgi* 'elder daughter') or *dhākṭā* 'younger'; in fact, these adjectives are often nominalized, so that *thorlā* and *dhākṭā* come to be equivalent to Tamil *aṇṇan* and *tambi*, and *thorli* and *dhākṭi* equivalent to Tamil *akkā* and *tange*.

Vocabulary replacement

The rate of replacement of a language's basic vocabulary falls in a rather narrow range for most languages. The departures (such as Icelandic) are in the direction of slower change, whereas Hall (1959) has found that the rate of replacement for Neo-Melanesian *vis-à-vis* English was wildly out of line in the other direction. Thus a glaring discrepancy in rate of replacement could be taken as supporting a hypothesis of pidginization. This line of investigation is valuable since it is one of the few indications we can get of the *rapidity* of change.

Comparing Marathi with Sanskrit the retention is on the order of 45%, which would indicate a time-depth of about four millennia. The retention figure for Hindi is about 65%, indicating a time-depth of only two millennia.[6] Both these percentages are probably biased on the high side, since the available sources for the vocabulary of Sanskrit lump together the vocabulary of different periods and probably different regional varieties as well. It is not possible to establish a single 200-word list, discrete in time and space, for the earlier period, and all words which have cognates in early Sanskrit texts have been counted as retentions. Thus the actual time-depths are probably higher.

[Compared with the 3,500 years derived from other estimates (see *Socio-historical background* above), the Hindi figure is, as expected, an underestimation, and perhaps not too great a one, considering also the persistence of Sanskrit in the same society, and hence lack of complete independence in the development of Hindi. The Marathi figure, on the other hand, already over-shoots the 3,500 year estimate, contrary to usual expectation with such figures. The overestimation is even more serious, in all likelihood, given the two sources of underestimation noted above (composite Sanskrit list, lack of independence). Marathi would thus seem to match Hall's finding for a known case of pidginization, Neo-Melanesian.]

If the Hindi figure can be taken as a norm, then the Marathi figure, and the discrepancy of 20% less retention, is perhaps deviant enough to support a hypothesis of pidginization, or some other abnormal transmission process. On the other hand, there are many uncertainties involved in this calculation; there remains, in addition, some doubt about the extent to which Sanskrit can be considered the direct parent of the modern vernaculars. A thorough study of this question would require a separate article. The most we can say at this point is that Marathi does appear deviant according to this measure.

Conclusions

In order to make a claim of prior pidginization plausible, it is necessary to show that the requisite social circumstances were in existence at the right time, and also that the characteristic linguistic effects of pidginization are in evidence. Mintz's discussion shows that pidginization requires a rather special set of circumstances; he also makes it clear that further comparative research will be necessary before agreement can be reached on the general social prerequisites. It seems, however, that the co-existence of interdependent but distinct hierarchically arranged social groups was a characteristic of all the Caribbean slave communities, as well as other situations which have given rise to European-based pidgins (e.g. in Melanesia and the Philippines). This characteristic, which would seem to be a crucial one, is also present in the multi-caste towns and villages of contemporary India, and has been a fundamental feature of society throughout the subcontinent from very early times.

As for the linguistic evidence, on balance the case is plausible but not conclusive. The evidence of deep structural penetration in *Grammatical changes* and *Semantic similarities* is necessary, but not sufficient, to show pidginization. The evidence of vocabulary replacement and of phonological irregularity is sufficient to show that something other than normal processes of change was at work, though not clear enough to prove pidginization decisively. Thus, there are conflicts in the data,[7] which in my opinion can be best resolved by recognizing that, whether or not Marathi qualifies as a true creole, its present characteristics are probably the result of a prolonged process of mutual adaptation between an Aryan language and a local pidgin-creole (or more likely, a series of pidgin-creoles). To spell it out more clearly, I believe the evidence points to the following series of events:

1. As the Aryan language spread into the indigenous (Dravidian and/or Munda) speech communities, pidginized forms of Indo-Aryan were created and stabilized in the context of trade and joint agricultural activities within multi-caste settlements. The creation of these pidgins may have in part coincided with the consolidation of these settlements.[8] In the initial stages the languages of such communities would have been: Sanskrit (confined mainly to ritual activities), Prakrit (i.e. a colloquial form of early Indo-Aryan), local language(s), and pidgin. The pidgin would have been the principal medium of communication between poor or middle-class cultivators and their superiors. From this starting point, the following developments took place gradually and (more or less) simultaneously:

2(a). The local language was given up in favor of Prakrit or pidgin. This development was probably a progressive one in the social (higher to lower) and geographical (north to south) senses. Note that for the lower castes the Prakrit or pidgin had higher prestige than the local language, whereas for the higher castes it was not particularly prestigious. (Obviously, where two languages are unequal in status, their influence on each other will not be mutual. In those cases where the higher language drives out the lower, it can only do so at the cost of drastic modifications in its structure.)

2(b). There was a gradual convergence between pidgin and Prakrit, to the point where they were no longer sharply distinguishable from each other, but were simply the extreme points of a continuum. (This would seem to parallel the development which DeCamp assumes for Jamaica (see his paper in this volume); in fact Marathi may well be an example of a post-creole speech continuum of much earlier origin than any discussed hitherto.) The result of this process would of course vary depending on the relative proportion of speakers of the different languages in each area; the same process was presumably taking place all over the present Indo-Aryan region, but with different degrees of pidginization in each place. Marathi (and particularly the lower-caste varieties of Marathi in the extreme south) apparently represents the most extreme, or most highly pidginized, of these developments.[9]

It may perhaps be useful to display some of the processes involved here, in diagrammatic form. If the normal development of a language is represented by the formula **Language X → Language Y** (e.g. Vulgar Latin → Italian, Proto-IE → Old Indo-Aryan), then perhaps an appropriate way to represent the process of pidginization would be:

$$\left.\begin{array}{c} \text{Language X} \\ + \\ \text{Language Y} \end{array}\right\} \to \text{X Pidgin Y (e.g.} \left.\begin{array}{c} \text{Chinese} \\ + \\ \text{English} \end{array}\right\} \to \text{Chinese Pidgin English)}$$

The development of a pidgin into a creole would be treated like a normal development (thus, Jamaican Pidgin English → Jamaican Creole English). The process which produces a quasi-creole, or semi-creole, like Marathi, could then be represented as follows:

$$\left.\begin{array}{c} \text{Language Y} \\ + \\ \text{X Pidgin Y} \end{array}\right\} \to \text{X creolized Y}$$

(the term *creolized* is meant to convey the notion of a language which is not quite a full creole, but modified in that direction). Regarding the appropriate labels for such languages, it is to be noted that most of the specific terms for hybrids combine an area name (Jamaican, Haitian, Philippine, Melanesian, etc.) with the name of the upper source language (English, French, Spanish, etc.); the lower language is usually not mentioned either because it is unknown

or because more than one lower language is involved. Using parallel termin-
ology for semi-creoles, Marathi could be called Maharashtrian creolized
Aryan (or Maharashtrian creolized Prakrit), and Mbugu would be called
Tanzanian creolized Bantu. (Another possibility would be Maharashtrian-ized
Prakrit, Tanzanian-ized Bantu.) Using these conventions, the development
of Marathi might be diagrammed as follows:

$$
\text{Old Indo- Aryan} \rightarrow
\begin{cases}
\text{Prakrit} & \begin{array}{l} \text{Upper-class} \\ \rightarrow\text{Maharashtrian} \\ \text{Prakrit} \end{array} \\
\begin{array}{l} \text{Prakrit} \\ + \\ \text{local} \\ \text{lgs.} \end{array} & \begin{array}{l} + \\ \text{Maharashtrian} \\ \rightarrow\text{Pidgin} \\ \text{Prakrit} \end{array}
\end{cases}
\rightarrow
\begin{array}{l} \text{Maharashtrian} \\ \text{creolized} \\ \rightarrow\text{Prakrit} \\ (=\text{'Marathi'}) \end{array}
$$

Thus, I am suggesting that Marathi, though perhaps not strictly a creole,
nevertheless has a pidgin in its past.[10] The only alternative would be to assume
that the Dravidian influence in Marathi was transmitted via a different kind
of bilingualism, involving fuller control of two languages on the part of a
substantial segment of the population. The validity of this alternative would
depend on evidence showing that this type of bilingualism has produced, or
does in general produce, the kinds of results presented in *Linguistic evidence*
above. In general, this does not seem to be the case: French-English bilingualism among the upper class in England led to profound effects on English (the
lower language), but not on French (the upper language). On the other hand,
it is clear that we have no satisfactory general picture of the relationships
between linguistic change and various types of contact situations; we have,
for example, very little understanding of the social processes which have led
to the linguistic convergence observed in such areas as western Europe or the
northwest coast of North America. Languages in contact imply social groups
in contact, and the study of the former implies an understanding of the
relationships among the latter.

It seems likely that if our total knowledge of Indian languages consisted of
Vedic Sanskrit, modern Marathi, and Tamil, Marathi would be unhesitatingly
classified as a creole. The reason why we hesitate to classify it as such, in the
light of present evidence, is that Marathi appears as an extreme case within
the matrix of Indo-Aryan, which also includes other cases (such as Hindi)
which show less clearly the signs of pidginization. Thus, if Marathi is classified
as a creole, then apparently Hindi must be regarded as a creole of lower degree,
a less pidginized creole. This would conflict with the notion of pidginization
and borrowing as distinct processes. This solution is not advocated here. The
hypothesis proposed here assumes that pidginization took place throughout
the Indo-Aryan area, but that its long-range linguistic effects were tempered
or reinforced by other social factors (caste structure, diglossia, and Sanskritiza-

tion); these factors have led, at the extreme end of the spectrum, to a result which is similar to the classic modern cases of pidginization known from the Caribbean and the Pacific.

NOTES

1 I wish to thank Dell Hymes and Joan P. Mencher in particular for their help in preparing the present version of this paper. Murray Emeneau and Walter Fairservis also read an earlier version and provided valuable suggestions.

2 I use the term *model language* for what Hall calls the *source language* and others (e.g. Samarin) call the *target language*, i.e. that language which the initial speakers of a pidgin are presumably trying to speak. Hall's term seems inappropriate for this because it could equally well be applied to the other partner in the hybridization process.

3 Standard Marathi is probably no more Sanskritized than, say, literary Malayalam, both in terms of the precentage of Sanskrit loanwords used and in the extent to which they appear in phonologically 'correct' form. Thus these features have no bearing on genetic affiliations, but are concerned rather with the Sanskritizing tendencies of the traditional educated class in these areas.

4 All of these except the Bengali and Nepali forms show agreement with a following noun, e.g. Hindi *rām kā bhāī* 'Ram's brother', *rām kī bahan* 'Ram's sister'.

5 The Marathi exclusive form *āmhi* is derived from the old Indo-Aryan first person plural pronoun, but the inclusive form *āpaṇ* derives probably from Sanskrit *ātman* 'self'.

6 These precentages are calculated on the basis of lexical elements present in the earliest Sanskit texts. They do not match the percentages given in discussing phonological irregularities, since these are based on all earlier forms regardless of antiquity. Several of the pronominal forms did not enter into that calculation, since the possibility of analogical change made them difficult to classify.

7 The survival of some of the nominal and verbal inflections of old Indo-Aryan in Marathi may also be construed as evidence against pidginization (e.g. the imperfective suffix -*t*- of Marathi *ho-t-o* 'he becomes', *za-t-e* 'she goes' reflects an old present participle ending -*ant*, as in Skt *bhav-ant*- 'being'). However, we should not assume that in genuine pidgins all such inflectional elements are invariably lost.

8 A modern parallel for such pidgins can be seen in Bazaar Hindustani, a reduced form of Hindi/Urdu used mostly by uneducated laborers and tradesmen of various linguistic backgrounds in the modern urban centers of India. The variety used by any particular group, such as the Tamil-speaking coolies in Delhi, is stabilized in a pidgin stage by the uniformity of their social and linguistic contacts with their employers or patrons, and by their lack of opportunity to learn 'good' Hindi.

9 Though the details of life two or three millennia ago are not fully known, it seems likely that social and linguistic communication between the highest and lowest groups was mediated by middle-rung individuals. This is the practice in agricultural activities in many areas today, and the existence of three socially-defined varieties of speech (Brahmin, high non-Brahmin, untouchable) which have been reported for Marathi (Apte), Kannada (McCormack), and Tamil (Pillai), probably correlates with this.

10 The type of bilingualism reported in Gumperz 1967, in which the local Indo-Aryan and Dravidian languages have converged except for morphophonemics, can also be explained in terms of an earlier stage of pidginized Indo-Aryan.

REFERENCES

Apte, Mahadev L. 1962. 'Linguistic acculturation and its relation to urbanization and socioeconomic factors', *Indian Linguistics* 23:5–25
Biligiri, H. S. 1965. *Kharia: Phonology, grammar and vocabulary*, Poona, Deccan College Postgraduate and Research Institute
Bloch, Jules 1919. *La formation de la langue marathe*, Paris, Edouard Champion
Boas, F. 1929. 'Classification of American Indian languages', *Language* 5:1–7
Chitnis, Vijaya Shridhar 1964. 'The Khandeshi dialect (as spoken by farmers in the village of Mohadi in the Dhulia Taluka)', University of Poona Doctoral Thesis (unpublished)
Dyen, Isidore 1956. 'Language distribution and migration theory', *Language* 32:611–26
Emeneau, Murray B. 1954. 'Linguistic prehistory of India', *Proceedings American Philosophical Society* 98:282–92
　　1956. 'India as a linguistic area', *Language* 32:3–16
　　1968. 'Dravidian and Indo-Aryan: the Indian linguistic area' (paper read at conference on Dravidian civilization, Austin, Texas, Dec. 1968)
Fairservis, Walter A., Jr. 1967. 'The origin, character, and decline of an early civilization', *American Museum Novitates* 2302:1–48
Ferguson, Charles A. and John J. Gumperz (eds.) 1960. 'Linguistic diversity in South Asia: Studies in regional, social, and functional variation' (Research Center in Anthropology, Folklore and Linguistics, Publication 13; *International Journal of American Linguistics* 26(3), pt. III), Bloomington
Gumperz, John J. 1958. 'Dialect differences and social stratification in a North Indian village', *American Anthropologist* 60:668–82
　　1961. 'Speech variation and the study of Indian civilization', *American Anthropologist* 63:976–88
　　1967. 'On the linguistic markers of bilingual communication', *Journal of Social Issues* 23(2):48–57
Gumperz, John J. and C. M. Naim 1960. 'Formal and informal standards in the Hindi regional language area', in Ferguson and Gumperz 1960
Hall, Robert A., Jr. 1943. *Melanesian Pidgin English: grammar, texts, vocabulary*, Baltimore, Linguistic Society of America and Intensive Language Program of the ACLS
　　1952. 'Pidgin English and linguistic change', *Lingua* 3:138–46
　　1959. 'Neo-Melanesian and glottochronology', *International Journal of American Linguistics* 25:265–7
　　1961. 'Pidgin', *Encyclopaedia Britannica* 17:905–7
　　1964. *Introductory linguistics*, Philadelphia, Chilton
　　1966. *Pidgin and creole languages*, Ithaca, Cornell University Press
Kennedy, Kenneth A. R. 1965. 'Man before history in India, Pakistan and Ceylon: An interpretation of recently discovered human skeletal remains from Late Stone Age sites' (Paper read at Cornell University, May 17, 1965)

Master, Alfred 1964. *A grammar of old Marathi*, Oxford, Clarendon

McCormarck, William 1960. 'Social dialects in Dharwar Kannada', in Ferguson and Gumperz 1960

Pandit, Prabodh B. 1963. 'Sanskritic clusters and caste dialects', *Indian Linguistics* 24:70–80

Panse, Murlidhar G. 1953. *Linguistic peculiarities of Jnanesvari*, Poona, Deccan College

Pillai, M. Shanmugam 1960. 'Tamil – literary and colloquial', in Ferguson and Gumperz 1960

   1965. 'Caste isoglosses in kinship terms', *Anthropological Linguistics* 7(3):59–66

Ray, Punya Sloka, M. A. Hai, and L. Ray 1966. *Bengali language handbook*, Washington, Center for Applied Linguistics

Southworth, Franklin C. 1958. 'A test of the comparative method: a historically controlled reconstruction based on four modern Indic languages', Yale University doctoral dissertation, Ann Arbor, University Microfilms

   1961. 'The Marathi verbal sequences and their co-occurrences', *Language* 37:201–8

   1968. 'Time and related categories in English, Marathi, and Tamil' (Paper read at American Anthropological Association, Nov. 1968)

Srinivas, M. N. 1962. *Caste in modern India and other essays*, Bombay, Asia Publishing House

Subbarao, Bendapudi 1958. *The personality of India*, Baroda, Maharaja Sayajirao, University of Baroda Press

[*Tamil* Lexicon]. 1936. Madras, University of Madras (reprinted 1962)

Wheeler, Sir Mortimer 1959. *Early India and Pakistan to Ashoka*, New York, Praeger

Zide, Norman H. 1958. 'Final stops in Korku and Santali', *Indian Linguistics*, Turner Jubilee Volume 1:44–8

STATEMENTS AND PRÉCIS

A REPORT ON CHINOOK JARGON[1]

TERRENCE S. KAUFMAN

Identification

Chinook Jargon (CJ) is a trade language which was used throughout the north-west of North America in the latter half of the nineteenth century. In the first half of the ninteeenth century, and in the first half of the twentieth century, it had considerably reduced spread. Its existence is documented with certainty for about 1834 on the Columbia River (Lee and Frost), but even Lewis and Clark collected words in 1805 which are only attested in CJ.

Origin and source of lexicon

There are six major lexical strata in CJ: Lower Chinook (Chinookan), Nootka (Wakashan), Chehalis (Salishan), English, French, and 'Jargon' (words of un-determined origin, which are known with fair certainty to have no analogues in languages of the area). These strata are attested in Hale 1842, the earliest scien-tific report on CJ. The English, French, and Chehalis strata are not represented in the earliest attestations of CJ.

It is likely that some sort of jargon existed on the Columbia River before English or American exploration, since Lewis and Clark in 1895 recorded a few words which are unique to CJ (e.g. wapto, saplil). Whether the jargon was pre-Columbian, or the result of a stimulus from European sailors who had probably already touched at the mouth of the Columbia by 1800 is uncertain and a matter for debate. Some of the upriver Indians knew some English swear words, and the Clatsop chief Concomly spontaneously spoke to Lewis and Clark – expecting to be understood – some Nootka words (kamtaks, wik) which later formed part of CJ. The spread of CJ is not well documented. Trappers were in the area by 1815. French and English traders used CJ, and the former often took Indian wives. Missionaries encouraged the spread of CJ. Yet the jargon as spoken by all Indians shows that it was spread by people who had completely mastered the complex phonologies of the NW Indian languages, and therefore that Indians largely learned it from other Indians. The only lexical stratum showing phonological mutilation is the Nootka, and it is quite probable that this stratum was introduced by Whites, since the Nootkas themselves were almost never involved in the situations where CJ was used, whereas the sailors and traders of the late eighteenth century, who first stopped at Nootka, learned some Nootka, and seemed to expect Indians at subsequently contacted points to know Nootka as well. This may explain the use of some Nootka words by Concomly.

Periods and distribution

In terms of documentation by independent witnesses, we can be sure of the use of CJ in the following areas with the indicated latest possible dates.

Mouth of Columbia	by 1834 (Lee and Frost); (cf. Lewis and Clark 1904–5)
Fort Vancouver	by 1838 (Parker)
Willamette Valley	by 1847 (Palmer)
Oregon generally	by 1850 (Lyonnet)
Western Washington	by 1855 (Gibbs)
Frazer River	by 1858 (Anderson)
Western Montana	by 1865 (Stuart)
British Columbia generally	by 1870 (Tate)
Eastern Washington	by 1870 (St Onge)

For most of these areas (down to maybe 1860) the actual dates of first use are probably considerably earlier. The relatively late earliest documentation has allowed people to propose that the jargon was invented by the Hudson's Bay Company; this is extremely unlikely, in view of the fact that most of the lexicon and all of the grammatical morphemes are Indian words and the phonology is uniform among all Indian users, having the same complexity as the native languages. Others have proposed that the early French missionaries invented it, but this falls under the same objections. Undoubtedly both Hudson's Bay Co. and French missionaries found the jargon in use and took advantage of its existence to spread its distribution still further. That both groups did foster its spread is known. Some of the more important historical periods for the area are: 1805–15 exploration; 1815–30 Hudson's Bay; 1830–60 Missions and Settlement in Oregon; 1858 Frazer River Gold Rush; 1860–70 Civil War and Aftermath. In 1870 CJ probably had its greatest spread and number of users. After 1870 new settlers poured into Oregon – mainly Midlanders, where the first settlers had been Northerners – and the Indian population rapidly declined, due to their land being appropriated by the new settlers. By 1900 CJ was effectively obsolete in Oregon. However during the same period CJ spread to parts of Alaska bordering on British Columbia.

Relexification

In its spread through western Washington into British Columbia, CJ picked up words from Nisqually, Halkomelem, and Clallam (all Salishan), as well as more English words. The nature of CJ lexicon is that there is a relatively small number of morphemes (c. 500), all of which are roots, some of which, to be sure, have some very general functions. Each root has a definable range of meanings, according to context. 'Complex lexical items' are formed by juxtaposing roots according to specifiable syntactic rules, but their identification as such depends on the construction having a meaning not predictable from the component parts. There are a large number of complex lexical items, idioms as it were. The lexicon of CJ is small, but not puny. In the process of picking up new lexicon, change has occurred in three ways: (1) a new morpheme supplants an old one, e.g. French words tend to be replaced by English ones; (2) a complex lexical item is replaced by a single new morpheme; (3) new concepts are introduced. Type (3) however, is not common, so that in comparing an earlier stage of CJ with a later one, we can consider the changes in lexical form as primarily involving relexification.

Potential creolization

Hale reports that in Fort Vancouver many children who were the offspring of French trappers with Cree wives spoke CJ equally as well as French, Cree, or occasionally English. He wondered whether a situation would ever develop where some people used only CJ as a linguistic medium. No such development is known to have occurred.

Structure

From different points of view both Boas and Silverstein have dwelt unnecessarily on the CJ speech of Mrs Howard, Jacob's Clackamas Chinook informant. Being a Chinook speaker, she undoubtedly Chinookized her Jargon in certain ways (reduplication, reduced forms of pronouns, and word order peculiarities). An examination of all other available CJ text material shows an extremely uniform grammar, bespeaking a formal structure learned along with the lexicon. This formal structure, though adequate, was to be sure minimal; no doubt CJ users had no special respect for it as a cultural phenomenon, and no doubt one's native language might influence his CJ speech, but rules existed, and I do not believe that CJ grammar is merely the lowest common denominator of all the grammars of the participating languages, nor the simplest possible grammar imaginable by the person using CJ at any one time.

Current research

I am engaged in preparing a dictionary of CJ, using all locatable written materials, published or manuscript, and separating them into 'primary sources' and 'pirated versions'. The primary sources are used for attestations of morphemes, lexical items, syntax, and phonology where appropriate. Etymologies will be given for all morphemes, and an attempt will be made to survey the lexical impact through borrowing of CJ on NW Indian languages. Some material collected by colleagues via field work will be included.

Barbara Efrat (University of Victoria) is doing field research on the CJ which was used by speakers of Straits Salish and other Salishan languages.

NOTE

1 Based on work in progress reported at the Mona conference, and also at the Third Salish Conference, Victoria, B.C., 26 August 1968.

REFERENCES

Anderson, Alexander Caulfield 1858. Hand-book and map to the gold region of Frazer's and Thompson's rivers, with a table of distances. (Chinook Jargon vocabulary, pp. 25–31), San Francisco, pp. 31

Boas, Franz 1933. 'Note on the Chinook Jargon', *Language* 9:208–13

Gibbs, George 1863. A dictionary of the Chinook Jargon, or trade language of Oregon (Smithsonian Miscellaneous Collection 161), Washington, D.C., Smithsonian Institution

Hale, Horatio 1846. 'The "jargon" or trade language of Oregon (pp. 635–50) of United States exploring expedition [1838–42, Wilkes]', *Ethnography and Philology*, Philadelphia
Jacobs, Melville 1932. 'Notes on the structure of Chinook Jargon', *Language*, 8: 27–50
  1936. 'Texts in Chinook Jargon', *UWPA* 7.1:1–27, November
[Lyonnet] Anon. 1853. *Vocabulary of the Jargon or trade language of Oregon*, Washington, D.C., Smithsonian Institution
Lee, D., and J. H. Frost 1844. *Ten years in Oregon* [*c*. 1834–44], New York, J. Collord, Printer
[Lewis and Clark] 1904–5. Original journals of the Lewis and Clark expedition 1804–6, ed. by Reuben Gold Thwaites, New York, Dodd, Mead, 7 vols. and atlas.
Palmer, Joel 1906. 'Journal of travels over the Rocky mountains, to the mouth of the Columbia river', in: Thwaites, *Early western travels 1748–1846* (= 'Palmer's journal'), Cleveland
Parker, Samuel 1842. Journal of an exploring tour beyond the Rocky mountains, (orig. publ. 1838), Ithaca.
St Onge, L. N., M. Demers, and F. N. Blanchet, 1871. *Chinook dictionary, catechism, prayers and hymns*, composed in 1838 and 1839 by Demers; revised in 1867 by Blanchet; modified by St Onge, Montreal
Silverstein, Michael 1965. 'Chinook Jargon: Language contact and the problem of multi-level generative systems', Ms.
Stuart, Granville 1865. *Montana as it is*, New York
Tate, Charles Montgomery 1889. Chinook as spoken by the Indians of Washington Territory, British Columbia and Alaska, Victoria

PROBLEMS IN THE STUDY OF
HAWAIIAN ENGLISH[1]

STANLEY TSUZAKI

There are two main problems connected with the study of the varieties of English spoken in Hawaii, their classification, and the provenience of their distinctive characteristics. Present-day Hawaiian English (HE) is best considered to comprise co-existent systems: an English-based pidgin, an English-based creole, and an English dialect, which as a whole have been changing rapidly in the direction of Standard American English (see paper in Part v). There are a number of possible sources for features not due to the base in English: Hawaiian, Japanese, Portuguese, Puerto Rican Spanish, Cantonese, Korean, Ilocano, possibly Bisayan, and other English-based pidgins and creoles. (See Reinecke 1969 on the immigration into Hawaii in the last quarter of the nineteenth century.) Both intralingual diffusion (from other English-based sources) and interlingual diffusion (from non-English sources) have been relatively neglected. HE shares features with Chinese Pidgin English, for example (Knowlton 1967: 230–1), and most of the principal differences between Jamaican Creole and English syntax (Bailey 1966:146) seem to obtain also between HE and English. Such resemblance is not likely to be due to chance, and points to influence of other English-based pidgins and creoles on HE, or a common influence (Afro-Portuguese) on all.

In tracing phonological and grammatical characteristics it is particularly difficult to determine which of several languages might be the source (or whether some languages might have reinforced each other). Hawaiian is by far the chief source, other than English, so far as is known, but it has been studied mostly in lexicon, and all possible language influences have not been equally investigated. Chinese in particular needs thorough study.

The most practicable course at present may be to undertake pair-wise comparisons, as Knowlton has done with regard to Portuguese influence (1960, 1967). A composite analysis might later be brought together.

NOTE

1 Summary of a paper of this title presented to the conference.

REFERENCES

Bailey, Beryl L. 1966. *Jamaican Creole syntax: a transformational approach*, Cambridge, Cambridge University Press.
Knowlton, Edgar C., Jr. 1960. 'Portuguese in Hawaii', *Kentucky Foreign Language Quarterly* 7:212–18
    1967. 'Pidgin English and Portuguese', *Proceedings of the symposium on historical, archaeological and linguistic studies on southern China, S.E. Asia and the Hong Kong region*, ed. by F. S. Drake, 228–37, Hong Kong, Hong Kong University Press
Reinecke, John E. 1969. *Language and dialect in Hawaii*, Honolulu, University of Hawaii Press

KONGO WORDS IN SARAMACCA TONGO[1]

JAN DAELEMAN

In Saramacca Tongo, a creole tone language spoken by descendants of fugitive slaves, now living mainly along the upper reaches of the Surinam River, there are a number of words of African origin. Words traced back to kiKóongo (a Bantu language spoken in the Lower Kongo) – but not necessarily to the exclusion of other Bantu languages – are studied in detail. The results are tabulated below. Table 1 shows relationships of tone with respect to the total of 1,694 independent Saramaccan entries in Donicie and Voorhoeve (1963); the 149 items represented in the table are 8·8% of the Saramaccan total. Table 2 shows comparison with respect to attestation in two early dictionaries, one of a Bantu language (Van Geel 1651), one of Saramacca Tongo (Schumann 1778), as well as with respect to Sranan Tongo, the main creolized language of Surinam. (On Sranan, see papers by Voorhoeve and Eersel in this volume.)

Kongo nominal forms belong to one of several tone-groups, each varying according to two tone-cases (1: subject before, or object after, absolutive verbal form; 2: isolated or predicative position). Kongo words of tone-groups A and D are taken in case 1 in Saramacca Tongo, words of tone-group E in case 2. It appears that in this way there is a maximal tonal agreement between Kongo originals and Saramaccan reflexes, some 65% (97 out of 149 comparisons). Of the 34 words taken from the dictionary by Laman (1936), 14 are hardly comparable in respect to tone and are consequently assembled under the heading 'tone not comparable'. Excluding the Laman data, the proportion of reflexes with identical tone rises to almost 75% (86 out of 115).

TABLE I

	Total	Identical	Different	Incomparable
Incontestable	97	73	11	13
Probable	15	7	3	5
Less probable	8	2	3	3
Possible	29	15	13	1
	149	97	30	22

The author discusses reasons why Saramaccan words which might be regarded as reflexes of Kongo are rejected or accepted. Two examples are cited here.

A Saramaccan word such as t'ɔdɔ 'toad, frog' could be related to Kongo ntòdi 'frog' (Laman: 'une petite grenouille qui coasse'). The meaning fits, but the tone does not and neither does the final vowel. What tips the scale is the fact that the English word *toad* seems closely related. Thus the word is to be rejected as African, unless the resemblance to the Kongo as well as the English word might have furthered its currency.

The Saramaccan word *tjali* 'regret, be sorry' could be connected with Sranan

K

sári, probably borrowed from English *sorry*. But as Saramaccan has other words that probably go back to the same English *sorry*, namely, *sái* 'sorrow, grief' and *sáa* 'sorrow, have pity', the comparison with Kongo *kyaadi* 'sorrow, grief, regret' seems more plausible. Both the meaning and the tone favor the supposed Kongo origin.

TABLE 2

	Geel 1651 (Bantu)	Schumann 1778 (S)	Sranan Tongo
Incontestable	31	42	23
Probable	5	5	5
Less probable	0	3	1
Possible	14	9	4
	50	59	33

Some items show only partial correspondence with Kongo words. A parallel may be drawn between Saramaccan *tótómboti* 'a large kind of woodpecker' and Kongo *thóto ǹti* 'woodpecker' (Laman: 'pic'), which is a compound of the deverbative of -*tóta* 'peck' and of *ǹti* 'tree'. On this hypothesis the two words would be compounds with a first element in common.

Saramaccan reflexes of Kongo vowels and consonants in different positions are discussed, and so are reflexes of Kongo prefixes. It is quite possible for the Saramaccan noun (without formal difference between singular and plural) to correspond to the plural noun in Kongo: *matutu* 'small rat' in Saramaccan corresponding to *matutu* 'mice' in Kongo (singular *tutu*); *bisaka* 'fish trap' in Saramaccan, corresponding to *bisaka* 'fish traps' in Kongo (singular *kisaka*).

Very few universal or basic items appear in the list of Kongo words in Saramaccan. Of the Swadesh lists only words for 'father', 'mother' and perhaps 'tie together' and 'vomit' have been observed among reflexes from Kongo words. Nouns for cultural items form the main body of words of Kongo origin, with ideophones and verbs. The nouns belong to the following semantic fields: kinship, community life; magic; fauna; flora; household, utensils, provisioning; body parts; diseases; atmosphere; place. (In appendices the words for 'banana', 'peanut' and 'monkey' are studied in greater detail.)

NOTE

1 Summary of a paper of the same title to appear in the *Journal of African Languages*. The summary has been prepared by Jan Voorhoeve, and approved with revisions by Father Daeleman.

REFERENCES

Donicie, Antoon, and Voorhoeve, Jan [1963]. *De Saramakaanse woordenschat*, Amsterdam, Bureau voor Taalonderzoek in Suriname van de Universiteit van Amsterdam

Laman, K. E. 1936. *Dictionnaire kikongo-français*, Brussel, Koninklijk Belgisch Koloniaal Instituut

Schumann, Chr. L. 1778. *Saramaccanisch Deutsches Wörterbuch*, Bambey. Cited from *Die Sprache der Saramakkaneger in Surinam*, ed. by Hugo Schuchardt (Verhandelingen Koninklijke Akademie van Wetenschappen, Afdeling Letterkunde, Nieuwe Reeks, Deel 14 (6), Amsterdam, 1914

Van Geel, Joris (Willems) 1651. 'Vocabularium P. Georgii Gelensis [title supplied by editors]. Cited from *Le plus ancien dictionnaire bantu – Het oudste Bantu-woordenboek*, ed. by J. Van Wing and C. Penders, S. J. Leuven, 1928

TONE AND INTONATION IN
SIERRA LEONE KRIO[1]

JACK BERRY

The paper outlines briefly the prosodic structure of Sierra Leone Krio. The conclusion reached is that Krio must be considered a tone language, though a tone language of the type in which sentence-related intonation and word-related tone conflict in many and special ways. The generally-accepted view (most recently stated by Strevens) that an original tonal system has been replaced in Krio by a sentence-stress and intonation system like that of English is now seen clearly to be untenable.

NOTE

1 Summary of a paper, 'Styles and registers in Sierra Leone Krio', presented orally at the conference, and to be published in *African language studies*, ed. by W. G. Atkins, London, School of Oriental and African Studies of the University of London.

A PROVISIONAL COMPARISON OF THE
ENGLISH-DERIVED ATLANTIC CREOLES[1]

IAN F. HANCOCK

The paper presents lexical comparisons for up to 450 items for six English-derived creoles of the Atlantic area: Krio (Sierra Leone), Sranan and Saramaccan (Surinam), Jamaican Creole (Jamaica), Gullah (Sea Islands off Georgia and South Carolina) and Cameroons Pidgin (Cameroons). The designation 'English-derived' is synchronic, being employed solely because the greater part of the lexicon in each creole as it exists today is clearly traceable to English and to no other language; however, the hypothesis presented also attempts to indicate that (with the exception of Saramaccan) this designation also pertains diachronically.

The interpretation of the comparisons is supported by an examination of the historical backgrounds of the languages in the areas in which they are now spoken. The object has been to demonstrate that each must be traced to an origin on the west coast of Africa, an origin which is both common and specific to each.

That these English-derived creoles share many points of syntax and lexicon in common has not gone unnoticed. One hypothesis maintains that resemblances may be accounted for by each creole having developed under similar circumstances. In the process of building up a lexicon, items basic to the situation of use would have been selected naturally along parallel lines in each case (thus accounting for the lexical similarity); that speakers of the incipient creoles shared a common West African linguistic background would account for phonological and syntactic similarities. Writers such as Rens (1953) and Turner (1949) who have worked on Sranan and Gullah respectively, have supported the claim implicit in this hypothesis, namely, that the African speakers of these languages came to the New World with no knowledge of any European tongue. The same idea of independent parallel development is upheld by Hall in his recent book (1966) – the first full-length volume on the general subject.

A more recent proposal is the relexification hypothesis, put forward by Stewart (1962). This view maintains that all the European-language-derived creoles – even those outside the Atlantic area – originated as varieties of an earlier pidgin, itself derived from Portuguese. In the process of creolization in different settings speakers would have drawn upon different languages (English, French, etc., or in Portuguese-controlled areas, still from Portuguese), for lexicon. The grammatical structure would have been already established with the original pidgin. Lexical and grammatical similarities would thus be retentions from the period of common origin before relexification began.

Neither hypothesis seems to be supported by the data examined in this paper for the English-derived creoles; this does not rule out the possibility that relexification from an earlier Portuguese-derived pidgin did give rise to, say, the French creoles, whose development appears to have gained impetus in the Caribbean rather than on the West African coast. French, being far more similar to Portuguese than is English, would have been more susceptible to relexification. Barbot (c. 1679) advised would-be travelers to both the Caribbean and the

Guinea Coast to learn the Portuguese trade-language – although he does not specify the areas in which it was employed.

Against the hypothesis of parallel independent development stands the specificity of the phonological and lexical resemblances among the English-derived creoles, especially their non-English-derived items. The comparisons and supporting historical evidence point to specific historical connections at relatively datable times. These facts militate against the relexification hypothesis as well, which would not explain the marked similarities among just these, as opposed to all, English-derived creoles. Moreover, if the relexification hypothesis were true, it is surprising that so few traces of Portuguese remain in these languages to-day. The grammatical structure shared by these creoles is no closer to Portuguese than it is to any other European language; Krio and Gullah have less than 1%, and Sranan 4% of their known vocabularies clearly traceable to Portuguese. Saramaccan, with 27% so traceable, may represent the only true example of relexification within the English-derived group.

A pidgin, however scant its lexicon may be, comprises sufficient essential vocabulary to cope with its immediate environment, and it seems unlikely that such basic items of vocabulary as the numerals and terms such as 'man', 'woman', 'work', 'eat', 'kill', etc. would need to be replaced wholesale. This is attested in such creoles as have a discernible pidgin substratum deriving from a language other than that which has provided the bulk of the lexicon during later creolization, i.e. Saramaccan, Papiamentu, Caviteño, etc. These languages can be said to have originated as varieties of a Portuguese pidgin, both by lexical content and by historical fact. One wonders why, therefore, other creoles do not exhibit these features if they had developed along similar lines.

A better term for the lexical change involved in the adaptation of pidgins would be *supralexification*, implying lexicon-building rather than lexicon-replacement.[2] In any case, where relexification does occur, supralexification must occur too, the new and the old item being used at first concurrently. This could involve (i) the original item gradually falling out of use (cf. Sranan *ánson* 'attractive', from English *handsome* gradually being superseded by Dutch-derived *moy* with the same meaning), (ii) retention of both words with the same meaning (cf. Saramaccan *baíka*, from Portuguese, and *bèéè*, from English, both meaning 'stomach'), or (iii) permanent supralexification through specialization of the differently derived items (cf. Krio *pikín*, derived from Portuguese and meaning 'baby', and *bebí*, derived from English *baby* but meaning 'doll'). The first type of supralexification (i), above, would in the first instance have been a fairly speedy process, examples such as Sranan *ánson* being the exception rather than the rule.

The English-derived creoles examined in this paper would seem to have originated neither as separate developments out of English in the areas they now occupy, nor from a prior Portuguese pidgin, but rather from an English-derived pidgin which was developed on the west coast of Africa during the sixteenth and seventeenth centuries. It would further seem that there were two periods of supralexification: firstly during the earliest years of pidgin-formation, and secondly during the process of creolization.

In the first instance English seamen must have stopped at African coastal communities where the inhabitants were already familiar with the Portuguese pidgin introduced several decades earlier by Lusitanian sailors (although whether the English recognized it as such is debatable, since this would pre-suppose that they knew Portuguese). As England defined her West African territories, those areas would have had increasingly less contact with the Portuguese language and more with English, thus the Africans would have supralexified their Portuguese pidgin, which was of little use in communicating with the English. The process of discarding Portuguese-derived items would have of necessity been rather quick; since this was still an intermittently used pidgin, and since the slave trade had not at that time reached a stage where great numbers of Africans of different linguistic backgrounds were being brought to-gether under confined circumstances, it would still have been flexible enough to allow for these changes. A century later, i.e. in the middle of the seventeenth century, the situation had changed sufficiently to have established the pidgin to such an extent that since being taken to Surinam it has been able to resist over three hundred years of Dutch-language influence.

In the second instance, supralexification occurred in the process of creoliza-tion. Separated from members of their own linguistic communities, Africans in the New World would have been forced to continue using the pidgin. Africans from the interior of West Africa, and therefore not likely to have been familiar with the pidgin, would have acquired a working knowledge of it during the time spent in the coastal forts while ships' captains assembled a full cargo of slaves, and during the trans-Atlantic voyage – a period often totalling more than a year. New generations of children, although in the first instance probably having some knowledge of the mother's language, would have had to converse with each other in pidgin. But since the very nature of a pidgin makes it in-adequate as a vehicle for expressing a very wide range of human experience, the children would have soon encountered difficulty in attempting to communi-cate their thoughts. It is not unlikely that under such circumstances the children turned to the adult slaves, who would be experiencing the same difficulties, for help. The adults, still being more familiar with the tribal tongues than with the pidgin, would have drawn upon them in order to 'expand' the pidgin, thus producing the extensive calquing and Africanization of the creoles, and the individual characteristics of each in the various areas. Had these languages been already creolized in Africa, they would be more similar than they in fact are. In the only area where the metropolitan language differs from that which initi-ated the creole, i.e. Surinam, the originally Portuguese-derived pidgin which has developed into Saramaccan had to supralexify from English, or more probably the English-based Sranan. If Surinam were a Portuguese colony, Saramaccan would have continued to supralexify from Portuguese, and would be a clearly definable Portuguese-derived creole to-day, and Sranan would contain a far higher percentage of Portuguese-derived items.

The idea that these Atlantic languages share a common origin was motivated by an examination of Sierra Leone Krio, a language which has until recently been neglected by scholars in this field. Krio seems to provide a link between the New World creoles and Africa, sharing with Sranan (and to a lesser degree Saramaccan) lexical and phonological similarities not found elsewhere in the Atlantic area. Such a link would date back to the years prior to 1667, when English control came to an end in Surinam.

Other features may be found which are peculiar only to Krio and Gullah; that a good many of the Gullah-speakers' descendants came from the Sierra

Leone area is indicated by the high proportion of African-derived items in the language originating from that part of West Africa – according to Turner's material, nearly 47% of the non-English-derived vocabulary.

The formation of these creoles extends over a time span of four centuries. Each has been subject to outside influences in differing degrees, contributing to their development. Guyana Creole, for example, demonstrates features from neighboring Sranan, others from Krio taken in during the 1840s by the liberated African labor force from Sierra Leone, and still others from Barbados Creole, representing a more recent influence. Krio has been influenced by Jamaican Creole, brought into Sierra Leone with the Maroons during the settlement of the colony during the early 1800s (however the effect of Jamaican Creole upon Krio has generally been overestimated; of the c. 900 Maroons who landed in Freetown only a few settled there; some returned to the West Indies and some fled to other parts of the coast fearing recapture. On the other hand over 5,000 Sierra Leoneans were sent to Jamaica and other parts of the Caribbean as a free labor force – mentioned above – between 1841 and 1850).

NOTES

1 Summary of a paper of this title, copies of which were made available to the Mona conference through the good offices of Jan Voorhoeve. The paper appears in the *African Language Review* (1970), expanded to include 570 items in eight creoles (Guyana Creole and Djuka (Surinam) being added).
2 With Mr Hancock's permission, the editor suggests *adlexification* as an alternative term.
3 The variety of English involved must itself have been in part something of a koiné. In the sixteenth century the crews of English ships would have included men speaking a gamut of widely differing English dialects. In Sierra Leone Krio there are preserved dialect forms from as far south as Cornwall and as far north as Scotland. Krio words such as *fitrí* (Yorkshire *fittery* 'with legs akimbo) and *gáŋga* (Y. *ganger* 'little girl's dress') are still used in Yorkshire today, and are quite unintelligible to a modern Devonian or Cornishman. Given also the likelihood of an admixture from non-English speakers in the crews, and the long history of specialized nautical lingo (cf. the realistic excerpt from Traven's *The Death Ship* at the beginning of Reinecke 1938), the form of English heard first by West Africans must have been itself a somewhat flexible compromise.

REFERENCES

Barbot, J. [*c*. 1679]. *Barbot's journal*, British Museum Add. Ms. xxviii, 788
Hall, R. A., Jr. 1966. *Pidgin and creole languages*, Ithaca, New York, Cornell University Press
Reinecke, J. E. 1938. 'Trade jargons and creole dialects as marginal languages', *Social Forces* 17:107–18. Reprinted in D. Hymes (ed.), *Language in culture and society* (New York, 1964), 534–42
Rens, L. L. E. 1953. *The historical and social background of Surinam Negro-English*, Amsterdam, North-Holland Publishing Company

Stewart, W. A. 1962. *Creole languages in the Caribbean. Study of the role of second languages in Asia, Africa, and Latin America*, ed. by Frank A. Rice, 34–53, Washington, D.C., Center for Applied Linguistics

Turner, Lorenzo Dow 1949. *Africanisms in the Gullah dialect*, Chicago, University of Chicago Press

GRAMMATICAL AND LEXICAL AFFINITIES
OF CREOLES[1]

DOUGLAS TAYLOR

In his *Comparative study of French creole dialects* (1964), Morris Goodman –
while recognizing the difficulty of rigorously defining the term *creole language* –
tells us that 'the languages dealt with herein have sufficient mutual similarity
not shared by any others to merit detailed investigation and comparison as a
group' (1964:14). And he goes on to say that these languages 'are those
traditionally known as *Creole* which derive the overwhelming portion of their
vocabulary from French' (*loc. cit.*). In what follows, I shall try to show that his
comparison, thus restricted to 'French-based creoles' treated as a family
(English-based creoles presumably constituting another), minimizes structural
differences between constituent members, and, of necessity, ignores striking
structural similarities between members of lexically differently based groups
which cannot be attributed to the 'source language'. (Moreover, the portion of
some creoles' vocabulary which clearly derives from one particular language is
not always 'overwhelmingly': roughly one third of the Saramaccan Creole's
vocabulary comes from English, one third from Portuguese, and the remainder
from various African, Amerindian and European sources.)

A small concrete example may make my meaning clearer: 'French-based'
Dominican Creole *mwẽ pa ka ni tã* and *mwẽ pa ni tã*, 'English-based' Sranan
(Taki-Taki) *mi nee (no +e) abi tẽ* and *mi no abi tẽ*, are all translatable alike by
Fr 'je n'ai pas le temps' or by Eng 'I haven't (got) time'. Yet in neither creole are
the two utterances equivalent. The first (containing DC *ka*, Sr *e*) may be called
'continuative'; it could be said by a visiting friend in reply to the question:
'Why don't you come to see me more often?' The second (without DC *ka*,
Sr *e*) may be called 'completive', refers to a particular occasion, and could be
said in answer to the invitation: 'Come and have a drink with me now.' For
speakers of these creoles, the distinction is clear and important, whereas that
between Eng *I have known that (for a long time)* and *I know that (now)* is not,
and is not made. The 'continuative' ≠ 'completive' distinction also is made by
'French-based' Cayenne Creole and by 'English-based' (?) Saramaccan, but not,
as we shall see below, by either 'French-based' Haitian Creole or by 'English-
based' Jamaican Creole.

Notice, that in this regard the 'English-based' and the 'French-based' creoles
both make a grammatical distinction unknown to either English or French.
It is often said, or implied, that the grammar of a creole language contains some
(but not all) of the distinctions made by that of its 'parent', and no others. The
example shows this not to be true, if the parentage of the creoles in question is
thought to be, respectively, English and French. The fact that the distinction
occurs in several creoles leads one to suppose, moreover, that it is a common
retention from some language other than French or English, rather than an
innovation in each.

Some features common to at least two lexically differently based groupings
(many others could be found), and seemingly characteristic of creole languages,
are listed below, and their occurrence tabulated (Table 1). Some may point to a

common source, others may help to show on what lines differentiation took place. The features are:

1. The third person plural pronoun serves as nominal pluralizer.
2. A combination of the markers of past and future expresses the conditional.
3. The word for 'give' also functions as dative preposition 'to' or 'for'.
4. Phrasal 'which thing/person/time/place?' are employed to express 'what?', 'who?', 'when?', 'where?'.
5a. A prepositional phrase is employed to express the possessive absolute ('mine' 'ours', 'the man's', etc.).
5b. A nominal phrase is so employed.
6. The demonstrative pronoun is postposed to its referent ('house this').
7. The definite article is postposed to its referent ('house the').
8. The pronominal determinant is postposed to its referent ('house my').
9. '(my) body' serves to express '(my)self'.
10a. The iterative (habitual) function is merged with the completive.
10b. The iterative (habitual) function is merged with the progressive.
10c. The iterative (habitual) function is merged with the future.
11. *na* is employed as a general locative: 'at; by; from; in; on; to'.
12. *ma* is employed as a disjunctive, 'but'.

Abbreviations employed for languages are: LC Louisiana Creole, HC Haitian Creole, LA Lesser Antillean (Guadeloupe, Dominica, Martinique, St Lucia, Grenada, Trinidad), CC Cayenne Creole, IO Indian Ocean (Mauritius, Réunion), JC Jamaica Creole, SR Sranan (Taki-Taki), SM Saramaccan, KR Krio (Sierra Leone), ND Negro Dutch (Virgin Islands; extinct), PP Papiamentu (Aruba, Bonaire, Curaçao), PG Portuguese Guinea Creole, GG Gulf of Guinea Creoles (Anobom, São Thomé, Principe).

An '×' denotes that the feature under which it is listed is attested for the creole (or in the cases of LA, IO and GG, at least one of the creoles) in whose line it is found. An ' − ' means that the feature is not attested for that particular creole. Under 11, the symbol '//' means that similar though non-identical forms with the same functions are attested for these creoles; viz.: LC and HC *nã, lã*, LA *ã* (besides *na* in St Lucia), CC *la* and JC *ina*. In São Thomé (and Principe?) *na* alternates with *ni*, but is not attested for Anobom. It may be noted that 'locative *na*' and disjunctive *ma* both occur in Ibo with the same range of functions as in the creoles, whereas neither Ptg *na* 'in the (fem.)' nor Dut *naar* 'to; after' has such a wide semantic range. Fr *mais* has given *mẽ* 'but' in all 'French-based' creoles; while Ptg *mas* [maš] 'but' has given GG [mãzi]. This last form should be compared with Anobom *káži*, Principe *káši*, São Thomé *kèè*, HC, LA and CC *kay*, all 'house', and perhaps ultimately from Ptg *casinha*.

The features listed under 10a, b and c may require explanation: In all these creoles except IO (where it has a form of its own), the iterative or habitual ('I drink beer'; 'I do/don't, always/never/often/sometimes drink beer') takes the same form as the completive ('I drank beer; I have drunk beer'), or as the progressive ('I am drinking beer'), or as the future ('I shall drink beer'; the distinction being made clear only by context. In this connection it is interesting to notice that such a 'French-based' creole as HC agrees with such an 'English-based' creole as JC, but differs from such a 'French-based' creole as LA, which agrees with such an 'English-based' creole as SR. Thus, HC *ki sa u fè?* and JC *a-wa yu du?* may both mean 'what do you do? whereas LA *(ki) sa u fè?* and SR *sã yu du?* can only mean 'what did you do?' or 'what have you done?'). On the

TABLE I

	1	2	3	4	5a	5b	6	7	8	9	10a	10b	10c	11	12	
LC:	×	×	×	×	—	×	×	×	—	—	×	—	—	//	—	French-based
HC:	×	×	×	×	—	×	×	×	×	×	×	—	—	//	—	
LA:	—	×	×	×	—	×	×	×	×	×	—	×	—	×,//	—	
CC:	×	×	×	×	—	×	—	×	—	×	—	×	—	//	—	
IO:	—	×	—	—	×	—	—	×	—	×	—	—	—	—	—	
JC:	×	—	×	—	×	—	—	—	—	—	×	—	—	//	—	English-based
SR:	×	×	×	×	×	—	×	—	—	—	—	×	—	×	×	
SM:	×	×	×	×	×	—	×	—	—	—	—	×	—	×	×	
KR:	×	×	×	—	×	×	—	—	—	—	—	—	—	×	—	
ND:	×	—	×	—	×	—	—	—	—	—	—	—	×	×	×	Dutch-based
PP:	×	×	—	×	×	—	×	—	—	—	—	×	—	×	×	Iberian (PTG/Sp)-based
PG:	—	×	—	×	×	—	—	—	—	—	—	—	×	×	×	
GG:	×	—	×	×	×	—	×	×	×	×	—	—	×	×	—	

other hand, whereas HC *ki sa w'ap-fè?* and JC *a-wa yu a du?* can only mean 'what are you doing?', LA (*ki*) *sa u ka fè?* and SR *san yu e-du?* may also mean 'what do you do?'. And similarly, in 'Dutch-based' ND as in 'Portuguese-based' GG creoles; the forms meaning 'what do you do?' are identical with those meaning 'what will you do?'

Another similarity between HC and JC is the replacement, after a negation, of the marker of future (HC *ava-* "*av-* "*va-* "*a-*; JC wi) by the aspect marker (HC *ap-*, etc; JC *a, da* or *de*). So: HC *y-ava-neye-l* 'they'll drown him' but *yo-p'ap-neye-l* 'they'll not drown him' (as well as, in a different context, 'they are not drowning him'). Likewise: JC *mi wi tel im di truut* 'I shall tell her the truth', but *mi naa* (<*no* + *e*) *tel im di truut* 'I shall not tell her the truth' (as well as, in a different context, 'I am not telling her the truth'). No such replacement takes place in LA (*yo ke neye-y* 'they'll drown him', *yo pa ke neye-y* 'they'll not drown him'), nor yet in SR; but Voorhoeve has reported its occurrence in SM and it would be interesting to know whether this restriction is found in yet other creoles.

It seems clear that structural similarities and differences among the various creoles are sufficiently independent of lexically determined groupings to justify us in ignoring the latter when we compare one creole language with another. And if we compare the following sentences of São Thomé Creole (Gulf of Guinea) with their equivalents in HC, PP and LA, we find not only rather striking if abstract patterns of resemblance, but also some concrete phonological and morphological correspondences (or at least some possible correspondences):

ST *pòtu kèè papá-m glãdi.* HC *pòt kay papa-m grã.* (both) '(the) door (of) my father's house (is) big'

ST *ke-kwa bo ka kumè?* PP *ki-ko bo ta kôme?* (both) 'what (lit.: which thing) do you eat?'

ST *ke-ŋe ka bali kèè se da bo?* LA *ki mun ka balie kay-la ba-u?* (both) 'who (lit.: what person) sweeps the house for (lit.: give) you?'

Note the reduction in this position of ST *mũ* and HC *mwẽ* 'my' to -*m*; the identity in form and (in this case) function of ST and LA *ka*; and compare with ST *kèè* and LA *kay*, their other GG equivalents, Anobom *kaži* and Principe *kaši*, all meaning 'house'.

NOTE

1 Expanded from a memorandum distributed to participants in the conference.

REFERENCE

Goodman, Morris 1964. *A comparative study of French creole dialects*, The Hague, Mouton

V

VARIATION AND USE: A RANGE OF ENGLISH-LINKED CASES

INTRODUCTION

Pidgins and creoles challenge conventional forms of linguistic description, just as they challenge conventional modes of linguistic history. How, and whether, processes of change have given rise to pidgins and creoles – the questions of origin – have attracted more attention, but the needs of language policy and education, together with new currents in linguistic theory, now bring descriptive questions rapidly to the fore.

The major topics are two: language situations and linguistic systems, or, varieties and variation. Once established, pidgins and creoles may give rise to further varieties, functionally specialized, and may give rise to individual and community linguistic systems of special complexity.

Perhaps the most vital thing for the future of a pidgin or creole is whether or not it continues adjacent (and subordinate) to a major source. Surinam shows the latter alternative, Hawaii and Jamaica show the former. In the one varieties of language are the salient concern, in the other variation.

The differential extent of English dominance, as between the coast and the interior, was already decisive in the few years in which the creoles of Surinam were formed. The Saramaccan of runaway tribes retains as much Portuguese as English, together with many words and tones of African origin, and is not mutually intelligible with the creole English that formed on the coast, and that now, as Sranan, is the lingua franca of the country. It is to be hoped that the work in Surinam of Voorhoeve and others will be intensively followed up. The possibilities of comparison, controlling for specific similarities and differences in linguistic and social factors, make the creoles of Surinam an important, indeed, crucial, case for general theory.

Voorhoeve sketches the dynamics of the social history (plantation slavery, formation of runaway tribes, rebellion, caste and its breakdown), and shows how Sranan, once formed, was elaborated in social role as well as in content. A new variety, duplicating within Creole itself the general Dutch-Creole diglossia, emerged, through the intervention of Moravian missionaries, acting as a third party without effective correction to their novel norm. Whereas Church Creole is differentiated primarily in phonology, there are also cult varieties of Creole, differentiated primarily by vocabulary replacement and special uses of the vocal channel (stuttering, throatiness) as mark of deities.

Voorhoeve notes that the differentiation of Church from Common Creole is not mechanical, that the features involved have intrinsic social meaning (e.g. absence of elision is a stylistic feature of both, with the same meaning in both – it is its ubiquity that stamps Church Creole). And he observes that the social valuation of the formal style has been reversed, from high seriousness to joke, among the younger generation.

Eersel takes up in greater detail the current situation in Surinam, where the development of Sranan has reached the stage of incipient standardization, as a

rival to the domination of Dutch.[1] It is striking that resistance to Dutch has led
to use of Spanish as an alternative source of new vocabulary, in sharp contrast to
the dependence of Jamaican and Haitian Creole on English and French respectively (cf. Craig in this part, and Hall 1953:222), and that one can name the
inventor of a plural suffix to nouns, and the book of poems in whose title it first
appeared. The situation recalls earlier cases of standardization of oppressed
national languages in Europe, such as Lithuanian, where Polish loanwords were
ejected after the First World War, and where conscious invention of new forms
by individuals is also documented. It will be important to follow the future of
Sranan in the context of language development in other countries of the Third
World today.

The social meaning of language choice in Surinam today is shown by Eersel
to involve two dimensions that appear to be both fundamental in human
relations and universal to sociolinguistic description, differential intimacy and
power (or, in transactional terms, exchanges involving affection and love, and
involving status). On either dimension, or on both combined, Sranan commonly
signifies relative absence, Dutch relative presence, of social distance. The present
pattern of code-switching in Surinam invites detailed analysis along lines such
as those marked out by Friedrich (1971), Blom and Gumperz (1971) and Rubin
(1968), and comparative study. The code-switching in Surinam between a
creole and an unrelated other language appears much more clear-cut than what
could perhaps be called the *style-ranging* between Creole and English in Hawaii,
Jamaica, Antigua, and the like. Not one or two, but all the Dutch features of
pronunciation together, are required to stamp a pronunciation as 'bakara'
(+Dutch). Sranan, indeed, is a particularly interesting case of the mutual
autonomy of the components of a grammar, associated with differential social
meaning, which pidgins and creoles highlight: appropriate competence for a
black Surinam citizen comprises Dutch grammar, Dutch lexis, and Sranan
pronunciation.

Although it is varieties rather than variation that comes to the fore in the
Surinam situation, no doubt detailed study of variation can and should be undertaken there. And, as Eersel indicates, there is a heritage of linguistic insecurity
and of ambivalence, such as underlie forms of variation elsewhere, in Surinam
too.

Ambivalence as to personal identity, and the creative development of a
language, born 300 years ago in slavery, are both shown in the Sranan poem
interpreted by Voorhoeve, the one in its theme, the other in its beauty.

Hawaii and Jamaica pose sharply the sheer difficulty of describing coherently
the complex variation that results when a creole develops, not against, but into,
as it were, a related dominant language. Whereas the historical problem involves
mixture in the formation of a language, the descriptive problem is one of mixture
in the formation of discourse, and in the underlying 'competence', or grammatical knowledge, that can be ascribed to an individual, a text, or a community.
Linguists wishing to treat their work as referring to an ideally fluent speaker-
listener in a homogeneous community (Chomsky 1965) often can ignore
variability as peripheral. In these cases variability is central.

Tsuzaki, Bailey and Craig all are members of the speech communities
(Hawaiian, Caribbean) they describe, and for each of them there are discrete
systems, which they perceive, inadequately perhaps from a purely 'objective'
standpoint, at the basis of the actual intermixture of speech (cf. Sapir 1921:58,

n. 19). They, and DeCamp, each adopt a different analytical construct to capture the underlying discrete system. Tsuzaki neatly sketches three coexistent systems: an obsolescent pidgin, a creole, and an English dialect (with standard and non-standard varieties), illustrated in terms of grammatical structures of the verb. Bailey considers continuous discourse, using a weighted scale to analyze texts in terms of their basis in, and departure from, two opposed norms as poles. DeCamp accepts the two poles, but analyzes the intervening range as rule-governed behavior in terms of a qualitative scale. Craig accepts the polar norms, and the continuum defined by DeCamp, but treats the intervening area as an 'interaction area' that contains mutation as well as mixing.

Together the papers well illustrate the kind of variation concretely found in such situations. And while all are primarily concerned to establish an underlying systematic basis for linguistic features *per se*, it is clear that to go from any underlying basis to what is sayable by a given person ('competence' in the strict sense) would require sociological features as well.

DeCamp's recognition of the post-creole continuum, dependent on jointly linguistic and social conditions (a dominant related language, breakdown of caste separation) is of the greatest importance, for creole studies, and for their contribution to general understanding of linguistic change in the modern world.[2] Here he is concerned to show that the variability of a post-creole continuum can be incorporated within the formal system of generative grammar, and offers examples from phonology, syntax and semantics. He concludes that the scalar continuum mirrors the sociolinguistic reality, that the one continuum (allowing for geographical variants) accounts for almost all the Jamaican variation, and that there is indeed a continuous scaled variation, rather than any particular number of levels ('pigeonholes') between extremes. Pursuing this view, DeCamp follows Chomsky (1965) in treating underlying competence (grammatical knowledge, or, sometimes, simply grammar) as a property of the speech community. (In Chomsky's formulation, competence at least is not distinct from a property of the speech community.) Thus competence must be continuous, and the discreteness intuited by Bailey and others, if it exists, must be assigned to 'performance', to behavioral realization.

Craig refers competence to the individual speaker, and seeks to *explain* the continuum in terms of the activity of a community, whose competencies extend over different ranges of a continuum between two norms; who are socially motivated to vary their speech along the continuum within the range they command; and whose competence is modified by feedback, sometimes imperfect, from attempts to move beyond their range. For Craig, then, the overt variation is partly a product of underlying competence, but it is also partly a product of imperfect performance. For Craig and Bailey, the polar types are underlying realities for each speaker, although for Craig the poles may be differently located along the continuum for different speakers.

Notice that both Bailey and Craig are concerned with educational realities and problems. Bailey finds her analytical construct essential for teaching children, and Craig finds his model essential to understanding the children taught, and hence for much needed increase in educational success.

In connection with educational issues, Craig points out the parallels between a creole-standard contrast, and Bernstein's contrast of restricted-elaborated codes. Bernstein has treated form of speech (morpho-syntactic means), reliance on context for interpretation of meaning, and cognitive orientation as interdependent, and as jointly serving to contrast the two types of code. Craig argues that morpho-syntactic means and use of context can change without a change in cognitive orientation, that there is no one-to-one relation between them, and that the cognitive significance of differences in the first two factors remains to be measured. The two types of code have been made much of in educational circles far removed from those for whose needs Bernstein undertook his research, and whereas Bernstein has related the differences primarily to differences in family modes of socialization, some educators have seized upon them to characterize (and stigmatize) racially linked differences in the New World. Craig's critique is thus of considerable importance.

The descriptive problem with post-creole continua is one not only of finding system in variation, but one also of finding the right system, and of gaining access to the necessary information. Dillard argues vigorously and inimitably that the development of creole studies has a vital contribution to make to the understanding of Negro Non-Standard English in the United States. American black speech, when viewed in the larger context of the New World, strongly suggests a much advanced process of decreolization. To view it in terms of ordinary dialect alone is quite inadequate. It has distinctive properties of its own that can have a structural basis of their own, that are not simply deviations from the standard. This is a message much needed in schools. If even in cases of undoubted Caribbean creole influence, as among some schoolchildren in Birmingham, differences are dismissed as 'dialectal' and 'bad English', it is not surprising that such differences are given short shrift in a post-creole continuum in the United States.

A broader creole perspective provides insight on two counts, that of the origin and place of such features in the dynamics of the specific process of decreolization, and that of the place of such features in the social subtleties and ambiguities of code-switching (or style-ranging) within the speech community. Without the creole perspective, Dillard argues, the provenience of features may be incorrectly assigned, and an invalid structure imposed on speech; critical evidence, indeed, may be overlooked or not obtained. Generations of oppression and disapproval hardly make people willing to volunteer or display facets of speech that have been disapproved and associated with resistance to oppression. The actual range of a person's speech is difficult enough to discover in any case, requiring methodology that goes beyond ordinary elicitation to natural observation and controlled variation of situations, even where no social barriers obtain.[3]

Dillard stresses age-grading, and masculine identity, as factors determining and helping to explain the variation found in young people's speech, and of great significance for schools. The central importance of self-identity is indicated in Craig's discussion, and in the work of Labov (1966; see his contribution in the final part), and is stressed in an article of great importance by Le Page (1969). In this article, which expresses methodological views he presented orally to the Mona conference, Le Page goes on from social interaction and identification as fundamental factors to the crucial distinction between (a) establishing the presence of linguistic features in a community, and (b) assigning them to any 'named' language (197, 206–7). With regard to variation in materials from his work in British Honduras, he concludes: 'It may conceivably be that the shift is best understood as into another register of a still-crystallizing indigenous educated dialect rather than as into Standard English; that the structure of the local Creole is and remains, even in this dialect, in some underlying way essentially different from that of English, and that a programme of universal education will stand far more chance of being effective both for the individual and for society if this is recognized' (1969:211).

Reisman briefly reports an important ethnographic study of the duality and ambiguity that may underlie speech in a creole situation, including the masking that may occur. His full study demonstrates the subtleties of behavior that require considerable patience and participation to understand or even to discover.

Carr describes work on the post-creole continuum in Hawaii that finds some five significant points from pidgin to English dialect. Finally, Wolfers describes the elaboration of an established pidgin into a prospective national language. In New Guinea, as in Haiti and Jamaica, the dominant source language remains a source of new lexicon, but the recency and relative decency of the circumstances of contact, the absence of a long history of severe exploitation and discrimination, permit a different outcome. Prejudice against Neo-Melanesian, as a pidgin language, plays some part, but political independence, coupled with the need for an internal lingua franca, seem to combine to ensure the language a future as national symbol. Whether Neo-Melanesian will prove to be subordinate to English in a diglossia situation, such as that of Sranan presently in relation to Dutch, or will have a quite different fate, remains to be seen.

NOTES

1 For an account of an analogous confrontation between Creole and Dutch in the Caribbean, see Wood 1969. The situation on the islands of Curacao, Aruba and Bonaire differs in that the creole, Papiamentu, now is dominantly Spanish, and is not identified with the black members of the community. The focus of the problem is in the schools, where native speakers of Papiamentu must teach other native speakers in a language foreign to both.

2 Cf. Dutton 1969, who describes what from its history (20), its largely mutual unintelligibility with standard Australian English (22), and a number of grammatical and lexical features (23–4, 34) can only be a creolized, or perhaps now de-creolizing, product of a former pidgin. Dutton interprets the Palm Island situation by analogy to De Camp's Jamaican analysis: 'The informal-formal dimension of Aboriginal English is a continuum or cline with a different range from that of the same dimension in Australian English. No two speakers' clines necessarily correspond exactly so that we get somewhat the same situation as has been described by DeCamp for Jamaican dialects . . .' (19). Palm Island would seem to have developed from a stage observable today in Northern Queensland (Jernudd 1969). Dutton (personal communication) agrees with this interpretation.

3 Cf. Dutton (1969:18): 'Normally this speech is never heard by non-Aboriginal Australians. Even the teachers at the two primary schools on Palm Island had never heard Aboriginal children speaking their variety of informal English.' Its existence was discovered by accident, through having left a tape-recorder running in a room where children were playing. When the existence of the speech was brought to the attention of school personnel, they showed little interest (Dutton, personal communication).

REFERENCES

Blom, Jan-Petter, and John Gumperz 1971. 'Social meaning in linguistic structures: code-switching in Northern Norway' *Directions in sociolinguistics*, ed. Dell Hymes and John Gumperz, New York, Holt, Rinehart and Winston

Chomsky, Noam 1965. *Aspects of the theory of syntax*, Cambridge, MIT Press

Dutton, T. E. 1969. 'The informal English speech of Palm Island Aboriginal children, North Queensland', *Journal of English Linguistics* 3:18–36

Friedrich, Paul 1971. 'Structural implications of Russian pronominal usage', *Directions in sociolinguistics*, ed. Dell Hymes and John Gumperz, New York, Holt, Rinehart and Winston

Hall, Robert A., Jr. 1953. 'Haitian Creole' (American Anthropological Association, *Memoir* 74), Washington, D.C.

Jernudd, B. 1969. 'Social change and aboriginal speech variation in Australia', *Working Papers in Linguistics* 4:145–67, Honolulu, University of Hawaii, Department of Linguistics

Labov, William 1966. *The social stratification of English in New York City*, Washington, D.C., Center for Applied Linguistics

Le Page, R. B. 1969. 'Problems of description in multilingual communities', *Transactions of the Philological Society* (1968), 189–212

Rubin, Joan 1968. *National bilingualism in Paraguay*, The Hague, Mouton

Sapir, Edward 1921. *Language*, New York, Harcourt, Brace

Wood, Richard E. 1969. 'Linguistic problems in the Netherlands Antilles'. *Monda Lingvo-Problemo* 1:77–85

VARIETIES OF CREOLE IN SURINAME[1]

Church Creole and Pagan cult Languages

JAN VOORHOEVE

Historical and social background

POPULATION GROUPS

The original population of Suriname was Amerindian, but their descendants today constitute only a small minority. Roughly half of the present population is of Asian background, the other half of African. The Asian proportion appears to be gaining rapidly, even though offspring of mixed Asian-African parentage are regarded as belonging to the Creole group. The Asians are descendants mostly of Indians and Indonesians whom the colonial government induced to immigrate during the last quarter of the nineteenth century and the first decades of this century to fill places on plantations left open after the emancipation of Negro slaves. Africans were brought as slaves from the beginning of the modern history of Suriname in the mid-seventeenth century.

CREOLE ORIGINS

Surinamese of African background are divided into Bush Negroes (descendants of runaways) and Creoles (descendants of slaves). The runaways founded separate tribes in the interior along the large rivers. There is a clear difference between the tribes occupying the Eastern part of the country (Djuka, Boni, Paramaccan), and those occupying the Central part (Saramaccan, Matuari, and perhaps also the small group of Kwinti). The Western part of the country has never been occupied by Bush Negro tribes.

The languages of the Eastern tribes have been much less studied than those of the Central tribes. The general impression, however, is that Djuka and related Eastern languages show a closer resemblance to the coastal Creole (Sranan).

The Central Bush Negroes speak Saramaccan and closely related dialects that have tonal distinctions (Voorhoeve 1959; Voorhoeve 1961a), and that show an almost even proportion of Portuguese and English-based items (Donicie and Voorhoeve 1963; cf. also Taylor 1965:369). A marked influence of Kongo on the vocabulary has been demonstrated by Daeleman (cf. the summary of his work in this volume). The Portuguese influence has been thought to have occurred in Africa, rather than subsequent to the arrival of slaves in Suriname. Runaways were recruited mainly from freshly imported slaves, who had not had time to adapt themselves fully to the linguistic habits of the slaves on the plantations (Herskovits 1931; cf. also Voorhoeve 1967: 104). If this is true, the linguistic difference between the Eastern and Central Bush Negroes (the greater affinity of the former to the Creole of the former plantation slaves) would force us to infer a distribution of runaways among the two groups of tribes according to two different stages of adaptation to plantation life. It seems only fair to mention here one counterindication to the theory of Herskovits. The coastal Creole word *barba* 'beard' seems to be derived from Portuguese. The Saramaccan equivalent *bia* must have been derived from English. If the English influence on Saramaccan has to be attributed exclusively to the influence of the slave language, the item *bia* presents a problem.

Little is known about the history of the separate Bush Negro tribes in Suriname. In the English period (before 1667), there had already been mention of a group of several hundreds of runaways under a headman named Jermes. In 1684 a peace treaty was concluded with this group. Another active group under a headman Ganimet attacked the plantations during the Amerindian revolt. This group was defeated in 1681. In 1690 a complete plantation force fled into the bush. The invasion of Jacques Cassard in 1712 has often been mentioned as the foundation of the first Bush Negro tribes. The total number of runaways was estimated in 1738 as 6,000. In 1761 peace treaties were concluded with the Djuka, Saramacca and Matuari. After these treaties the slavemasters became engaged in a new war against the troops of Boni, operating in the coastal areas. They were chased to French Guayana, and finally defeated in 1791. There is reason to believe that the Boni Negroes consisted of slaves that had run away after 1761. (Most of this information has been taken from De Groot 1963:7–15; cf. also Van der Linde 1966:95 and Abbenhuis 1964.)

It may be that the Central Bush Negro tribes consisted of the first waves of runaways (up until 1712), and that the Eastern tribes were founded afterwards. During this second period, the influence of Portuguese Pidgin on the African coast might have been diminished to the benefit of English-based Pidgin.

Sranan (also called Negro-English, Taki-Taki, or Coastal Creole) is spoken by descendants of the slaves. It is clearly an English-based creole (cf. Hancock's work, summarized in this volume). Geographical varieties exist. The major differences seem to be between the old plantation area in the Eastern and Central part of Suriname (including the city of Paramaribo) and the new plantation area (Coronie and Nickerie, occupied after 1800). The district of Nickerie must have undergone some recent English influence. These dialectal differences, however, are not very important. On the whole, there is a remarkable uniformity in Sranan throughout the area. As Sranan is also the *lingua franca* of Suriname as a whole, there also exist Asian varieties of it. Finally, some social variations can be observed. Creoles from higher social classes are completely bilingual and may even learn the Creole (Sranan) as a second language. Their creole may be affected by Dutch, and often is (cf. Voorhoeve 1961b:100–11, and Eersel, following).

In his work on the subject, Rens (1953:10) starts from the assumption that the slaves entered the colony without an active linguistic background, and tried to learn their masters' language as best they could. The English ruled the country from 1651 to 1667. When the Dutch took over in that year, they tried to keep English planters on the spot. They lacked competent Dutch colonists. Barbados, which always feared competition from Suriname in the sugar industry, even during the English rule, tried to ruin the country by withdrawing all English inhabitants. They were quite successful. Not many Englishmen stayed in Suriname after 1678, and the English planters were allowed to take with them all slaves acquired before 1667.

The slave language, however, remained essentially English. This must mean either that the English-based creole had already been acquired on the African coast, and was reinforced by the new influx of slaves after 1667 (but there has not been much historical support for this hypothesis), or that the new slave language had been already firmly established in Suriname by 1667, so that it could be effectively passed on to the new slaves between 1667 and 1678. The social conditions which gave rise to the birth of a new language in about 25 years have been analyzed in Voorhoeve (1964). The withdrawing of English from the scene left the slave language remarkably intact. So did the continuing colonial society, based as it was on an almost complete distinction between masters and slaves.

MAINTENANCE OF CREOLE

In the time of slavery, Suriname society was structured as a two-caste society of masters and slaves. The language and culture of the two groups were separated as much as possible. Slaves could not wear shoes, could not become Christians, could not learn Dutch, etc. Regulations for manumission were strict. The manumitted slave should be baptized. Intimate contacts with the slave society were strictly forbidden. The manumitted slave even risked loss of his freedom after two official warnings. The society tried hard to keep both groups as distinct as possible. In addressing the slaves, the masters had to use Creole, the slave language, but for the rest each group stuck to its own language. This explains the relatively slight influence of Dutch on the slave language.

When in 1863 all slaves became free, this caste system (deeply embedded in language and culture) broke down from one day to the next. The government tried hard to indoctrinate the former slaves into the language and culture of the former masters. They were free people now and should adhere to the language and culture of the free. Compulsory education was introduced in Suriname in 1873, a very early date, but execution of the law had to be postponed for some years for practical reasons. However, at the beginning of the twentieth century, so much progress had been made, that education officers were very optimistic about being able to eradicate the Creole language in one generation. Co-operation of the parents was requested to observe strict rules at home for the benefit of their children. Children should not be allowed to use Creole at home or at school.

The result of these efforts has not been the eradication of Creole language and culture, but participation of almost the whole population in both cultures. It is quite obvious to observers that Creoles are able to switch codes with the greatest ease and skill. According to the pressure of the situation, one can as well practise a kind of voodoo religion as pray in church, one can as well behave in a European as in a Creole way. Even within the scope of one minute, one can switch between codes which are in actual competition.

Formerly, both cultures were related to each other in a hierarchical system, the one (belonging to the former masters) having higher value than the other (belonging to the former slaves). Somatic features were included in this hierarchy: straight hair was called 'good' hair, and marrying a person of brighter complexion was called 'raising' one's colour. In this same hierarchy of values, speaking Creole was regarded as vulgar. Even as late as 1956 I used to practice Creole with Asians rather than Creoles, because one risked difficulties in addressing Creoles in Creole. They did not like to be considered as vulgar, uneducated people. I remember one occasion, on which I was forced to speak Dutch on the telephone, while I was sure not to be understood. I tried to get my message through by translating literally from Creole into Dutch.

I realize that there is more to it than has been described in this paper. I do not want to deny the warm, intimate feeling that goes with this so called 'vulgar' language. A more subtle appraisal of the sociolinguistic setting can be found in Reisman's paper (cf. the summary in this volume). I do not try to describe the situation in a more subtle way, because I want to focus on one special feature of the Suriname setting, which has not been found elsewhere, I mean the existence of a distinct intermediate layer between the two extremes of Dutch and (common) Creole. Here is used a special kind of Creole, which will be called church Creole in this paper. Church Creole definitely is a variety of Creole, but one which is not regarded as vulgar, and can be used on formal occasions. I have heard it used at political gatherings, in formal addresses, in election speeches, and of course in church.

Church Creole

The Moravian Missionaries started about 1780 to use Creole in church. They translated the Bible, compiled a hymnbook (for use in church), and a collection of Christian songs (for use in Christian homes). They published a monthly paper (1852–1932) and countless pamphlets, tracts and edifying stories (Voorhoeve and Donicie 1963; Voorhoeve 1957). In fact, a complete program for alphabetization was carried out in the nineteenth century, gradually diminishing in the twentieth century. When the mission schools were forced by government to switch over to Dutch, the program lost its original impetus, but Creole remained the most important language in the Moravian church up till the present day.

Foreign missionaries have not always been gifted language learners. Their pronunciation of Creole was not always correct. The Moravian orthography was partly based on etymology, and many missionaries used to pronounce Creole as it had been written down. The word *tem* (time) was pronounced [tɛm] according to the rules of Dutch and German pronunciation, although the correct Creole pronunciation would have been [tẽ]. The missionaries were not corrected by the Creoles (as would have occurred in normal situations) but imitated. So, by institutionalized mispronunciation the foreign missionaries created a Creole variety, rather different in phonology from the common Creole, used in everyday life. The church style of speaking was imitated by others as the more fashionable style, which got superior status, because it was used on solemn occasions by people belonging to the former caste of the masters. It has been used since on all occasions demanding a language of higher prestige than everyday Creole, but in which communication by means of Dutch was not efficient. One might say that this variety of Creole was used on all formal occasions where the active presence of lower-class people was essential. The linguistic situation described above has been termed diglossia (cf. Ferguson 1959). The Suriname setting is more complex, because of the possibility of a third linguistic choice (Dutch), linguistically not related to the other two possible choices (church Creole and common Creole). A speech in parliament would necessarily be given in Dutch, but a political speech could be in Dutch or church Creole, and after 1956 also in common Creole. Indeed, the process of the raising of the status of common Creole after 1956 is by far the most interesting phenomenon in the Suriname situation.

About 1956 the younger generation began to question the old hierarchy. The new ideas have generally been associated with a cultural-nationalistic movement under the name of *Wie Eegie Sanie* ('Our own things'), founded by students abroad, but soon also planted in Suriname (Voorhoeve and Van Renselaar 1962). The following kinds of questions have been discussed in this group: Why should Dutch be a superior language? What is wrong with

Creole dances? Why should voodoo religion be inferior to Christian ritual? Could polygamy be a more suitable form of marriage?

The cultural-nationalistic movement definitely raised the status of common Creole. The first book of Creole poetry by Trefossa produced a real shock (Trefossa 1957). Creole performances soon became popular in the theater. Creole was used in broadcasting. A Creole version of the national anthem was approved officially by the government. Creole became increasingly popular and fashionable. People came to see the beauty and efficiency of just plain, common Creole. The existence of church Creole was no longer necessary. Now the style of old-fashioned preachers was only imitated by youngsters who wanted to have a good joke. Church Creole almost ceased to exist outside church.

It was in this period that I had the task of translating the New Testament into Creole. It was quite clear at that time, that, if Creole survived, it would not be in the form of church Creole. So I started to translate into common Creole, as used in poems and elsewhere. This was not very difficult, because church Creole relied heavily on literal pronunciation of orthography for its distinctiveness (rather than on anything more substantial). But by the same token, in changing the orthography to reflect actual speech, one threatened already the very life of church Creole.

I succeeded in bringing all interested groups together and in getting a change in orthography. It was followed in principle by a government commission later on. I then measured the reactions in the Moravian church. On the whole, there has been a rather unfavourable reaction from church officials. They had adopted with considerable difficulty this special style of speaking. Their position in church often was based on their ease in handling church Creole. They liked the solemn swing, and stood a bit outside the secular movement in favour of common Creole. They would not be in favour of a drastic change. I then started to use common Creole in church services, and the reaction of church members on the whole was favourable. The common reaction was: Why, this is not a change, this is just the way we speak ourselves. As, however, the written text of the Bible is almost exclusively used in church by the officials, I must say that the new translation has not been very popular.

Linguistic characteristics of church Creole

I have already pointed out that the main differences between the two kinds of Creole are to be found in phonology. There is some specialized vocabulary too. Christian concepts such as *gnade* (grace), *tolnaar* (taxgatherer), *disciple* (disciple) are mostly loans from Dutch or German. There are some dated expressions like *meli* (to touch) and *fika* (to leave behind), which would not be used by modern Creole speakers, but are understood by most of them. Syntactic differences are extremely rare. I have found some instances of the use of the all-purpose preposition *na* after or instead of the auxiliary verb *gi* (to give, to), but this has been found in written texts only. I do not think it is common in spoken church Creole.

In phonology, the differences between the two styles of Creole, however, are considerable. I will try to illustrate the differences on three points:

NASALIZATION

Most syllables in Suriname Creole end on oral or nasal vowel. There are some exceptions as p.e. [mɛf] 'menstruating', [sɛm] 'same', and [jaf] 'to show off, to brag'. But these are rather slangy expressions.

Final nasal vowel, followed by pause, shows a slight velar nasal constriction: cf. [ma] 'but' and [mãⁿ] 'man'. The final nasal vowel loses its nasal feature before oral vowel: /sã ede/ 'why' is realized as [sayde], /dẽ e go/ 'they are going' is realized as [deego].

A few morphemes share all realizations with other morphemes on final nasal vowel, except the last one. Before vowel initial object these transitive verbs end on [m]: [mi fɔm a boy] 'I beat the boy', [mi krim a jari] 'I cleaned the garden', [mi ñam a sani] 'I ate the thing', [mi brɔm a fɔtɔ] 'I burned the town'. Before pause these verbs are realized like all other morphemes on final nasal vowel: [fɔ̃ⁿ] 'to beat', [krĩⁿ] 'to clean', [ñãⁿ] 'to eat', and [brɔ̃ⁿ] 'to burn'. Final [m] has no clear etymological justification. The etymology of [fɔ̃ⁿ] is not clear, but final [m] also appears in Jamaican English (Cassidy and Le Page 1967: s.v. FUM). [ñãⁿ] has final [m] in West African languages like Wolof But [krĩⁿ] and [brɔ̃ⁿ] definitely reflect English items with final [n]. Church Creole makes a distinction between *krin* (clean) and *krini* (to clean). It is a remarkable fact, that [krĩⁿ] only shows final [m], when used as a transitive verb preceding vowel initial object. All other items mentioned here are monosyllabic transitive verbs. It is not possible for me at the moment to prove that this class 'monosyllabic transitive verb' is important. The verb [krẽⁿ] 'to climb' seems to be used in both ways: [mi kre a bɔ̃ⁿ] ~ [mi krem a bɔ̃ⁿ]. But this difference might reflect intransitive and transitive use of the verb respectively: 'I climbed on a tree' versus 'I climbed a tree'. I have not found intransitive verbs showing the same final [m]; cf. [kɔ̃ⁿ] 'to come' in [mi k a skɔrɔ] 'I came to school'.

The above will illustrate the fact that a final nasal consonant is an exceptional phenomenon in coastal Creole. In church Creole final nasal consonants are frequent, as the following provisional list will show: *dem* (pers. pron. 3 pl., pl. article], *hem* (pers. pron. 3 sg.), *ben* (indicator of past tense), *tem* (time), *nem* (name, to be called), *kom* (to come), *pikin* (small child), etc. All these items have high frequency in texts. The final nasals are pronounced in church

Creole as written, while in common Creole they end on nasalized vowel and loose nasality before vowel.

VOWEL QUALITY

Common Creole has a five-vowel system, and a fairly complete range of vowel combinations. This means that there is no phonemic distinction between [e] and [ɛ]. The last allophone is used in closed syllables only. But as closed syllables are extremely rare, the allophone might only be heard in the two slangy expressions mentioned before: [mɛf] 'menstruating' and [sɛm] 'same'. In church Creole closed syllables are rather common, especially with final nasal consonant. In all these items [ɛ] is used, p.e. [tɛm] 'time' in church Creole as against [tẽⁿ] in common Creole. Cf. also other items as p.e. [hɛlpi] 'to help' for common Creole [yepi].

Items like [bɛlə] 'belly' and [spɛlə] 'of different kinds' pose a different problem. Common Creole pronunciation is [bere] and [speri]. There are no closed syllables here. I should like to propose [lə] as an allophonic variation for word final /l/ in church Creole. This might be an old Creole phenomenon, preserved in church Creole only. The oldest Creole text in Suriname (published in 1718) contains the expression *belle wel* for 'very well' (cf. Rens 1953:142).

For other strange vowels, compare the following provisional list:

Church Creole	Common Creole	
[ɛyxən]	[eyji]	'own'
[dröwfi]	[drɔyfi]	'grape'
[zürdegi]	[srudeci]	'leven'
[bürti]	[birti]	'environment'
[rɔ̃stə]	[lɔstu]	'to rest'
[bowtskɔpu]	[bɔskɔpu]	'message'
[ɔwru]	[owru]	'old'

VOWEL ELISION

Vowels in unstressed syllables are often elided in common Creole. No special research has been carried out to solve the problems of vowel elision in common Creole. H. Eersel has pointed out to me that vowel elision involves syntactic features. Final unstressed vowel is generally elided in verbs, but not in nouns. The extent of the elision partly depends on the speed of utterance. In rapid speech one may hear: [maaksmefmaññãⁿ] 'but he asked me if I had food'. In church Creole, one would certainly pronounce: [ma a haksi mi efu mi habi ñañam].

Vowel elision does not depend on syntactic class and speed of utterance only, but also on emphasis. Emphasis involves two operations in Creole:

1. A syntactic operation: the emphasized part of the utterance is displaced to the very beginning, and preceded by a presentative morpheme /na/, e.g. /na lɔ̃ mi wani lɔ̃ gɔwe/ 'it is running I want to run away'.

2. A phonological operation: vowel elision is avoided in the elements which get special emphasis.

In church Creole vowels are never elided. This produces the impression that every element of the complete utterance gets special emphasis.

Cult languages in pagan religion

In the voodoo-like pagan religion of Suriname Creoles, different groups of Gods use different languages, i.e. their adepts use different languages when they are possessed. Three different languages are used in town services: the language of the Indian Gods, the language of the snake God Fodu, and the language of the Kromanti Gods. It is claimed by religious specialists, that as many as seven Kromanti languages can be distinguished, but I could not get any proof for this statement. Some very deviant Bush Negro cult languages have been observed, but a study of these phenomena proved impossible.

The Kromanti cult language had become increasingly popular among lower class youngsters, when we carried out our research (H. C. van Renselaar and myself in 1960). A complete religious service takes several days. Generally, the Kromanti Gods are invoked in the early Sunday morning hours (around 2 a.m.). The services are held outside town. Youngsters used to drop in after midnight, and almost completely took the show out of the hands of the older people, who gradually retired to their sleeping places. These youngsters did not show any interest in Indian Gods, or Fodu, or earth Gods, but concentrated exclusively on Kromanti. The service got in their hands a definitely violent character. The youngsters became possessed, walked proudly around the scene, danced the violent Kromanti dances, and sang and talked in Kromanti. It was quite clear that these Kromanti dances offered them an outlet for latent aggression, and that they needed it.

Fancy pronunciations are used to characterize different Gods: a certain amount of stuttering indicates possession by Fodu, a certain throatiness of the voice possession by Kromanti Gods. In phonology there is some difference too. Kromanti-possessed may try to imitate Bush Negro pronunciation. But the clearest differences may be found in the domain of vocabulary. The general sentence structure does not deviate from the Creole one, but lexical items are replaced by keywords from the cult languages, or by lexical items from Bush Negro languages in the case of Kromanti.

Indian Gods may use Indian words like *pitani* (child). Fodu uses words like *frojaja* (clothes), *fiye* (child), *mey* (woman), *honto* (snake), *gwela* (water, river), *akaya* (machete), *mado* (house), *hankou* (to talk), *yagaza* (to change), *daome*

L

(to be well). Kromanti Gods use words like *hodani* (house, but I also noted down *danivo* and *dani*, so *hodani* might be a complex item), *ameleku* (woman), *okreswa* (egg), *busnu* (water), *toloki* (to talk, cf. also Sranan *troki*, to lead the chorus), *grebu* (to call out), *bantivo* (cruel). The analysis of an utterance is not always easy. An expression like Fodu *alada fiye mey fu mi honto* (Alada – praise name of the God – daughter of me, the snake) can be analyzed, an expression like Kromanti *ajamsi mdasi* (thank you) can not. In Kromanti a suffix -*ini* has been observed without any other functions apparently than to embellish the utterance.

Conclusions

Special forms of coastal Creole are used in Suriname under special conditions. They are essentially based on common Creole grammar. Church Creole is characterized primarily by differences in phonology, the pagan cult languages by differences in vocabulary. Both remain, I think, essentially Creole.

REFERENCES

Abbenhuis, M. F. 1964. 'Bonni'. *Biografiën (in remembrance of) Emancipatie 1863–1963*, 23–9.
Cassidy, F. G. and R. B. Le Page 1967. *Dictionary of Jamaican English*, Cambridge, Cambridge University Press
De Groot, Silvia W. 1963. 'Van isolatie naar integratie. De Surinaamse marrons en hun afstammelingen', Officiële documenten betreffende de Djoeka's (1845–63), (Verhandelingen Koninklijk Instituut voor Taal-, Land- en Volkenkunde 41), 's-Gravenhage
Donicie, Antoon and Jan Voorhoeve [1963]. *De Saramakaanse woordenschat*, Amsterdam, Bureau voor Taalonderzoek in Suriname
Ferguson, Charles A. 1959. 'Diglossia', *Word* 15:325–40
Herskovits, Melville J. 1931. 'On the provenience of the Portuguese in Saramacca Tongo', *De West-Indische Gids* 12:545–57
Rens, L. L. E. 1953. *The historical and social background of Surinam Negro-English*, Amsterdam, North-Holland Publishing Company
Taylor, Douglas 1965. 'Review of Morris F. Goodman, *A comparative study of Creole French dialects*', *International Journal of American Linguistics* 31:363–70
Trefossa 1957. *Trotji, puëma. Met een stilistische studie over het gedicht Kopenhagen, vertalingen en verklarende aantekeningen door Dr Jan Voorhoeve*, Amsterdam, North-Holland Publishing Company
Van Der Linde, J. M. 1966. *Surinaamse suikerheren en hun kerk. Plantagekolonie en handelskerk ten tijde van Johannes Basseliers, predikant en planter in Suriname*, Wageningen, H. Veenman en Zonen
Voorhoeve, Jan 1957. 'Missionary linguistics in Surinam', *The Bible Translator* 8:179–90
        1959. 'An orthography for Saramaccan', *Word* 15:436–45
        1961a. 'Le ton et la grammaire dans le Saramaccan', *Word* 17:146–63

1961b. 'A project for the study of Creole language history in Surinam', *Proceedings of the conference on creole language studies* (1959), ed. by Robert B. Le Page, 99–106 (Creole Language Studies 2), London, Macmillan

1964. 'Creole languages and communication', *Sympósium on multilingualism* (*Brazzaville*, 1962), 233–42 (CSA/CCTA Publication No. 87), London, Commission de cooperation technique en Afrique

1967. 'Review of Robert A. Hall, Jr., *Pidgin and creole languages*', *Lingua* 18:101–5

Voorhoeve, Jan and Antoon Donicie 1963. *Bibliographie du Négro-anglais du Surinam, avec une appendice sur les langues créoles parlées à l'intérieur du pays* (Koninklijk Instituut voor Taal-, Land- en Volkenkunde, Bibliographical series, 6), 's-Gravenhage

Voorhoeve, Jan, and H. C. Van Renselaar 1962. 'Messianism and nationalism in Surinam', *Bijdragen tot de Taal-, Land- en Volkenkunde* 18:193–216

VARIETIES OF CREOLE IN SURINAME

Prestige in Choice of Language and Linguistic Form[1]

CHRISTIAN EERSEL

The language situation

Amerindian languages, Hindi and Javanese, and the Bush Negro Creoles, are spoken only within their respective ethnic groups. Since 1667 the official language of the country has been Dutch, and since 1876 there has been compulsory education with Dutch as the only medium of instruction from elementary school on. Dutch is the language of the Christian churches with the exception of the Moravian Brethren, who traditionally use Sranan in their services and edifying books (see Voorhoeve, preceding). Dutch has a written and spoken standard form. The other main language of Suriname, Sranan, is the *lingua franca* of the country. Because the Amerindian and Bush Negro groups are not fully integrated into the society, questions of prestige do not play an important part in their relations with other groups. They use Sranan as a *lingua franca*, but for them it is just that. For the descendants of Asian immigrants, the question of status of Sranan relative to Dutch does arise, as also the question of supporting efforts to develop it as a national language. Even though they use Sranan within their own groups, however, it has little standing for them, relative to Dutch (and to the standardized forms of their own native languages). Their preference for Dutch, because of its prestige, reflects general long-standing patterns of language choice and evaluation, rooted in the master-slave relation of slavery and the stratified, European-dominated society of the colonial era. I shall describe these patterns, while indicating also changes that emerge as Sranan is being standardized and revaluated now.

Language choice

As a consequence of the inherited means and forms of social differentiation, command of Dutch is almost the only secure way to win prestige and success in Suriname. One may be socially judged according to one's fluency in Dutch. Among elites the choice of language is determined by the subject of conversation, the situation, and the degree of intimacy between the speakers. Accepted equality is manifested by speaking Sranan to each other. To an inferior Dutch is spoken generally. But sometimes it is rewarding to speak Sranan to inferiors, and it is preferable to do so during elections.

In terms of social position, the general patterns of language choice are as follows:

1. High – High. Dutch and Sranan, with a preference for Sranan in intimate relations between males. Females belonging to the elite group show a somewhat conservative attitude in language choice. Relations between the sexes linguistically correlate with this conservative attitude.

2. High – Low. Nearly always Dutch, when speaking to bilinguals. In time of political campaigning, or for some obvious reason, Sranan.

3. Low – Low. Mostly Sranan.

4. Low – High. Sranan or Dutch, depending on the nature of the relation and the social distance between speakers. Choice here is not like that when a high status speaker addresses one of low status. In some instances it is considered bad behaviour to speak in Dutch to one's superior, although in other instances the reverse is true.

The relation of parents to their children is analogous to that between persons of different status, regardless of the actual social position of the parents. Because all parents want their sons and daughters to climb high on the social ladder, they insist that they speak Dutch. Sometimes parents speak Sranan to their children but expect them to answer in Dutch, even when they, the parents, do not completely understand Dutch. Children have to speak Dutch to each other, at least in the presence of their parents. In higher social circles nearly monolingual Dutch-speaking children can thus be found. This type of monolingualism disappears as the children's field of social contacts widens. The number of truly monolingual Dutch-speaking native adults is negligible. In contrast, monolingualism is very common among Sranan speakers.

The new elite, not having other means of demonstrating their position – colour of the skin does not serve – have to take refuge in Dutch, even in situations in which Sranan would be the only adequate vehicle of communication. An illustration: in a meeting with the chief of one of the Bush Negro tribes a high government officer will speak in Dutch and have his talk translated into the language of that tribe. The chief's answer will be translated back into Dutch. But both men are able to use Sranan as a *lingua franca*! Yet for this ceremony two interpreters are required. The officer's words go in Dutch to the government interpreter, from him in a variety of the language of the tribe to the chief's interpreter, and finally from this man to the chief in the pure form of the language of the tribe. The chief's words come back the other way round. Of course there is much pomp in the manner in which the chiefs organize their meetings, but for the government officer, surely, reasons of prestige have led him to choose Dutch. He then is sure to receive almost the same appreciation from the tribesmen as the white officer of colonial times used to get.

Choice of language in social interaction is not always in accord with one's expectations. There are cases of asymmetry or dissimilarity of choice that may cause difficulties, or even disturb the pattern. The superior or the parents may consider it as not fitting when an inferior or a child speaks Sranan to them. The unexpected use of Dutch can also produce confusion or even irritation when it comes from the lower placed.

Asymmetric language choice is symptomatic of the disturbance of the established social relations and makes visible the uncertainty within the society. For the last ten to fifteen years the Dutch language and its position of prestige have been under attack, due to the activities of the nationalistic cultural movement. Sranan speakers are becoming proud of their language and culture, so clearly different from those of the Dutch. In a way Sranan is in a privileged position, compared to many other creole languages. It is completely different from Dutch, and its speakers can easily develop independently a standard of their own.[2] Sranan speakers have to do so when using the language on a literary or scientific level. Actually there is a flowering in poetry and drama. Dutch has lost much of its former prestige and glory – much, but not all. For Sranan is not the official language of the country, and it is not (yet) fully standardized. The process of imposing Dutch as the only language of prestige, begun more than a century ago, cannot be stopped overnight. Dutch will remain for a long time the most important language of Suriname and, notwithstanding the new cultural ideals, paradoxically enough, a good command of Dutch will still pave the way to positions of prestige.

Asymmetric language choice may be, therefore, also an indication of some ambivalence in Suriname's multilingual society. Ambivalence is characteristically a product of the insecurity in a changing social system. Dutch is accepted as the official language, but its Surinamese speakers have no emotional ties with it. They will not stand up in praise of this national language. Many take a stance of purely pragmatic efficiency in their preference for Dutch. They will never acknowledge Dutch as their mother tongue, even when they are nearly monolingual in it. They will only confess that because of their education in Dutch they are not able to speak Sranan properly. For some Surinamers, who have rejected Sranan, the situation is hopeless, for they have no language of their own. An open acceptance of Dutch as one's mother tongue is considered a betrayal of the growing national consciousness. A Surinamer does not want to be called a Dutchman. Consequently, Dutch is not his language, although he will not go so far as to say that Sranan is. His pragmatic attitude leads him to learn Dutch in order to study at a Dutch university, to be able to carry on business and politics and by doing so to gain prestige in the society. This ambivalence is certainly one of the causes of the lack of substantive creative writing in Dutch. In the end, the nationalistic attitude and the linguistic ambivalence produce the same result: weakening of the prestige position of the Dutch language.

Choice of linguistic forms

DUTCH

Notwithstanding the high position of Dutch and its function as the official language of the country, the accepted standards for it are not the same as in Europe. The written European standard is accepted, and in syntax and lexicon the ideal norms are more or less the same as in Holland; so also for the spoken language. In pronunciation, however, the ideal is definitely not European. The velar /r/, for example, and the typically European intonation are not accepted when coming from a coloured mouth. This attitude can create serious problems for students who have stayed for a long time in Holland when they return home with an unconsciously acquired European pronunciation. They often encounter charges of talking affectedly and artificially, these charges coming mostly from their friends and relatives. Popular comedy is full of characters satirizing these 'coloured Europeans'!

We have here an indication of the coming into existence of an indigenous pronunciation standard, negatively, through rejection of the European pronunciation. Thus a Surinamer may gain prestige with a good command of Dutch, so long as his sounds are not too European. The black 'bakara' [Dutchman] is not generally accepted. As an illustration, here are a few of the differences between the two norms:

European Dutch	Suriname Dutch
velar /r/	front /r/
labio-dental /w/	bilabial /w/
vowels always oral	vowels slightly nasalized before nasals

There are furthermore marked differences in stress and intonation patterns, in the way in which diphthongs are handled, and in the types of liaison and reduction in sequences of sounds. Some European Dutch oppositions do not exist in Surinamese Dutch:

v : f	f
z : s	s

It is not the occurrence of some one or more of the European Dutch features that constitutes a European pronunciation. There are teachers who zealously teach their pupils to pronounce the labio-dental /w/, while at the same time themselves having the front /r/, or nasalized vowels. It is the appearance of all features together that marks the 'bakara' pronunciation that is not accepted from native Surinamers. This shows why a student who speaks Dutch in perfectly formed sentences, choosing words from a well-stocked thesaurus, and without a Dutchman's pronunciation, is highly praised: a man without affectation!

SRANAN

Influences from Dutch upon Sranan, and conversely, are normal and to some extent predictable in such a multilingual situation, from linguistic considerations alone. There are some cases in which prestige clearly has determined the choice, or avoidance, of forms in Sranan.

Examples

1. In creolized Dutch words the voiced and voiceless fricatives are replaced by Sranan /k/, as in *gevaarlijk* : *kefarlek, gulden* : *koloe*. For some speakers the Dutch fricative has greater prestige than their /k/ in such words, and they introduce it into their speech in Sranan: *gulle* ('guilder'), *growte* ('excrements') instead of *kole, krowte*. In their Dutch this preference for the fricative can cause hypercorrect forms, e.g. *dochter* (= Dutch 'daughter'!) instead of the intended *dokter* ('doctor').

2. Reduction of full vowels to schwa or to zero does occur in Sranan, but its distribution is different from that in Dutch. In some words the Dutch pattern is followed, because the full Sranan vowels in those positions are felt to be crude (by some speakers): *fiadoe* becomes *fiade, fronsoe* becomes *fronse*. This happens frequently with initial syllables, as in *fri* : *fer, pri* : *per, kri* : *ker* ('e' representing schwa). In the last case it is not always clear whether prestige has been the determining factor or not, but certainly *fri-, pri-, kri-* are found more in the language of the lower class.

3. Sranan taboo words (some names of parts of the human body, etc.) may be replaced by loan translations from Dutch, or by creolization of new Dutch words, as in *gogo→bakasé* (another Sranan word) 'buttocks'; *pio→brak* 'to vomit'; *kara→growte* 'to relieve oneself'.

Lexical substitutions are not always for prestige reasons. Lack of knowledge of one's own language plays a role as well. Some Sranan words are paired with Dutch equivalents, mostly in the case of syntactic words: *oo* : *toe* 'that', *tak* : *dat* 'that'. It is not certain whether these doublets are to be ascribed to prestige.

Nationalistic purists warn against these and other Dutch influences on Sranan. They for their part look to Spanish when they need a new word, and so a few Spanish words have come into Sranan: *puwema* 'poem', *problema* 'problem'.

One case will demonstrate how deep (unconsciously) and strong the inferiority feelings of Sranan speakers still are, and at the same time show how even in matters of structure Dutch is in higher esteem. The plural of nouns is shown in Sranan not by suffixes, but by the form of the article, somewhat as in French, thus, *a mati* 'the friend' : *den mati* 'the friends'. When the Sranan noun is used without an article, it is to be taken as a class-name. In Dutch a noun is always either in the plural or in the singular. This leads some Sranan

speakers to look upon the Sranan noun without a number marker as inferior
to Dutch. They believe also that the only way to mark a plural noun is by
using suffixes (as in Dutch). In December 1967 a young Surinamese poet
published a collection of poetry with a subtitle containing *puwemas* 'poems',
that is, with an -s suffix for the plural. In an interview with one of his colleagues
he declared that he wanted to start a discussion on the need for a plural in
Sranan. That is why he introduced it on the title-page of his book![3]

Conclusion

Dutch, in its Surinamese variety, is still in a prestige position in Sranan.
Unconsciously an indigenous standard of Dutch is being developed. The
prestige position of Dutch not only affects choice of language but also choice
of forms in Sranan. The nationalistic revaluation of Sranan, and the ambivalence concerning the national language of the country, are complicating
factors that cause asymmetric linguistic behaviour and uncertainty in multilingual social contacts. The system is in change.

NOTES

1 The present paper omits the sketch of the historical background of Sranan
in the original paper, 'Questions of prestige in language choice in a multilingual
setting', presented to the Mona conference. For this background, see the first
section of Dr Voorhoeve's paper, preceding.
2 Unlike, for example, the situation in Jamaica, where the creole, English-based
as is Sranan, has remained subordinate to English and is perhaps being re-
absorbed by it (cf. DeCamp's paper on post-creole continuum in this volume).
3 The book is: *Sibiboesi, Powemas foe Jozef Slagveer*, Paramaribo, 1967.

VARIETIES OF CREOLE IN SURINAME

The Art of Reading Creole Poetry[1]

J. VOORHOEVE

Poetry is universal, because man is man in all times and all cultures. Every form of poetry in the world can be appreciated everywhere else, how remote the source of the poetry might be, culturally or racially. This does not mean, however, that the ears of every listener are tuned in to the beauties hidden in a special poem. Shakespeare lived in a different world. He refers to and reacts on situations, unknown to us now. The same is true for poems which do not lie far behind us in time, but which still refer to a different world. I should like to demonstrate this by reading a poem, written by a Creole from Suriname.

The poem is written in Suriname Creole (Sranan). To overcome the language difficulties I reproduce the poem with a quasi literal translation in English. I do not think the language used creates special problems. It is the poem itself which needs annotation.

The poem consists of four stanzas, of which the first three show a peculiar symmetrical structure. They have recurrent lines 1 3 4 5 and variant lines 2 6 7. The last stanza goes its own way, but shows internal symmetry. Line 1 is repeated with slight alternation in lines 6 and 7, line 3 is repeated in line 5. If not for line 2, the stanza would show a mirror image starting from the middle line *ala mi mati* (all my friends). This is a structure of great complexity, reminiscent of the structure of songs.

The title introduces a person in the first person singular pronoun. This man or woman has gone away (formerly) and is coming back (now). In the first three stanzas this person imagines the dry season wind on three different places putting before him the same question: Creole, how? This is the rather meaningless question people use in meeting each other. It certainly does not refer to a long absence, as suggested by the title. The Creole then imagines himself answering all three times with the same peculiar statement: Here I am. The question 'How?' would rather ask for the same meaningless answer: 'Not too bad.' Instead of this, the Creole answers: 'Here I am.' This peculiar statement makes us suspect more behind the simple question of the dry season wind than we thought before. This new interpretation is reinforced by the variant lines, added to the statement. These lines in fact contain a subtle comparison between Europe and Suriname. In three different stanzas the Creole throws in three different arguments in favour of his home country:

his life as a small boy, listening to the old stories of his granny; the cotton-trees, lively with spirits, as against the dead technical miracles of Europe; and the cake his Creole love used to prepare, as against the potatoes from Holland.

The simple meaningless question of the dry season wind now gets a bitter flavour. By going abroad the Creole has created serious doubts about his roots in life. One does not know where he really belongs. He is welcomed three times as if he was a stranger, by the most indifferent greeting formula in the language. But in asking 'how' the wind also asks about the place where he really belongs. Therefore he has to affirm three times: I am here, I belong to this country. He confirms this statement by telling in a very subtle way about his experiences abroad.

Then, the fourth stanza opens with the title line, which refers to a well-known song. In a more subtle way the whole poem refers to songs. I already mentioned the song-like structure of the poem. The words *trotji* and *pitji* also are technical terms in the musical culture of Suriname Creoles, referring to the roles of soloist and chorus in Creole songs. The dry season wind starts the song as a soloist, the Creole answers each time with his chorus. One of the most remarkable achievements in this poem is, that the Creole succeeds to answer each time in a different recognizable dance rhythm. So the last lines of the first three stanzas offer a display of Creole dance rhythms. The most fascinating point, however, is that the third stanza uses a closing rhythm, especially because the rhythmic repetition is for the first time absent in the third stanza. Every Creole listener will now realize that the dance is over.

The dance is over, the answer has been given. Imagination stops and reality begins. At that same moment a new song starts, a song, used in Suriname long ago to advertize a popular skeleton-show on the yearly fancy-fair. It suggests the spell visitors are in after witnessing the show: they go away, but they must come back to see the next performance. By a subtle change of tense of the first verb, it is suggested here: I have gone away, I tried to escape, but I failed, I realize now that I must come back.

But now the Creole realizes also the dangers ahead, which might prevent him from coming back: the sea is wide. He calls urgently on his friends back home to evoke the old magical words to help him overcome the dangers. These magical words prove to be no other than the same line of the advertizing song, but now in a shortened staccato way, almost whispered: I've gone, I come . . . Small dots indicate that the words continue to be whispered, till he will be safely home.

Poem by Trefossa (in Suriname Creole)

mi go – m' e kon

te dreeten winti sa trotji
na Mawnidan:

– krioro fa?
m' sa pitji:
– dja mi de,
– banji fu ba-m'ma seti keba:
– ertintin . . . ertintin . . .

te dreeten winti sa trotji
na kankantri:
– krioro fa?
m' sa pitji:
– dja mi de,
– Eifeltoren hee pasa,
– m'a n'a jorka, a n'a jorka . . .

te dreeten winti sa trotji
na Moi-bon fu Bose:
– krioro fa?
m' sa pitji:
– dja mi de,
– s'sa Mina, ptata bun,
– ma bojo fu ju tjir-tjiri . . .

mi go – m' e kon,
sootwatra bradi.
tak wan mofo,
ala mi mati,
tak wan mofo.
m'go,
m' e kon . . .

I've gone – I come

if the dry season wind starts singing
in Mahogany Street:
– Creole, how?
I'll answer:
– here am I
– granny's bench has been set ready
– once upon a time . . . once upon a time . . .

if the dry season wind starts singing
in the cotton-tree:
– Creole, how?
I'll answer:
– here am I
– Eifel Tower is much higher,
– but has no spirits, has no spirits . . .

if the dry season wind starts singing
in Big Tree of Bose:
– Creole, how?

I'll answer:
– here am I
– Sister Mary, potatoes are all right,
– but your cake is just the best . . .

I've gone – I come,
the sea is wide.
say the words,
you all my friends,
say the words.
I've gone,
I come . . .

NOTE

1 Dr Voorhoeve presented this poem and its interpretation at the 'Creole evening' preceding the conference discussions. It is reprinted here from Nomen: *Leyden studies in linguistics* (The Hague, Mouton, 1969) by permission of the publishers.

COEXISTENT SYSTEMS IN LANGUAGE VARIATION

The Case of Hawaiian English

STANLEY M. TSUZAKI

The classification of Hawaiian English (HE) or English as spoken by natives of Hawaii has been a favorite source of controversy locally (documented, for example, in Tsuzaki and Reinecke 1966). The basic issue is whether HE should be designated a pidgin, a creole, or a dialect of English. The positions taken on this question have been very divergent, ranging all the way from the pidgin to the dialect interpretations, and including various 'combinatory' analyses. The differences of opinion seem to be attributable largely to two factors: (1) the relatively wide range or latitude of variation found in the structure of HE, apparently in all stages of its development, including the present, and (2) the general failure on the part of many analysts and observers to keep the synchronic aspects of HE separate from the diachronic. For example, the latter confusion is manifested in its elementary form in the pidgin view of current HE which is based on and defended in terms of the diachronic fact that HE was originally a pidgin. The following discussion is aimed at treating the problem of variation in present-day HE from a strictly synchronic point of view.[1]

The dialect interpretation of HE has been a very popular one (indeed, perhaps the most popular), in all probability because it has had a relatively long and reputable, though somewhat peculiar, history. That is, the tradition dates back some three decades to Reinecke's work on 'language and *dialect* in Hawaii' (Reinecke 1935) and on the 'English *dialect* of Hawaii' (Reinecke and Tokimasa 1934). At that time (when the difference between pidgins and creoles — not to mention dialects — was not nearly as clear as it was to become a decade or so later, primarily in the works of Robert A. Hall, Jr.), Reinecke could be said to have taken the dialect position. While this may be true enough, it is also incontestably true that the main thrust of Reinecke's work on HE and on language in general has been motivated by an interest in historical and sociological considerations, as evidenced by his M.A. thesis (Reinecke 1935) and his Ph.D. dissertation (Reinecke 1937). In other words, I think that the position he took on the synchronic nature of HE at the time was ancillary to his views on diachronic and extralinguistic problems. In spite of this fact, his position on the taxonomic question of HE has been utilized repeatedly as the cornerstone of identical or very similar points of view taken by subsequent students of HE. The result of this situation has been a rather peculiar state of affairs. While many subscribe to this point of view, very few have adduced supporting evidence beyond that offered originally by Reinecke (e.g. Reinecke and Tokimasa 1934), but only in an incidental and tentative sense.

This relative lack of evidence, it seems to me, has been and still is the principal weakness of the point of view under consideration. To the extent that such evidence can be and is mustered, the position will become more tenable. For example, if the existence of an English 'language mastery continuum'[2] in HE could be demonstrated or if the use of the so-called 'pan-dialectal' or 'over' grammar approach (see C. Bailey [1968], DeCamp [1968], Labov [1968]) indicates a close relationship between HE and other dialects of English, the position will be strengthened and consequently should attract many more adherents. The fact remains, however, that to date practically nothing has been done along the lines just indicated; hence the interpretation still suffers from the lack of a very fundamental ingredient — linguistic evidence.

Another popular position (though perhaps not nearly so as the first) has been one which in fact posits the existence of multiple systems (i.e. coexistent systems) within HE. As it is typically stated, all HE speakers are said to be classifiable into pidgin, creole, and/or dialect speakers. Couched in terms of HE as a set of coexistent systems, the equivalent statement would be that HE is partly a pidgin, partly a creole, and partly a dialect. Like the dialect explanation, however, this interpretation has suffered from a relative lack of supporting evidence, particularly evidence of a linguistic nature. This deficiency, coupled with my feeling that it was basically a very good interpretation of the HE situation, prompted me several years ago to publish a short note (Tsuzaki 1966), in which I argued in favor of this point of view and presented some substantiating evidence. The present article may be viewed as an elaboration of that note.

The use of coexistent systems in explaining linguistic structures, particularly phonological structures, has had its proponents as well as opponents. Among the former are Fries and Pike (1949:49), who summarize their position as follows:

Some languages contain phonemic arrangements which are not completely in balance; they contain conflicting elements which may be analyzed as coexistent phonemic systems. The points of conflict can be determined by first studying the sounds of a language on the assumption that they compose a single completely systematic unit, and by then looking for elements of the postulated system which contradict evidence separately obtained by analysis of the objectively observable reactions of native speakers to the writing or analysis of their own language or to the speaking of a foreign language. Sounds are pertinent only as they are parts of a system, so systems must be compared with systems. Coexistent systems may include, among other types, a vernacular (1) with sounds borrowed from other languages, or (2) with relics or advance elements of linguistic change, or (3) with special segments of an interjectional type, or (4) with general differences of quality, style, or speed. Monolingual and bilingual speakers may have an identical pronunciation of the vernacular but different reactions to it . . .

Others in this camp include Firth (1948: esp. 127–8, 150–1) and Francescato (1959).

In the opposing group is Bloch (1950:87),[3] who expresses the negative point of view as follows:

The presence of recent loanwords in Japanese, as in many other languages, complicates the analysis; but there is no purely descriptive test by which they can be identified, and no valid excuse for excluding them – so far as the analyst can recognize them through his accidental knowledge of other languages – from the total vocabulary. The view set forth by Fries and Pike, . . . that loanwords may constitute a separate phonemic system coexisting with one or more other systems in the same dialect, is unacceptable. What we are able to discern as the phonemic system of a dialect is necessarily single, not multiple: the total network of relationships among all the sounds that occur in the dialect; and the analyst's task is to describe the system in a way that is correspondingly single, in a coherent set of general statements which will enable him to predict the phonetic shape of utterances that have not yet occurred . . . All the details that make up a language have an equal claim to be used as evidence for the system; whatever occurs in the utterances of those who speak the language is for that reason a part of the total structure . . . The question how to treat loanwords can have only one answer: treat them as words.

Others who have also opposed the use of the concept are Diebold (1962:45), Hockett (1950:74–7), and Wonderly (1946).

The position taken in this paper with respect to the concept of coexistent systems will be a favorable one. To wit, it will attempt to show that the concept is useful in explaining the HE situation – i.e. that its use results in a better interpretation of the HE situation than any others I have examined to date based on other concepts. It will also suggest by extension that the concept might conceivably be useful in explaining other similar situations in the world.

Since the concept as utilized in this paper derives most directly from the formulation by Fries and Pike (1949), it is perhaps only fair that divergencies from the original model be stated explicitly. The following are among the most significant deviations:

1. It is assumed that for certain purposes (such as for purposes of the present discussion) it is possible to do a synchronic description of a merged or mixed system and to have a reasonably complete synchronic description of such a system without taking into account the direction of change, which, in my opinion, is better viewed as a diachronic question (cf. Fries and Pike 1949:42).

2. The component systems of HE, though fragmentary, comprise sizeable

partials (see n. 10) and the locus of the systems is not so firmly attached to the idiolect (cf. Fries and Pike 1949:31).

3. The applicability of the concept of coexistent systems is not restricted to the phonological level; it is assumed to be applicable at all levels. Practically all of the examples to be cited will in fact come from the grammatical (i.e. syntactic) level.

4. Questions pertaining to procedures and assumptions for analyzing language/dialect mixture are incidental to the main question concerning the immediate utility of the concept as an explanation for the HE situation (cf. Fries and Pike 1949:32–44).

In my version of the coexistent view, the basic systems of HE consist of (1) an English-based pidgin, (2) an English-based creole, and (3) a dialect of English, which in turn is divisible into (a) a non-standard, and (b) a standard variety. System (1) will be referred to as Hawaiian Pidgin English (HPE); (2) as Hawaiian Creole English (HCE); (3) as Hawaiian Dialect English (HDE); (3a) as Non-standard Hawaiian English (NSHE); and (3b) as Standard Hawaiian English (SHE).

The principal justification for calling HPE a pidgin is that it meets certain linguistic and social criteria specified in current definitions of the term, such as the following (Hall 1966:xii): 'For a language to be a true pidgin, two conditions must be met: its grammatical structure and its vocabulary must be sharply reduced . . . and also the resultant language must be native to none of those who use it.' That is, HPE is designated an English-based pidgin because its structure is greatly simplified in comparison with English, the language on which it is based, and because it has no native speakers, since those who use it speak other languages as their native tongues – e.g. dialects of Chinese, Hawaiian, Japanese, Korean, and the Philippine languages.

Furthermore, HPE manifests many of the characteristics attributed to other pidgins of the world, especially those based on English (cf. Hall 1966:8). The following are representative features:

(i)   Copulaless equational clauses (e.g. *Me/I too much happy* 'I am/was very happy')
(ii) Juxtaposition of nouns without the possessive suffix or the preposition *of* (*My husband house kaukau no good* 'The food at my husband's house is not good')
(iii) Lack of the definite and indefinite articles (*Outside door me/I see my husband* 'Outside the door I see/saw my husband')
(iv) The generalized third person pronoun *em* as direct object of the verb (*No can fool em* 'One cannot fool him/her/it/them')
(v)   Lack of inflectional suffixes, which makes for an extremely simple morphological system (*One day me/I see some mountain* 'One day I see/saw some mountains')

(vi) A small inventory of prepositions, the usage of which is highly restricted (. . . *if me/I come stay for hanahana rice field* '. . . if I came/had come to work in the rice fields')

In view of the foregoing evidence I think the important question is not so much whether HPE is or is not a pidgin but rather whether or not it needs to be taken into account in a synchronic description of present-day HE. The negative view on the latter question seems to be based on the argument that with the expiration of the first generation immigrants, who originally came to Hawaii to work on the sugar cane plantations, HPE has been expiring or that indeed it has expired and that therefore it should not be taken into account. While I agree that it has been rapidly losing ground in terms of numbers of speakers and is therefore a dying language, I do not agree that it is completely dead. It is my opinion (based on personal observation) that there are sufficient numbers of the original plantation immigrants still living today who have occasion to use HPE that the latter must be considered as a component of HE. Without giving up this basic position on the current status of HPE, I would freely admit that it is by far the least significant (i.e. the smallest, the least influential, the least prestigious) component of the three major ones posited.

There are several kinds of justification for calling HCE an English-based creole. The ultimate test in classifying a language as a creole is a historical one, according to Hall (1966:122–3):

Whereas a pidgin is identifiable at any given time by both linguistic and social criteria, a creole is identifiable only by historical criteria – that is, if we know that it has raisen out of a pidgin. There are no structural criteria which, in themselves, will identify a creole as such, in the absence of historical evidence.

If this criterion is valid, HCE could be said to have passed the test many years ago when Reinecke (1935) demonstrated quite conclusively that a 'nonmakeshift' type of HE was evolved from a 'makeshift' type. The fact that he used the terms 'pidgin' and 'creole' to refer to the makeshift language and 'dialect' for the nonmakeshift is a terminological question that is not germane to the problem at hand. There is hardly any question then that the historical base of HCE was HPE, a pidgin; there is a question as to whether or not the resultant language was a creole.

Turning to definitions again, one finds such statements as the following: 'A creole language arises when a pidgin becomes the native language of a speech-community' (Hall 1966:xii). 'In the development of a creole language out of a pidgin, . . . the main change is in the direction of re-expansion of both structure and vocabulary' (*ibid*. p. 25). In such definitions one finds further evidence corroborating the creole interpretation, for the language in question can be defined as a pidgin which has been expanded in structure and 'nativized' by a large segment of the speech community as a first language.

The criterion of mutual intelligibility also gives support to the creole analysis.[4] The fact that English-speaking newcomers to Hawaii have difficulty understanding certain varieties of HE (i.e. HPE, HCE, and perhaps even NSHE), a well-known phenomenon locally,[5] would lead one to the conclusion that at least a part of HE is a creole, rather than a dialect. Cases in which this problem of communication does not arise or does not seem to be as serious as I have indicated it to be do not invalidate the conclusion. It simply means that whatever the reasons may be, some newcomers are exposed predominantly or exclusively to SHE and/or Standard English (SE). This situation should not be too difficult to understand if one bears in mind that the majority of HE speakers restrict their English to SHE or SE when communicating with non-HE speakers, even in an indirect sense as when they are within earshot of non-HE speakers.

In short, the application of the criterion of mutual intelligibility to HCE, a mutually unintelligible but English-appearing variety of HE, implies creolization, particularly when coupled with the fact that HCE cannot be viewed as a highly deviant dialect of English (like Cockney or Lancashire) simply because the English language has not been present in Hawaii long enough for it to have developed mutually unintelligible dialects. The unintelligibility involved seems to depend partly on structural factors (viz. pronunciation, vocabulary, and syntax) and partly on nonstructural considerations (i.e. choice of topic, organization of discourse, attitudes, and the like).

Perhaps the strongest type of evidence that I have been able to find in support of the creole interpretation, however, lies in the similarities between HCE and other creole languages of the world, especially English-based creoles. The extent of similarity is such that one could take a set of characteristics for a creole other than HCE (e.g. Jamaican Creole as characterized by B. Bailey (1966:146) or Antiguan as characterized by Reisman (1964:112–15)) and by making a few alterations, construct a fairly representative list of characteristics for HCE.

A more convincing illustration of the similarities involved may be found in a more pinpointed example, for which the verbal system will serve admirably. Basically the HCE verbal system[6] shows a remarkable resemblance to those reported in many other creoles by various scholars – e.g. Voorhoeve (1957), Taylor (1956:408ff.), Thompson (1961:108–10). In terms of 'positional analysis of categories' (see Hymes 1955, 1956 and Taylor 1956), the following verbal categories (and markers, referred to here as 'particles') occur in HCE in the order given:

(i)   Negative (*no/never*)
(ii)   Auxiliary (*can/might*(?)/*must*(?)/etc.)
(iii) Past tense (*been/went/had*)
(iv)   Future or contingent mood (*go*)
(v)   Progressive aspect (*stay*)

(vi) Habitual aspect (Ø [= unmarked stem])

(vii) Verb stem, nucleus, or base

All of the prestem particles do not seem to occur within a single verbal construction, suggesting co-occurrence restrictions. For example, (i) (*never*) and (iii) are usually mutually exclusive, since *never*, which is usually used as a past negator, indicates past time. Similarly categories (ii) and (iii), (iv), and (v) are usually mutually exclusive. The use of up to three preposed particles in any given verbal construction is the rule (e.g. *I no eat* 'I don't eat'; *I no go eat* 'I am not going to eat/I will not eat'; *I no go stay eat* 'I am not going to be eating/I will not be eating'). Four particles are possible, but unusual (e.g. *I no been go stay eat* 'I wasn't/hadn't been eating'); five seem to be impossible (i.e. sentences of the type **I no could been go stay eat* are not grammatical sequences).

The foregoing sketch of the verbal system of HCE, which basically seems to be of the pan-creole type, is a strong justification for setting up a creole component for HE. *It also seems to provide a base from which on the one hand a pidgin variety of HE, i.e. HPE, could be established and a dialect on the other, i.e. NSHE and SHE.* That is, that variety of HE which for the most part does not use the system of preposed particles just outlined (with the exception of categories (i), (ii), (vi), and (vii) but instead relies almost exclusively on lexical items to signal the semantics of the verb (e.g. *yesterday, now, suppose*) is HPE. That variety which makes use of a modified version of the creole system in the direction of SE is NSHE; and the one in which the SE verb system is utilized is SHE.

By way of illustration let us consider two sets of sentences, each set representing alternative ways of 'saying the same thing' in HE:

(1a) Me/I kaukau/eat

(1b) I stay eat/kaukau

(1c) I stay eating

     I eating

(1d) I am eating

(2a) Me/I kaukau/eat

(2b) I been eat/kaukau

(2c) I ate

(2d) I ate

In the coexistent view of HE under discussion, sentences of the type (a) are considered to be part of HPE; those of type (b), of HCE; those of type (c), of NSHE; and those of type (d), of SHE. The overlap, especially the partial overlap, between contiguous sentences representing different varieties of HE is of some significance and will be discussed presently.

This brings us to HDE, the third variety of HE, which is considered a dialect of English primarily on the basis of structural similarities with other dialects of English. To continue the argument via the verb analysis, one could say that a basic difference between the HCE and the HDE verbal systems is that the former uses a series of particles preposed to the verb stem whereas the latter uses inflection – i.e. suffixes and replacives. The combination of these two types of verbal systems gives rise to such non-standard phrases as *stay eating*, in which the *stay* is clearly a carryover from HCE and the *eating* is ultimately modelled after the SE form. It is the existence of such combinations, which literally seem to partake of both types of systems, that makes it convenient to posit a non-standard variety of HDE. The NSHE variant *eating* could be derived from either NSHE *stay eating* or SHE-SE *am eating* by deleting the *stay* and the *am*, respectively; in either case the resultant structure would be the same, a non-standard pattern. The verbal system of SHE seems to be very similar, if not identical, with that of SE. In fact, grammatically it seems to share a great deal with SE; what makes it peculiarly Hawaiian is probably its phonology and lexicon.[7] Because of its similarities with SE, SHE is mutually intelligible with other dialects of English. To some extent, I think this is also true of NSHE.

Leaving the discussion of the component systems of HE, we should now turn our attention briefly to natural corpora, or specific bodies of data, an examination of which might verify or refute the coexistent interpretation. A cursory inspection of my HE materials, consisting of tapes and texts, suggests an immediate refutation, for there seem to be no convincing examples of the component systems occurring in their pure forms, or as completely discrete systems occurring independently of one another. While I cannot disregard shortcomings in my collection of materials as a possible explanation for this problem, and though I do not deny the existence of HE speakers who might utilize the component systems in their pure forms, I strongly suspect that a more systematic and comprehensive collection of data would lead to the same general conclusion. Even a detailed examination of the verbal systems of HE leads to an initial disconfirmation of the coexistent interpretation because the several systems are not to be found occurring in their unadulterated forms but rather in combinations of different proportions with one another, often in the same corpus and even in apparently identical contexts and styles.

From certain vantage points in linguistics – e.g. structural linguistics, this situation poses a serious problem – the problem of being faced with an analysis which does not seem to account for a sufficient proportion of the corpus to be considered seriously as a solution. In the case of HE the problem is complicated further because I find that the initial analysis in terms of coexistent systems still appeals to me. That is, it is a relatively neat and simple explanation of the HE situation which is basically in accord with my native intuition – I feel it is essentially correct and sense a kind of reality to the three-fold scheme posited above which the right approach to the data ought to justify. Further, I think an empirical accounting for the combinations or intermixtures of the component systems will prove possible, through discovery of the linguistic and social conditions that govern their realization.

The problem is a familiar one in work dealing with bilingualism, language contact, linguistic acculturation, and pidgins and creoles, where, in my estimation, the 'single system' or 'monosystemic' solution to analytical problems caused by foreign influences predominates. So long as the influences attributed to one linguistic system on another are numerically small or structurally slight,[8] the single system scheme seems to be workable, as demonstrated in numerous studies on English influences in the immigrant languages of the New World (see bibliographies in Haugen (1956) and Weinreich (1953), including my own work on the Spanish of Mexicans in Detroit, Michigan (Tsuzaki 1963)). However, when the extent of these influences is relatively great or more accurately when the analytical scheme used forces recognition of the extent of influence to reach sizeable and significant proportions, I think the approach becomes hardly tenable because the results obtained in fact reduce the concept of system or structure to an absurdity.[9] Whatever the reasons may be, linguistic systems do not seem to admit of wholesale borrowing of the type that would cause drastic changes in their basic structures. There appears to be some unspecifiable point in the process of borrowing at which they become incapable of achieving homeostasis, at which time they are usually displaced by other more stable, viable, and balanced systems. As Sapir (1921:206) put it almost half a century ago: 'Language is probably the most self-contained, the most massively resistant of all social phenomena. It is easier to kill it off than to disintegrate its individual form.'

I think that a much better alternative, at least in the HE situation, is to take the 'multiple systems' or 'polysystemic' approach but to de-emphasize the roles of the idiolect and the criterion of accountability insofar as 'surface' grammar is concerned. Except for the use of coexistent systems, this change of focus seems to be quite justified in terms of recent work done in transformational-generative grammar and sociolinguistics. The unreliability of the idiolect as a basis for extracting (a simple, coherent) system has been demonstrated quite convincingly by Labov (1966); the principle of accountability as applied to surface structures alone seems to run counter to the goals of transformational-generative grammar.

From such a vantage point, the inexplicability of a given corpus in its entirety in terms of any single component system of HE becomes relatively unimportant. To the extent that the same corpus, and by extension all other HE corpora, can be explained in terms of a set of coexistent (very imperfectly documented here but *known* or at least *posited*) systems, one has a better model for explaining situations like HE, in which as a result of relatively rapid linguistic changes, coexistent systems emerge from a synchronic analysis (cf. statement by Fries and Pike (1949:41) regarding linguistic change and coexistent phonemic systems).

Such a scheme of coexistent systems for HE (now viewed as a hyper or super system) as I envisage it at the present time would consist of a set of three basic overlapping, rather than completely independent, structures. Exactly how the three systems overlap or how great the overlap is or to what extent they are in conflict is not very clear to me. Within idiolects these overlapping systems would probably have to be partial (defective or fragmentary) as well, partaking, so to speak, of two contiguous systems (i.e. the pidgin and the creole or the creole and the dialect) in various proportions. An important (indeed crucial) point to keep in mind about these partial, overlapping systems within idiolects is that in most cases enough of the whole component systems are preserved in the partials so that the latter cannot be disregarded nor can they be incorporated easily into a monosystemic scheme.[10]

To conclude, the coexistent systems interpretation of HE has both its merits and demerits. I think its principal merit is that it represents a more adequate and valid analysis of the status of current HE than any other interpretation I have examined to date – i.e. one which accounts for a great deal of variation in strictly synchronic terms.[11] Its principal drawback at present lies in the lack of definitive delineations among the component systems. To obtain such delineations, one would need to have a fairly complete analysis of each of the three major types of HE.

NOTES

1 For an excellent historical as well as sociological treatment of HE up to the mid-1930s, see Reinecke 1935.

2 Which is characterized as follows (Reinecke 1935:34): 'At one end of the scale is the uneducated laborer who can barely make known his elementary wants in atrociously mispronounced and extremely simplified English; at the other end is the exceptional immigrant, or more likely the son or grandson of an immigrant, who expresses himself in fluent, idiomatic, and adequate English, but who retains a scarcely perceptible smack of the "foreign accent" and peculiar idioms of his language group.'

3 The original passage contains three footnotes which the interested reader might want to consult since they have been omitted in the present quote.

4 For an entirely different conclusion based on the same criterion, see Voegelin and Voegelin (1964:25).

5 See Dulaney and Dulaney 1962 for a short published account illustrating the problem.

6 The data presented here are taken from an ongoing study of the verbal system of HE begun in the summer of 1968. Since the study has not been completed as of this writing, the results should be treated cautiously.

7 For some peculiarities in the suprasegmental phonology, see Vanderslice and

Pierson 1967; for peculiarities in the lexicon, see Tsuzaki 1968 and Reinecke and Tsuzaki 1967. For other relevant sources, see Tsuzaki and Reinecke 1966.

8 See Haugen (1956:65) for a corroborating statement as to the actual extent of influence in such studies.

9 See Meyerstein (1959:54–6) for a contrary view, in which so-called 'unassimilated loans' (i.e. linguistic elements which are imported or borrowed from another language but which are not adapted to the structure of the borrowing language) are considered to be 'an integral part of the corpus analyzed' because they occur in 'spontaneous responses to certain situations'.

The only real exception to this apparent rule of parsimony in borrowing seems to be the case of pidgin and creole languages. However, it should be noted that with these languages it is customary to treat them as separate systems, divorced synchronically from the structures of their 'parent' or 'foster parent' languages. It should also be noted that they are characteristically treated as single systems.

10 A preliminary count of my HE verb concordances shows that the percentage ratio of HCE verb forms to non-HCE forms varies from 75:25 to 25:75. In other words, the minimum percentage of creole verb forms in the corpora counted to the total number of forms in those corpora is 25% – a very sizeable proportion indeed.

11 There seem to be some diachronic advantages attached to this interpretation as well. For example, I think that HCE structures could be utilized as bridges to connect HPE and HDE, thus making it possible to trace the historical 'drift' of HE in the direction of SE.

REFERENCES

Bailey, Beryl Loftman 1966. *Jamaican creole syntax: a transformational approach*, Cambridge, Cambridge University Press

Bailey, Charles-James N. 1968. 'Optimality, positivism, and pan-dialectal grammars' (Paper, originally entitled "The uses that can be made of sociolinguistic data for linguistic theory', read at a sociolinguistic forum of the Chicago Linguistic Society, 29 March, 1968)

Bloch, Bernard 1950. 'Studies in colloquial Japanese IV: phonemics', *Language* 26:86–125

DeCamp, David [1968]. 'Toward a generative analysis of a post-creole speech continuum' (in this volume)

Diebold, A. Richard, Jr. 1962. 'A laboratory for language contact,' *Anthropological Linguistics* 4(1):41–51

Dulaney, Walter F., and Ele Dulaney 1962. 'I hear you talking, but you don't make sense,' *The Honolulu Advertiser*, 27 April, 1962

Firth, J. R. 1948. 'Sounds and prosodies', *Transactions of the Philological Society* (1948) 127–52

Francescato, Giuseppe 1959. 'A case of coexistence of phonemic systems', *Lingua* 8:78–86

Fries, Charles C. and Kenneth L. Pike 1949. 'Coexistent phonemic systems', *Language* 25:29–50

Hall, Robert A., Jr. 1966. *Pidgin and creole languages*, Ithaca, New York, Cornell University Press

Haugen, Einar 1956. *Bilingualism in the Americas: a bibliography and research guide* (Publication of the American Dialect Society, 26). University, Alabama, University of Alabama Press for the American Dialect Society

Hockett, Charles F. 1950. 'Peiping morphophonemics,' *Language* 26:63–85

Hymes, D. H. 1955. 'Positional analysis of categories: a frame for reconstruction', *Word* 11:10–23

1956. 'Na-Déné and positional analysis of categories', *American Anthropologist* 58:624–38

Labov, William 1966. *The social stratification of English in New York City*, Washington, D.C., Center for Applied Linguistics

[1968]. 'Contraction, deletion, and inherent variability of the English copula' (Paper distributed at the Conference on pidginization and creolization of languages, University of the West Indies, April, 1968; also presented in abbreviated form at the LSA annual meeting, December, 1967)

Meyerstein, Goldie Piroch 1959. 'Selected problems of bilingualism among immigrant Slovaks', Unpublished Ph.D. dissertation, University of Michigan

Reinecke, John E. 1935. 'Language and dialect in Hawaii,' Unpublished M.A. thesis, University of Hawaii (Revised version published by the University of Hawaii Press, 1969)

1937. 'Marginal languages: a sociological study of creole languages and trade jargons,' Unpublished Ph.D. dissertation, Yale University

Reinecke, John E. and Aiko Tokimasa 1934. 'The English dialect of Hawaii', *American Speech* 9:48–58, 122–31

Reinecke, John E. and Stanley M. Tsuzaki 1967. 'Hawaiian loanwords in Hawaiian English of the 1930's', *Oceanic Linguistics* 6:80–115

Reisman, Karl M. L. 1964. ' "The isle is full of noises": a study of creole in the speech patterns of Antigua, West Indies', Unpublished Ph.D. dissertation, Harvard University

Sapir, Edward 1921. *Language: an introduction to the study of speech*, New York, Harcourt, Brace & World [Reprinted, Harvest Books, HB7, 1963]

Taylor, Douglas 1956. 'Language contacts in the West Indies', *Word* 12:399–414

Thompson, R. W. 1961. 'A note on some possible affinities between the creole dialects of the Old World and those of the New', *Proceedings of the conference on creole language studies*, ed. by R. B. LePage, 107–13 (Creole Language Studies II) London, Macmillan

Tsuzaki, Stanley M. 1963. 'English influences in the phonology and morphology of the Spanish spoken in the Mexican Colony in Detroit, Michigan', Unpublished Ph.D. dissertation, University of Michigan (Revised version to be published by Mouton & Co.)

1966. 'Hawaiian English: pidgin, creole, or dialect?' *Pacific Speech* 1(2):25–8

1968. 'Common Hawaiian words and phrases used in English,' *Journal of English Linguistics* 2:78–85

Tsuzaki, Stanley M. and John E. Reinecke 1966. *English in Hawaii: an annotated bibliography*' (Oceanic Linguistics Special Publication 1). Honolulu, Hawaii, Pacific and Asian Linguistics Institute, University of Hawaii

Vanderslice, Ralph and Laura Shun Pierson 1967. 'Prosodic features of Hawaiian English', *The Quarterly Journal of Speech* 53:156–66

Voegelin, Carl F. and Florence M. Voegelin 1964. 'Hawaiian pidgin and mother tongue', *Anthropological Linguistics* 6(7): 20–56

Voorhoeve, Jan 1957. 'The verbal system of Sranan', *Lingua* 6:374–96
Weinreich, Uriel 1953. *Languages in contact: findings and problems* (Publications of the Linguistic Circle of New York, 1), New York, Linguistic Circle of New York
Wonderly, William L. 1946. 'Phonemic acculturation in Zoque,' *International Journal of American Linguistics* 12:92–5

JAMAICAN CREOLE

Can dialect boundaries be defined?

BERYL L. BAILEY

Early American structural linguistics concentrated its energies on establishing the 'system' of a language, the implication being that for each code there was a fixed set of rules or 'patterns' to which members of a given language community regularly conformed for purposes of interaction and communication. The concept has in recent years been seriously challenged, and it is now a matter of general acceptance that for any given language there exists not one, but a number of closely related subsystems on which native speakers draw at will.

From this point of view there would seem to be some justification for the stand taken by David DeCamp[1] (among others), who would have the term creole applied not just to one form of speech, but to the entire language spectrum as it exists in Jamaica, including even the form of standard English peculiar to the island. This may be a very useful concept for the sociolinguist, and I, for one, would not deny him this right provided it helped clarify issues for his own purposes, and he clearly stated the specific limits within which his definition of the word 'creole' holds. For my part, I have steadily resisted this definition on the grounds that far from helping to solve the problems to which my energies must be directed, namely the pedagogical ones, it merely serves to obfuscate them. The situation is analogous to that of the blind men of Hindustan, for whom the elephant had sharply irreconcilable associations. The pedagogue must work with neat, clearly defined patterns of behavior. He must be constantly aware of where he finds his students, and equally well defined must be the target to which he must lead him.

In our zeal for linguistic truth and our search for better methodology for representing these truths we must not lose sight of some very practical problems, such as the very mundane one of teaching the standard to speakers of some non-standard variant. If, therefore, I have preferred to operate with two distinctly divergent poles, and to regard all performances which occur within the continuum as belonging to one or the other of these poles, it is because contrastive analysis remains the single most valuable tool with which linguistics has provided the pedagogue. It is interesting that despite the modern tendency to denigrate the contributions of structural linguistics, we have really not been able to find an alternative to contrastive analysis. Indeed the best we have been able to do has been to modify (even though considerably in some cases) the uses to which it has been put. Jamaican Creole (JC) is, therefore, in my frame of reference, that form of language used in Jamaica which is syntactically, phonologically, and lexically farthest removed from the Jamaican standard (SJE). It is the idealized construct which I described in *Jamaican Creole Syntax* (Bailey 1966), the construct which I here assume lies at the core of all borrowing and interference as manifest in the continuum. The speakers of unadulterated JC are rare indeed, but the pedagogue or the text-book writer must deal with maximal situations, and it would seem that optimal effects will be achieved only when all possible divergencies are taken into consideration.

For some time I have felt a compelling need for some system which would enable the linguist and the teacher alike to determine whether a given specimen of language was standard with incursions from the creole, or creole with incursions from the standard. I was first led to this by the uncanny feeling that the narrator of the four stories in *Creole Language Studies I* (Le Page and DeCamp 1960) used language which was at some point midway in the continuum, and that some means had to be found for justifiably assigning them to the creole rather than the standard end of the continuum.

In the search for a linguistic procedure capable of producing results which would somewhat approximate a native speaker's intuitive sense of the place in the continuum to which a specimen of the language belonged, I was encouraged by my former colleague, John Gumperz, to attempt some kind of translatability measure, similar to that used by him in his Hindi–Punjabi and Kannada–Marathi studies. Gumperz unfortunately could not see the justification for trying to determine whether a given text was JC or SJE, on the grounds that such a procedure would have to rely too heavily on speaker performance. Consequently, he suggested that the translatability measure be applied to determining how a given text differs from educated speech. This approach, despite the apparent crudeness of the method, I have found to be not only intriguing, but useful. Expanding on the idea, I have applied the measure in both directions, that is, I have found the ratio of the number of rules necessary to convert a text to SJE and JC respectively, with the aim of discovering precisely to which pole it belongs. An arbitrarily designed scale was devised in such a way as to favor syntactic items over morphophonemic ones, and morphophonemic over purely phonological ones; while phonological and lexical items were equally weighted.[2] A single case of change in sentence type is given a score of 5; change in embedding process 4; phrase structure change 3; morphophonemic change 2; phonological and lexical change 1.

In this paper I have analyzed three texts along these lines. I am presenting the results here because they are very close to what I would have predicted on the basis of native speaker intuition only. The significance of the approach is even more far-reaching when in examining stylistic variation we find that a JC speaker who attempts to switch to SJE does no more than switch from one set of behaviors to another, invariably modifying the surface structure only, namely the phonological and lexical items. Thus he will introduce some SJE items to add elegance to his performance, but to the acute ear his performance is still recognizably creole. The reverse is also true: the introduction of a few creole items will not make a text JC; it will still be recognizably at the SJE end of the continuum.

PROCEDURES

For the sake of uniformity in the presentation of the text, the phonemic orthography first employed by Cassidy in *Jamaica Talk* (1960) and since established in the *Dictionary of Jamaican English* (Cassidy and Le Page 1967) is used for all three texts. The first of these is a fragment told by a 60-year-old grandmother in an isolated hill village in the middle of the island. Two translations of this story are given, the JC version in the Cassidy orthography, and the SJE version in standard English orthography. In order to facilitate the analysis and discussion, the sentences in each version have been correspondingly numbered. Needless to say, since there are many ways of translating a given sentence of one language into the sentences of another, some restraints had to be introduced into the methodology. Care has therefore been taken to retain all features shared by the language of the text and that of the translation, and only when the two are irreconcilable are changes made.

STORY A

1. Wans opan a taim die woz a jengklman huu had wan uondli daata.
2. Har niem woz Pini.
3. Shi woz a gie an dandi gorl.
4. Shi didn laik tu taak tu eni an eni man.
5. Shi laik a gie fain man tu taak tu.
6. Shi staat tu taak tu a man.
7. θingkin ðat it woz soch a wandaful man
8. hantil aaftaword shi gat kalops bai taakin to di man,
9. and aafta taakin tu di man, di man slipt har.
10. Shi muon an krai aal die antil aaftaword, shi get in toch wit anada man
11. huu shi fiil dat dat woz muor wandaful dan di fors wan.
12. Bot luo, aafta shi gat mari, insted it woz a man, it woz a bul-kou.
13. And evribadi telin har ðat dat woznt a gud man,
14. bot shii huol aan opan di man an biliiv
15. dat dat wan woz muor wandaful dan di forst wan.
16. Wel, dier woz a man huu kup plie fidl,
17. and anað a wan pliez a gitaa.

18. Buoθ miit tugeða an ði spat.
19. An wen di die of ði wedin kom
20. an ði man staat tu plie hiz fidl
21. and ði aða wan staat tu plie hiz gitaa,
22. ði wan wit ði fidl staat pliein an singin:
     23. Pini Pini mi dier, Pini Pini mi lov yu marid a fain man, m-m.
24. Di ada gitaa man se:
     25. Pini Pini mi dier, Pini Pini mi lov yu marid a fain man, m-m.
     26. yu marid a bul-kou, m-m.
     27. yu marid tu bul-kou, m-m.
28. So a dat onggli.
29. Plenti muo, bot mi no rimemba.

Even before attempting translation and analysis the following observations can be made. The narrator uses JC phonology throughout, although there are occasional occurrences of θ and ð which are incursions from the standard. But were it not for the fact that our technique requires it, there would be no necessity to gloss the story, for the lexicon and syntax are obviously English and not creole. The story begins with the English formula *once upon a time* rather than the JC *wantaim*. There are two occurrences of the existential phrase *there was* which does not occur in JC; the sentence type *her name was* —— rather than the construction based on the naming verb is used; regular past tense forms of the verb occur, as in *was, didn't, got, could*, etc.; the negator is regularly *not* and not *no*; the infinitive particle is *tu* and not *fi*; the pronoun is inflected for gender and case, hence the forms *she, her,* and *his*, in place of *im*; the indefinite article *a* appears instead of *wan*. The impression is that this is a bilingual speaker who uses SJE for story-telling purposes, but shifts immediately to JC in her final comment to the field worker; 'so a dat onggli. Plenti muo, bot mi no rimemba'.

STORY A (SJE Version)

1. Once upon a time, there was a gentleman who had an only daughter.
2. Her name was Peony.
3. She was a gay and dandy girl.
4. She didn't like to talk to just any man.
5. She liked (wanted) a gay, fine man to talk to.
6. She started to talk to a man,
7. thinking that he was a very wonderful man.
8. But she got pregnant by talking to the man,
9. and after talking to the man, the man slipped her.
10. She moaned and cried all day, until afterwards she met another man
11. who she felt was more wonderful than the first one.

12. But lo, after she got married, instead of its being a man, it was a bull.
13. And everybody kept telling her that that wasn't a good man,
14. but she held on to the man and believed
15. that that one was more wonderful than the first one.
16. Well, there was a man who could play the fiddle,
17. and another one played a guitar.
18. Both met together at the spot.
19. And when the day of the wedding came,
20. and the man started to play his fiddle,
21. and the other one started to play his guitar,
22. the one with the fiddle started playing and singing:
    23. Peony, Peony, my dear, Peony, Peony, my love
      You've married a fine man, hm-hm.
24. The other guitar man said:
    25. Peony, Peony, my dear, Peony, Peony, my love
      You've married a fine man, hm-hm
      You've married a bull, hm-hm
    26. You've married a bull, hm-hm
    27. You've married a bull, hm-hm.
28. So that's all.
29. (There's) plenty more, but I don't remember (any more).

The following syntactic rules are needed for translation:

(i) A rule effecting change of sentence type from inverted to direct sentence, as in No. 28 [*a dat onggli* > *that is all*] (Index = 5).

(ii) A rule to change the form of embedding in No. 12 [*instead*+clause > *insted* + prepositional phrase] (Index = 4).

(iii) A rule to change the structure of the generic phrase in No. 16 [*plie fidl* >*play the fiddle*] (Index = 3).

(iv) A rule to shift the past form of the verb (V_{past}) from optional to obligatory category (Index = 2).

(v) A rule inserting the carrier verb *do* in negative sentences such as No. 29 (Index = 2).

This gives a score of 16 for syntactic changes only. On the phonological scale the following changes will be made:

(i) Change dental stop to dental fricative in *there, that, with,* etc. (1, 7, 10).

(ii) Change velar stop to dental in *gentleman* (1).

(iii) Change rising diphthong to falling in *gay, day, only,* etc. (3, 10).

(iv) Change dental nasal to velar as in *thinking* (7).

(v) Change low central vowel to mid central as in *her* (2).

(vi) Delete intrusive stops in -nl- cluster as in *only*; (1, 28)

(vii) Delete intrusive initial aspirate as in *until* (8).

M

(viii) Substitute long for checked final vowel in monosyllabic words, as *she*, *you* (3, 23).

The total phonological score is 8. An examination of the lexical items yields the following:

(i) *wan* must be changed to *an* (1).

(ii) *eni an eni* becomes *just any* (4).

(iii) *laik* becomes *wanted* (5).

(iv) *kalops* becomes *pregnant* (8).

(v) *bulkou* becomes *bull* (12).

(vi) *huol aan opan* becomes *held on to* (14).

(vii) *onggli* becomes *all* (28).

(viii) *no* becomes *not* (29).

(ix) *mi* becomes *I* (29).

The lexical score is 9, giving a total of 33 as the index of the distance of the text from SJE. We can now compare this with the distance from the JC version.

STORY A (JC Version)

1. Wantaim, wan man en ha wan gyal-pikni nomo.
2. Im en niem Pini.
3. Im ena wan priti gyal fi-truu.
4. Im neba laik fi taak tu eni an eni man.
5. Im laik a nais buosi man fi taak tu.
6. Im taat taak tu wan man,
7. tingk se a soch a wandaful man;
8. Bot im get kalops aafta im taak tu di man.
9. An aafta im taak tu di man, di man slip im.
10. Im muon an krai aal die so tel aaftawod im get iin wid wan neda man
11. we im tingk se im muor wandaful dan di fors wan.
12. Bot luo, afta im marid, steda man, a bulkou im marid.
13. Ebribadi tel im se a no gud man,
14. bot im huol aan pan di man an biliib
15. se dat im muor wandaful dan di fors wan.
16. Wel, wan man kuda plie figl,
17. an aneda wan plie gitaa.
18. Di tuu a dem miit op a di spat.
19. An wen di wedn die kom
20. an di man taat plie im figl
21. an teda wan taat plie im gitaa,
22. di wan wid di figl taat plie an sing
23. Pini, Pini, mi dier, Pini, Pini, mi lob, yu marid a fain man m-m;

24. Di eda gitaa man se:
25. Pini, Pini, mi dier, Pini, Pini, mi lob, yu marid a fain man, m-m.
26. Yu marid a bulkou, m-m,
27. Yu marid tu bulkou m-m.
28. So a dat nomo.
29. Nof muor, bot mi no memba.

The analysis gives the following results: Syntactic score = 53; phonological score = 16, and lexical score = 4, yielding a total of 73. The ratio for the text is therefore 33:73, indicating that it is well within the SJE end of the continuum, and far removed from the JC end. This is, of course, what we would have predicted from an initial reading of the text. It confirms native speaker intuition.

The second text is a story told by the thirteen-year-old grandson of the narrator of the first story. At the time of telling the story he lived with his grandmother, and attended the local elementary school. He was therefore not unschooled, and yet he tells his tale in a language which is recognizably JC.

STORY B

Wans opan a taim Bra Anansi an Bra Aligeta miit op. So Bra Aligeta aaks Bra Anansi ef im an im a famili. So im se yes. Sins az mi an yu a famili ai gwain bwail wan hat korsiin pan a parij, an if yu dringk aaf i nou, mi an yu a famili. Im bwail di hat korsiin pan a parij, an im tek out fi im an gi Bra Anansi di balans. Bra Anansi ties i. So wen i bon Bra Anansi so, Bra Anansi se: Laad, Bra Aligeta, a disaya yu kaal hat, man? Mek mi put i out a son an mek i likl hata. Den a stor i miinwail, den mek i likl hata. Wen im put i out de, a stor i, a stor i, dat taim it a kuol, miinwail a kuol. Den miinwail im stor, wen im ties i an si se i kuol, im se: Laad, Bra Aligeta, a nou i hat. An im dis pik op i an mek so, wups. Dat finish nou.

When the text was translated into SJE and the technique described above applied to it, a score of 77 was obtained, to be broken down as follows: syntactic score = 54, phonological score = 10, and lexical score = 13. We are not surprised at the high score, because with the exception of the introductory formula *once upon a time* and a single use of *I* insted of *mi*, the story is told in unadulterated creole. Indeed it was not necessary to translate the text into JC, because only the two items mentioned here, both lexical in nature, would require translation. The ratio is therefore 77:2 placing the text at the very end of the continuum. Its claim to being JC is much more decisive than that of the first text to SJE membership.

The third text I shall examne is the beginning of one of the four stories recorded by DeCamp in *Creole Language Studies I* (Le Page and DeCamp 1960:150, 2–18). It covers the second to the thirteenth sentences of *Blamblam, Cindy, and Dido*. The style in which the story is told is literary, and it consequently posed many problems in the translation into JC. Frozen forms do not lend themselves to translation techniques or translatability rules. Given, for instance, a formula such as *der waz a yong man*, it is impossible to translate into JC without destroying the tone and distorting the text. Should it be treated as a borrowing, and excluded from the subsequent analysis? For the moment, at least, this is the course pursued.

An analysis of the text resulted as follows. Translated into SJE, the index was 50 – syntactic score = 37, phonological score 7, and lexical score 6. Translated into JC the index is 45 – syntactic score = 31, phonological score = 6, and lexical score = 8. The ratio is therefore 50:45, placing the text somewhat in the middle of the continuum, but tipped to the JC end. The uneasiness which I have always felt about these four texts can now be empirically explained, and a means can now be found to describe explicitly, behaviors found at various points in the continuum; they are justifiably regarded as JC even in a system which requires an SJE/JC dichotomy.

As I have mentioned before, the technique is still in a very crude state, but it holds tremendous promise for the dialectologist interested in defining dialect boundaries. There are clearly three social dialects represented here, the two most extreme represented by a single household, with the grandmother, and not the grandson, manifesting the socially more accepted behavior. The indication is that the kinds of stories being told were a significant linguistic variable, and that the different speakers were obviously capable of controlling several different styles.

NOTES

1 DeCamp's position is well illustrated in his contribution to this volume, in which, quite fortuitously, he addresses himself to the same question, albeit from a different point of view. See also DeCamp (1964).
2 As was pointed out by DeCamp in the discussion which followed the presentation of this paper, other weightings can and should be tested also. No such alternate weighting has been attempted here.

REFERENCES

Bailey, Beryl Loftman 1966. *Jamaican Creole syntax: a transformational approach*, Cambridge, Cambridge University Press
Cassidy, Frederic G. 1960. *Jamaica talk: three hundred years of the English language in Jamaica*, London, Macmillan
Cassidy, Frederic G. and Le Page, Robert B. 1967. *A dictionary of Jamaican English*, Cambridge, Cambridge University Press
DeCamp, David 1964. 'Creole language areas considered as multilingual communities', Symposium on multilingualism (Brazzaville 1962), 227–31 (Commission de cooperation technique en Afrique, publication No. 87), London
Le Page, Robert B. and DeCamp, David (eds.) 1960. 'Jamaican creole', Creole language studies 1, pt. 2, London, Macmillan

TOWARD A GENERATIVE ANALYSIS OF A POST-CREOLE SPEECH CONTINUUM

DAVID DECAMP

The life-cycle theory of pidgin-creole, for which Robert A. Hall, Jr., has argued so long and so eloquently (1953, 1966, and especially 1962) is now generally accepted: A pidgin may develop, often rapidly, from a mere auxiliary vehicle for minimal interlingual communication into the native language of most of its speakers.

Unfortunately, the beginning and end of this cycle are shrouded in uncertainty. There is no resolution in sight to the debate between the proponents of polygenetic theories (e.g. Reinecke, Hall) and of monogenetic theories (e.g. Whinnom, Taylor, Stewart) of the initial stage, the origin of pidgins. The final stages of the creole life-cycle are equally unknown and have attracted the attention of fewer scholars. The basic alternatives seem clear enough. A creole can continue indefinitely without substantial change, as Haitian French seems to be doing. It may become extinct, as Negerhollands and Gullah are doing. We say that it may further evolve into a 'normal' language, though we are hard put to find documented examples of this, and even harder to define what we mean by a 'non-creole' or 'ex-creole' language. Finally it may gradually merge with the corresponding standard language, as is happening in Jamaica. As yet, however, we cannot identify the sociolinguistic factors that determine which of these four alternative courses a creole will take. And we know very little about the fourth alternative: merger with a standard language.

This paper will deal with what I have elsewhere (1968) called *post-creole* speech communities, i.e. communities in which a creole is in the process of merging with a standard. I will briefly describe the sociolinguistics of a post-creole society, outline some of the theoretical linguistic problems which it poses, and suggest a way in which we might reconcile the apparently inconsistent approaches taken toward these problems by sociolinguists and by theoretical linguists (specifically, generative-transformationalists).

Creoles vary greatly in their degree of distinctness from one another and from their corresponding standard languages. All the French creoles are mutually intelligible, even including those of the Indian ocean, as has been often cited. None of them, however, is mutually intelligible with standard French. To an educated Haitian, the frequently necessary switching back and forth between creole and standard French has most if not all the psychological and social characteristics of switching between totally foreign languages, a classic example of Ferguson's *diglossia* (1959). For as yet unknown reasons, the English creoles are less uniform. Even Sranan and Saramaccan, both spoken in Surinam, are mutually unintelligible. At the same time both contrast sharply with standard English. In Jamaica (and apparently also in Hawaii (see Tsuzaki's paper in this volume) and in much of the formerly Gullah area), the situation is yet again different. The varieties of Jamaican English themselves differ to the point of unintelligibility; but some Jamaican English is mutually intelligible with standard English.

Admittedly this claim of mutual unintelligibility within Jamaican English is based on only one empirical test, the inability of two small groups of speakers to understand one another's tape recordings, and the subject requires further and more rigorous investigation. But no one can deny the extreme degree of variability of Jamaican English. There are many middle-class St Andrew housewives who claim that they can speak the broad creole because they can converse with their maids, yet they can understand very little of the conversation if they overhear the maid talking with the gardener. Further, in Jamaica there is no sharp cleavage between creole and standard. Rather there is a linguistic continuum, a continuous spectrum of speech varieties ranging from the 'bush talk' or 'broken language' of Quashie to the educated standard of Philip Sherlock and Norman Manley. Many Jamaicans persist in the myth that there are only two varieties: the patois and the standard. But one speaker's attempt at the broad patois may be closer to the standard end of the spectrum than is another speaker's attempt at the standard. The 'standard' is not standard British, as many Jamaicans claim; rather it is an evolving standard Jamaican (or perhaps standard West Indian) English which is mutually intelligible with, but undeniably different from, standard British. Each Jamaican speaker commands a span of this continuum, the breadth of the span depending on the breadth of his social contacts; a labor leader, for example, commands a greater span of varieties than does a suburban middle-class housewife.

Creolists have reacted in different ways to this Jamaican speech continuum. Stewart (1962), Taylor (1963), and Alleyne (1967) have for this reason called it an English dialect system rather than a true creole. Stewart goes so far as to make clear separation from standard, i.e. a structural gap between the two at some point, a defining criterion of a creole. Bailey (1966) defends the creole status of Jamaican English by restricting the term *creole* to the extreme non-standard end of the spectrum. What she describes in her book is an abstract ideal type, a composite of all non-standard features, a combination which is actually spoken by few if any Jamaicans. (See her paper in this volume.) The Cassidy–Le Page dictionary (1967) is equally ideal–typical in approach: I am sure that Cassidy is the only living Jamaican familiar with all the fifteen thousand 'Jamaicanisms' contained in it. I would not have wanted Bailey,

Cassidy, and Le Page to do otherwise, for it is precisely the idealized extreme variety which had to be accurately described before we could begin on the many varieties intermediate between it and the standard. But I contend that these books represent a useful linguistic abstraction, not the sociolinguistic reality.

Following Bailey, we would conclude that there are few if any speakers of 'pure' creole in Jamaica. Following Stewart, we would throw Jamaica out of the creole field entirely, and we might well then ask why this conference is held in Mona at all. I believe, however, that the Taylor-Stewart restrictions on the term creole are unjustifiably arbitrary and severe. As early as 1934, Reinecke and Tokimasa were pointing out from the Hawaiian case that continuing pressures from schools and other institutions can turn any creole community into a dialect continuum. Jamaica is therefore only a creole community in a late stage of development.

For some time now I have been calling a speech continuum like that of Jamaica a *post-creole* speech community in order to distinguish it from the diglossia of creole areas like Haiti. Not every creole has a post-creole stage in its life-cycle. I suggest that both of the following conditions must be present: First, the dominant official language of the community must be the standard language corresponding to the creole. Thus Sranan or the French of St Lucia and Grenada have not developed a post-creole continuum, because there is no continuing corrective pressure from standard English in Surinam or from standard French in St Lucia and Grenada. Second, the formerly rigid social stratification must have *partially* (not completely) broken down. That is, there must be sufficient social mobility to motivate large numbers of creole speakers to modify their speech in the direction of the standard, and there must be a sufficient program of education and other acculturative activities to exert effective pressures from the standard language on the creole. These corrective pressures do not operate uniformly on all the creole speakers. Otherwise the result would be merely a uniform narrowing of the gap between creole and standard, not a linguistic continuum. Rather these acculturative influences impinge on different speakers with varying degrees of effectiveness, drawing some of them more than others toward the standard. The degree of acculturation varies with such factors as age, poverty, and isolation from urban centers.

Let us assume that we have a linguistic description of both ends of this linguistic continuum. In fact, much more research is needed, but in the Bailey syntax, Cassidy's *Jamaica talk*, and the Cassidy–Le Page dictionary we at least have the basic outlines of the creole extreme; and the standard Jamaican English is close enough to standard British (at least as close as are standard American and Canadian varieties) so that we can now profitably turn our attention to the intermediate varieties in the continuum, the speech actually used by almost all Jamaicans. But how can we describe a continuum within the

framework of present linguistic theory? Will we need ten grammatical descriptions, or perhaps a hundred, or perhaps one for every perceptibly different
variety along the continuum?

Linguistic description has always tended to be normative, postulating an
ideal speaker-hearer with a complete yet unvarying knowledge of a uniform
language structure. A certain degree of indeterminacy was provided for by
the concept of free variation, but until recently there was little theoretical
attention given to systematic variation, switching phenomena, etc. Such
phenomena were merely described empirically without incorporating them
into the theory. An unfortunate split thus developed in the field of linguistics,
separating the dialectologist and sociolinguist from the theorists. In a paper
presented at the 1961 meeting of the Linguistic Society of America but not
published then (DeCamp 1969), I demonstrated the inadequacy of earlier
attempts to bridge this gap and proposed a new approach based on generative
theory. The 'common core' approach, I claimed, merely relegated all linguistic variation to the area of indeterminacy. The 'overall pattern' of Trager
and Smith was only a superimposition of two or more separate descriptions,
which obscured the structures of the individual varieties without cap-
turing any generalizations about the 'language' except for a composite
taxonomic inventory of potential grammatical devices which might be found
in any or all of the varieties. Weinreich's 'diasystems' were only an arbitrary
juxtaposition of separate descriptions, an elaborate system of notation to convey
just the same information (though perhaps in a more abbreviated and
efficient form) as would be found in a whole shelf of separate grammars of
each variety, each in its own volume. None of these approaches, I argued,
really described the functional correspondences between analogous features in
different dialects. None of them enabled us to convert sentences in one dialect
into equivalent sentences in another. *If the ability to make such conversions is a
part of the native speaker's competence, then it must be accounted for in the theory.*

Chomsky's distinction between competence and performance has often been
misinterpreted as excluding all linguistic variation from theory. A performance model, if one is ever constructed, would have to include such considerations as the speaker's incomplete knowledge of his language, the limitations on
his memory span, his momentary lapses and reformulations, etc. The ratio of
passive to active sentences in my speech on a given day, the median length
and complexity of my sentences, the frequency with which I deviate from
grammatical well-formedness, these are performance features and cannot be
reduced to the same type of rules found in generative grammars. But some
kinds of variation are indeed rule-governed behavior. If I shift into a formal,
oratorical style, several rule-predictable things happen to my grammar: the
contraction transformation is blocked, so that I say *is not* and *he has* instead of
isn't and *he's*; the ordering of the rules for case marking and for relative

attraction is reversed, so that *whom* appears in my surface structures; conversely an otherwise dormant rule of disjunctive pronominalization makes me sprout *it is he* and *it is I*: several phonological rules of assimilation and vowel reduction are blocked. I am not then using a totally new grammar, as if I were shifting into Chinese, nor am I merely varying freely and randomly within the confines of some overall grammar. Rather I am performing a complex but related set of switching activities, all triggered by the presence of one stylistic feature [+ oratorical]. Because I am able to perform these switches consistently, they are a part of my linguistic competence and therefore must be described in the grammar.

These stylistic changes affect the lexicon, the transformations, the semantics, and the phonology, every component of a generative grammar except the branching rules, which are possibly a language universal and almost certainly a constant within a dialect system. Within earlier formulations of generative theory, such switching rules entailed serious theoretical problems. Permuting the order of transformations or changing the structural description of a transformation, for example, then required the use of 'second-order' rules, i.e. rules which operate on rules. The addition of syntactic features to the newer version of the theory and the substitution of replication and erasure for permutation within the theory have largely eliminated these obstacles. A feature may be opted in the base rule whose presence triggers all the necessary changes which the subsequent components of the grammar must make in any derivation marked with that feature, just as the selection in the base rules of an element (or feature) Q or NEG as a sentence qualifier triggers all the changes necessary to produce an interrogative or a negative sentence. The application of any rule may be blocked by the presence or absence of that feature in its structural description. Thus there is no need for a set of 'super-rules' which change the rules of the grammar in order to account for linguistic variation; rather the potential variation is built into the rules themselves and is controlled by the device of features, selected in the base.

For a simple shift between two uniform styles, a single binary feature (e.g. [± oratorical]) would be sufficient. For a linear continuum, a whole scheme of such binary features would be essential ($[\pm 1]$, $[\pm 2]$, $[\pm 3]$, ..., $[\pm n]$). A redundancy convention could be formulated whereby the presence of any index feature implied the presence of all other index features of lower number. Thus it would be unnecessary to specify within each rule the entire list of speech varieties (i.e. points on the continuum) which activate or block that rule. It would be sufficient to identify the point on the continuum beyond which the rule does or does not operate.

To the extent that a linguistic continuum is linear, this approach thus provides a very economical and meaningful way of incorporating many linguistic varieties into one grammatical description. Even if a continuum should be multidimensional rather than linear, a similar approach could be followed, but then two or more simultaneous sets of index features would be required, and both the rules and every derivation based on them would be correspondingly complicated. Fortunately, a linguistic continuum of the type found in Jamaica does seem to be linear. (I will discuss later the apparent exception of geographical variation.) Of course the sociological correlates of the linguistic variation are multidimensional: age, education, income bracket, occupation, etc. But the linguistic variation itself is linear if described in linguistic terms rather than in terms of those sociological correlates.

At this point, before demonstrating such rule-governed variation with some examples from Jamaican English, I must stop to explain my proposed technique for ordering into a linear series the set of empirical observations of linguistic variations which is then to be accounted for by the theory. The linguistic variation in Jamaica is, of course, not literally a continuum, for the number of speakers is finite. Furthermore, the number of variable linguistic features is limited. By calling it a continuum I mean that given two samples of Jamaican speech which differ substantially from one another, it is usually possible to find a third intermediate level in an additional sample. Thus it is not practicable to describe the system in terms of two or three or six or any other manageable number of discrete social dialects. Assume that we have n number of empirically different samples, where n is finite but large (my own collection includes more than two hundred speakers, no two alike). Assume too that each sample is relatively homogeneous, or may be subdivided into homogeneous sub-samples; this is a necessary but indeed questionable assumption, for a speaker's stylistic level keeps varying during an interview, no matter how hard the interviewer tries to keep the atmosphere of an interview constant. The problem now is how to arrange the members of n in a meaningful order.

Sociolinguists have traditionally approached this problem by assuming a priori that certain socioeconomic characteristics of the informants could serve as criteria for sorting. Thus C. C. Fries (1940) divided his informants into three groups, primarily according to level of education. Hans Kurath (1939) doubled the number of pigeonholes by subdividing the three educational groups into older vs. younger subgroups of informants. Such techniques are questionable for two reasons. First, we cannot presume that any one socio-economic characteristic (or even any set of two or three such characteristics) will be the true co-variable with language. One can indeed make several such sortings with different sets of pigeonholes and choose that which gives him the neatest groupings of his linguistic data, but this can obscure the complex interplay between different socioeconomic co-variables. Furthermore it is dangerous to assume that the same co-variable will be primary throughout the distribution: educational level might be more important at one end of the linguistic continuum, but income bracket might be more important at the other.

The second objection to the pigeonhole technique is that it does not provide for continuous variation in the socioeconomic characteristics. Why only three educational levels for informants? Is it not possible that a difference between eleven and twelve years of formal schooling might be just as linguistically significant as a difference between twelve and thirteen years? A linguistic geographer would be properly horrified at the following suggestion: Let us use state boundaries as preconceived pigeonholes for sorting the data from an American linguistic atlas, and then merely indicate the percentage of New York state informants who say *pail* as opposed to *bucket*, the equivalent percentages for Pennsylvanians, for Virginians, etc. The linguistic geographer would quite properly insist on treating the provenience of his informants as continuous phenomena, on mapping the exact location of each response and on drawing his isoglosses on the basis of the linguistic data, not of any geographical preconceptions such as state boundaries. Why, then, have sociolinguists so often correlated their linguistic data to preconceived categories of age, income, education, etc., instead of correlating these non-linguistic variables *to* the linguistic data?

Both the varieties and the defining features of a linear linguistic continuum can be ordered without recourse to the sociolinguistic data, so that these data may then be used to interpret the continuum without circularity of reasoning. As a demonstration, Table 1 presents a 'continuum' consisting of seven speakers, each of which differs from the other six by one or more of six

TABLE I

Features		Speakers
+A child	−A pikni	1. +A +B +C −D +E +F
+B eat	−A nyam	2. −A +B −C −D +E +F
+C /θ~t/	−C /t/	3. −A +B −C −D −E −F
+D /ð~d/	−D /d/	4. −A −B −C −D −E −F
+E granny	−E nana	5. +A +B +C +D +E +F
+F didn't	−F no ben	6. +A +B −C −D +E +F
		7. −A +B −C −D +E −F

features. This mini-continuum is not hypothetical. The seven informants are selected from those interviewed in my survey of 142 Jamaican communities, and the six features are among the many which define the continuum of Jamaican English. The feature [+A] indicates habitual use of the word *child*; [−A] indicates use of *pikni* or *pikini* in equivalent contexts. [+D] indicates a phonological contrast in such pairs as *den/then*; [−D] indicates a lack of this contrast. [+F] indicates the use of *didn't* in negative past-tense constructions, [−F] the use of various alternatives such as *no ben, no did*.

My technique is based on the co-occurrence of features within each idiolect. First let us sort the informants into two groups according to their usage on any one feature. The following horizontal line bisected by a single vertical represents the fact that informants 1, 5, and 6 used the form *child* (i.e. [+A]), while informants 2, 3, 4, and 7 all used *pikni* ([−A]).

	+A	−A	
	1, 5, 6	2, 3, 4, 7	

Next let us divide the same group of informants according to their usage on feature B. This division separates informant 4 (the only one who said *nyam*) from the other six informants, all of whom used *eat*.

	+A	−A	+B	−B
	1, 5, 6	2, 3, 7		4

Notice that the two classifications we have so far made are mutually compatible, so that we can represent them by two vertical cuts on the same horizontal line. Our seven informants are now sorted into three groups: [+A, +B]: 1, 5, 6, [−A, +B]: 2, 3, 7, and [−A, −B]: 4. The fourth possibility, [+A, −B], simply does not occur. It is more than just chance that it does not occur. The reason is that *nyam* is a word much farther down the social scale than is *pikni*, much more a shibboleth of Quashie speech. Any speaker of sufficient social status and in a sufficiently formal speech situation to say *child* instead of *pikni* would normally not say *nyam*.

Continuing with the analysis, we find that sorting the informants according to their usage on feature C separates informants 1 and 5 from the others, and the classification is still mutually compatible.

	+C	−C	+A	−A	+B	−B
	1, 5	6		2, 3, 7		4

Following the same procedure for features D, E, and F results in the following line:

+D	−D	+C	−C	+A	−A	+F	−F	+E	−E	+B	−B
5	1		6		2		7		3		4

If more than seven informants and more than six features were considered, this line could approach a continuum. The seven informants have now been arranged in the order 5, 1, 6, 2, 7, 3, 4, on no criteria other than the co-occurrences of linguistic features, and the six features have been similarly arranged in the order D, C, A, F, E, B. If all the *n* varieties of a speech continuum are thus arranged in an ordered series such that the difference between any variety and its neighbors is minimal, the result is a significant spectrum, just as if one were to arrange a large number of different-colored blocks in a row with minimal color differences between adjacent blocks, the sequence of colors produced would be that of the color spectrum.[1]

I will anticipate one obvious objection. With the seven informants I have selected, the divisions have always been mutually compatible, and I have said that the speaker who says *child* would normally not say *nyam*. However, a few speakers do exactly that. Let us consider speaker 8, whose usage is as follows: [−A, +B, −C, −D, −E, +F]. If informant 8 were substituted for informant 7 in the data, the relative positions on the continuum of features E and F would be reversed. If both informant 7 and informant 8 were included, but no additional informants beyond the eight presented here, there would be no way to decide the relative position of these two features. In fact, however, I have many more informants who agree with 7 than who agree with 8.

As would be expected, for every variable feature which is a part of the linear continuum, there is a clear consensus on its position along that continuum. Of all the variables which cannot be clearly located on the continuum by this method, most are geographically determined. The amount of linguistic variation in Jamaica which is neither a part of the continuum nor a matter of simple word geography is surprisingly small. That is, relatively few features vary with age, sex, occupation, ethnic group, etc., except to the extent that these co-variables are themselves a part of the linear continuum; e.g. the very old and the very young tend more toward the creole end of the continuum than do young adults. Geographical variation in Jamaica is of two types: first, there are localisms and regionalisms; second, there are the geographical patterns produced by acculturative diffusion, e.g. the common pattern of urban forms which have diffused to a varying degree through the central part of the island, leaving conservative areas in the east and west. The linguistic variables in such diffusion are generally part of the same linear continuum, for isolation from Kingston is merely one of the socioeconomic co-variables of the continuum. The true localisms and regionalisms are indeed incompatible with the linear continuum, but they are not difficult to sort out. They are almost entirely lexical. There are indeed a few western and north-coast characteristics in intonation; 'h-dropping' is slightly more frequent in the vicinity of Kingston; there is a western preference for *de* rather than *a* as the continuative aspect particle; but generally the regional variables of Jamaican English would be adequately described by a word geography, and they do not seriously interfere with the analysis of the linear continuum by the methods which I propose.

Now that we have established this seven-point linguistic spectrum on the basis of linguistic evidence alone, we can add to it at the appropriate position for each informant any social and economic data which we believe may be relevant. We may note, for example, that informant 5, at one end of the line, is a young and well-educated proprietor of a successful radio and appliance shop in Montego Bay; that informant 4, at the other end of the line, is an elderly and illiterate peasant farmer in an isolated mountain village; and that the social and economic facts on the other informants are roughly (not exactly) proportional to these informants' positions on the continuum. For example, informant 6 has had fewer years of formal schooling than has informant 7, but her responsible position as a market clerk gives her a higher income, more social prestige, and more opportunity to observe the speech of educated speakers, and this helps to explain her relative position on the continuum. The ideal types at the extremes of the continuum can now be given meaningful names: We can call them *standard* and *creole*.

These and similar interpretations can be read directly from the base line, or, if we are certain that our sampling of informants is adequate, we can quantify the data and use correlation techniques. Again if our sampling is adequate, we can examine the quantitative distribution of the informants along the continuum to determine whether there are social isoglosses. That is, if the informants were not evenly distributed along the line but were bunched up at certain positions (if, for example, 30 other informants could be located at the same place as informant 7, 30 more at the same place as informant 1, but few or no additional informants at the same places as informants 6 and 2), then we would have evidence of dialect groupings within the continuum. Preliminary analysis of my field data, however, gives little evidence of such grouping. Without a considerably larger sample, I would not be justified in any conclusion except that Jamaican speakers seem to be fairly normally distributed along the continuum.

To return now to the question of incorporating multiple varieties along such a continuum within the same set of generative rules. In my 1961 paper at the Linguistic Society, I presented the data in Table 2. These are somewhat-normalized phonetic transcriptions of the syllabic nuclei of three varieties of Jamaican English (using symbols developed by Bernard Bloch and published in Kurath (1939); barred-o represents New England short unrounded *o*). What I have arbitrarily labeled dialect H is spoken by many, but not all, speakers of higher and upper-middle classes in Jamaica. Dialect M is spoken by many, but not all, speakers of middle class. Dialect L is spoken by many, but not all, speakers of lower class – laborers and peasant farmers. I pointed out that a bi-unique taxonomic analysis such as a Tragerian overall pattern would require the recognition of a fourfold contrast before in-glides for both the front vowels and the back vowels of dialect M (the sequence [æ ǝ] only occurs marginally as *baa*, the name for the sound made by a goat). There is

TABLE 2

Dialect H								
[ɪ] bit		[ʊ] book	[ɪə̯] beer		[ʊə̯] tour	[iɪ] beat		[uʊ̯] boot
[ɛ] bet	[ʌ] bud		[ɛə̯] bear	[ɜ:] bird	[ɔə̯] tore	[eɪ] bay		[oʊ̯] toe
[æ] bat	[a] father	[ɔ] pot	[æə̯] baa	[aə̯] lard	[ɔə̯] lord		[aɪ] bite	[ɔɪ] boil
							[aʊ̯] bout	
Dialect M								
[ɪ] bit		[ʊ] book	[ɪə̯] beer		[ʊə̯] tour	[iɪ] beat		[uʊ̯] boot
			[eə̯] bay		[oə̯] toe			
[ɛ] bet	[ʌ] bud		[ɛə̯] bear	[ɜ:] bird	[ɒə] tore			
[æ] bat	[a] father	[ɔ] pot	[æə̯] baa	[aə̯] lard	[ɔə̯] lord		[aɪ] bite	[ɔɪ] boil
							[aʊ̯] Bout	
Dialect L								
[ɪ] bit		[ʊ] book	[ɪə̯] beer bay bear		[ʊə̯] tour toe tore	[iɪ] beat		[uʊ̯] boot
[ɛ] bet		[Θ] bird bud						
	[a] pat pot father			[aə̯] lard lord			[aɪ] bite boil	
							[aʊ̯] bout	

only a threefold contrast in the equivalent vowels of dialect H, and no such contrast at all for dialect L. An overall pattern would require ten vowels to accommodate the contrasts of dialect M. To impose such a pattern on the other varieties would distort and obscure the eight-vowel system of dialect H and the five-vowel system of dialect L. Independent analyses of the three varieties, even if presented in the notation of Weinreich's diasystems, would obscure the functional equivalence of the lexically-corresponding transcriptions in the three varieties. *For some speakers these three vocalic systems are only functional varieties*, i.e. a man may converse with his friends in dialect M, deliver a lecture in dialect H, and then talk to his gardener in dialect L. All three systems and the processes of switching from one to another must therefore be described in the grammar. This was simply an impossible task for a rigidly bi-unique autonomous phonology.

TABLE 3

/i/ bit		/u/ book	/ir/ beer		/ur/ tour	/i:/ beat		/u:/ boot
/e/ bet	/ə/ bud		/er/ bear	/ər/ bird	/or/ tore	/e:/ bay		/o:/ toe
/æ/ bat	/a/ father	/ɔ/ pot	/ær/ baa	/ar/ lard	/ɔr/ lord		/ay/ bite	/ɔy/ boil
							/aw/ bout	

In a generative phonology, however, it is immediately apparent that dialect H and dialect M are morphophonemically identical, differing only on the phonetic level. That is, those troublesome higher-mid diphthongs [eə] and [oə] of dialect M correspond functionally to the diphthongs [eị] and [ou] of dialect H. The homophony of dialect L is simply the result of collapse of some of the contrasts retained in dialects H and M. All three varieties can be derived from the same underlying representation (Table 3). The relations between dialect H and dialect M are now fully accounted for by the following phonetic rule:

$$/:/ \longrightarrow \left\{ \begin{array}{l} [ə] \; / \; \left\{ \begin{array}{l} [e] \\ [o] \end{array} \right\} \underline{\qquad} \ldots \qquad\qquad [+M] \\ [i] \; / \quad [e] \qquad \underline{\qquad}_\bullet \ldots \\ [u] \; / \quad [o] \qquad \underline{\qquad}_\bullet \ldots \end{array} \right\} [+H] \right\}$$

The fact that [ɹ] can be a phonetic representation of either /:/ or /r/ would, of course, have outlawed such a solution in an autonomous phonology with a bi-uniqueness condition. For dialect L, the following three additional rules are necessary:

$$1. \quad \begin{Bmatrix} e \\ o \end{Bmatrix}_{1} + \begin{Bmatrix} : \\ r \end{Bmatrix} \longrightarrow \begin{Bmatrix} ir \\ ur \end{Bmatrix}_{1}$$

$$2. \quad \begin{Bmatrix} æ \\ ɔ \end{Bmatrix} \longrightarrow a$$

$$3. \quad ə(r) \longrightarrow \begin{Bmatrix} o/\text{—}́ \\ a/\text{—}̆ \end{Bmatrix}$$

Rule 1 collapses /e:, er, ir/ to /ir/, and /o:, or, ur/ to /ur/. Rule 2 collapses /æ, a, ɔ/ to /a/. Rule 3 collapses /ə, ər/ to /a/ or /o/, depending on stress. The result of application of these three rules is the following derived representation of dialect L (Table 4).

TABLE 4

/i/	/u/	/ir/	/ur/	/i:/	/u:/
bit	book	beer	tour	beat	boot
		bay	toe		
		bear	tore		
/e/	/o/				
bet	bird				
	bud				
	/a/		/ar/		/ay/
	pot		lard		bite
	pat		lord		boil
	father				/aw/
					bout

This solution not only accommodates all three varieties and accounts for the switching operations from one to another. It also permits the solution of an otherwise difficult problem of 'linking *r*'. Although the words *beer*, *bear* and *bạy* are homophones in dialect L (and similarly *tour*, *tore*, and *toe*) when these words are spoken in isolation or are followed by a juncture or a consonant, a 'linking' retroflexion often occurs when *beer*, *bear*, *tour*, and *tore* (but not *bay* or *toe*) are followed by vowels. That is, retroflexion occurs in *the beer all the time cold* but not in *the bay all the time cold*, even though *beer* and *bay* are pronounced identically in isolation. In this generative analysis, the underlying representations of *beer, bear, tour,* and *tore* contain /r/, but those of *bay* and *toe* do not. All that is needed, therefore, is a rule to attach a final /r/ to a following vowel:

$$\text{Vr V} \longrightarrow \text{Vr rV}$$

In the ordering of rules, this *r*-linking rule precedes rule 1 (above), which rewrites /:/ as /r/, making *bay* a homophone of *bear*.[2]

This is of course only one example of the use of phonological rules to capture generalizations about multiple varieties of a language and the speaker's ability to shift from one to another. Some of the alleged syntactic differences within Jamaican English may yield to similar treatment on the phonological level. At the 1967 meeting of the Linguistic Society of America, William Labov presented a paper on copula-deletion in non-standard American Negro English. His conclusions seem to be equally applicable to copula-deletion in Jamaican English. He demonstrated convincingly that the domain of copula-deletion in non-standard Negro English was identical with that of copula-contraction in standard English. This difference between the two dialects could therefore be stated in phonological terms. It is interesting that only three days earlier, at the meeting of the American Dialect Society, Marvin D. Loflin offered a very different solution to this same problem of copula-deletion, one which attributed it to differences in the basic syntax of the two dialects. If we wish to include multiple varieties of the language within the same set of grammatical rules, then Labov's solution is preferable to Loflin's because it accounts for the same phenomena at a lower level of the grammar: the phonology. The advantage is simplicity. The higher the level of the grammar at which a rule appears which allows for switching between speech varieties, the greater will be the number of subsequent lower-level rules whose structural descriptions will have to be complicated in order to make them apply to both alternative outputs of the higher-level switching operation. Consequently, the more complex the grammar will be.

Of course some of the variable features in the Jamaican continuum are indeed syntactic. Most of these, however, are only differences in the syntactic features in lexical entries. For example, all levels of Jamaican (like all other varieties of English) have inchoative constructions such as *the water is boiling, John frightens easily,* and *the eggs are selling well.* These are normally matched with corresponding causative constructions: *the cook is boiling the water, something frightens John,* and *the farmer is selling the eggs* (for a generative analysis of such inchoatives and causatives, see Lakoff 1965:IV:4–18). In standard English, including standard Jamaican, only a small number of verbs can appear in such inchoative constructions. As we approach the creole end of the spectrum, however, we find that almost every transitive verb is so privileged: *the tree will cut, the ground can plant*, etc. In fact, beyond a certain point on the continuum, the passive transformation is blocked, and this construction is the only means of translating the standard English passive. If we were considering only the extremes of the continuum, a simple conversion rule would suffice: $[+ \underline{\hspace{1cm}} NP] \longrightarrow [+ \underline{\hspace{1cm}} [+\text{inchoative}]_v]/[+\text{creole}]$. Such a rule would enable all transitive verbs to participate in inchoative constructions, so special marking might be necessary for the few exceptional

TABLE 5

Dialect	5–7 a.m.	11–noon	Time 4–6 p.m.	7–8.30 p.m.	10.30– midnight
UM	*breakfast* medium	*lunch* medium	*(tea)* light	*dinner* heavy	*(supper)* light
LM	*breakfast* medium	*dinner* heavy	*supper* medium ~	*supper* light	
EL	*tea* light	*breakfast* medium		*dinner* heavy	
PF	*tea* light	*breakfast* heavy	*dinner* medium	*(supper)* light	

transitives such as *buy*, which apparently does not occur with inchoatives. If we consider the entire continuum, however, we find that the switch of the inchoative feature occurs at different points on the continuum for different verbs. In a complete grammar of the entire system, therefore, it would probably be necessary to include in the lexical entry of every transitive verb the appropriate cutting number as an index feature to indicate at what point on the continuum the inchoative switch takes place.

Even semantic variation within the continuum can be incorporated into the generative grammar, though not enough is known about generative semantics at present to permit more than programmatic suggestions. As an example, I offer Table 5, a semantic analysis of names for meals in four varieties of Jamaican English (basically an extension of a schema first presented in

DeCamp 1963). The level labeled UM in Table 5 represents upper middle class usage. Level LM represents certain lower middle class speakers (tradesmen, small shop owners, etc.). EL represents many of the estate laborers, and PF many peasant farmers. Parentheses indicate optional meals; e.g. the peasant farmer may have a late 'supper' only on special occasions. The tilde ~ separates alternatives; i.e. the LM speaker may take either a medium-sized meal in late afternoon or a light meal later in the evening, but in either case he would call it his *supper*.

The meanings, at least those aspects of meaning essential to defining the contrasts within this composite system, consist of five different times of day and three relatives sizes of meal, all of which can be reformulated in terms of the following five binary features:

[+H] the heaviest meal of the day
[+L] the lightest meal, normally without hot food
[+P] peripheral daylight hours, i.e. 5–7 a.m. or 7–8.30 p.m.
[+M] morning, i.e. before noon
[+N] night-time

Thus the data of Table 5 can be rewritten as Table 6 (see p. 365). Note that the alternatives for the LM *supper*, which were marked by ~ in Table 5, are indicated by the variable coefficient α, meaning that if feature L is plus, so is P; if L is minus, so is P. Note also that this system, like phonological and syntactic feature representations, contains redundancies. For example, the meaning of a meal name cannot be both [+H] and [+L], though it can be both [−H] and [−L], indicating that it is neither the heaviest nor the lightest meal of the day – hence medium. As in phonology and syntax, the semantic representation can be simplified by leaving redundant features unspecified and providing redundancy rules:

$$
\begin{array}{lll}
1. & [+H] & \longrightarrow [-L] \\
2. & [+L] & \longrightarrow [-H] \\
3. & \left\{ \begin{array}{l} [+P] \\ [+M] \end{array} \right\} & \longrightarrow [-N] \\
4. & [+N] & \longrightarrow \left[\begin{array}{l} -P \\ -M \end{array} \right]
\end{array}
$$

The array in Table 6 is still only a juxtaposition of four separate analyses. As with the phonology and the syntax, we can construct conversion rules, both to simplify the total description and also to capture significant generalizations about the process of switching from one level to another. For example, we can represent the semantic features of the UM level as in Table 6, and then provide

TABLE 6

Dialect — Features — Names	UM					LM					EL					PF				
	H	L	P	M	N	H	L	P	M	N	H	L	P	M	N	H	L	P	M	N
breakfast	+	+	−	−		−		+			−		+			+			−	
lunch	+	−	−	+		+		−	α			+	+	+		+		+	−	
tea	−	−	+	+		+		−	α		−	+	+	−		−		+	−	+
dinner				−	+	+		−		−										
supper				+	−	+		−								+			−	−

the following three sets of rules to convert level UM to LM, LM to EL, and EL to PF:

UM⟶LM	LM⟶EL	EL⟶PF
1. $[+H] \longrightarrow \begin{bmatrix} -P \\ +M \end{bmatrix}$	3. $\begin{bmatrix} \alpha M \\ -P \end{bmatrix} \longrightarrow [-\alpha M]$	5. $\begin{bmatrix} +P \\ +H \end{bmatrix} \rightarrow \begin{bmatrix} -P \\ -N \end{bmatrix}$
2. $\begin{bmatrix} +L \\ +N \end{bmatrix} \longrightarrow \begin{bmatrix} -H \\ \alpha L \\ \alpha P \\ -M \\ -N \end{bmatrix}$	4. $[\alpha P] \longrightarrow [-\alpha P]$	6. $\begin{bmatrix} -H \\ -M \end{bmatrix} \longrightarrow \begin{bmatrix} +L \\ +P \end{bmatrix}$
		7. $\begin{bmatrix} -L \\ \alpha H \end{bmatrix} \longrightarrow [-\alpha H]$

Rules 1 and 2 would be triggered by the presence of a dialect feature [+LM]. The first four rules would be triggered by [+EL], and all seven rules by [+PF]. Alternatively, we could write such conversion rules in such a way as to convert level UM directly to EL or to PH without passing through intermediate varieties.

UM⟶LM	UM⟶EL	UM⟶PF
1. $[+H] \longrightarrow \begin{bmatrix} -P \\ +M \end{bmatrix}$	3. $\begin{bmatrix} -H \\ \alpha P \end{bmatrix} \longrightarrow [-\alpha P]$	5. $\begin{bmatrix} -M \\ +L \\ -N \end{bmatrix} \longrightarrow [+M]$
2. $\begin{bmatrix} +L \\ +N \end{bmatrix} \longrightarrow \begin{bmatrix} -H \\ \alpha L \\ \alpha P \\ -M \\ -N \end{bmatrix}$	4. $[+L] \longrightarrow [+M]$	6. $[\alpha P] \longrightarrow [-\alpha P]$
		7. $\begin{bmatrix} \alpha H \\ -P \end{bmatrix} \longrightarrow [-\alpha H]$
		8. $[\quad] \longrightarrow [-N]$

In this alternative, the dialect feature [+EL] would trigger only rules 3 and 4. The feature [+PF] would trigger only rules 5, 6, 7, and 8. The latter alternative would thus simplify the derivation of sentences, especially in level PF. The former, however, provides simpler grammatical rules, and it presents all these conversions as a single set of related operations; e.g. note in the latter alternative how rules 3 and 4 have to be essentially repeated in rules 5 and 6. The former alternative is therefore probably preferable.

These examples from phonology, syntax, and semantics are only demonstrations of the potential applicability of generative rules to a post-creole continuum. They are not yet a complete or even a representative description of the sociolinguistics of Jamaica. Although this theoretical approach seems the most promising, we are still a long way from that goal. We need much more empirical evidence on the intermediate varieties of the continuum, especially on the co-occurrences of variable features at different stylistic levels. Rules must be written, empirically tested, and then rewritten if invalidated. No such composite grammar will ever be so complete as to account for every sociolinguistic variable in Jamaica. Even a grammar sufficiently detailed to account for the main outlines of the Jamaican continuum, however, would give us a better theoretical model of a complex speech community than any now available. Meanwhile we can profitably study within this framework many special subjects of immediate relevance, e.g. the creole auxiliary and the problems it poses for education not only in Jamaica but in other creole-affected areas. The fact that many scholars now see in the United States a Negro cultural and linguistic spectrum analogous to the Jamaican continuum (or perhaps even part of the same larger New World post-creole phenomenon) gives our work a significance beyond the description of the sociolinguistics of one island in the Caribbean (see Dillard's paper in this volume). And the fact that generative theory is applicable to the entire variable continuum, not just to one uniform idiolect such as the 'pure creole' extreme, can eliminate the unfortunate gap between sociolinguistics and linguistic theory.

Two interesting questions are raised by this approach, both with important theoretical implications. First, what is the locus of a language: in the mind of the individual speaker, or in the community at large? A grammar is a theoretical construct like a geometry, not a collection of empirical observations. If it is a 'useful' grammar rather than a mere intellectual exercise, it mirrors a human linguistic competence which manifests itself in empirically observable behavior. But where does this competence reside? The observable behavior, i.e. the linguistic performance, is both individual and social. The sociologist sees no objection to speaking also of the linguistic competence of a community as well as of that of an individual. The psychologist usually objects and insists that this competence is a property of the individual members of the community, not the community itself; otherwise we would have to assume some sort of mystical collective intelligence.

This is not a new argument. At the 1951 Linguistic Institute, for example, A. L. Kroeber and Harry Hoijer debated the same issue with Bernard Bloch and argued that a language, like a kinship system, was neither an artifact nor an attribute of an individual brainpan, but was a communal competence. One

of my generative colleagues recently approved my generative treatment of the
post-creole continuum only to the extent that the span of speech varieties lay
within the range of an individual speaker's ability to switch stylistically from
one level to another. A continuum too broad to fall entirely within the stylistic
range of the individual speaker could indeed be described, he granted, but I
could not call such a description a 'grammar'. He quipped that I might
instead call it a 'diagrammar'.

It happens that most generative theorists are psychologically oriented rather
than sociologically or anthropologically, but I believe that this is due to
historical accident rather than to anything essential to the theory. One could
well argue that the individual speaker's limitation to a span of the continuum,
the fact that no one speaker can command the entire range of varieties, is
a matter of performance rather than competence, analogous to his inability to
speak sentences beyond a certain level of complexity. The theoretical competence of the 'ideal speaker-listener' could be defined as spanning the entire
continuum, including full command of all the switching rules between any
one point and another. We could then look for socioeconomic explanations
of the manner in which the actual performance of real speakers falls short
of this ideal competence. It indeed seems arbitrary to hold that of the n
varieties in this continuum, levels 7 through 23 legitimately belong in the same
grammar because we can find speaker A who commands them all, but to
exclude level 24 because it is beyond his range, even though speaker B may
command levels 8 through 24. The issue of social versus psychological 'reality'
of language will not be soon settled, but there is nothing in generative theory
which outlaws the social definition. The only relevant issue is whether a
generative approach provides any valuable insights into the linguistic behavior
of the community.

The second question raised by this approach does indeed concern performance: What factors govern the individual speaker's switching behavior
within that span of the continuum which he commands? What constitutes a
stimulus sufficient to make him switch upward or downward stylistically? If
we count his utterances during a 'normal' day or week, classifying them
according to level, will the result be an even distribution over the span which
he can command? Will it be a bell-shaped curve, thus defining a single
norm for his usage? Or will it perhaps be a trimodal curve, indicating separate
norms for his habitual, unselfconscious speech, his attempts to approach the
standard, and his attempts to 'talk down' to his social inferiors? On the level
of performance there may indeed be some basis to the persistent myth of a
two-dialect system in Jamaica. That is, the quantified verbal behavior of the
individual may turn out to be discrete, even though the composite behavior
of the community, like the spectrum of competence features, is continuous.
Such questions can be answered only by means of empirical studies, with

large samples and rigorous experimental procedures. If sociolinguistics is to make further useful contributions to creole studies, then both theoretical research and empirical studies are needed, and the two must be planned in close coordination with each other.

NOTES

1 I developed this technique of analysis in 1959 and presented it at two national professional meetings and in several public lectures as my original discovery. It was not until the summer of 1968, after the Mona conference, that I discovered that I had been anticipated. My colleague Walter Stolz then informed me that the general procedure has been known to psychologists for more than twenty years as the Guttman scalogram analysis (Guttman 1944; Torgerson 1957), though I believe that I was indeed the first to apply it to linguistic data. Stolz has now also prepared a paper on the application of scalogram analysis to the standard-nonstandard dimension of central Texan. The fact that so many psychologists and sociologists have for so long been unaware of the applicability of scalogram analysis to language data, and that so many linguists have been unaware of the very existence of this useful procedure is a cogent argument for increased exchanges of information and ideas between linguistics and related disciplines.

2 These special phonological rules for Jamaican English are not only ordered with respect to each other; they are also generally ordered after the phonological rules for general 'standard' English. That is, an optimal set of synchronic rules tends to recapitulate the sociolinguistics of a language just as it tends to recapitulate the history of that language. Rules applicable only to all varieties of Jamaican English tend to follow rules applicable to general English but to precede rules applicable only to one level of Jamaican English. I am indebted to Stanley Peters for pointing out what appears to be the only exception: the central diphthongization rule, which generates [ə] inglides in dialects M and L, must precede the vowel shift rule. Otherwise the [+compact] feature which defines the environment of the diphthongization rule will have been changed by the vowel shift rule. Thus at least one rule which applies only to dialects M and L precedes a rule which applies to all varieties of English.

REFERENCES

Alleyne, Mervyn 1967. 'Review of *Jamaican creole syntax*, by Beryl Bailey', *Caribbean Studies* 6:92–4
Bailey, Beryl 1966. *Jamaican creole syntax: a transformational approach*, Cambridge, Cambridge University Press
Cassidy, F. G. 1961. *Jamaica talk: three hundred years of the English language in Jamaica*, London, Macmillan
Cassidy, F. G. and R. B. Le Page 1967. *Dictionary of Jamaican English*, Cambridge, Cambridge University Press
DeCamp, David 1963. 'Review of *Jamaica talk*, by F. G. Cassidy', *Language* 39:536–44
    1968. 'The field of creole language studies', A background paper prepared for the 1968 conference on pidginization and creolization of languages; pub-

lished 1968, *Latin American Research Review* 3:25–46, and 1969, *Studia Anglica Posnaniensia* 1:29–51

    1969. 'Diasystem vs. overall pattern: the Jamaican syllabic nuclei', *Studies in the language, literature, and culture of the middle ages and later*, ed. by E. Bagby Atwood and A. A. Hill, Austin, University of Texas Press. Originally presented as a paper before the 1961 winter meeting of the Linguistic Society of America

Ferguson, Charles A. 1959. 'Diglossia', *Word* 15:325–40

Fries, C. C. 1940. *American English grammar*, New York, Appleton-Century-Crofts

Guttman, Louis 1944. 'A basis for scaling qualitative data', *American Sociological Review* 9:139–50

Hall, Robert A., Jr. 1953. 'Haitian creole' (American Anthropological Association, Memoir 74), Washington, D.C., American Anthropological Association

    1962. 'The life cycle of pidgin languages', *Lingua* 11:151–6

    1966. *Pidgin and creole languages*, Ithaca, Cornell University Press

Kurath, Hans, *et al.* 1939. *Handbook of the linguistic geography of New England*, Providence, Brown University Press

Lakoff, George 1965. 'On the nature of syntactic irregularity', Report No. NSF-16, The Computation Laboratory, Harvard University, Cambridge, Mass.

Reinecke, John, and Aiko Tokimasa 1934. 'The English dialect of Hawaii', *American Speech* 9:48–58, 122–31

Stewart, William A. 1962. 'Creole languages in the Caribbean', *Study of the role of second languages in Asia, Africa, and Latin America*, ed. by Frank A. Rice, 34–53, Washington, D.C., Center for Applied Lingustics

Taylor, Douglas 1963. 'Review of *Jamaican creole*, by Robert B. Le Page and David DeCamp', *Language* 39:316–22

Torgerson, Warren 1957. *Theory and methods of scaling*, New York, Wiley

EDUCATION AND CREOLE ENGLISH IN THE WEST INDIES

Some Sociolinguistic Factors

DENNIS R. CRAIG

The newly emerging nations of the former British West Indian colonies – Guyana, Trinidad, Barbados, Jamaica, the rest of the English-speaking Windward and Leeward Islands, and Belize (British Honduras) – face social and educational problems directly attributable to the fact that forms of English creole speech are the everyday language of the majority of their populations. Of such speech, that of Jamaica is best known (cf. Le Page and DeCamp (1960), Cassidy (1961), Bailey (1962, 1966), and Cassidy and Le Page (1967)). The differences between Jamaican Creole and other varieties of English creole in these nations are minor, and Bailey's summary of the principal differences between Jamaican Creole and English syntax (Bailey 1966:146) can stand as a summary of known differences between English and most West Indian English creoles. In addition to the basic similarity of speech there is a corresponding similarity in social structure. The social traditions and institutions have evolved from common origins in seventeenth- and eighteenth-century British colonial plantation systems based on Negro slavery, and at present all the territories remain small societies with large, poor, coloured working classes, small middle-classes mainly in bureaucratic occupations, seriously underdeveloped economies, and social status requirements, including language, patterned on the British model. These similarities between individual territories lend some justification to the ensuing attempt to consider the West Indian creole language situation as a whole with regard to some of the sociolinguistic phenomena it has produced.

The interaction area between creole and standard

In recognizing the existence of the creoles, it has been necessary to recognize also what has been referred to as the 'continuum' between creole and West Indian Standard English. This fact needs no treatment here, having been adequately dealt with in the works cited above, and in Bailey (1964) and the papers by Bailey and DeCamp in this volume. A theoretical model for Jamaica (Craig 1966), one which seems relevant also to the other territories, conceives the language situation as a dynamic interrelationship of forms of speech, such as shown in (1a, 1b):

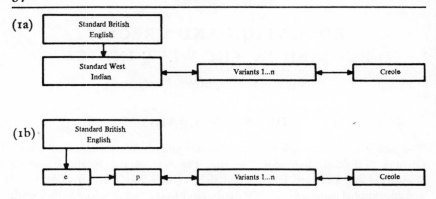

In the second diagram Standard West Indian speech, as accepted in formal social situations, is analyzed into two components; p represents the ways in which such speech differs from Standard British English. There is a one-way channel of influence from SBE to SWI and to p, but p is linked to the rest of the system by two-way channels. The rest of the system consists of a range of linguistic variation (variants 1, 2, 3, . . . *n*), which, together with p, represents an *area of interaction* between the community's social standard and creole speech. Influence flows both ways.

This area of interaction is intermediate between the extremes of the continuum defined for Jamaica by Bailey and DeCamp. I refer to it as 'interaction' because its existence has been, and continues to be, dependent on the cross-influences from the two extremes.

DeCamp (1968) points out that 'given two samples of Jamaican speech which differ substantially from one another, it is usually possible to find a third intermediate level in an additional sample'. In thinking of the continuum as 'interaction', however, it becomes possible to formulate a social corollary:

(2) A speaker aiming to produce a significantly less familiar, but socially required system of speech usually produces a system intermediate between his most familiar one and the one aimed at.

The importance of this formulation is that it emphasizes individual behavior and the individual acts of speech that go to make up a continuum; the origin of the continuum in varying social requirements for language; and that what otherwise might have been a stratification of a few discrete kinds of speech is indeed made into a continuum by the cumulative results of mutual *interference* or 'interaction' between linguistic systems. In brief, the end of the processes outlined in (1) and (2) is a continuum, one compatible with the analyses of Bailey and DeCamp, but one whose existence and sociolinguistic implications cannot be adequately accounted for except in terms of interaction and mutual interference. (A linguistic 'system' here denotes any given set of interrelationships among linguistic forms, irrespective of the extent of over-lapping in features with other such sets.)

There seem to be two main ways in which interaction between linguistic systems creates a continuum. The first is well illustrated in DeCamp's Table 1, and may be called 'simple mixing'. In simple mixing, different speakers use different combinations of the contrasts provided by two relatively widely separated systems. DeCamp's examples show six contrasts and seven combinations of these, and demonstrate that the combinations are rule-governed.

The second mode of interaction also involves mixing, but before mixing occurs, the original contrasts seem to be mutated in various ways, sometimes through interference of one system with the other. I refer to this second type as 'mutation with mixing'. Examples can be seen in the following:

(3)

Some socially significant contrasts

Standard extreme	Intermediate	Creole extreme
'didn't'	/din/, /in/, no/, /na/	/no ben/, /na bin/
'it's'	/iz/	/a/
'want to go'	/waan(t) guo/	/waan fi(fo) guo/
'bay' [beı̯]	/beə̰/	/bIə̰/*
'potato' [puteı̯toṵ]	/puteto:/, /putetə/	/pəteta/, /pitie̯ta/

* See De Camp, Table 2.

Mutated items, such as those in the intermediate column of (3), would be subject to the rules of social selection mentioned by DeCamp. A speaker who uses /in/ for 'didn't', for example, would not have the same combined substitutions (of the type of DeCamp's Table 1) as a speaker who uses /na/ or /no/. The combined processes of mutating and mixing produce the extreme complexity of the so-called continuum and express the social relationships that underlie it.

The complexity would be even more apparent if segments of discourse, rather than isolated lexical items, were contrasted. Thus, two contrasting, and referentially equivalent statements, from the extremes, such as:

(4) 'He's her uncle'   /shi a fi(fo) kaal im(i) oŋkl/

would be represented by a lengthy range of socially significant variants, including a pronunciation of 'She is to call him uncle' that many speakers would unhesitatingly accept as belonging to West Indian Standard English.

Language and social mobility

The situation outlined above reflects a striving on the part of a former creole-speaking population toward a model provided by Standard British English and the social mobility it confers, a striving that has created the specific forms of West Indian Standard English to be found in the different territories. Bailey's comment (1966b:106) about Jamaica is as true for the entire West Indies today as it has undoubtedly always been:

It is possible to move from one social class to another by changing one's linguistic norm. This is of course due to another factor, the correlation between a good education and acceptable English, which makes it possible to assume that ability to manipulate SJE (Standard Jamaican English) is indicative of a good education, in addition of course, to birth in a higher caste or class.

In this striving for social status through English, the axiom stated in (2) above becomes reality, and speakers create the interaction area. Younger people encounter this upward social striving at an early age. It is a long-standing practice in many places for children who do not 'talk proper', or who 'talk bad', to be scolded into producing a 'better' kind of speech. Many parents, who may be able to shift somewhat into the interaction area, but whose own repertoire is normally creole, do this. I have had experience of this in Guyana and have witnessed such scolding in Jamaica, St Vincent, Grenada, and Trinidad. The result is that by early school age some children have become able to shift their speech into the interaction area, even though their home is mostly creole-speaking. The speech of most other children is brought into this area by formal schooling and the influence of the mass media. At present it would seem that the spontaneous as well as careful speech of a majority of school-age children lies entirely within the interaction area. That is, it is neither creole nor standard West Indian, nor yet again does it represent a discrete, stable speech norm of its own.

The examples in (5) below are typical of the responses teachers have been observed to obtain when trying to get children to 'correct' spontaneous utterances. Each of the sets 5(i) to 5(viii) comes from a different child, usually in a different place (since these items are only chance records made by the writer in visits to schools in Jamaica, Trinidad and Guyana). The children range in age from 7 to 12 years.

(5)

Spontaneous utterance and attempts of the same child at 'careful' standard-language replacement	Creole and Standard versions not heard
(i) /a mi buk dat/	/a fi mi buk dat/
/iz mi buk/	'It's my book.'
/iz mai buk/	
(ii) /a bin tu di stuor/	/mi bin a stuor/
/ai did guo tu di stuor/	'I went to the store.'
(iii) /we i de/	/a we i de/
/wier hi iz/	'Where is he?'
(iv) /shi brokop di pliet/	(This seems already to be the creole form)
/shi briek di pliet/	'She's broken the plate.'

(v)	/a waan letout/ /ai waant tu letout/	/mi waan (fu) letout/ '*I want to be let out*' i.e. .... *to be allowed to go outside.*
(vi)	/a in get non/ /ai didn get non/	/mi na bin get non/ '*I didn't get any.*'
(vii)	/iz kot yu waan kot it/ /yu waan kot it/	/a kot yu waan (fu) kot i/ '*Do you want to cut it?*'
(viii)	/yu in si yu a mash mi fut/ /sii yu mash mai fut/	/yu na bin, si se yu a mash mi fut/ '*Don't you see you are mashing (stepping on) my foot?*'

Note that the attempt to switch from one level of speech to another is sometimes accompanied, as is to be expected, by a reduction in expressiveness, as in (iv), (vii) and (viii). Apart from this, however, the kind of ability displayed by most children as in (5) results on the whole in a surprising paradox. For a vast majority of young people, this ability fails to develop any further, so that they leave school and attain adulthood without being able to shift out of the interaction area into the highly-prized standard-language extreme of the continuum. The apparent facility with which these young speakers operate within the interaction area seems incompatible with the apparently difficult barrier that they find between this facility and the highly-prized goal of standard language. The likely reason for this and the important educational implications that arise will be shown in the next section.

The early age at which children learn to switch linguistic forms in the presence of elders, teachers and strangers in general, given the evidently vital social significance of language in the West Indies, seems to indicate that the stages of 'social perception' and 'stylistic variation' *begin much earlier and at the same time are probably more prolonged for West Indian children* than for the New York children described by Labov (1964:91). Much more research, however, needs to be done. (The methods of Labov (1963 and 1966) for correlating linguistic and social variables would undoubtedly be fruitful in the West Indies.)

Academic interest in the interaction between creole and standard language has an importance which goes beyond the mere perfecting of sociolinguistic theory, important as the latter is. Such interest in the West Indies is essential to the provision of guidelines for social action, specifically educational action in respect of language. The language situation in the West Indies is intimately involved in economic and social development. Large sectors of the non-standard-speaking population (estimated at about 70% of the total population) have to be educated, and rapidly so, for functioning in a modern economy; and Standard English, by way of text-books, instructors, examinations etc., is the medium through which this is being attempted. The societies in all territories are, in a way, trapped within their Standard English traditions;

widespread inability to use the standard language is resulting in increasing wastage in expanding educational systems, a wastage which poor economies cannot afford. Official government statements in all the territories, apart from putting increasing emphasis on the social-mobility value of English and condemning school examination results (which often give a failure rate at all levels of between 60–85% in English in most territories) show very little insight into the real nature of the problem.

Consequences for language teaching

The factors so far outlined place the West Indian child in the kind of language-learning situation discussed by Stewart (1964) in which *English is neither a native language nor a foreign language*. It has been shown elsewhere (Craig 1966, 1967) that this unique language-learning situation is directly related to the interaction area discussed above and that, because of this, the language, Standard English, to be learned may be theoretically analyzed into four strata:

(6)

Class A: Patterns actively known. That is, creole or other non-standard speakers know how to use these spontaneously in their own informal speech.

Class B: Patterns used only under stress. These may have been learned, without becoming firmly habitual, through school teaching, through short contacts with Standard English speakers, through intermittent exposure to mass media, etc.

Class C: Patterns known passively. That is, creole or other non-standard speakers would understand these owing to context, if used by other speakers, but non-standard speakers would not themselves be able to produce them, except as mutations within the interaction area or 'errors' relative to Standard English.

Class D: Patterns not known.

The evidence for this stratification in the English-language repertoire of West Indian children comes from studies of the abilities of speakers under several conditions:

(7)

(i) Talking spontaneously with friends. (Samples of over 300 Jamaican children, and smaller numbers of children in Grenada and St Lucia, recorded in small peer-groups.)

(ii) Talking in social situations requiring formal or 'careful' speech. Transcriptions of children talking on given topics to an interviewer in classroom situations in Jamaica, Trinidad, Guyana and some of the smaller territories. (In addition, corroborative evidence is supplied by samples of written composition of older children and young adults.)

(iii) Comprehending standard speech. (Evidence from the results of classroom exercises in oral and reading comprehension and reported classroom observations of practising as well as trainee teachers.)

From 7(i) and 7(ii) it is possible to ascertain the range of children's speech within the interaction area and to divide this range into two sets of features corresponding to Classes A and B of illustration (6). Class A features (actively known) are those common to both 7(i) and 7(ii). Class B features are those which appear only under condition 7(ii). Standard English features appearing as mutations under condition 7(ii) would belong to Class C, but these as well as other features belonging to Classes C and D would be further revealed under condition 7(iii). In practice, especially when older learners are involved, it is not always possible to make a clear separation of Class C (passively known) from Class D (unknown) features since some linguistic contexts are so helpful to speakers that the presence of an unknown feature has little or no effect on comprehension, except in very well controlled tests of a kind which it has not been possible to conduct up to now in the West Indies. It is sometimes convenient therefore to treat the two classes as one (Class C/D) in teaching methods, while acknowledging the theoretical difference between them. (See Appendix for illustration of stratification.)

The special implication of the stratification of the Standard English being learned is that *the learner is able all the time to recognize Standard English far out of proportion to his ability to produce it.* This happens chiefly because of Class C features which are either inherently redundant, or, as pointed out before, may be rendered so by the context, or which are recognizable because of resemblance to mutations actually possessed by the speaker. These features, when combined with Classes A and B, create within the learner the illusion that the target Standard English is known already. This is reminiscent of the well-known distinction between the production and recognition levels of a learner's control of language (cf. Fries 1963) but the implications are not identical. Under normal circumstances a foreign learner's production and recognition repertoires of English are both initially non-existent. When acquired, they do not form a part of his native language repertoire; they remain separate and distinct. In the case of the creole or other non-standard speaker, however, a basis for both already exists when he comes to learn Standard English, and they become, within the speaker, the *area of interaction* between his familiar speech and Standard English.

It was mentioned earlier that the apparently difficult speech barrier that some learners find between the interaction area and the Standard-English extreme of the continuum seems inconsistent with the ability of most speakers to use language from the interaction area. This situation is explainable in terms of the nature of the passively known (Class C) features relative to the rest of the stratification. The learning of Standard English can become arrested at a point where the quantity of unknown features (Class D) has become

N

negligible, relative to formal social requirements, but at the same time the quantity of features known passively (Class C) has remained relatively large and significant. The speaker in this situation would possess an adequate 'recognition' of Standard English and a consequently strong sense of knowing the language. These dispositions would reduce both his motivation to modify his language as well as his ability to perceive contrasts between what language he actually produces and what he aims to produce. Only the social consequences of his Standard English efforts would be apparent to him. That this is the frustrating position in which many non-standard-speaking learners find themselves seems abundantly clear from the examinations and other reports on English-language proficiency that appear in the West Indies year after year.

Owing directly to the high level of recognition mentioned above and to the fact that the *context* of speech, as a variable element, can always act to convert an unknown feature of Standard English into a passively known feature, the learner reacts in the following ways to normal *foreign language* teaching procedures:

(8)

   (i) The learner often fails to perceive new target elements in the teaching situation.

   (ii) The reinforcement of learning which derives from the learner's satisfaction at mastering a new element, and knowing he has mastered it, is minimal.

   (iii) Because of the ease of shifting from Standard English to Creole or other non-standard speech and vice-versa, the learner resists any attempt to restrict his use of Standard English within the Standard English patterns known to him in the teaching situation.

At the same time, *native-language* methods, because they assume that the learner already knows the language being taught, fail to give him an active command over language patterns of Classes C and D. The West Indies have been committed to such methods in schools by history and social tradition, and abundant evidence of the results is to be perceived not only in linguistic but in social terms, in the complaints about school-leavers' proficiency and the general social anxiety referred to earlier.

English-teaching methods appropriate for the kind of language situation here discussed have been outlined in greater detail in sources cited already. The salient points about such methods are as follows:

(9)

   (i) Foreign-language teaching techniques of grading and pattern drill can be used successfully mostly for unknown and only to a lesser extent for passively known patterns.

   (ii) Since the learner's native speech and Standard English co-exist in the same everyday environment and since the aim of English-teaching, unlike that in a true foreign-language situation, is to replace the child's original language in the expectation that the child would switch to Standard

English in most social situations, grading and pattern practice need to be integrated, more closely than in a normal foreign-language situation, with the learners' normal everyday requirements for language. This means that grading has to be strongly guided by the maturity, interests and experiences of specific learners, and contextual orientation on the whole plays a bigger role than it does in normal foreign-language teaching.

(iii) Because of (ii), and high recognition, pattern drills are of less importance than they are in normal foreign-language teaching. The major method of teaching therefore needs to consist of a meaningful repetition of language through a *repetition of controlled situations naturally requiring such language*. Methods such as the 'situational' methods of Hornby (1950) and the use of role-theory (cf. Biddle and Thomas 1966) seem important.

(iv) For effective use of situational methods, the patterns of Standard English must be grouped in such a way that a teaching-set would consist of an unknown or passively known element as target, together with such Class A or B elements as are necessary to create a simulated language 'situation'.

Such methods, when used with young, extreme or intermediate Creole-speakers, produce results which seem to support the theoretical position here discussed as to the interaction area between Creole and Standard English and the stratification of the learner's English repertoire that arises out of this. An illustration follows.

LANGUAGE ACQUISITION AND ATTITUDES

The learning of English by children possessing Creole or other non-standard speech appears to proceed not in clearly definable steps, but as a gradual process of linguistic change through the 'interaction area' earlier described. The process was studied with regard to five groups:

(10)

E_1, E_2, E_3, E_4 = Four groups of rural Creole-speaking children who entered school for the first time at age $6\frac{1}{2}$–7.

E_{10}, E_{20}, E_{30}, E_{40} = The same groups of children after 6 months of learning English

C_1, C_{10} = A control group of children at the beginning (approximately) and end respectively of the experimental period.

The children's learning was measured at regular intervals by language-production tests which required each child to talk freely about a given picture-card. The E groups were taught by the procedures stated in (9). The control group was taught by traditional native-language methods, but possessed an advantage over the experimental-groups in that it had previously had 2–3 years of infant education and had been involved in special native-language infant school projects. It was felt necessary to give the control group this advantage over the experimental groups in order to counterbalance a possible 'Hawthorne' effect in the experimental children. The criteria measured by the tests were a few which experience has shown to differentiate Creole and

Standard-speaking children. These were:

(11)

 (i) The average proportion of clauses containing non-standard verb-phrases or non-standard relationships between nominative and verb.
 (ii) The average proportion of 'and' - linked clauses.
 (iii) The average number of words per clause.
 (iv) The quantity of intentionally formal speech (i.e. total number of words spoken) on a given occasion.

Criterion (i) is concerned with purely syntactic characteristics. (ii) is a stylistic characteristic related to the fact that the creole makes extensive use of /an/, 'and', in place of other types of linkage or terminal junctures within connected discourse. (iii) probably reflects a stylistic characteristic as well (i.e. many short co-ordinated clauses instead of longer clauses structured otherwise). The possibility that (ii), (iii) and (iv) together probably reflect some characteristics of a restricted code as postulated by Bernstein (1961) would need to be considered, since there is some indication, as will be discussed subsequently, that middle class Jamaican children rate higher on (iii) and (iv) but lower on (ii) than lower class children. Little or no change occurred in the control group, while the experimental groups changed significantly.* For the experimental children, the attempt to learn English resulted in a gradual increase of their ability to move towards the standard-language extreme within the area of variation already described and *not in a restriction of their discourse (in formal social situations) to the purely standard forms they had learned*; this is shown by reduction without elimination of the Creole features with respect to criterion (i) especially. *The incipient English repertoire of the individual is evidenced as variation arising from a Creole/Standard English interaction.* In terms of the stratification illustrated in (6), this process of learning may be envisaged as a progressive movement from any given stratum of the target repertoire to the one next above it.

 This movement within the area of variation was accompanied by a normal growth in fluency and verbal planning ability as indicated by the increases shown with respect to criteria (iii) and (iv).

 The children studied in (10) are Jamaican, but the situation they illustrate seems representative of the rest of the English-standard Caribbean as well, even though it is sometimes felt, especially in the absence of intensive linguistic study, that in the rest of the West Indies the Creole end of the 'continuum' is not as far removed from the English end as it is in Jamaica. However this may be, there is some evidence that the reduction of Creole characteristics just described is unusual for similar children in some other territories and that this is due to the specially controlled teaching methods (based on the stratifi-

* See Table 18 in Appendix.

cation shown in (6)) used with the Jamaican children. Comparable Trinidadian children from six schools in or around Port of Spain were tested and matched with the pooled Jamaican samples $E_{10} + E_{20} + E_{30} + E_{40}$, of (10). The following is the result of the comparison:

(12)

	Jamaican special-tuition samples	Trinidad normal samples	Standard error	Level of significance
(i) Total number of words spoken (11, iv)	72·48	69·47	10·55	Not
(ii) Mean number of words per clause (11, iii).	4·94	4·66	0·50	Not
(ii) Proportion of non-standard verb phrases (11, i)	0·175	0·372	0·054	0·01

This shows that the proportion of non-standard verb-phrases in the Trinidadian children without special tuition, is significantly more than the proportion in the Jamaican children after tuition, even though the former were attending school a year earlier. West Indian children on the whole are unlikely to react very much differently from the children studied so far. This seems to support the conclusions earlier reached about the nature of the inter-action area between English and Creole and its significance in the total language situation.

The examples come from young school children mainly because, in relation to the specific phenomena we refer to here, there is a paucity of data evidence from adult language. Given the accelerating economic development of the region and the relatively rapid social changes being brought about, however, the language of school children and young adults will most strongly be subject to the stresses which motivate linguistic change. This in itself is ample justification for more intensive and less superficial studies of young people's language than those producing the evidence discussed above.

Young people's motivation for linguistic change is related to their attitude to the language to be learned. It is likely that attitudes towards Standard English, though not necessarily clearly overt, will be strong and deep-seated. This matter has hardly been studied but there is some evidence that children as young as those studied may have the beginnings of definable attitudes toward standard speech. In one or two instances boys, when not aware of being observed by teachers, etc., amused themselves by a somewhat exaggerated mimicry of girlish voices conveying bits of standard speech. The point of the mimicry seemed to be *that femininity or lack of toughness was to be associated with standard speech*. In the groups studied in (10), girls' speech changed more extensively towards the prestige norms than boys did, although both changed. Thus when the groups E_{10}, E_{20}, E_{30}, E_{40} were pooled and analysed into boys and girls, the results were as follows:

(13)

Proportions of non-standard verb-phrases		Standard error	Significance of difference
Boys	Girls		
0·29	0·075	0·065	0·01

The proportion of non-standard verb-patterns differed significantly between boys and girls. The girls showed the smaller proportion although initially there were no significant differences between boys and girls or between these children and control groups (Craig, 1967b). The preceding result could be due to differential rates of learning between boys and girls, as are sometimes evidenced in educational studies, but even so differential learning usually results from differences in underlying motivations. Attitudes and motivations of creole speakers learning Standard English need much further investigation.

Relevance of the theory of restricted and elaborated codes

The presumed origins of Creole and the conditions perpetuating it in the West Indies are such as should have resulted in a syntactic structuring of creole along the lines of a restricted code in the sense of Bernstein (1961, 1964, 1965, 1966). The kind of shared referential situations postulated by Bernstein as giving rise to restricted codes seem to correspond closely with what must have applied in the original contact situations producing the pidgin language which finally became creole English. The working-class urban and rural conditions providing the social environment of creole speech today likewise correspond with the postulated social contexts of restricted codes. When furthermore the syntactic structure of West Indian creole speech is compared with that of Standard English it becomes evident that the main differences between the two correspond with some of the main predicted structural differences between restricted and elaborated codes. Some illustration of this correspondence is set out in (14).

(14)

Main peculiarities of English creole syntax	Predicted tendencies of speakers (in terms of a restricted code)
(i) (a) No subject-verb concord (b) No case in pronouns (c) No sex in pronouns (Jamaica).	Considered together with (iii) below, clauses or sentences would need to be shorter rather than longer, simple preferably, have a referential domain known to speaker and listener so that subject-predicate relationships may be easily perceptible.

(ii) No passive form of the verb.
'A syntactic form stressing the active voice.' (Bernstein 1961.)

(iii) No marking to indicate tense in the verb except by the use of a particle specifying 'past' and sometimes one specifying 'continuous'.
Reinforcement of predicted tendencies as for (i) with the burden of tense relationships being taken over by context.

(iv) (a) Predication of adjectives
Modifications of English in the direction of implicit rather than explicit meaning.

/Jan sik/ = John
(is)
(was)
(etc.) sick.

(b) Associative plurals
/Mieri-dem/ =
Mary and her friends.
/Di piipl dem/ = all the people.

(v) (a) Reduplication.
/wan-wan/ = a few here and there.
/taak-taak/ = talk all the time
/huoli-huoli/ = full of holes.
Use of repetition resulting in a reduction in the range of required lexis. Reinforcement of the tendency in (iv).

(b) Some uses of the 'inverted' sentence.
/a ded im ded/ = he's really dead.

There can be little doubt that, viewed as in (14), creole speech relative to Standard English would represent a decrease in the quantity of formal devices available for the organization and explicit treatment of subject-matter and in this respect it would be, by Bernstein's terms, a restricted code. This point will be further discussed subsequently. At the moment there is a related aspect of the matter which needs to be considered. This is that movement from the Creole end of the continuum towards Standard English would represent a progressive increase in the available formal devices of the kind mentioned. In learning Standard English, a Creole speaker or a speaker within the interaction area would experience this increase. That the latter might indeed be so has already been evidenced incidentally; three of the variables (12(ii) 'and'-linked clauses; 12(iii) length of clauses; 12(iv) quantity of speech) usually studied in the Bernstein type of investigations (cf. Bernstein 1962 (a and b), Lawton 1963 and 1964 and Robinson 1965) were noted to change from restricted to elaborated-code proportions as the learning of Standard English progressed. Further, the children studied in the group E_4/E_{40} of (10) possessed relatively less of 12(ii) and relatively more of 12(iii) and (iv) than the other children both at the beginning and end of the experimental period. The children of E_4/E_{40} came predominantly from relatively well-provided homes in an area where most parents, even though of working-class occupations, were well-paid employees of a large bauxite company. Thus the group in E_4/E_{40} of (10) would possess a background of middle-class influences not present in the other groups and this by the Bernstein theory might account for the advantage it displays in the variables stated. It would thus seem that some of the variables postulated as differentiating between social-class codal systems also differentiate creole from Standard English, and decrease or increase progressively over the range of the continuum, viewed either for the language community taken as a whole or for the individual passing from one point of the continuum to another through learning.

The preceding conclusions however, if valid, imply a contradiction in terms since codal differences, of the kind postulated in the Bernstein theory, should not be merely functions of different syntactic systems and be variable in the way they appear to be in the Creole/Standard English continuum. It is true that the individual syntactic and stylistic variables in (14) and (10) are only a very few of those considered in codal experiments so far, but as types they seem related to a large proportion of the variables postulated as differentiating codal systems (if we exclude for the moment certain lexical variables which appear different in nature, as will be indicated below). Thus, the assumed differences between restricted and elaborated codes may be analyzed into three main types:

(15)
   (i) differences between discrete morpho-syntactic systems.
   (ii) differences in the use made of the context of speech.
   (iii) differences in cognitive orientation.

These three kinds of difference interact and influence each other, but they are quite distinct, and failure to distinguish between them seems to be a difficulty in the theory of restricted and elaborated codes.

Differences between discrete morpho-syntactic systems (15(i)) are evident to some extent in the Creole/Standard English continuum, but not in the type of situation so far assumed in Bernstein's theory. It seems doubtful, however, that such differences can be ruled out in considering social class differences in language, certainly at this stage of our knowledge. Differences in use made of the context of speech have to do with the contrast between situations in which meaning must be explicitly elaborated and situations in which shared understanding allows or requires it to be left implicit. Most of the differences between restricted and elaborated codes belong to these two categories, or to the second alone. As shown earlier, the same differences are found between points in the creole language continuum and Standard English.

What is important about these two sets of differences is that they can be reduced and no doubt eliminated by the learning of linguistic conventions. All that these two sets of differences represent is an adjustment in the use of morpho-syntactic and lexical elements to correspond with adjustments in the use of speech-context. In a situation such as that assumed in Bernstein's theory, where there are no dialectal differences, the learning of these adjustments consists of learning to make a social adaptation. In situations of creole, Creole/Standard-English interaction, or other non-standard speech, the learning of these adjustments proceeds, or ought to proceed with appropriate teaching, as a consequence of learning the morpho-syntax of the standard language concurrently with the necessary situational adaptations. This would account for the indications in the work of Lawton (1963, 1964) and Robinson (1963), that working-class English children probably have an elaborated code available for selected use and that working-class children who were Robinson's subjects, evinced more signs of restricted coding in 'informal' uses of language than middle class children did in the same, but that differences between the two classes of children were inconclusive when the 'formal' use of language was considered. Differences of the last sort seem likely because the working class children in the last instance had probably learned the necessary situational adaptations for formal-language usage, but at the same time, being more habituated than middle-class children in using the context of speech for conveying meaning, their informal use of language betrayed this habituation.

The third kind of codal difference, cognitive orientations, is the most fundamental, if it exists. These are differences which may be expected to arise because members of different socio-cultural identifications may be differently habituated in the kinds of situations demanding language, the kind of life-experiences that language treats as content, and the ways in which such experiences are apprehended and cognitively mediated through language. The prime importance of the Bernstein theory is that it relates this kind of human disposition to behavioral norms of social class. It is not often realised, however, that in this respect the theory is an intra-cultural version of the Whorfian hypothesis, corresponding to one of the two types of linguistic relativity discussed in Hymes (1966). The theory is of this kind because it seeks to make inferences from language, which is directly evidenced, to cognitive processes which are not, and the relationship between the two is a part of a cyclical process such as is diagrammed in (16).

It is precisely the linguistic-relativity aspect that makes it necessary for differences to be analyzed as in (15). The assumed social-class codes approximate in form to the Creole/Standard-English continuum, but there one can postulate a range of discrete morpho-syntactic systems, each of which make as lesser or greater use of the context of speech. In such systems, a particular meaning or type of meaning that is mediated in one way in one system may

(16)

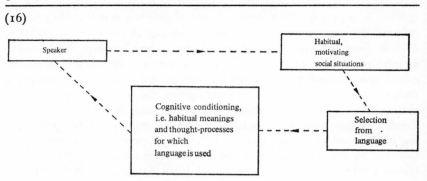

be mediated in another way, but with a minimum of morpho-syntactic variation, in another system. In such an assumed range of systems, it would be possible for different systems to give different functional loads to identical morpho-syntactic devices, or to eliminate or maintain different proportions of the natural redundancy of language; and these variations can occur without the possibility of doubt that the speakers involved are exercising equivalent linguistic capabilities, merely with different proportions of the two elements involved in the combination: 'morpho-syntax + context'. If our theory then makes inferences about the cognitive orientation of speakers, there must be observable criteria other than the two already mentioned. There must be independent evidence that differences in cognitive orientation are involved. I refer to this third set of necessary criteria as *semantic* criteria, because it seems that this kind of concern can only be answered by relating selections of language to the sum of meanings that the speaker aims to convey, or is in the habit of conveying or is at all capable of conveying.

In the codal studies cited already, the concern to study certain lexical variables shows that the relevance of semantic considerations has been felt. The question at issue in testing the theory of restricted and elaborated coding was never, it seems to me, the form of the language used, nor exclusively whether one form of code used the context of speech to a greater extent than the other, but rather *the cognitive purposes to which language is applied.* Yet the methods of such study up to now, while permitting some attention to semantic variables, seem to attempt the measurement of cognitive purposes mainly in terms of the presence or absence of lexical and morpho-syntactic elements without being able to make any measurement of the possible *semantic equivalence* of different combinations of lexis, morpho-syntax and the use of context. When the samples of speech tested for codal differences are, on the one hand, an extreme or intermediate form of creole and, on the other, Standard English, and are thus close enough to be compared as social-class codes, though differing sufficiently to justify a search for semantic equivalences of the kind mentioned, then the need for more penetrating methods of language analysis becomes evident. Until recently, methods of studying semantic relationships held little promise of providing efficient tools for the study of codal systems. Over the past few years, however, the work of Katz and Fodor (1964) and Chomsky (1965) in studying how selectional features of lexical items function in grammatical relationships, of Frake (1962) and Southworth (1967) in studying hierarchical systems in lexis, of Halliday (1967) in analysis of the cognitive and situational options available to speakers, and of Mathiot (1967, 1968) and Garvin, Brewer and Mathiot (1967), in the semantic analysis of lexis and the cognitive study of language hold out several new approaches which may be adaptable to the investigation of restricted and elaborated coding. Such investigation in relation to the West Indian creole language continuum is an urgent task, in view of the rapid changes being attempted by means of education in a society where the relationship between language and social class is so significant.

APPENDIX

A very short, selected list of Standard English features and the stratification of these that was apparent for two sets of Jamaican learners is shown in (17), where the plus sign within a column under the heading Stratification . . . indicates the stratification-class occupied by the relevant Standard English feature. Each pair of contrasts in 17 (i) to (iv) is meant to be taken as a unit of knowledge possessed by the speaker of Standard English, so that each pair is regarded as a single feature occupying a place in the stratification. 17 (v) and (vi) give examples of phrase-structure combinations which are meant to be taken in the same sense as the examples preceding. The first set of learners, consisting of 7-year-old children are some of the subjects in the experiment outlined on pp. 379–382; the second set consists of an illustrative, typical class of training college students taught by myself in 1963. From (17) it is possible to observe the stratification for each set of learners separately and also to observe the changes attributable to the process of education and age-differences between younger and older learners. On the whole, progress in education and in age leads to a movement from D towards A within the stratification; it will be shown subsequently that this same movement occurs in the individual learner over a period of time and is not just a phenomenon observable between different groups.

(17)

Examples of standard features (Note: *con.* = 'in contrast with')	Rural children in the first grade of primary school at age 7 years				1st-year teacher training college students, with local educational qualifications only at age 18 – 20 years			
	Stratification of features as in illustration (6)							
	A	B	C	D	A	B	C	D
(i) $\left\{ \begin{array}{l} /(r)st/\ con./s/ \\ /nd/\quad con./n/ \end{array} \right\}$ /Vowel –			+				+ ——	
(ii) (a) 'I' *con.* 'me'		+ ——				+ ——		
(b) 'me' *con.* 'my'	+ ——				+ ——			
(c) 'John' *con.* 'John's'	+ ——				+ ——			
(iii) $\left\{ \begin{array}{l} \text{'who'} \\ \text{'which'} \end{array} \right\}$ *con.* 'what'		+ —				+ ——		
(iv) [PRESENT *con.* PAST]/-Verb								
(a) PAST→ $\left\{ \begin{array}{l} \text{Affix } /d/, /t/ \\ \text{Internal} \\ \text{change} \end{array} \right\}$		+ ——				+ ——		
(b)				+				+ ——
(v)								
(a) AUX→ PAST + Modal + 'have' + en				+				+ ——
(b) NP→ Pre-Art. + Art. + Adj. + Noun	+ ———————				+ ——			
(vi)								
(a) S₁→The man liveø in the tree	+ ———————				+ ——			
(b) S₂→The man* stealø meø food	+ * ——				+ ——			
(c) S₃→The S₁ +man PAST + come + ⤷T-adjectivalization + PLACE + TIME + PURPOSE + S₂— T-Purpose Infinitive ← Example: 'The man living in the tree came here yesterday to steal my food.'				+				+ ——

* Indicates that the particular lexical item is responsible for the position occupied by the whole combination in the stratification. Creole /tiif/ = 'steal'.

(18)

	Samples	Means compared	Standard error	Level of significance
Criterion (i)	E_1/E_{10}	0.647/0.140	0.130	0.01
	E_2/E_{20}	0.666/0.200	0.115	0.01
	E_3/E_{30}	0.630/0.186	0.163	0.02
	E_4/E_{40}	0.347/0.164	0.111	0.10 (not)
	C_1/C_{10}	0.586/0.480	0.093	Not
Criterion (ii)	E_1/E_{10}	0.621/0.011	0.089	.01
	E_2/E_{20}	0.196/0.032	0.085	.05
	E_3/E_{30}	0.628/0.112	0.171	0.01
	E_4/E_{40}	0.299/0	0.128	.05
	C_1/C_{10}	0.250/0.326	0.084	Not
Criterion (iii)	E_1/E_{10}	2.78/4.91	0.75	0.01
	E_2/E_{20}	3.48/5.15	0.53	0.01
	E_3/E_{30}	2.92/4.40	0.62	0.05
	E_4/E_{40}	4.95/5.30	0.91	Not
	C_1/C_{10}	4.27/4.48	0.42	Not
Criterion (iv)	E_1/E_{10}	31.5/ 53.6	8.99	0.05
	E_2/E_{20}	24.1/ 70.6	12.21	0.01
	E_3/E_{30}	21.0/ 50.8	10.49	0.01
	E_4/E_{40}	50.6/114.9	25.75	0.05
	C_1/C_{10}	48.8/ 42.0	8.34	Not

REFERENCES

Bailey, Beryl 1962. *A language guide to Jamaica*, New York, Research Institute for the Study of Man

1964. 'Some problems involved in the language teaching situation in Jamaica', *Social dialects and language learning*, ed. by Roger Shuy, pp. 105–11, Champaign, National Council of Teachers of English

1966. *Jamaican Creole syntax*, Cambridge, Cambridge University Press

[1968] 'Jamaican Creole: can dialect boundaries be defined'. Paper presented at the Conference on pidginization and creolization, Mona, April 1968

Bernstein, Basil 1961. 'Social structure, language and learning', *Educational Research* 8(3):163–76

1962a. 'Linguistic codes, hesitation phenomena and intelligence', *Language and Speech* 5:31–46

1962b. 'Social class, linguistic codes and grammatical elements', *Language and Speech* 5:221–40

1964. 'Family role systems, socialization and communication', Paper presented at Conference on cross-cultural research, University of Chicago

1965. 'A socio-linguistic approach to learning', *Social Science Survey*, ed. by J. Gould, London, Pelican

1966. 'Elaborated and restricted codes, an outline', *Explorations in sociolinguistics*, ed. by S. Lieberson, *Sociological Inquiry* 36:254–61

Biddle, B. and E. Thomas (eds.) 1966. *Role theory*, New York, John Wiley

Cassidy, F. 1961. *Jamaica talk*, New York, Macmillan

Cassidy, F., and R. Le Page 1967. *A dictionary of Jamaican English*, Cambridge, Cambridge University Press

Chomsky, Noam 1965. *Aspects of the theory of syntax*, Cambridge, Mass., M.I.T. Press

Craig, Dennis, R. 1966. 'Teaching English to Jamaican Creole speakers', *Language Learning* 16(1–2)

   1967a. 'Some early results of learning a second dialect', *Language Learning* 17(3–4)

   1967b. *An experiment in teaching English*, Mona, University of the West Indies, Institute of Education

DeCamp, David [1968]. 'A generative analysis of the post-creole continuum', Paper presented at the Conference on pidginization and creolization of languages, Mona, April 1968

Frake, C. O. 1962. 'The ethnographic study of cognitive systems', *Anthropology and human behavior*, ed. by T. Gladwin and W. C. Sturtevant, 72–85, Washington, D.C., Anthropological Society of Washington

Fries, C. C. 1963. *Teaching and learning English as a foreign language*, Ann Arbor, University of Michigan Press

Garvin, Paul, J. Brewer, and M. Mathiot 1967. 'Predication-typing,' *Language* 43(2), pt. II

Halliday, M. A. K. 1967. 'Notes on transitivity and theme in English', *Journal of Linguistics* 3 (1–2)

Hornby, A. S. 1950. 'The situational approach in language teaching', *Teaching English as a second language*, ed. by H. B. Allen, New York, McGraw-Hill

Hymes, Dell 1966. 'Two types of linguistic relativity', *Sociolinguistics*, ed. by W. Bright, pp. 114–158, The Hague, Mouton

Katz, J. J. and J. A. Fodor 1964. 'The structure of a semantic theory', *The structure of language*, ed. by J. A. Fodor and J. J. Katz, Englewood Cliffs, N.J., Prentice-Hall

Labov, William 1963. 'The social motivation of a sound change', *Word* 19: 273–309

   1964. 'Stages in the acquisition of English in New York City', *Social dialects and language learning*, ed. by Roger Shuy, Champaign, National Council of Teachers of English

   1966. *The social stratification of English in New York City*, Washington, D.C., Center for Applied Linguistics

Lawton, David 1963. Social class differences in language development. *Language and Speech* 6:120–43

   1964. 'Social class language differences in group discussions', *Language and Speech* 7:182–204

Le Page, Robert 1957–58. 'General outlines of Creole English in the British Caribbean, *Orbis* 6:373–91; 7:54–64

Le Page, R. and D. DeCamp 1960. 'Jamaican Creole' (*Creole Language Studies I*, pt. 2), New York, Macmillan

Mathiot, Madeleine 1967. 'The place of the dictionary in linguistic description', *Language* 43:703–24

   1968. *An approach to the cognitive study of language* (Publications of the

Research Center in Anthropology, Folklore, and Linguistics), Bloomington, Indiana University

Robinson, W. P. 1965. 'The elaborated code in working class language', *Language and Speech* 8(4): 243–52

Southworth, Franklin, C. 1967. 'A model of semantic structure', *Language* 43:342–61

Stewart, W. A. (ed.) 1964. *Non-standard speech and the teaching of English*, Washington, D.C., Center for Applied Linguistics

THE CREOLIST AND THE STUDY
OF NEGRO NON-STANDARD
DIALECTS IN THE CONTINENTAL
UNITED STATES

J. L. DILLARD

To the apparently increasing number of areas with which the creolist can profitably concern himself, amply documented in this volume, must be added that of the study of Non-Standard Negro dialects in the continental United States – an area which, despite the clearly creole nature of Gullah and of one variety of Louisiana French, has been until recently almost exclusively the domain of the dialect geographer.[1] It is, as a matter of fact, no longer necessary to establish the significance of the creolist for American Negro dialect studies; Stewart 1967 and 1968 and Bailey 1965 do that quite well, and Loflin 1967 contributes in an indirect fashion by demonstrating the deep structure difference between Negro Non-Standard English (NNS) and Standard English (StE). There remain, of course, individual items of structural resemblance which have hardly been treated at all.[2] It seems, however, that, if serious work on the functioning of NNS in an at least partly alien culture is to be done without such interruptions as the cancelling of research grants, a vast bulk of comparative work is necessary. With only a few exceptions, only creolists seem capable of doing this kind of work.[3]

It is of some theoretical and of great practical importance to establish the validity of relationships implied in terms like code switching, diglossia, etc., when the varieties involved are not so clearly different, on the surface at least, as in the familiar treatments. For political more than for scholarly reasons, it will probably remain impossible to do very much until acceptance has been won for the concept of different grammatical systems and different historical backgrounds for NNS and StE. Here the creolist, with his familiarity with grammatical patterns which are strange to the dialect geographer in the United States, is apparently the only one likely to make a significant contribution. It is quite obvious when a speaker of both Sranan Tongo and English switches from one to the other; but some knowledge of the historical relationships may be necessary to establish switching behavior on the part of those speakers who are masters of NNS and parts of StE. The experience of Turner (1949) stands as a warning to investigators who may be misled by such switching behavior. Turner, in addition to establishing almost incidentally the creole nature of Gullah, was able, through his rapport with the Sea Islanders, to obtain hard evidence of the persistence of a mass of forms of African origin. These forms had eluded earlier writers who had naively dismissed Gullah as just the sort of 'bad English' one would expect such (inferior) people to have. Unfortunately, the real feat which Turner performed has been misinterpreted as discovery of the dialect itself; this misinterpretation, in turn, has supported the erroneous belief that Gullah developed in isolation. Actually, as Turner himself carefully pointed out (pp. 5–14), Gullah had been known and (unprofessionally) studied for a long time. It was the very contact with – not isolation from – StE which enabled the Gullah speakers to engage in code-switching enough to fool non-professional investigators (although not enough to make anyone think that the Sea Islanders spoke Standard English).

In the absence of clear lines of separation of the two varieties, Reisman's suggestion that one exploit the ambiguities resulting from the type of dual value system frequently encountered in the Caribbean seems especially pertinent (see his précis of work on Antigua, this volume). Although extensive systematic work has not been done with NNS, a few occurrences indicate the possibilities. A quasi-bidialectal 12-year-old boy, confronted, almost by accident, with the written sentence *Here go a man and a lady*, refused to say 'what it means' until speakers were specified, and then gave two interpretations, different in syntax and semantics, the statement itself being repeated with phonological variation:

(a) [hIə^(or hIr) go . . .], paraphrased 'A man and a lady are walking here', in the context of his mother (a university professor) as speaker;

(b) [hIgo . . .], translated 'Here are a man and a lady', in the context of his playmates ('disadvantaged' Negro boys), as speakers.

Research on any such matter may be hindered by the conditions that make it possible that any researcher on Afro-American varieties, whether Afrikaans, Haitian Creole, or Negro Non-Standard, may be subject to political reprisals. In some cases, like the three above, even recognition of the historical background may cause resentment; in Hawaii, according to Loban 1968, it is all right to report the differences in Hawaiian 'Pidgin' but not to treat it with respect. Establishment attitudes are often that these languages or dialects derive from Dutch, Northern French in some super-archaic version, or Standard (presumably British) English by some mysterious process which is known as Selective Cultural Differentiation (McDavid 1967) and which both explains historical divergence and is synonymous with it. There is the added complication that a certain Romanticism with regard to African survivals, which has colored some of the best work (Herskovits 1941) but which has in the past constituted the only opposition to the Establishment position, easily rubs off on the creolist. It provides a convenient straw man which is easily knocked down by defenders of the Received Position. What is being said that is really new is hardly being heard.

Currently, transformational-generative theory, itself potentially the greatest ally which this approach can have, provides some areas of apparent conflict. This is especially true of that part of the theory which inclines to relate dialects of the 'same' language by low-level (essentially phonological) rules. No real conflict exists, however, once linguists within the transformational-generative approach recognize the 'quasi-foreign language' nature of the problem. NNS should disturb the 'low-level' relationship between mainstream English dialects no more than the special case of Papiamento would affect the pattern of Iberian-derived Spanish dialects. Loflin (1967b) points out the difference between the 'quest for, and justification of, formal and substantive universals' and the formulation of Standard English as a 'super grammar' from which NNS (his NNE) must be derived (p. 24). NNS must surely relate to a universal grammar in the same way that Standard English does – not derive from universal grammar at an extra remove *through* Standard English. In this way, the creolists' fierce defense of the languages they study as full peers of other languages with different kinds of historical development can be seen to be fully compatible with the new emphasis on language universals. Whatever psychological universals concerning language acquisition and language competence can be abstracted from transformational-generative study of Standard English simply apply in the same way and to the same degree to NNS (and to the creole languages).

Perhaps because American Negro speakers have their own folk taxonomies of speech and language swamped by the lore of the schools more completely than do, say, the residents of Antigua studied by Reisman, the 'community's own theory of code repertoire and code switching' (Hymes 1967) is even less well known in the United States than on the islands. Even the Black Separatist movement has, apparently, found as yet no formal place for NNS, preferring to stress ethnic slang or to organize classes in Swahili. An occasional cosmopolitan Ph.D., nevertheless, is aware enough of his own switching between NNS and StE to teach it to a child who had been born overseas; and when an article on the Washington project on urban language appeared in the Washington *Post*, a caller proudly demonstrated his switching ability to me over the telephone. Only one community term for such ability has ever been suggested to me: *dentist*; it is said to be in wide use in at least part of the Washington black community. Because of the submerged and unrecognized nature of NNS, conventional terms such as *interpreter* and *translator* would obviously not be felt to be applicable. *Dentist*, with its suggestion of oral proficiency, really is not half bad.

As long as pidgin or creole characteristics – or African language characteristics with the possible exception of vocabulary items[4]–are taken up one by one, it is possible, with the requisite exercise of ingenuity, to trace them to something in the present or past of the standard language, especially if one utilizes varieties of the European language widely separated in space and time, thus increasing one's chances. This is not to say that there are not dialect features from English, etc., in pidgins and creoles that come as a surprise to the linguist who knows only the standard language, or that there is not a great deal that is controversial and still to be learned about specific historical provenience. It is to say, however, that more ingenuity seems to have been exercised in providing European origins than energy been spent in mastering relevant African data. In effect, only one term of the comparison – the European – has been at all thoroughly explored. Turner (1949) and Daelemann's work (see précis, this volume) indicate how much of importance there is to be done.

The inconclusiveness of other evidence seems to give special importance to such treatments of the verb system of NNS as Loflin (1967) and Stewart (1966). Even as complete a treatment of an individual item (the zero copula) as Ferguson provides for comparative purposes seems to leave things where they were with regard to language relationships and language differences. If both the standard European languages and the presumably influential or analogical 'exotic' languages have conditions under which either a copula must be used or contraction is permitted – corresponding to those conditions in the creoles and NNS under which some lexico-phonemic realization of the copula is obligatory – what is the advantage of explaining the creole or NNS form either by one more phonological rule (deletion of the contracted form, presumably) or by a history of creolization and decreolization? Where is either monogenesis or polygenesis? The standoff which existed for some time has apparently been reached again.

The creolist is so accustomed to this particular kind of standoff, insofar as any one grammatical structure or etymology is concerned, that he would unhesitatingly proceed to the comparison of other features – not, after all, a linguistically unorthodox procedure. In the case of the copula, he would certainly consider features other than those paralleling the contractable and non-contractable features of Standard English. Part of this would be due to the realization that (e.g.) Haitian Creole (HC) has at least some syntactic features which are similar (Goodman 1964:58), and that it would be absurd to derive the HC zero copulas from contracted StE verbs.

Fortunately, it is not necessary to look very far in search of the kind of fuller information needed to resolve this particular standoff. The forms of English *be* associated with V-*ing* in the StE 'present progressive' are often considered to be related to the copula *be* and may even be considered to be identical (Stewart 1968: n. 4).
In addition to

StE	NNS
He is good	He good

we have

He is being good	He bein' good
He is eating pie	He eatin' pie

Considered as 'present' (or non-past) forms, these look like more proof of the same thing – *is* in StE before V-*ing* is as contractable as the copula which links noun and adjective. The important complication is that NNS *He bein' good* and *He eatin' pie* are not necessarily present (or non-past).[5] Stewart 1968 cites NNS

We was eatin' – an'·we drinkin', too

corresponding to StE

We were eating – and drinking, too.

Contraction as a source for the NNS sentence would presumably have had to involve the insertion of the pronoun *we*. Even working from some kind of compounding of

We were eating. We were drinking.

there would still have to be *were* in the source, and contraction of *were* is surely not a feature of StE.[6] The possibility of treating zero copula as a further phonological step after contraction seems to be eliminated by sentences like

(1) I mean Doris makin' a man wif some stupid little eye glasses

or

Doris stupid.

This is not to suggest that the relationship between StE contracted copula and NNS zero copula is not significant. If the creole which preceded NNS had a more restricted set of overt copulas, and if a great deal of the behavior of NNS speakers, particularly older informants, is influenced by StE, the imitation of the overt copula may be much easier where StE does not permit contraction. When the speaker of NNS does produce overt copula (whether the same as the StE form or, as in very many cases, a different form) in an 'unexposed' position, the simplest and indeed almost the only explanation – without violence to the grammatical system – is that of code switching, from NNS to StE. Stewart (1964) and Bailey (1965) have said so, and have evoked a storm of protest – presumably because of the close relationship between the varieties involved. The relationship, however, is no closer than that between Urban Haitian French and Urban Creole treated by Stewart (1962a). Apparently, it is all right to write of code switching in the 'exotic' environment of Port-au-Prince, but unacceptable to find it under the noses of researchers who have devoted their professional lives to the non-grammatical study of dialects.

The concept is certainly not new, even as applied to NNS; Lanier (1879) used it (although not, of course, with the linguist's terminology) to explain his intentional inconsistency in writing Negro dialect, and specifically attributed it to Negro speech after the Civil War.

Looked at otherwise than as a deviation from Standard English, NNS V-*in'* is not a present or present progressive tense. Neither Stewart (1966) nor Loflin (1967) analyzed it as such, and their approaches differed greatly. There are frequent utterances like

(2) An' when I come back they came back, they was outa school an' so I comin' down an' she out there blabbin' her mouth told her sister I was playin' hookey from school.

where both *I comin'* and *she out there* are past from the viewpoint of StE.[7] Or consider *we fishin'* in

(3) . . . an' one time we got through an' we fishin' an' then we went back to the tent an' didn't come back out.

In the range of sentences offered by Stewart (1968), it would have been perfectly possible to include

We sat dere an' we drinkin'.

Thus, to deal uncritically in terms of deletions may be to miss the grammatical point completely; it may lead one to miss the stylistic shift in *she was* [wɪ] . . . or *we was* [wɪ] . . . ; and it does not allow for the simple insight into incomplete or inaccurate code-switching which is easily attained by other means for such well-attested (see, again, Botkin 1945 or any one of thousands of literary sources) forms as *She am drinking*.

Given the strong evidence of the forms presented by Stewart (1967 and 1968) and the somewhat weaker evidence of such overt statements as are recorded,[8] tending toward proof of a different history for NNS and StE, there is a pressing need to determine exactly how much NNS resembles the English Creoles of the present and has resembled their earlier stages in the past. So new is this line of investigation that even fragmentary evidence continues to be of interest. Forms quoted by Craig (this volume) like

/wer hi iz/

from Jamaican Creole (JMC) may be paralleled by NNS

(4) What your name is?

Since

(5) Arthur, Arthur, where you?

is an attested form, it seems fairly safe to assert that

Arthur, Arthur, where you is?
Where he is?

are also grammatical. A major difference is that the Washington youngster who produced (4) would not under any conditions produce

/we i de/

but, in spontaneous recordings and therefore apparently without any special urging, will produce

What is your name?
What's your name?
Where is you?
Where are you?

If he is young enough, he will also produce

Yes, Im is.
Yes, Im am.

and he will frequently use the copula marker or a homophonous form as a generalized question marker:

(6) Is you in Shirley's room?
Is dey been dere?

The same little Washington girl (age group 6–8), said to the same addressee, within seconds of each other:

(7) You ain' know who Brenda Weston is.
(8) You don' know who is Brenda Weston.

Apparently, the speech of Washington Negro children has the same continuum characteristics (DeCamp 1968: 27–8) as those cited from Jamaica by Craig, but at a 'higher' level. They frequently produce utterances which are identical, or nearly identical, with StE, and they can fool a linguist who is obviously meddling in their speech affairs; compare, again, Reisman on Antigua. But they apparently never say

/a fi mi buk dat/
/a mi buk dat/
etc.

If Gullah of the Sea Islands, Georgia and South Carolina is considered as the 'lowest' level (thereby being the only instance in which the conventional geographical ordering of dialects has much relevance for NNS), the continuum analogy is even better – although still not perfect. The position of any speaker on the continuum is complicated by age- and class-grading in Washington, but there is some evidence (Dillard 1968a) that the same is true in the West Indies. There are enough apparent correlations to hold out the very promising hope that social grading and decreolization might profitably be studied concurrently, in the same speech community.

It happens that neither creolized varieties nor decreolization is unfamiliar within the boundaries of the continental United States. Morgan 1959 contains at least rudimentary study of decreolization along with more orthodox structural study of Louisiana French Creole. Commercial recordings[9] and accounts by former residents of Charleston indicate that there are clearly varieties of Gullah in different stages of decreolization, although no such indication is to be found in the Linguistic Atlas materials. But the really interesting phenomena are those which are localized in age grades rather than in geographic areas.

To ride a mock horse a bit further,[10] what would happen if the syntactic rules of Haitian Creole were hooked onto the lexicon and (for the sake of argument) phonology of Standard English? Well, a Haitian woman working in the American Embassy in Port-au-Prince said to me, in the context of discussing whether a certain Dr X Dillard might have been confused with Dr J. L. Dillard

He a woman doctor.

The interpretation 'The man is a gynecologist' is hardly possible, since the receptionist had no way of knowing that I was not one. Clearly the StE equivalent would be something like 'The doctor is female'. Here, zero copula and absence of pronoun gender have their obvious source in the syntax of HC. (I refuse to admit the possibility that the woman was simplifying her English in order to enable me to understand.) Compare these sentences from Washington pre-schoolers:

(9) He a nice little girl. (Answer to question, 'Why do you like Shirley?' A check revealed that there was only one Shirley – a girl – at this summer school project.)
(10) I don't know her name. (Said of a male linguist.)

For more such examples, see Stewart 1968. Among older speakers, the only evidence of this structural characteristic is a kind of 'stumbling' under emotional stress which does not seem to be accounted for by the invoking of the magic terms *competence* and *performance*. Craig has called this variable factor in JMC 'no sex in pronouns'.

Somewhat less sporadic, and not so completely confined to the lower age grades but still characteristic of them, are structures like

(11) Me help you?
(12) Her paintin' wif a spoon.

The context makes it clear that (12) is not a gerund with its subject. As a matter of fact, the occurrence of this construction among younger Negro children is now widely recognized among workers with this dialect (Stewart 1968; Loban 1968).

Even less sporadic, and generally characteristic of somewhat older children (although the 14–15 year-old informant to whom a vast amount of attention was given on the Washington project did not use such a form in working with the linguists) is the use of the undifferentiated pronoun, especially *he*, for possession. This is apparent evidence of what Craig calls 'No case in pronouns'. Although perhaps 'low level' grammatically, this feature is bizarre enough from the viewpoint of StE to attract a great deal of attention – and to motivate at least one authoritative pronouncement that nobody would say it. In nouns, there are abundant parallel cases; the notorious *Mary hat* has become known as the structure which causes a Washington, D.C. teacher to draw a picture of a hat and of Mary, in order to give her students visual proof that the hat belonged to Mary! Pedagogy, too, might profit from an occasional creole insight.

With some allowances for the greater degree of decreolization (or 'leveling' or 'merger') in the United States, most of the items in Craig's list, or from a comparable list like those of Herskovits 1936 or Stewart 1968, can be matched from NNS. We might profitably substitute 'non-redundant plurals' (*sixteen bottle* but *the bottles*) for Craig's 'associative plurals'. 'Reduplication' is the most problematic of all. There is some not entirely conclusive evidence from recordings and from my personal experience, but nothing consonant with rigorous proof.

'No marking to indicate tense' can hardly be applied to NNS, but there are certainly great differences between its use of the category of tense and that of StE; any treatment of the NNS auxiliary must make tense optional, or perhaps dominated by another category like aspect. There is the rather clear evidence of utterances like those in Bailey 1968 and the following:

(13) She said . . . She kep' on laughin'. An' den we say, 'Nikki, we can't sleep down dere in a tub an' bathroom an' everythin' else.' An' she say . . .

(See also note 5.) Superficially related is the 'difficulty with *-ed* verb endings' reported by numberless teachers and reasonably well documented in Loban (1966).

'No subject-verb concord' is the most obvious of all, having led to McDavid's (1967) notorious comparative map of East Anglia.[11] So far as I know, every serious linguist who has described the verb system of NNS has concluded that *he go*, is not the grammatical equivalent of StE *he goes*. There must, then, be something more than the phonological process of deletion of final *-s* involved. In like manner, the classification 'lack of subject-verb concord' is for every creolist merely a preliminary to a casting of the verb system into categories different from those of StE (French, Portuguese, etc.).

There is abundant indication in my corpus concerning a supernumerary structure, the large number of forms which are transcribed by *a*, as in

I'a draw a man.

Transcription practices on the Washington project, strongly influenced by the systematic phonological theories of the transformational-generative school, resulted in the use of /l/ for this schwa-like vowel when a phonemic notation was utilized, and even of orthographic -ll, on the assumption that the sentence was a form of *I'll* (*I will*) *draw a man*. The transcriptional practice worked sometimes, but came a real cropper in

(14) Well, my father, he'*ll* talkin' bout get some gloves an' things, little boxin' gloves.

Read with the schwa vowel – among several other sentences, real and spurious in NNS, in an attempt to disguise intentions – to two quasi-bidialectal informants, this sentence produced acceptance from one with the explanation 'it means he *was* talking', and scornful rejection from the other (whose post-creole continuum soared higher into Standard English) on the grounds that 'Nobody talks like that'. The analysis as *l*, assuming a derivation from StE *will*, also is a bit stretched in

(15) Ima put a sweater on her.

The forms *Ia*, *Ima*, *Imo* occur with great frequency in texts from younger children, especially from the small girls in the 6–8 age range which furnished most of these examples. In this case, the girls were put to drawing with crayons and paper and naturally proceeded to talk about what they were drawing and would draw. (It is impossible to choose among these two alternatives (were ...ing, would) merely by listening to the recordings.) These forms (along with, e.g. *Im put*, from 5–6 year olds) function as *purposive futures*, in other words, some of the time. There is an almost inevitable tendency for the linguist to treat these forms as reductions of *I am going to*, despite the problem of the variation between *Ia~Ima* and its suggestion of the variation *I is~Im is*. There are, of course, in the English Creoles verb forms (*de*, *di*, *duh*, *a*, etc.) which can stray into a kind of future time reference although not basically futures. (It was apparently something like this that led Bailey (1965) to analyze the *be* forms from the speech of the 14-year old Harlem boy in Warren Miller's *The Cool World* as futures, whereas other linguists who have worked on NNS have not so described them.)

Stewart (1938, n. 25) compares the 'preverbal *a*- in some southern Negro dialects' to 'preverbal *a* in J[amaican] C[reole]', which he calls 'a modern reduction of older *da*, obviously related historically to GUL[lah] *duh* and SRA [Saramaccan] *de*'. It is tempting to see at least a relic of this preverb in the Washington forms, and perhaps in the very widespread *you a lie*. (Much more data than can be indicated here emerged from the Washington project, but little could be done in the way of analysis.)

In more than grammatical structure there are parallels between NNS and less-than-deepest JC – or HC, if a not entirely facetious comparison be kept up for dramatic effect. For example, Craig (this volume) reports, 'It was noticed in one or two instances that boys tended to associate femininity or lack of toughness with "more English" forms of speech.' Stewart (1962a) clearly shows an equivalent association of Creole with masculinity and French with femininity in Port-au-Prince, and he has frequently pointed out that the same is true in Washington. In fact, a writer with an entirely different purpose in mind (Hurst 1965) inadvertently points up the truth of the last assertion when his graphs show (although he suppresses the discussion in his text) *femininity* as a personality factor in acquiring StE for both his male and female subjects. The curves in Loban (1966), which show progressively fewer 'errors' in StE for Negro boys from 7 to about 14 and then an increase for boys around 14, undoubtedly reflect the use of NNS forms for a display of masculinity (something like Reisman's 'dramatic low status assertion' for Antigua) on the part of boys reaching puberty.

A matter that Craig seems almost apologetic about – the age of his inform-ants – seems rather one of the very strongest points of his presentation. The question of age-grading is very probably going to be one of the most important socio-linguistic topics for post-creolization communities, and there is no surplus of data from very young informants. Stewart 1965 awakened such interest in age-grading in the NNS community as is to be found; Stewart 1968a discusses the same subject in broader terms. Dillard 1968a hazards the guess that age-grading will be most marked where there is language contact between a pidgin, creole, or post-creolized variety of a language and the standard variety of that same language – that is, more age-grading (overt at least) in Jamaica, Antigua, urban Port-au-Prince, or the Washington ghetto than in Dominica, rural Haiti, the Suriname bush, or the Gullah-speaking Sea Islands before Emancipation. It may be that children speak the 'deepest' creole. Here is surely one of the most important and most ignored of socio-linguistic topics, and pidgin-creole communities may be the most advantage-ous places in which to work on it. Needless to say, such work can be done within the United States only under the condition that the difference between the two varieties – something more basic than differences involving the pro-nunciation of post-vocalic /r/ and the choice between *dragon fly* and *snake doctor* – is recognized. Probably it would be preferable for pilot studies to be done in the Caribbean and then followed up in the United States, considering the more favorable political atmosphere for research in the West Indies.

This is one of the several areas in which pilot studies by creolists, especially in the Caribbean but perhaps also in Hawaii, might point the way to signifi-cant work on American Negro dialects. It is felt that the creolists have the most significant contribution to make to such dialect work inside the con-tinental United States; more conventional dialectologists apparently just can't see the structures which one with even a modicum of exposure to the English Creoles spots automatically. Obviously, it is not going to occur to the linguist who does not know the structural significance of *He tell me say* . . . (it has even been confusedly regarded as a 'deletion' from *He tell me to say!*) to test for the significance of the frequent occurrence of locutions like *He tell me, he say* . . . in the 'decreolized' community.

There are, of course, not many creolists – and plenty of work to keep them busy elsewhere. But unless they involve themselves, the study of American Negro dialects is in danger of being left to a discipline which Hymes (1967:9) describes thus:

Dialectology in the United States until recently was almost an abstraction of language from interaction with its immediate social setting, having primarily a geographical and reconstructive orientation of little relevance to contemporary American society.

Even this evaluation is charitable. To *abstraction from interaction with its immediate social setting* Hymes might have added *separation from all grammatical considerations*; and *reconstructive orientation* apparently refers to the attempt to trace all American English forms back to some corner of England. That attempt has resulted in perhaps the greatest mess in the annals of historical linguistics.

Somewhat more recently, adherents of the dominant school of American dialect geography have offered ecological explanations for NNS forms which border on the creation of myths. Even if no attempt to establish a causal connection is made, the concentration of studies in the larger cities at a time when there is much talk of urban problems in the United States could imply to the unwary that the dialect differences are the result of urban blight. Stewart (1968) now provides a convincing demonstration to the contrary, and it seems incredible that anyone could give an even fairly careful reading to such a well-known Southern author as Sidney Lanier without noticing that Negro dialect differences and Negro code switching behavior have been recognized since long before the period of Negro migration to the North and to the cities. A quick impression of how widespread in rural areas are the dialect characteristics being found in the big city ghettos today can be gained by looking in works like Botkin (1945), where Negro residents in all the scattered Southern states are quoted as using just those grammatical structures. Works like Botkin and sociologist Johnson (1934) provide – because the authors, with all their innocence of phonology, transcribed more or less what their interviewees said rather than presenting questionnaires which were biased toward the belief that it is only necessary to discover certain items of vocabulary and of pronunciation – better evidence as to how Negroes talked than any of the works of the dialect geographers. An occasional dissertation by one of the latter is usable, almost in spite of itself, because texts appended to the dissertation proper show the relevant grammatical features. Treatments of the geographical distribution of items like *rain worm* and *whiffletree* (or, in an especially daring modernization, the name of some part of the automobile) are never of any real use.

If the dialect of the American Negro who makes eighty dollars a week is the *result* of deprivation – 'communication barriers' brought on by poverty and slum-dwelling – what must be true of the Haitian peasant who makes eighty dollars a year? Would he not truly be speaking, in the words of *The Voice* of St Lucia, 'A patois . . . not a language'? If one's language has an unusual amount of variation but nothing like code switching because there is no second code, is there not linguistic evidence for one's 'unreliability' or even 'shiftlessness'? Does one automatically acquire copulas with increased income and attendant respectability – overnight in the case of a sudden inheritance? If the historical antecedents which we grant to any human language be denied to Afro-American dialects – if they are indeed only the result of skewing by the American caste system (McDavid 1965) – what conclusion can be drawn? No one seems to have summoned them yet, but the spectres of stereotypes about sub-human language lurk in the shadows. We may yet hear, 'Come closer to the middle class so I can see what you're saying'.

NOTES

1 Dell Hymes professed to like my whimsical summary of the paper presented at the Conference: 'My creolist can lick your dialect geographer.' The comment is included, more or less at his request. I am grateful to Professor Hymes for several suggestions concerning the revision of this paper. It would be impossible to estimate the extent of my debt in all these matters to William A. Stewart. Responsibility for the materials, and particularly for mistakes, remains of course my own.
2 One of these is clearly the use of *say* as a clause introducer, particularly in the structure *N tell Pn say* . . . The occurrence is apparently so restricted except in Gullah, where occurrence with a large number of verbs (*e.g., N tink say* 'N thinks that') is possible. Both Stewart and I observed this structure to be limited to somewhat older informants in Washington, D.C., although *N ran out the house say*, which occurs in one of the transcriptions, may be a blending of this and another construction. Examples are everywhere – except, of course, in the Dialect Atlas. Alan Lomax's 1952 field recordings reproduced on United Artists UAL 4027 contain an example from adult informants; my tapes made in Beaumont, Texas, in 1965–6, with adults, contain many; so do such unprejudiced transcriptions as those of Botkin 1945. Joel Chandler Harris's *Brer Rabbit says, sezzee* . . . seems suspiciously similar to me. For Pidgin and Creole use of the same structure, see any treatment (e.g. Cassidy 1961, Schneider 1964).
3 See the unpublished proposals of the Urban Language Study, done in 1966 and early 1967, and the subsequent history of that project.
4 Of course, unless some limits are placed, even the most obvious vocabulary items are not safe. The most extreme case known to me comes from a Spanish dictionary of Fernando Poo pidgin (1938), which derives *poto poto* from English *putty putty*. The latter compound, is of course, not unknown in Standard

English; about 1940, a Tin Pan Alley song had the line 'Cement mixer, putty putty'. Etymologies of this sort could open up a whole new field of pidgin studies! They recall Turner's discovery (1949) that, whereas an earlier investigator had taken the Gullah word for 'fat' to be a corruption of English 'done for fat', commenting amusedly on the folk psychology revealed in considering a fat man to be done for, the Gullah form was actually *da fa*, with a clear African etymology (tones and all); the earlier investigator's informant had simply been glossing it for his interlocutor: '*da fa* "fat" '.

5 Neither, for that matter, is *He good*. The meaning is rather like that cited for English Creole by Craig, except that *John was sick* is widely used when there is some explicit reason for placing the action in the past (a category of Tense is optional at sentence level). See the locative construction in (2) below. The NNS zero copula, like the base form of the verb, may frequently be translated into StE as a present tense; but there are cases in which such translation is inaccurate: 'Her husband came [kĕy] home an' drink some of it and left his [lehf Iz] dime an went back to work.'

6 For the sake of argument, it might be maintained that *was* in 'He was eating – and he was drinking, too' has a White Non-Standard contracted form spelled *uz* in dialect fiction. This, impressionistically considered, does not seem to be the same kind of contraction. And in any case *were* remains unaccounted for.

7 The pull of StE on the analysis is so strong that one linguist on the Washington project, in the early stages of work, presented a list of allomorphs of an NNS preterite which included *in*. The same project linguist later circulated a mimeographed list of suggestions, including the possibility of a frequent 'shift to the historical present'. I know nothing to disprove a statement like 'Six to ten-year-old speakers of NNS have a marked tendency to use the stylistic device of the historical present', except that it seems absurd.

8 Such statements, insofar as is now known, never take the form 'The slaves speak Pidgin (or Creole) English', but rather something like 'Their language is broken, but they understand each other, and the whites may gain their ideas' (Leland 1790). Yet non-linguists seldom if ever make more explicit statements about even Sranan Tongo or Liberian or WesKos Pidgin. In fact, Leland's wording is remarkably like the usual description of those languages.

9 Dick Reeves, *Gullah* (Lenwal Enterprises, Charleston, S.C., 1963).

10 Still, there is precedent for such comparisons. Read (1956:482) says that Louisiana French Creole 'bears about the same relation to pure French as our Southern Negro talk does to English purely spoken'. Leyburn (1941) made extensive comparisons between HC and Southern U.S. Negro speech, assuming that such a demonstration would reduce the concept of African – and presumably any non-Gallic – influence on HC to absurdity, and would prove his contention that Norman was the matrix of HC.

11 For polemic and hostile criticism, see Dillard (1968b).

REFERENCES

Bailey, Beryl L. 1965. 'Toward a new perspective in Negro English dialectology', *American Speech* 40(3):171–7

    1968. 'Some aspects of the impact of linguistics on language teaching in disadvantaged communities', *Elementary English* 45:570–9

Bloomfield, Leonard 1933. *Language*, New York, Holt

Botkin, B. A. 1945. *Lay my burden down: a folk history of slavery*, Chicago

Cassidy, Frederic G. 1961. *Jamaica talk*, London, Macmillan

DeCamp, David [1968]. 'The field of creole language studies', Paper circulated to Conference on pidginization and creolization of languages

Dillard, J. L. 1964. 'The writings of Herskovits and the study of New World Negro language', *Caribbean Studies* 4(2):35–43

  1967. 'Negro children's dialect in the inner city', *The Florida FL Reporter* 5(3):7–10

  1968a. 'Review of proceedings of the 1964 Mona conference', *Caribbean Studies* 8(1):62–5

  1968b. 'Non-standard Negro dialects – convergence or divergence?' *The Florida FL Reporter* 6(3):9–12

Goodman, Morris F. 1964. *A comparative study of Creole French dialects*, The Hague, Mouton

Hall, Robert A. 1966. *Pidgin and creole languages*. Ithaca, Cornell

Herskovits, Melville J. 1936. *Suriname Folk Lore*, New York

  1941. *The myth of the Negro past*, New York

Hurst, Charles 1965. *Psychological correlates in dialectolalia*, Washington

Hymes, Dell 1967. 'Models of the interaction of language and social setting', *Journal of Social Issues* 23(2):8–28

Johnson, Charles Spurgeon 1934. *The shadow of the plantation*, Chicago.

Lanier, Sydney 1879. Letter to *Scribner's Monthly*, November 23, 1879, Sidney Lanier Centennial Edition, Baltimore, 1945

Leland, John 1790. *The Virginia Chronicle*, Norfolk

Leyburn, James G. 1941. *The Haitian people*, New Haven, Yale University Press

Loban, Walter 1966. 'Problems in oral English', National Council of Teachers of English, Research report 5, Champaign

  1968. *Teaching children who speak social class dialects*. Elementary English

Loflin, Marvin D. 1967a. 'A note on the deep structure of non-standard English in Washington, D.C.', *Glossa* 1(1):1–7

  1967b. 'On the structure of the verb in a dialect of American Negro English', Center for Research in Social Behavior, Technical Report 26, Columbia, University of Missouri

McDavid, Raven I. 1965. 'American social dialects', *College English* 26(4):254–60

  1967. Historical, regional, and social variation', *Journal of English Linguistics* 1:1–40

Marcano De Zarco, R. P. 1938. *Dialecto Inglés-Africano, o broken-English de la Colonia Española del Golfo de Guinea*, 2nd ed., Turnhout

Morgan, Raleigh, Jr. 1959. 'Structural sketch of St Martin Creole', *Anthropological Linguistics* 1(8):20–4

Schneider, Gilbert A. 1964. *First steps in Weskos*, Hartford, Hartford Seminary Foundation

Stewart, William A. 1962a. 'Functional distribution of Creole and French in Haiti', Thirteenth annual round table on languages and linguistics (Monograph series, No. 15) ed. by E. E. Woodworth, 149–62. Washington, D.C., Georgetown University Press

  1962b. 'Creole languages in the Caribbean', *Study of the role of second languages in Asia, Africa, and Latin America*, ed. Frank A. Rice, pp. 34–53, Washington, D.C., Center for Applied Linguistics

1964. 'Foreign language teaching methods in quasi-foreign language situations', *Non-standard speech and the teaching of English*, ed. W. A. Stewart, Washington, D.C., Center for Applied Linguistics

1965. *Urban Negro speech: sociolinguistic factors affecting English teaching*, Champaign, National Council of Teachers of English

1966. 'Impressions of non-standard verb paradigm', Unpublished

1967. 'Sociolinguistic factors in the history of American Negro dialects', *The Florida FL Reporter* 5(2):11–29

1968. 'Continuity and change in American Negro dialects', *The Florida FL Reporter* 6(1):3–14

Turner, Lorenzo Dow 1949. *Africanisms in the Gullah dialect*, Chicago, University of Chicago Press

STATEMENTS AND PRÉCIS

CULTURAL AND LINGUISTIC AMBIGUITY: SOME OBSERVATIONS ON THE ROLE OF ENGLISH-BASED CREOLE IN AN ANTIGUAN VILLAGE[1]

KARL REISMAN

English-based Creole on the island of Antigua exists and finds its identity *not* in any system of bi- or multi-dialectalism (or -lingualism), nor even in a system that can be characterized as a simple scale or continuum. Creole plays its role as part of a more general way of handling cultural symbols which maximizes and plays with ambiguities of cultural reference and of expressive and moral meaning.

There is a duality of cultural patterning, both of Creole versus English speech and of 'African' versus English culture. But this underlying basis is denied and covered, and the two cultural strands are woven into a complex garment of cultural and linguistic expression.

This system of 'remodelling' (Taylor 1964) has its roots in certain fundamental values, first systematically noted by Herskovits, which in their West Indian form can be seen as fundamentally African. Herskovits' notions can be summed up in the terms *respect, reticence,* and *indirection.* (A section of the paper seeks to explore these notions in their Antiguan expression and to give them a broader and fuller content.) Associated with respect is the discipline of resignation, accepting things as they are and adjusting oneself to them. Associated with reticence is discretion, the avoidance of any act or gesture that would arouse the envy or jealousy of others or any expression of direct antagonism or hostility. Both of these are tied to indirection; looking first to see what the situation and its forms and conventions are, then masking one's actions and expressions in these forms, transvaluing or remodelling them to be closer to one's own forms and meanings. 'When in Rome', say the Antiguans, 'do as the Romans do.'

In the Antiguan situation one 'accepts' with 'respect' both the status system – with its concomitant self-definition as 'low' – and the total superiority of the standards and values of English culture, all other values and forms of expression being described in terms of an *absence* of the quality under discussion. Yet the gamut of negative terms which result are transvalued into one way of referring to a whole set of informally held alternate values.

By this process Creole becomes 'broken language' or simply the absence of language. To talk Creole is to 'make noise'. On the other hand Creole also symbolizes that which is natural. It is what one 'breaks away' into. It accompanies and marks expressions of deep and genuine feeling. To 'make noise', in a variety of Antiguan contexts, is to express oneself.

Like other alternate underlying values the norms of Creole cannot be found by asking questions involving translation from English. They must be found

o

indirectly within Creole contexts, or through cases of misunderstanding and confusion. Creole contexts are, of course, not clearly marked off. The Creole content of speech may 'fade in' – sometimes for purposes of disguise or expression – or it may 'fade out' without any sharp break in the code being used.

Features of Creole phonology aid the ambiguation process by lending themselves to the production of multi-meaning utterances which may be taken by the hearer in the way to which he is predisposed, without his ever becoming aware of the alternatives. Other aspects of the speech system share in these processes and serve to dramatize this interplay of cultural meanings in contexts in which alternation between English and Creole forms plays a symbolic role.

NOTE

1 Summary of a paper to appear in Whitten and Szwed (1970).

REFERENCES

Taylor, Douglas 1964. 'Review of *De Saramakaanse Woordenschat*, by Donicie and Woorhoeve', *International Journal of American Linguistics* 30:434–9
Whitten, Norman, and John Szwed (eds.) 1970. *Afro-American Anthropology: contemporary perspectives*, New York, Free Press.

THE ENGLISH LANGUAGE IN HAWAII[1]

ELIZABETH CARR

The English language in Hawaii has been considerably influenced by mass immigrations of laborers from a number of different countries, most of them brought to the Islands between 1886 and about 1930 to provide workers for the sugar plantations. The impact of so many foreign languages upon the English of Hawaii can be guessed, at least, when we know that even today more than 50% of the population of Hawaii is made up of these aging immigrants, their children, their grandchildren, and their great-grandchildren. In a technical sense, it was only the immigrant group who spoke pidgin. With strong pressure from the schools and the public, their children began the slow route from pidgin through creole and on to the present-day patterns, some of which are very similar to those of the western part of the United States or to other 'standard' American dialects. I have come to group this movement along the spectrum from pidgin to standard into five types or stations, and to try to collect evidence for the kinds of changes made from station to station. In my studies I have been concerned with the influences of other languages upon Hawaii's English, particularly in respect to phonology, loanwords, and what I have called *Hawaiian-isms*. Because of my intense interest in intonation, I have usually tape-recorded the stream of speech (in interviews and dialogues) rather than lexical items only. I have a collection of recordings on disc and tape of the young people of Honolulu extending over three decades.

Realizing that the early immigrants to Hawaii (in the 'sugar migrations') would soon be gone, I undertook the making of a collection of tapes of the spoken English of these elderly persons in the Chinese, Portuguese, Japanese, Puerto Rican, Korean, and Filipino ethnic groups. Their speech provides us with the nearest thing we have today to our early plantation pidgin. In this project I have been assisted by one of the local foundations in Honolulu. Assistance in recording has come occasionally from other sources, as when in 1961 two members of the Robinson family (owners of the inaccessible Island of Niihau) allowed me to record a number of residents of that island, where the influence upon English comes from the Hawaiian language only.

Selections and transcriptions from my collection of tapes, with analytical studies and a large glossary of Hawaiianisms make up the main portion of my book (Carr 1971). Among my published articles, two of the most pertinent are the most recent (Carr 1968), and a paper read before the Tenth Pacific Science Congress, held in Honolulu in 1961 (Carr 1961–2).

NOTE

1 Summary of work presented in discussion at the conference, and partly reported in articles circulated to the participants.

REFERENCES

Carr, Elizabeth 1961–2. 'Bilingual speakers in Hawaii today', *Social Process in Hawaii* 25:53–7
    1968. 'Pidgin English and dialects in Hawaii', *Thrum's Hawaiian almanac – all about Hawaii* 90:199–203
    1971. *Hawaii's English – from pidgin to standard American speech*, Honolulu, University of Hawaii Press

A REPORT ON NEO-MELANESIAN[1]

EDWARD WOLFERS

In a number of very important respects, the single most important element in the socialization of many New Guineans, as New Guineans, is the learning of Pidgin. It is Pidgin more often than English that helps to break down the old barriers between once hostile communities, that makes communication possible not only with Europeans but with other-language-speaking New Guineans too.

Pidgin, Pidgin English, once referred to in a derogatory way as *tokboi*, and now officially known as Neo-Melanesian, is spoken by at least 530,000 New Guineans. It is thought to be the only language known to about 10,000 New Guineans, who have, largely, been brought up away from their home areas. They have not, therefore, learnt their own vernaculars, but live in surroundings where English is not widely spoken. Pidgin is in fact the *lingua franca*, the principal means of inter-racial and inter-language-group communication throughout New Guinea, and the Southern Highlands of Papua. It is also used increasingly even among speakers of a common vernacular in some (usually modern) situations, and when discussing certain, especially non-traditional, matters.

Pidgin (spelt *Pisin* in its own dictionaries) has a vocabulary which finds its principal roots in English, German and Kuanua, the language of the Tolai of the Gazelle Peninsula of New Britain. Its syntax, according to linguists, has features of a Melanesian kind, and certainly bears but little external resemblance to that of either of its Western European forebears. Its vocabulary, its special expressions, even its grammatical structure, vary quite widely from place to place throughout the territory, very largely under the influence of the particular traditional local languages, and the special linguistic and social history of the local people. Nonetheless, Pidgin is spoken and understood throughout the Trust Territory of New Guinea, the British Solomon Islands Protectorate, and, to a lesser extent, the New Hebrides. Its use in Papua is growing, as it gradually displaces Police Motu, a pidginized version of the Motu language of the coast around Port Moresby, which was officially sponsored by the pre-war Papuan Administration as the principal Papuan *lingua franca*. In fact, Sir Hubert Murray went to very great pains indeed to exclude the use of Pidgin from Papua, a resolve that was only rendered entirely futile after the war, when the two pre-war Administrations were amalgamated. The Southern Highlands of Papua were entered and administered after the war by Pidgin-speaking Europeans and indigenous assistants, and Pidgin has become the *lingua franca* there too.

It is necessary, however, to distinguish between the pidgin as a social phenomenon, and its role as a subject of continued political and academic debate.

Briefly, the use of Neo-Melanesian has been a political issue since the early 1950s. Successive resolutions were then passed by the United Nations Trusteeship Council, and unfavourable observations made by United Nations Visiting Missions to New Guinea, all opposing its further growth, and certainly any official encouragement of its use. The United Nations seemed to feel that the rapid expansion of the pidgin seriously retarded the official fostering of English as the Territory's principal, and official, language, and in some way served to perpetuate the indigenes' inferior status to Europeans in colonial society. The pidgin was regarded simply as a form of bastardized English, not as a language in its own right.

Scholars have disagreed very widely as to the status of the language. Perhaps its most notable protagonist has been Professor Robert A. Hall, Jr., of Cornell University, who has written numerous articles and at least one book defending it, and taking direct issue with the United Nations' verdict, quite apart from his more serious, academic studies of its linguistic characteristics. There has, however, been no paucity of scholars and politicians, both indigenous and foreign, who have attempted to controvert his arguments.

In large part the debate has been purely academic. Since the mid-1950s, the Territory's Administration has refused assistance to mission schools (the major element in the Territory's primary and secondary education system) that do not teach in English. Neo-Melanesian is not used as a medium of instruction, much less is it taught as a school subject in its own right in Administration and Administration-assisted schools. The language is still taught, however, in many, especially the more backward, areas of the Territory, but only in mission-run schools. It remains the principal means of communication between European officials in the bush and their indigenous charges, and between indigenes from different language groups. (The Administration has never provided any financial inducement for its officers to learn local languages, even in areas where the latter may be understood by great numbers of people.) Indeed, the ability at least to speak and understand the pidgin is a virtual prerequisite for a Papuan or New Guinean in search of a job. Comparatively very few of the Christian missions even have encouraged their European workers to learn local languages.

Still, the language remains a matter of controversy for politicians and academics, as evidenced, for example, by Dr Wurm's recent articles in its defence (1966, 1966–7), and the long and eloquent plea by the new Professor of English at the University of Papua and New Guinea in his inaugural lecture, that English remain the official language, and the medium of instruction in schools throughout the Territory.

Several standard criticisms have been levelled at Neo-Melanesian, and reasonably uniform sorts of answers returned:

(a) that it is a vulgar and degrading way of speaking; that it is, in fact, no language at all, but serves only to preserve the vocabulary and attitudes of colonialism;
(b) that it is inadequate as a means of communication in a modern society;
(c) that its official encouragement would only serve to complicate yet further the Territory's already complex linguistic problems.

It does seem true that some Motu-speakers and Europeans do, in fact, feel that Neo-Melanesian is really but a species of baby-talk, a debased form of English which no self-respecting European chooses to use. Some Papuans and New Guineans feel that it perpetuates social relationships and ways of thinking more appropriate to the colonial past than to the modern society that is emerging in the Territory. In large part, this sort of argument reflects the legitimate pride that many of the Motu people especially feel for their own language, and their feeling that the Territory's indigenes should preserve their pride and refuse to take second-best linguistically. John Guise, probably the most prominent present-day Papuan politician, even before he became well known in politics, achieved a measure of renown during the 1950s for his letters to the press attacking the use of Neo-Melanesian. For those who do not yet speak English, and for whom communication with the outside world would therefore be impossible without the pidgin, such arguments may have about them the ring of educated arrogance, or of a proto-nationalism without much real point. In fact, many New Guineans regard the learning of the pidgin as a most important turning-point in their lives, when, for the first time, they are able to look for work outside their home areas. A knowledge of the language is still one sure way of gaining prestige as an educated man, and one capable of dealing with Europeans, in some of the areas of the Territory.

Certainly, Neo-Melanesian contains many words that were in their original English form 'unladylike', or simply obscene. The language grew up in an environment not particularly renowned for its gentility, the world of the late nineteenth-century canefields, plantations and mines. Fortunately, the allegedly rude words in which the language abounds do not carry their less pleasant connotations over from English, but have often less conventional, but more useful, day-to-day meanings. Thus, *as lo bilong gavman* simply means 'constitution', and *mi bagerap* means 'I'm tired' or 'I've had it'. Some quite innocent-sounding English expressions, however, have a meaning all of their own.

A brief example from an Administration political education pamphlet entitled 'The Representatives' Responsibilities' may demonstrate at least the superficial dissimilarity of Neo-Melanesian and English. This document, unfortunately, lacks, as do most Europeans, the eloquence and true feeling for colloquial expression that the language may gain when used by men of considerable oratorical ability in their own language, and to whom the pidgin is, very often, therefore, simply an alternative, rather than a secondary, means of communication:

'Ol wok o diuti em Memba i mas karim o mekim insait long House of Assembly em hevi moa long sampela wok em wusat man i holim long dispela kantri. Emi bikpela samting moa long save gut long dispela. Wonem ol dispela diuti o wok?

'I tru Memba i gat diuti o wok long elektoret bilong em. Em i mas toktok bilong ol pipal long dispela elektoret bilong em insait long House of Assembly, long wonem em i sanap bilong ologeta pipal long dispela elektoret, na i mas save gut long ol samting em ol dispela pipal i laikim. Bihain long taim miting i pinis, em yet i mas go bek long elektoret bilong em na tok klia long wok em i House i mekim pinis na wonem ol tingting ol i bin oraitim na watpo ol i bin oraitim ol dispela tingting . . .'

The official translation reads:

The responsibilities that a Member of the House of Assembly must bear are among the heaviest carried by any person in this country. It is important to understand this. What are those responsibilities?

'Of course an Elected Member has responsibilities to his electorate. He must speak for his electorate in the House, because he represents all the people in that electorate, and he must fully understand what those people want. After each meeting, he should return to his electorate and explain the work the House has done and tell the people what decisions were made and why these decisions were made . . .'

Although the foregoing passage dealt with something alien to the experience of most New Guineans, at least until very recently, and was rather stodgy and repetitive in presentation, as well as so literal and faithful to the English original as to be almost completely graceless, it should be clear that Neo-Melanesian is more than a particular local form of Simple English. If anything, the orthography of the foregoing passage is rather more anglicized than usual. Neo-Melanesian has as yet no standardized spelling system, and the spelling of a particular word quite often varies quite haphazardly even within the one article or letter.

It is true that much of the vocabulary of Neo-Melanesian did in the past, and partly still does, echo the sorts of inter-racial relationships that exist in colonial society. The ubiquitous use of *boi* when addressing an indigenous New Guinean, and *kanaka* when speaking of him, as well as his reply of *masta*, reflect the colonial heritage of the pidgin. *Boi* is now being very rapidly displaced by 'mate', or, more usually, the indigene's name, while 'New Guinean' is becoming the noun used to refer to the indigenes, or they are referred to by the names of their home areas such as 'Tolai', 'Chimbu' or 'Buka', for example. Even during the last eighteen months, I have noticed the very rapid displacement of *masta* by 'sir' in personal conversation, and by 'European' or *wetman* ('white man') in the third person. *Kanaka* is now used mainly by New Guineans themselves as a derogatory term to describe their more backward compatriots in the bush. In a very real sense, the vocabulary of Neo-Melanesian is changing with the structure of race and social relationships generally throughout the Territory.

Argument over the adequacy of the vocabulary of Neo-Melanesian properly belongs to the linguist, but the argument on this point has been even more wildly assertive and less satisfactory than is the case on other points. It has been said many times that the vocabulary, like that of almost every other living language, is constantly increasing to cope with new situations, phenomena, and ideas. Some of the words used in the above quotation, especially such a word as 'elektoret', would have been quite meaningless to most New Guineans until the first House of Assembly elections were held in 1964. It has now entered the vocabulary of the language in such a way that it apparently requires no explanation or amplification at all when used. Similarly, the word 'ba'azet', variously spelt, has become the regular word for 'budget'; in fact, the list of similar new creations is immense. Very skilled speakers seem quite capable of expressing fine shades of meaning in the language, and to explain, then employ, relatively specialized concepts, though the Territory's lawyers insist that legal draughting in the pidgin is simply impossible. The Department of District Administration has recently been unable, for example, to translate 'majority rule' precisely into Neo-Melanesian. 'Bihainim tingting bilong planti moa pipal', its final compromise, means no more than 'supporting the opinion of many people', and is inadequate for the task. The concept can be explained through lengthy circumlocution and demonstration, but the problem of finding an accurate, short means of translation still remains.

It does seem true, nevertheless, that Neo-Melanesian is quite adequate for conveying the day-to-day thoughts and observations of the average New Guinean. The language will expand its vocabulary as more sophisticated and technical means of expression are sought from it. It is currently inadequate as a means of expression only in the way in which the languages of pre-literate societies are inadequate as means for the communication of modern ideas and their wide dissemination in the world. It simply is the case that the need for New Guineans to make highly complex and technical decisions will rapidly outstrip the educational advancement of the broad mass of the Territory's population, and that, therefore, the daily vocabulary of Neo-Melanesian will prove inadequate in a manner that English would not. In other words, if the rate of political and technological progress in the Territory continues to proceed at the present tempo, one can imagine a situation in which the educated and political elites will speak either English or a form of the pidgin with rather more foreign words in it than is the case even now. Perhaps, however, this phenomenon will simply resemble the present dichotomy between the day-to-day vocabulary of English and the emerging international jargon of science.

Perhaps the third criticism of Neo-Melanesian is the most important. If it were to spread rapidly throughout the Territory and displace English almost completely as the official language and the most used medium of instruction, then the Territory's population would be effectively cut off from the literature and text-books of the rest of the world. The cost of translating even a fraction of the necessary technical and literary materials into Neo-Melanesian would be astronomical. On the other hand, while it may marginally slow some individuals' progress when they later come to learn English, Neo-Melanesian is of immense importance as the primary means of intra-Territorial communication.

Neo-Melanesian has not only helped to break down the old barriers of linguistic isolation within the Territory, and between the races, but it has, in fact, given birth to a whole sub-culture of its own. Although S. W. Reed pointed to the emergence of such a phenomenon already in the early 1940s, no serious study has so far been made of the social importance of the pidgin, and especially of the community of songs, expressions, poems, in fact the entire set of social bonds created by the simple act of speaking a common language, that have grown up in New Guinea.

Neo-Melanesian now serves as a simple bond among indigenous New Guineans when they seek to set themselves apart from Europeans or even coastal Papuans, when they share no other common language. The concept of a *wantok*, i.e. a speaker of one's own language, did not exist in pre-contact society, where men fought against other speakers of their own language as often as they fought against linguistic outsiders. Nowadays *wantok* is used as an expression of friendship to speakers of one's own language in an otherwise linguistically alien environment, although its use also expands at times to mean 'friend' generally. In bar fights I have seen *wantok* used to express a measure of unity amongst the indigenous combatants when a group of Europeans attempted to interfere. In a rather strange way, the common bond of Pidgin gave a sense of solidarity to those who had been fighting, as they sought to keep the conflict within their own group, and to exclude the alien intruders. Thus, the pidgin very often provides a sense of unity among New Guineans, where none previously existed, both against Europeans, and, very often, against non-Pidgin-speaking Papuans. Pidgin-speakers in the more primitive areas of the Territory, where as yet but few people may speak it, are well-known for the scorn which they may show for their less well-educated compatriots even on quite public occasions.

Two years ago, Neo-Melanesian was rarely heard in Port Moresby. Europeans here refused to speak it, though very few indeed could speak Police Motu. The local Motuans stuck proudly to their own language, and despised those who found it necessary to speak Police Motu to them.

By early 1966, it was noticeable that things had changed a little since the

year before. The pidgin was used far more than ever before, as increasing numbers of New Guineas came to work in, perhaps simply to see, the big town.
The pidgin had always been used on the local plantations as the principal
means of communication with the workers who came here under the Highlands Labour Scheme. By 1966, the pidgin was used as a bond among the less
well-educated and sophisticated, as a means, for example, for passing rude
sexual comments about passing Motuan women who usually did not understand
the language, and even about uncomprehending Papuans generally. Few women
at all, anywhere in the Territory, speak anything other than their own *tokples* or
local language – probably a symbol of their generally lower social status
traditionally, and now educationally. The women have never needed to learn
pidgin as have the men, for there is also very little employment available for
them outside their villages except in more skilled occupations, as teachers,
nurses, etc.

Now, although still not widely used in Papua, and insulting if employed in
conversation with English-speaking Papuans and New Guineans, Neo-
Melanesian is being increasingly used on signs and in conversations in the Port
Moresby area. The cultural ethos that one inescapably associates with it has
come too. In fact, some extremely fluent, if politically-minded, English-speakers
use Neo-Melanesian in order to create a special sort of bond with their less
sophisticated friends, even from their own home areas. The language, then,
is used as a sort of proto-nationalistic means of distinguishing New Guineans
from nearby Europeans, and, less frequently, Papuans. It enables the urban
sophisticate and the illiterate labourer in town to converse as linguistic equals.
Papuans now use it much more readily than before in order to communicate and
establish some common bonds of identification with their New Guinean compatriots. In the House of Assembly, for example, Motu is now used less than
ever, and many a well-prepared speech in English is interrupted by a shouted
request to speak in the pidgin instead. Despite the provision of a simultaneous
translation service in the house, for English, Neo-Melanesian and Motu, Neo-
Melanesian is now almost universally used by the indigenous members, and by
many of the European elected members. Most of the ten official members,
however, have remained faithful to the United Nations' will, if not the house's,
and either cannot or do not speak anything other than English in the house.
A few official members have, however, bowed to the requests of the elected
members. As the translation of official documents and bills is often inadequate,
and many of the members are illiterate anyway, much of the house's proceedings
remain almost incomprehensible to many of the indigenous members, who,
therefore, rely upon the official members' speeches for explanation of many
bills and other documents. The simultaneous translation into Neo-Melanesian
of as complex a document as the annual budget is such a difficult matter as almost
to defy the best attempts at intelligibility of the most conscientious interpreters.

The new Administrator, Mr D. O. Hay, has recognized the growing importance of Neo-Melanesian in the Territory, and has broken with his predecessor's
stand on the matter. The response to his speeches in the pidgin has been so
favourable that one wonders at the persistence of the old policy which preferred
the silence of incomprehension or the frequent interruptions that accompanied
translation to the present gratitude at the new ease of communication with
Nambawan Gavman.

Neo-Melanesian, then, whatever one may argue as to its intrinsic merits, has revolutionized New Guinea society. It has broken down old barriers, and allowed for direct inter-racial and inter-language-group communication where this was not previously possible. It has made a national radio news-service feasible, and a newspaper, the *Nu Gini Toktok*, available to the relatively unsophisticated. The pidgin has been one of the most important elements in the Territory's slow and hesitant groping towards nationhood. Its very history, its origins on the plantations and in European employ generally, have allowed for, if not encouraged, the growth of that common set of experiences and attitudes from which a nation grows. One only hopes that the scholars' and overseas politicians' arguments will not be allowed to subsume the sociological importance of the language, which will, in a sense, probably remain whatever they may say. Indeed, the matter may have been decided already, for the Territory's two largest indigenous political parties have advocated the adoption of Neo-Melanesian as Papua and New Guinea's national language. Its use as the common language of daily discourse, one party feels, must not be confused with the official use of English. Interestingly enough, the same body, the PANGU Pati, has a strong Papuan, English-speaking membership. The United Democratic Party, also, advocates the use of Neo-Melanesian as the national language. Indeed, for a time, the United Democrats combined their support for it with a policy advocating the Territory's eventual incorporation as the seventh state of the Australian federation.[2]

NOTES

1 Slightly revised from a report submitted to the Institute of Current World Affairs, New York, of which Mr Wolfers is a Fellow, on 18 June 1967. The editor is grateful to Mr Wolfers and the Institute for permission to publish it here, and to Dr Joshua Fishman for bringing it to his attention.
2 The linguistic situation in Oceania as a whole, with reference to pidgins, creoles and lingue franche, is treated by Wurm (in press); on New Guinea, see also Wurm (1966, 1966–7, 1969). See also Salisbury (1967).

REFERENCES

Salisbury, R. F. 1967. 'Pidgin's respectable past: a matter of New Guinean pride', *New Guinea and Australia, the Pacific and South-East Asia* 2(2):44–8
Wurm, Stefan A. 1966. 'Pidgin – a national language', *New Guinea and Australia, the Pacific and South-East Asia* 7:49–54
  1966–7. 'Papua-New Guinea nationhood: the problem of a national language', *The Journal of the Papua and New Guinea Society* 1(1):7–19 [Reprinted in *Language problems of developing nations*, ed. Joshua Fishman, Charles A. Ferguson and Jyotirindra Das Gupa, 345–64, New York, John Wiley]
  1969. *Handbook of New Guinea pidgin* (Linguistic Circle of Canberra, Series C, 2), Canberra
  19–. 'Pidgins, creoles and lingue franche', *Oceanic linguistics*, ed. Thomas A. Sebeok *et al.* (Current trends in linguistics, 8), The Hague, Mouton (In press)

VI

DISCIPLINARY PERSPECTIVES

INTRODUCTION

In some areas of research it may appear possible to separate the linguistic from the socio-cultural, the synchronic from the diachronic, or historical. Certainly it is not possible to do so in the study of pidgin and creole languages. Given the present apportionment of skills and knowledge among disciplines, adequate study of pidgin and creole languages thus must have a multidisciplinary base. The need for such a base poses two kinds of question: the relations of disciplines to each other, taken as they are, and ways in which disciplines may need to change, if the new relationships show them to be overlooking aspects of their own domains, or if domains of some importance are found to be lying untended between them.

The dimensions synchronic/diachronic, and linguistic/sociocultural, define between them four foci of concern. Four scholars, each a specialist in one of these, and concerned with its relation to the others, were asked to discuss the conference and its subject from their respective vantage points: comparative sociology (Grimshaw), linguistic analysis (Labov), language history (Hoenigswald) and social history (Mintz).

In relations among disciplines, ignorance may breed respect. A historian may hesitate to speak for fear of naiveté in linguistics, while across from him a linguist is silent out of respect for the other's command of history. Of the four contributors here, only Grimshaw ventures a critique across disciplinary lines. Having emphasized the value of linguistics to comparative studies of society and history, he goes on to point out scientific naiveté, one might say, and shaky empirical foundations, for many generalizations in conventional linguistics. Labov develops a related critique from within linguistics, linking study of pidgins and creoles to study of English in the urban United States.

Most work on pidgin and creole languages has been limited to a single case at a time. As DeCamp points out in his introduction to this volume, the bringing together of scholars in consciousness of a common field is as recent as it is vital. The main extension has been along a line familiar to linguists, historical relationship – tracing the connections and reconstructing, if possible, the earlier characteristics of French-based creoles, English-based Atlantic creoles, and the like. Such historical research is indispensable, but Grimshaw shows the need for a comparative perspective as well – a typology of cases, and the sort of controlled comparison, getting at covariations and causes, for which the relevant experience is in social science, rather than linguistics.

To need for extension by comparison of cases, Labov adds need for extension in the range of phenomena studied in a single case. Variability has been taken to be a characteristic that sets pidgins, and to some extent creoles apart. Labov shows – and this is the first of the two points that make his essay so important – that the variability of pidgins and creoles is a difference in degree, not in kind. Variability is *normal* in language. The apparent division has been an artefact of method. In pidgins and some creole situations variability is so salient that it cannot be ignored. In study of English in the United States, say, variability is set aside as epiphenomenal. To be sure, not only degree of variability may be involved. Expectations may also play a part. In considering it normal for pidgins and creoles to be variable (even if also structured), and normal for other languages not to be, linguists may unwittingly perpetuate an ethnocentric, colonial heritage.

Labov shows also – this is the second main point – that variability is not only normal, but also *systematic*. He shows that linguistic rules can and must be extended to account for it.

Hoenigswald starts from the pervasiveness of historical considerations through all the topics of the conference, and shows the social aspects of history to be inseparable from the linguistic. He cuts to the heart of the question of genealogical relationship. There are two processes, or, one could say, two attitudes on the part of speakers: massive borrowing into a language that is being retained, and imperfect learning of a language that is being adopted. Crucial cases – those in which creolization is known or suspected – may be defined as those in which the outcomes of the two processes are difficult to distinguish. The criterion of last resort is basic vocabulary – that sector of vocabulary whose elements designate universal features of experience (parts of the body, natural conditions and elements, and the like). Such elements are both unlikely to be borrowed and in common use. Generally, basic vocabulary is the part of a language last to be borrowed, first to be learned, most likely to persist through periods of cultural change. Hoenigswald makes explicit and precise what has been in fact the practice of historical linguistics, faced with a crux in which the usual twin criteria of lexicon and grammar do not point in the same direction; but in pushing genealogical classification to the limit of its applicability, he also shows it to mean much less than had once been thought. Such classification had initially been thought to provide a key to history, to show the origin and continuity of languages, and even of cultures and peoples. In favorable cases, it still does, but modern linguistic prehistory, and the study of pidgin and creole languages, combine to show that under the erosion of time, or under drastic social change, such a history of language reduces to the history of a set of terms. Classification of languages needs a broader base than what has been meant by genealogy. In part this requires a history of languages as structural types and as products of diffusion, but it requires as well a history of languages as functional varieties. Viewed as transmitted stocks of lexical and grammatical resources, languages may display a specious continuity. Viewed as resources organized and adapted to social purposes, they take on a different aspect. The emergence of pidgins and creoles, as of standard languages, makes inescapable the recognition of discontinuity, and forces us to think seriously of what it means for a language, as ways of speaking, to come into being, and to end. Languages must be classified as to their use, as socially recognized entities, as well as to the provenience of their features.

From his analysis of genealogical relationship, and his consideration of the papers of the conference, Hoenigswald is led to a view of change that parallels Labov's view of variability. Creolization may not set creoles apart. Its characteristics are normal in linguistic change. It is the particular historical circumstances, jointly linguistic and social, that determine the outcome, just as the circumstances may determine whether or not variability reaches, or remains, at the level of saliency considered typical of pidgins and some creole situations.

Hoenigswald and Labov would both seem to conclude that the processes at work in pidginization and creolization are universal; that under certain circumstances the results are distinct, but not apart; and that the distinctive cases must be understood in terms of what they share with all language and language change, as well as in terms of the circumstances that individuate them.

The special circumstances of the Caribbean are set forth by Mintz. Within the Caribbean, his approach is comparative, bringing to bear on individual cases an understanding of both common and differentiating traits. The attention with which his oral presentation was received at Mona, and the written essay here, show how essential social history is to explanation, especially when interpreted with anthropological insight. Mintz is able to harness rich detail to analytical purpose, and he notices what is *not* there, in the Caribbean-pidgins, as a key to the story. He suggests a set of testable conditions for the emergence of creole languages of the Caribbean type. Pidgin and creole languages, he concludes, may attest not only the limits to which men can be driven, but also human resiliency and creative power.

SOME SOCIAL FORCES AND
SOME SOCIAL FUNCTIONS
OF PIDGIN AND CREOLE LANGUAGES[1]

ALLEN D. GRIMSHAW

Introduction

As is the case with all interdisciplinary meetings in attractive settings, participation in the Mona Conference reflected a variety of motives. My interests,
as a comparative sociologist, were no more and no less parochial than those
who attended because of solely linguistic concerns with the internal structure
of pidgin and creole languages or because of ideological concerns with the
international political and literary status of those languages. As a sociologist
I am interested in identifying the ways in which differently constituted social
structures differentially influence the patterning of social behavior. I view
language behavior as a particularly useful source of data for such study;
speech in particular is valuable because it is more accessible to careful
observation and measurement than many other varieties of social behavior.
I believe, however, that the value of data from the study of pidginization and
creolization can be fully realized only if linguists themselves attend more
carefully to relevant sociological consideration. I have two purposes in this
paper: (1) the demonstration, to sociologists, of the value of linguistic material
on pidgins and creoles, and; (2) to suggest, to linguists, ways in which attention to social variables (and, more briefly, to certain aspects of research design)
can make their work more useful both to themselves and to social scientists
more generally.

I begin with a brief statement on sociology and some possible sociological
perspectives on language. I turn then to a discussion of some social sources of
pidgin and creole languages, including in my discussion a highly tentative
taxonomy of some important social variables influencing language outcomes
in contact situations. I turn next to a consideration of some social functions
of these languages, a consideration which includes a very incomplete attempt
to indicate their importance on both micro- and macro-societal levels. Finally,
and too briefly, I have incorporated some comments on research design and
methods — suggesting some aspects of current linguistic work on creoles and
pidgins which make the use of data provided problematic for social scientists
who are potential consumers.

A sociological perspective

The principal aim of sociology is the understanding of how membership in groups and location in differentiated social structures patterns human social behavior in recurrent and predictable ways. This emphasis on differential human experience has led sociologists to look for explanations of variations in social behavior rather than for invariant behavior characteristics of all humans or even of all members of particular society. Historically, sociologists have been interested in the interactional analogs of linguistic 'performance' rather than those of 'competence'.[2] The expression of interest in pidginization and creolization by a sociologist and the increasing awareness of social constraints on, and meanings of, differentiated linguistic performance among their users, by linguists, together reflect fairly fundamental shifts in the disciplinary perspectives of the two disciplines. Sociologists, who formerly have been primarily interested in systematic variations in social behavior as revealed through correlational studies, are beginning to ask whether there may not be some invariant patterns of social behavior — some interactional universals.[3] Some sociologists believe they have discovered, in speech behavior, a possible source of data which can be employed in the search for such universals.[4] At the same time, some linguists are beginning to interest themselves in aspects of language behavior which they had previously treated as non-universal 'free variation', as a residual congeries of 'grammatically irrelevant conditions', which govern a speaker's performance as contrasted to his competence in the narrow sense.

These shifts reflect substantive theoretical reassessments which are taking place in the two disciplines; they have either precipitated or have been precipitated by, other changes which have been occurring. There are two such changes which are of particular relevance for my discussion here and I will limit my attention to them. One of these changes is a decline in parochialism among American sociologists, who have become increasingly interested in doing work outside of the United States. At the same time that sociologists have been attempting to overcome the parochialism of recent decades, linguists have been turning increasingly to the sampling of speech in natural settings as contrasted to earlier practices which emphasized elicitation techniques applied to intensive work with individual informants. This latter shift, while it has been overshadowed by the occasionally disputatious dialogue between structuralists and generative grammarians, may, in the long run, have an equally revolutionary impact on linguistic theory.

Comparative sociology is not fundamentally different from other sociologies in either its goals or its methods. All sociological research involves description, explanation, and/or replication. Comparative sociology involves attempts to explain similarities or differences in social behavior occurring in different societies through reference to differences in structured social relationships and, through replication, to test the limits of generalizations or propositions derived from research in different societies. The purpose of such work is the movement from contingent propositions of the, 'when a and b and c, then, if x, then y' variety to propositions which state, 'if and whenever x, then y'. This is possible only through trans-societal replication. Most past 'comparative' research, whether in sociology or in linguistics, has been primarily anecdotal.[5] As a comparative sociologist I see in the papers presented at the conference a variety of data resources which can help people in my discipline move toward the statement of some 'if and whenever if' propositions. I see, moreover, data which clearly underlines, for linguists, the importance of attending to social variables in understanding linguistic performance.

Before turning to a more explicit discussion of the topic of this volume, viz., sociolinguistic perspectives on pidgins and creoles, I should like to make one additional comment of a general theoretical nature. In the paragraphs above I have suggested the possibility of complementary relationships between sociologists and linguistics. I should like here to suggest (following Hymes, 1966b) that there are four possible perspectives on causal relationships between social structure and language.[6] Briefly, it can be argued: (1) that language structure or behavior causes social structure or behavior; (2) that the reverse is true; (3) that the two sets of behaviors and structures co-occur and mutually influence each other, or; (4) that both sets are determined by some third factor, whether that third factor be the organization of the human brain or the necessities of the human condition. Most of the papers above which have attended at all to this question have emphasized the importance of social variables (primarily prestige considerations) in repertoire selection. In the discussion below – there will be an opportunity to review examples which support each of the first three perspectives.[7] First, however, I want to say something about apparent problems in defining pidgin and creole languages.

The origins of pidgin and creole languages

Many students of social behavior, unfamiliar with the details of linguistic work, have accorded to linguistics a status as the most precise, rigorous and scientific of the social science disciplines. This reputation rests in part upon the fact that linguists, in contrast to some other social scientists, deal with a level of behavior which is simultaneously inaccessible to common-sense description and interpretation and so patterned as to invite rigorous logical and inductive analysis. Linguists have done little to disabuse their colleagues about possible errors in this stereotype and have not infrequently been admired as masters of an arcane art who are, additionally blessed with polyglottal fluency. It was a shock for me, therefore, to discover that the linguists at the Jamaica meeting seemed not even to share common definitions of the terms creole and pidgin, let alone agree on the origins or social consequences of these languages.

In practice the problem of assigning definitions to these terms is obviously related to questions about the origins of the language to which they refer. There seem to be three kinds of questions about the origins of these languages, the several questions and their possible answers are richly inter-implicated. The first question asks how these languages originate, the answers are either that they have independently evolved as a response to similar contact situations — or — that the pidgin and creole solutions to situations of linguistic contact have (in all the cases in which one of the contact languages was that of a European imperialist power) derived from a common origin. If the common origin argument is accepted, and many scholars believe that the similarities among geographically quite distant language codes can be explained in no other way, there are still additional dimensions to the question. Is there *one* common source for all such languages or are there, rather, common origins for sets of languages — for example, a common base for English-related creoles, another for French-related creoles, and so on?

Whatever the 'ultimate' source of pidgins and creoles, once initiated they are subject to the same processes of linguistic change as other languages are. The second set of questions has to do with the processes by which pidgins and creoles take on their individual identities. The first of the diffusionist perspectives, that of *one* common source, asserts that the principal process involved is that of relexification (Stewart 1962). Another, more recent view, suggests far more complex processes in which linguistic differentiation and development are associated with and a part of over-all processes of acculturation and continuing contact — contact involving not only Europeans and creole speakers in one contact setting but also that involving continuing, if intermittent, interaction among speakers of the several European and creole languages (Alleyne, this volume). Students who believe that pidgins and creoles have arisen independently in a number of different contact situations, however, have tended variously to propose theories emphasizing simple mixture or amalgamation; simplification (in the sense of 'baby-talk' or 'foreigner-talk'), or 'hybridization' (for details on these several perspectives see DeCamp, Introduction, this volume).

The apparent confusion over answers to questions on sources, processes of differentiation, and the current social and linguistic positions of pidgin and creole languages underlines the necessity for systematic comparative and contrastive analysis across the entire range of cases. While the task of creating an adequate typology of *languages* is clearly the responsibility of the linguists who work on them, it is hard to avoid the conclusion that the several typological perspectives currently extant have been based on intensive examination of individual languages along with somewhat uncritical acceptance of anecdotal materials on other cases — insofar as theoretical conclusions already developed are not challenged.[8] Something is wrong when common origin interpretations of one type (viz. that of a single European language (Hancock and Daelman in this volume), can simultaneously co-exist with both contradictory common origin interpretations (common African base for French and English creoles) and the independent evolution thesis still supported by Hall (1966). And none of these perspectives would be helpful in explaining Chinook Jargon!

The mandate for linguists interested in the generation of adequate theory on these languages (including typologies) seems clear. They must attend to social and historical variables, examining them both across cases and longitudinally within cases. As Hymes has suggested (1969) '*solution* (of these theoretical and taxonomic problems) *requires knowing who was speaking what, when and where*'.

The third question asks whether each of these languages falls on some continuum which has a standard language at one pole and a continuously changing, unstable collection of idiolectical variants at the other or whether there are, rather, discrete languages (or dialects, or repertoires) such that individual speech patterns can be located in terms of greater or lesser approximation to ideal type standards (or creoles, or pidgins).

The dominant theoretical perspective on the origins of these languages has been that of Bloomfield (1933, see also Hall 1966) who saw both types of languages as simplified and reduced versions of 'upper' (usually European) languages and creoles as pidgins which had somehow gone through a process of at least partial standardization (or at least stabilization). The presentations and discussions in this volume demonstrate that Bloomfield's own position was an example of a simplified and reduced version of a much more complex and difficult reality. Although a tremendous amount of difficult work remains to be done, many new ways of looking at pidgins and creoles have emerged in the nearly four decades since Bloomfield published – the new perspectives increasingly reflect a responsiveness to sociolinguistic and comparative considerations. Alleyne points out, for example, that the contact situations producing pidgins and creoles are fundamentally different. In the pidgin-producing situation the two (or more) contact cultures maintain their integrity – creoles, on the other hand, represent one of several outcomes of acculturation (cf. Southworth's paper on Marathi and Hoenigswald's comment on Goodman's Mbugu case). Moreover, it seems that there may be instances in which pidgins move directly to standardization without first becoming creolized (cf. Lawton, this volume). Bahasa Indonesian may well have gone through such a direct standardization, Wurm (1968) has suggested that this may now be happening with Neo-Melanesian in New Guinea. These several interpretations, and the definitional distinctions they imply, suggest several varieties of sociological questions – some about the preconditions for the development of one or another variety of contact repertoire, others about the interaction of social and linguistic variables in the development of contact languages once they have first achieved some modicum of uniformity.

In his thought-provoking report Mintz examines the social contexts which contributed to the development of the several creole languages of the Caribbean area. In the remarks I prepared for the Kingston conference I attempted to identify some of the economic, political, social and educational contexts of the development of pidgins and creoles more generally. Among the contextual situations I suggested were: (1) latifundiary *versus* mercantile systems; (2) colonial domination *versus* culture contact; (3) intersection of multiple spheres of colonial domination (this could be concurrent or serial, e.g. the Spanish and English conflict over the Antilles or the German and English influences in New Guinea and Papua as contrasted to the English-Dutch sequence in Surinam or the French-English sequence in Louisiana), and; (4) the efficiency or lack thereof of pidgins and/or creoles for involvement in industrializing labour forces. Stewart in the discussions at the conference specified three types of conditions, all of which were sociolinguistic prerequisites for pidginization. They were: (1) situation of culture contact with multilingualism; (2) social — primary and secondary speakers of a language with the secondary users: (a) concerned only with communication, (b) socially marginal to the primary speakers, and, (c) in agreement with their characterization as being marginal, and; (3) linguistic — the languages in contact must differ sufficiently to ensure that there will be interference. As a comparative sociologist I must ask myself the question — what is it about the differential experience of language contact sites that has sometimes resulted in pidginization (variously culminating in creolization, in the maintenance and continued renewal of the pidgin, in the disappearance of the pidgin, or, in some few cases, the stabilization [standardization?] of the pidgin) and, in other cases has produced no special contact language at all? Where *creolization* does occur, what is it about the differential experience of language contact that variously determines the disappearance of the creole, its emergence as a new standard, or its stabilization as a mutually intelligible dialect of one of the source languages?

In reviewing what had been said about these differences in experience it became clear that three sets of variables were of great importance. The first of these was the patterns of conflict relations, first between the dominant group of prestige language speakers and the subordinated population and secondly, among the subordinated groups. Equally important, it appears, are the industrial and commercial contexts within which contacts have occurred, viz. trading or agriculture, farm or plantation, and so on. This variable also includes the social organization of work — indenture, slavery, contract, free. Finally, the mundane matter of the numbers involved, the demographic variable, has obvious implications for the maintenance of these languages, if not for their appearance.

Any comparative sociolinguistic study of pidgins and creoles will have to investigate not only the variables just listed, but others as well. While there is no space in this paper for a complete review of even some of the more obvious of the variables I have suggested; it is possible to identify, in an extremely rough and preliminary manner, a few of the relationships which will have to be investigated in the course of the sociolinguistic study of these languages. In Chart 1[9] I have attempted to identify some of the more obviously salient of these variables, and some possible outcomes of their interaction. It is obvious, for example, that in order for contact to occur, speakers of one or more languages must travel to an area where there are speakers of one or more different languages.[10] Moreover, in each case of new language contact one or some languages will have higher prestige than the other(s). Host societies (or countries, or cultures) can have one or more languages, they either will or will not have the high prestige languages(s) in the contact situations.

CHART 1. *Interaction of linguistic repertoires of contact societies and prestige of languages*

		Linguistic characteristics of host society			
		MONOLINGUAL		MULTILINGUAL	
		Status of language (s)			
		High	Low	High	Low
MONOLINGUAL — High		(1) Cocoliche Russenorsk	(2) Romans in Britain Chinese Pidgins	(3) French in Eastern Europe in 19th century	(4) Europeans in Africa, Melanesia (Neo-Melanesian; Police Motu)
MONOLINGUAL — Low	Status of language (s)	(5) Mongol invasions of China Gypsies in, e.g. England	(6)	(7) Gypsies in, e.g. Austro-Hungary	(8)
MULTILINGUAL — High		(9) Crusades?	(10) Open door period in China?	(11) Chinook Jargon Marathi-Kannada (Sanskrit)? *Wontok*	(12) Immigrants to Israel?
MULTILINGUAL — Low		(13) Caribbean slavery American immigrants (19th, 20th centuries)	(14)	(15) African migrations into South Africa	(16)

(Left margin label: Linguistic repertoires of immigrants or visitors (or conquerors))

Chart 1 is meant to be suggestive and evocative. I am interested in a possible taxonomy of relationships, not in unimpeachable assignment of cases within the taxonomy itself. I have used language names or descriptions interchangeably, my principal concern being to demonstrate the value of a comparative look at different contact situations. I am not interested in arguing about misassigned cases. I do hope that readers will see that different combinations of only two variables, those of mono- and multi-lingualism and of status of host and visitor language(s), can have very substantial impact on the development of language situations. The variables suggested are coarse in the extreme. Language status, for example, may variously reflect considerations of prestige of languages with high literary traditions or simply the power of its speakers.[11] The fact that they do discriminate, in spite of their coarseness, seems to me to indicate a greater analytic strength which would become available if the variables were refined and actual contact situations more closely scrutinized.[12]

I do believe that entries in some cells are somewhat more persuasive than entries in others. I have more confidence in the exemplary cases in the upper right and lower left (cells 4 and 13) than in those in the lower right and upper left. In those situations in which high prestige languages are brought to host societies with many local languages (cell 4) it does not seem likely that a creole will develop.[13] What happens instead is that the contact code (pidgin) can develop directly into a *second* language which has prestige intermediate between the local languages and the high prestige non-indigenous language. In time such a language may replace the original prestige language (as it has in Indonesia and seems to be doing in Melanesia). Users of the emergent language continue to be bilingual. This appears to contrast with the high prestige language contact with a monolingual host society where, as in China, the pidgin is variously reported as dying out or as continuously renewed but never as moving toward standardization (cell 2).[14]

In those situations in which speakers of many low prestige languages have brought them to host societies with a single high prestige language (or a clearly dominant language with residual multilingualism), emergent pidgins have quickly been supplanted by fairly uniform and increasingly standardized creoles. In such cases a group of monolingual creole speakers appears, other persons (native speakers both of the prestige language and of the low prestige non-local languages) become bilingual (in the prestige standard and in the creole). A combination of demographic, social and political variables then determines whether, in the process of standardization, the creole emerges as a new language or as a dialect of the standard – or whether it simply merges with the latter. Which of these outcomes occurs depends upon such considerations as whether the host society is a modern industrialized or industrializing society and the immigrants voluntary (twentieth-century USA and Argentina, for example), or a latifundiary society with involuntary (slave) or semi-involuntary (indentured) immigrants. The massive numerical preponderance and concurrent powerlessness and restricted mobility of the slaves or contract workers in a society with few opportunities constrains them to experiences quite different from those of the Hymie Kaplans of the United States or the *cocoliche* speakers of the Argentine.

The question as to whether pidgins and creoles (particularly the latter) are discrete languages or whether, instead, there is some continuum of speech patterns representing different degrees of standardization is a sociolinguistic as well as a linguistic question. There are, for the linguist, interesting methodological implications to this issue. There are a number of sociological questions as well. Beryl Bailey, if I understand her position correctly, seems to be saying that there is one ideal-typical (and perhaps even 'ideal') creole language and that speakers more or less approximate to the ideal-typical pattern. Variation from the norm is quantitatively measureable but neither linguistically nor sociolinguistically to the point – at least Bailey does not suggest any way of organizing the variations linguistically (e.g. in terms of markers, covariation and so forth).

Whinnom, in emphasizing his notion of 'hybridization' seems to suggest that there are very large numbers of ways in which the speech of individual speakers can be patterned and that there are only very general rules for the combinations which occur (see, e.g. Whinnom's footnote predicting AB, Ab, aB and ab combinations of *nyam* and *tick*, *eat* and *thick*. He calls this secondary hybridization). Finally, DeCamp asserts the variation in speech patterns which can be observed in the linguistically complex populations under consideration are *linguistically predictable* (viz. that co-occurrence rules determine whether, in Whinnom's example, the AB pattern is followed by Ab or aB) and *sociologically relevant*. While DeCamp has not analyzed the speech of sufficiently large samples of speakers to assure himself that the Guttman-scalogram type of pattern that he has identified is not violated by some speakers (and some errors are to be expected), the direction of his findings is considerably more persuasive than the suggestion that speech variations constitute random error. I would feel quite confident in making the prediction, moreover, that speakers in one or another scale-type (viz. collections of individuals for whom certain co-occurrence rules apply) will be characterized by other socio-economic similarities and that ability to shift from one scale-type to another will characterize speakers whose social horizons are more open, and so on.[15]

The resolution of these definitional problems will require the application of measurement techniques available only to professional linguists. Given the principle of parsimony, however, my interpretation is that the methodological evidence and the sociological implications of the several definitions collectively lend support to arguments for continua of varieties or contextual styles in situations of pidginization and creolization (as in standardization more generally). It must be further noted, however, that within a single social setting individual speakers may variously simply move along continua or, more sharply, shift from one speech variety to another quite different one. This seems to be the case, for example, with university students returning to Hemnesberget as contrasted to locals (Blom and Gumperz 1970). It is clear that there are dangers of projecting middle-class standards onto populations; of selecting populations and data on ideological grounds; of failing to sample variations in actual speech behavior. The populations studied are crucial, proper sampling and the elicitation of natural speech are necessary prerequisites for answers to any of the questions raised in this section.

The functions of language

Each of the four perspectives on the causal relationships between social structure and language mentioned above attends with particular care to one or more of the many varieties of functions of languages. Scholars, for example, who subscribe to the perspective that whatever is of interest in language structure and speech behavior *and* social structure and social interaction is determined by the characteristic organization of the human mind are not interested – as are sociologists, anthropological linguists or experts on mass communication – in how language and speech variously serve as media of communication, as mechanisms for the maintenance and enhancement of prestige, as agency of social control or weapon in social conflict.[16] Many linguists are simply not interested in the ordering of social structures and social behavior. Those linguists who seek to find in linguistic evidence insights into the characteristic organization of the human mind have a perspective on relations between speech and social interaction (if they attend to that relation at all) which is both difficult to prove and of little interest to the student of society.[17]

SOCIAL STRUCTURAL INFLUENCES

There is no difficulty in finding, in data on the use of pidgin and creole languages, comparative confirmation of patterns in which social structure influences code or repertoire selection and where language choice reflects rules for social interaction. The phenomenon of switching, for example, is reported for a tri-lingual case by Polomé (he reports that in Katanga the several mother-tongues are spoken in the intimacy of the home, that Swahili is used for communication, and French is used for elegance and communication of status claims) and, in a situation more reminiscent of that described by Gumperz (1964b) in his pioneering report on Hemnesberget, as institutionally constrained choice between creoles in Voorhoeve's and Eersel's accounts (in this volume) on varieties of creole in Surinam. Eersel suggests that there are multilingual societies 'where there is no correlation between social stratification and the language used in the multilingual social contacts', where the factors in language choice are simply 'topic . . . situation and so on'. In such societies (none of which he names) prestige questions are associated only with intra-language differentiation, according to Eersel. Insofar as there seem to be prestige considerations involved in any· choice of language for multilingual contact it is difficult to imagine what situations Eersel has in mind. Insofar as most situations involving creoles are characterized not by identifiable groups of speakers speaking discrete, bounded, languages, but rather by a population of speakers controlling varying segments of differentiated linguistic continua, it is difficult to imagine *any* case in such a society where code choice does not weigh heavily in status and prestige considerations.[18]

SPEECH CLUES TO SOCIAL RULES

In relatively structured settings, it is clear that code selection is constrained, and that the ways in which people talk tell us both about their status and about the social situation in which interaction is taking place. It is not always so obvious that people frequently experience situations where they do not know what is going on and what expectations there may be for their behavior — until conversation has been initiated. When a person enters an ongoing social interaction he obtains cues not only for expected demeanour and speech styles but also for deferent or authoritative behavior by discovering the topics being discussed and, particularly, that way in which others are speaking. In defining a situation, how someone talks may be more important that what he talks about. The speaker of Jamaican creole who controls a substantial segment of the linguistic spectrum on the island knows when he meets an acquaintance with the same control speaking with another speaker who controls a lesser range, that if his friend uses *nyam* and *tick* he is defining the situation on the axis of solidarity and shared identity whereas if he is using *eat* and *thick* he is interested in the maintenance of social distance and formality. The newcomer to the ongoing social interaction is constrained not only to use the same speech pattern but to adopt congruent social attitudes, gestures, and so on, as well. Usages with pidgins and creoles appear to be identical with those of repertoire selection generally and to be congruent with the findings reported in studies of honorifics and pronominal usage (Stewart 1962). The functions of language in social control and, potentially, for conflict, can be clearly seen in such situations.

CO-DETERMINATION

A considerably more complex case of language influence on social development can be found in those situations where new languages have become vehicles for the development of a sense of social cohesion, shared identity, and nationalism. As a sociologist I am not competent to join in the arguments over the nature of creoles and pidgins, particularly as to whether the latter are 'simplified' or 'reduced' languages. I am not sure I am even interested in the answers. Whatever the answers may be to those, for me, surprisingly controversial questions, it is obvious to the sociological observer that these languages have had what must be considered as an indispensable role in making it possible for groups of great intitial – and sometimes continuing – linguistic diversity, to replace fearful hostility first with halting communication and ultimately with a sense of common identity and unity. This seems to have been a function of Bahasa Indonesian both before and after Independence. A number of observers believe that Neo-Melanesian – or *wontok* – may be performing a similar function in facilitating communication and mutual awareness in that even more linguistically diverse area of Melanesia constituted by New Guinea and Papua (Wurm 1966a and 1966b; Wolfers 1967). While linguists have apparently not yet decided on how it is to be labelled linguistically, it is clear that non-standard Negro English has some analogous functions in the mobilization of American black people in the USA for their struggle for full equality (or perhaps for independent nationhood). However these languages are classified it seems obvious that their presence has a direct impact on the social structure and the course of social events.

A closer scrutiny of the cases mentioned, however, may reveal a far more complex interaction – these events may be instances of the mutual influence and co-determination of language and social structure which scholars interested in working toward an integrated theory of sociolinguistic description see as being the most interesting of the possible causal relationships. And – a closer examination of even the three cases so vaguely sketched reveals that differences in power and conflict relations in the societies in which pidgins and creoles variously flourish may constrain or encourage the development (and the standardization or lack of it) of these languages in quite different ways. It would seem legitimate to speculate on the different linguistic outcomes in creole Jamaica and 'soul-talking' USA where the languages have originated in slavery and conflictful relations and matured in contexts of searches for group identity as contrasted to the pidgins which originated primarily from communicative needs and which acquired roles in political and social mobilization only after some unmeasured but specifiable level of communication had been reached. I believe that fuller exploration of these differences will provide added dimensions to the discussion of origins already completed.

Few of the papers prepared for the Kingston conference seem to provide substantial support for the perspective of co-determination. It is unfortunate that Karl Reisman's stimulating paper is not available in full for publication in this volume. Amongst the papers presented it seemed to me that his more than others has made claims of substantial magnitude about the social, structural (cultural, if the reader prefers) determination of semantic shifts and about the use of speech in social control. Reisman suggests that there is something in the set of social relationships of the group he studied that has shaped language and language use, and, at the same time, there has been mutual reinforcement because some terms come to be more easily available to some (kinds of) speakers than to others and that an outcome of this is differential constraint on social interaction. This again underlines the importance of language functions other than the communication of information (viz. as ritual or as 'put down'). This is true even in the cases of languages or codes sometimes characterized as inadequate for communication (e.g. in the richness of 'rifting' or 'the dozens', see Kochman 1969); I strongly recommend that readers of this volume read Reisman's article.

There are two articles which have implications for the co-determination perspective which were not fully discussed by the authors themselves and which in their present form are suggestive rather than definitive. Dillard mentions, anecdotally and almost in passing, that urban Haitian boys tend disproportionately to speak creole and girls of the same age and social class to speak French. He suggests that this pattern, like similar patterns reported for English creoles and non-standard Negro English in the USA, is related to concepts of masculinity and femininity. Given some 'popular' sociological views about the conservatism of females and the male role in cultural innovation, a number of interesting sociological and linguistic questions would seem to be raised.

The other suggestive case, and the author explicitly remarks on his inability to explain it, is found in Frake's very interesting discussion of the Zamboaguneo dialect of Philippine Creole Spanish. He observes that in much of the lexicon there is no particular patterning in the occurrence of Philippine or Spanish forms. However, when Spanish and Philippine-derived forms occur together in a contrast set — 'the Philippine form will designate the marked category: it will signify lesser magnitude, shorter distance, worse evaluation, female sex, junior generation, or plurality'. A glotto-archaeology of colonial relations?[19]

On research design and method

I had the impression, in reading papers prepared for the conference and in listening to the discussions at Mona, that some linguists are far more demanding of rigor in logical and deductive theory construction than in research design. It is true that fewer linguists than in the past feel that they can study a language successfully by painstaking work with one or two individual informants. While the desirability of sampling natural speech seems to have been widely accepted; this acceptance has frequently resulted in a rhetoric of rigor rather than in sophisticated research design. Much of the 'documentation' presented in Jamaica was anecdotal; there is no way an outsider can learn whether or not selective remembering has occurred so that only cases which fit theoretical presuppositions are recalled — some anecdotal exchanges at the conference made this seem a plausible hypothesis. The notion of controlled research; of holding variables constant and of manipulating variables systematically to determine why something happens in one case and not in another — rather than taking an individual case (or a small, selected set of cases) and expecting it (or them) to provide answers to questions of great complexity — has not yet been adopted by substantial numbers of linguists.

SAMPLING

At least some linguists label as 'sample' any collection of speakers (or words, or sentences, and so on), regardless of whether that collection was constituted by probability sampling, because of convenience of access, or through purposive selection to maximize the presence or absence of some population characteristic. The purpose of probability sampling is to determine whether observed differences could occur by chance. There is a question in my mind as to whether some linguists who use the term sample are familiar with this and other fundamental tenets of sampling theory. Thus, it is not possible to tell whether differences reported are a consequence of an imagined 'independent' variable or whether they result simply from characteristics of the 'sample' examined. In the case of studies of educational influences on use of creoles, for example, differences in socio-economic characteristics of pupil populations and differences in the location of institutions studied (urban-rural, industrial-tourist and so on) would be expected to affect outcomes. As the term sample was used by some conference participants, however, both the population characteristics of the universe to be studied and the sampling techniques were left undiscussed.

RESEARCH DESIGN

The ideal experimental design is as follows:

	Before (Time 1)	After (Time 2)	
Experimental group (stimulus)	x_1	x_2	$d = x_2 - x_1$
Control group (no stimulus)	x_1'	x_2'	$d' = x_2' - x_1'$

Behaviors x_1 and x_1' should be the same. The researcher's interest is in whether the difference between d and d', a difference which can be attributed to the experimental (or natural experimental) stimulus, is too large to have occurred by chance. In other words, such a design makes it possible to isolate the experimental treatment as having been plausibly responsible for the differences in the two groups at Time 2. If this is not done, if there is no control group, causal attribution may be made erroneously — school programs may be labelled as successful when actually student performance is responsive to industrial opportunities. Similarly, the simple co-occurrence of events cannot be taken as causal evidence unless some controls are present – viz. are there any cases where contacts of a Type A have *not* resulted in a language of Type B. Amongst those who made presentations it seemed to me that Stewart and Labov emphasized the need for controls and that other participants were only occasionally aware of any such necessity.

Related to the problem of controls is that of the effect of the interviewer or experimentor, something which has been labelled as the 'Hawthorne effect'. In a series of industrial studies it was found that workers' output improved when lighting was improved, when it was made worse, when more time off was given, when less was given, and so on. The conclusion was that it was not the things that were being done for or to the workers but that they were simply responding to the fact that somebody was interested in them and paying attention to them. Linguists doing research on languages with particularly salient prestige implications might well keep these effects in mind.

MEASUREMENT

The problems of measurement in the area of language use, whether the interest be in phonology, syntax or lexicon, are problems of linguistic methodology. Problems of semantics are probably problems for joint work by linguists and psychologists. Problems of measuring differences in social status and prestige and in social response to language use are problems for sociologists.[20] Without elaborating, I should simply like to suggest that DeCamp has provided an excellent model for other linguists in the increasing precision he has brought to measurement of the creole continuum – it seems logical to expect that other language phenomena will be equally amenable to innovations in measurement. (Labov 1968, suggests a number of new ways of attacking measurement problems in sociolinguistics.)

Coda

Sociologists are interested in recurrent patterns of human social behavior. The comparative sociologist is interested in checking assertions about such consistency by looking at similarly oriented behavior in different social contexts. Pidginization and creolization are persistent social processes. It is evident, moreover, that variations in contact situations and in the social functions of languages in such situations determine the different patterns which occur in post-contact periods. As a sociologist, I am convinced that the study of these languages can be most helpful, with linguistic data providing both clues to the understanding of processes of social change and a useful variety of data for the direct analysis of social interaction and social structure.

Anthropological and sociological students of culture contact and accompanying processes of acculturation have, for nearly a century, been carefully

P

studying the consequences of the meeting of different political, religious and technological systems. In spite of the elusive character of values as an object of study they have learned much about the persistence, syncretism and adaptation of beliefs and attitudes as well as of the socially patterned behavior associated with varying social structures and their value systems. The greater accessibility of linguistic behavior, particularly speech, to objective observation and measurement, should recommend it to social scientists as a superb source of data for the study of social processes, particularly those processes related to social change.

Linguists, in their turn, by viewing those linguistic processes which are socially determined as social processes analogous to social systemic acculturation (and resistance to acculturation), can enrich their attempts to gain theoretical understanding of linguistic behavior by drawing on the substantial corpus of work done by social scientists. This literature can be helpful to linguistic students of pidgins and creoles (and other language phenomena) in two ways. First, the interimplications of such social variables as power and loyalty (seen both historically and contemporaneously), are the same for outcomes of language contact as they are for other systems of social behavior — and language behavior *is* social behavior. Second, while there are some differences in the procedures for specification of evidence in linguistic as contrasted to, e.g. sociological research, the canons of research design and theoretical interpretation are identical. This congruence holds not only for criteria of reliability, validity and control but also for sampling and for imperatives for systematic consideration of comparative cases. An understanding of 'grammatically irrelevant conditions' will, perhaps, reveal that they are not so irrelevant as some linguists believe. Certainly, insofar as linguists increasingly concern themselves with linguistic performance they will find understanding of social variables essential.

NOTES

1 As a traditionally trained sociologist I continue to be pleasantly surprised by the long-neglected richness of language behavior as data for sociological research (although I realize that an earlier exposure to Everett Hughes would have reduced my sense of wonderment). I am continually grateful to my colleagues on the Social Science Research Council Committee on Sociolinguistics for their labors in introducing me to language as data, and for their continuing efforts to restrain me from over-enthusiasms resulting from my trained incapacities. I am particularly grateful to Dell Hymes for involving me in the Mona Conference and for his unselfish efforts to reduce those incapacities through long conversations and an unflagging zeal for editorial and educational correspondence. Thanks are also due to John Gumperz for a careful reading of this paper – even if I obstinately refuse to learn some important distinctions; to Gertrud Buescher and the University of West Indies (Mona) for gracious hospitality, and to other participants in the Conference for a number of insights and suggestions.

2 I am here making the distinction between competence as tacit knowledge of grammar and performance as actual speech behavior as that distinction is currently made by generative grammarians. Hymes (1966) argues, however, I believe with great cogency, that such tacit knowledge exists for other aspects of communication conduct. Hymes (1969) extends his argument to state that there may be *universal* aspects of language behavior in addition to the grammatical (universal conditions and relations of interaction through speech) and that *interactional* universals may be tacitly known. Performance may not be the residual and secondary (and irrelevant) behavior that some linguists imply that it is.

3 Sociologists have been looking for such universals on several different levels. See, variously, Homans (1950) and Berelson and Steiner (1964).

4 This is clearly one direction in which the work of the ethnomethodologists is moving. They, themselves, are extremely cautious in making claims about the generality of their findings. For interesting examples of work which has implications for questions about such universals see, e.g. Garfinkel (1967, in press) and Schegloff (in press).

5 There have been exceptions of course. It would be difficult to dispose of Weber as being 'primarily anecdotal'. Among linguists Greenberg and Pike engage in comparative research; members of the Prague school were interested in trans-societally relevant propositions.

6 John Gumperz has commented that these are less differences in perspectives on the direction of causal relationships than on what is to be defined as linguistic and what as social.

7 For a somewhat fuller exposition and supporting documentation see Grimshaw (1969).

8 Reinecke (1938) anticipated many of these questions. When originally published, however, his article seems to have had little impact.

9 The purpose of Chart 1 is to illustrate the range of possible variations in contact situations; I make no claims either for exhaustiveness or for accuracy of assignments within the chart. Linguists and area specialists will want to shift some cell entries, to add others, to refine the marginal labels. I do believe, however, that while my typology is primitive, it does indicate the kind of thing that is needed – *ad hoc* response to individual cases has not provided a viable base for theoretical development. Fortunately I do not have to stake my professional reputation on the adequacy of the suggested typology or the accuracy of its application. I *am* willing to take the risk of stating unambiguously that the questions noted above will not be satisfactorily answered until linguists and sociolinguists systematically examine the entire range of relevant cases.

10 There are, of course, situations of stable language contact across established national (or other) boundaries. In many such instances it can be argued that the languages are more or less equal in status. Bilingualism is a more likely outcome in such cases than is the development of a new pidgin or creole—though many schoolchildren may learn Franglais or some similar patois.

11 Chinese *literati* were unlikely to learn pidgin.

12 The relative and absolute sizes of the populations in contact should be included as a variable. Members of a group which constitutes five per cent of a population are far more likely to be 'exposed' to speakers of another language than are members of a group constituting 50%. However, once groups have passed some demographic threshold (the magnitude of which is unknown) it

444 ALLEN D. GRIMSHAW

will be easier for it to provide opportunities for internal interaction so that the need for interaction with speakers of other languages is reduced. For an examination of the importance of some of these demographic variables see Lieberson (1964, 1965).

13 Krio would seem to be an exception.

14 Since the linguistic record is not available it is not possible to tell whether some such monolingual-monolingual contact as that of Latin with languages under Roman control may have resulted in a pidgin→creole→standard development. Southworth provides an interesting example of an attempt to reconstruct a similar linguistic situation in India.

15 This is a point which Gumperz (1964a; 1964b) and Ervin-Tripp (1964) have been making for some years.

16 See Grimshaw (1969). More generally, see Duncan (1968).

17 For a fuller discussion see Grimshaw (In press).

18 Some linguists talk about social patterns with a casualness they would never adopt in linguistic discussions. Stratification clearly affects speech behavior, as do other social structural aspects of the speech setting. As more good sociolinguistic fieldwork is completed (the work of pioneers like Gumperz and Labov is exemplary in this respect), it is likely that more care will be taken by linguists in making sociological generalizations.

19 Frake's paper highlights the real interests of sociolinguists. Linguists deal with grammars – and languages are produced by grammars. But languages are *always* socially defined.

20 See, however, the work of psychologist Wallace Lambert and his students.

REFERENCES

[References to Alleyne, Daelman, Hancock, Lawton, and Wolfers are to their contributions represented in this volume]

Berelson, B. and Steiner, G. 1964. *Human behavior: an inventory of scientific findings*, New York, Harcourt, Brace

Blom, J. P. and J. J. Gumperz 1971. 'Social meaning in linguistic structures: code-switching in Norway', *Directions in sociolinguistics*, ed. by J. J. Gumperz and D. H. Hymes, New York, Holt, Rinehart and Winston

Bloomfield, L. 1933. *Language*, New York, Holt

Duncan, H. D. 1968. *Symbols in Society*, New York, Oxford University Press

Ervin-Tripp, Susan M. 1964. 'An analysis of the interaction of language, topic, and listener', *The ethnography of communication*, ed. by J. J. Gumperz and Dell Hymes, pp. 86–102 (*American Anthropologist* 66(6), pt. 2), Washington, D.C.

Garfinkel, H. 1967. *Studies in ethnomethodology*, Englewood Cliffs, New Jersey, Prentice-Hall

1971. 'Remarks on ethnomethodology', *Directions in sociolinguistics*, ed. by J. J. Gumperz and D. H. Hymes, New York, Holt, Rinehart and Winston

Grimshaw, A. D. In press a. 'Sociolinguistics and the sociologist', *The American Sociologist* 4(4):312–321

In press b. 'Sociolinguistics', *Handbook of communication*, ed. by W. Schramm, I. Pool, N. Maccoby, E. Parker, F. Frey and L. Fein, Chicago, Rand McNally and Co.

Gumperz, J. J. 1964a. 'Religion and social communication in village North India', *Journal of Asian Studies* 23:89–97

1964b. 'Linguistic and social interaction in two communities', *The ethnography of communication*, ed. by J. J. Gumperz and D. H. Hymes, 137–53 (Special publication, *American Anthropologist* 66(6), pt. 2) Washington, D.C., American Anthropological Association

Hall, R. A., Jr. 1966. *Pidgin and creole languages*, Ithaca, New York, Cornell University Press

Homans, G. C. 1950. *The human group*, New York, Harcourt, Brace and World

Hymes, D. H. 1966a. 'Two types of linguistic relativity (with examples from Amerindian ethnography)', *Sociolinguistics: Proceedings of the UCLA sociolinguistics conference*, 1964, ed. by W. Bright, 114–67, The Hague, Mouton and Co.

1966b. 'On communicative competence', *Report of the research planning conference on the language problems of disadvantaged children*, 1–16, New York, Yeshiva University, Dept. of Educational Psychology and Guidance. Also, an enlarged and revised version to appear in *Proceedings of a conference on mechanisms of language development*, ed. by E. Ingram and R. Huxley, London, Centre for Advanced Study in the Developmental Sciences and Ciba Foundation, 1969

1969. Personal communication

Kochman, T. 1969. ' "Rapping" in the black ghetto', *Trans-action*, 6, 26–34

Labov, W. 1968. 'A proposed program for research and training in the study of language in its social and cultural setting', Unpublished manuscript

Lieberson, S. 1964. 'An extension of Greenberg's linguistic diversity measures', *Language*, 40:526–31

1965. 'Bilingualism in Montreal: a demographic analysis', *The American Journal of Sociology*, 71:10–25

Reinecke, J. E. 1938. 'Trade jargons and Creole dialects as marginal languages', *Social Forces*, 17:107–18. Reprinted in *Language in culture and society*, ed. by D. H. Hymes, 534–46, New York, Harper and Row, 1964

Schegloff, E. A. 1971. 'Sequencing in conversational openings', *Directions in sociolinguistics*, ed. by J. J. Gumperz and D. H. Hymes, New York, Holt, Rinehart and Winston

Stewart, W. A. 1962. 'Creole languages in the Caribbean', *Study of the role of second languages in Asia, Africa and Latin America*, ed. by F. A. Rice, 34–53, Washington, D.C., Center for Applied Linguistics

Wurm, S. A. 1966a. 'Language and literacy', *New Guinea on the threshold*, ed. by E. K. Fisk, 135–48, Canberra, Australian National University

1966b. 'Papua-New Guinea nationhood: the problem of a national language', *The Journal of the Papuan and New Guinea Society*, 1:7–19. Reprinted in *Language problems of developing nations*, ed. by J. A. Fishman, C. A. Ferguson and J. D. Gupta, 345–64, New York, John Wiley and Sons, Inc., 1968

THE NOTION OF 'SYSTEM'
IN CREOLE STUDIES

WILLIAM LABOV

If one concept were to be named as central to linguistic theory and practice, it would probably be that of 'system'. In linguistics, this notion has developed with much greater clarity than in other studies of human behavior. By a *system* we commonly mean a set of elements which are so tightly organized that one cannot change the position of one without changing the position of the others. Or we may look at systems from the standpoint of resistance to change: that pressure exerted upon one member of a system produces less movement because it is anchored in a set of relations with other items; this is the concept of a 'system in equilibrium' as presented by Homans (1951:291). It seems to be well established that in general the central structures of linguistic systems – for example, verbal tense and aspect – resist influence from other languages, while peripheral elements of the vocabulary are freely borrowed. The older notion that a language can have only one parent reflects this notion that linguistic systems follow their own internal logic in the course of evolution, and when they react to outside influences, do so as a whole.

The pidgins and Creoles described in this volume offer a number of tests and challenges to this concept of system. First, there are pidgins which show such a fluctuating and unsystematic character that one can question whether or not they are systems in the sense given above. Secondly, there are Creoles described here which show such profound overlapping of historical sources in their central sub-systems that we can no longer assert that any area of linguistic structure is immune to hybridization and outside influences. Thirdly, the complex 'continuum' in many post-Creole communities raises the difficult question as to whether we are dealing with one variable system or several co-existent systems. Questions of segmentation and classification which have been extensively discussed for phonemes and morphemes have not yet been applied successfully to the higher level notion of system itself. We have yet to develop a procedure for arguing 'one system or two'.

The observations which I shall make in this paper are from a standpoint just outside of the field of Creole Studies. For a number of years I have been engaged in the study of language in monolingual speech communities in which there were many second and third generation speakers, and the indirect influence of a foreign sub-stratum was never far distant. These studies of the speech community involved a direct confrontation with the facts of variation;

variation was found to exhibit a far higher degree of structure and order than had been suspected previously. In some cases, such variation could best be described as an integral part of a single system. In other cases, particularly in studying non-standard Negro English NNE within a number of Northern cities, there were clearly two separate but closely related systems. It was in this study of non-standard Negro English that I first was drawn into contact with Creole studies, through Stewart's contention that this dialect showed the effects of a past Creole history.

I did not find these arguments convincing as they were first stated, in terms of direct parallels between non-standard Negro English of the United States and the Creole English of Jamaica and Trinidad or the Creole French of Haiti. It quickly became apparent that NNE was much closer to standard English, and the extremely stable vernacular spoken by Negro youth 8 to 17 years old showed very indirect relations with Creole grammars. In Jamaican English, for example, we find no present copula for predicate adjectives, an obligatory copula with predicate nouns, and an optional one (de) with locatives (Bailey 1966). There is no direct parallel for this in NNE; in any of these environments the present copula forms *is* and *are* can be deleted wherever standard English can contract. Our analysis of the speech used by vernacular peer groups shows clearly that these forms are removed by a deletion rule dependent upon contraction, governed by almost the same constraints as the standard contraction rule.

The tense system of NNE was similarly found to be far more closely related to standard English than to Creole grammars. Trinidadian English, for example, shows no *-ed* suffix in the preterit, and no irregular ablaut types either: the past is the simple unmarked form *Mi give* . . . (Solomon 1966). But NNE on the other hand, shows the *-ed* deleted by a variable rule which is constrained by phonological and grammatical factors: there are no speakers of NNE who always delete the *-ed*; furthermore, verbs such as *give, tell, keep,* show their irregular past forms even more regularly than in non-standard white dialects.

At the same time, NNE is much more different from standard English than any of the white non-standard dialects with which it is in contact. It forms a clearly separate *sub-system* on the basis of evidence to be outlined below. There are many characteristic rules within this system operating upon the raw material of English grammar in a distinctive way, leading to a set of stable differences which are persistent and well established. Furthermore, as noted by Stewart, there are forms found in various areas of the South, and among young Negro children, which may be best interpreted as indirect evidence of an earlier grammar which was far *more* different from standard English than the grammar we find today. For example, many Negro children have difficulty in re-constituting the full form of *am* from the common contracted form *I'm*; and Negro children use only one form of certain pronouns in subjective and objective positions more often and later than other children. Together with the evidence from the nineteenth century accounts which Stewart has compiled (1967, 1968) one must take this as a strong invitation to pursue the Creole hypothesis. No one who is interested in explaining and accounting for the structural differences between NNE and SE can afford to neglect Creole studies. We seem to see the results of extensive 'remodelling' in the sense outlined by Reisman in this volume, by which many of the original rules of nineteenth century Negro English have been adapted and reinterpreted in the light of the northern variety of standard English.

It is also worth noting that much of the behavior of young children which can be cited as possible evidence for a Creole substratum shows *non-systematic* linguistic behavior. For example, although it seems to be the case that more Negro children than white have trouble with *I am*, some say *I'm*, some say *I'm is*, and others say *I is*. There is no regular rule to predict which of the various forms will be selected or distinguished. There are children who say *he* for both *he* and *him*, and there are children who say *her* for both *she* and *her*, but they are not necessarily the same children – nor can we say in advance which child will do what. As Stewart has pointed out (personal communication), there have been fluctuations in the history of American Creoles as to which of the two forms would be chosen. The fact that important and significant linguistic behavior can be non-systematic, not predictable by rule and without regular norms, makes it all the more important to look for empirical evidence of a system in the early development of pidgins. The use of a form of language for communication does not make it automatic that it forms a system in the sense outlined above; the degree of systematicity is an empirical matter.

This conference demonstrates that there are enormous implications for linguistic theory in Creole studies; for developing our concept of system, and for the treatment of systematic variation. In the following discussion, I will focus on these concepts as they recur in the various papers, drawing certain parallel illustrations from my own work in other non-standard dialects. By way of further introduction, two methodological notes may be in order.

A newcomer to Creole studies is struck by the great wealth of data and expert knowledge in this field. It is a highly professional area: there are a great many scholars who know the Creole communities by first-hand experience, who actually control an enormous amount of the linguistic data (Polomé's dissection of Katanga Swahili for example). On the other hand, we see very little of the Creole speakers themselves in these papers. Hymes' basic proposals that we should seriously study the use of language (1962) have not yet reached the Creolists as a whole, who have been trained to report invariant grammar or phonology of the language to the exclusion of its other aspects. A notable exception is the paper of Karl Reisman, which contains a number of important observations on the larger Caribbean tendency to develop a covert, underlying set of values, and on the importance of this over-all set for the problem of isolating linguistic systems.

In all of the Creole systems, we are dealing with a subordinate dialect in contact with a superordinate standard. In this situation, one cannot hope to elicit reliable data by direct questioning. The general sociolinguistic principle that has emerged from our own work applies here: *Whenever a subordinate dialect is in contact with a superordinate one, linguistic forms produced by a speaker of the subordinate dialect in a formal context will shift in an unsystematic manner towards the superordinate.* Although one can predict the general magni-tude of the shift, social correction of this sort operates unpredictably upon particular forms, and furthermore, we have no guaranteee that there will not be reverse hyper-correction: what Le Page calls 'Hypercreolization'. An edu-cated informant who senses what the linguist is looking for may show 'hyper-incorrect' forms, and over-differentiate the non-standard dialect in a stereo-typed manner. Under 'formal context' we must include any situation where more than the minimal attention is being paid to language, for whatever reason.

Many of the authors point out that there are systematic reasons why the basic vernacular or Creole is not freely used. Creolists who are aware of this problem may therefore attempt to internalize the data themselves, or work from texts collected in semi-formal situations. Neither approach is entirely satisfactory, and more sophisticated sociolinguistic methods for solving this problem will undoubtedly be used in the future. One possibility, of course, is for linguists who are native speakers of a Creole to contribute their own intuitive knowledge. Certainly Creole studies are fortunate in having a num-ber of well-trained linguists such as Eersel and Bailey contributing to the work; there are no linguists who have a native knowledge of the non-standard Negro or Puerto Rican vernaculars of the mainland United States. But if we are to judge from the sociolinguistic situation in other areas, it is extremely unlikely that anyone can acquire a perfect command of the standard without affecting the form and stability of his vernacular rules. In moving between two closely allied systems, it seems inevitable that the learning of one rule will affect the form of similar rules in the underlying Creole. Certainly the intuitive insight of native Creole speakers is an invaluable asset in these investigations; but given the sociolinguistic situation that prevails, it cannot serve as hard evidence on the grammar and phonology of the vernacular. The principal limitation of these papers is that we have no direct contact with the data: there is no reflection of work done by recording creole speakers con-versing, arguing, swearing, worrying, boasting, or singing. Many of my com-ments must therefore represent extrapolations and analogies from other studies of speech events.[1] But there is every indication that Creole studies are moving in the direction of greater accountability to the data, and I believe that we can expect some of the most realistic and reliable studies of language from this field in the near future.

System

The linguistic concept of *system* involves a set of relations; these relations may appear as rules for the formation of sentences or the embedding of sentences, as the processes of word formation: as paradigms for tense or number; or as a structured set of relations between vowels – that some vowels are 'higher than' or 'fronter than' other vowels. Such relations form an *array*: that is, a fixed configuration with one-to-one matching in two or more dimensions. In the case of ordered rules, linguistic relations are matched with the positive integers. Vowels, grammatical paradigms, and semantic arrays are matched with each other, mutually determining their own position.

$$A_1 \rightarrow B_1 \rightarrow C_1$$
$$\downarrow \quad \downarrow \quad \downarrow$$
$$A_2 \rightarrow B_2 \rightarrow C_2$$

This mutual determination is the source of the stability of the system. If there is a tendency to move one element (raise a vowel, delete a dual, etc.) we find (1) that there is more resistance to this tendency than to the loss of an isolated word, and (2) that the tendency is reflected in a simultaneous movement of parallel or opposing relations in the array. Ordered rules mutually determine their positions by referring to their mutual outputs, and/or by applying to the same word classes, so that a generalization (or a lowering) of one rule leads to changes in the over-all output of the system and necessarily in the operation of other rules. The terms *structure* and *system* are used in much the same way: the chief difference is that *structure* focuses on the elements or categories, and *system* upon their relations (Labov 1966:230).

It would be meaningless to say that linguistic relations are systematic if there were not also forms of communication which were *unsystematic*. We will raise a similar question in relation to variation: that to assert that there are variable rules is meaningless if one cannot locate invariant rules by contrast. It may be going too far to assert that there are 'unsystematic' languages, but the description of several pidgins in this volume strongly indicates that in some sense they may be less than languages. Whinnom's account of Argentine *cocoliche*, and Samarin's account of Sango raise this question explicitly: in the absence of fixed standards of pronunciation and grammatical form, the notion of syntax begins to give way.

Samarin deals most explicitly with this problem in questioning whether Sango has two distinct codes, and therefore shows the same type of style shifting as more complex, full-fledged languages. He concludes that the existence of one respect feature in the pronoun system is not enough to satisfy the requirement of a distinct code: 'a clearly defined and integrated array of linguistic features, opposed to another similar array.' The concept of a code is plainly equivalent to that of a 'sub-system' as introduced here.

The notion of systematic and unsystematic relations can be illustrated by an example from New York City. In a complex set of words centered around the 'broad *a*' class of *ask, dance*, etc., short /æ/ was tensed to ǣ, and this tense, ingliding vowel has been gradually raised over the past sixty years to [ɛ:ᵊ], [e:ᵊ] and [ɪ:ᵊ], to equal the height of the word classes of *there* and *here*.[2] The systematic character of the vowel system appears in a parallel raising, several decades later, of the tense ingliding vowel of *Paul, lost*, etc. eventually reaching [ʊ:ᵊ] and merging with *sure*. By the same rule, the nucleus of *boy* was simultaneously raised to [ʊⁱ]; this was followed by a backing of the nucleus of *buy* and of the low tense vowel in *god* and *guard*. This and further changes show how a tightly related system will respond to the movement of one of its members (Labov 1966:553 ff). But overt social correction of such movements is far less systematic. The raising of ǣ is stigmatized, but one cannot predict which members of the tense ǣ class will be lowered in any given sentence to [æ:], nor which members of the tense ɔ̄ class will be lowered; furthermore, one cannot even specify the target vowel to which ɔ̄ will be corrected: it may be [ɔ] [ə] or even [ɑ]. Nor does this correction include the nucleus of *boy*, which is systematically identical with that of *Paul*, but not perceived as such under overt social processes. Thus the corrected form of language used in formal situations is unsystematic, although the vernacular is highly systematic.

The rules for the 'double negative', or negative concord, in non-standard English dialects show a series of systematic relations among the rules that emphasize or strengthen the negative element. For all dialects, the negative is attracted to the first indefinite if it is in subject position: *No one sits there* instead of **Anyone doesn't sit there*. But there is an optional rule for moving the negative rightward. In formal style, *He can't sit anywhere→He can sit nowhere*. In various non-standard dialects, this is the rule of negative concord that gives *He can't sit nowhere*. In non-standard Negro English, negative concord within the clause has become practically obligatory, so that it has lost its emphatic or contrastive character. The function of emphasizing the negative is carried out by two extensions of the negative rules: (1) the negative particle is duplicated in a following clause, so that NNE *It ain't nobody can't sit there* means the same as white non-standard *There ain't nobody can sit there*; (2) the negative is inverted with an indefinite subject, so that *Can't nobody do nothing about it* is the emphatic form of *Nobody can't do nothing about it*. Thus the shift of negative concord to obligatory status in one rule is compensated for by extensions of a similar function in other rules: in this sense, we are justified in saying that NNE forms a separate sub-system from other dialects of English.

Another set of systematic relations can be seen in the treatment of the finite forms of *be*. In various Southern dialects, the non-standard deletion of post-vocalic schwa operates so that the form *are*, when contracted, disappears entirely, to yield *You gettin' tired*. In NNE, there is a further extension of contraction which completely removes the lone /z/ of *is* to give also *He gettin' tired*. There is in NNE a compensating difference in the verbal system which introduces invariant *be*, immune to these phonological processes, with the semantic mark of habitual or general aspect, as in *He be foolin' around* (Labov 1969).

Such systematic relations contrast with the kind of unsystematic behavior we observe when speakers of NNE attempt to insert an -*s* in the present tense of the verb in formal styles: one cannot predict exactly what person or number will be affected. It is very common for some speakers to say *I gots to go, We likes it here*, as well as *He can gets hurt*. The amount of such hypercorrection shows a great deal of individual variation: some speakers do it a great deal, others not at all. Systematic rules of a language are not at the mercy of such idiosyncratic development, and we can further distinguish between systematic and non-systematic communication systems on this basis. Language systems are social in nature: a collection of idiolects is not a language.

In almost any language, we can locate unsystematic 'sub-systems' simply by moving down in the age range until we reach speakers whose grammars are in flux. While six-year-old children have indeed mastered a large part of the adult language, there are many areas where no fixed norm can be located. One would be ill-advised to make a study of the on-going vocalization of -*l* and -*r* in a speech community by the speech of six-year-olds, for it is difficult to distinguish between those who have learned a vocalic form and those who have not mastered the consonantal form. We noted above that Negro children have difficulty with uncontracted *I am*, and with the case distinction in pronouns: the distribution of these features is quite idiosyncratic. That is not to say that such behavior does not reflect real social and historical factors; it is simply that the end result at this point in their development is not a well-defined set of social norms.

It is therefore an empirical matter to determine the amount of systematicity in any linguistic sub-system. The Greek and Arabic diglossia outlined by Ferguson (1959) show the oppositions of two well-formed systems; although speakers can and do move in between the two levels, the vernacular and classical models seemed to have been clearly defined by the speech community. The same might be said for the London opposition between Received Pronunciation and Cockney. In New York City, the vernacular is a well-defined system as far as phonology is concerned, but there is no fixed standard available to middle-class speakers. The same range of possibilities seems to prevail in Creole communities. Valdman shows variable Haitian Creole opposed to a reasonably well-defined standard French. In Jamaica, there is some question as to how firmly fixed the Creole vernacular is; Bailey and Cassidy both emphasize the variation which was once neglected, yet their earlier outlines of Jamaican Creole strongly suggest that this variation is systematic (see below) and that Jamaican Creole is indeed a well-defined system.

Tsuzaki would like to resolve Hawaiian English into a set of co-existent sub-systems, and recent field work confirms his analysis. At the other end of the spectrum, we have the pidgins described by Whinnom. In the case of Argentine *cocoliche* and Hong Kong pidgin, he indicates that there are no fixed standards for any set of speakers. In fact, Whinnom argues that such pidgins can be formed only when the native speakers of the model language are removed from the scene, and with them the well-defined norms which control the system: that pidgins are defective in that they are removed from the original source of normative behavior.

Pidgins thus seem to be unsystematic in both senses noted: the absence of well-defined norms and the high degree of individual variation. Reinecke points out that standard French speakers used French phonology in speaking the Tây Bôi pidgin, while Vietnamese speakers 'completely Vietnamized' the French morphemes. Whinnom notes that in *cocoliche* one adds *s*'s in a non-systematic, almost random manner, parallel to the unsystematic correction of third singular -*s* in NNE.

If it is the case that pidgins were originally formed in a period when the standard language was not immediately available, this removal was only temporary. Reinecke gives us no indication that the Vietnamese pidgin speakers were removed from the influence of standard French, though admittedly this is only the briefest of sketches. The various Creole situations discussed here all show that some contact with a standard or modified standard is available. The problem for the Creole is in locating a well-defined set of norms at the vernacular end – to demonstrate that the language actually used is more than a set of deviations from the standard. Reisman points out that there are good reasons why this is not a simple task. Because the research methods used in the past did not include recording the vernacular in casual speech, the analyst usually extrapolated from his mixed texts to a hypothetical, homogeneous Creole structure. Continuous penetration of the Creole system by prestige items, and inherent variation within the Creole system, were impossible to represent; we will consider the theoretical innovations necessary to overcome this difficulty in the next section.

There is another basis for denying full linguistic status to pidgins, and perhaps to some Creoles: that they are too *simple*. Not only were the inflections of the model language lost, but also severe limitations in vocabulary found in pidgins such as Sango are taken as evidence that these are not full-fledged languages. But a purely structural notion of simplicity is of no value to us. By counting words or inflections we cannot hope to establish that the pidgin is indeed restricted as a potential means of communication. Inflectional simplification may give way to fixed word order; synthetic constructions may give way to analytic ones; the dictionary may be simplified in favor of peri-phrastic forms. But let it be noted that these processes are also used to yield Ogden and Richard's *Basic English*, with only 850 words. In *Basic English* verbs give way to a small set of operators and prepositions; almost any complex term can be paraphrased by an ingenious translator. Granted that many pid-gins are used to convey simple ideas, the same can be said of colloquial English: if pidgins are limited by their structural simplicity, this must be shown by studies of the pidgin in actual use, where speakers are struggling to express certain ideas which can take form in their native language but not in pidgin.

Samarin and others note that pidgins are characterized by a limited range of functions as compared to full languages. But though colloquial English has become increasingly limited by the growth of a literary English, one would not say that it is no longer a full language. Again, we need studies of speakers trying to adapt the available pidgin structure to these other functions to see if the mechanism is indeed too simple. Ferguson suggests that observations of 'foreigner talk' will give us a strategic point from which to study pidginization. Conceivably there are things that cannot be explained to foreigners – points too subtle for such an incipient pidgin which no one would attempt to convey.

It is certainly not difficult to show that some forms of languages lack the means of expressing certain distinctions. We have good reason to think that children's grammars are limited by tactical constraints which prevent them from expressing ideas which the speakers have clearly formed. For example, Lois Bloom (1970) shows that 21-month-old children may say in rapid succession 'Lois read', 'Read book', and 'Lois book', yet their grammars do not seem to permit 'Lois read book'. But at a later age children do find means of expressing complex ideas despite the limitations in their grammar. For example, a six-year-old Negro girl in Harlem defined a fence as 'To keep the cow . . . don't go out of the field'. Here her inability to form the nominaliza-tion *from going out of the field* did not prevent her from saying what she knew about fences, and it would be hard to prove that her syntactic device, a second finite verb, is not doing the job of communicating her meaning.[4]

On the other hand, some conditioned sound changes can lead to loss of such basic distinctions as singular-plural. In modern French, one cannot distin-guish number in several preposition and article combinations, nor in most nouns. In a public address De Gaulle once found it necessary to express his intention of using the plural by a meta-comment, since the language could

not do it for him: 'Je m'addresse aux peuples – au pluriel – . . .'⁵ This is a
minor limitation in French, for in general the plural has been preserved despite
the loss of final -s. But if certain pidgins are to be declared less than languages,
it is this type of limitation which must be demonstrated, on a larger scale.

CO-EXISTENT SYSTEMS

Throughout this conference, a number of writers refer to a plurality of systems, but it is Tsuzaki who makes the most explicit case for an analysis into
co-existent systems in Hawaiian English. He sees evidence of a pidgin, a
Creole, and a dialect of English. This is the paradigmatic case of what Creolists and dialectologists have been doing for some time – accounting for the
fluctuations and irregularities in their data by dialect mixture. Bailey (1966)
has done this in Jamaica, and Sivertsen in her study of Cockney English
(1960). In fact, Stewart (1967, 1968) makes such a polysystemic situation
criterial for a Creole situation. Eersel's and Voorhoeve's accounts of Sranan
leave no doubt that the Dutch and Sranan phonologies are preserved, at
least in part, as separate sub-systems; we see that they are combined in discrete
ways in different sociolinguistic contexts.

It is not enough, however, to claim that there are separate systems. What
must be done to establish one system, must now be done for two; it must be
shown that there are separate, internal constraints operating within each sub-
system. For those who have attempted to identify structure with homogeneity,
the mere existence of variation was enough to establish the presence of two
separate systems. But more realistic studies of change in progress have led
us to the realization that homogeneous systems are probably not functional
at all (Weinreich, Labov and Herzog 1968): that working systems must encompass means of style shifting and internal variation. Another basis for
isolating separate systems was to identify elements like recent loans which are
clearly not integrated with the older elements, and declare that their inclusion
or exclusion formed separate, co-existent systems. Indeed, Fries and Pikes'
original paper was based upon this marginal sense of 'system' (1949). Yet
surely we must set up more exacting standards for establishing the existence
of two systems.

Ideally, one would want to show that there are relations in equilibrium in
one system which are inconsistent with the corresponding set in the other.
Thus Denis Solomon argued that in Trinidadian Creole English, one had an
unmarked past *He give* and a marked present *He does give*, while the system
for any English dialect will show a marked past *He gave* and unmarked present
He give(s) (Solomon 1966). It was suggested that the passage of one system
into the other could not be a gradual affair, since both items must give way
at the same time, but this has not yet been established as an empirical fact.

It seems fairly easy to establish that in most situations French and English are co-existent systems using the kind of strict co-occurrence model that Gumperz first relied on in his studies of social code-switching (1964):

	Rule E$_2$	Rule F$_2$
Rule E$_1$	x x x x x x x x x x x	
Rule F$_1$		x x x x x x x x x

The absence of any mixed forms gives us a strong demonstration of the separateness of the two systems. In fact, bilingual speakers do produce strange mixtures of the two languages, as in this example from a New York Puerto Rican speaker:[6]

Por eso cada, you know it's nothing to be proud of, porque yo no estoy proud of it, as a matter of fact I hate it, pero viene Vierne y Sabado yo estoy, tu me ve haci a mi, sola with a, aqui solita, a veces que Frankie me deja, you know a stick or something, y yo equi solita, queces Judy no sabe y yo estoy haci, viendo television, but I rather, y cuando estoy con gente yo me . . . borracha porque me siento mas, happy, mas free, you know, pero si yo estoy com mucha gente yo no estoy, you know, high, more or less, I couldn't get along with anybody.

So far, however, no one has been able to show that such rapid alternation is governed by any systematic rules or constraints, and we therefore must describe it as the irregular mixture of two distinct systems.

The kind of implicational scale which DeCamp suggests here establishes a range of dialects but not the existence of two distinct sub-systems.

$$R_1 \text{ implies } R_2 \text{ implies } R_3 \text{ implies } R_4$$

Any cutting points on such an implicational scale would be quite arbitrary; the mere ordering of rules does not lead to the presumption that each combination of rules forms a separate sub-system. The only sound approach to this question is to demonstrate, by quantitative or qualitative means, that there are two sets of compensating, mutually balanced relations. This is what I have sketched above in several examples comparing NNE to other white nonstandard dialects. The basic argument must take the form:

System A has a set of rules R_1 R_2 R_3 R_4 . . .
System B has a set of rules R_1 r_2 R_3 r_4 . . .

and the combination of r_2 and r_4 carries out the same expressive function as R_2 and R_4, in a way that r_2 and R_4 or R_2 and r_4 would not. A single lexical example can of course appear trivial, as for example, one dialect of English can use *porch* and *piazza* where another uses *kitchen* and *porch* respectively or one uses *hydrant* and *plug* where the other uses *faucet* and *hydrant* respectively.[7] But in phonology, such relations can be impressive evidence of different sub-systems. For example, one dialect of Scots Gaelic opposes tense and lax finals as voiceless versus voiced, while another opposes them as pre-aspirated versus unaspirated voiceless consonants. Mixtures of such systems would be disastrous.

	Sutherland East Coast	West Coast
final /t/	[-t]	[-ʰt]
final /d/	[-d]	[-t]

A single pair of rules can be even more impressive evidence in the intersection of phonological and morphological patterns. Most English dialects show optional consonant cluster simplification in monomorphemic clusters only, but various Scots dialects (including standard Scots) have extended this rule categorically to the point where no clusters in -*pt* or -*kt* are permitted (Grant and Dixon 1921). This would have meant the loss of the regular preterit except for a change in the epenthesis rule:

	Standard English (colloquial)	Standard Scots (all styles)
act funny	[ækfʌni]	[ækfʌni]
packed full	[pæktfʊl]	[pakɪtfʊ]

The case is thus quite parallel to the NNE example of negative concord given above. Whereas the SE preterit is preserved by a constraint upon the simplification rule, the Scots preterit is preserved by a different means: English preserved the preterit by a constraint upon grammatical bimorphemic clusters; the Scots epenthesis rule differs from the English and the net result is the preservation of the preterit in both dialects.

THE COMPONENTS OF A LINGUISTIC SYSTEM

The standard view of language is that it is an assemblage of sub-systems, each closely interrelated with each other; that a language is one over-all system where 'tout se tient'. The recent development of generative grammar has shown us how deeply syntax is involved in the phonological output; for example, the low-level rule of contraction operates only when the tense marker is incorporated in the auxiliary (Labov 1969). The lexicon is now shown as the repository of a vast amount of syntactic information: each lexeme will show a number of categorical and selectional restrictions such as [+——NP, -Det——, +——S, +[+anim]——, . . .]. All of these developments show the various components of the linguistic system inextricably involved with each other, and it is often argued that a simplicity metric cannot be applied to only one of them: that the 'simplest grammar' will necessarily require calculation over the entire system.

All of these developments are deeply satisfying to those who feel that system is a good thing, and that we cannot have too much of it. But it should be pointed out that many of the statements made about systematic inter-connections are made on faith rather than evidence. For example, it is asserted that if two phonemes fall together, the value of every other phoneme in the system is instantaneously altered (Hockett 1958:448): 'a change *in any part* of a phonemic system alters the structural position of *every* form in the language.' This highly improbable assertion is made on the *a priori* notion that each phoneme is defined by its oppositions with every other element in the system. Instead of asking what evidence there is for such interrelations, and what observable consequences might result, it is normal to make such assertions on the basis of deductive principles, such as:

1. Every phoneme is related (by an opposition of mutual exclusion) to every other phoneme.
2. The value of a phoneme consists of its relations to all other phonemes.
3. When a phoneme merges with another, its relation to all other phonemes changes.
4. Therefore the merger of two phonemes changes the values of all other phonemes.

The empirical evidence we are gathering on sound changes in progress indicates that various sub-sections of the phonemic system may be related more directly than others; it may take many generations for the effects of change to spread throughout the system (Labov 1966:560). And there is now accumulating comparable evidence that the various sub-components of the linguistic system may be relatively independent: that it is possible for one to be completely replaced, while the others remain relatively intact.

There are three main bodies of evidence, all represented in this volume, which indicate that the various components of a linguistic system are relatively independent, and which challenge the notions that languages form coherent, highly integrated systems which are influenced only marginally from the outside.

(1) Evidence of the extreme similarity of Creole grammars in widely separated areas to support the relexification hypothesis advanced by Taylor, Whinnom, and Stewart.

(2) Evidence that languages like Zamboangueño and Mbugu can be put together from a number of highly diverse components (Frake, Goodman).

(3) Evidence that languages in close contact over long periods of time can become identical in some components but very different in others (Gumperz).

The relexification hypothesis requires that the lexicon of a language can be split off from the grammar – not just once, but many times, in the course of the development of a Creole. The notion that there are such 'dotted lines' in a language, and that one can tear out one component and throw it away, is in direct opposition to the idea that languages form inseparable wholes. Yet there is increasing evidence that such re-lexification has taken place.

Goodman's account of Mbugu shows the results of such relexification at an earlier time, with a Bantu grammatical base rather than a Creole grammar. Those who do not believe in relexification, or in 'hybrid' languages, will have a great deal of difficulty in accounting for Mbugu. The description of Zamboangueño given by Frake is an even more startling example of hybridization. The penetration of one language by another, in lexicon and grammatical subsystems, is shown to be much deeper than most linguists would have been willing to believe possible. For both Mbugu and Zamboangueño it can be said that this restructuring took place during a specific period when certain social and cultural conditions permitted it: but since that time, these linguistic systems have been no more open to the influence of surrounding languages than any other. Therefore it is not some structural weakness or liability of Mbugu or Zamboangueño culture which led to this hybridization, but rather a specific set of social conditions which are no longer available for our inspection: conditions which might conceivably affect any language.

Gumperz' work in Kupwad is a major step forward in answering this condition. He selected this site for his research into bilingualism because it was archetypical for certain specific conditions: a rural, bilingual community in which languages from two different genetic stocks had been in undisturbed and intimate contact, almost on an equal basis, for several hundred years. Gumperz finds that the two languages, Dravidian Kannada and Indo-European Marathi have become practically identical in their deep structure and semantics, on the one hand, and in their phonetic output on the other, while they have consistently remained distinct in lexicon and grammatical formatives. When he first presented his results, the objection could be raised that standard Marathi and standard Kannada, as spoken in large cities, would show much the same approximation, in line with the well-known convergence of Dravidian and Indo-European on the South Asian peninsula: but Gumperz' present paper is a conclusive demonstration of his argument. In point after point, he shows that the local varieties of the two languages converge where the standard languages differ. The importance of Gumperz' work for linguistic theory can hardly be overestimated: we see linguistic evolution moving in two different directions within the same languages.[8] One can hardly doubt, after Gumperz' research, that the lexical components of a language can be divorced from the underlying grammatical sub-structure. It is not only the results, but the model of research followed by Gumperz which should be instructive to us. He has not confined his linguistic interest to a particular region or specialty, but rather focused on the general problems of communication in the speech community. He first isolated the problem of code-switching and convergence in stable bilingualism; located a strategic research site; then carried out empirical research by direct observations of the language in use. Gumperz' work gives the strongest theoretical support to the relexification hypothesis, and it also provides a model of research which Creole studies can follow with profit in the future.

Variation

One of the main themes which connects this conference with other socio-linguistic discussions is the prominence of *variation* as an ever-present aspect of the creole situation. Almost all the papers deal with it: Reisman, Bailey, Valdman, Samarin, DeCamp, Whinnom, Le Page, Tsuzaki, Cassidy, Voorhoeve, Eersel and Craig. This situation heightens the interest of the conference for me, since I have sometimes approached sociolinguistic analysis primarily as a means of dealing with variation in a principled way.

It is of course not sufficient to merely mention variation, or to worry about it. Linguists have devised countless means of disposing of variation, so that they could reconstruct the homogeneous, invariant systems which could be described within the traditional categorical view. Sometimes variation is simply recognized and given a name ('free variation', 'social or expressive variants','the variphone'); sometimes the field of research is contracted to the 'idiolect' or expanded ('overall pattern') to do away with variation.

More serious approaches to the problem recognize the systematic nature of variation, and attempt to account for it within the framework of categorical, invariant rules. The variants can be assigned to separate, co-existent systems as Tsuzaki and Reisman have done. But the actual work of separating such systems can only be done on a body of vernacular conversation, and this step Creolists have not yet taken. The statement that the opposing variants belong to different systems is not enough: it is necessary to show how the speaker moves from one system to another, and under what conditions. When actual conversation is examined, it usually appears that oscillation between the two takes place many times within a sentence, and to explain all variation as code-switching becomes increasingly artificial. It is equivalent to asserting that the speaker switches systems within a single utterance many times, unpredictably, without apparent motivation or conditioning. Let us consider what such a treatment would look like, applied to the language of Boot, one of the leaders of the 'Thunderbirds', a pre-adolescent group in Harlem. Boot is as characteristic an NNE speaker as one can find, as far as phonology and grammar are concerned, yet to account for his variation on the basis of co-existent NNE and SE systems, we would have to posit such eccentric code switching as shown below. ('NNE' would be in lower case, 'SE' in capitals; Boot is describing the rules for 'Skelly', a street game played with weighted bottle tops.)

Well, i's long line, y'start off, an' y'shoot – y'shoot into skellies. An' 'en ef you make in in skellies, you shoot de onesies. An' den like IF YOU MISS ONESIES, de OTHuh person shoot to skelly; ef he miss, den you go again. An' IF YOU GET IN, YOU SHOOT TO TWOSIES. An' IF YOU GET IN TWOSIES, YOU GO TO tthreesies. An' IF YOU MISS tthreesies, THEN THE PERSON tha' miss skelly shoot THE SKELLIES an' shoot in THE ONESIES: An' IF HE MISS, YOU GO from tthreesies to foursies.

We would have to posit sixteen switches of code in this short passage. Boot begins with NNE [ɛf], and switches to SE [ɪf]; this is countermanded by [də] for *the*, and immediately followed by standard [ð] in *other* (and not 'NNE' [d] or [v]); yet the low open vowel which ends this word is characteristically NNE, as is the absence of third singular -*s* on *shoot*. Where *th* is spelled in the standard fashion, it is a fricative [θ]; otherwise, it is an affricate or stop as indicated. In this short passage, we can see three examples of systematic and inherent variation which cannot be resolved into separate sub-systems without yielding an irrational scheme. There are also shown here categorical, semi-invariant rules of NNE which differ from SE; note that there is no third singular -*s* in *Other person shoot, he miss, that miss*, etc. – altogether, six instances of this NNE feature which do not vary at all.

If Creolists were to examine their data in such detail, I believe that they would find both inherent variation and regular, invariant rules characteristic of each sub-stratum. The variation shown here is not without structure, but it is not the strict co-occurrence demanded by the model above. Instead, Boot's use of consonant clusters or affricates would show a pattern such as:

	Casual style	Formal (reading) style

'SE' prestige form		x x
		  x x x x
		    x x x x x x x x

'NNE' vernacular form	x x x x x x x^x x^x x x	x x x

This is what we call 'co-variation' – the type of irreducible and regular variation which is rule-governed, but cannot be reduced to categorical form. Any attempt to resolve such behavior into the co-existent systems is bound to fail; we will be left only with the notion of 'dialect mixture' – that is, without any regularity, rhyme or reason in the speaker's behavior. In some ways, the traditional notion of 'mixture' as used by Le Page and Cassidy, is a more accurate statement of our knowledge if no accountable analysis has been carried out.

Among the scholars represented here, Valdman, Le Page, DeCamp and Craig are the only ones who attempt to deal directly with variations as we have done in other areas. Valdman notes that variation in Creole systems goes back to the earliest times that we have been able to record, and he gives some detailed and persuasive examples of such variation. He justly criticizes the 'dialect mixture' tag by noting that 'too often analysts attribute aberrant features of languages existing in a contact situation to bilingual interference, and fail to consider the alternative possibility of retention from an older stage'. The existence of an inherited variation of front rounded versus unrounded vowels is the case in point. If we see that inherited variation is characteristic of all linguistic systems, then one need not feel that this is too strong an inference at all.

DeCamp's recent contributions to Creole work and sociolinguistics generally have been among the most thoughtful, and his emphasis on the need for theory rather than 'mere' description is certainly in order. To my way of thinking, sociolinguistics as a descriptive discipline is a hopeless task; there is no limit to the number of correlations between linguistic and social factors which might be described. An interdisciplinary sociolinguistics, divorced from the theoretical problems of linguistics, anthropology and sociology, is not likely to make significant contributions to our knowledge of language or social behavior. DeCamp's paper in this volume has many original and productive suggestions for the development of sociolinguistic theory which I hope will be developed further. His positive orientation towards generative grammar seems to me equally appropriate, since it is within that framework that we have been able to make progress in formalizing sociolinguistic statements. It is in the light of these positive aspects that I would like to submit certain criticisms; DeCamp also seems to have adopted some of the major defects of generative grammar, so that his many good notions are offset by some backward steps for the study of language in its social context.

One well-known weakness is in the relation of theory to data. DeCamp's approach to 'sociolinguistic theory' seems to be the translation of small amounts of data – essentially fragmentary examples – into the terminology devised by Chomsky and Halle for their treatment of standard English. Those who have been carrying out sociolinguistic work within the speech community – including Gumperz, Shuy, Wolfram, Fasold and myself – have been motivated by a keen awareness of the limitations of current linguistic theory. Our intention was to use this rich data on change and variation to repair the obvious weaknesses of theories which are incapable of dealing with it – and so to provide new and better solutions to traditional problems of synchronic analysis. The categorical rules of generative grammar, for example, are no better adapted to deal with the actual use of language than the categorical statements of the structural linguistics of the 1940s. The binary notation of Chomsky and Halle has been shown inadequate to deal with the kind of movements in phonological space we are dealing with (Labov 1966:531–7). No generative grammar or semantics has yet shown a capacity for dealing with discourse beyond the sentence. To import generative phonology in its present form into the sociolinguistic arena would be self-defeating: the advantages of the data will be lost, and the defects of the theory will remain.

One of the serious limitations of current generative grammar is not in the form of the rules, but rather in the mode of work, and the relation of the analyst to the data. DeCamp has the knowledge, the data and the capacity to go far beyond the stage of rewriting a small number of examples in a novel framework. The now accepted paradigm is to develop an idea on the basis of a few small examples, without any serious consideration of what would happen if all of the available data were to be treated in this way. The implicational scale which DeCamp suggests is an important means of dialect classification: on what basis were they selected? What will happen when the six items used by DeCamp are expanded to the hundreds of dialect differences in his data, and how does one classify people who vary in their usage? If it is to be useful, this technique must certainly be adapted to variable rules, as Stolz and Bills have done in their Texas studies of 1968. Their ordering of sociolinguistic variables included, for example, whether or not a speaker used more or less than a certain frequency of the *got* passive.

In response to DeCamp's proposals, one might say that it is perhaps a good idea to apply generative grammar in its present form to sociolinguistic data and see just how far it will take us. This is a point of view quite appropriate for those who have some interesting data and are searching for a theory which will help explain it for them; or for a newly created interdiscipline like psycholinguistics which looks to linguistics for hypotheses to test. But a socially realistic linguistics should be all too conscious of the limitations of current linguistic theory; we turn to the speech community because we know that better data is needed, and we hope to derive theory which is accountable to that better data. To lean parasitically upon generative grammar for theoretical support will inevitably lead to the rejection of the data itself, and we will find Creolists publishing papers based upon mere fragments of their own wide competence, simply because the larger bodies of data do not fit the model.

DeCamp curiously asserts that Chomsky's position in *Aspects* (1965:3) has been misunderstood – that he did not intend to exclude social and stylistic variation from the theory of competence. I find it difficult to follow DeCamp on this point. Chomsky is a serious writer, who is always at pains to say exactly what he means; in his opening pages he states in the plainest terms the position he has always taken: that general linguistic theory (necessarily a theory of 'competence') takes as its object a homogeneous speech community in which everyone speaks the same and learns the language instantly. Those who work in the sociolinguistic field and hope to gain Chomsky's approval are due for a rude awakening: they may finally succeed in making his pronouncements seem ambiguous, but he in turn will have no hesitation whatsoever in brushing aside their work as irrelevant to linguistics. As I hope to show below, we can use Chomsky's insights and profit tremendously from generative grammar, but not if we allow him to define for us the limits of linguistics and the shape of linguistic rules. Hymes has taken a firm position on this matter in his insistence that we consider 'communicative competence' (1968), and there is reason to think that Chomsky's formulation will have to give way to this broader conception.

In the field of semantics, Creole studies would be equally well advised to avoid dependence upon generative models which are now being put forward. Most depend upon the manipulation of a small number of semantic features expressed in binary notation, as DeCamp has done in his analysis of Jamaican terms for meals. First, it should be noted that all of these presume that there is a finite set of semantic features which will some day be defined by their mutual exclusions, but no one has ever demonstrated or even proposed such a set. Given the absence of a well-formed semantic theory, I think we should try in each case to be sure that our statements are adding some clarity to the data, and making the situation clearer for us rather than more complex. There are a few evident regularities in the Jamaican use of these terms which apply to usage of the three lower classes which DeCamp lists, but not to the highest group, which seems to follow a foreign model.

(a) *Supper* is the term for the meal after *dinner*.

(b) *Breakfast* is the term for the meal before *dinner*.

(c) If there is a meal before *breakfast*, it is called *tea*.

In addition to these facts, we have to specify when each group takes its dinner, and which is the heaviest meal of the day. The elaborate treatment which DeCamp provides for these terms would be an admirable exercise, if it were based upon a set of features which shared some of the stability and intersubjective status of phonetic features; lacking this, it has all the disadvantages of manipulating unknowns to achieve unknowns.

VARIABLE RULES

In all of our recent work in the speech community (Labov, Cohen, Robins and Lewis 1968; Labov 1969) we have been concerned with the formalization of sociolinguistic data in a manner consistent with our recognition of inherent and systematic variation. At present, generative grammar can handle variation only through the distinction between obligatory and optional rules. It might seem, at first glance, that inherent variation can be 'accounted for' by an optional rule. Valdman's example of variation in front rounding in Haitian French might then be shown as

$$V \rightarrow \langle [+\text{back}] \rangle / \overline{[+\text{round}]}$$

The angled brackets indicate that the rule is optional, equivalent to the label

Top for a transformation. One would then be left with the problem of explaining who uses this rule more often and who less often, in what stylistic context, and so on. DeCamp's approach would here suggest an additional context, say /[-urban] after the linguistic environment. But this would not account for the facts of the matter at all, for no categorical statement will fit the situation. If it is true that far more rural speakers than urban speakers use the rule, and in less formal contexts, we would not gain any precision by stating that all rural speakers use it in casual speech, and implying that urban speakers never use it.

Leaving aside the broader social context, there are many linguistic relations which cannot be signalled within the framework of optional and obligatory rules. This can clearly be seen in the development of the rules for contraction and deletion in NNE (Labov 1969), phonological rules which operate to give

contraction   deletion
He is wild   ——→   He's wild   ——→   He wild

We show that these are parallel phonological rules by establishing the following sets of relations between the variable constraints on contraction and deletion:

(1) They show the same constraint from the preceding grammatical category: both rules are used more often after a pronoun then after other noun phrases.

(2) They show the same constraints from the following grammatical category: both are used most often before *gonna*, then before verbs, and least often before predicate nouns.

(3) They show parallel but opposite effects from the following phonological environment: contraction is more frequent before vowels, and deletion before consonants. This reversal of the effects fits in with the way that these two rules differ in their operation: contraction is the removal of a vowel, while deletion is the removal of a consonant. The variable constraints show that both operations are favored when they produce a CVC syllable structure.

It should be apparent that optional rules would not capture the fine-grained quantitative relations which permit such arguments. An even more abstract set of variable relations shows us that these are distinct but separate rules of the same form, with contraction preceding deletion. We find that each of the parallel variable constraints under (1) and (2) above are sharpened or intensified when deletion is added to contraction (Labov 1969).

The basic operation in formalizing these relationships is to assign to every rule a quantity ϕ which represents the proportion of cases in which the rule applies out of all those cases in which it might have applied. If the rule goes to completion, then $\phi = 1$. If not, it may be considered to be restrained by a factor k_0, so that $\phi = 1 - k_0$. The variable constraints mentioned above are conceived as modifications of this limiting factor k_0. They are most simply indicated in the environment of the rule by the use of angled brackets. When these brackets occur in connection with angled brackets around the output expression, immediately to the right of the arrow, they indicate that the bracketed conditions favor the application of the rule. Thus for the NNE rule which deletes the already contracted copula:

$$[+\text{cons}]— <\text{ø}>/<+\text{pro}> \#\#——\#\# <+\text{Vb}>$$

Informally, this rule states that a lone consonant, all that remains of a word, is deleted variably – more often when the subject is a pronoun, and more often when a verb follows. It is sometimes useful to show the relative strengths of these constraints, by the use of Greek letters (Labov 1969) or Arabic numerals (Fasold 1970, Bailey 1970). But such relations among the constraints vary from dialect to dialect, and shift as the language evolves. The simpler expression just given describes conditions which hold for English generally, and for many Creole continua.

A Creole grammar may have no copula at all, but sometimes we find the copula before noun phrases and/or locatives, but not before verbs or predicate adjectives. This is the case in Jamaican Creole, and when speakers shift along the continuum towards Jamaican English we can expect to find their use of the copula governed by such a rule as this. If we consider that adjectives are fundamentally verbal predicators, marked with [+Vb], then the rule just given will account for the speech of a Jamaican in formal style who shows zero copula most often before adjectives and verbs under the influence of the underlying Creole grammar. It might be more realistic to write a rule for the variable insertion of the copula with converse constraints; but in all such situations we find that more contracted or deleted forms are found with pronoun subjects. We do not have such data on Jamaican variation as yet; but recent work of Richard Day on Hawaiian English Creole shows variable constraints similar to those of other English dialects for speakers moving between the basic Creole grammar and Standard Hawaiian English. The basic Creole (as identified by Tsuzaki in this volume) is moving closer towards English, although the status of the copula is still insecure. In our data we find *stay* used with locatives (*Look where they stay!* = SE *Look where they are*) and sometimes we have zero where NNE or other English dialects would demand a copula (*I show you where the lion*). But for most varieties of Hawaiian English we can write a variable rule for the copula with *is* and *are* controlled by a set of constraints similar to those just shown.

There has been some misunderstanding of the role proposed for variable rules in grammatical analysis. It is not suggested that all rules be variable – nothing could be farther from the spirit of linguistic procedures. The fundamental problem of linguistics is to eliminate the superficial variation which we first encounter in the language: our analysis normally explains away such variation as the product of invariant rules of environmental conditioning which were not perceived at first. Those who hunt for variables as if they were the goal of analysis are reversing the normal intent of linguistics for no good reason. But it is equally illusory to believe that all cases of variation can be resolved into invariant rules, dialect mixture, or free variation. In some cases the variation we find can be resolved into a set of invariant rules which vary from individual to individual in an implicational array of the sort that DeCamp suggests. And in some cases we can account for the observed variability with the conventional categories of obligatory and optional rule. But more often, we find that the optional or variable rules show considerable internal structure, and only by describing such structure in the form of variable constraints can we solve the historical or analytical questions that we are faced with.

As a final argument to avoid the incorporation of variable relationships in our grammars, one might say that these are matters of 'performance' rather than 'competence'. It is now evident to many linguists that the primary purpose of this distinction has been to help the linguist exclude data which he finds inconvenient to handle – that is, to further the restricted definition of linguistics set out by Chomsky in *Aspects* (1965:3). As a whole, the distinction between competence and performance has never proved to be particularly helpful for our work, and it becomes more and more unclear as we consider its general implications. If performance involves limitations of memory, attention, and articulation, then we must consider almost the entire English grammar to be a matter of performance.

We see that the syntax, morphology and phonology of a language is a means of transforming a complex, multi-dimensional network of semantic features into a linear sequence. The basic problem is that we cannot *say* our intention without organizing it into a sequence of overlapping articulations. There are many steps along this route which lead to the surface organization of subject, finite verb, and complement with most modifications in the form of right hand branching. Typical of such processes is extraposition:

> It (John hits George) is easy →
> It is easy for John to hit George

The first sentence might have produced, 'For John to hit George . . . ', a formal expression not characteristic of colloquial speech. We note that adolescent youngsters rarely if ever use such subject nominalizations: no doubt a matter of performance. But the very existence of the extraposition transformation is plainly motivated by the same performance factor which makes it obligatory for many speakers. We could show that almost every transformation of English – relatives, coordination, reflexives – all have the effect of making sentences easier to say, easier to grasp, and easier to remember. If we take this larger view of grammar, the present distinction between grammatical competence and performance collapses.

The formal rules developed here are designed to give full support to those Creolists who recognize variation as an inherent property of the linguistic situation, not an accident of an aberrant, mixed, or degenerate speech community. The more deeply we examine speech communities, even the supposedly homogeneous communities of Hemnes, Norway, or Chilmark, Martha's Vineyard, the more we become convinced that the existence of a uniform, homogeneous dialect is problematical at best. We argue that such homogeneity, if it existed, would no doubt be dysfunctional, and would give way to more heterogeneous language forms. The major theoretical move required is to abandon the identification of structure with homogeneity (Weinreich, Labov and Herzog 1968). Creole studies may benefit from this step more than any other branch of linguistics.

The variable relations mentioned in section 2 may be looked at as part of the typical phenomena of de-creolization. As noted in the introduction, it is not impossible to say with Stewart and Dillard that NNE represents a grammar converging with standard English – that earlier forms were more different, closer to the Creole grammar of the Caribbean. In such an earlier stage, we would still expect to find inherent variation, as we find it in Jamaican Creole English, in Trinidadian English, in Haitian Creole, or in the Gullah transcribed by Lorenzo Turner (1949:254–89). In many rules, we see the gradual development of phonological conditioning – as the underlying forms come closer to those of the surrounding English dialects (Labov, Cohen, Robins and Lewis 1968:240–95). There is no doubt that speakers will re-interpret forms in the light of their current data, and one can trace gradual shifts of this type which can be called de-creolization. At the same time, we observe some elements in the current grammar which remain categorically different from those of other dialects (such as the absence of the third person singular -*s*, attributive -*s*, or use of invariant *be*) so that it is not true that all elements of the original grammar are being re-interpreted. If all the rules peculiar to NNE which we discover were variable, then we might say that this sub-system is nothing but a transition stage of some more stable grammar, now being de-creolized. But we find that some NNE rules are invariable where the corresponding white non-standard rules are variable: negative concord is a good example. There is no reason to think that the NNE grammar we are describing is any more in flux than the grammar which might have been used by field hands in the eighteenth century. It is therefore not legitimate to extrapolate backwards in time, without further evidence, to argue that the currently variable rules were once invariant rules maximally different from the English dialects now influencing them.

The processes of pidginization and creolization are viewed by most of the writers in this volume as continuous processes. It is obvious from the study of Mbugu and Zamboangueño that there are discrete periods of change in the past history of languages, and these can be terminated. But the study of change in progress shows us that a uniformitarian doctrine for linguistics is not unreasonable. In geology, this is the point of view which has replaced the earlier notion that most of the physical features we see around us are the results of sudden catastrophes at unstable periods in the past; geologists now feel that they are the result of the same kind of ongoing processes which we can observe around us. In a given region, there are periods when one or the other type of change prevailed, but these earlier movements are not viewed as different in kind from those taking place today. This seems to be a reasonable approach to the historical problems of Creole languages: close studies of variation and change in present-day Creole communities will no doubt give us a good indication of what has happened in the past.

NOTES

1 The empirical studies referred to here include those of Gumperz in Khalapur and Hemnes (1964), and in Kupwad discussed in this volume; of Shuy *et al.* (1967) and Wolfram (1969) in Detroit; of Fishman, Cooper and Ma in Jersey City (1968); my own work in New York City (1966); and that of myself, Cohen, Robins and Lewis in Harlem (1968). One aspect of the study of non-standard Negro English is developed in detail in Labov (1969). A preliminary draft of this paper was circulated at this conference as an illustration of the ways in which generative grammar and quantitative sociolinguistic analysis may be used to deal with extensive variation in a formal manner.

2 The complex tensing rule, which selects members of the lax /æ/ class, shows widespread geographic variation from New York to Philadelphia and Baltimore, but no clear social significance. The raising rule, on the other hand, is a distinct process of a much simpler kind which raises all tense æ with (eventually) very sharp social response. See Cohen (1969).

3 This analysis of negative inversion fits the more general pattern in which modals are also inverted: *Can't nobody do it*. But the *ain't* construction is also subject to an analysis from an underlying *it ain't nobody knew he did*. See Labov, Cohen, Robins and Lewis (1968:3.7).

4 The example is drawn from the work of Professor Jane Torrey, of Connecticut College, who is currently investigating the language of Negro children 4 to 8 years old as an extension of our work in Harlem.

5 The example is cited by Sauvageot, (1962:73).

6 The example is taken from exploratory interviews in the West Side Puerto Rican community of New York City, carried out by Pedro Pedraza of Columbia University. Similar examples are given in Fishman *et al.* 1968 from their work in Jersey City.

7 The first example is drawn from Atwood (1962), and the second from my own observations on Martha's Vineyard.

8 Bright and Ramanujan (1964) show opposing directions of linguistic change within the same language (Tulu) as the result of social differentiation of Brahmins and non-Brahmins. But these deal with relatively small scale changes as compared with Gumperz' findings.

REFERENCES

Atwood, E. Bagby 1962. *The regional vocabulary of Texas*, Austin, University of Texas Press

Bailey, Beryl 1966. *Jamaican Creole syntax*, New York, Cambridge University Press

Bailey, C.-J. 1970. 'Studies in three-dimensional linguistic theory', *Working Papers in Linguistics*, Hololulu, University of Hawaii

Bloom, Lois M. 1970. *Language development: form and function in emerging grammars*, Cambridge, Mass:. M.I.T. Press.

Bright, William and A. K. Ramanujan 1964. 'Sociolinguistic variation and language change', *Proceedings of the 9th International Congress of Linguists*, 1107, The Hague, Mouton

Cohen, Paul 1969. 'The tensing of short /æ/ in the New York City area', New York, Columbia University Master's essay

Fasold, Ralph W. 1970 'Two models of socially significant linguistic variation', *Language* 46:551–563

Ferguson, C. A. 1959. 'Diglossia', *Word* 15:325–40

Fishman, Joshua A., Robert L. Cooper, Roxanne Ma *et al.* 1968. *Bilingualism in the Barrio*, Final Report on OEC-1-7-062817, Washington, D.C., Office of Education. 2 vols.

Fries, C. C. and K. Pike 1949. 'Coexistent phonemic systems,' *Language* 25:29–50

Grant, W. and J. Dixon 1921. *Manual of modern Scots*, Cambridge, Cambridge University Press

Gumperz, John J. 1964. 'Linguistic and social interaction in two communities', *The ethnography of communication*, ed. by John Gumperz and Dell Hymes, 137–53. (*American Anthropologist* 66(6), 2), Washington, D.C.

Hockett, Charles F. 1958. *A course in modern linguistics*, New York, Macmillan

Homans, George C. 1951. *The human group*, New York, Harcourt, Brace

Hymes, Dell 1962. 'The ethnography of speaking', *Anthropology and human behavior*, ed. by T. Gladwin and W. C. Sturtevant, 13–53, Washington, D.C., Anthropological Society of Washington

[1968]. 'On communicative competence', Mimeographed [To be published, Philadelphia, University of Pennsylvania Press, 1970]

Labov, William 1966. *The social stratification of English in New York City*, Washington, D.C., Center for Applied Linguistics

1969. 'Contraction, deletion and inherent variability of the English copula', *Language* 45:715–62

Labov, William, Paul Cohen, Clarence Robins and John Lewis 1968. *A study of the non-standard English of Negro and Puerto Rican speakers in New York City* (Cooperative Research Report 3288), New York, Columbia University

Sauvageot, A. 1962. *Français écrit, français parlé*, Paris

Shuy, Roger, Walter A. Wolfram and William K. Riley 1967. *Linguistic correlates of social stratification in Detroit speech* (Final report, Cooperative Research Project 6–1347), Easi Lansing, Michigan State University

Sivertsen, Eva 1960. *Cockney phonology*, Oslo

Solomon, Denis 1966. 'The system of predication in the speech of Trinidad: a quantitative study of decreolization', New York, Columbia University Master's essay

Stewart, William A. 1967. 'Sociolinguistic factors in the history of American Negro dialects', *The Florida FL Reporter* 5(2)

    1968. 'Continuity and change in American Negro dialects', *The Florida FL Reporter* 6(1)

Stolz, Walter and Garland Bills 1968. 'An investigation of the standard-non-standard dimension of Central Texan English', Mimeographed

Turner, Lorenzo Dow 1949. *Africanisms in the Gullah dialect*, Chicago, University of Chicago Press

Weinreich, Uriel, William Labov and Marvin Herzog 1968. 'Empirical foundations for a theory of language change', *Directions for historical linguistics: a symposium*, Austin, University of Texas Press

Wolfram, Walter A. 1969. 'Linguistic correlates of social stratification in the speech of Detroit Negroes', Washington, D.C., Center for Applied Linguistics

LANGUAGE HISTORY AND CREOLE STUDIES

HENRY M. HOENIGSWALD

There is not a paper submitted for this conference which does not have some historical implications. In some papers these implications are more directly spelled out than in others. Both explicitness and reticence have their merits. The historian of language who considers the problem (and not for the first time, either) and who finds it difficult to decide where to begin and where to draw the line may be excused to start from a framework of his own devising.

The historian is accustomed to asking two fairly separate questions when confronted with 'marginal' languages. He is interested (1) in their genesis and their subsequent behavior in time, and he wants to know (2) to what extent pidgins and creoles are indeed marginal or (to use Whinnom's phrase) 'special' cases of language. Really, of course, he wants to combine the two. If (1) matters of origin, change, and disappearance are more essentially on the surface of things in the case of pidgins and creoles than they are in the case of other forms of speech, but if it were also true (2) that the difference is only one of degree and not of kind, it would require no more than a fairly safe extrapolation to furnish the theory of linguistic change — so largely speculative in character — with a quasi-empirical foundation.

We must remember that the theory of linguistic change is often viewed as though there existed the following intellectual choice: between one approach in which only formal relationships within 'the language' are considered ('seule la causalité interne intéresse le linguiste' (Martinet 1960:81)), and another in which change is 'reduced' to the social phenomena of contact, multilingualism, hypercorrection and the like. It is easy to see the affinity between the latter viewpoint and the generalizations obtainable from a study of marginal languages. Just for this reason, however, it is interesting to note Whinnom's reference to the 'mechanical barrier' that differences in sound, grammar, or semantics may set up between any two languages in contact, however close. The internal and the external factors in linguistic change are densely intertwined, but not, as the phrase goes, inextricably so. On the contrary, their connection can be understood. It is one of the benefits to be derived from our increasing familiarity with the so-called special languages that some of the entities which historical interpretation has identified on speculative grounds can be observed in their synchronic functioning. It may therefore be useful to take stock of some of these entities.

Q

There is, first, the variable of contact *intimacy*. That this variable should have been so frequently discussed in the exclusive terms of (non-colonial) conquest, or of immigration, is probably just bad ethnocentric bias. Now that the study of bilingualism and diglossia is being pursued more independently, the complexity of potential and actual contact situations is more evident than it used to be. Many participants, and Alleyne and Mintz in particular, have said a good deal on this point, though they have also reminded us how much needed knowledge is still in the future. Without wishing to embark on detailed comment, the historical linguist cannot forbear calling attention to Mintz' tentative comparison between the French-based creoles of Haiti (politically independent since the beginning of the nineteenth century) and of Martinique-Guadeloupe (still under French sovereignty) where

the precise significance of the closeness or remoteness of ties to the metropolis . . . may turn out to be far less important than the initial conditions under which a creole language does or does not become stabilized, or than the particular demographic conditions at the time.

Note the three important elements: (1) once again, the special role of pidgin languages as clearly outlined surface objects; (2) the idea that demographic (hence speech community) history, so far from passively taking place in the flow of time, is rather a history of crises and their consequences; and, more incidentally, (3) the special factual virtue possessed by the Caribbean area with its rather sharply defined colonial communities, and the relatively small-scale but also relatively neat differentiation among the economic and legal systems imported by the different European powers.

Next, there is the *prestige* differential. The 'upper-lower' relationship usually recognized through its effects (prestige-induced replacement rather than need-filling borrowing and loan translating; Hockett 1958:404) seems to be at work constantly and significantly in most situations of language contact, imparting to them the characteristic non-symmetrical character to which we shall return below. Again, the marginal languages tend to occur in a maximally clear setting in which the term 'prestige' may almost be said to have its rather brutal everyday meaning. We are perhaps too seldom reminded, however, that things are not necessarily all that obvious; witness the Chinook Jargon.

We have already touched upon the factor of *mutual structure* (no longer a strictly internal factor!) when we cited the 'mechanical barrier'. It is fairly generally agreed that the very strangeness of the language structures which come into contact will contribute decisively to the creation of a pidgin with the special traits of a pidgin, whatever these may be; that, in other words (and to take the other extreme) contact between two forms of speech which are mere dialects of each other would never lead to a pidgin recognizable as such, even if the contact occurred under conditions that would otherwise call forth a pidgin language. Whinnom believes that only phonological traits count, and that there is no 'morphological barrier'. On the other hand, Sapir (1921:210) had hinted at the existence of such barriers as well, implying that they bring about (in 'normal', non-marginal language histories) the choice between outright borrowing of loanwords and loan-translating. According to Whinnom important structural differences pose no impediment to pidgin-formation because the population is one 'of speakers in a state of cultural shock'. In fact it is doubtful whether 'the puzzle of why pidgins arise in certain places and at certain times' is really closer to a solution than the general and familiar historic-linguistic question why certain changes take place when and where they do.

On the view (unproved and unprovable, of course) that situations of contact *always* contain the germs of pidginization, this process perhaps becomes simply a particular case of the issue of *survival*. In the philological tradition it is customary to consider two possibilities. One is that of the 'upper' language only surviving, as in the case, say, of Gaulish Latin. The symptoms of contact that survive are minimal because interference from lower to upper is relatively restricted, and any 'imperfect learning' (that is, roughly, any 'substratum effect') is erased through subsequent acts of interference from a persevering and triumphant upper model. Contrariwise, if the lower language survives, it shows the marks of the struggle in the form of loanwords and loan-translations of varying depth and subtlety. In a sense, the marginal languages demonstrate their customary usefulness as possibly aberrant cases. While they are of course not just 'upper languages imperfectly reproduced' and nevertheless surviving in that shape, there is enough in them to suggest their affinity to such objects.

In most essentials the mechanics of pidgin formation and those of language switching are, after all, of a piece (Alleyne). Pidgins arise where an effort at learning is made, and not where borrowings swamp a lower language. We are here dealing with the famous attitudinal factors to which Meillet, Weinreich, and many others have called attention. Concern for purity (Whinnom) at one extreme, and shock-like non-resistance at the other, are not necessarily the best labels, considering the specialized and often utilitarian incentives for 'learning' in a pidgin situation. One may indeed further argue that 'learning' and 'massive borrowing' are less extremes on a scale than quantitatively different, incompatible attitudes. But what is the story about the survival of the pidgin itself? That the continued presence of the ('upper') model may not be important is already clear. In the discussion it seemed to be Reinecke's point that the withdrawal of standard speakers has had two opposite effects in China and in Vietnam. In China the very event of withdrawal kept the pidgin in being inasmuch as Chinese pidgin English was actively used among various groups of Chinese speakers. In Vietnam, pidginized French is disappearing as French disappears.

There is enough in the literature to illustrate the natural truth that pidgins undergo subsequent change, although probably not enough to show whether there is anything peculiar to the change processes that affect pidgin languages without changing their status as pidgin languages. More than in the case of natural languages one expects to run into problems of identity from stage to stage. It is difficult enough to be quite sure, both in theory and in practice, when a given ordinary language is a descendant (under change) rather than a collateral relative of a given older language. It has been said that to discover a line of descent is to discriminate what has gotten handed down from mother to infant over the generations from what has passed through other channels. If this is true, the pidgins, with their special mechanism of exclusively secondary transmittal (?) should indeed be troublesome to place on a family tree. And if it is further the case that pidgins are typically born and then again dropped from use in shortlived bursts of activity, the whole linear notion of 'gradual' change is not even a superficially useful approximation to the truth, as it is for normal, primary languages. Still, the altering complexion of a pidgin-using *area* (say, the Caribbean) over the generations and centuries is surely an important and fit subject for diachronic study.

To be sure, there is one kind of change process which is unique to pidgin languages by definition, namely, the very step of alleged creolization. There is remarkable agreement about the degree of reality attaching to this step. This is because our belief in the specificity of the initial, uncreolized pidgin is so firm in the first place.[1] The crucial attributes have been called by many names: simplicity, reduction, impoverishment, deficiency; peculiarities in matters of information-bearing and functional load have been used as defining factors. The disagreement seems to be about the manner in which such simplification comes about as the pidgin is formed. Some look upon it as a retreat to the particular area of language structure in which the contact languages overlap. This notion calls for at least some elaboration before it can account for the rather uniform cast of the pidgin languages known; pidgins do not, as they should if they were the results of mere overlap, look like concentrates of language universals with embellishments here and there in the form of a specific overlap. Nor is 'relexification' by itself sufficient as a mechanical principle. Special attention should, on the other hand, be given to Ferguson's plea for a study of *simplification* as a specific mode of linguistic conduct. What a speaker does when he simplifies depends presumably on language universals, on contingent structure in terms of the typological class to which the speaker's language belongs, as well as on the effects on the community's past history of exercising its capacity for producing simplifications, be they 'baby talk' or special styles for contacts with speakers of different languages. It is all very well to disabuse naval personnel serving in the Pacific of the notion that Melanesian Pidgin (in its present historically conditioned form) conforms to their idea of 'baby talk' and thus needs no formal study. But this does not mean that individuals do not behave in structured fashion when they strive for some sort of skeleton language. We may be sure that rules could be written for the production of such skeleton devices. It is this factor which tends to be forgotten in the formulae about the 'substrate speakers imitating the superstrate speakers' imitation of the substrate speakers' imitation of the superstrate language' examined by Whinnom.

Thus, pidgins are recognizable as such; creolization is a change process unique to pidgins because pidgins are unique. But here picturesqueness ends because creoles *are* ordinary languages except in the sight of the antiquarian. Whinnom, to be sure, questions this. But he does so in a way hardly destructive enough to suggest cutting off the familiar query about the essential identity of creolization with natural diversification and descent. Closely connected with this is the discussion about so-called mixed languages. Goodman makes the point most sharply: 'the grammar' — and this means both the grammatical structure (seen either as a table of contrasts or, presumably, as a sequence of rules) and the affixes serving it — of Mbugu is 'overwhelmingly Bantu', while the 'basic' vocabulary has 'almost no Bantu roots'. The specific connections of the latter do not matter here. Goodman thinks it 'clear that at some time a Bantu and a non-Bantu language came into contact'; that 'the Bantu language incorporated a number of non-Bantu words and adapted them to the Bantu grammatical system'. So far so good. He then also says that 'on the other hand, Bantu words were borrowed into the non-Bantu progenitor of Mbugu with some variation in their affixes according to grammatical function' and that 'the Bantu and the non-Bantu language may have gradually become ever more alike until they were little more than stylistic variants, depending on who was speaking to whom'. Finally he asks if Mbugu is not, therefore, a true mixed language. 'This would depend on one's definition, but it clearly refutes the presupposition that one can unambiguously determine the antecedence of every language.' (This is of course a reference to an accepted view such as Hall has often formulated with emphasis and with special reference to the role of creolization in normal language history; e.g. Hall 1966.) Goodman concludes that Mbugu developed as a result of a particularly intense contact situation which has subsequently disappeared, and that since then change has been normal and gradual.

The case *is* interesting, for several reasons. Above all, there is the discrepant behavior reported for precisely the two kinds of language material which one considers crucial for the business of genealogical classification; namely, the 'grammar' and the 'basic' vocabulary. One usually expects both to point in the same direction. In the case of Mbugu, and often enough with other creolized languages, evidence is presented that the two lines point in different directions. It is even suggested that this fact may be a criterion of creolization (Taylor).

The problem is not merely one of choosing or weighting certain kinds of evidence as against others. It is, as we have hinted before, a matter of the nature of the process of change that has given rise to the evidence. Ultimately we would like to know whether speakers of language A continued to use their own language or shifted to language B. More precisely, the historian's problem is whether or not the outcome of nearly total lexical borrowing from language B into language A can be distinguished, and is therefore distinct, from the outcome of acquisition of B by speakers of A with 'substratum' effects from their former language. In the one case, the outcome could be said to be a continuation of A, despite the B vocabulary; in the second case, the outcome could be said to be a continuation of B, despite the A grammar.

As we have indicated above, if A and B differ only as dialects to begin with, the answer may well be negative: where there are no 'mechanical barriers' to speak of it may be typical for the attitudinal opposites mentioned above to collapse as well. The question is, however, whether there are not some conditions of 'intimate' contact, even between grossly different A's and B's, that lead to excessive borrowing of loanwords and creating of calques and loantranslations (process 1) with effects that would resemble rapid 'learning' uncorrected by any ironing-out of flaws (process 2). Perhaps this possibility is characteristic of the turbulence and instability attributed to periods of creolization.

Herein might lie the resolution (or insolubility) of the issue posed between those who see creoles in terms of their French, or English, relationship (implying the predominance of imperfect learning) and those who see the grammatical links that cut across French or English affiliation as evidence that at least some creoles arose in a way that implies a much more important role for what conditions those 'imperfections'; in the latter case, the 'lower' traits loom so large that their presence jeopardizes the orthodox distinction between genealogical and only typological significance.[2]

If this is what is characteristic of the formation of creoles, then Whinnom may be more right than he knows in stressing the rare, specific nature of the circumstances in which a pidgin may crystallize as a new, recognized norm of speech. The formation of true pidgins may not be a frequent enough event for all creoles to be based on them. Moreover, the circumstances enabling a pidgin to form may be most likely either to perpetuate it or, if they fail, to let it disappear suddenly, as in the case of Vietnamese pidgin French. Perhaps when we recognize a creole we essentially recognize cases in which either process, massive borrowing or imperfect learning, has gone so far as to pose serious problems in distinguishing it from its opposite. Some of the languages which have entered into situations giving rise to creoles no doubt have been pidgins, but we may not need to assume so in every case. If many of the world's creole languages do go back in some way to an early Portuguese-based pidgin, then that fact may reflect a very specific, perhaps unique, set of historical circumstances and not in itself provide a general definition.

However this may be, the sector of language that should serve to distinguish the two processes longest, permitting assignment in a genealogical classification, is the basic vocabulary. The 'total borrower' from B presumably borrows other, more 'cultural' vocabulary first – semantic items found in the other language and not in his own – giving up his core vocabulary last. The 'imperfect learner' of B presumably acquires its basic vocabulary first; he will have immediate need of it. It should be noted that grammatical morphs should by rights belong in the basic vocabulary, while 'grammar' in the abstract structural sense (i.e. the presence of certain grammatical categories, no matter how represented morphically) must be considered fully vulnerable to loan translation and innovation by diffusion. On the other hand we shall do well to remember that the grammatical morphs in question are affixes (the independent pronouns are precisely non-Bantu in Mbugu!), and that the borrowing of affixes may be a process which is fundamentally different from the incorporation into a language of free forms.

Since the alleged mixture of Bantu and non-Bantu in Mbugu is not even and random, but occurs along a qualitative boundary line involving the basic vocabulary, the picture of two symmetrical histories, each affecting one partner language but both ending up identically, cannot be complete. If Goodman entertains this notion, his familiarity with African sociolinguistics must suggest to him the plausibility of a setting in which 'prestige' differentials are so small, or so fleeting and reversible, as to cancel each other out. Perhaps it is this possibility, with the opportunities for re-borrowing the same material in opposite directions, which explains the aberrancies of the case. This recalls the instances in which lexical items from the secondary partner in a pidgin relation (e.g. Chinese words) are said to have entered the pidgin (Chinese Pidgin English) typically, or primarily, because they had first penetrated the base language (the local, or sailors', or traders' English) as cultural loans.

When Samarin insists both on the special status of pidgins and on the features which link marginal languages with phenomena of reduction and simplification in general, he also maintains that such reduction need be neither 'drastic' nor 'sharp'. But it is precisely the 'sharpness' of change which to Southworth assumes a special role in the theory of change processes where some scholars incline to contrast it with 'normal transmission'. He suggests of course that the dichotomy is not the last word. His final guess that 'creolization may have taken place much more frequently in the past than historical linguists have generally recognized' may, in fact, not go far enough. Possibly all change processes partake of the characteristics of creolization, with the *particular* historical circumstances making the crucial, but essentially quantitative, difference.

NOTES

1 But see Alleyne's discussion, and our own doubts about the inevitability of positing a pidgin for every creole, below.
2 See, e.g. Greenberg (1966:1–5).

REFERENCES

Greenberg, Joseph H. 1966. *Languages of Africa*, 2nd revised edition, Bloomington and The Hague, Indiana University and Mouton & Co

Hall, Robert A., Jr. 1966. *Pidgin and creole languages*, Ithaca, Cornell University Press

Hockett, Charles F. 1958. *A course in modern linguistics*, New York, Macmillan

Martinet, Andre 1960. *Éléments de linguistique générale*, Paris, Colin

Sapir, Edward 1921. *Language*, New York, Harcourt, Brace

THE SOCIO-HISTORICAL BACKGROUND
TO PIDGINIZATION AND CREOLIZATION[1]

SIDNEY W. MINTZ

I am impressed by the wide range, the richness of detail and the originality displayed in the Conference papers and in the comments upon them. To do all of this justice would be impossible even for a linguistically-sophisticated listener, which I am not; my remarks are confined to socio-historical and anthropological matters. Nor can I presume to comment upon materials dealing with cases or with geographical regions other than the Caribbean area. Moreover, much of what I had intended to say has been dealt with already by Dr Alleyne's paper and by others, far better than I could do so. For instance – and I do not propose to review these points exhaustively – Dr Alleyne's comments on differences in metropolitan colonial policy, and in regard to the masters' use of the same language forms as their slaves (especially in the colonies of England and France) are provocative and, I think, important. In this and other regards, I hope that what there remains for me to do has been happily abbreviated.

Nonetheless, it may be of some use if I try to sketch in briefly a few of the major socio-historical characteristics of the Caribbean region, as background to the processes of pidginization and creolization whose history has been so lengthy and so complex in this part of the globe.[2] I wish to suggest that, among the background conditions that may have affected the ways that creole languages arose and took shape, there are three whose effects may have been especially important in the Caribbean region. The first of these conditions would be the relative proportions of Africans, Europeans and other groups, over time, present in particular Antillean societies. The second would be the codes of social interaction governing the relative statuses and the relationships of these differing groups in particular societies. And the third such condition would be the specific sorts of community settings, within which these groups became further differentiated or intermixed.

Generally speaking, the Hispano-Caribbean colonies were never dominated demographically by inhabitants of African origin; moreover, in those colonies movement from the social category of 'slaves' to that of 'freemen' was almost always *relatively* rapid and *relatively* continuous.

Such a generalization can be advanced only with considerable caution. But it appears to hold, on the whole, for the Hispanic Caribbean (which, until the second decade of the seventeenth century, meant *all* of the Caribbean);

and thereafter for the Hispanic Greater Antilles (which, until 1655, meant all of the Greater Antilles). Economic development was very uneven in the Spanish islands before the late eighteenth century, and frequent manumissions were probably the consequence of this unevenness, at least in part. After the late eighteenth century, when slavery became important in Cuba and Puerto Rico (but not in Spanish Santo Domingo), and the importation of African slaves rose, there was already in these islands a large Spanish-speaking population of mixed physical antecedents. It seems very probable that, at various periods in the histories of the Hispanic Caribbean islands, pidgins (or possibly some 'less than standard' dialects of Spanish) were used; but in all of those islands that remained in Spanish hands, a standard dialect of Spanish came to prevail. (On this process, see Reinecke's interesting comments in Reinecke 1938 [1964].) Perhaps these cases might be compared to the cities of the United States Northeast at the turn of the century, when massive influxes of foreign language-speakers undoubtedly affected the English being spoken at that time.

In quite marked contrast, the Anglo-Caribbean colonies repeatedly *supplanted* their European settlers with African slaves, while the movement of persons from slavery to a free status was severely hampered and discontinuous. This assertion is not attributable solely to the presence of a more rigid system of slavery. In the British Leeward and Windward Islands, and in British (i.e. post-1655) Jamaica, the establishment of the plantation system drove small-scale yeomen off the land, while the profitability of slave plantations led to high slave mortality, high rates of slave importation, and rare manumission.

In French Saint Domingue and, to a lesser extent, in other Franco-Caribbean colonies, the proportion of African slaves to free Europeans early became very high; but passage from slave to free status was generally quite rapid. Saint Domingue became French by treaty in 1697; in 1790, Moreau de St Méry estimated that the colony had 452,000 slaves, 40,000 whites and 28,000 *affranchis*. The *affranchis*, who were of course free and of mixed ancestry, are believed to have owned up to one-third of the land and one-fourth of all of the slaves in the colony. Even if these estimates are much exaggerated, they imply that the history of Saint Domingue during the century preceding 1790 must have been remarkable, in terms of the relationships of free men to slaves, and of whites to non-whites (Leyburn 1941:18). With regard, then, to the first two of the suggested background conditions – demographic proportions, and the codes of social relations – it is possible that the Spanish, English and French Caribbean colonies may offer some useful contrasts.

As far as the particular sorts of community setting are concerned, several principal distinctions might be drawn. The first is that between plantation and non-plantation rural settings; the second between rural and urban settings;

and the third, the distinctions among predial, domestic and other categories of slaves, and among free and slave populations within the same colony. Dr Alleyne has touched on these matters, as has Dr Voorhoeve (1964), and they have been dealt with in many other sources, including Patterson's recent book, *The Sociology of Slavery* (1967), and Professor LePage's earlier *Jamaican Creole* (1960).

Caribbean social history has been a history of colonialism, massive immigrations, plantations and the extensive use of slave and contract labor. The islands and their surrounding shores constituted the first really convincing instance of European overseas capitalism; but it was an emergent agricultural capitalism based on forced labor, rather than on a wage-earning proletariat. The principal form of organization, the plantation, involved the use of large masses of imported (or, rarely and early, locally-enslaved aboriginal) labor, under the control of small numbers of European masters. The Spaniards introduced African slaves, the sugar cane, and plantation organization to the New World through the Greater Antilles (Cuba, Española, Puerto Rico and Jamaica), in the early sixteenth century; but this pattern had begun to decline within fifty years. It was reinitiated first in Barbados by the English, who employed indentured English laborers, but soon replaced them with African slaves. The growth of the plantation there, as in many Anglo-Caribbean colonies, also drove out free European small-scale cultivators (cf. Mintz 1961).

A similar process occurred at about the same time in the French colonies of Martinique and Guadeloupe. The system was transferred to Jamaica after 1655; it was developed by the French in Saint Domingue (the western third of Española) beginning in the third quarter of the seventeenth century; and it spread through some of the Lesser Antilles under the sponsorship of the Dutch and the Danes. Following the Haitian Revolution and the outlawing of the slave trade by Great Britain, the plantation system soon disappeared in newly-independent Haiti, and declined noticeably in Jamaica and in many of the smaller islands. Great Britain outlawed slavery in 1834, France and Denmark in 1848, the Netherlands in 1863.

The pioneer slave-based plantation system in the Hispanic Antilles had declined after about 1550. Much later, it was revived in the remaining Hispanic islands, first in Cuba, beginning about 1770, and then in Puerto Rico (though not in eastern Española). In spite of laws against the slave trade, Cuba and Puerto Rico received large numbers of African slaves in the nineteenth century; the trade only ended definitively with emancipation (Puerto Rico: 1873; Cuba: 1880). Meanwhile, after Emancipation in the British and French colonies and accompanying a second decline of traditional plantation forms in Cuba and Puerto Rico, large numbers of Asians — particularly Indians, Chinese and Javanese — were imported as contract laborers. Cuba received the bulk of Chinese immigrants; Trinidad and (then British)

Guiana the bulk of Indians; and Surinam (Dutch Guiana) the bulk of Javanese – this last group continuing to arrive well into the present century. Substantial numbers of free Africans and South Europeans, particularly Portuguese, also reached the Antilles and the Guianas as contract laborers after the end of slavery. And subsequent intra-Caribbean migration has occurred in this century as well – nearly a quarter of a million Haitians and Jamaicans, for instance, migrated to Cuba between 1912 and 1924, in response to North American plantation development in that island.

I am stressing the uneven but massive movement of new populations into and among these islands over the centuries, since such movement undoubtedly had significant socio-linguistic implications, and because the main impulse to these migrations has been one particular form of agro-social development: the plantation system.

A thorough description of that system is not practical here; moreover, adequate sociological analyses of local variants of the system have only now begun to appear. But a few general characteristics may be enumerated, as background to the linguistic processes that must have typified such social settings. Each plantation, at the outset, would be manned by a substantial number of enslaved Africans (less commonly, and particularly in the Hispanic Caribbean, of enslaved American Indians), who were politically powerless, and controlled by a very small number of free Europeans. The political basis of plantation organization was physical force, and all of its institutional arrangements facilitated the rapid and unhampered use of force to achieve desired results: the profitable production of agricultural staples for foreign investors. Typically, Caribbean slave plantations engaged two migrant groupings – the masters and the slaves – neither of which was able to transfer more than a portion of its cultural traditions to the islands. One may suppose that, initially, pidginization of the masters' language would be part of the process of mutual adjustment necessary to carry on plantation operations. In some cases pidgin languages disappeared, being supplanted by dialectal forms of the language of the masters. In other cases, pidgin languages must have evolved into creole languages. In all *Caribbean* cases, however, pidgin forms failed to persist – or, at any rate, we have no evidence of their persistence, nor any way at present to determine when, in any particular case, a creole language on the one hand or a stable dialectal variant of a European language on the other may be said to have first appeared. While each island situation was different from every other, and while each such situation clearly changed over time, the pattern of social encounter of a small, powerful, monolingual European minority with a large, powerless multilingual African majority typified most of Caribbean post-Conquest history. Periods of social stabilization on one island – for instance, the post-Emancipation epoch in Jamaica – sometimes coincided with periods of rapid change in another; as Jamaica emerged from the slave-plantation epoch, Puerto Rico was busily entering upon just such an epoch (Mintz 1959). Yet the sociolinguistics of these two cases differed dramatically, since they involved populations of different proportions, living by different social codes, and with significantly different historical backgrounds. On the one hand, important sociological and historical differences made each such case unique. Yet on the other, the colonial and immigrant character of the Caribbean area, and the remarkably rigid nature of the social systems engendered by plantation colonialism, undoubtedly affected in certain common ways the processes of language learning and linguistic differentiation. Under these general conditions, almost every Caribbean colony has been typified historically by the growth of a bipolar social structure — masses of illiterate newcomers from other world areas, dominated by tiny minorities of Europeans, with very limited opportunities for upward social or economic mobility for the laboring classes.

The early extirpation or genetic assimilation of aboriginal populations is yet another important background factor in the social history of the Antillean area. In the Caribbean, everyone but the native Indians was a newcomer. Though the general significance of this fact has been noted in comparisons between the coastal lowlands of Latin America and the highland areas of dense aboriginal concentration (Service 1955), its particular meaning in the case of the Caribbean islands has received too little attention. In other world areas, the cases most likely to come to mind are those of Australia – where essentially only one European migrant population eventually settled – and the Mascarene Islands, including Mauritius, with which some useful comparisons with the Caribbean may be made (Valkhoff, 1966; Benedict, 1961).

In effect, the European conquerors of the Antilles scourged those lands of their native inhabitants, creating vacuums within which European, African (and later, Asian) migrant populations could be accommodated. One is reminded of Mannoni's image of the European conqueror as one motivated by 'the lure of a world without men'; Mannoni (1964:101) had Madagascar in mind, but the Caribbean islands would have fitted his argument far better. I have suggested elsewhere that:

This scourging of the human landscape enabled the Europeans to set the terms of their future colonialism in the Caribbean area in ways very different from those available to them in the densely occupied areas of the non-western world. The significance of this distinction is real; the next stage in Antillean history was set in the absence of subject peoples, for the European colonist had transformed himself from guest into host simply through having eliminated his native predecessors (Mintz 1966:918).

It was within the population 'vacuums' (in the Antilles created by European arms, European economics and European diseases) that the plantation system flourished. In many cases, the plantation system was so pervasive and long-lasting that only the sparsest economic alternatives were available to settlers, and those who broke out of the plantation mold had serious difficulties in establishing other modes of existence. But while the plantation system vertebrated the entire social structure of many islands, it did not function so overwhelmingly in all of them. In every colony, some measure of peasant development occurred: before the mid-seventeenth century, in the French and British Lesser Antilles; after the revolution, in Haiti; before the rise of late eighteenth- and early nineteenth-century plantations in Cuba, Puerto Rico, and Trinidad; and at various times on islands too small or too arid to encourage plantation development, such that alternative economic forms and different kinds of communities were established. Moreover, even in the classic plantation societies — beginning with Barbados in the mid-seventeenth century, and Jamaica, Martinique, Guadeloupe and Saint Domingue later in that century — social systems underwent differentiation, changing these societies to some degree away from the rigid plantation model.

One such sort of differentiation involved the growth of a stratum intermediate between the dominant minority and the laboring masses — a stratum genetically intermediate among other things, born of slave mothers and — usually – free European fathers. The linguistic significance of this social differentiation was of course considerable, particularly in those Antillean societies in which the number of slaves was much greater than that of free (and usually European) inhabitants. A second sort of differentiation was linked in particular to the failure of the plantation system to encourage the growth of self-sufficient island economies. Since the plantation was a European invention, hinged to a mercantilist philosophy which ordained complete economic dependence upon the industrial metropolis, most products consumed by the plantation society had to be imported. But the system never worked perfectly; and much Caribbean social history is concerned with the growth and distinctiveness of various kinds of non-plantation community in some way complementary to the plantation system, and of the social groupings that functioned outside the boundaries of that system. I have in mind here such developments as the Maroon (runaway slave) communities of the Guianas, Jamaica, Cuba, Española, and Puerto Rico; fishing communities in all (or almost all) of the islands; 'internal frontier', squatter-type peasantries in societies such as Cuba and Puerto Rico and, at a later stage, the British and French islands and the Guianas; communities on islands too small or unpromising ever to evolve a plantation economy; and so on. In each case, it seems fair to assume that some sociolinguistic concomitants to such growth may at least have been possible.

Beyond this, however, it is necessary to discuss the particular contexts within which language learning or language use took place -- insofar as one may generalize about such matters. To clarify these contexts, I wish to revert to an earlier point — the relevance of the codes of social relations governing the statuses and social interactions of different groups in each society. I can only make three general points in this connection, though many more might be relevant. To begin with, one notes that the European powers differed significantly in their insistence on control of colonial political structures and decision-making. It seems clear that Spanish policy was most grudging of local autonomy, while British policy was most generous; other colonial systems seem to have fallen somewhere between these extremes. Again, the slavery codes themselves also varied greatly. Though I insist that these codes cannot be compared nationally — that is, for example, the Spanish code with the British code, as if there were no important local or temporal distinctions — it might be correct to claim that, on the whole, the Spanish code was most liberal, the British code probably least so. The significance of distinctions in the application of slavery codes — to the extent that I am justified in drawing them — is twofold. First, social participation of slaves and free men in the same institution, such as the church, would matter significantly. Second, where the codes encouraged (or at least permitted) the growth of an intermediate free group, the presence and increase of such a group would certainly affect the subsequent social environment.

My third point has to do with the ideology of the dominant group *vis à vis* its participation in metropolitan and in insular affairs. In each colony, the dominant classes constituted the links between the governing power and the colonial society, and the attitudes and ideologies of these classes toward their roles in the colonies varied greatly. Too little is known to allow us to view different groups of colonists along some spectrum of greater or lesser identification with the colonies in which they lived; generally speaking, however, it appears that the Spanish colonists in the Caribbean area came to identify more rapidly and more completely with their new homes than did the French or English colonists. This may seem paradoxical since, as noted earlier, Spanish administrative control over the colonies was more rigid than that of the French and English. But one may hazard the guess that rigid colonial administration by the metropolis resulted in the swifter growth of a local or 'creole' identity. Whereas the Spanish settlers in Cuba and Puerto Rico soon came to view themselves as Cubans and Puerto Ricans, the French and British colonists apparently tended more to see themselves as Europeans in temporary exile. Admittedly, there was growth of a 'creole identity' throughout the Caribbean area; but there are good grounds for seeing this process comparatively and differentially. Among the factors that may have influenced this differentiation were: the types of local economic development; the presence or absence of colonial institutions within which all colonists could participate; the relative proportions of different social groupings, particularly of slaves and freemen; the distinctions of privilege established by the metropolis, to separate 'creoles' from 'homelanders'; and the sexual and mating codes and practices in each colony. On the whole, it appears that these factors worked to encourage the emergence of local loyalties and identities most rapidly and firmly in the Spanish islands, as I have suggested. In the French possessions, where metropolitan control was perhaps intermediate in effectiveness between that of typical Spanish and typical English colonies, the presence of a universalistic religion, early frequent manumission and considerable interracial mating probably accelerated cultural creolization.

Though we are not in a position to confirm these assertions with confidence, they may be worthy of reflection. In cultural terms, the emergence of a 'creole culture', borne by the colonial powerholders, would mean that newcomers and the socially subordinate groups in a particular colony would be provided with some sort of acculturational — and, possibly, linguistic — model. In such colonies as Cuba, where one may suppose that a pidgin language did exist, at least briefly and in those periods when the influx of multilingual slave shipments was considerable, Spanish would provide a continuing medium of communication for culturally creolized slaves and for freemen of all physical types. For the greater part of Cuba's and Puerto Rico's post-conquest history – that is, from the Discovery until at least the late eighteenth century – the relative proportions of slaves to freemen were low, and the rates of manumission apparently high. In such colonies as Saint Domingue, where the importation of slaves after 1697 was both massive and rapid, the stabilization of a pidgin and the emergence of a creole language thereafter would be expectable, even though manumission was common, and the growth of an intermediate and economically influential free mulatto class – probably bilingual — was swift. Revolution and independence at the close of the eighteenth century, and the substantial elimination of the French colonists, may have contributed powerfully to the full stabilization of Haitian Creole thereafter. (Yet admittedly, a French-based creole language also typifies Martinique, Guadeloupe and other French Antilles, with markedly different histories.) In the British possessions, rapid slave importations and the substantial lack of a firm creole culture, a numerous intermediate group, or insular institutions that could unify the colonial population, probably contributed to the particular linguistic situations typical of these colonies.

Any careful evaluation of such factors in sociolinguistic terms is quite impossible, at least at the present time; yet their relevance, I think, is real. We have been hearing about target-languages affecting the nature of linguistic change; we may ask ourselves about target-cultures, affecting the nature of cultural change. At any rate, I would argue that the more a Cuban slave were to identify with his master, the more Cuban he became; whereas the more a Jamaican slave were to identify with his master, the less Jamaican he would become. Such an argument has to do with the social continuities or discontinuities typical of the colonial social structure in each case, and also with those which typified the relationships of the colony to the motherland. Presumably if social linkages between the bottom-most and top-most groupings in the colony were close, and those to the metropolis were weaker, the colonial language picture was likely to be one of a regional dialect. In contrast, if the social linkages between the top-most colonial groupings and the motherland were closer than ties among groups within the colony, the more likely that the colonial language picture would be one of a regional dialect spoken by the ruling group, and of a pidgin language becoming a creole language for the remainder of the population.

Haitian Creole is in some ways the most interesting Antillean case in this connection. Though a French colonial society had begun to form in western Española even before the 1697 cession to France, only after that year did the colony begin its brilliant career as the world's richest European possession. Less than a century later, it lay in ruins; by the time that the Revolution had ended in 1804, the slave population is believed to have fallen substantially, the European population had practically disappeared, and the free colored population had declined very sharply. Thereafter, Haiti was largely isolated from the world outside for more than a century. French remained the official language, while Haitian Creole remained the language of the people.

Our knowledge of the language history of pre-revolutionary Haiti is, at best, slight. But surely the Revolution radically altered the relationship between the French of Haiti and the language (or languages) of the slaves. After 1804, the impact of French — of any dialect of French — on the speech of the ordinary folk was sharply reduced, at least until recent decades. This is a very different picture from what is known for Martinique and Guadeloupe, for instance, which remain closely tied to metropolitan France — and which, as I have admitted, continue to use a French-based creole language to this day. The closeness or remoteness of ties to the metropolis, in other words, will very probably turn out to be far less important than the initial conditions under which a creole language does or does not become stabilized.

Hoetink, the Dutch sociologist-historian, has given an interesting interpretation of the relationship between language and society in the Caribbean, by suggesting that the readiness to mix racially (or the absence of that readiness) determines the extent of 'cultural homogenization' (which I would see as a somewhat different matter from 'cultural creolization') and accordingly what happened linguistically.

The best illustration of this homogenization is probably provided by the fact that in all Latin Caribbean societies the language of the Iberian mother country became the commonly spoken and written language, while in virtually none of the societies of the North-West European variant is one language the official as well as the common language. In Haiti, French is the official language,

Créole the common one; in the British West Indies English is the official language and Anglo-Créole or French Créole the common one; in the French islands French and French-Créole, respectively; in the Dutch Windward Islands, English or Dutch and Anglo-Créole; in Surinam, Dutch and Sranang (apart from the Asian languages); in the Dutch Leeward Islands, Dutch and Papiamentu. The linguistic situation in the North-West European variant reflects the cleavage which has always existed between the original dominant segment and the great majority of non-whites, while in the Iberian variant the linguistic situation reflects the linking function of the coloured group (1967:178).

Clearly, specific sociological, attitudinal and demographic details did matter tremendously. But the analysis of particular historical events or trends may throw light upon the language situation in each case, and illuminate as well our usages of such terms as 'ambiguity', 'ambivalence', 'code-switching', 'inter-ference', and the like, in discussing these cases from the past.

If we turn from this level of generalization to somewhat less abstract and more contemporary cases, it may be worth suggesting that the study of par-ticular kinds of communities in the Caribbean region could contribute to our understanding of the way historical forces may have affected linguistic change. I am thinking of events occurring at the time of, and after, the emancipation of the slaves in Jamaica, with regard to rural populations in that country. Jamaica stands almost alone among Anglo-Caribbean possessions in the establishment of a numerous peasant class after Emancipation (but cf. Farley 1953 and 1954). This partial reconstitution of Jamaican society on a yeoman basis was accomplished largely through the activities of the non-Establishment missionary churches, especially the Baptist and Methodist groups, who arranged to purchase 'ruinate' sugar and cattle properties and to settle their parishioners upon them. I have contended elsewhere that this process was of considerable sociological and economic significance for Jamaica; it seems to me that it may also have had certain sociolinguistic implications. In each such case, the peasant community included in its formation a church and a school, and all (or nearly all) of the parishioners thus settled were at least partly literate. Though we do not know precisely how many Jamaican freed-men were settled in this fashion, between 1838 and 1844, 19,000 ex-slaves and their families removed themselves from the estates and obtained land in free villages (Paget n.d. [1951?]). Quite possibly, almost half of the former field slaves in Jamaica were affected; and since most of the original church-founded free villages are still identifiable, it is curious that no careful socio-logical study has been made of them, much less a study of their linguistic peculiarities, if any (cf. Cumper 1954, and Mintz 1958). Other distinctive communities that might reward sociolinguistic study include fishing villages (cf. Price 1966), and what were originally runaway (Maroon) communities. It is not at all clear that local speech would reflect sociological or occupational differences in these cases; but it would be interesting to know.

These comments upon Caribbean social history are intended only to suggest the relevance of that history to the study of pidgins and creoles. I would like to make several additional general observations in this connection. Without joining the argument over the precise classification of pidgins, creoles and other such 'poorly-fitting' languages, I would suggest that the Caribbean region has many languages that may be creoles, and that have usually been described in this way, but absolutely no language — if I understand correctly — that can be regarded today as a pidgin.

If it is correct to claim that the Caribbean region has creole languages but not pidgins, then it should follow that in the early colonial history of this region, wherever speakers of (probably three or more) different languages interacted, some single language soon emerged as a new native tongue for the subordinate group, at the same time that its members would be forsaking their former native tongues.

I am implying that language usage in the Caribbean region probably never for long involved three or more different language communities, all of which retained their own languages while employing a pidgin as well.

Dr Cassidy has suggested that the transformation of a pidgin into a creole can probably take place very swiftly. And in an earlier comment, Dr Joos submitted that, in the formalization of pidgins, linguistic 'defects' — I think he used that term — emerge inevitably from a lack of solidarity and of any prospect of solidarity between speakers and addressees. Speakers and addressees, in other words, are not — and probably are not encouraged to expect to become — members of the same social group; learners are not learning to be part of a single community with those from whom they are learning. Dr Joos went on to say that, under severe circumstances, pidgin languages come swiftly into some kind of equilibrium, due to needs that are not general community needs. We have seen how the plantation system created non-communities upon the Caribbean landscape — socially artificial collocations of slaves and masters — of a sort that would presumably hasten just such a process of linguistic stabilization.

Thus we appear to be dealing with historical circumstances that led repeatedly to the emergence of pidgin languages — but that also led either to their swift conversion into creoles, or to their replacement by the language of the dominant social group. Pidgin languages apparently did not survive anywhere in the Caribbean region, but were instead supplanted — one supposes quite swiftly, in at least some cases — by creole languages on the one hand, or by more or less standard dialects of the masters' language, on the other.[3] When I stress the marked presence of surviving creole languages in the Caribbean region, and the marked absence of surviving pidgin languages, I think I am making a less obvious sociological or historical point, as well as a more obvious linguistic one. The relationship to demographic factors is worth remarking, and one wonders whether parallel demographic and linguistic processes could be documented elsewhere.

Yet another relevant feature of the Caribbean situation, however, has to do with the Hispanic Caribbean in particular. Dr Lawton noted in his paper that there is no evidence of a pidgin language in the history of Puerto Rico, nor of a creole language in that country (though there were influences from creole languages). I think one can go further. Spain was unchallenged in these islands for nearly a century; and there were no European attempts to settle there, in defiance of Spanish claims, for much longer than that. Spain's control of Puerto Rico, Cuba, and the eastern two-thirds of Santo Domingo persisted, virtually uninterruptedly, until the mid-nineteenth century, and until the brink of the twentieth, in the case of Puerto Rico and Cuba. Yet I know of no irrefutable evidence of any pidgin or creole language, past or present, in any of these Greater Antillean Spanish possessions.

Santo Domingo is perhaps especially striking in this regard, when compared with contiguous Haiti, where the largest national creole-speaking population in the world is to be found. It needs mentioning that absence of evidence of the prior existence of any pidgin language in these Hispanic islands by no means proves that there never were any such languages there, however; in fact, it would be surprising if pidgin languages did not at one time exist in those colonies. This question has been discussed in Reinecke's (1938 [1964]) pioneering paper.

We need to ask ourselves why there appear to be no surviving pidgin languages in the Caribbean (Tagliavini's 1931 reference to 'Negro Spanish' in Cuba remains obscure); and we must also wonder why there are no clearly-defined creole languages in the Hispanic Caribbean. On the one hand, such apparent non-occurrences suggest other questions about the social history of the region; on the other, where a creole language has embedded itself deeply in the social fabric of Caribbean societies, we are moved to wonder how this could have come about. I have made inconclusive reference to the Haitian case; let me now touch briefly on one other.

In a socio-historical study of Curaçao, Hoetink briefly compares that society with Surinam, in terms of linguistic creolization (Hoetink 1958:148–9). In Surinam, the development of Sranan Tongo and of the Bush Negro creole languages (Voorhoeve 1962) probably shared some of the sociological features of the pidginization and creolization processes characteristic of what Reinecke (1938 [1964]:539–42) has called 'plantation creoles'. The European metropolitan languages (English, Portuguese and Dutch) were the languages employed by the uppermost strata of Surinam society at different times in that colony's history; but at no time did a creole language serve as a *lingua franca* among them. Surinam creole languages became stabilized as the idioms of subordinate groups, including those descendants of runaway slaves who became the Bush Negroes; they did not supplant the languages of the upper strata, though they became second languages in certain cases for members of those strata.

The pidginization and creolization processes in the case of Curaçao occurred under different social conditions, however, and had — Hoetink tells us — very different linguistic consequences. In Curaçao, Papiamento served typically as a means of communication between groups of different social levels (although Curaçao was never a typical plantation colony). But in Curaçao, there were two upper stratum groups: the Portuguese-speaking Jewish colonists from Brazil; and the Dutch-speaking Protestant colonists from the Netherlands. Cultural interpenetration of these two groups was slight. Both groups learned and employed Papiamento, not only to communicate with their social subordinates, but also in order to communicate with each other. There is a strong socio-historical suggestion here that the presence of two 'master-groups' speaking mutually unintelligible languages, in contact with a subordinate group speaking a creole language, may well lead to the adoption of the creole by the master-groups as a common tongue. Naturally, we would want to know more of the specific circumstances in these cases; but Hoetink has given us a valuable socio-historical hint for the study of Caribbean (and possibly other) pidginization and creolization.

In approaching my conclusion, I would like to suggest that, in spite of the obvious difficulties, some useful purpose may be served by attempts to formulate the conditions under which pidgin languages may develop, as well as those under which pidgin languages may be transformed into creole languages. In my own first attempts at such formulations, I found myself restricted by my own ignorance to the Caribbean region -- essentially, that is, to but one portion of Reinecke's 'plantation creole' category. While I want to be the first to admit that the conditions here set forth are contradicted by non-Caribbean cases (and perhaps by some Caribbean cases, as well), I hope that this exercise will lead to others of a more refined and telling sort. In my view, Caribbean creole languages were produced under particular historical circumstances, including:

(1) the repeopling of empty lands;
(2) by more than two different groups;
(3) one of which was smaller and socially dominant;
(4) and the other of which was larger, socially subordinate, and included native speakers of two or more languages;
(5) under conditions in which the dominant group initiates the speaking of a pidgin that becomes common to both groups — that is, conditions under which the dominant group, at least, is bilingual, and the subordinate group multilingual; and

(6) there is no established linguistic continuum including both the pidgin and the native language of the dominant group; and

(7) the subordinate group cannot maintain its original languages, either because the numbers of speakers of any one of its languages are insufficient, or because social conditions militate against such perpetuation, or for both reasons.

To be sure, each one of these suggested conditions would have to be tested against each Caribbean case for which the data are researchable; and I remain quite uncertain as to the relevance of these conditions for non-Caribbean cases. I offer these suggestions with considerable tentativeness.[4]

Whether it can be reasonably argued that qualitatively different linguistic processes are involved in the emergence of pidgins and creoles from those governing other sorts of linguistic change is of course much in doubt. Nevertheless, more linguists than before are beginning to take account of the unusual sociological circumstances surrounding the emergence of at least some creole languages. Lounsbury, for instance, has recently (1968:205–6) written:

There is a possibility that gross typological differences reflect, if not thought or culture, then something of the accidents of the social histories of speech communities, as these have created periods and circumstances in which traditional linguistic structures were, one might say, destroyed, and language rebuilt, putting (as Powell and so many others expressed it) 'old materials to new uses.' It may be of interest in this connection that the purest 'analytic' and 'isolating' languages known are the Pidgins and Creolized languages. These have long been the unwanted stepchildren of linguistic science. But it is in these that one can see most clearly something like the first principle in the building of grammar that was posited by the evolutionary typologists. One may note that the historical circumstances that gave birth to the Pidgins and Creolized languages were far more drastic and destructive of continuity of tradition in language than were those that gave impetus to change in the modern 'analytic' Romance vernaculars, or in early modern English.

Thus put, pidgin and creole languages may be in some way testaments to the remarkable psychic and intellectual resiliency of mankind; certainly the New World plantation slavery experience tested the human spirit to the limit. From this perspective, surely one ought to be encouraged by the concern shown at the Mona Conference for the practical implications of the phenomena we study. Our human future, viewed as an understanding reconstitution of the past, must certainly include some redressing of the balance, some reintegration, some serious attempt to bring into being new kinds of organic, humanly rewarding social entities.

NOTES

1 Revised from remarks prepared for the Mona conference. The writer is indebted to Jacqueline W. Mintz for essential criticisms and suggestions, to

Drs Dell Hymes, John Reinecke and Keith Whinnom for their useful comments on an earlier draft, and to Dr Jan Voorhoeve for advice and information.

2 I have attempted to treat some of these background aspects in three previously published papers, but without particular reference to language history. Cf. Mintz 1966, 1967, and 1968.

3 Parenthetically, one may note Dr Alleyne's hypothetical linguistic acculturational situation in West Africa, near the European slave stations where, he believes, Africans were motivated to learn a European language – but presumably not at the cost of giving up their own. I think the presumption would further be that these Africans did form language communities, for whom any version of a European language could be considered a second language.

4 Following the oral presentation of my remarks, Dr Joos handed me a series of handwritten hypotheses concerning the creation and modification of pidgin languages. I thought the hypotheses unusually insightful and provocative, and included them in a footnote in an earlier draft of my report; my own statement of criteria for the formation of creoles in the Caribbean was partly stimulated by them. Though Dr Joos did not intend these hypotheses for publication, he consented to their use in this volume on the understanding that their impromptu origin, not representing a complete, deliberated presentation, be made clear. Because of their length and their relevance to the first section of this book, the editor has wished to transfer them there.

REFERENCES

Benedict, Burton 1961. *Indians in a plural society* (Colonial Office, Colonial Research Studies 34), London, Hull Printers Ltd for H.M.S.O.

Cumper, George 1954. 'Labour demand and supply in the Jamaican sugar industry, 1830–1950', *Social and Economic Studies* 2(4):37–86

Farley, Rawle 1953. 'The rise of the village settlements of British Guiana', *Caribbean Quarterly* 3(2):101–9

    1954. 'The rise of the peasantry in British Guiana', *Social and Economic Studies* 2(4):87–103

Hoetink, Harmannus 1958. *Het patroon van de oude Curaçaose samenleving*, Assen, Van Gorcum

    1967. *The two variants in Caribbean race relations*, Oxford, Oxford University Press

Le Page, Robert 1960. 'Jamaican Creole. An historical introduction to Jamaican Creole. And four Jamaican Creole texts with introduction, phonemic transcriptions and glosses by David DeCamp', *Creole Language Studies No. 1* (R. B. Le Page, ed.) London, Macmillan and Co. Ltd., and New York, St Matin's Press

Leyburn, James 1941. *The Haitian people*, New Haven, Yale University Press

Lounsbury, Floyd G. 1968. 'One hundred years of anthropological linguistics', in Brew, J. O. (ed.), *One hundred years of anthropology*, 153–225, Cambridge, Harvard University Press

Mannoni, O. 1964. *Prospero and Caliban*, 2nd ed., New York, Frederick A. Praeger

Mintz, Sidney W. 1958. 'The historical sociology of the Jamaican church-founded free village system', *De West-Indische Gids* 38:46–70

    1959. 'Labor and sugar in Puerto Rico and Jamaica', *Comparative Studies in Society and History* 1(3):273–80

1961. 'The question of Caribbean peasantries', *Caribbean Studies* 1(3):31–4

1966. 'The Caribbean as a socio-cultural area', *Cahiers d'histoire mondiale* 9(4):912–37

1967. 'Caribbean nationhood in anthropological perspective', *Caribbean Integration: Third Caribbean Scholars' Conference (Georgetown)*, ed. by S. Lewis, and T. G. Matthews 141–54

1968. 'Caribbean society', *International Encyclopedia of the Social Sciences* 2:306–18

Paget, Hugh [1951?]. 'The free village system in Jamaica', *Caribbean Quarterly* 1(4):7–19

Patterson, Orlando 1967. *The sociology of slavery*, London, MacGibbon and Kee

Price, Richard 1966. 'Caribbean fishing and fishermen', *American Anthropologist* 68:1363–83

Reinecke, John 1938 [1964]. 'Trade jargons and creole dialects as marginal languages', *Social Forces* 17:107–18 [Reprinted in Hymes, D. (ed.) 1964. *Language in Culture and Society*, 534–46, New York, Harper and Row]

Service, Elman 1955. 'Indian-European relations in colonial Latin America', *American Anthropologist* 57(3):411–25

Tagliavini, Carlo 1931. 'Creóle, Lingue', *Enciclopedia Italiana* 11:833–5

Valkhoff, Marius 1966. *Studies in Portuguese and Creole*, Johannesburg, Witwatersrand University Press

Voorhoeve, Jan 1964. 'Creole languages and communication', *Symposium on multilingualism (Brazzaville 1962)*, 233–42 (Second Meeting of the Inter-African Committee on Linguistics) (Committee for Technical Co-Operation in Africa, Publication 37), London

VII

APPENDICES
A: RESEARCH MEMORANDA

RESEARCH MEMORANDA

Memoranda outlining leading questions for research were distributed to participants before the conference by Hoenigswald, Hymes, Reinecke, Samarin and Voorhoeve, as was a paper by Figueroa containing related material. Professor Voorhoeve's memorandum, 'The problem of English-based pidgins and creoles', called attention to the work of Daelemann and Hancock (now represented by précis in this volume), and to the difficulties posed by the relations among the English-based creoles. The memoranda by Hoenigswald and Samarin are absorbed in their formal contributions, and that by Hymes is noted in his preface. Reinecke's memorandum, and part of Figueroa's paper, are published here.

Dr Reinecke was the first American to make a systematic study of pidgin and creole languages, and it is to be hoped that his *Marginal languages* (New Haven, Yale University dissertation, 1937) may yet be published in full. (For an article based on it, see J. Reinecke, 'Trade jargons and creole dialects as marginal languages', *Social Forces* 17:107–18 (1938); reprinted, *Language in culture and society*, ed. by Dell Hymes, 534–42 (New York, Harper and Row, 1964).) While pursuing a career in the trade union movement in Hawaii, he has maintained a comprehensive and concerned knowledge of the field, which his memorandum succinctly reflects.

Professor Figueroa, a host of the conference, and organizer of the evening of poetry with which it began, here expresses ways in which the scientific importance of research on these languages is at the same time of great human importance, especially in an area such as the West Indies, where the languages are so bound up with cultural and personal identity.

SOME SUGGESTED FIELDS FOR RESEARCH[1]

JOHN E. REINECKE

1. *Regional bibliographies.* Because so much of the material about and in these languages is difficult to locate (provincial journals and newspapers, devotional pamphlets, unpublished theses, radio broadcast scripts, mss. in archives, etc.), we need a series of detailed and annotated bibliographies like the Voorhoeve-Donicie bibliography on Surinam (1963).

2. *Choice of areas* for detailed scientific description of creole and pidgin languages. (And encouragement and scholarships for persons working in those areas!) Thus far the description of these languages has been on pretty much a chance basis. Some languages, e.g. the Creole of Haiti and the English of

Jamaica, have been described by several competent hands, sometimes according to advanced linguistic techniques. Others have been left to the amateurs or have not been described at all, only mentioned. Without more studies in detail of particular dialects, comparisons will be inexact and incomplete, or cannot be made at all. (Work like that of Göbl-Gáldi (1934) and Goodman (1964) would hardly be possible for the Caribbean English dialects, for instance.) There is danger that some dialects may pass from use without ever having been adequately analyzed – as has probably occurred with some of the Indo-Portuguese dialects about which Schuchardt wrote.

3. *Pidginization and perhaps creolization of African languages.* Apparently Africa is the area where pidginization and incipient creolization is taking place on the largest scale (always excepting New Guinea). Africa offers a rewarding range of pidginization, from very simplified pidgins such as Fanagalo to the slightly simplified 'Town Bemba' of the Zambian Copperbelt briefly discussed by I. Richardson (1961). Further, the wealth of material at hand in Africa for comparative purposes should free us from preoccupation (sociological as well as linguistic) with pidgins and creoles of Indo-European base. Still further, except for Sango and Fanagalo, most of the pidgins and semi-pidgins still await detailed description.

4. *Semi-pidginization.* Under what circumstances do some languages undergo extreme simplification (Cantonese Pidgin English, Neo-Melanesian, Chinook Jargon), while others are only slightly simplified (Town Bemba, probably Kingwana Swahili, Bazaar Hindustani, Low Malay)?

5. Circumstances under which languages suffer a rapid simplification of the sort which we generally attribute to trade contacts or similar superficial contacts in the case of recognized pidgins, but where speakers of the simplified languages are in intimate, continuous, and non-discriminatory contact; e.g. the Kerewa and Koriki languages of Papua reported by Capell in his Linguistic Survey of the south-west Pacific (1962).

6. Circumstances under which some creole languages go out of use rapidly, almost abruptly, e.g. the Creole Portuguese of Príncipe as described by Valkhoff (1966), while others remain in use although the odds would appear against them, e.g. the Creole Portuguese of Malacca.

7. Does cultural and linguistic pluralism play a significant part in the formation and perpetuation of a creole language – or does it not? Does government by a state using a language other than the base language of the creole play a significant part?

8. What circumstances inhibit development of a pidgin, especially in plantation countries, and later development of a creole? For example, why has there been no Pidgin Hindi or Pidgin Fiji reported from the Fiji Islands? Here belongs also the still unsettled question of why no permanent creole dialects developed in Baía and Cuba, although these places were in many respects highly Africanized (survival of African languages and religions in Baía, survival of Yoruba (Lucumí) in Cuba).

9. Carry-over of 'pidgin' habits from one language to another. Vatuk (1964) says that Indians of Guyana simplify their Hindi along the lines of 'Creolese' English (besides mixing English with the Hindi). Does the same thing happen in other places, for example with the Hindi of Surinam? (So far as I know, it has not happened with the immigrants' languages in Hawaii; and in Trinidad the Hindi, instead of being creolized, is going out of use.)

10. Circumstances which give rise to secular literary use of a creole or even a pidgin language, thus increasing its prestige and sometimes making it a symbol of nationalism; and conversely, circumstances which condemn a creole to remain a patois.

11. Differing attitudes toward pidgin or creole languages on the part of rulers and ruled, e.g. the extremely low prestige of Neo-Melanesian among Australians and its high prestige among the Abelam as reported by Laycock (1966), who borrow extensively from the Neo-Melanesian at the expense of their own native words; or among the Manus Islanders reported by Capell (1962), who are adopting it as a creole language in place of their own languages.

12. Inquiry into pidginization (and perhaps partial creolization) in contact on the Spanish and Portuguese frontiers in Latin America. Is the paucity of reported instances due to actual absence or (more probably in my opinion) to poor reporting?

13. Comparative analysis of pidgins and creoles with different bases (not Indo-European alone) to try and discover if there are any general rules of simplification. In other words, given a situation which produces a pidgin, can the form of that pidgin be more or less predicted regardless of the structure of the base language and the other language(s) involved?

NOTE

1 A memorandum distributed to participants preceding the conference.

REFERENCES

Capell, A. 1962. *A linguistic survey of the south-western Pacific* (New and revised edition), Nouméa, New Caledonia, South Pacific Commission

Göbl-Galdi, L. 1934. 'Esquisse de la structure grammaticale des patois français-créoles', *Zeitschrift für franzosische Sprache und Literatur* 58:257–95

Goodman, Morris 1964. *A comparative study of creole French dialects*, The Hague, Mouton

Laycock, Donald C. 1966. 'Papuans and Pidgin: aspects of bilingualism in New Guinea', *Te Reo* 9:44–52

Richardson, Irvine 1961. 'Some observations on the status of town Bemba in Northern Rhodesia', *African Language Studies* 2:25–36

1963. 'Examples of deviations and innovations in Bemba', *African Language Studies* 4:128–45

Valkhoff, Marius F. 1966. *Studies in Portuguese and Creole, with special reference to South Africa*, Johannesburg, Witwatersrand University Press

Vatuk, Ved Prakash 1964. 'Protest songs of East Indians in British Guiana', *Journal of American Folklore* 77:220–35

Voorhoeve, Jan and Antoon Donicie 1963. *Bibliographie du négro-anglais du Surinam avec une appendice sur les langues créoles parlées à l'interieur du pays* (Koninklijk Instituut voor Taal-, Land- en Volkenkunde, Bibliographical Series, 6), 's-Gravenhage, Martinus Nijhoff

CREOLE STUDIES[1]

JOHN J. FIGUEROA

Need for continued study

I would not like to give the impression that I think that the question of Creole languages should be studied merely because it would be beneficial to the Caribbean. I have gone into great detail above (with regard to previous activities at the University of the West Indies (UWI) and in the Caribbean) because I feel that the kind of creole studies which we have in mind is bound to make marked contributions to pure linguistics.

Creole studies will throw light on, and very often ask awkward questions about, our theories of the origin of languages, and of their relationships in families; and on the whole question of language universals. It should also throw light on the question of whether the formation of a new language moves by a slow uniform evolution, or whether in fact there are not sudden appearances of high plateaux, in fact sudden Lamarckian 'jumps'. The whole question of socio- and psycho-linguistics has very much to learn from the creole field. Moreover much that can be learned here will, undoubtedly, have direct relevance to the situation which arises in many parts of Latin America where indigenous Indian languages exist alongside the 'official' language of the area.

It is of course, true, and has to be stressed, that – from the point of view of Caribbean territories – a real study of the creole situation will help us to correct our ever outward looking tendencies. So far in the Caribbean we have found it difficult to believe in any of our own achievements, or even to study carefully our own development, including the very kind of language (or languages) which we use. So far our education has tended to be completely outward looking, so in the end, to quote Roach (1969):

> We take banana boats
> Tourist, stowaway,
> Our luck in hand calypsoes in the heart:
> We turn Columbus' blunder back
> From sun to snow, to bitter cities;
> We explore the hostile and exploding zone.

But in the Caribbean our education system, and the practices of the classroom, must teach us that 'the hostile and exploding zone' which most needs our exploration is that zone not only of our inner selves but also, and most emphatically, of the societies from which we look to the archipelago and to the wider world.

From this inward examination and outward look we must come to decide whether the present values of the developed countries are necessarily those which we wish to adopt. Or are we to assume that Mafia type organizations, to mention but one North American blight, are the necessary price which we will have to pay for development?

I am maintaining, then, that the study of the creolization of language in the Caribbean area is not only to be considered as an adjunct to the study of the teaching of language, but in fact has a real contribution to make to the study of pure linguistics. It will contribute also to the study of socio- and psycho-linguistics and to the whole communications complex, of the Caribbean area, and of other places, of which there are many in Latin America, which have similar social structures, similar economic and political problems, similar emotional problems, all arising in part out of the total situation of languages and cultures in contact. I would further like to suggest that a study of our recent fiction will show that it is a mistake to emphasize only the problems that arise – although they must be studied – it is as important to realize that we in fact have a rich language heritage which can be exploited by authors like Derek Walcott, Vidia Naipaul and George Lamming.

Further work

What work then do I suggest that we in PILEI undertake or at least strongly encourage? First of all, I should like to say that I would be very happy to have the Department of Education at the UWI act as a clearing house for information about creole studies and their relation to teaching problems and social problems in the area. Next I would like to refer you to an outline of plans developed for a Joint Communications Centre between UWI and Indiana University (the centre to be at Mona).

(a) Archives of creole studies, including archives of oral examples of speech and of what one might call oral literature in the vernacular. Associated with the archives should be a plan of disseminating information about work already done, and about further work as it proceeds.

(b) Further descriptive work on the creoles to include the study of both the popular language and the oral and written imaginative literature in the creoles.

(c) The encouragement of further analytical work to include:

(1) Theory of origin of creoles.
(2) Socio- and psycho-linguistic aspects of creole.
(3) The political aspects in the broadest sense of 'political'. How, for instance, to get into our model of democracy the necessary inter-communication between all citizens, between the grass-roots and those developing the country economically and industrially. The communication referred to has to be a two-way communication and there is some evidence to suggest that the language continuum as it exists inhibits this communication, as does the inadequate and unimaginative use being made of TV and radio.

(d) (i) A study of how the learning and teaching of English (or the official language) and also of European foreign languages, are affected by the presence of creole speakers in the schools. In this connection it is worthwhile quoting the final resolution of a conference on the English-based creoles of the Caribbean, and on the teaching of English in the special language and social circumstances of the Caribbean, that I convened and chaired in Jamaica in 1964 (*Proceedings*, 1965).

'It was fully realized by the Meeting that although the complexities of the language situation in the Caribbean made teaching and communication difficult at various levels, it offered a unique opportunity for increasing our pedagogical and linguistic knowledge. The language situation is one in which acceptable English cannot easily be described either as a mother tongue or a foreign language. The methods devised abroad both in teaching and in language study have therefore to be applied with care in the English-speaking Caribbean, and their application and re-thinking might well lead to further theoretical and pedagogical discoveries. The realization of this situation, which is at the same time one of difficulty and of opportunity, should encourage those working in the English-speaking Caribbean.'

(ii) The effect on the whole education system, from the primary to the university, of the existence of creole, and of the socio- and psycho-linguistic implications of this situation.

It is well worth pointing out that creole situations differ within themselves. For instance, in Jamaica what we really have is a continuous unbroken continuum between something that is very nearly standard received British speech, to the most creolized of Jamaican speech. This situation contrasts with that of Surinam where the English-based creole does not have side by side with it a language in any way resembling standard southern British English. It is most important to keep in mind this difference. The problem of teaching English in Surinam is not quite like the problem of teaching English in Jamaica. Moreover, the psycho- and socio-linguistic implications are quite different. One gathers that in Paramaribo, for instance, the Creole based on English is entirely accepted as a language, just as Papiamento is accepted in Curacao. One of the complications of the Jamaican situation is that, because of the unbroken continuum, what might be called the lower ends of the language spectrum – i.e. the more creolized sections – are not accepted in many circles as constituting a language. Many people do not realize that what they call 'broken' English has a system all its own. Furthermore in the continuum situation the likeness between almost any part of the continuum and standard British, or standard Jamaican, speech makes the teaching of a standard form of English *more* not less difficult. In much the same way (I understand from a prominent Brazilian linguist) a person who has grown up speaking Portuguese often finds that he makes less mistakes in speaking English (once he has learned it) than he does in speaking Spanish, because Portuguese is so much closer to Spanish than it is to English.

(e) The whole socio-economic and pedagogic aspects of communication are also to be studied.

I should also like to recommend very strongly that in all these areas work be done to determine what might be considered a linguistically and socially acceptable standard. Many teachers, for instance, as well as businessmen and professional men are confused about what should be the target language of the schools and the community. I think that this matter is neither completely linguistic nor, as some linguists have tried to maintain, purely social. The matter needs study both from the point of view of the tendencies which are clear in the language situation, and from the empirical facts about what is likely to be accepted by employers and leaders in the community.

A good comparative study, yielding much interesting information, might well be done between the situation in a place like Jamaica and that of a place like Surinam. This is with reference to the existence on the one hand of a far stretching continuum and on the other to a creole which exists in a situation where one of its original parents, at least, does not appear on the scene at all.

As I have already hinted the creolization of language did not take place only in the Caribbean but wherever African slaves were brought to the New World. (And wherever 'trade' took the European adventurers, particularly the Portuguese; cf. Whinnom (1956) on languages in contact in the Philippines.) In the United States of America at the present one of the social consequences of slave history is being felt through problems that arise in the so-called Inner Cities.

R

One knows that these problems are not solely problems of Negro Americans; they are indeed problems of minority groups. However, in the case of descendants of African slaves one of the clear symptoms, and at the same time cause of the problems is the kind of English now being called in certain circles 'Negro English'. In fact William Stewart, a member of the PILEI, is at present focussing on the problem of 'Negro English' in the States, knowledge of which he has gained from his work on Creole in the Caribbean. A fruitful field for collaboration is to be found in this question of the study of the linguistic, sociolinguistic and pedagogical aspect of Negro English. Without a doubt work in the Caribbean would throw light on the problems that are arising in Inner America (cf. Stewart 1967 and Dillard's paper in this volume). PILEI are encouraging collaboration between those working on creole in the Caribbean and those studying the linguistic problems of the so-called 'disadvantaged' in the United States of America.

Finally, I would press strongly for the use of imaginative literature in the study of the creole situation and in the teaching of languages. The latter point I have made at length in a paper published in the proceedings of the Bloomington Symposium (Figueroa 1966). About the former I wish to say this. By careful study of old literary texts we can learn more about the origin and consistencies of various creoles; by a study of modern literary texts, such as the poems of Walcott, or the novels of Lamming, we can come to a fuller realization of the resources, flexibility and limits of the creole languages. We can also help to work towards some acceptable standard; because the creative artist might help us to see not the problems, linguistic and pedagogic, of the creole situation, but the richness of the language resources which exist all around us – resources which are likely to be left by us in the state of unappreciated raw material. Our creative artists will show us how to turn this raw material into real resources for our spiritual, emotional and political development.

NOTE

1 Expanded from part of a paper of the same title read at the PILEI Conference, Mexico City, January 1968. The paper is to appear in the *Proceedings* of the conference, and was distributed to participants in the Mona conference.

REFERENCES

Figueroa, John 1966. *El uso de textos literarios en enseñanza del idioma* (Report of the second PILEI conference, Bloomington, Indiana 1964), Bogota, Instituto Carvo y cuervo

[Proceedings] 1965. *Language teaching, and the teaching of English in a multi-lingual society*, Mona, University of the West Indies, Faculty of Education

Roach, E. M. 1969. *Love overgrows rock. Blue horizons:* an *anthology of West Indian verse*, ed. with an introduction, by John Figueroa, London, Evans Brothers

Stewart, William A. 1967. 'Sociolinguistic factors in the history of American Negro dialects', *Florida FL Reporter* 5(2)

Whinnom, Keith 1956. *Spanish contact vernaculars in the Philippine Islands*, Hong Kong, Hong Kong University Press

B: A MAP AND LIST OF PIDGIN AND CREOLE LANGUAGES

A SURVEY OF THE PIDGINS AND CREOLES OF THE WORLD

IAN F. HANCOCK

Note: Not discussed in this survey are the various African languages which have survived in the New World (Lucumí, Lángu, Bríkamu, etc.) and which appear to have some features of pidginization, or the mixed languages of the Slavo-German or Slavo-Italian type, as described by Hugo Schuchardt, *Dem Herrn Franz von Miklosich zum 20 Nov. 1883. Slawo-deutsches und Slawo-italienisches* (Graz 1884).

1. Hawaiian Pidgin English, used as a first language by many of its *c.* 500,000 speakers. English-derived, with possible influence from Chinese, Japanese, Hawaiian and various Philippine languages. A Neo-Melanesian-like substratum seems to be discernible. Well documented, but see especially J. E. Reinecke, *Language and dialect in Hawaii* (Honolulu, University of Hawaii Press, 1969), and Tsuzaki and Carr, with references, in this volume.

2. Pitcairnese Creole English, spoken today by *c.* 150 people, descendants of the mutineers from H.M.S. *Bounty* who settled on the island in 1790. The language appears to have more in common with the English-derived creoles of the Atlantic than with those spoken elsewhere in the Pacific. Extensive Tahitian influences. See A. Wiltshire, 'The local dialects of Norfolk and Pitcairn Islands', *Journal of the Royal Australian Historical Society* 25:331–7 (1939), A. Ross and A. Moverley, *The Pitcairnese language* (London 1964), and D. Woods, *Pitcairn Island dialect* (Georgetown University, 1967, unpublished).

3 (a). Chinook Jargon, based mainly on Chinook proper but with considerable lexicon from Nootka, French, English and Salishan dialects. Gained maximum currency during the late nineteenth century, being spoken by an estimated 100,000 people from southern Oregon to Alaska. Thought to have been creolized in some areas. Now known only by some older generation speakers. See Kaufman, with references, in this volume (pp. 275–8).

(b). Pidgin Eskimo; a number of varying Eskimo pidgins used in trading with whites, and a quite different Eskimo pidgin used in dealing with Athapaskan Indians, are reported by V. Stefánsson, 'The Eskimo trade jargon of Herschel Island', *American Anthropologist* (n.s.) 11:217–32 (1909). Stefánsson provides a Herschel Island vocabulary 'adopting the MacKenzie River Eskimo pronunciation as used in dealing with whites' (218).

4 (a). Pachuco or Pochismo, a Spanish-English contact language in waning use between English and Spanish speaking Americans, and used as an argot by some youths of Mexican ancestry in Arizona and parts of southern California. See George C. Barker, *Pachuco: An American Spanish Argot and its social functions in Tucson, Arizona* (Tucson, 1950). A related argot in Texas is referred to as 'the language of the tirilones', or as the *caló*; see L. Coltharp, *The tongue of the Tirilones* (University, Alabama, 1965), and discussion in the Introduction to Part III, n. 4.

(b). Trader Navaho, a name applied to forms of Navaho in Arizona Although reported earlier as a pidgin (cf. C. F. Voegelin, 'An expanding language, Hopi',

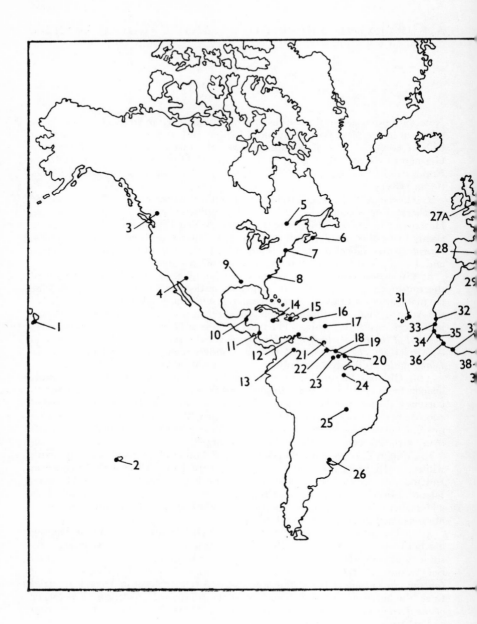

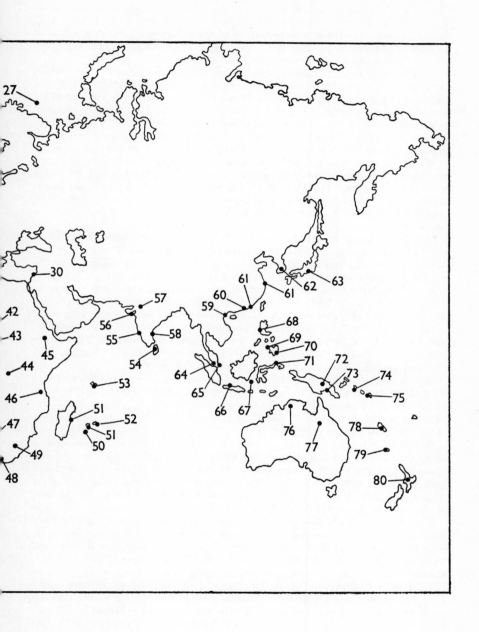

Plateau 32(2):33–9 (1959), it has been found to be spoken only by traders, to Navahos, not conversely, and to consist of idiosyncratically varying forms of limited knowledge of Navaho. See O. Werner, *A typological comparison of four Trader Navaho speakers* (Bloomington, Indiana, 1963).

5. The long-extinct Franco-Amerindian contact vernacular ('un certain baragouin'), reported as having been in use between Frenchmen and the indigenous population in and around Montreal. Recorded in a letter sent to his superiors by the missionary Paul le Jeune in 1632: 'The Frenchmen who spoke it supposed it to be good Indian, and the Indians believed it to be French.' Mentioned in J. H. Trumbull, 'Words derived from Indian languages of North America', *Transactions of the American Philosophical Society* (1870), 19–32, p. 20.

6. Souriquoien, now extinct but at one time in use between French fishermen and the local population in Nova Scotia. Reported by Lescarbot in his *Histoire de la Nouvelle France* (1612), p. 694: 'the local people, to accommodate themselves to us ... speak to us in a language with which we are more familiar, wherein there is much Basque mingled.' Also mentioned in Trumbull, *op. cit.* 5 above, p. 20.

7(a). New Jersey Amerindian trade pidgin, now extinct, based lexically on the Munsee, Unami and Unalachtigo (Delaware Algonquian) dialects of that region, and with a grammatical structure resembling English. Used between the local population and visiting English and Dutch traders. See J. D. Prince, 'An ancient New Jersey Indian jargon', *American Anthropologist* 14:508–24 (1912). Cf. now F. T. Siebert, 'The earliest Algonquian general vocabulary and the Atlantic Jargon', *International Journal of American Linguistics* 36: (1970).

(b). An Amerindian-based pidgin, Mogilian, derived mainly from Choctaw, was formerly used by all tribes along the Gulf coast and along the Mississippi as far as the Ohio river. Now extinct, it is mentioned in E. H. Thomas, 'The Chinook Jargon', *American Speech* 2:377–84 (1927), p. 377.

(c). General Amerindian Pidgin English is discussed by D. Leechman and R. A. Hall, Jr., 'American Indian Pidgin English: attestations and grammatical peculiarities', *American Speech* 30:163–71 (1955), and by Mary R. Miller, 'Attestations of American Indian Pidgin English in fiction and non-fiction', *American Speech* (May 1967), 142–7.

8. Gullah (Goolah, Geechee, Geedgee), an English-derived creole spoken along the coastal strip and offshore Sea Islands from northern Florida to South Carolina by some 125,000 Americans of African descent. Many syntactical and lexical features in common with English-derived creoles and pidgins of West Africa, especially Krio (35, below). Well documented, but see L. D. Turner, *Africanisms in the Gullah dialect* (Chicago, 1949).

9. Louisiana Creole French, occasionally known as 'Gumbo', spoken by a dwindling population in eastern Louisiana and at one time in parts of communities in Mississippi. For the dialect of one community, see R. Morgan, 'Structural sketch of Saint Martin Creole', and 'The lexicon of Saint Martin Creole', *Anthropological Linguistics* 1(8):20–4 (1959) and 2(1):7–29 (1960).

10. Creole English of British Honduras. Fairly conservative, with many features in common with Jamaican dialects. A first language for a mainly urban population, rural Hondurans using a variety of languages (Spanish, Mayan, Cariban) with the creole as a *lingua franca*. Poorly documented, but see 'A note on the behaviour of Creole verbs' *Inquiry* 1:13–18 (1956) (Journal of the Dept. of Extramural Studies, U.W.I., Belize).

11(a). Pidginized variety of various Caribbean Creole English dialects in use in ports and coastal settlements along Nicaragua's Mosquito Coast. Most closely related to the creoles of Jamaica and British Honduras, and spoken as a first language by settlers from these countries. Mentioned in Ernst Schultze, 'Die Sklaven and Dienersprachen', *Sociologus* 9:389–418 (1933), pp. 396–7, section v, 'Die Ersatzsprache der Moskitoküste'.

(b). A creolized Nahuatl-Spanish was established in Nicaragua during the sixteenth century, but now is probably extinct. See A. M. Elliot, 'The Nahuatl-Spanish dialect of Nicaragua', *American Journal of Philology* 5(1).

12(a). Papiamentu (Papiam, Papiaments, Papiamento, Curaçoleño, Curassese). Spanish creole derived from an earlier Portuguese pidgin, much influenced lexically by Dutch. Spoken in three main dialects by upwards of 200,000 people in Curaçao, Bonaire and Aruba. Reportedly once spoken in Cuba. Well documented, but see R. Lenz, *El papiamentu, la lengua criolla de Curazao, la gramàtica mas sencilla* (Santiago 1928).

(b). For Africanisms and creole elements in modern Cuban Spanish, see J. I. de Armas, *Orijenes del lenguaje criollo*, 2nd ed. (Havana 1882), and F. Ortiz, *Glosario de afronegrismos* (Havana 1924). For those in nineteenth-century Puerto Rican Spanish, see M. A. Nazario, 'Notas sobre el habla del negro en Puerto Rico durante el siglo XIX', *Revista del instituto de cultura puertorriqueña* 2:43–8 (1959).

13(a). Pidgin Spanish, used principally by two Amerindian tribes inhabiting western Venezuela, in their dealings with traders in the area. See O. L. Riley, 'Trade Spanish of the Piñaguero Panare', *Studies in Linguistics* 2(1):6–11 (1952).

(b). A creolized variety of Spanish is reported from Bolívar, Colombia, by Germán De Granda, 'Sobre el estudio de las hablas "criollas" en el area hispanica', *Thesaurus* 23:1–15 (1968). de Granda bases himself on José Joaquín Montes, 'Sobre el habla de San Basilio de Palenque (Bolívar, Colombia)', *Thesaurus* 17:446–50 (1962), and believes that there are probably a number of other creolized forms of Spanish, used mostly by Amerindians, in South America. See now D. Bickerton and A. Escalante, 'Palanquero: a Spanish-based creole of northern Colombia', *Lingua* 24:254–67 (1970).

14. Jamaican Creole English (Bungo, Quashee, Jagwa-Taak), spoken in several closely related forms by most of the country's over one million inhabitants. Well documented, but see especially F. Cassidy and R. Le Page, *Dictionary of Jamaican English* (Cambridge, 1967), containing a bibliography of all major works on the language to that date. See also Cassidy, Bailey, DeCamp, and Craig in this volume. On Caribbean creoles generally, see bibliographies by Vera Rubin and J. L. Dillard, *Caribbean Studies* 2(4):51–61, 3(1):84–95 (1962, 1963).

15. Haitian Creole French, spoken in three main dialects by over four million Haitians. Well documented. See André Marcel d'Ans, *Le créole français d'Haïti* (The Hague 1968), with extensive bibliography, and Valdman (this volume).

16. Virgin Islands Dutch Creole, now practically extinct, but at one time having sufficient speakers to warrant a New Testament translation (1818). See E. Pontoppidan, 'Einige Notizen über die Kreolensprache der Dänischwestindischen Inseln', *Zeitschr. für Ethnologie* 13:130–8 (1881), D. C. Hesseling, 'Het Negerhollands der Deense Antillen', Leiden (1905), and H. Schuchardt, 'Zum Negerholländischen von St Thomas', *Tijdschr. voor Nederlandse Taal- en Letterkunde* 33:123–42 (1941).

17. French Creole dialects of the Antilles, spoken in Guadaloupe, Desirade, Marie Galante, Les Saintes, Saint Barthélemy, Dominica, Martinique, Saint Lucia, Grenada, the Grenadines, Trinidad and Tobago. For these, and other French-derived pidgins and creoles, see K. J. Hollyman, 'Bibliographie des créoles et dialectes régionaux français d'outre-mer modernes', *Le Français moderne* 33:117–32 (1965).

18. Sranan, the creole English of coastal Suriname also known as Taki-Taki, Ningre Tongo, Krioro, etc Spoken as a first language by *c.* 80,000 people, and as a second language by many thousands more both in the interior of the country and in the ports along the Guiana coast. See Rens (1953), Voorhoeve (1962), and other references in Voorhoeve (this volume).

19. The English-derived 'Bush Negro' dialects of Suriname: Boni or Aluku, and Djuka or Aucan, all mutually intelligible. Djuka has at least three sub-dialects, Ojo, Bilo, and Cottica River. All three are probably early offshoots from Sranan. Poorly documented, but see M. Kahn, *Djuka, the Bush Negroes of Dutch Guiana* (New York 1931), esp. 161–74, and J. Voorhoeve, 'A project for the study of creole language history in Surinam', *Creole language studies II* (London 1961), 99–106. Djuka is unique amongst the creoles in that it has developed a syllabic writing system, one having remarkable similarities with the various indigenous scripts of West Africa. Consult T. D. P. Dalby, 'The indigenous scripts of West Africa and Surinam: their inspiration and design', *African Language Studies* 9:156–97 (1968).

A Pidgin Djuka is used between Djuka Bush Negroes and the Trio Indians. Modelled upon Djuka Creole, it has a heavy influx of Trio vocabulary, including grammatical morphemes. See C. H. de Goeje, *Verslag der Toemoekhoemak-expeditie (Tumuchumac-expeditie)* (Leiden 1908), Bijlage 11, Taal, 204–19 (J. Dillard, personal communication).

20. French Creole of French Guiana, spoken by less than 50,000 people inhabiting Cayenne and other smaller coastal settlements. Some Portuguese-language influence discernible. See A. de Saint-Quentin, 'Notice grammaticale et philologique sur le créole de Cayenne', a 70-page appendix to A. de Saint-Quentin, *Introduction à l'histoire de Cayenne* (Antibes 1872); A. Horth, *Le patois guyanais* (Cayenne 1949); and C. G. Rowe and A. Horth, '*Dolos*, Creole proverbs of French Guiana', *Journal of American Folklore* 64:253–64 (1951).

21(a). English Creole of Trinidad ('Bouriki', 'Banana English'), and the more conservative dialect of Tobago. The Trinidad variety exhibits influences from Barbardian Creole English as well as from various immigrant languages such as Spanish and Hindi. In both islands Antilles Creole French is still spoken, but appears to be dying out. A Krio-based variety, or Krio influence, must have been important in the nineteenth century; see J. J. Thomas, 'Essay on the philology of the Creole dialect', *Trübner's American and Oriental Literary Record*, 31 December 1870, 57–8. For the English-derived creole of Tobago, see H. B. Meikle, 'Tobago villagers in the mirror of dialect', *Caribbean Quarterly* 4:154–60 (1956); for Trinidad Creole French, see J. J. Thomas, *The theory and practice of Creole grammar* (London 1869, reprinted London 1969), and A. T. Carr, 'Pierrot Grenade', a fairly long phoneticized text, *Caribbean Quarterly* 4(3/4):281–314 (1956).

(b). On Antiguan Creole English, see Reisman in this volume.

22(a). Guyana Creole English, or 'Creolese'. Various contributing elements discernible, including the creoles of Barbados and Sierra Leone (brought in with the free African labor force during the mid-nineteenth century). There are dubious reports of much more conservative English-derived creole similar to Sranan having survived in eastern Guyana; this may be the speech of settlers from neighboring Surinam, however. See J. van Sertima, *The Creole tongue of British Guiana* (New Amsterdam 1905), J. G. Cruickshank, *Black talk, being notes on the Negro dialect in British Guiana, with a chapter on the vernacular of Barbados* (Demerara 1916), and S. R. Allsopp, 'The English language in British Guiana', *English Language Teaching* 12:59–66 (1958).

(b). In the interior of Guyana, near the Brazilian border, a 'much corrupted Portuguese, almost unintelligible to speakers of genuine Portuguese' is spoken by Nikari Karu Amerindians as a first language. This may be creolized. See E. F. Thurn, 'A journey in the interior of British Guiana', *Proceedings of the Royal Geographic Society* 8:481 (1880).

(c). A Pidgin Dutch, spoken far inland on the rivers in Guyana, is reported by Charles D. Dance, *Chapters from a Guyanese log book* ... (London 1881), pp. 32, 58, 99.

23. The Portuguese-derived 'Bush Negro' dialects of Surinam, i.e. Saramaccan and Matuwari. Originally developing from a Portuguese pidgin, these dialects now have a high English-derived lexical content, probably via Sranan. They also appear to have retained a far higher proportion of African (especially Kikongo) derived words than any other Surinam creole. The total number of 'Bush Negro' language speakers, including those listed under (19) above, does not exceed 20,000. See H. Schuchardt, *Die Sprache der Saramakkaneger in Surinam* (Amsterdam 1914), and A. Donicie and J. Voorhoeve, *De Saramakaanse woordenschat* (Amsterdam 1962).

24. Brazilian Creole Portuguese, still retained in varying stages of decreolization by some Brazilians of African ancestry living in rural areas, and known as Tabarenho, Matutenho, or Caipiranho. A rudimentary creole known as Fazendeiro exists in São Paulo, and is spoken by some Brazilians of mixed Italian and Negro ancestry. See I. S. Révah, 'La question des substrats et des superstrats dans le domaine linguistique brésilien: les parlers populaires brésiliens, doivent-ils être considérés comme des parlers "créoles" ou "semi-créoles"?', *Romania* 84:433–50 (1963), and M. J. Valkhoff, *Studies in Portuguese and Creole*, esp. chs. I, II (Johannesburg 1966). For material on Fazendeiro, see A. Nardo Gibele, 'Alcune parole usate dalla popolazione mista italiana e negra nelle fazende di São Paulo nel Brasile', *Archivio per lo studio delle tradizioni popolari* 19:18–24 (1900).

25. Lingoa Gêral, sometimes known as Ava'–neē, a rudimentary pidgin based on the Tupi-Guarani languages of central South America and at one time in extensive use in coastal and inland Brazil. Now fast losing ground to Portuguese. See C. F. Hartt, 'Notes on the Lingoa Gêral or modern Tupi of the Amazonas', *Transactions of the American Philological Association* 3:58–76 (1872).

26(a). Cocoliche (Lunfardo, Rioplatense), an Italianized Spanish in use in the Buenos Aires area. May be rudimentarily pidginized (but see Whinnom, this volume). See R. Donghi de Halperín, 'Contribucion al estudio del italianismo en la República Argentina', *Cuadernos de la facultad de Filosofía y Letras de la Universidad de Buenos Aires* 1:183–98 (1925), and G. Meo-Zilio, 'Fenomeni stilistici del cocoliche rioplatense', *Lingua Nostra* 17:88–91 (1956).

(b). A Franco-Spanish contact language is also used in Buenos Aires; see A. Rigaud, 'Le Fragnol', *Vie et Langage* 96–9 (1959).

(c). A German-Portuguese contact language has also been reported from Brazil; see A. W. Sellin, 'Deutschbrasilianisches', *Magazin für die Literatur des Inn und Auslandes* 34:496 (n.d.).

27. Russenorsk, the Russian-Norwegian contact language, now practically extinct, but in frequent use between Scandinavian, Lappish and Russian fishermen in the Barents and Norwegian Seas towards the end of the nineteenth century. See notes on the language, with references, in O. Broch, 'Russenorsk', *Archiv für Slawische Philologie* 41:209–262 (1927), and G. Neumann, 'Russenorwegisch und Pidginenglisch', *Nachrichten der Giessener Hochschulgesellschaft* 34:219–34 (1965).

27A. Anglo-Romani (*pogado jib*, 'broken talk') is known to perhaps a majority of British Romanichals in what now appears to be a creolized form. Evidence for its origin as a pidgin is discussed in Ian F. Hancock, 'Is Anglo-Romanes a creole?', *Journal of the Gypsy Lore Society* 49(1–2):41–4 (1970).

An Anglo-Irish pidgin, used principally by Irish tinkers and known as Sheldru or Shelta, appears structurally based on English with lexicon from Irish. See R. A. S. MacAlister, *The secret languages of Ireland* (Cambridge 1937), 130–224.

28. Inglés de Escalerilla, a Spanish-English pidgin reportedly in use in the Mediterranean seaports of Almería, Malagá, La Linea, etc. Mentioned in Meillet and Cohen, *Les langues du monde* (1952), 63.

29. Pidgin French, or 'Petit Mauresque', of North Africa. Sometimes wrongly referred to as Sabir or Petit Nègre. See A. Lanly, 'Notes sur le français parlé en Afrique du nord', *Le français moderne* 23:197–211 (1955), and A. Dupuy, 'Le français d'Afrique du nord', *Vie et langage* (1960), 2–11.

30. The extinct Sabir or Sabeir, which gained impetus in the Middle East during the time of the Crusades, and which existed in various forms in many Mediterranean ports for several centuries. Known also as the Lingua Franca. Basically a pidginized variety of Provençal, influenced lexically by French, Catalan, Italian, etc., and various languages of the eastern Mediterranean. See H. Schuchardt, 'Die Lingua Franca', *Zeitschrift für Romanische Philologie* 33:441–61 (1909), P. Fronzaroli, 'Nota sulla formazione della lingua franca', *Atti e memorie dell'Accademia Toscana di Scienze e Lettere 'La Colombaria'* 20:211–52 (Florence 1955), and H. R. Kahane and A. Tietze, *The Lingua Franca in the Levant. Turkish nautical terms of Italian and Greek origin* (Urbana 1958).

31. The Portuguese-derived creole of the Cape Verde Islands, in two main dialects, Sotavento and Barlavento. See B. Lopes da Silva, *O dialecto crioulo de Cabo Verde* (Lisbon 1957). The Cape Verde creole is spoken by a community of Afro-Americans near New Bedford, Massachusetts, descended from nineteenth century immigrants, known locally as 'Bravas'. See Mary L. Nunes, 'The phonologies of Cape Verdean dialects of Portuguese', *Boletim de Filologia* 7:1–56 (Lisbon 1963). Contact with Standard Portuguese has apparently resulted in considerable decreolization both in Massachusetts and in California (where communities are also reported to speak it).

32. Senegal Creole Portuguese, or Kryôl, closely related to the preceding, and with *c.* 57,000 speakers. See A. Chataigner, 'Le créole portugais du Sénégal', *Journal of African Languages* 2(1):44–71 (1962).

33. Creole English of Bathurst, the Gambia, where it is known as Aku, Krio or Patois. Spoken as a first language by some 3,500 Creoles or 'Akus', descendants of freed Yoruba slaves, and traders from Sierra Leone. Spoken by many

more as a second language. No literature available for Gambian Krio, but material for the Freetown variety useful.

34. Guiné Creole Portuguese, or Crioulo. Similar to the Cape Verde and Senegal creoles, and forming a larger unit with them (as distinct from the Portuguese-derived creoles of the Gulf of Guinea, 39 below). Employed as a *lingua franca* by most of the country's population of 500,000. Creolized in the larger townships. See W. A. A. Wilson, *The crioulo of Guiné* (Johannesburg 1962).

35. Krio, the English-derived creole of Freetown and nearby villages in Sierra Leone. Spoken as a first language by an estimated 120,000 people, and used as a *lingua franca* throughout the country by many thousands more. Some evidence to suggest that Krio might be the product of double creolization, the second involving an earlier English-derived creole and Yoruba, brought in with liberated Africans during the nineteenth century. See E. Jones, 'Sierra Leone Krio', in J. Spencer (ed.), *The English language in West Africa* (London 1970).

36 (a). Liberian English ('Americo-Liberian', 'Kwásai', 'Brokes' or 'Waterside' English), characteristic of the Liberian settlers in Monrovia and other towns along the Liberian coast, and representing a variety of nineteenth-century United States Negro English creole, arrested in its 'pendulum swing' back to English, and carried to West Africa. Poorly documented, although samples of Liberian English may be found in W. Stewart, 'Foreign language teaching methods in quasi-foreign language situations', *Non-standard speech and the teaching of English*, Center for Applied Linguistics, Language information series 2:1–15 (Washington, D.C. 1964), and I. F. Hancock, 'The English-derived pidgins and creoles of the Atlantic area', *African Language Review* 8 (1969).

(b). Kru fishermen, whose tribal home is in Liberia, employ a highly conservative form of English-derived pidgin in their dealings with other African communities along the West African coast. Known as Kru (or Kroo) English, this speech appears to be most closely related to Freetown Krio. The Kru may have been instrumental in establishing some of the common syntactic and lexical features shared by the various English-derived pidgins and creoles on the coast. No available literature on this speech.

37. Pidgin French, Petit-Nègre or Pitinègue, spoken in the Ivory Coast and other former French possessions on the West African coast. Used mainly by soldiers, the pidgin contains many words of nautical French provenance. Very inadequately documented, but consult M. Delafosse, *Vocabulaires comparatifs*, 263–5 (Paris 1904), and 'Parlers négro-européens de la Guinée', in Meillet and Cohen, *Les langues du monde* 843–4 (Paris, 1952), and R. Mauny, *Glossaire d'expressions et termes locaux employés dans l'Ouest africain* (IFAN-Dakar 1952).

38. Fernando Po Creole, spoken by *c.* 4,000 people at Santa Isobel and San Carlos, sometimes known as 'Porto' or 'Porto Talk'. English-derived, and originally the speech of Sierra Leone Creole and West Indian Maroon settlers who arrived there in 1830. Appears to have retained several features now archaic in Freetown Krio; Spanish being the official tongue of the island, English has not exerted a standardizing effect on the creole, as has been the case in Sierra Leone. Cameroons Pidgin is also spoken in the island. See R. P. Mariano de Zarco, *Dialecto inglés–africano o broken-english de la colonia española del Golfo de Guinea: epitome de la gramatica seguido del vocabulario español-inglés y inglés-español*, 2nd edn. (Turnhout 1938).

39. The Gulf of Guinea Portuguese Creoles, spoken on the islands of Anno-

bon, São Tomé and Príncipe (this latter variety highly lusitanized, and therefore, like Liberian English, representing a vestigial creole rather than a rudimentary creole, such as Afrikaans (q.v.)). Some similarities with the northern
group of West African Portuguese creoles (nos. 31, 32, 34 above), reinforced by
Capeverdian migrants settling in São Tomé and Principe. See M. Valkhoff,
Studies in Portuguese and Creole, ch. 3 (Johannesburg 1966).

40. Cameroons Pidgin English, also known as Bush English, Cameroons
Creole, West Coast, Wes Kos, Broken English, etc., used by over one million
speakers as a second language in the Cameroons, and by many others in Eastern
Nigeria and on Fernando Po. Well documented, but see especially D. Dwyer
and D. Smith, *An introduction to West African Pidgin English* (East Lansing,
Michigan 1966), and G. D. Schneider, *West African Pidgin-English* (Athens,
Ohio 1970).

41(a). Ewondo Populaire, an African-derived pidgin in use over a large area
of the French Cameroun, between inland tribes of differing linguistic backgrounds. Also known as Bulu des chauffeurs, Bulu bediliva, and Pidgin A70. See
P. Alexandre, 'Aperçu sommaire sur le pidgin A70 du Cameroun', *Symposium
on multilingualism*, 251–6 (London 1964).

(b). A Pidgin Hausa, called Barikanci, grew up around the European barracks
in northern Nigeria and was used as a *lingua franca* in the armed forces, sometimes taught by English-speakers to speakers of diverse Nigerian languages.

42(a). Tekrur or Pidgin Arabic, employed as a *lingua franca* over a wide
area to the east of Lake Chad, and in the Bodélé region. Mentioned in L.
Homburger, *The Negro-African languages* (London 1949), p. 35.

(b). Sudan-Arabic (Southern Arabic, Mongallese, Bimbashi Arabic), which
flourished in the southern provinces of the then Anglo-Egyptian Sudan from
about 1870 to 1920; see A. N. Tucker, 'The linguistic situation in the Southern
Sudan', *Africa* 7:29 (1934).

(c). Hausa speakers report the presence of a pidgin Arabic in northern Nigeria
also (personal communications).

(d). Galgaliya, a pidgin Arabic used by the Kalamáfi tribe in northeastern
Nigeria; noted by F. W. Taylor, *Fulani-English dictionary* (Oxford 1932), p. 62.

43. Sango, a pidginized variety of the Ngbandi language (also known as
Sango). Extensively used in the Central African Republic, as well as in some
areas of the Cameroun and Chad. Many lexical adoptions from French.
Creolized in some areas, notably in the capital, Bangui. See W. Samarin,
A grammar of Sango (The Hague 1967), and Samarin (this volume).

44. Several pidginized forms of indigenous African languages current in the
Congo area, including Kituba (also known as Kibulamatadi, Munukutuba,
Kisodi, Fiote, Ikeleve, Kileta, Commercial Kikongo, Commercial Kikwango,
etc.), derived from Kikongo and used by perhaps two million speakers as a second
language; Ngbandi or pidginized Swahili, spoken in the eastern Congo;
Pidgin Chiluba, employed extensively in Kasai Province; and Bangala or
Lingala, a pidginized Ngala used in and around Léopoldville. See E. Nida,
'Tribal and trade languages', *African Studies* 14:155–8 (1955), J. Berry,
'Pidgins and creoles in Africa', *Symposium on multilingualism* 219–25 (1962),
W. Samarin, '*Lingua francas*, with special reference to Africa', *Study of the
rôle of second languages in Asia, Africa and Latin America* 54–64 (Washington
1962), and especially B. Heine, *Afrikanische Verkehrssprachen* (Cologne 1968).

45. Asmara Pidgin Italian, originally developed whilst Eritrea was in Italian

hands, and still current in that part of Ethiopia (Professor F. G. Cassidy, personal communication.)

46. Swahili, itself the result of Arabic-Bantu contact and inter-marriage, has given rise to various pidginized forms widely spoken in eastern Africa. Perhaps the most aberrant variety is the so-called Kisetta (< 'Settler') spoken in Kenya between Europeans and Africans. See G. W. Broomfield, 'The development of the Swahili language', *Africa* 3:516–22 (1930), W. H. Whiteley, 'Swahili as a *lingua franca* in East Africa', *Symposium on multilingualism* 183–7 (London 1969), and Whiteley, *Swahili, the rise of a national language* (London, 1969).

47. Pidginized Afrikaans, employed by Hottentots and Afrikaners in the Namaland region. See. J. H. Rademeyer, *Kleurling-Afrikaans, die taal van die Griekwas en Rehoboth-Basters* (Amsterdam 1938).

48. Afrikaans, 'Taal' or 'Cape Dutch', sometimes referred to in colloquial Dutch as 'Baby-Hollands'. May be said to be a rudimentary creole, its formation involving only semi-creolization away from the metropolitan language. Pidgin Portuguese was spoken at the Cape until the nineteenth century. On Afrikaans as a creole, see Valkhoff, *op. cit.* (39, above).

49(a). Fanagaló (also called Isikula, Silunguboi, Isilololo, Chilapalapa, Isipiki, Chikabanga, Mine Kaffir, Kitchen Kaffir, Basic Bantu, etc.), a pidginized Zulu employed by migrant African mine workers around Johannesburg. Also reportedly spoken in parts of Rhodesia.

(b). Several simplified indigenous African languages are in use in the Rhodesia copperbelt area, the most widespread being Town Bemba (or 'Chikopabeluti'). For Fanagalo, see D. T. Cole, 'Fanagalo and the Bantu languages in South Africa', *African Studies* 12(1): 1–9 (1953); for Fanagalo and Town Bemba, A. L. Epstein, 'Linguistic innovation ... on the Copperbelt, Northern Rhodesia', *South-western Journal of Anthropology* 15:235–53 (1959); for Town Bemba, I. Richardson, 'Linguistic change in Africa, with special reference to the Bemba-speaking area of Northern Rhodesia', *Symposium on multilingualism* 189–96 (London 1964).

50. Réunion French Creole, Réunionnais, or (formerly) Bourbonnais, spoken by over 200,000 people. In earlier years several dialects were discernible, including that of the original Creole population, and the Malagasy and Mozambique immigrant varieties. Many of the latter group were probably familiar with Barracoon, a contact vernacular in use during the nineteenth century in the Mozambique ports, and comprising elements from Arabic, Swahili, Portuguese, Malagasy, Makua and Hinzua. See A. Vinson and P. Duclos, 'Du patois créole de l'île Bourbon', *Bulletin de la Société des Sciences et des Arts* (1884), notes on Mozambique French Creole of Réunion by J. Vinson in *Revue de Linguistique* 15:330–2 (1882), and Mozambique Barracoon speech, mentioned on p. 2 of I. Richardson, 'Evolutionary factors in Mauritian Creole', *Journal of African Languages* 2(1):2–14 (1963).

51(a). Mauritian French Creole, similar to Réunionnais. Spoken by most of the population of *c.* 600,000 in Mauritius, and by several hundreds more (with Réunionnais) in Madagascar, especially at Tamatave, where Mauritius and Réunion migrants have settled. Also understood as a trade language in the Comorro Islands. See I. Richardson, *op. cit.* (50, above), and P. Baker, 'The language situation in Mauritius', *African Language Review* 8 (1969).

(b). A Swahili-Malagasy contact language is reported as having been in use along the north-western Madagascar coast (in I. Richardson, *op. cit.* p. 2); a Portuguese Pidgin speaking community was established during the sixteenth and seventeenth century on Vinany-Bè Island, near Fort Dauphin.

52. Rodrigues French Creole, similar to the Mauritian and Réunion dialects, spoken by *c.* 17,000 people. No material available for this creole, but literature on the preceding dialects useful.

53. Seychelles French Creole, or Seychellois. Spoken by over 40,000 people in the Seychelles Islands, and in Chagos and Agalega. The French-derived creole dialects of the Indian Ocean area are sometimes grouped together under the heading 'Mascarenian'. Data on Seychellois sparse, but see S. Jones, 'The French patois of the Seychelles', *African Affairs* 51:237–47 (1952).

54(a). Creole Portuguese of Ceylon. Spoken (or formerly spoken) by Indo-Portuguese Christians settled at Mannar, Negumbo, Colombo, Calaturey, Galle, Batticaloa, Trincomalee and Jaffna. See H. Schuchardt, 'Allgemeineres über das Indoportugiesische (Asioportugiesische)', *Zeitschrift für Romanische Philologie* 13:476–516 (1889), and S. R. Dalgado, *Dialecto indo-português de Ceylao* (Lisbon 1900). In a recent dialect survey, Professor D. Hettiaratchi (Nugegoda University) has found numerous speakers in various towns, e.g. the village of Uppordai near Batticaloa, and has obtained several old books in the language (personal communication).

(b). A semi-creolized form of Dutch was possibly once spoken in Ceylon.

55. Goanese, the Creole Portuguese of Goa, now probably extinct. See Schuchardt, *op. cit.* (54 above).

56. Creole Portuguese of Diu and Daman (Damao), both possibly extinct. With Salsette Creole, these constituted the Norteiro group of Indo-Portuguese dialects. Creole Portuguese was formerly spoken in many ports along the Indian coast, including Cambay, Surat, Thana, Bassein, Bombay, Chaul, Dabul, Rajapur, Angediva, Onnore, Baticalá, Barsalore, Mangalore, Cannanore, Tallicherry, Mahé, Callicut, Cranganore, Cochin, Mampulim, Anjengo, Manapar, Tuticorin, Karaikal, Nagapattinam, Trankenbar, Cuddalore, Devanapattinam, Pondicherry, Sadras, Kowalam, Madras, Palliacat, Masulipatnam, Vishakhapatnam, Bimili, Balasore, Pipli, Calcutta, Chandernagore, Hugli, Cassinbassar, Dacca and Chetigan. Not shown on the map are the Portuguese pidgin dialects of Saint Helena (off the south-western African coast), Gammeron (Iran), Basra (Iraq), Mecca, and the Further Indian group on the Burma-Thailand coasts, at Arakan-Yoma, Pegu, Siriam, Tanasarin, and Jonsalan, none of which is spoken today. See Schuchardt, *op. cit.* (54 above), 478–9 and 506.

A Pidgin English on St Helena is cited by A. Zettersten, *The English of Tristan da Cunha* (Lund Studies in English, 37) (Lund 1969), 134.

57(a). Hobson-Jobson, 'Babu English' or 'Chhi-Chhi'. A rudimentary pidgin employed during the period of British rule in India. Some Hindi influence. See H. Schuchardt, 'Das Indo-Englische', *Englische Studien* 15:286–305 (1890), H. Yule and A. Burnell, *Hobson-Jobson* (London 1903 and 1968), and J. Spencer, 'The Anglo-Indians and their speech', *Lingua* 16:57–70 (1966).

(b). The question of creolization in Indo-Aryan is raised by Southworth (this volume).

58. Madras English Pidgin, or 'Butler English'; similar to the preceding in form and function, but with strong Dravidian influence. See Schuchardt, *op. cit.* 292–3, and Yule and Burnell, *op. cit.* 133–4 (both 57, above).

59. Tay Boi, Franco-Annamite, or Indo-French Pidgin, now practically extinct, but widely used in Tonkin, Haiphong and most of coastal Annam during the period of French control. During the middle of the nineteenth century the area was settled by colonists from Réunion (then Bourbon), hence the similarities between, Franco-Annamite, Pidgin and the Mascarenian creoles. See Reinecke's paper in this volume, with references to Schuchardt (1888) and Stageberg (1956). [It would be interesting to know if a contact language using English has developed since 1956.]

60. Makista or Macauenho, the Portuguese-derived creole of Macao. Steadily approximating to metropolitan Portuguese, also spoken in the island. A more conservative form of Makista has been retained by the *c.* 2,000 Creoles who settled in Hong Kong (and thereby away from Portuguese-language influence) during the years following 1841. Some Chinese lexical adoptions. See G. N. Batalha, 'Estado actual do dialecto macaense', *Revista portuguesa da filologia* 9:177–213 (1959), and R. W. Thompson, 'O dialecto português de Hongkong', *Boletim de filologia* 19:289–93 (1960).

61(a). China Coast Pidgin English, sometimes called Business English ·or just 'Pidgin'. Developed during the eighteenth century and at one time in extensive use along the Chinese coast. Now no longer used in Communist China, where it is remembered only by a few old people in Shanghai and other seaport communities; giving way to metropolitan English in Hong Kong. See R. A. Hall, Jr., 'Chinese Pidgin English: grammar and texts', *Journal of the American Oriental Society* 64:95–113 (1944).

(b). A pidginized Chinese is reportedly in use as a contact language on the northwest frontiers of Laos and Vietnam (reference in K. Whinnom, *Spanish contact vernaculars in the Philippine Islands* (Hong Kong 1956), viii, n. 5).

(c) For a Sino-Russian pidgin, see Günter Neumann, 'Zur Chinesich-russischen Benelfssprache von Kjachta', *Sprache* 12:237–51 (1966).

62. Korean Pidgin English, or 'Bamboo English', which gained maximum currency during the Korean War in the 1950s. See J. T. Algee, 'Korean Bamboo English', *American Speech* 35:117–23 (1960), and G. Webster, 'Korean Bamboo English once more', *American Speech* 35:261–65 (1960).

63(a). A Japanese Pidgin English was apparently in use during the latter years of the nineteenth century, similar to 61(a) above. Cf. F. J. Daniels, 'The vocabulary of the Japanese ports lingo', *Bulletin of the Society for Oriental Studies* 12:805–23 (1948).

(b). A Japanese Pidgin English came into existence in the Hamamatsu area during the period of American occupation, but has fallen out of use. Also known sometimes as 'Bamboo English'. See J. S. Goodman, 'The development of a dialect of English-Japanese Pidgin', *Anthropological Linguistics* 9(6):43–55 (1967).

(c). The Korean and Japanese varieties of Pidgin English have shaped the Pidgin English now used by U.S. military personnel in Vietnam. Many of its forms are used in K. Melvin, *Sorry 'Bout That* (Tokyo: Wayward Press 1966), 46–8. Its use is described by J. B. Treaster, 'G-Eye view of Vietnam', *New York Times Magazine*, 30 October 1969, p. 108 (S. Broudy, personal communication).

64. Malacca Portuguese Creole, also known as Papia Kristang, Lusoatian, Serani, Malaqueiro, Malaquenho, Malaquense, Bahasa Gragu, etc., is still the first language of about 3,000 people in Western Malaysia.

Although the only 'home' of the Creoles today is in Malacca, a Portuguese community was at one time established further north on the Kedah coast

522 IAN F. HANCOCK

(according to Schuchardt, *op. cit.* (54, above), p. 479). See A. da Silva Rêgo, *O dialecto português de Malaca* (Lisbon 1942).

65. Singapore Portuguese Creole, similar to the Malacca dialect. Speakers of the creole are not centered in any one area of the city, but much of their social life revolves around their church, St Joseph's, where sermons are sometimes preached in the language. Some lexical and grammatical influence from Malay and English. See A. Coelho, 'Os dialectos românicos ou neo-latinos na Africa, Asia, e América', *Boletim da Sociedade de Geográfia de Lisboa* 2:129–96 (1880–1), 3:451–78 (1882), and 6:705–55 (1886); and 'O indo-portuguez de Singapura', 6:718–23.

66. Portuguese Creole of Jakarta (formerly Batavia) and nearby Pekan Tugu. During the early years of the present century the Creole communities in these towns dispersed, and the language is by now probably almost extinct. With 64 and 65 above, this creole forms a Malayo-Portuguese group, other dialects of which are (or were) spoken at Banda Atjeh, Padang, Djambi, Bangkahulu and Palembang (all in Sumatra), in Martapura (Borneo), Solor (Flores), Timor, Banda and Ambon (Ceram), Ternate and Tidor (Moluccas) and Macassar (Celebes). See H. Schuchardt, *op. cit.* (54, above), and 'Über das Malaioportu-giesische von Batavia und Tugu', *Sitzungberichte der Phil.-hist. classe der K. Akademie der Wissenschaften in Wien* 122:1–256 (1890).

67. Pasá or Bazaar Malay, a pidginized variety of High Malay in widespread use in Malaysia and Indonesia. Well documented, See R. Le Page, 'Multi-lingualism in Malaya', *Symposium on Multilingualism* 133–46 (London 1964).

68. Caviteño, and the closely-related Ermitaño, Spanish creoles spoken in the Manila area. Originally a Portuguese Pidgin–Spanish contact language brought into the Philippines from Ternate (71, below). See K. Whinnom, *op. cit.* (61, above).

69. Zamboangueño or Chabacano, spoken in Zamboanga City and originating mainly from Caviteño, with strong influences from Tagalog and Cebuano. See K. Whinnom, *op. cit.* (61 above), H. P. McKaughan, 'Notes on Chabacano grammar', *Journal of East Asiatic Studies* 3:205–26 (1954), R. O. Ing, 'A brief outline of Chabacano phonology', *Le Maître Phonetique* 128: 26–33 (July-December 1967); and especially Frake (this volume).

70. Davaueño or 'Abakay Spanish', spoken in Davao and representing an offshoot of Zamboangueño. A pidgin known as 'Bamboo Spanish' is reportedly in use in the area by older generation Chinese shopkeepers. Originally developed by the local Japanese community, its use has been perpetuated by the Chinese in Davao since the expulsion of the Japanese in 1945. See K. Whinnom, *op. cit.* (61 (b), above), 16–17.

71. Ternateño, once spoken in Ternate in the Moluccas. The progenitor of the Philippine Creoles, this language developed out of contact between Spanish/ Mexican soldiers and the local Portuguese Pidgin speaking community. Two hundred families from Ternate settled in Manila in 1659. See Whinnom, *op. cit.* (61, above), 7–11.

72. New Guinea or Papuan Pidgin English, creolized in some areas. Some lexical and structural influence from indigenous Papuan languages, but inter-intelligible with 74 and 75 below. See G. Landtman, 'The Pidgin English of British New Guinea', *Neuphilologische Mitteilungen* 19:62–74 (1918), and D. C. Laycock, 'Papuans and Pidgin: aspects of bilingualism in New Guinea', *Te Reo* 9:44–51 (1966).

73(a). Police Motu, a pidginized variety of Hanuabada Motu with considerable lexical adoption from 72, above. Used extensively in the Port Moresby area. See S. Wurm and J. Harris, *Police Motu, an introduction to the trade language of Papua* (Canberra 1963).

(b). Use of a pidgin form of the Siassi language as a *lingua franca* in Astrolabe Bay, New Guinea, is reported by T. Harding, *Voyagers of the Vitiaz Strait* (Seattle, 1967), p. 203.

74. Melanesian Pidgin English, also known as Neo-Melanesian, Sandalwood English, Bêche-de-mer, Beach-la-mar, etc.; originally an offshoot of China Coast Pidgin, this language now has over 1,000,000 speakers (including speakers of Papuan Pidgin English, with which it is usually classified). Becoming nativized in some areas. See R. A. Hall, *Melanesian Pidgin English: grammar, texts, vocabulary* (Baltimore 1944). F. Mihalić, *Pidgin English (Neo-Melanesian) dictionary and grammar*, Techny and Westmead (1957), and Wolfers (this volume).

75(a). Solomon Island Pidgin English or Neosolomonic, similar to the preceding. See R. A. Hall, 'Notes on British Solomon Islands Pidgin', *Modern language notes* 60:315–18 (1945).

(b). A now extinct English-derived pidgin was spoken in the Micronesian islands during the nineteenth century. Mentioned in R. A. Hall, 'English loanwords in Micronesian languages', *Language* 21:214–19 (1945).

76. Bagot Creole English, spoken on the Bagot Aboriginal Reserve near Darwin, Northern Australia. Originally a variety of Australian Pidgin English, with possible influence from 72 and 74, above. (Professor R. W. Thompson, personal communication.)

77. Australian Pidgin English, a direct development of Neo-Melanesian. Similarities shared by this group of pidgins are in part due to the illegal practice of 'blackbirding', whereby inhabitants of widely separated areas were pressed into plantation work, use of the pidgin then becoming necessary for mutual comprehension. See R. A. Hall, 'Notes on Australian Pidgin English', *Language* 19:283–7 (1943), and S. J. Baker, *The Australian language*, containing a chapter on pidgin (Sydney and London 1945).

78. New Caledonia Pidgin French, sometimes referred to by French writers as 'Bichelamar'. Some similarities with Réunion Creole due to settlers from that island who arrived in New Caledonia during the eighteenth and nineteenth centuries. See K. J. Hollyman, 'L'ancien pidgin français parlé en Nouvelle Calédonie', *Journal de la Société des Océanistes* 20:57–64 (1964).

79. Norfolkese, an offshoot of Pitcairnese (2, above), spoken by the descendants from H.M.S. *Bounty* who settled on the Australian island of Norfolk from Pitcairn in the nineteenth century. Today, only about half of the island's population of about 1,000 is of the original stock and speaks the language. See Ross and Moverley, *op. cit.* (2, above), B. F. Brazier, 'Norfolk Island', *Journal of the Historical Society of Queensland* (1920), and H. Holland, 'The Norfolk Island patois', *ABC Weekly* (1946), reproduced in S. J. Baker, *Australia Speaks*, 204–6 (London and Sydney, 1953).

80. Maori Pidgin English, now no longer spoken, but current during the early years of colonization. Similar to Neo-Melanesian, Australian Pidgin English, etc. See ' "Pidgin" English in New Zealand', ch. 9, in S. J. Baker, *New Zealand slang, a dictionary of colloquialisms*, 71–92 (Christchurch [*c.*] 1941).

INDEX

NOTE: The numbers in parentheses following certain language names refer to the position of that language on the map on pages 510 and 511, and to the the notes between pages 509 and 523